Fodor's **2001**

London

D0190546

Fodor's Travel Publications • New York, Toronto, London, Sydney, Auckland

CONTENTS

Destination London 5

Great Itineraries 26

Fodor's Choice 30

1 EXPLORING LONDON 33

Westminster and Royal London 39

St. James's and Mayfair 59

Soho and Covent Garden 69

Bloomsbury and Legal London 77

The City 85

The East End 100

The South Bank 107

Chelsea and Belgravia 118

Knightsbridge, Kensington,
and Holland Park 123

Hyde Park, Kensington Gardens,
and Notting Hill 131

Regent's Park and Hampstead 135

Greenwich 144

Upstream from London 149

2 DINING 155

3 LODGING 192

4 NIGHTLIFE AND
THE ARTS 221

5 OUTDOOR ACTIVITIES
AND SPORTS 238

6 SHOPPING 244

7 SIDE TRIPS FROM
  LONDON 272
    Bath 273
    Cambridge 274
    Oxford 276
    Stratford-upon-Avon 277
    Windsor 279

8 BACKGROUND
  AND ESSENTIALS 282
    Portrait of London 283
    Books and Videos 288
    Chronology 290
    Smart Travel Tips A to Z 293

  INDEX 323

  ABOUT OUR WRITERS 336

MAPS

CENTRAL LONDON
36–37

Westminster and
Royal London 42

Westminster Abbey 56

St. James's and Mayfair 62

Soho and Covent Garden 72

Bloomsbury and
Legal London 80

The City 89

St. Paul's Cathedral 94

The Tower 96

The East End 103

The South Bank 111

Chelsea and Belgravia 121

Knightsbridge, Kensington,
and Holland Park 126

Hyde Park, Kensington
Gardens, and
Notting Hill 133

Regent's Park and
Hampstead 138

Greenwich 147

DINING 158–159

Dining in Mayfair,
St. James's, Soho, Covent
Garden, and Bloomsbury
160–161

Dining in South Kensington,
Knightsbridge, and
Chelsea 175

Dining in Kensington
and Notting Hill Gate 180

Dining in the City
and the South Bank 184

LODGING 194–195

Lodging in Mayfair,
St. James's, Soho, and
Covent Garden 198

Lodging in Kensington,
Knightsbridge, Chelsea,
Belgravia, and
Westminster 206

Lodging in Bayswater
and Notting Hill Gate 214

Lodging in Bloomsbury 217

THEATERS AND
CONCERT HALLS 230

SHOPPING

Shopping (Map A):
Mayfair, Soho, and Covent
Garden 248–249

Shopping (Map B):
Kensington, Knightsbridge,
and Chelsea 250

Shopping (Map C):
Notting Hill 251

Circled letters in text correspond to letters on the photographs. For more information on the sights pictured, turn to the indicated page number Ⓐ⟩ on each photograph.

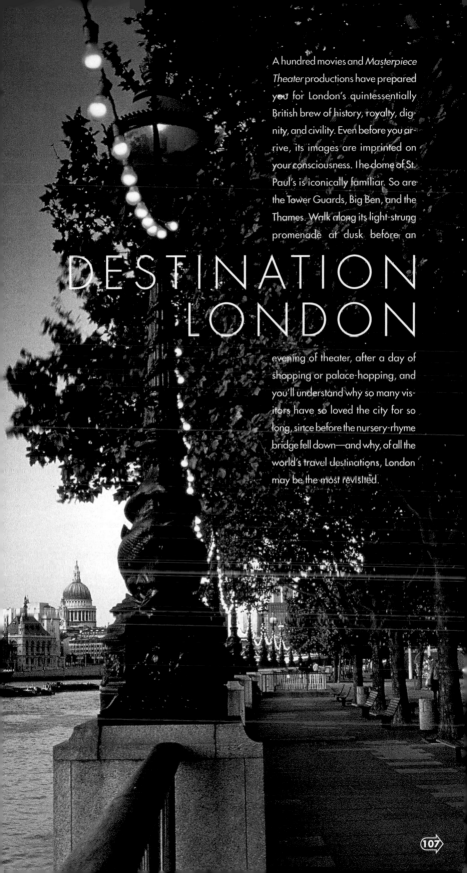

A hundred movies and *Masterpiece Theater* productions have prepared you for London's quintessentially British brew of history, royalty, dignity, and civility. Even before you arrive, its images are imprinted on your consciousness. The dome of St. Paul's is iconically familiar. So are the Tower Guards, Big Ben, and the Thames. Walk along its light-strung promenade at dusk before an

DESTINATION LONDON

evening of theater, after a day of shopping or palace-hopping, and you'll understand why so many visitors have so loved the city for so long, since before the nursery-rhyme bridge fell down—and why, of all the world's travel destinations, London may be the most revisited.

Ⓐ 93

After the Great Fire of 1666, London's dominant architectural element was the charred beam. But then, upon the city's

ARCHITECTURE

ashes, Sir Christopher Wren fashioned a new city and left a mark that seems indelible, if only because of his Ⓐ**St. Paul's Cathedral,** whose majestic dome humbles all modern buildings nearby. Of late, architecture has become a hot topic among Londoners, who are fortunate heirs to a rich legacy in stone that includes Westminster Cathedral, Ⓒ**Westminster Abbey,** the Ⓔ**Royal Courts of Justice,** and the Houses of Parliament, whose clock tower holds Ⓓ**Big Ben.** Prince Charles is a keen critic, a fervent advocate of the traditional. Members of the architecture establishment sometimes roll their eyes at his pronouncements (and if they *like* the prince, bite their tongues). The modern and postmodern booms sweeping the city have kindled heated

Ⓑ 90

debates. Most Londoners, however, admire new buildings such as the Ⓑ**Lloyd's of London** headquarters created by the same Richard Rogers who designed the Millennium Dome in Greenwich and set the French to quarreling over the Pompidou Center. With its complex structure boldly arrayed on the outside, it's a cool

Ⓒ 55

D▷46

setting for so august an institution. Sir Norman Foster's Millennium Bridge connecting St. Paul's Cathedral with the new Tate Modern quite literally brings together the old and the new. But that, too, is London for you: traditional and edgy at the same time.

E▷83

ROYAL
LONDON

Trappings of royalty set London apart not only from the rest of Britain but from all the cities of the world. Even in places such as Stockholm and Madrid, where kings and queens still make a living embodying their nation's heritage, royals are simply not such a big deal. Almost more than any other people, the English nurture an emotional investment in their sovereigns and the proud legacy they represent—despite the controversy that rages over the viability of the monarchy. Britons still snap up tabloids when royals are in the headlines, congregate for processions of the Royal Livery from the Ⓐ**Royal Mews,** and throng the streets on the Queen's birthday for the parade known as Trooping the Colour. Pilgrimlike, they visit Ⓑ**Kensington Palace,** former home of Diana, Princess of Wales. The royal warrant in the windows of fine shops signals

Ⓑ 127

Ⓐ 52

Ⓒ 43

wares of the highest quality. The royalty connection and the castles, palaces, and collections of paintings left by royals through the centuries fill the imagination of travelers, as well. Who could fail to gawk at the incomparably regal State Dining Room in ©**Buckingham Palace** or to marvel at the Ⓓ**Changing of the Guard** outside? Everyone wants to inspect the splendid Crown Jewels in the Ⓔ Ⓕ**Tower of London,** once the final stop for unlucky royals, children included, on the outs with their kinsmen on the throne. A chat with one of its Yeoman Warders, who have guarded the Tower for 500 years, yields a fascinating look at British history— and gives you a sense of just how much the Crown has meant through the centuries to the people of Shakespeare's "sceptered isle."

Ⓔ▷96

Ⓕ▷96

A 174

In the 1980s any commentary on dining in London might have ended right about *here*. Today restaurants are London's new passion, and newcomers are always bursting onto the scene, often with amazing chefs hanging their toques in the kitchen. In restaurants such as the ©**Sugar Club,** inventive cuisine is the irresistible draw. Sometimes the setting is as original as the food—that's notably true at South Kensington's Ⓐ**Bibendum** and at Notting Hill's

DINING OUT

B 180

prescriptions

C 169

10

Ⓓ〉270

ⒷPharmacy. Or the glitterati may come for the romance of a stellar panorama like the one at the South Bank's **ⒻOXO Tower Brasserie and Restaurant.** Meanwhile, as gastrodomes serving world cuisines proliferate, local traditions endure. The Savoy Grill remains the power dining room par excellence, Fortnum & Mason's Fountain lives on, endearingly frumpy, and simply excellent fish-and-chips pack 'em in at Ⓔ**Geales,** although it lacks both theme and clever concept. Stylish snacking is everywhere—witness the options at Ⓓ**Leadenhall Market,** a fine Victorian arcade. More than anything else this decade, London's exuberant food scene has infused the city with excitement and has become one more facet to celebrate.

Ⓔ〉183

Ⓕ〉184

SHOPPING

Ⓐ⟩ 270

You would have, as Brits say, "a brilliant holiday" if you spent your entire stay in London shopping—even if you went no farther afield than ⒹHarrods, one of the world's great shrines to mankind's acquisitive drive. If clothing is your thing, London's got it; designers like Alexander McQueen and Vivienne Westwood are hotter than ever. Check out stores such as ⒷBrowns and ⒸJigsaw, purveyors to the beautiful, as well as true stalwarts such as Marks & Spencer and the redone Selfridges. Men willing to spring for a shirt or suit from Turnbull & Asser, Kilgour, or another of London's bespoke tailors

Ⓑ⟩ 261

Ⓒ⟩ 262

Ⓓ 252

Ⓔ 63

Ⓕ 266

place themselves in the hands of true artists—and are treated like peers from first fitting to last. Elegant enclaves like Mayfair's Ⓔ**Burlington Arcade** are good places to commission the best suit you'll ever own.

Ⓐ**Portobello Market,** for many the best of London's famous bazaars, stretches farther than you can see, overflowing with ephemera, silver, porcelain, and other appurtenances of merry old England. For the loveliest shopping experience of all, stop in at Ⓕ**Floris,** whose perfumes were a favorite of Queen Victoria's. If consumerism is allowed in heaven, this is what it must look like.

MUSEUMS
AND MARVELS

(A)>82

A blizzard of blue plaques all over town proclaims the historic importance of structures as wide-ranging as Dennis Severs's House, the Geffrye Museum, and the (A)**Dickens House Museum** and turn London itself into something of a museum. High culture and low, it's here. The (B)**National Gallery** holds Bronzino's *An Allegory with Venus and Cupid* and a flurry of masterworks that are instantly familiar. Hertford House showcases the splendid Wallace Collection, stuffed

(B)>49

with old masters and fine French furniture. Gracious England lives on here and in wonderful stately homes such as Spencer House and Leighton House. If you had defeated Napoléon, saving Europe in the process, you might have hung your medals in an imposing structure like gilded ©**Apsley House** (where the Duke of Wellington's trophies remain). Farther afield are Chiswick House and Ham House, and ®**Hampton Court Palace,** where Henry VIII gamely battled gout and a rotation of subsequent monarchs took up residence, having fallen in love with the place. Visit and you will instantly see why: the grounds are beautiful beyond description, the palace is extraordinary, and, in the best English tradition, it is reputedly frequented by a royal ghost. Sightings are free. Then there's the ®**Natural History Museum,** very much of the 19th century outside but totally 21st within. Many of its ingenious displays are animated and as delightful to grown-ups as to kids.

®⟩129

®⟩153

Of all of London's great museums, the ⒻBritish Museum is preeminent. Think of it as a jumbo time capsule. The full scope of human endeavor is represented here, including the Rosetta Stone and the Magna Carta, as well as such exquisite, if controversial, treasures of antiquity as the Elgin Marbles of ancient Greece. Impressive in its own right is the ⒽVictoria and Albert Museum, whose whimsically eclectic collections might someday, conceivably, include a hat from one of the schoolchildren who tour it regularly. At the Tate Gallery's renovated Millbank site, ⒾTate Britain focuses on British artists, displaying art

Ⓗ ▷ 130

from the past five centuries together in new theme galleries. As a break from sheer beauty or just to see what attracts millions every year, make a beeline for ⒼMadame Tussaud's and commune with a forever-young and toothy Dudley Moore and dozens of other celebrities both dead and alive.

Ⓐ ⇨ 134

If you spend all your time in central London, you'll go home having seen . . . central London. A stroll in one of the city's many neighborhoods makes a fine break from more purposeful sightseeing. Each has its attitude and style: Knightsbridge and Kens-

CITY OF VILLAGES

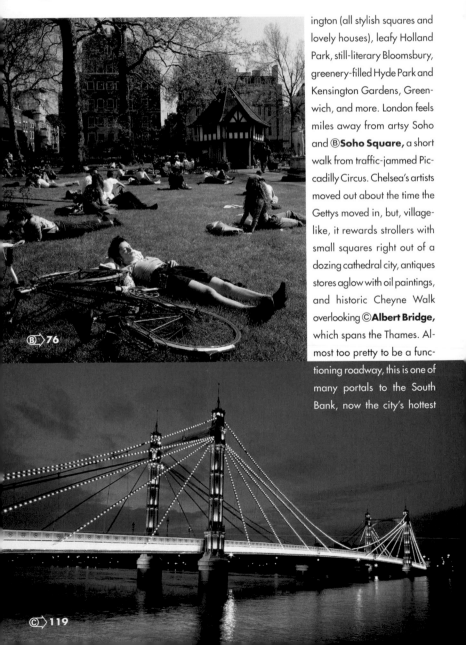

Ⓑ ⇨ 76

ington (all stylish squares and lovely houses), leafy Holland Park, still-literary Bloomsbury, greenery-filled Hyde Park and Kensington Gardens, Greenwich, and more. London feels miles away from artsy Soho and Ⓑ**Soho Square,** a short walk from traffic-jammed Piccadilly Circus. Chelsea's artists moved out about the time the Gettys moved in, but, villagelike, it rewards strollers with small squares right out of a dozing cathedral city, antiques stores aglow with oil paintings, and historic Cheyne Walk overlooking Ⓒ**Albert Bridge,** which spans the Thames. Almost too pretty to be a functioning roadway, this is one of many portals to the South Bank, now the city's hottest

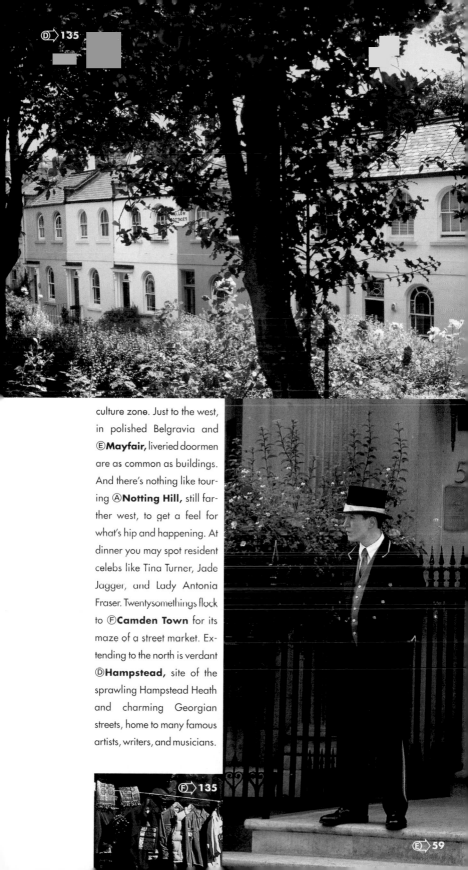

culture zone. Just to the west, in polished Belgravia and Ⓔ**Mayfair,** liveried doormen are as common as buildings. And there's nothing like touring Ⓐ**Notting Hill,** still farther west, to get a feel for what's hip and happening. At dinner you may spot resident celebs like Tina Turner, Jade Jagger, and Lady Antonia Fraser. Twentysomethings flock to Ⓕ**Camden Town** for its maze of a street market. Extending to the north is verdant Ⓓ**Hampstead,** site of the sprawling Hampstead Heath and charming Georgian streets, home to many famous artists, writers, and musicians.

Ⓕ> 135

A 151

Londoners love greenery and flowers—madly, if you consider the acreage devoted to things horticultural. Parks are said to be a city's lungs; in London they are also the city's heart—abloom, successively, with crocuses, azaleas, rhododendrons, daffodils, tulips, lilacs, roses, water lilies, and heather. In May don't miss the prestigious Chelsea Flower Show. Of all London's green spaces, the best known may be Ⓕ**Hyde Park,** whose famed Speaker's Corner, with its soapbox orators, can bring out the heckler in any-

PARKS AND GARDENS

B 52

C 132

(D) 143

body. ⒶKew Gardens is a mandatory stop for all those who, back home, enjoy getting soil under their fingernails. Its sprawling Royal Botanic Gardens both dazzle and edify. By Buckingham Palace, and property of the monarchy, ⒷSt. James's Park is a favorite of bird lovers (some bird lovers become favorites of the birds). You'll even find pelicans here. In adjoining ⒸGreen Park, also part of the Queen's backyard, daffodils rule in spring. On summer days, Londoners love to laze the afternoon away in ⒹRegent's Park. The formal, fountained Italian parterres at ⒺKensington Gardens are perhaps a touch exotic, think Brits, who favor the more natural look of the English garden (after all, they invented it).

(E) 134

(F) 132

Several nations have monarchs. Many nations play cricket (some better than England). But none comes close to matching the most British institution of all: the pub. Sir Arthur Conan Doyle used to unwind from mystery writing at what is now the ®**Sherlock Holmes.** If Charles Dickens had frequented all the pubs claiming him for a patron, he would have died young and unpublished. (The ©**George Inn** is one that can truly call him its own.) Pubs are the seat of England's soul, and in London there's a local on every corner, with names charming enough to inspire pub crawls—the

PUBS

Ⓐ190

Ⓑ190

©189

Pheasant and Firkin, Ye Olde Cheshire Cheese, the Ⓐ**Lamb & Flag,** the ©**Albert,** the Ⓓ**Three Greyhounds.** By all means, try meeting the English in a pub. Nowhere else do you get to know them so well. Think of the pub as a common hearthside, where locals, sometimes with kids in tow, come to affirm community. In summer, when some pub keepers set up tables on the sidewalk or in a patio or garden, you may also think of the pub as a community park that serves refreshments. Thick, chocolatey stout or bitter, served warm, may be an acquired taste, even when gently brewed the traditional way, but most travelers acquire it quickly, and pub grub—hearty fare like shepherd's pie and often, lately, more ambitious cuisine—enhances the experience.

Ⓓ191

Ⓔ189

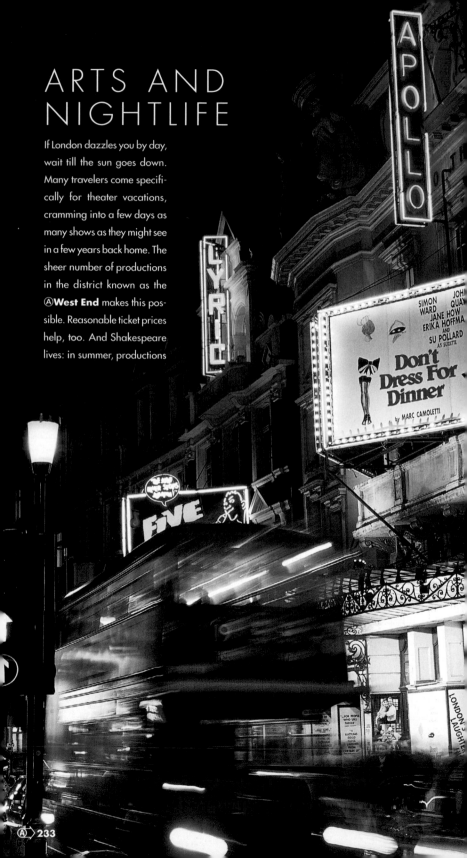

ARTS AND NIGHTLIFE

If London dazzles you by day, wait till the sun goes down. Many travelers come specifically for theater vacations, cramming into a few days as many shows as they might see in a few years back home. The sheer number of productions in the district known as the Ⓐ**West End** makes this possible. Reasonable ticket prices help, too. And Shakespeare lives: in summer, productions of his plays are a cherished tradition at Ⓑ**Regent's Park Open-Air Theatre** and are becoming so at the reconstructed Globe on the South Bank. Audiences at the Globe experience living history as well as great drama. The theater clones the Elizabethan original, right down to the standing-room pit, and the Bard's work (and his humor) seem all the more topical. Also in summer, between July and September, ticket prices are slashed at Ⓒ**Royal Albert Hall** for its Proms series. Then and during the rest of the year, performances by local and international musicians fill the concert calendar, divas draw sellout crowds, and dancers of the Royal Ballet, English National Ballet, and other stellar companies jeté across a handful of stages. As for nightlife, the scene ranges from casinos to karaoke, comedy to drag cabarets, heavy metal to world-beat clubs, and there's plenty of good jazz. Think of it like this: when you dance all night at clubs like the Ⓓ**Sound Republic,** you get an early start on your next London day.

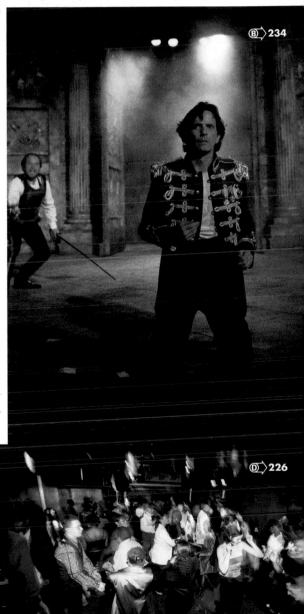

Ⓑ〉234

Ⓒ〉231

Ⓓ〉226

GREAT ITINERARIES

London in 5 Days

In a city with as many richly stocked museums and matchless marvels as London, you risk seeing half of everything or all of nothing. So use the efficient itineraries below to keep you on track as you explore both the famous sights and those off the beaten path. Although you'll need those familiar red double-decker buses and the Underground to cover long distances, you'll soon discover how London rewards those who stroll its streets. So that you don't show up somewhere and find you've missed the boat, shuffle the itinerary segments with the closing hours, listed below, in mind.

DAY 1

Spend your first day in Royal London, which contains much that is historic and traditional in British life. Beat the crowds and get an early start at magnificent, medieval Westminster Abbey—if Prince Charles becomes king, this is where he will be crowned. After an hour exploring the abbey, make the 15-minute walk (or tube it from Westminster to St. James's Park) to catch the Changing of the Guard at 11:20, outside Ⓐ Buckingham Palace. Don't dawdle—optimally you need to get there by 10:45. In season an alterna-

Ⓐ 43

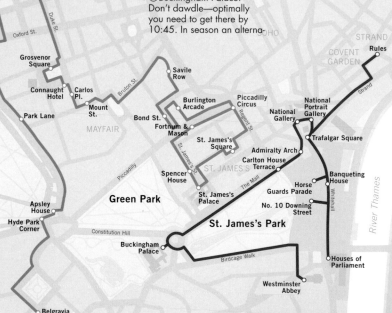

Ⓑ 79

tive option is to tour Buck House itself, as the British quippingly call it. Next stroll down the Mall, enjoying the very view the monarch sees when she rides in her gilded coach to open Parliament every year. Passing King George IV's glorious Carlton House Terrace, walk through the Admiralty Arch into Trafalgar Square, the very center of the city. Spend an hour or two in the National Gallery, the finest art museum in the land. If you're interested in history or you'll have time on another day for the National Gallery, go instead to nearby St. Martin's Place and the National Portrait Gallery, a visual who's who of England. From Trafalgar Square, head south to Whitehall, which is lined with grand government buildings, the Baroque-era Banqueting House, outside of which King Charles I was beheaded, and the Horse Guards Parade (Her Majesty's mounted guardsmen make a great photo-op). Head past 10 Downing Street—the Prime

Tuesday or Wednesday. But remember that between mid-July and April, the Changing of the Guard (usually a daily event) occurs only every other day; check schedules before you plan. Buckingham Palace is open daily in season—from late August to early October. Between October and June, when the Houses of Parliament are open to visitors, the House of Lords is closed from Thursday to Sunday, the House of Commons from Friday to Sunday; optimal times are complex, so check the Houses of Parliament schedule in Chapter 1. On Sunday the Banqueting House is closed, and Westminster Abbey (except for the museum) is open only to those attending services.

DAY 2

Think of this day as London 101—a tour of the city's postcard sights. Begin at the Ⓑ British Museum—home to the Elgin Marbles, Rosetta Stone, and Magna Carta— and explore the adjacent treasures of bookish Blooms-

the Thames to Southwark and Shakespeare's Globe for a play by the Bard performed in the most famous theater in the world. At day's end, journey along old Father Thames east to Le Pont de la Tour or west to the OXO Tower to enjoy a riverside dinner with London spectacularly illuminated at your feet. ☽ *Don't plan on doing day 2 on Sunday, when both the Dickens House Museum and Sir John Soane's Museum are closed. Note that Shakespeare's Globe stages plays in the open-air theater only from May to September.*

DAY 3

Explore St. James's and Mayfair, the core of London's West End, the smartest and most atmospheric central area of the city. From Piccadilly Circus go west on Piccadilly to splurge on breakfast at the Queen's grocers, Fortnum & Mason.

For a brush with royalty,

Fleet St.
St. Paul's Cathedral
Blackfriars
THE CITY
Blackfriars Bridge
River Thames
Shakespeare's Globe Theatre
OXO Tower
Southwark St.
Tooley St.
Tower Bridge
Le Pont de la Tour

Minister's residence—to the Houses of Parliament. To see them, you have two options: either wait in line for the limited seats available in the Strangers Gallery of either house (use the St. Stephen's Entrance opposite the abbey), or prebook a tour, which shows off all the State Rooms. Eventually you'll hear ©Big Ben signaling the approaching dinner hour, just in time for your reservation at Rules, London's most beautiful restaurant, and a feast in the same salon where Lillie Langtry and the Prince of Wales once dined.
☽ *It's best to do this tour on*

bury, including the Dickens House Museum and the British Library (on Euston Road, 10 blocks north), then perhaps track the spirit of Virginia Woolf on verdant Bedford, Russell, and Bloomsbury squares. Now head southeast toward the Thames to visit the Regency delight that is Sir John Soane's Museum at Lincoln's Inn. Continue south to Fleet Street, then east to 17th-century St. Paul's Cathedral, the city's presiding spirit. Wander south through the crooked streets of Blackfriars to Blackfriars Bridge and cross

maybe even with Wills and Harry, detour several blocks to Prince Charles's Tudor-era home, St. James's Palace near St. James's Square, then continue on to palatial Spencer House, once home to the ancestors of the late Princess of Wales. From Piccadilly travel north for some ritzy window-shopping on Bond Street, in the 19th-century Burlington Arcade, and along Savile Row, continuing on through beautiful Mayfair via Mount Street,

Carlos Place—tea at the Connaught Hotel, anyone?—and Grosvenor Square. From here take Duke Street north to view the Fragonards and Halses at the Wallace Collection on Manchester Square. Keep going south to Park Lane and just before Hyde Park Corner visit Apsley House, flanked by the Wellington Arch and a statue of Achilles pointing to the Duke's time-burnished mansion. To the southwest is the splendidly aristocratic enclave of Belgravia, London at its most *Upstairs, Downstairs*. ⊘ *Apsley House is closed on Monday and Spencer House is open only on Sunday.*

DAY 4

London legends populate this itinerary. First take a break from the city and travel up to its most famous "village,"

tube stop to pick up a spine-chilling Jack the Ripper Theme Walk through the East End. ⊘ *Note that the East End Jack the Ripper tours begin at 7 PM.*

Knightsbridge and shopping at Harrods or Harvey Nichols. Afterward you can go north or south. To the north, in Kensington Gardens, you can salute the Peter Pan statue, then visit historic Kensington Palace, childhood home of Queen Victoria and repository of the Royal Dress Collection. Continuing on

Hampstead. After taking in the picturesque houses, chic cafés, and Church Row—London's most complete Georgian street—move on to (if you're a Beatlemaniac) Abbey Road, in nearby St. John's Wood. Then tube it down to Baker Street, visit the Sherlock Holmes Museum or Madame Tussaud's (a must for kids), then go north to Regent's Park and its swooningly elegant Cumberland Terrace and Chester Terrace (*101 Dalmatians'* Dearly family, the "pets" of Pongo and Perdita, lived here on the Outer Circle). In the afternoon take the tube to Tower Hill and the legendary Ⓓ Tower of London to see the Crown Jewels and the eight Tower Ravens. At dusk cross the street to the Tower Hill

DAY 5

This segment of your itinerary is all about shopping, history, and priceless art. Begin at the "museum mile" of South Kensington. See either the Victoria and Albert Museum, or, if you have children in tow, opt for the Natural History Museum. Head up Brompton Road for lunch in

Kensington High Street to Holland Park you will come to Leighton House, home of the noted 19th-century orientalist painter Lord Leighton, and lovely Victorian-era Linley Sambourne House. Have dinner in sassy and sophisticated Notting Hill. Alternatively from Knightsbridge you might head south to historic Chelsea to charming Cheyne Walk and the Tate Britain. It

Map labels:
To Hampstead, Church Row
Abbey Road
St. John's Wood Tube Station
ST. JOHN'S WOOD
Abbey Rd.
St. John's Wood Rd.
REGENT'S PARK
Cumberland Terrace
Chester Terrace
York Terrace
Baker Street Tube Station
Great Portland Street Tube Station
Madame Tussaud's Wax Museum
Marylebone Rd.
Baker St.
Sherlock Holmes Museum
MARYLEBONE
BAYSWATER
Notting Hill Gate
Notting Hill
Peter Pan Statue
Kensington Palace
Kensington Gardens
HOLLAND PARK
Linley Sambourne House
Kensington High St.
Holland Park
Leighton House
KENSINGTON
MAYFAIR
ST. JAMES'S PARK
Kensington Rd.
Harvey Nichols
Harrods
KNIGHTSBRIDGE
Brompton Rd.
Sloane St.
BELGRAVIA
Victoria and Albert Museum
Natural History Museum
BROMPTON
SOUTH KENSINGTON
Chelsea
Kings Rd.
PIMLICO
Chelsea Embankment
Cheyne Walk

you go this route you can ensure a gala finale for your stay by booking tickets to a play or musical in the West End's Theatreland. But by now you will have learned that London is the most wonderful free show in the world.

☉ *Every season mandates different timing for this segment of the itinerary. Between April and September you must choose between the two mansions. Any day but Sunday you can tour Leighton House, and on Wednesday or Sunday afternoon you might opt to see Linley Sambourne. Between November and February, make this tour Wednesday through Saturday. On Wednesday in October and March all the sights on this itinerary are open.*

Court Palace, half rose-red Tudor brick, half serenely classical, still buried deep in parkland.

If You Have 3 Days

Touring the largest city in England in the space of three days sounds difficult, but it's long enough to give you a tempting taste of the city. Follow the itineraries for days 1 and 2 above, then begin your third day at the legend-haunted Tower of London. After a morning tour, take the tube or a taxi to Hyde Park Circle to see one of London's most spectacular town houses, Apsley House. You're in posh Mayfair now, so stroll to the Burlington Arcade and

Bond Street for some world-class shopping, then head north to view the treasures at the Wallace Collection. From Marble Arch take the tube to Kensington High Street and Kensington Palace. After touring the historic palace, repair to its Orangery for tea and a well-deserved time-out. Try the best of contemporary British cuisine in nearby Notting Hill or book an evening in Theatreland.

the lively presentation about the Thames in the Tower Bridge. Cross to the south bank and hang a left toward Butler's Wharf for lunch. If you have teens, stop on Tooley Street at the goriest museum in town: the London Dungeon, a hoot of a horror waxworks show. Recross the river to catch a ferry at Tower Pier for a thrilling 15-minute cruise to Waterloo Pier (or, as far as Westminster Pier, from which you can walk across Westminster Bridge and then backtrack to Waterloo Pier; if it's raining, tube it from Tower

Hill to Waterloo Station). On the way explore the Museum of the Moving Image, where special effects appear to let your child soar like Superman over the Thames, ride British Airways London Eye, England's tallest Ferris wheel, and tour the London Aquarium. At day's end take the tube back to Piccadilly and have tea at Fortnum & Mason.

If You Have More Time

Spectacular day trips lie upriver and down. Easily reachable by boat along the Thames to the east is Greenwich, whose 18th-century streets form a striking contrast to what's being called the "Stonehenge of the 21st Century," the Millennium Dome. Westward on the Thames from London lie destinations that take you back, not forward, in time: Chiswick House, Kew Gardens, Syon House, and the 17th-century Ⓔ Hampton

A Kid's Day Out

Although children can't fly over the town as Peter Pan and Wendy did so thrillingly, this tour will show them a London packed with wonders. Get an early start with a tube ride to the Tower of London, home to the fabled Beefeater guards (plus its eight resident ravens; be sure to say hello to Thor, who talks). Across the street see

Map labels:

Piccadilly Circus
Piccadilly
Fortnum & Mason
ST. JAMES'S
SOHO
STRAND
THE CITY
Waterloo Pier
Museum of the Moving Image
SOUTH BANK
SOUTHWARK
London Eye
Westminster Pier
London Aquarium
Waterloo Station
Westminster Bridge
Westminster Abbey
WESTMINSTER
River Thames
LAMBETH
Vauxhall Bridge Rd.
Grosvenor Rd.
Bus St.
Tate Britain
Lower Thames St.
Tower Hill Tube Station
Tower Pier
Tower of London
Tower Bridge
London Dungeon
Tooley St.
Butler's Wharf
Whitechapel (Jack the Ripper tour)

Ⓔ❯153

29

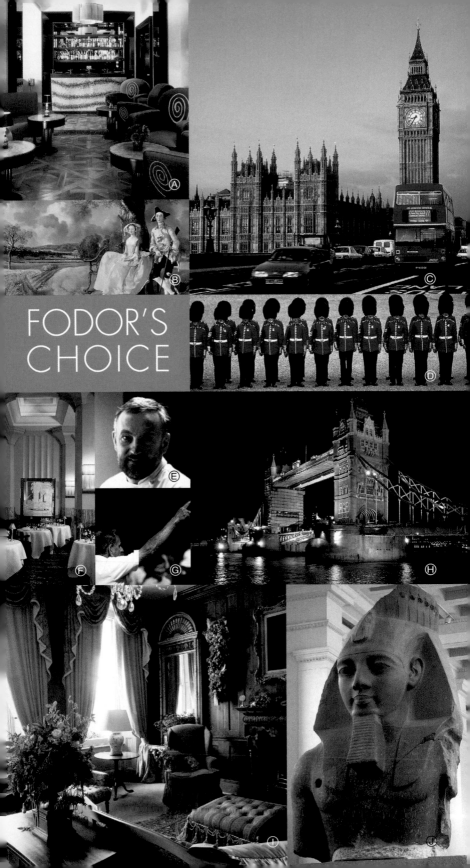

FODOR'S
CHOICE

Even with so many special places in London, Fodor's writers and editors have their favorites. Here are a few that stand out.

QUINTESSENTIAL LONDON

Afternoon Performance at Shakespeare's Globe. London at its Wellsian time-machine best, this open-to-the-skies reconstruction of Shakespeare's beloved "Wooden O" transports you back to Elizabethan London. ☞ p. 116

Beatles' Magical Mystery Tour. This wonderful stroll down Memory Lane offered by Original London Walks includes the London Palladium, No. 3 Savile Row—the Fab Four's London headquarters—and Abbey Road. Yeah, yoah, yeah! ☞ p. 137

ⓓ Changing of the Guard. Adding a dash of red to the gloomiest of London days, the Life Guards and the Guard of Color march in front of Buckingham Palace as the band plays (they have been known to cut loose to Billy Joel when Her Majesty is away). ☞ p. 44

ⓒ Houses of Parliament at Sunset. Cross the Thames to Jubilee Gardens to see this view of London at its storybook best. ☞ p. 46

ⓖ Sunday Afternoon at Speakers' Corner, Hyde Park. A space especially reserved for anyone with anything to say that *must* be said publicly makes for great entertainment. Speakers seem to be most oratorical on Sunday afternoons. ☞ p. 67

ⓗ Tower Bridge at Night. A dramatically floodlighted Tower Bridge confronts you as you come out of the Design Museum on a winter's night. Have your camera ready. ☞ p. 95

MAGNIFICENT MUSEUMS

Apsley House. Known as No. 1 London, this was the residence of the Duke of Wellington, fabled conqueror of Napoléon. The house's centerpiece, the Waterloo Gallery, is one of the grandest rooms in Europe. ☞ p. 61

ⓙ British Museum. You could move into this grand pile and never tire of all that it has to

offer, from the Rosetta Stone to the sublime Elgin Marbles from ancient Greece. ☞ p. 79

ⓑ National Gallery. Da Vincis, Rubenses, and Rembrandts fill the rooms here—the richest trove of old-master paintings in Britain. ☞ p. 49

Sir John Soane's Museum. Eccentric architect of the Bank of England, Sir John left his house to the nation on the condition that nothing be changed. The result is a Regency-era phantasmagoria of colors, unusual perspectives, and objets d'art. ☞ p. 83

Spencer House. The London house to end all London houses, this glamorous Palladian mansion was built by Princess Diana's ancestors and proves that even the 18th-century Spencers were no slouches in the flash department. ☞ p. 67

COMFORTS

The Beaufort. Use this set of Victorian houses, run by an all-female staff, as a home away from home, especially if you plan to spend all your time next door at Harrods. ££££ ☞ p. 208

ⓕ Claridge's. The same fine qualities that attracted the king of Morocco, among many others, to this world-renowned Mayfair hotel are sure to make you feel right at home, too. ££££ ☞ p. 197

Covent Garden Hotel. Discerning travelers now call this the most stylish hotel in London. ££££ ☞ p. 203

The Savoy. Secure a river suite at this historic, late-Victorian hotel overlooking the Thames, and you'll get one of the best stays—and views—in London. ££££ ☞ p. 204

ⓘ The Pelham. Designed to capture the essence of English country housedom, this boutique hotel is a tranquil country retreat in the center of South Kensington. £££ ☞ p. 211

Dorset Square Hotel. Tim and Kit Kemp, hoteliers extraordinaire, decanted the English country look into a fine pair of Regency town houses and then turned up the volume in the first of their four London addresses. ££ ☞ p. 201

Abbey House Hotel. Rooms at this popular B&B in a pretty, white-stucco Victorian town house—home to a bishop and an MP—have both wash-basins and color TVs. £ ☞ p. 207

FLAVORS

ⓐⓔ La Tante Claire. Pierre Koffmann may be London's best chef, and he is practicing his seemingly effortless art in new surroundings at the Berkeley Hotel. The service is impeccable and the French wine list impressive, but food is the point. ££££ ☞ p. 176

Oak Room. Marco Pierre White enjoys Jagger-like fame as he ventures where few chefs have gone before. His kitchen is dizzyingly creative: expect grand style—foie gras, caviar, and truffles—and truly adventurous preparations. ££££ ☞ p. 163

Le Caprice. This glamorous place has stood the test of time—the food is great, the ambience even better. The other reason everyone comes here is that everyone else does, which leads to the best people-watching in town. £££ ☞ p. 166

Rules. Come, escape from the 21st century. London's answer to Maxim's in Paris, Rules enjoys an incomparably delicious 19th-century setting, one that has welcomed everyone from Dickens to the Duke of Windsor. £££ ☞ p. 171

The Cow. Notting Hillbillies and other stylish folk adore this luxe "gastro-pub." A serious chef whips up Tuscan-British specialties, but some diners prefer the half-dozen Irish rock oysters with a pint of Guinness. ££ ☞ p. 182

Quality Chop House. The food at this gorgeous, converted greasy spoon is a glorious parody of "caf" food (bangers and mash, egg and chips); the seats are Victorian pews. ££ ☞ p. 185

The Eagle. This superior pub, with wooden floors, a few sofas, and art on the walls, serves amazingly good-value Goan/Portuguese/Spanish food. £ ☞ p. 183

1 EXPLORING LONDON

If London contained only its landmarks—
Buckingham Palace, Big Ben, the Tower of
London—it would still rank us one of the
world's top destinations. But England's
capital is much more. It is a bevy of British
bobbies, an ocean of black umbrellas, and
an unconquered continuance of more than
2,000 years of history. A city that loves to
be explored, London beckons with great
museums, royal pageantry, and historic
delights: call on the Duke of Wellington's
house, track Jack the Ripper's shadow in
Whitechapel. East End, West End, you'll
find London is a dickens of a place.

Updated by
Jacqueline
Brown and
Anna Jefferys

ONDON IS AN ANCIENT CITY whose history greets you at every turn. To gain a sense of its continuity, stand on Waterloo Bridge at the hour of sunset. To the east, the great globe of St. Paul's Cathedral glows golden in the fading sunlight as it has since the 17th century, still majestic amid the towers of glass and steel that hem it in. To the west stand the mock-medieval ramparts of Westminster, home to the "Mother of Parliaments," which has met here or hereabouts since the 1250s. Past them both snakes the swift, dark Thames, as it flowed past the first Roman settlement nearly 2,000 years ago.

For much of its history, innumerable epigrams and observations have been coined about London by both her enthusiasts and detractors. The great 18th-century author and wit Samuel Johnson said that a man who is tired of London is tired of life. Oliver Wendell Holmes said, "No person can be said to know London. The most that anyone can claim is that he knows something of it." Simply stated, London is one of the most interesting places on earth. There is no other place like it in its agglomeration of architectural sins and sudden intervention of almost rural sights, in its medley of styles, in its mixture of the green loveliness of parks and the modern gleam of neon. Thankfully, the old London of Queen Anne and Georgian architecture can still be discovered under the hasty routine of later additions.

Discovering it takes a bit of work, however. Modern-day London still largely reflects its medieval layout, a willfully difficult tangle of streets. This swirl of spaghetti will be totally confusing to anyone brought up on the rigidity of a grid system. Even Londoners, most of whom own a copy of the indispensable A–Z street finder (they come under different names), get lost in their own city. But London's bewildering street pattern will be a plus for the visitor who wants to experience its indefinable historic atmosphere. London is a walker's city and will repay every moment you spend exploring on foot. The visitor to London who wants to penetrate beyond the crust of popular knowledge is well advised not only to visit St. Paul's Cathedral and the Tower but also to set aside some of his or her limited time for random wandering. Walk in the city's back streets and mews, around Park Lane and Kensington. Pass up Buckingham Palace for Kew, the smallest royal palace, beautifully situated in the botanical gardens. Take in the National Gallery, but don't forget London's "time machine" museums, such as the 19th-century homes of Linley Sambourne and Sir John Soane. For out-and-out glamour, pay a call on the palatial Wallace Collection and Apsley House, the historic abode of the Duke of Wellington. Abandon the city's standard-issue chain stores to discover unique shopping emporiums, such as the gentlemen's outfitters of St. James's. In such ways can you best visualize the shape or, rather, the various shapes of Old London, a curious city that engulfed its own past for the sake of modernity but still lives and breathes the air of history.

Today, that sense of modernity is stronger than ever. Everyone is talking about swinging-again London. It is still, as *Vanity Fair* recently proclaimed, "the coolest, hottest city in the world." Millennium fever left its trophies on the capital—a panoply of new buildings, none larger than the Millennium Dome—and London is now more than ever the *only* place to be, as *Newsweek* declared. The boom economy of the mid-'90s helped the city's art, style, fashion, and dining scenes make headlines around the world. London's chefs have become superstars; its fashion designers have conquered Paris (John Galliano, Alexander McQueen, and Stella McCartney hold the reins at Dior, Givenchy, and Chloë); avant-garde artists have caused waves at the august Royal

Academy of Arts; the city's raging after-hours scene is packed with music mavens ready to catch the next big thing; and the theater (including the National Theatre) continues its tradition of radical, shocking productions, which barely seem to turn most hairs. Even Shakespeare is ready for the millennium: the Bard's own, reborn Globe—the fabled "Wooden O"—is going swimmingly on the banks of the Thames just 200 yards from where it stood in the 16th century. Tellingly, when the troupe here presents *Two Gentlemen of Verona*, cast members even sport Ray-Ban sunglasses and sneakers.

On the other hand, while the outward shapes may be altered and the inner spirit may be warmer—the 1997 funeral of Diana, Princess of Wales, was far removed from the conventional picture of a somewhat staid city of people who don't display their emotions—the bedrock of London's character and tradition remains the same. Deep down, Britons have a sense of the continuity of history. Even in the modern metropolis, some things rarely change. The British bobby is alive and well. The tall, red, double-decker buses still lumber from stop to stop, though their aesthetic match at street level, the glossy red telephone booths, is slowly disappearing. And, of course, teatime is still a hallowed part of the day, with, if you search hard enough, toasted crumpets still honeycombed with sweet butter. Then, of course, there is that greatest living link with the past—the Royal Family. Don't let the tag of "typical tourist" stop you from enjoying the pageantry of the Windsors, one of the greatest free shows in the world. Line up for the Changing of the Guard and poke into the Royal Mews for a look at the Coronation Coach. Pomp reaches its zenith in mid-June when the queen celebrates her official birthday with a parade called Trooping the Colour. Royalty-watching is by no means restricted to fascinated foreigners. You only have to open London's tabloid newspapers to read reports of the latest rumors. Then again, more and more people are feeling that what goes on inside Buckingham Palace is no one's affair but the queen's.

In the end, the London you'll discover will surely include some of our enthusiastic recommendations, but be prepared to be taken by surprise as well. The best that a great city has to offer often comes in unexpected ways. Armed with energy and curiosity, and the practical information and helpful hints in the following pages, you can be sure of one thing: to quote Dr. Johnson again, you'll be able to find "in London all that life can afford."

New & Noteworthy

From the vantage point of mid-2000—and after the frenzy (some would say "yawn") of the heralding of Y2K—it seems that the millennium bug did not bite London. All the exciting new works and events (and more importantly, transport to them) that should have opened, did, and in style. The epicenter of the celebrations, the awesome Millennium Dome in Greenwich, opened on December 31, 1999. The Dome's exhibits will close December 31, 2000, and plans for what to do with the enormous monument to the new millennium remained thoroughly unsettled at press time—in fact, the building was up for sale. The new lines of underground tube transport to and from the millennium borough almost didn't make it, after months of industrial turbulence and setbacks, but the directive from the top was to get it done whatever the cost. Now, Londoners on their way to Greenwich have rail and tube alternatives to that time-honored mode of transport called old Father Thames and the ferry from the new streamlined Charing Cross Pier, now called Embankment Pier. This new landmark was the brainchild of the "new" Labour party, propelled by the prime

Central London

Belsize Rd.
Abbey Rd.
Acacia Rd.
St. John's Wood Ter.
Crowndale Rd.
Pancras
Abercorn Pl.
Wellington Rd.
Circus Rd.
Prince Albert Rd.
Regent's Park
Eversholt St.
Maida Vale
Randolph Rd.
Hall Rd.
Grove End Rd.
St. John's Wood
Outer Circle
Inner Circle
Chester Rd.
Albany St.
Hampstead Rd.
Euston Station
Clifton Rd.
Bloomfield Rd.
Edgware Rd.
Lisson Grove
Park Rd.
Balcombe St.
Dorset Square
Marylebone Rd.
MARYLEBONE
Euston Rd.
BLOOMS
Gower
Harrow Rd.
Marylebone Flyover
Seymour Pl.
Gloucester Pl.
Baker St.
Marylebone High St.
Harley St.
Portland Pl.
Gt. Portland St.
Maple St.
Tottenham Court Rd.
Telecom Tower
Berners St.
Bishop's Bridge Rd.
Paddington Station
Praed St.
Sussex Gdns.
Edgware Rd.
Manchester Square
Wigmore St.
Oxford Oxford Circus
SOHO
St.
Queensway
Craven Hill
BAYSWATER
Oxford St.
Duke St.
New Bond St.
Shaftesb
Brewer St.
Bayswater Rd.
N. Carriage Dr.
Grosvenor Square
Brook St.
Grosvenor St.
Regent St.
Jermyn St.
Piccadilly Circus
Regent St.
market
Bayswater Rd.
U.S. Embassy
Berkeley Square
Sth. Audley St.
Royal Academy
Dover St.
Pall Mall
Kensington Gardens
Hyde Park
The Serpentine
Park Lane
MAYFAIR
Curzon St.
Piccadilly
Green Park
St. James's
St. James's Park
The Mall
Round Pond
W. Carriage Dr.
Kensington Palace
S. Carriage Rd.
Knightsbridge
Constitution Hill
Buckingham Palace
Birdcage Walk
Kensington Rd.
Kensington Gore
Kensington Rd.
Royal Albert Hall
Sloane St.
Belgrave Square
Grosvenor Pl.
Victoria St.
Horseferry Rd.
Palace Gate
Prince Consort Rd.
Exhibition Rd.
Science Museum
Victoria and Albert Museum
Brompton Rd.
Pont St.
BELGRAVIA
Eaton Square
Buckingham Palace Rd.
Victoria Station
VICTORIA
Regency St.
Cromwell Rd.
Queen's Gate
Natural History Museum
KNIGHTSBRIDGE
Cadogan Pl.
Wilton Rd.
Vauxhall Br.
Gloucester Rd.
Old Brompton Rd.
Sloane Ave.
Warwick Way
Belgrove Rd.
SOUTH KENSINGTON
Fulham Rd.
Sydney St.
CHELSEA
King's Rd.
Royal Hospital Rd.
Pimlico Rd.
Lupus St.
PIMLICO
Redcliffe Gdns.
Finborough Rd.
Fulham Rd.
Old Church St.
Oakley St.
Chelsea Br. Rd.
Grosvenor Rd.
Redcliffe Gdns.
Beaufort St.
Cheyne Walk
Chelsea Embankment
Chelsea Br.
Nine Elms
River Thames
Battersea Park

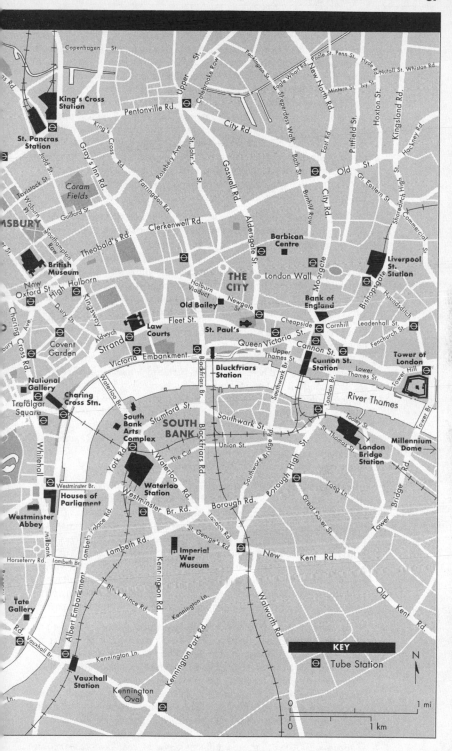

Copenhagen St.

King's Cross Station

Pentonville Rd.

St. Pancras Station

City Rd.

Upper St.

Colebrooke Row

Poole St. Penn St. Hyde Rd. Nutall St. Whiston Rd.

Packington St.

Eagle Wharf Rd. Shepherdess Walk

New North Rd.

Mintern St. Ivy St.

Hoxton St. Kingsland Rd. Hackney Rd.

Shoreditch High St.

Commercial

King's Cross Rd.

Gray's Inn Rd.

Rosebery Ave. St. John's St.

Goswell Rd.

East Rd. Pitfield St.

Old St.

Gt. Eastern St.

Judd St.

Tavistock St. Woburn

Southampton Row

Coram Fields

Guilford St.

Farringdon Rd.

Clerkenwell Rd.

Aldersgate St.

Bunhill Row

City Rd.

Moorgate

Bishopsgate

Liverpool St. Station

Houndsditch

BLOOMSBURY

Theobald's Rd.

British Museum

New Oxford St. High Holborn

Kingsway

Drury Ln.

Holborn Viaduct

THE CITY

London Wall

Barbican Centre

London Wall

Bank of England

Leadenhall St.

Fenchurch St.

Old Bailey

Newgate St.

Cheapside

Cornhill

Charing Cross Rd.

Covent Garden

Aldwych

Strand

Law Courts

Fleet St.

St. Paul's

Queen Victoria St.

Cannon St.

Tower of London

Tower Hill

National Gallery

Charing Cross Stn.

Victoria Embankment

Waterloo Br.

Blackfriars Br.

Blackfriars Station

Upper Thames St.

Cannon St. Station

Lower Thames St.

London Br.

Southwark Br.

Tower Br.

River Thames

Trafalgar Square

South Bank Arts Complex

Stamford St.

SOUTH BANK

Southwark St.

Blackfriars Rd.

Tooley St.

Millennium Dome →

Whitehall

York Rd.

The Cut

Waterloo Rd.

Union St.

Southwark Bridge Rd.

Borough High St.

St. Thomas St.

London Bridge Station

Westminster Br.

Waterloo Station

Westminster Br. Rd.

Borough Rd.

Long Ln.

Great Dover St.

Tower Bridge Rd.

Houses of Parliament

Westminster Abbey

Lambeth Palace Rd.

Westminster Br. Rd.

Kennington Rd.

Lambeth Rd.

Imperial War Museum

St. George's Rd.

Lovelby Rd.

New

Kent Rd.

Old Kent Rd.

Horseferry Rd.

Lambeth Br.

Millbank

Tate Gallery

Albert Embankment

Black Prince Rd.

Kennington Ln.

Kennington Park Rd.

Walworth Rd.

Vauxhall Br.

Vauxhall Station

Kennington Ln.

Kennington Oval

N

0   1 mi

0   1 km

minister, Tony Blair. His energetic enthusiasm is reflected in the exciting projects unveiled by some of London's most venerable museums.

Every museum, in fact, has been part of this whirlwind of activity (and some are still in the thick of it). Classicism spearheaded by innovation is the byword for the offerings: the glittering new Great Court of the British Museum; the latest technological gizmos at the staid British Library; the state-of-the-art new branch of the Tate Gallery—"Tate Modern" (with a new look at the old Tate, or "Tate Britain")—now installed at the futuristic Bankside Power Station; the multimillion-pound makeovers of the Sadlers Wells Theatre and the Royal Opera House; the new face of the National Portrait Gallery; and the scintillating space-age Earth Galleries at the Natural History Museum. Thanks to these attractions, swinging-again London now outranks its neighbors as Europe's most future-forward spot.

The big talking point, in every sense of the word, at the beginning of last year, was the **Millennium Dome.** Prominently close to Greenwich and its association with time and the meridian line, it played host to the turn of the century in grand pyrotechnic style. Whether it was one of the most expensive multimillion-pound white elephants in history or a great achievement will probably never be reconciled. In terms of a great day out, visiting the 14 theme zones is certainly a memorable experience, if you are in London before the last day of 2000.

Other major building projects in London include the new **Tate Modern,** being installed in the former Bankside Power Station. Culturally, London is making a bid to catch up with its overseas rivals in terms of modern art, and the word here is that big is beautiful—opening in May 2000, the Tate Modern will house the huge numbers of works of art formerly hidden from public view due to lack of space in the old Millbank Gallery. Also on the south side of the Thames is the **British Airways London Eye**—which finally wheeled into action in February 2000. Although it missed the magic of the new year opening, no less excitement was generated when the public finally got to see the unrivaled views of London and beyond from the see-through, podlike capsules.

Among London's other attractions, check out the new **British Library,** which already offers selected services to researchers. The less academic can revel in its public-friendly offerings: the Italianate piazza-style entrance, the touch-screen access to subjects ranging from the Magna Carta to mega rock stars, and the glass edifice that houses King George's library. At the **Victoria & Albert Museum,** the Spiral, a dramatic new exhibit space designed by Daniel Libeskind, is now slated to rise with "a facade forming a glittering non-repeating fractal pattern of great mathematical sophistication and beauty." At press time the building has a go-ahead with a projected opening date of 2004. Watch this space.

At the staid bastion of the **British Museum,** claim and counterclaim about the Elgin Marbles flew between the Greek and British historical experts—in heated discussions in the very gallery containing the contentious spoils—at the close of 1999. The Brits refuse to return the marbles. These controversial treasures are now shown in a grand, modern setting and their history brought up-to-date with a tactile, interactive display in the Parthenon Galleries. There are other new galleries to house the defunct Museum of Mankind ethnographic collection, and the whole place will be blasted into the future (projected completion date is autumn 2000) with the magnificent glassed Great Court palazzo entrance—the grandiose plan of architects Foster and Partners—for an enclosed area for restaurant, bookshop, information, and exhibition space. The beautifully restored Reading Room will be at the core, under the largest glass roof in London (about the equivalent of 200 greenhouses). The **Natural History Museum** has opened its biggest project since it opened in 1881, the Earth Galleries, which examine earthly phenomena, like volcanoes, tornadoes, and deserts, and then take you out into space and onto other planets.

Now on display at **Somerset House** (☞ Courtauld Institute of Art, *below*) are ancient treasures from a royal palace, recently discovered under the parking lot. Also at Somerset House in 2000, members of the public have for the first time been given access to the original navy chambers. The **Tower of London** is the top tourist attraction year after year. Its latest (and 10 years in the making) enhancement is the redisplay of the Royal Armouries in the White Tower. All you ever wanted to know about the increasing size of Henry VIII's armored suits is here. And finally, polished and ready to meet the world after four years' restorative work, the **Albert Memorial** in Kensington Gardens was revealed in all its newly gilded glory in late 1998. The George Gilbert Scott monument has not been seen in its true color since 1915, when it was given a dull coat of black to avoid its becoming a moonlit landmark for nearby Kensington Palace, a target for zeppelins. Amid a fanfare of floodlighted fireworks, the queen declared it to be magnificent. Quite so. Like the Albert Memorial, all of London is putting on a bold new face worthy of the momentum of the new millennium.

White Card Museum Pass

If museums are at the top of your sightseeing list, check out the **White Card** (☎ 020/7923–0807), which offers free admission into 15 major museums for one basic fee. The museums are Apsley House; the art gallery at the Barbican; Courtauld Institute of Art (Somerset House); Design Museum; Hayward Gallery; Imperial War Museum; London Transport Museum; Museum of London; Museum of the Moving Image; National Maritime Museum, Old Royal Observatory, and Queen's House in Greenwich; Natural History Museum; Royal Academy of Arts; Science Museum; Theatre Museum; and Victoria and Albert Museum. The basic fee is £16, for three days; also available are seven-day tickets and family tickets. The White Card is available at any of the museums listed above.

WESTMINSTER AND ROYAL LONDON

This tour might be called "London for Beginners." If you went no farther than these few acres, you would see many of the most famous sights, from the Houses of Parliament, Big Ben, Westminster Abbey, and Buckingham Palace to two of the world's greatest art collections, housed in the National and Tate galleries. You can truly call this area Royal London, as it is neatly bounded by the triangle of streets that make up the route that the queen usually takes when journeying from Buckingham Palace to the Abbey or to the Houses of Parliament on state occasions. The three points on this royal triangle are Trafalgar Square, Westminster, and Buckingham Palace. If you have time to visit only one part of London, undoubtedly this should be it. There is as much history in these few acres as in many entire cities, as the statues of kings, queens, soldiers, and statesmen that stand guard at every corner attest—this is concentrated sightseeing, so pace yourself. The main drawback to sightseeing here is that half the world is doing it at the same time. So, even if you're tired after a long day on your feet, try to come back in the evening, after the crowds have dispersed, to drink in the serenity and grandeur at your leisure. You'll get to see it in a new light, literally, as much of Royal London is spectacularly floodlighted at night.

Westminster is by far the younger of the capital's two centers, post-dating the City by some 1,000 years. Edward the Confessor put it on the map when he packed up his court from its cramped City quarters and moved it west a couple of miles, founding the abbey church of Westminster—the minster west of the City—in 1050. Subsequent kings continued to hold court here until Henry VIII decamped to Whitehall Palace in 1512, leaving Westminster to the politicians. And here they are still, not in the palace, which burned almost to the ground in 1834, but in the Victorian mock-Gothic Houses of Parliament, whose 320-ft-high Clock Tower is as much a symbol of London as the Eiffel Tower is of Paris.

Numbers in the text correspond to numbers in the margin and on the Westminster and Royal London map.

A Good Walk

Trafalgar Square ① is the obvious place to start for several reasons. It is the geographical core of London and home to many political demonstrations, a raucous New Year's Eve party, and the highest concentration of bus stops and pigeons in the capital. After taking in the instantly identifiable **Nelson's Column** ② in the center (read about the area on a plaque marking its 150th anniversary), head for the **National Gallery** ③, on the north side—this is Britain's greatest trove of masterpieces. Detour around the corner to see the **National Portrait Gallery** ④—a parade of the famous that can be very rewarding to anyone interested in what makes the British tick. East of the National Gallery, still on Trafalgar Square, see the much-loved church of **St. Martin-in-the-Fields** ⑤; then, stepping through grand **Admiralty Arch** ⑥ down on the southwest corner, enter the royal pink road, the **Mall,** with St. James's Park on your left. On your right is the **Institute of Contemporary Arts** ⑦, known as the ICA and housed in the great Regency architect John Nash's **Carlton House Terrace** ⑧. At the foot of the Mall is one of London's most famous sights, **Buckingham Palace** ⑨, home, of course, to the monarch of the land and punctuated by the ornate, white marble **Queen Victoria Memorial** ⑩. Turning left and left again, almost doubling back, follow the southern perimeter of St. James's Park around Birdcage Walk, passing the **Queen's Gallery** ⑪—in the midst of complete renovation and scheduled to reopen in 2002, with changing exhibitions from Her Majesty's vast art collection—and the HQ of the Queen's Guard, the **Wellington Barracks** ⑫ on your right and, in turn, the hulking Home Office and **Queen Anne's Gate** ⑬. Cross Horse Guards Road at the eastern edge of the park and walk down Great George Street, with **St. Margaret's Church** ⑭ on your right. Continue across Parliament Square to come to another of the great sights of London, the **Houses of Parliament** ⑮. A mock-medieval extravaganza down to the last detail (neo-Gothic umbrella stands), it was designed by two celebrated Victorian-era architects, built along the Thames, and includes the famous Clock Tower, known the world over as Big Ben. Try to stick around for the sonorous chiming of the bell: for millions of citizens of the British empire, the sound of Big Ben's chimes is a link with the heart and soul of the commonwealth. A clockwise turn around the square brings you to yet another major landmark, breathtaking **Westminster Abbey** ⑯. Complete the circuit and head north up Whitehall, passing the **Cabinet War Rooms** ⑰, where you'll see a simple monolith in the middle of the street—the Cenotaph (☞ Downing Street, *below*), designed by Edwin Lutyens in 1920 in commemoration of the 1918 armistice. The gated alley on your left is **Downing Street** ⑱, where England's modest "White House" stands at Number 10. Soon after that, you pass **Horse Guards Parade** ⑲, the setting for the queen's birthday celebration, Trooping the Colour, with the perfect classical Inigo Jones

Banqueting House ⑳, scene of Charles I's execution, opposite. It's well worth it to backtrack a little ways down Whitehall and Abington Street, to Millbank and the **Tate Britain** ㉑, the new name for the expanded collection that can now be displayed at the site of the old Tate Gallery—now that the new Tate Modern at Bankside Power Station branch has recently opened in Southwark.

TIMING

You could achieve this walk of roughly 3 mi in just over an hour, but you could just as easily spend a week's vacation on this route alone. Allow as much time as you can for the two great museums—the National Gallery requires at *least* two hours; the National Portrait Gallery can be whizzed round in less than one. Westminster Abbey can take half a day—especially in summer, when lines are long—both to get in and to get around. In summer, you can get inside Buckingham Palace, too, a half day's operation increased to a whole day if you see the Royal Mews and the Queen's Gallery or the Guards Museum. If the Changing of the Guard is a priority, make sure you time this walk correctly.

HOW TO GET THERE

This is an easy neighborhood to access, especially if you start at Trafalgar Square, where many buses stop. The central neighborhood tube stop, Charing Cross (on the Jubilee, Northern, and Bakerloo lines), exits at the beginning of Northumberland Avenue, on the southeast corner. Practically all buses stop around here, including Buses 3, 9, 11, 12, 16, 24, 29, 53, 88, 139, and 159. Just to the north of Trafalgar Square on Charing Cross Road is Leicester Square tube stop (on the Northern and Piccadilly lines), which is just behind the national galleries. Alternative tube stations on the south side are St. James's Park (on the District and Circle lines), which is the best for Buckingham Palace, or the next stop, Westminster, which deposits you right by the bridge, in the shadow of Big Ben.

Sights to See

⑥ Admiralty Arch. Gateway to the Mall—no, not an indoor shopping center but one of the very grand avenues of London—this is one of London's stateliest urban set pieces. Situated on the southwest corner of Trafalgar Square, the arch, which was named after the adjacent Royal Navy headquarters, was designed in 1910 by Sir Aston Webb as part of a ceremonial route to Buckingham Palace. As you pass under the enormous triple archway—though not through the central arch, opened only for state occasions— the atmosphere changes along with the color of the road, for you are exiting frenetic Trafalgar Square and entering the Mall (rhymes with shall)—the elegant avenue that leads directly to the palace. ⊠ *The Mall, Cockspur St., Trafalgar Sq., SW1. Tube: Charing Cross.*

⑳ Banqueting House. This is all that remains today of the Tudor Palace of Whitehall, which was (according to one foreign visitor) "ill-built, and nothing but a heap of houses." James I commissioned Inigo Jones (1573–1652), one of England's great architects, to do a grand remodeling. Influenced, during a sojourn in Tuscany, by Andrea Palladio's work, Jones brought Palladian sophistication and purity back to London with him. The resulting graceful and disciplined classical style of Banqueting House must have stunned its early occupants. In the quiet vaults beneath, James would escape the stresses of being a sovereign with a glass or two. James I's son, Charles I, enhanced the interior by employing the Flemish painter Peter Paul Rubens to glorify his father all over the ceiling. As it turned out, these allegorical paintings, depicting a wise monarch being received into heaven, were the last thing Charles saw before he was beheaded by Cromwell's Parliamentarians in 1649.

Westminster and Royal London

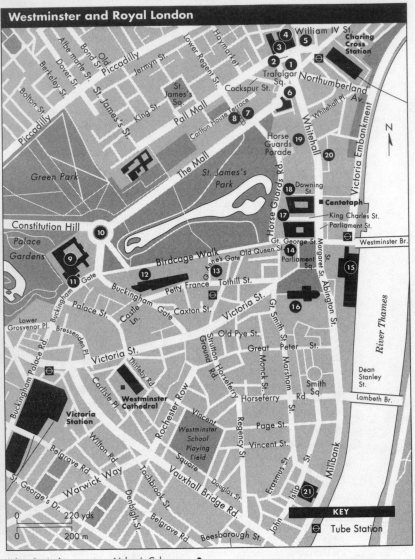

Admiralty Arch **6**

Banqueting
House **20**

Buckingham
Palace **9**

Cabinet War
Rooms **17**

Carlton House
Terrace **8**

Downing Street **18**

House Guards
Parade **19**

Houses of
Parliament **15**

Institute of
Contemporary Arts
(ICA) **7**

National Gallery . . . **3**

National Portrait
Gallery **4**

Nelson's Column . . . **2**

Queen Anne's
Gate **13**

Queen Victoria
Memorial **10**

Queen's Gallery . . . **11**

St. Margaret's
Church **14**

St. Martin-in-the-
Fields **5**

Tate Britain **21**

Trafalger Square **1**

Wellington
Barracks **12**

Westminster
Abbey **16**

But his son, Charles II, was able to celebrate the restoration of the monarchy in this same setting 20 years later. ⊠ *Whitehall, SW1,* ☎ *020/7930–4179.* ⊡ *£3.60, includes free audio guide.* ⊙ *Mon.–Sat. 10–5; closed on short notice for banquets, so call first. Tube: Westminster, Embankment, Charing Cross.*

⑨ Buckingham Palace. Supreme among the symbols of London, indeed of Britain generally and of the Royal Family, Buckingham Palace tops many must-see lists—although the building itself is no masterpiece and has housed the monarch only since Victoria (1819–1901) moved here from Kensington Palace at her accession in 1837. Its great gray bulk sums up the imperious splendor of so much of the city: stately, magnificent, and ponderous. When Victoria moved in, the place was a mess. George IV, at *his* accession in 1820, had fancied the idea of moving to Buckingham House, his parents' former home, and had employed John Nash, as usual, to remodel it. The government authorized only "repair and improvement"; Nash, that tireless spendthrift, overspent his budget by about half a million pounds. George died, Nash was dismissed, and Edward Blore finished the building, adding the now familiar east front (facing the Mall). Victoria arrived to faulty drains and sticky doors and windows, but they did not mar her affection for the place, nor that of her son, Edward VII. The Portland stone facade dates only from 1913 (the same stone used for the Victoria Memorial outside the Palace, and Admiralty Arch at the foot of the Mall), and the interior was renovated and redecorated only after it sustained World War II bomb damage. Indeed, compared to other great London residences, this is very much a Johnny-come-lately affair.

The palace contains 19 state rooms, 52 royal and guest bedrooms, 188 staff bedrooms, 92 offices, and 78 bathrooms—a prerequisite for the 450 people who work there, and the mere 50,000 who are entertained during the year. The state rooms are where much of the business of royalty is played out—investitures, state banquets, and receptions for the great and good. The royal apartments are in the north wing; when the queen is in residence, the royal standard is raised. Until fairly recently all the quarters were off-limits to the public, but funds to pay for the reparations after the 1992 fire at Windsor Castle had to be found. And so the state rooms are on show from August to early October, a period when the Royal Family is away. A visit to the palace's west wing is a fascinating glimpse into another world: the fabulously gilded interiors are not merely museum pieces but pomp and pageantry at work. A tour starts from the Ambassadors' Court entrance, through to the **Entrée**, where portraits of past kings look down. The classical tone is set with Ionic columns in honeyed Bath stone, marble pillars in cool Carrara white, fine French and English furniture, and Chinese vases. Once through the **Grand Hall,** the **Grand Staircase,** and **Guard Room** (too small for the royal bodyguards—Yeoman of the Guard and Gentlemen-at-Arms in their traditional red and gold uniforms), the superlatives for the richness and elegance before your eyes could begin to wane. Prepare to be completely and utterly gilded out as Nash's ornate designs unfold through the numerous drawing rooms—each more jaw-dropping and neck-craning than the last—decorated with awesome ceilings and chandeliers, and magnificent objects brought from the Prince Regent's original palatial home, Carlton House. (Some of the most precious Sèvres porcelain in the world found its way here after the French Revolution.) The **Throne Room** is opulent with gilded Baroque decor and the original 1953 Coronation throne chairs. Queen Victoria used to hold balls here, but today it is the backdrop for royal wedding photographs and presentations. By now, when eyes are becoming gilded, the **Picture Gallery** is a restful feast of renowned art. The collection was begun by Charles I, and the works are periodically rearranged. Highlights among the many masterpieces are pieces by Rubens, Vermeer, Van Dyck, Cuyp, and Canaletto. The state rooms are graced with some of Her Majesty's most famous old-master paintings, but other artwork is sometimes on view in special temporary exhibitions held at the **Queen's Gallery** (☞ *below*), near the south side of the palace (closed until 2002 for a grand new entrance and internal renovation for increased exhibition space and updated facilities). The palace tour continues through more galleries and drawing rooms filled with exquisite paintings and tapestries, culminating with the **State Dining Room** and its overly elaborate Blore ceiling. The table is sadly not set for a banquet with its usual gilt, silver, and gold ware, but a solitary pair of ewers stands to attention.

From here there are views across the sweeping gardens. But without an invitation to one of the queen's summer garden parties, you won't see more of the magnificent 45-acre grounds. The **Changing of the Guard,** with all the ceremony monarchists and children adore, remains one of London's best free shows and culminates in front of the palace. Marching to live music, the Queen's Guard proceeds up the Mall from St. James's Palace to Buckingham Palace. Shortly afterward, the new guard approaches from Wellington Barracks via Birdcage Walk. Once the old and new guards are in the forecourt, the old guard symbolically hands over the keys to the palace. The ceremony usually takes place on schedule (☞ *below*), but the guards sometimes cancel owing to bad weather; check the signs in the forecourt or phone. Get there by 10:30 AM to grab the best viewing section at the gate facing the palace, since most of the hoopla takes place behind the railings in the forecourt. There are those who may scoff at this clockwork ceremony, but for the Briton who treasures the continuity of history, pageantry means permanence. Be sure to prebook tour reservations of the palace with a credit card by phone. ⊠ *Buckingham Palace Rd., SW1,* ☎ *020/7839–1377; 020/7799–2331 24-hr information; 020/7321–2233 credit-card reservations.* ▣ *£10.* ☉ *Early Aug.–early Oct., daily 9:30–4:15 (confirm dates, which are subject to Queen's mandate). Changing of the Guard Apr.–July, daily 11:30 AM; Aug.–Mar., alternating days only 11:30 AM. AE, MC, V. Tube: St. James's Park, Victoria.*

⑰ Cabinet War Rooms. It was from this small maze of 17 bomb-proof underground rooms—in back of the hulking Foreign Office—that Britain's World War II fortunes were directed. During air raids, the Cabinet met here—the Cabinet Room is still arranged as if a meeting were about to convene; in the Map Room, the Allied campaign is charted; the Prime Minister's Room holds the desk from which Winston Churchill (1874–1965) made his morale-boosting broadcasts; and the Telephone Room has his hot line to FDR. The great man only slept here on a number of occasions; he preferred the comfort of Downing Street, even at the height of the German blitz. ⊠ *Clive Steps, King Charles St., SW1,* ☎ *020/7930–6961.* ▣ *£4.80.* ☉ *Apr.–Sept., daily 9:30–5:15; Oct.–Mar., daily 10–5:15. Tube: Westminster.*

⑧ Carlton House Terrace. This is a glorious example of Regency architect John Nash's genius. Between 1812 and 1830, under the patronage of George IV (Prince Regent until George III's death in 1820), Nash was the architect for the grand scheme of Regent Street (☞ *below*) and the sweep of neoclassical houses encircling Regent's Park. The Prince Regent, who lived at Carlton House, had plans to build a country villa at Primrose Hill (to the north of the park), connected by a grand road—hence Regent Street. Even though it was considered a most extravagant building for its time, Carlton House was demolished after the prince's

JUST REMEMBER TO ADDRESS HER AS "YOUR MAJESTY"

YOU'VE SEEN BIG BEN, THE TOWER, and Westminster Abbey. But somehow you feel something is missing: a close encounter with Britain's most famous attraction—Her actual Majesty. True, you've toured Buckingham Palace, but the Windsors are notorious for never standing at a window (the London *Times* once suggested that the palace mount a full-scale mechanical procession of royal figures to parade in and out of the palace, on the hour, in cuckoo-clock fashion), and the odds are that you won't be bumping into Elizabeth II on the tube. But at a surprisingly wide variety of royal events, you can catch a glimpse of her, along with many other Windsor personages. Fairs and fetes, polo matches and horse races, first nights and banquets galore—her date book is crammed with such events and, on one of them—who knows?—you might even meet her on a royal walkabout.

The queen and the Royal Family, in fact, attend approximately 400 functions a year, and if you want to know what she and the rest of the Royal Family are doing on any given date, turn to the *Court Circular*, printed in the major London dailies. You might catch Prince Charles launching a ship, Princess Margaret attending a film premiere, or the queen at a hospital's ribbon-cutting ceremony. But most visitors want to see the Royals in all their dazzling pomp and circumstance. For this, the best bet is the second Saturday in June, when the Trooping the Colour is usually held to celebrate the queen's official birthday. This spectacular parade begins when she leaves Buckingham Palace in her carriage and rides down the Mall to arrive at Horse Guards Parade at 11 exactly. (Well, occasionally the clock has been timed to strike as she arrives and not vice versa!) If you wish to obtain one of the 7,000 seats (no more than two per request, distributed by ballot), enclose a letter and stamped, self-addressed envelope or International Reply Coupon—from January to February 28 only—to **Ticket Office** (✉ Headquarters Household Division, Horse Guards, London SW1A 2AX, ☎ 020/7414-2479). Of course, you can also just line up along the Mall with your binoculars!

Another time you can catch the queen in all her regalia is when she and the Duke of Edinburgh ride in state to Westminster to open the Houses of Parliament. The famous gilded coach that became such an icon of fairy-tale glamour at Elizabeth II's coronation parades from Buckingham Palace to Parliament, escorted by the brilliantly uniformed and superbly mounted Household Cavalry—on a clear day, it is to be hoped, for this ceremony takes place in late October or early November, depending on the exigencies of Parliament. As the queen enters the Houses, the air shakes with the booming of heavy guns, and all London knows that the democratic processes that have so long protected England from oppression have once again been renewed with all their age-old ceremony. But perhaps the nicest time to see the queen is during Royal Ascot, held at the racetrack near Windsor Castle—just a short train ride out of London—usually during the third week of June (Tuesday–Friday). After several races, the queen invariably walks down to the paddock on a special path, greeting race-goers as she proceeds. Americans wishing a seat in the Royal Enclosure should apply to the **American Embassy** (✉ 24 Grosvenor Square, London W1), before the end of March. But remember: you must be sponsored by two guests who have attended Ascot at least seven times before! (Fashion note: the big party hats come out on Ladies Day, normally the Thursday of the meet.) If you're lucky enough to meet the queen (contrary to her stodgy public persona, she's actually a great wit), just remember to address her as "Your Majesty."

accession to the throne. Nash's Carlton House Terrace, no less imposing, with white-stucco facades and massive Corinthian columns, was
built in its place. It was a smart address, needless to say, and one that
Prime Ministers Gladstone (1856) and Palmerston (1857–75) enjoyed.
Today Carlton House Terrace is home to the Royal College of Pathol-
ogists (Number 2), the Royal Society (Number 6, whose members numbered Isaac Newton and Charles Darwin), the Turf Club (Number 5),
and, at Number 12, the **Institute of Contemporary Arts** (☞ *below*), better known as the ICA. ⊠ *The Mall, W1. Tube: Charing Cross.*

⑱ Downing Street. Looking like an unassuming alley but barred by iron
gates at both its Whitehall and Horse Guards Road approaches, this
is where **Number 10 Downing Street,** London's modest version of the
White House, stands. Only three houses remain of the terrace built circa
1680 by Sir George Downing, who spent enough of his youth in America to graduate from Harvard—the second man ever to do so. **Number 11** is traditionally the residence of the chancellor of the exchequer
(secretary of the treasury), although Prime Minister Blair and his
young, growing family are installed here, having found the quarters
next door too small; **Number 12** is the party whips' office. Number
10 has officially housed the prime minister since 1732. (The gates were
former prime minister Margaret Thatcher's brainstorm.) Just south of
Downing Street, in the middle of Whitehall, you'll see the **Cenotaph,**
a stark white monolith designed in 1920 by Edward Lutyens to commemorate the 1918 armistice. On Remembrance Day (the Sunday
nearest November 11) it is strewn with red poppies to honor the dead
of both world wars and all British soldiers killed in action since, with
the first wreath laid by the queen. ⊠ *Whitehall, SW1. Tube: Westminster.*

⑲ Horse Guards Parade. Once the tiltyard of Whitehall Palace, where
jousting tournaments were held, the Horse Guards Parade is now notable mainly for the annual Trooping the Colour ceremony, in which
the queen takes the Royal Salute, her official birthday gift, on the second Saturday in June. (Like Paddington Bear, the queen has two birth-
days; her real one is on April 21.) There is pageantry galore, with
marching bands—the occasional guardsman fainting clean away from
the heat building up under his weighty busby—and throngs of onlookers.
Covering the vast expanse of the square that faces Horse Guards Road,
opposite St. James's Park at one end and Whitehall at the other, the
ceremony is televised. Visitors may also attend the queenless rehearsals
on the preceding two Saturdays. At the Whitehall facade of Horse
Guards, the changing of two mounted sentries known as the **Queen's
Life Guard** provide what may be London's most frequently exercised
photo opportunity. ⊠ *Whitehall, SW1.* ⊘ *Queen's Life Guard Ceremony Mon.–Sat. 11 AM, Sun. 10 AM. Tube: Westminster.*

★ ⑮ Houses of Parliament. Overlooking the Thames, the Houses of Parliament are, arguably, the city's most famous and photogenic sight, with
the Clock Tower—which everyone calls Big Ben—keeping watch on
the corner and Westminster Abbey ahead of you across Parliament
Square. The most romantic view of the complex is from the opposite
(south) side of the river, a vista especially dramatic at night when the
storybook spires, pinnacles, and towers of the great building are floodlighted green and gold—a fairy-tale vision only missing the presence
of Peter Pan and Wendy on their way to Never-Never Land.

The Palace of Westminster, as the complex is still properly called, was
established by Edward the Confessor during the 11th century, when
he moved his court here from the City. It has served as the seat of English administrative power, on and off, ever since. In 1512, Henry VIII
(1491–1547) abandoned it for Whitehall, and it ceased to be an offi-

cial royal residence after 1547. At the Reformation, the Royal Chapel was secularized and became the first meeting place of the Commons. The Lords settled in the White Chamber. These, along with everything but the **Jewel Tower** and **Westminster Hall,** were destroyed in 1834 when "the sticks"—the arcane abacus beneath the Lords' Chamber on which the court had kept its accounts until 1826—was incinerated, and the fire got out of hand. This great hall, with its remarkable hammer-beam roof, was the work of William the Conqueror's son, William Rufus. It is one of the largest remaining Norman halls in Europe, and its dramatic interior was the scene of the trial of Charles I.

After the 1834 fire, architects were invited to submit plans for new Houses of Parliament in the grandiose "Gothic or Elizabethan style." Charles Barry's were selected from among 97 entries, partly because Barry had invited the architect and designer Augustus Pugin to add the requisite neo-Gothic curlicues to his own Renaissance-influenced style. As you can see, it was a happy collaboration, with Barry's classical proportions offset by Pugin's ornamental flourishes—although the latter were toned down by Gilbert Scott when he rebuilt the bomb-damaged House of Commons after World War II. The two towers were Pugin's work. The **Clock Tower,** now virtually the symbol of London, was completed in 1858 after long delays due to bickering over the clock's design. (Barry designed the faces himself in the end.) It contains the 13-ton bell known as Big Ben, which chimes the hour (and the quarters). Some say Ben was "Big Ben" Caunt, heavyweight champ; others, Sir Benjamin Hall, the far-from-slim Westminster building works commissioner. At the southwest end of the main Parliament building is the 336-ft-high **Victoria Tower,** newly agleam from its recent restoration and cleaning. The rest of the complex was scrubbed down some years ago; the revelation of the honey stone under the dowdy, smog-blackened facades, which seemed almost symbolic at the time, cheered London up no end.

The building itself is a series of chambers, lobbies, and offices, joined by more than 2 mi of passages, which cover 8 acres. There are two Houses, the Lords and the Commons. The former has undergone a radical reform by Mr. Blair's Labour party. On November 5 (somewhat symbolically, on the night that Guy Fawkes tried to blow up the Houses of Parliament in 1605), more than 100 hereditary peers (earls, lords, viscounts, and other aristocrats) failed to win the right to continue to be elected to their seats in the House of Lords. This much-downsized House of Lords is part of the Labour Party's drive to democratize and modernize the ancient institution. The House of Commons is made up of 659 elected Members of Parliament (MPs). The party with the most MPs forms the government, its leader becoming prime minister; other parties form the Opposition. Since 1642, when Charles I tried to have five MPs arrested, no monarch has been allowed into the House of Commons. The state opening of Parliament in November consequently takes place in the House of Lords. Visitors aren't allowed many places in the Houses of Parliament, though the Visitors' Galleries of the House of Commons do afford a view of the best free show in London, staged in the world's most renowned ego chamber. The opposing banks of green leather benches seat only 437 MPs—not that this is much of a problem, since absentees far outnumber the diligent. When MPs vote, they exit by the "Aye" or the "No" corridor, thus being counted by the party whips. When they speak, it is not directly to each other but through the Speaker, who also decides who will get the floor each day. Elaborate procedures notwithstanding, debate is often drowned out by the amazingly raucous and immature jeers and insults familiar to TV viewers for more than a decade, when cameras were first allowed into the House of Commons.

Other public areas of the 1,100-room labyrinth are rather magnificently got up in high neo-Gothic style and punctuated with stirring frescoes commissioned by Prince Albert. You pass these en route to the Visitors' Galleries—if, that is, you are patient enough to wait in line for hours (the Lords line is shorter) or have applied in advance for the special "line of route" tour (open only to overseas visitors) by writing to the **Parliamentary Education Unit** (⊠ House of Commons Information Office, House of Commons, London, SW1A 2TT) at least a month in advance of your visit. The tour takes you through the Queen's Robing Room, Royal Gallery, House of Lords, Central Hall (where MPs meet their constituents—the lucky ones get to accompany their MP to a prestigious tea on the terrace), House of Commons, and out into the spectacular Westminster Hall. Watch for the "VR" (Victoria Regina) monograms in the carpets and carving belying the "medieval" detailing as 19th-century work. Permits for tours of up to 16 people are available Friday afternoons between 3:30 and 5:30 while the House is sitting. The time to catch the action is "Question Time"—when the prime minister defends himself against the slings and arrows of his "right honorable friends" on Wednesday between 3 and 3:30 PM. Foreigners are required to secure tickets from their respective embassies. The next best time to visit is either chamber's regular "Question Time," held Monday–Thursday 2:30–3:30. The easiest time to get into the Commons is during an evening session—Parliament is still sitting if the top of the Clock Tower is illuminated.

For a special exhibition devoted to "History of Parliament: Past and Present," head to the **Jewel Tower,** across the street from Victoria Tower, on Abingdon Street (also called Old Palace Yard), just south of Parliament Square. Not to be confused with the other famed jewel tower at the Tower of London, this was the stronghold for Edward III's treasure in 1366. It's also one of the original parts of the old Palace of Westminster and still retains some original beams; part of the moat and medieval quay still remain. (The tower is run by English Heritage, with a small charge for entry.) The **Lord Chancellor's Residence,** within the Palace of Westminster, has recently reopened after a spectacular renovation; be sure to have your name placed in advance on the waiting list for the twice-weekly tours—press coverage of the refurbishment has generated great demand. ⊠ *St. Stephen's Entrance, St. Margaret St., SW1,* ☎ *020/7219–3000, 020/7219–4272 Commons information, 020/7219–3107 Lords information, 020/7222–2219 Jewel Tower, 020/7219–2394 Lord Chancellor's Residence.* ▣ *Free.* ☉ *Commons Mon.–Thurs. 2:30–10, Fri. 9:30–3 (although not every Fri.); Lords Mon.–Thurs. 2:30–10; Lord Chancellor's Residence Tues. and Thurs. 10:30–12. Closed Easter wk, July–Oct., and 3 wks at Christmas. Tube: Westminster.* ✎

❼ Institute of Contemporary Arts (ICA). Behind its incongruous white-stucco facade, at Number 12 Carlton House Terrace, the ICA has provided a stage for the avant-garde in performance, theater, dance, visual art, and music since it was established in 1947. There are two cinemas, an underused library of video artists' works, a bookshop, a café and a bar, and a team of adventurous curators. ⊠ *The Mall, W1,* ☎ *020/7930–3647.* ▣ *1-day, weekday membership £1.50; weekend, £2.50; additional charge for entry to specific events.* ☉ *Daily noon–9:30, later for some events. Tube: Charing Cross, Piccadilly Circus.*

NEED A BREAK?　　The **ICAfé** is windowless but brightly spotlighted, with a self-service counter offering good hot dishes, salads, quiches, and desserts. The bar upstairs, which serves baguette sandwiches, has a picture window overlooking the Mall. Both are packed before popular performances and are subject to the £1.50 one-day membership fee.

The Mall. This street was laid out around 1660 for the game of *pell mell* (a type of croquet crossed with golf), which also gave Pall Mall its name, and it quickly became the place to be seen. Samuel Pepys, Jonathan Swift, and Alexander Pope all wrote about it, and it continued as the beau monde's social playground into the early 19th century, long after the game it was built for had gone out of vogue. Something of the former style survives on those summer days when the queen is throwing a Buckingham Palace garden party: hundreds of her subjects throng the Mall, from the grand and titled to the humble and hard-working, all of whom have donned hat and frock to take afternoon tea with the monarch—or somewhere near her—on the lawns of Buck House. The old Mall still runs alongside the graceful, pink, 115-ft-wide avenue that replaced it in 1904 for just such occasions. ⊠ *The Mall, SW1. Tube: Charing Cross, Green Park.*

★ ❸ **National Gallery.** Jan Van Eyck's *Arnolfini Portrait,* Leonardo da Vinci's *Madonna of the Rocks,* Velázquez's *Rokeby Venus,* Constable's *Hay Wain* . . . you get the picture. There are about 2,200 other paintings in this museum—many of them instantly recognizable and among the most treasured works of art anywhere. The museum's low, gray, colonnaded neoclassic facade fills the north side of Trafalgar Square. The institution was founded in 1824, when George IV and a connoisseur named Sir George Beaumont persuaded a reluctant government to spend £57,000 to acquire part of the recently deceased philanthropist John Julius Angerstein's collection. These 38 paintings, including works by Raphael, Rembrandt, Titian, and Rubens, were augmented by 16 of Sir George's own and exhibited in Angerstein's Pall Mall residence until 1838, when William Wilkin's building was completed. By the end of the century, enthusiastic directors and generous patrons had turned the National Gallery into one of the world's foremost collections, with works from painters of the Italian Renaissance and earlier, from the Flemish and Dutch masters, the Spanish school, and of course the English tradition, including Hogarth, Gainsborough, Stubbs, and Constable.

In 1991, following years of wrangling and the rehanging of the entire collection, the Sainsbury Wing was opened. It had been financed by the eponymous British grocery dynasty to house the early Renaissance collection and designed—eventually—by the American architect Robert Venturi after previous plans were abandoned. (Prince Charles didn't like these modernist designs. "A monstrous carbuncle on the face of a much-loved friend" was his headline-making comment.) Occasionally, this wing hosts noted temporary exhibitions; in 2000, a beautiful, un-missable exhibition on masterpieces from Renaissance Florence heralds in the millennium.

The collection is really too overwhelming to absorb in a single viewing. It is wise to acquaint yourself with the layout—easy to negotiate compared with that of other European galleries—and plot a route in advance. The **Micro Gallery,** a computer information center in the Sainsbury Wing, might be the place to start. You can access in-depth information on any work here, choose your favorites, and print out a free personal tour map that marks the paintings you most want to see. Careful, though—you could spend hours in here scrolling through this colorful if pixelized history of art.

The following is a list of 10 of the most familiar works, to jog your memory, whet your appetite, and offer a starting point for your own exploration. The first five are in the Sainsbury Wing. In chronological order: (1) **Van Eyck** (circa 1395–1441), *The Arnolfini Portrait.* A solemn couple holds hands, the fish-eye mirror behind them mysteriously illuminating what can't be seen from the front view. (2) **Uccello** (1397–1475), *The Battle of San Romano*. In a work commissioned by the Medici family, the Florentine commander on a rearing white warhorse leads armored knights into battle with the Sienese. (3) **Bellini** (circa 1430–1516), *The Doge Leonardo Loredan*. The artist captured the Venetian doge's beatific expression (and snail-shell "buttons") at the beginning of his 20 years in office. (4) **Botticelli** (1445–1510), *Venus and Mars*. Mars sleeps, exhausted by the love goddess, oblivious to the lance wielded by mischievous putti and the buzzing of wasps. (5) **Leonardo da Vinci** (1452–1519), *The Virgin and Child*. This haunting black chalk cartoon is partly famous for having been attacked at gunpoint, and it now gets extra protection behind glass and screens. (6) **Caravaggio** (1573–1610), *The Supper at Emmaus*. A cinematically lighted, freshly resurrected Christ blesses bread in an astonishingly domestic vision from the master of chiaroscuro. (7) **Velázquez** (1599–1660), *The Toilet of Venus*. "The Rokeby Venus," named for its previous home in Yorkshire, has the most famously beautiful back in any gallery. She's the only surviving female nude by Velázquez. (8) **Constable** (1776–1837), *The Hay Wain*. Rendered overfamiliar by too many greeting cards, this is the definitive image of golden-age rural England. (9) **Turner** (1775–1851), *The Fighting Téméraire*. Most of the collection's other Turners were moved to the Tate Britain (☞ *below*); the final voyage of the great French battleship into a livid, hazy sunset stayed here. (10) **Seurat** (1859–91), *Bathers at Asnières*. This static summer day's idyll is one of the pointillist extraordinaire's best-known works.

Glaring omissions from the above include some of the most popular pictures in the gallery, by Piero della Francesca, Titian, Holbein, Bosch, Brueghel, Rembrandt, Vermeer, Canaletto, Claude, Tiepolo, Gainsborough, Ingres, Monet, Renoir, and van Gogh. You can't miss the two most spectacular works on view—due to their mammoth size—Sebastiano del Piombo's *Sermon on the Mount* and Stubbs's stunning *Whistlejacket*. These great paintings aren't the only thing glowing in the rooms of the National Gallery—thanks to government patronage and new lottery monies, salons here now gleam with stunning brocades and opulent silks. Rubens's *Samson and Delilah* has never looked better.

New Dutch rooms in the North Galleries, completed in September 1999, mark the final phase of refurbishment. The collection of Dutch 17th-century paintings is one of the greatest in the world, and pieces by Hals, Hooch, Ruisdel, Hobbema, and Cuyp are shown in renewed natural light and gracious decor. There is also a program of temporary themed exhibitions where key works are loaned from other galleries of world renown. If you visit during the school vacations, there are special programs and trails for children that are not to be missed. Neither are the Ten Minute Talks, which illuminate the story behind a key work of art. Check the information desk, or Web site, for details. ⊠ *Trafalgar Sq.*, *WC2*, ☎ *020/7747–2885*. ⊠ *Free; charge for special exhibitions.* ⊙ *Mon.–Sat. 10–6, Sun. 10–6; June–Aug., Wed. until 9, Sainsbury Wing until 10; 1-hr guided tour starts at Sainsbury Wing weekdays at 11:30 and 2:30, Sat. 2 and 3:30. Tube: Charing Cross, Leicester Square.* ✎

NEED A BREAK? The **Brasserie** in the Sainsbury Wing of the National Gallery offers a fashionable lunch—mussels, gravlax, charcuterie, salads, a hot special—plus baguette sandwiches, pastries, tea, coffee, and wine, in a sophisticated, spacious room on the second floor.

★ ❹ **National Portrait Gallery.** An idiosyncratic collection that presents a potted history of Britain through its people, past and present, this museum is an essential visit for all history and literature buffs. The gallery has also been given a complete rejuvenation by the architects Jeremy Dixon and Edward Jones, who have been responsible for the Royal Opera House renaissance. In May 2000, the previously dark, dingy stairways and rooms were opened to reveal new galleries and spaces that are light, bright, and more easily accessible. The new entrance lobby has an escalator directly to a skylit gallery displaying the oldest works. Here you'll see one of the best landscapes for real: a panoramic view of Nelson and the backdrop along the Mall to the Houses of Parliament. A rooftop restaurant with classy British cuisine (Searcy's, which has long delighted diners at the Barbican), open beyond gallery hours, will satiate skyline droolers. Back in the basement is a new lecture theater, computer gallery, bookshop, and café. The National Portrait Gallery has the largest cache of portraits in the world and, with the architectural face-lift, has doubled its exhibition space. Throughout the gallery, the subject, not the artist, is the point; and there are numerous notable works. In the Tudor Gallery—a modern update on a Tudor long hall—is a Holbein cartoon of Henry VIII; Stubbs's self-portrait (in the refurbished 17th-century rooms; and Hockney (in the modern Balcony Gallery) mixed up with photographs, busts, caricatures, and amateur paintings. (The miniature of Jane Austen by her sister Cassandra, for instance, is the only likeness that exists of the great novelist.) Many of the faces are obscure and will be just as unknown to English visitors because the portraits outlasted their sitters' fame—not so surprising when the portraitists are such greats as Reynolds, Gainsborough, Lawrence, and Romney. But the annotation is comprehensive, the layout is easy to negotiate—chronological, with the oldest at the top—and there is a new, separate research center for those who get hooked on particular personages. Don't miss the new Victorian and early 20th-century portrait galleries nor the photography gallery. ⊠ *St. Martin's Pl., WC2,* ☎ *020/7306–0055.* ⊒ *Free.* ☉ *Mon.–Sat. 10–5:45, Sun. noon–5:45. Tube: Charing Cross, Leicester Sq.* ⌂

❷ **Nelson's Column.** Trafalgar Square takes its name from the Battle of Trafalgar, Admiral Lord Horatio Nelson's great naval victory over the French, in 1805. Appropriately, the dominant landmark here is this famous column, a 145-ft-high granite perch from which E. H. Baily's 1843 statue of Nelson (1758–1805), one of England's favorite heroes, keeps watch; three bas-reliefs depicting his victories at Cape St. Vincent, the Battle of the Nile, and Copenhagen (and a fourth, his death at Trafalgar itself in 1805) sit around the base. All four bas-reliefs were cast from cannons he captured. The four majestic lions, designed by the Victorian painter Sir Edwin Landseer, were added in 1867. The calling cards of generations of picturesque pigeons have been a corrosive problem for the statue; this may have been finally solved by the statue's new gel coating. ⊠ *Trafalgar Sq., WC2. Tube: Charing Cross, Leicester Sq.*

⑬ **Queen Anne's Gate.** Standing south of Birdcage Walk, by St. James's Park, are these two pretty 18th-century closes, once separate but now linked by a statue of the last Stuart monarch. (Another statue of Anne, beside St. Paul's, inspired the doggerel "Brandy Nan, Brandy Nan, you're left in the lurch, your face to the gin shop, your back to the church"—proving that her attempts to disguise her habitual tipple in a teapot fooled nobody.) ⊠ *Queen Anne's Gate, SW1. Tube: St James's Park.*

⑩ **Queen Victoria Memorial.** You can't overlook this monument if you're near Buckingham Palace, which it faces from the traffic island at the west end of the Mall. The monument was conceived by Sir Aston Webb as the nucleus of his ceremonial route down the Mall to the Palace, and it was executed by the sculptor Thomas Brock, who was knighted on the spot when the memorial was revealed to the world in 1911. Many wonder why he was given that honor, since the thing is Victoriana incarnate: the frumpy queen glares down the Mall, with golden-winged Victory overhead and her siblings Truth, Justice, and Charity, plus Manufacture, Progress-and-Peace, War-and-Shipbuilding, and so on—in Osbert Sitwell's words, "tons of allegorical females . . . with whole litters of their cretinous children"—surrounding her. ⊠ *The Mall and Spur Rd. Tube: St. James's Park, Victoria.*

⑪ **Queen's Gallery.** This is the former chapel at the south side of Buckingham Palace, which has been open to visitors since 1962 for special, temporary exhibitions (focusing on small parts of the collection, such as Her Majesty's Michelangelo drawings). From October 1999 to 2002, however, the gallery will be closed for a complete renovation, expansion, technological update, and splendid Nash-style entrance, in tune with the grandeur of the collection, to replace the previous nondescript side door. The opening is to coincide with the queen's Golden Jubilee. Sign-of-the-times note: now that HRH is a taxpayer, her artwork, along with all her other possessions (for example, Buckingham Palace), is officially part of a business known as Royal Collection Enterprises. ⊠ *Buckingham Palace Rd., SW1,* ☎ *020/7799–2331.* 🎫 *£4, combined ticket with Royal Mews [☞ below] £6.70.* ⊘ *Mar. 5–Dec. 23, Tues.– Sat. 9:30–4:30, Sun. 2–4:30. Tube: St. James's Park, Victoria.*

☾ **Royal Mews.** Unmissable children's entertainment, this museum is the home of Her Majesty's Coronation Coach. Standing nearly next door to the Queen's Gallery (☞ *above*), the Royal Mews were designed by famed Regency-era architect John Nash. Mews were originally falcons' quarters (the name comes from their "mewing," or feather shedding), but horses gradually eclipsed birds of prey. Now some of the magnificent royal beasts live here alongside the fabulous bejeweled glass and golden coaches they draw on state occasions. ⊠ *Buckingham Palace Rd., SW1,* ☎ *020/7839–1377.* 🎫 *£4.20, combined ticket with Queen's Gallery [☞ above] £6.70.* ⊘ *Mon.–Thurs. noon–4, until 4:30 in summer (call for months), last admission 30 mins before closing. Closed royal and state occasions; call ahead. Tube: St. James's Park, Victoria.*

St. James's Park. With three palaces at its borders (the ancient Palace of Westminster, now the Houses of Parliament; the Tudor **St. James's Palace** [☞ St. James's and Mayfair, *below*]; and Buckingham Palace), St James's Park is acclaimed as the most royal of the royal parks. It is also London's smallest, most ornamental park, as well as the oldest; it was acquired by Henry VIII in 1532 for a deer park. The land was marshy and took its name from the lepers' hospital dedicated to St. James. Henry VIII built the palace next to the park, which was used for hunting only—duelling and sword fights were forbidden. James I improved the land and installed an aviary and zoo (complete with crocodiles). Charles II (after his exile in France and because of his admiration for Louis XIV's formal Versailles Palace landscapes) had formal gardens laid out, with avenues, fruit orchards, and a canal. Lawns were grazed by goats, sheep, and deer. The Mall (☞ *above*), alongside, also became used for the French croquet-type game of *paille-maille,* or pell mell. Its present shape more or less reflects what John Nash designed under George IV, turning the canal into a graceful lake (which was cemented in at a depth of 4 ft in 1855, so don't even think of swimming) and generally naturalizing the gardens. St. James's Park makes a spectacular frame for the towers of Westminster and Victoria—especially at night, when the illuminated fountains play and the skyline beyond the trees looks like a floating fairyland.

About 17 species of birds—including flamingos, pelicans, geese, ducks, and swans (which belong to the queen)—now breed on and around Duck

Island at the east end of the lake, attracting ornithologists at dawn. Later on summer days the deck chairs (which you must pay to use) are crammed with office workers lunching while being serenaded by music from the bandstands. But the best time to stroll the leafy walkways is after dark, with Westminster Abbey and the Houses of Parliament rising above the floodlighted lake, and peace reigning. ⊠ *The Mall or Horse Guards approach, or Birdcage Walk, SW1. Tube: St. James's Park, Westminster.*

St. John's, Smith Square, completed around 1720, charmingly dominates Smith Square, an elegant enclave of perfectly preserved early 18th-century town houses that still looks like the London of Dr. Johnson. The Smith Square address is much sought after by MPs, especially of the Tory persuasion; Number 32 is the Conservative Party Headquarters. The Baroque church is well known to Londoners as a chamber-music venue; its popular lunchtime concerts are often broadcast on the radio. ⊠ *North of Horseferry St., end of John Islip St., SW1,* ☎ *020/7222–1061.* ☉ *Weekdays 10–5, Sat. for concerts only. Tube: Westminster.*

NEED A BREAK?

In the Crypt of St. John's, Smith Square, is the **Footstool**—about the only place to find refreshments around here. It has an interesting and reasonably priced lunchtime menu and also serves evening meals on concert nights, Monday–Saturday 11:30–2:30 and 5:30–10.

⑭ **St. Margaret's Church.** Dwarfed by its northern neighbor, Westminster Abbey, this church was founded during the 12th century and rebuilt between 1486 and 1523. St. Margaret's is the parish church of the Houses of Parliament and much sought after for weddings: Samuel Pepys married here in 1655, Winston Churchill in 1908. The east Crucifixion window celebrates another union, the marriage of Prince Arthur and Catherine of Aragon. Unfortunately, it arrived so late that Arthur was dead and Catherine had married his brother, Henry VIII. Sir Walter Raleigh is among the notables buried here, only without his head, which had been removed at Old Palace Yard, Westminster, and kept by his wife, who was said to be fond of asking visitors, "Have you met Sir Walter?" as she produced it from a velvet bag. ⊠ *Parliament Square, SW1. Tube: Westminster.*

❺ **St. Martin-in-the-Fields.** The small medieval chapel that once stood here, probably used by the monks of Westminster Abbey, was indeed surrounded by fields. These gave way to a grand rebuilding, completed in 1726, and St Martin's grew to become one of Britain's best-loved churches. James Gibbs's classical temple-with-spire design became a familiar pattern for churches in early Colonial America. Though it seems dwarfed by the surrounding structures of Trafalgar Square, the spire is actually slightly taller than Nelson's Column, which it overlooks. It is a welcome sight for the homeless, who have sought soup and shelter here since 1914. The church is also a haven for music lovers; the internationally known Academy of St. Martin-in-the-Fields was founded here, and a popular program of lunchtime (free) and evening concerts continues today. The church's musty interior has a wonderful atmosphere for music making—but the wooden benches can make it hard to give your undivided attention to the music. St. Martin's is often called the royal parish church, partly because Charles II was christened here. His mistress, Nell Gwynne, lies under the stones, alongside William Hogarth, Joshua Reynolds, Nicholas Hilliard (the painter of miniatures), Thomas Chippendale (the cabinetmaker), and Jack Sheppard (the notorious highwayman). Also in the crypt is the **London Brass-Rubbing Centre**, where you can make your own souvenir knight from replica tomb brasses, with metallic waxes, paper, and instructions provided for about £1; and the **St. Martin's Gallery**, showing contemporary work.

There is also a crafts market in the courtyard behind the church. ⊠ *Trafalgar Sq., WC2,* ☏ *020/7930–0089; 020/7839–8362 credit-card bookings for evening concerts; Mon.–Sat 10–5.* ☼ *Church daily 8–8; crypt Mon.–Sat. 10–8, Sun. noon–6. Tube: Charing Cross or Leicester Sq.*

NEED A
BREAK?
St. Martin's **Café-in-the-Crypt** serves full meals, sandwiches, snacks, and even wine by the glass, Monday–Saturday 10–8 and Sunday noon–8.

★ ㉑ **Tate Britain.** The gallery previously known as the Tate has been given a new name and direction. Although its fabulous new offspring, Tate Modern (☞ The South Bank, *below*), opened across the river at Bankside in May 2000, the original has not flagged in its wake. The gallery, which first opened in 1897, funded by the sugar magnate Sir Henry Tate, was relaunched with a fresh new face—and theme galleries—in March 2000. As the bold new name proclaims, great British artists from the 16th century to the present day are the focus. It's a brilliant celebration, and it's been done in an entirely new way. The galleries, organized around themes (Family and Society, Literature and Fantasy, and Home and Abroad) display key works from different eras alongside one another. This strategy also rescues from storage many important pieces that rarely saw the light of day. The Family and Society section, for instance, charts a sequence from religious art to the popular portraits and scenes of domesticity (works by Van Dyck, Hogarth, and Reynolds rub shoulders with Rossetti, Sickert, and Bacon) and poverty in cities (works by Frith, Lowry, Gilbert, and George). Literature and Fantasy conjures together such artists as Barry, Millais, Stanley Spencer, and Blake, the original mindblower. The Home and Abroad gallery covers the breadth of country landscape (Stubbs, Gainsborough, Turner, Nash). Other galleries explore themes such as Nudes (Freud, John, and Leighton); Painters in Focus (from Joshua Reynolds to Stanley Spencer); and British Artists in Focus (from Gainsborough to Hockney, with a special Constable section).

The Turner Bequest consists of J. M. W. Turner's personal collection; he left it to the nation on the condition that the works be displayed together. The James Stirling–designed **Clore Gallery** (to the right of the main gallery) has fulfilled his wish since 1987, and it should not be missed. The annual Turner Prize gets artists and non-artists into a frenzy about where art is at—or going to.

You can rent a "Tateinform," a handheld audio guide, with commentaries by curators, experts, and some of the artists themselves. About a 20-minute walk south of the Houses of Parliament, the Tate is also accessible if you tube it to the Pimlico stop, then take a five-minute, signposted walk. A new shuttle bus and boat service links Tate Britain with Tate Modern at Bankside across the river. ⊠ *Millbank, SW1,* ☏ *020/7887–8000.* 🎟 *Free; special exhibitions £3–£7.* ☼ *Daily 10–5:50. Tube: Pimlico.* 🚇

➊ **Trafalgar Square.** This is the center of London, by dint of a plaque on the corner of the Strand and Charing Cross Road from which distances on U.K. signposts are measured. It is the home of the **National Gallery** (☞ *above*) and of one of London's most distinctive landmarks, **Nelson's Column** (☞ *above*). Permanently thronged with people—Londoners and tourists alike—and roaring traffic, it remains London's "living room." Great events, such as New Year's Eve, royal weddings, elections, and sporting triumphs will always see the crowds gathering in the city's most famous square.

The square is a commanding open space, built on the grand scale demanded by its central position in the capital of an empire that once reached to the farthest corners of the globe. Long ago, however, the site housed the Royal Mews, where Edward I (1239–1307) kept his royal hawks and lodged his falconers (not the numberless Edward the Confessor of Westminster Abbey fame, who died in 1066; this one, known as "Longshanks," died of dysentery in 1307). Later, all the kings' horses were stabled here, in increasingly smart quarters, until 1830, when John Nash had the buildings torn down as part of his Charing Cross Improvement Scheme. Nash cleverly exploited the square's natural incline—it slopes down from north to south—making it a succession of high points from which to look down the imposing carriageways that run dramatically away from it toward the Thames, the Houses of Parliament, and Buckingham Palace. Upon Nash's death, the design baton was passed to Sir Charles Barry and then to Sir Edwin Lutyens.

There's a pathetic history attached to the **equestrian statue of Charles I,** which stands near Whitehall on the southern slope of the square (on a pedestal *possibly* designed by Sir Christopher Wren and *possibly* carved by Grinling Gibbons). After Charles's High Treasurer ordered it (from Hubert le Sueur), the Puritan Oliver Cromwell tumbled Charles from the throne and commissioned a scrap dealer with the appropriate name of Rivett to melt the king down. Rivett apparently buried the statue in his garden and made a fortune peddling knickknacks wrought, he claimed, from its metal, only to produce the statue miraculously unscathed after the restoration of the monarchy—and to make more cash reselling it to the authorities. In 1767 Charles II had it placed where it stands today, near the spot where his father was executed in 1649. Each year, on January 30, the day of the king's death, the Royal Stuart Society lays a wreath at the foot of the statue.

Today, street performers enhance the square's intermittent atmosphere of celebration, which is strongest in December, first when the lights on the gigantic Christmas tree (an annual gift from Norway to thank the British for harboring its Royal Family during World War II) are turned on and then, less festively, when thousands see in the New Year. ⊠ *Trafalgar Square, SW1. Tube: Charing Cross.*

⑫ **Wellington Barracks.** These are the headquarters of the Guards Division, the queen's five regiments of elite foot guards (Grenadier, Coldstream, Scots, Irish, and Welsh) who protect the sovereign and patrol her palace dressed in tunics of gold-purled scarlet and tall fur "busby" helmets of Canadian brown bearskin. (London fact: the two items together cost more than £4,000.) If you want to learn more about the guards, you can visit the **Guards Museum;** the entrance is next to the Guards Chapel. ⊠ *Wellington Barracks, Birdcage Walk, SW1,* ☎ *020/7930–4466 ext. 3430.* ◱ *£2.* ◷ *Daily 10–4. Tube: St. James's Park.*

★ ⑯ **Westminster Abbey.** Marked by the teeming human contents of tour buses, off the south side of Parliament Square, this is where nearly all of England's monarchs have been crowned amid great heraldic splendor; most are buried here, too. The main nave is packed with atmosphere, crowds, and memories, as it has witnessed many splendid coronation ceremonies, royal weddings, and, more recently, the funeral of Diana, Princess of Wales. As the most ancient of London's great churches, the place is crammed with spectacular medieval architecture. Other than the mysterious gloom of the vast interior, the first thing to strike most people is the fantastic proliferation of statues, tombs, and commemorative tablets: in parts, the building seems more like a stonemason's yard than a place of worship. But it is in its latter capacity that this landmark truly comes into its own. Although attending a service is not something to undertake purely for sightseeing reasons, it provides a glimpse of the abbey in its full majesty, accompanied by music

Belfry
Tower 17

Chapel of St.
Edward the
Confessor;
Henry V's
Chantry 14

Chapter
House 21

Coronation
Chair. 15

Henry VII
Chapel 9

High Altar . . 12

Norman
Undercroft and
Museum. . . . 20

North
Entrance . . . 16

Organ Loft . . . 5

Poet's
Corner. 8

Pyx
Chamber . . . 19

Royal Airforce
Chapel 12

St. George
Chapel 4

Sanctuary . . . 6

Sir Winston
Churchill
Memorial 2

Stairs to
Library 18

Tomb of
Elizabeth I . . 13

Tomb of
Henry II 11

Tomb of
Mary, Queen
of Scots 10

Tomb of the
Unknown
Warrior 3

West Entrance
and
Bookshop. . . . 1

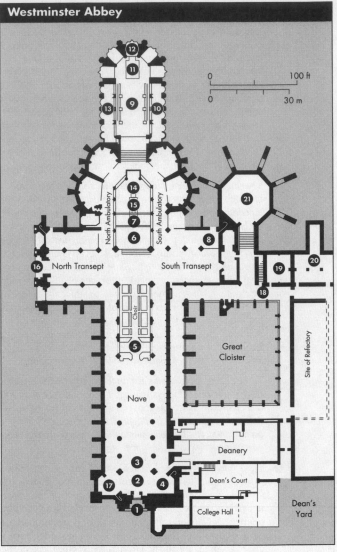

Westminster Abbey

from the Westminster choristers and the organ that Henry Purcell once played. During a service, you won't be bothered by the frequent and jarring loudspeaker announcements made during peak hours, requesting "a minute of silence" from the noisy masses. Note that some parts are closed on Sunday except to worshipers.

The origins of Westminster Abbey are uncertain. The first church on the site may have been built as early as the 7th century by the Saxon king Sebert (who may be buried here, alongside his queen and sister); a Benedictine abbey was established during the 10th century. There were certainly preexisting foundations when Edward the Confessor was crowned in 1040, moved his palace to Westminster, and began building a church. Only traces have been found of that incarnation, which was consecrated eight days before Edward's death in 1065. (It appears in the Bayeaux Tapestry.) Edward's canonization in 1139 gave a succession of kings added incentive to shower the abbey with attention and improvements. Henry III, full of ideas from his travels in France, pulled it down and started again with Amiens and Rheims in mind. In fact, it was the master mason Henry de Reyns ("of Rheims") who, between 1245 and 1254, put up the transepts, north front, and rose windows, as well as part of the cloisters and Chapter House; and it was his master plan that, funded by Richard II, was resumed 100 years later. Henry V (reigned 1413–22) and Henry VII (1485–1509) were the chief succeeding benefactors. The abbey was eventually completed in 1532. After that, Sir Christopher Wren had a hand in shaping the place; his West Towers were completed in 1745, 22 years after his death, by Nicholas Hawksmoor. The most riotous elements of the interior were, similarly, much later affairs.

The nave is your first sight on entering; you need to look up to gain a perspective on the truly awe-inspiring scale of the church because the eye-level view is obscured by the 19th- (and part 13th-) century choir screen, past which point admission is charged. Before paying, look at the poignant **Tomb of the Unknown Warrior,** an anonymous World War I martyr who lies buried here in memory of the soldiers fallen in both world wars. Nearby is one of the very few tributes to a foreigner, a plaque to Franklin D. Roosevelt.

There is only one way around the abbey, and as there will almost certainly be a long stream of shuffling visitors at your heels, you'll need to be alert to catch the highlights. Pass through the choir, with its mid-19th-century choir stalls, into the north transept. Look up to your right to see the painted-glass rose window, the largest of its kind; on the left is the first of the extravagant 18th-century monuments in the north-transept chapels. For a fee, you can then proceed into one of the architectural glories of Britain, the **Henry VII Chapel,** passing the huge white marble tomb of Elizabeth I, buried with her half sister, "Bloody" Mary I; then the tomb of Henry VII with his queen, Elizabeth of York, by the Renaissance master Torrigiano (otherwise known for having been banished from Florence after breaking Michelangelo's nose). Close by are monuments to the young daughters of James I; Sophia, who only lived for three days, is remembered by a single alabaster candle. An urn holds the purported remains of the so-called Princes in the Tower— Edward V and Richard. All around are magnificent sculptures of saints, philosophers, and kings, with wild mermaids and monsters carved on the choir-stall misericords (undersides) and with exquisite fan vaulting above—one of the miracles of Western architecture. (Keep an eye open for St. Wilgefort, who was so concerned to protect her chastity that she prayed to God for help and woke up one morning with a full growth of beard.)

Next you enter the **Chapel of Edward the Confessor,** where beside the royal saint's shrine stands the **Coronation Chair,** which has been briefly graced by nearly every regal posterior. Edward I ordered it around 1300; it used to shelter the Stone of Scone (pronounced "Skoon"), upon which Scottish kings had been crowned since time began, but this precious relic was returned in 1996 to Scotland's Edinburgh Castle for good.

The tombs and monuments with which Westminster Abbey is packed (some would say stuffed) began to appear at an accelerated rate starting in the 18th century; newest additions are ten 20th-century figures, including Martin Luther King, over the West Door. One earlier occupant, though, was Geoffrey Chaucer, who in 1400 became the first poet to be buried in **Poets' Corner.** Most of the other honored writers have only their memorials here, not their bones: William Shakespeare and William Blake (who both had a long wait before the dean deemed them holy enough to be here at all), John Milton, Jane Austen, Samuel Taylor Coleridge, William Wordsworth, Charles Dickens. All of Ben Jonson is here, though—buried upright in accord with his modest demand for a 22-ft grave site. ("O rare Ben Jonson," reads his epitaph, in a modest pun on the Latin *orare,* "to pray for.") Sir Isaac Newton, James Watt, and Michael Faraday are among the scientists with memorials. There is only one painter: Godfrey Kneller, whose dying words were "By God, I will not be buried in Westminster."

After the elbow battle you are guaranteed in Poets' Corner, you exit the abbey by a door from the south transept. Outside the west front is an archway leading into the quiet green **Dean's Yard** and the entrance to the **Cloisters,** where monks once strolled in contemplation. You may do the same and catch a fine view of the massive flying buttresses above in the process. You may also, for a modest fee, take an impression from one of the tomb brasses in the **Brass-Rubbing Centre** (☎ 020/7222–2085). Also here is the entrance to Westminster School, formerly a monastic college, now one of Britain's finest public (which means the exact opposite to Americans) schools; Christopher Wren and Ben Jonson number among the old boys. The **Chapter House,** a stunning octagonal room supported by a central column and adorned with 14th-century frescoes, is where the King's Council and, after that, an early version of the Commons, met between 1257 and 1547. Underfoot is one of the finest surviving tiled floors in the country. In the **Undercroft,** which survives from Edward the Confessor's original church, is the abbey's collection of deliciously macabre effigies made from the death masks and actual clothing of Elizabeth I, Charles II, and Admiral Lord Nelson (complete with eye patch) and the battle kit of shield, saddle, and helmet of Henry V at Agincourt, among other fascinating relics. Finally, the **Pyx Chamber,** or Chapel of the Pyx, next door, contains the abbey's treasure, just as it did when it was the royal strong room during the 13th century. In fact, the columns date back to the 11th century and the pyx was the name for the monk's box of gold and silver. Note that photography is only permitted on Wednesday 6–7:45 PM. ⊠ *Broad Sanctuary, SW1,* ☎ *020/7222–5152.* ⌑ *Abbey £5; Undercroft Museum, Pyx Chamber treasury, and Chapter House £2.50, £1 if you have bought a ticket to the abbey.* ⊙ *Mon.—Sat. 9–3:45 (last admission Sat. 1:45). Undercroft Museum, Pyx Chamber treasury, and Chapter House daily 10:30–4. Abbey closed weekdays and Sunday to visitors during services. Tube: Westminster.* ⌘

Westminster Cathedral. This massive cathedral is hard to miss—once you are almost upon it, that is. It's set back from the left side of the street in a 21-year-old paved square that has fallen on hard times. The cathedral is the seat of the Cardinal of Westminster, head of the Roman Catholic Church in Britain; consequently it is London's principal Roman Catholic church. The asymmetrical redbrick Byzantine hulk, dating only from 1903, is banded with stripes of Portland stone and abutted by a 273-ft-high campanile at the northwest corner, which you can scale by elevator. Faced with the daunting proximity of the heavenly Westminster Abbey, the architect, John Francis Bentley, flew in the face of fashion by rejecting neo-Gothic in favor of the Byzantine idiom, which still provides maximum contrast today—not only with the great church but with just about all of London. The interior is partly unfinished but worth seeing for its atmosphere of broody mystery, its mosaics, and its noted Eric Gill reliefs depicting the stations of the cross. Just inside the main entrance is the tomb of the much loved Cardinal Basil Hume, who died on June 17, 1999, after holding the seat for more than 25 years. ⊠ *Ashley Pl.,* ☎ *020/7798–9055.* ⌑ *Tower £2.* ⊙ *Cathedral daily 7–7. Tower Apr.–Sept., daily 9–5; Oct.–Mar., Thurs.–Sun. 9–5.*

ST. JAMES'S AND MAYFAIR

St. James's and Mayfair form the very core of London's West End, the city's smartest central area. No textbook sights here; rather, these neighborhoods epitomize much of the flavor that is peculiarly London's—the sense of being in a great, rich, (once) powerful city is almost palpable as you wander along its posh and polished streets. Here is the highest concentration of grand hotels, department stores, exclusive shops, glamorous restaurants, commercial art galleries, auction houses, swanky offices—all accoutrements that give this area an unmistakable air of wealth and leisure, even on busy days.

A late-17th-century ghost in the streets of contemporary St. James's would not need to bother walking through walls because practically none have moved since he knew them. Its boundaries, clockwise from the north, are Piccadilly, Haymarket, the Mall, and Green Park: a neat rectangle, with a protruding spur satisfyingly located at Cockspur Street. The rectangle used to describe "gentlemen's London," where Sir was outfitted head and foot (but not in between, since the tailors were, and still are, north of Piccadilly in Savile Row) before repairing to his club. In fact, this has been a fashionable part of town from the first, largely by dint of the eponymous palace, St. James's, which was a royal residence—if not *the* palace—from the time of Henry VIII until the beginning of the Victorian era. In 1996, St. James's once again became a truly royal residence, as Prince Charles took up quarters here, shortly after leaving the Kensington Palace digs he once shared with his then wife.

Mayfair, like St. James's, is precisely delineated—a trapezoid contained by, respectively, Oxford Street and Piccadilly on the north and south, Regent Street and Park Lane on the east and west. Within its boundaries are streets both broad and narrow, but mostly unusually straight and gridlike for London, making it fairly easy to negotiate.

Numbers in the text correspond to numbers in the margin and on the St. James's and Mayfair map.

A Good Walk

Look at any street map and you'll quickly see what a random pattern the streets of St. James's and Mayfair form. The easiest approach would be the serendipitous one—follow your instincts and see where they take you. Here, however, is a tour that incorporates all the highlights. Starting in Trafalgar Square, you'll find Cockspur Street off the southwest corner; follow it to the foot of **Haymarket.** On your right is London's oldest shopping arcade, the splendid Regency Royal Opera Arcade, which John Nash finished in 1818. Now you come to **Pall Mall** ①, a showcase of 18th- and 19th-century patrician architecture and home to such famous gentlemen's retreats as the Reform Club, halfway along on the right, from which Phileas Fogg set out to go around the world. At the end of Pall Mall, you collide with the small, Tudor brick **St. James's Palace** ②. Continue along Cleveland Row by the side of the palace to spy on York House, home of the Duke and Duchess of Kent; then turn left into Stable Yard Road to Lancaster House, built for the Duke of York in the 1820s but more notable as the venue for the 1978 conference that led to the end of white rule in Rhodesia (now Zimbabwe); and Clarence House, designed by John Nash and built in 1825 for the Duke of Clarence (who became William IV) and now home to the Queen Mother. Now, head north up along St. James's Street to St. James's Place, where, if you turn left, you can spot, at Number 27, one of London's most spectacular 18th-century mansions, **Spencer House** ③, home of Diana's ancestors; the interior can be viewed on tours given on Sunday only throughout the year (except August and January).

Cross back over St. James's Street to King Street—Number 8 is Christie's, the fine art auctioneers who got £25 million for van Gogh's *Sunflowers*; Duke Street on the left harbors further exclusive little art salons—but straight ahead is **St. James's Square** ④, one of London's oldest and home of the London Library. Leave the square by Duke of York Street to the north, and turn left on **Jermyn Street** ⑤, the world center of gentlemen's-paraphernalia shops. Set back from the street is the lovely **St. James's Church** ⑥. A right on Duke Street brings you to Piccadilly. Turn right again, and you'll pass the exclusive department store that supplies the queen's groceries, Fortnum & Mason, on the right, and the **Royal Academy of Arts** ⑦, opposite, with famous **Piccadilly Circus** ⑧ ahead. Turn around—Wellington Arch and **Apsley House (Wellington Museum)** ⑨, the gloriously opulent mansion the Duke of Wellington once called home, are ahead in the distance. Cross the street and head north up the shopping mecca of **Bond Street** ⑩, with **Burlington Arcade** ⑪ to the right. You could detour by turning right before you reach Oxford Street into Brook Street (the composer Handel lived at Number 25), which leads to Hanover Square. Turning right down St. George Street brings you to the porticoes of St. George's Church, where Percy Bysshe Shelley and George Eliot, among others, had their weddings. A right turn after the church down Mill Street brings you into Savile Row, the fashionable center for custom-made suits and coats since the mid-19th century. Number 3 is mecca for Beatlemaniacs: the former headquarters of Apple Records and the site of John, Paul, George, and Ringo's legendary rooftop concert (the building now houses a financial institution and is not open to the public). Continuing from Savile Row to behind the Royal Academy is Albany, one of the smartest addresses since the turn of the 19th century. You can peer through the railings at the posh Henry Holland apartments built for fashionable bachelors, which included Byron, Prime Ministers Gladstone and Heath, Graham Greene, and latterly actor Terence Stamp. From Savile Row, head west on Grosvenor Street to Duke Street: slightly to the south, you'll find one of Mayfair's beauty spots—Carlos Place (site of the Connaught) and neighboring Mount Row, both adorned with some veddy, veddy elegant residences. Here, too, is Mount Street, a pedigree-proud shopping avenue; take South Audley Street one block south to discover St. George's Gardens, a fine place for a picnic. Head over to Hyde Park to take in **Speakers' Corner** ⑫ and **Marble Arch** ⑬. Shop-till-you-droppers can then explore Oxford Street (**Selfridges** ⑭ and **Marks & Spencer** are here), while art lovers will want to continue north to Manchester Square for the magnificent **Wallace Collection** ⑮. TV aficionados should, instead, make a beeline for the new **BBC Experience** ⑯.

TIMING

Although this walk doesn't cover an enormous distance, you'll probably do a lot of doubling back and detouring down beckoning alleys—and into interesting shops. If you want to do more than window-shop, we suggest most emphatically a weekday jaunt, starting in the morning, so you get time for visits to the Royal Academy and the Wallace Collection or perhaps some of the commercial art galleries in and around Cork Street. The walk alone should take less than two hours. Add at least an hour for Apsley House, and another two for the Wallace Collection. Any of those could easily consume an afternoon, if you have one to spare. Shopping could take all week.

HOW TO GET THERE

You could start walking around this area from Trafalgar Square (☞ Westminster and Royal London, *above*), or get the Piccadilly or Bakerloo Line to the Piccadilly Circus tube stop, the Piccadilly to the Hyde

Park Corner stop, or the Central Line to any of the stops along Oxford Street—Marble Arch, Bond Street (also Jubilee Line), Oxford Circus (also Victoria and Bakerloo lines), or Tottenham Court Road (also Northern Line). The Green Park stop on the Piccadilly, Victoria, or Jubilee Line is also central to many of this neighborhood's sights. The best buses are 8, 9, 14, 19, 22, and 38 along Piccadilly, especially the 8, which loops around via New Bond Street to Oxford Street and skims the eastern border of Green Park down Grosvenor Place.

Sights to See

★ ⑨ **Apsley House (Wellington Museum).** For Hyde Park Corner read "heroes corner"; even in the subway, beneath the turmoil of traffic, the Duke of Wellington's heroic exploits are retold in murals. The years of war against the French, and the subsequent final defeat of Napoléon at the Battle of Waterloo in 1815 made Wellington—Arthur Wellesley—the greatest soldier and statesman in the land. The house is flanked by imposing statues: opposite is the 1828 Decimus Burton **Wellington Arch** with the four-horse chariot of peace as its pinnacle. Cast from captured French guns, the legendary **Achilles** statue points the way with thrusting shield to the ducal mansion from the tip of Hyde Park. Once known, quite simply, as Number 1, London, this was long celebrated as the best address in town. Built by Robert Adam and later refaced and extended, this was home to the Duke of Wellington from 1817 until his death in 1852. As the Wellington Museum, it has been kept as the "Iron Duke" liked it—even the railings outside are painted pale green as the duke once had them—his uniforms and weapons, his porcelain and plate, and his extensive art collection are displayed heroically. Unmissable, in every sense (and considered rather too athletic for the time), is the gigantic Canova statue of a nude (but fig-leafed) Napoléon Bonaparte, Wellington's archenemy, which presides over the grand staircase, leading to the many elegant reception rooms. The most stunning is the Waterloo Gallery, where the annual banquet for officers who fought beside Wellington was held. With its heavily sculpted and gilded ceiling, feast of old master paintings on red damask walls, and commanding gray candelabra, it is a veritable orgy of opulence. Apsley House installed iron shutters in 1830 after rioters, protesting the duke's opposition (he was briefly prime minister) to the Reform Bill, broke the windows. Yes, the British loved him for defeating Napoléon, but mocked him with the name Iron Duke—referring not only to his military prowess but to his indomitable will. ✉ *149 Piccadilly, W1,* ☎ *020/7499–5676.* ☞ *£4.50; free sound guides.* ☉ *Tues.–Sun. 11–4:30. Tube: Hyde Park Corner.*

⑯ **BBC Experience.** For those who have been weaned on a steady diet of *Masterpiece Theatre* presentations, the BBC is the greatest television producer in the world. These fans, and those of the BBC's countless other programs, will be happy to know that the BBC opened the doors of its own in-house museum to celebrate the group's 75th anniversary in 1997. There's an audiovisual show that traces the BBC's history, an interactive section—want to try your hand at commentating on a sports game, presenting a weather forecast, or making your own director's cut of a segment of *EastEnders?*—and, of course, a massive gift shop. Tickets can be purchased at the front door, or you can prebook a tour with a credit card. ✉ *Broadcasting House, Portland Pl., W1,* ☎ *020/7765–1109.* ☞ *£6.95.* ☉ *Daily 9:30–5:30. Tube: Oxford Circus.*

Berkeley Square. As anyone who's heard the old song knows, the name rhymes with "starkly." Not many of its original mid-18th-century houses are left, but look at Numbers 42–46 (especially Number 44, which the architectural historian Sir Nikolaus Pevsner thought London's finest terraced house) and Numbers 49–52 to get some idea of

St. James's and Mayfair

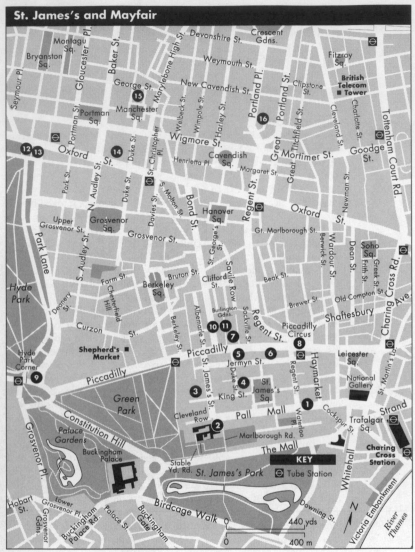

Apsley House
(Wellington
Museum) 9

BBC Experience . . . 16

Bond Street 10

Burlington
Arcade 11

Jermyn Street 5

Marble Arch 13

Pall Mall 1

Piccadilly Circus 8

Royal Academy
of Arts 7

St. James's
Church 6

St. James's Palace . . . 2

St. James's
Square 4

Selfridges 14

Speaker's
Corner 12

Spencer House 3

Wallace
Collection 15

why it was once London's top address—not that it's in the least humble now. Snob nightclub Annabels is one current resident. ⊠ *Berkeley Square, W1. Green Park.*

⑩ Bond Street. This world-class shopping haunt is divided into northern "New" (1710) and southern "Old" (1690) halves. New Bond Street boasts **Sotheby's,** the world-famous auction house, at Number 35, but there are other opportunities to flirt with financial ruin on Old Bond Street: the mirror-lined Chanel store, the vainglorious marble acres of Gianni Versace and the boutique of the more sophisticated Gucci, plus Tiffany's British outpost and art dealers Colnaghi, Léger, Thos. Agnew, and Marlborough Fine Arts. **Cork Street,** which parallels the top half of Old Bond Street, is where London's top dealers in contemporary art have their galleries—you're welcome to browse, but dress appropriately. ⊠ *Bond Street, Green Park.*

⑪ Burlington Arcade. Perhaps the finest of Mayfair's enchanting covered shopping alleys is the second oldest in London, built in 1819 for Lord Cavendish, to stop the flotsam and jetsam throwing rubbish into his garden at Burlington House, which is behind the arcade. It's still patrolled by top-hatted beadles, who prevent you from singing, running, or carrying open umbrellas or large parcels (to say nothing of lifting English fancy goods from the mahogany-front shops). ⊠ *Piccadilly, W1. Tube: Green Park, Piccadilly Circus.*

Faraday Museum. In the basement of the Royal Institution is a reconstruction of the laboratory where the physicist Michael Faraday discovered electromagnetic induction in 1831—with echoes of Frankenstein. ⊠ *21 Albermarle St., W1,* ☎ *020/7409–2992.* ⊡ *£1.* ☉ *Weekdays 10–5. Tube: Green Park.*

Grosvenor Square. This square (pronounced "*Grove*-na") was laid out in 1725–31 and is as desirable an address today as it was then. Americans certainly thought so—from John Adams, the second president, who as ambassador lived at Number 38, to Dwight D. Eisenhower, whose wartime headquarters was at Number 20. Now the ugly '50s block of the U.S. Embassy occupies the entire west side, and a British memorial to Franklin D. Roosevelt stands in the center. The little brick chapel used by Eisenhower's men during World War II, the 1730 Grosvenor Chapel, stands a couple of blocks south of the square on South Audley Street, with the entrance to pretty **St. George's Gardens** to its left. Across the gardens is the headquarters of the English Jesuits as well as the society-wedding favorite, the mid-19th-century Church of the Immaculate Conception, known as Farm Street because that is the name of the street on which it stands. ⊠ *W1. Tube: Bond Street.*

Heinz Gallery. The gallery of the Royal Institute of British Architects has a changing program of exhibitions and interesting, often cutting-edge, evening lectures. ⊠ *21 Portman Sq., W1,* ☎ *020/7580–5533.* ⊡ *Free.* ☉ *Sept.–July, weekdays during exhibitions 11–5, Sat. 10–1. Tube: Bond St.*

⑤ Jermyn Street. This is where the gentleman purchases his traditional fashion accessories. He buys his shaving sundries and hip flask from Geo. F. Trumper; briar pipe from Astley's; scent from Floris (for women, too—both the Prince of Wales and his mother are customers of Floris), whose interiors are exceedingly historic and beautiful, or Czech & Speake; shirts from Turnbull & Asser; and deerstalkers and panamas from Bates the Hatter. Don't forget the regal cheeses from Paxton & Whitfield (founded in 1740 and a legend among dairies). Shop your way east along Jermyn Street, and you're practically in Piccadilly Circus. ⊠ *SW1. Tube: Piccadilly Circus.*

⑬ Marble Arch. The name denotes both the traffic whirlpool where Bayswater Road segues into Oxford Street and John Nash's 1827 arch, which moved here from Buckingham Palace in 1851. Search the sidewalk on the traffic island opposite the cinema to find the stone plaque that marks (roughly) the place where the Tyburn Tree stood for four centuries, until 1783. This was London's central gallows, a huge wooden structure with hanging accommodations for 21. Hanging days were holidays, the spectacle supposedly functioning as a crime deterrent for the hoi polloi. It didn't work, alas. Oranges, gingerbread, and gin were sold, alongside "personal favors," to vast, rowdy crowds, and the condemned, dressed in finery for his special moment, was treated more as hero than as villain. Cross over (or under—there are signs to help in the labyrinth) to the northeastern corner of Hyde Park to Speakers' Corner (☞ *below*). Believe it or not, there are two tiny apartments in Marble Arch, rented out by the National Trust. ⊠ *Park Lane, W1. Tube: Marble Arch.*

NEED A BREAK?   Smarter than the usual street café, **Sotheby's Café** (⊠ 34–35 New Bond St., W1) is a cut above, as you would expect of this classy auction house in the chic shopping quarter of Bond Street. Lunches, such as the lobster club sandwich, aren't terribly cheap, but service is included within the tab.

❶ Pall Mall. Like its near-namesake, *the* Mall, Pall Mall rhymes with "shall" and derives its name from the cross between croquet and golf that the Italians, who invented it, called *pallo a maglio* and the French, who made it chic, called *palle-maille*. In England it was taken up with enthusiasm by James I, who called it "pell mell" and passed it down the royal line, until Charles II had a new road laid out for it in 1661. Needless to say, Catherine Street, as Pall Mall was officially named (after Charles's queen, Catherine of Braganza), was *very* fashionable. Number 79 must have been one of its livelier addresses, since Charles's gregarious mistress, Nell Gwynne, lived there. The king gave her the house when she complained about being a mere leaseholder, protesting that she had "always conveyed free under the Crown" (as it were); it remains, to this day, the only privately owned bit of Pall Mall's south side. Stroll slowly, the better to appreciate the creamy facades and perfect proportions along this showcase of 18th- and 19th-century British architecture.

Notable examples are two James Barry–designed buildings, the **Travellers' Club** and the **Reform Club,** both representatives of the upperclass gentleman's retreat that made St. James's the club land of London. The Reform is the most famous club of all, thanks partly to Jules Verne's Phileas Fogg, who accepted the around-the-world-in-80-days bet in its smoking room and was thus soon qualified to join the Travellers'. And—hallelujah—women can join the Reform. The RAC Club (for Royal Automobile Club, but it's never known as that), with its marble swimming pool, and the Oxford and Cambridge Club complete the Pall Mall quota; there are other, even older establishments—Brooks's, the Carlton, Boodles, and White's (founded in 1736, the oldest of all)—in St. James's Street around the corner, alongside *the* gentleman's bespoke (custom) shoemaker, Lobb's, and, at Number 6, *the* hatter, James Lock, which has one of the most historic store facades in the city—you half expect Lord Byron or Anthony Trollope to walk out the door. Waterloo Place, around the corner, is a continuation of this gentleman's quarter (☞ *below*). ⊠ *SW1. Tube: Piccadilly Circus.*

❽ Piccadilly Circus. New York has its Times Square, in Venice it's Piazza San Marco, and London has Piccadilly Circus. As natives say, if you stand here long enough, you will meet everyone you know. The name came into use during the early 17th century, when a humble tailor on

VACATION COUNTDOWN

Your *checklist for a perfect journey*

WAY AHEAD

- Devise a trip budget.

- Write down the five things you want most from this trip. Keep this list handy before and during your trip.

- Make plane or train reservations. Book lodging, rental cars, and other transportation.

- Arrange for pet care.

- Submit your passport application, or check that your existing passport is valid.

- Photocopy important documents and store in a safe place.

A MONTH BEFORE

- Make restaurant reservations and buy theater and concert tickets. Visit fodors.com for links to local events and news.

- Familiarize yourself with the local language or lingo.

TWO WEEKS BEFORE

- Replenish your supply of medications and contact lenses if necessary.

- Create your itinerary.

- Enjoy a book or movie set in your destination to get you in the mood.

- Develop a packing list. Shop for missing essentials. Repair and launder or dry-clean your clothes.

A WEEK BEFORE

- Stop newspaper and mail deliveries and pay bills.

- Acquire local currency and traveler's checks.

- Stock up on film and batteries.

- Label your luggage.

- Finalize your packing list— always take less than you think you need.

- Create a toiletries kit filled with travel-size essentials.

- Get lots of sleep. You don't want to get sick or run-down before your trip.

A DAY BEFORE

- Drink plenty of water.

- Check your necessary travel documents.

- Get packing!

DURING YOUR TRIP

- Keep a journal/scrapbook as a personal souvenir.

- Spend time with locals.

- Take time to explore. Don't plan too much. Let yourself get lost and use your Fodor's guide to get back on track.

HOW TO USE THIS GUIDE

Think of this guide as your tool kit for a perfect trip. It's packed with everything you need—color photos, insider advice on hotels and restaurants, practical tips, essential maps, and more.

COOL TOOLS

As you're planning your trip, be on the lookout for our favorite features.

Fodor's Choice Look for entries marked with a star. Although all listings in this guide come highly recommended, these deserve special mention.

Great Itineraries Not sure what to see in the time you have? Mix and match our easy-to-follow itineraries to create a trip that suits you.

Good Walks Let us be your guide to the must-see sights. Follow the numbered bullets and you won't miss a thing.

Need a Break? Looking for a quick bite to eat or a spot to rest? These sure bets are along the way.

Off the Beaten Path Some lesser-known sights are definitely worth a special trip. We tell you which to detour for.

POST-IT® FLAGS

Note your favorite spots with these handy Post-it® flags.

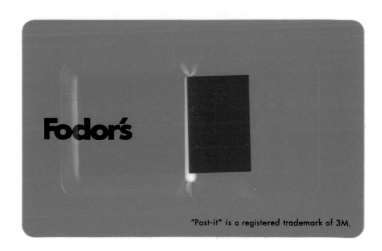

"Post-it" is a registered trademark of 3M.

ICONS AND SYMBOLS

Look for these icons and symbols throughout the guide. Price charts for dining and lodging are strategically located—check the index to find the one you want.

★   Our special recommendations
✗   Restaurant
⊡   Lodging establishment

✗⊡   Lodging establishment whose restaurant warrants a special trip
☃   Good for kids
☞   Sends you to another section of the guide for more information
⊠   Address
☏   Telephone number
☉   Opening hours
☜   Admission prices
✎   Sends you to www.fodors.com/urls for up-to-date links to the property's Web site

the Strand named Robert Baker sold an awful lot of picadils—a collar ruff all the rage in courtly circles—and built a house with the proceeds. Snobs dubbed his new-money mansion Piccadilly Hall, and the name stuck. As for "Circus," that refers not to the menagerie of backpackers and camera-clickers clustered around the steps of **Eros** but to the circular junction of five major roads.

Eros, London's favorite statue and symbol of the *Evening Standard* newspaper, is not in fact the Greek god of erotic love at all, but the angel of Christian charity, commissioned in 1893 from the young sculptor Alfred Gilbert as a memorial to the philanthropic Earl of Shaftesbury (the angel's bow and arrow are a sweet allusion to the earl's name). It cost Gilbert £7,000 to cast the statue he called his "missile of kindness" in the novel medium of aluminum, and because he was paid only £3,000, he promptly went bankrupt and fled the country. (Not to worry—he was knighted in the end.) Eros has lately done his best to bankrupt Westminster Council, too, owing to some urgent leg surgery and a new coat of protective microcrystalline synthetic wax. Around Eros, London roars on—this hub is home to a very large branch of Tower Records, the tawdry Trocadero Centre (video arcades, food courts, chain stores, the Guinness World of Records), a SegaWorld, and a perpetual traffic jam. Beneath the blight, however, is beauty: just behind the modern bank of neon advertisements are some of the most elegant Edwardian-era buildings in town. ⊠ *W1. Tube: Piccadilly Circus.*

Portland Place. The elegant throughway to Regent's Park was London's widest street during the 1780s, when brothers Robert and James Adam designed it. The first sight to greet you here, drawing the eye around the awkward corner, is the curvaceous portico and pointy Gothic spire of **All Souls Church,** one part of Nash's Regent Street plan that remains. It is now the venue for innumerable concerts and Anglican services broadcast to the nation by the British Broadcasting Corporation. The 1931 block of Broadcasting House next door is home to the BBC's five radio stations and the new **BBC Experience** (☞ *above*). It curves, too, if less beautifully, and features an Eric Gill sculpture of Shakespeare's Ariel (aerial—get it?) over the entrance, from which the playful sculptor was obliged to excise a portion of phallus lest it offend public decency—which the modified model did in any case. At Number 66, opposite the Chinese Embassy, the Royal Institute of British Architects has a small exhibitions gallery devoted to shows from its esteemed members. Here, too, if you need a break, is a tasteful branch of a Patisserie Valerie café. ⊠ *W1. Tube: Oxford Circus, Great Portland St.*

Regent Street. This curvaceous thoroughfare was conceived by John Nash and his patron, the Prince Regent—the future George IV—as a kind of ultra-catwalk from the Prince's palace, Carlton House, to Regent's Park (then called Marylebone Park). The section between Piccadilly and Oxford Street was to be called the Quadrant and lined with colonnaded purveyors of "articles of fashion and taste," in a big PR exercise to improve London's image as the provincial cousin of smarter European capitals. The scheme was never fully implemented, and what there was fell into such disrepair that, early this century, Aston Webb (of the Mall route) collaborated on the redesign you see today. It is still a major shopping street. Hamleys, the gigantic toy emporium, is fun; and since 1875 there has been Liberty, which originally imported silks from the East, then diversified to other Asian goods, and is now best known for its "Liberty print" cottons, its jewelry department, and—still—its high-class Asian imports. The stained glass–lighted mock-Tudor interior, with beams made from battleships, is worth a look. ⊠ *W1. Tube: Piccadilly Circus, Oxford Circus.*

❼ Royal Academy of Arts. Burlington House was built in the Palladian style for the Earl of Burlington around 1720, and it is one of the few surviving mansions from that period. The chief occupant today is the Royal Academy of Arts (RA), which mounts major art exhibitions, usually years in the planning. Old Masters are the basic bill of fare, but in 1997 the academy mounted a show of Britain's leading enfants terribles, called "Sensation," which caused just that. One can only imagine what Sir Joshua Reynolds—whose statue is in the academy courtyard—would have made of Damien Hirst's formaldehyde-preserved tiger-shark sculpture. The academy's own fabled collection has unfortunately been dispersed to other museums, notably the Tate and the National Gallery; the latter got the prize—the *Taddeo Tondo* (a sculpted disk) by Michelangelo of the Madonna and Child. But the return is that major exhibitions plunder other collections heavily to produce barnstorming exhibitions. The mammoth Monet in 1998 broke all attendance records and saw the gallery open for 24 hours on the final weekend to squeeze in ticketholders. For 2001 a grand Turner Watercolours exhibition is planned. Every June, the RA mounts the **Summer Exhibition,** a mishmash of sculpture and painting, with about 1,000 things crammed into every cranny. Art-weary now? Try the shop; it's one of the best museum stores in town. The restaurant is also highly recommended. The White Card is accepted. ✉ *Burlington House, Piccadilly, W1,* ☏ *020/7300–8000 or 020/7300–5760 recorded information.* 🎟 *Admission varies according to exhibition.* ☉ *Sat.–Thurs. 10–6, Fri. 10–8:30. Tube: Piccadilly Circus, Green Park.*

❻ St. James's Church. Recessed from the street behind a courtyard, the church is filled most days with a crafts market. Completed in 1684, this was the last of Sir Christopher Wren's London churches and his own favorite. It contains one of Grinling Gibbons's finest works, an ornate limewood reredos (the screen behind the altar). The organ is a survivor of Whitehall Palace and was brought here in 1691. A 1940 bomb scored a direct hit here, but the church was completely restored, albeit with a fiberglass spire. It's a lively place, offering all manner of lecture series—many on incongruously New Age themes—and concerts, mostly Baroque, as well as a brass-rubbing center. ✉ *Piccadilly, W1. Tube: Piccadilly Circus, Green Park.*

NEED A BREAK?   The **Wren** at St. James's, attached to the church, has not the faintest whiff of godliness, as the cake display proves. Hot dishes at lunchtime are vegetarian, very good, and very inexpensive. There are tables outside in spring and summer.

---

❷ St. James's Palace. With its solitary sentry posted at the gate, this surprisingly small palace of Tudor brick was once home to many British sovereigns, including the first Elizabeth and Charles I, who spent his last night here before his execution. Today, it is the residence of another Charles—the future King Charles III (that is, if the current Prince of Wales makes it to Westminster Abbey). His front door actually debouches right onto the street, but he always uses a back entrance. Matters to ponder as you look (you can't go in): the palace was named after a hospital for women lepers, which stood here during the 11th century; Henry VIII had it built; foreign ambassadors to Britain are still accredited to the Court of St. James's even though it has rarely been a primary royal residence; and the present queen made her first speech here. Friary Court out front is a splendid setting for Trooping the Colour, part of the Changing of the Guard ceremony (☞ Buckingham Palace *in* Westminster and Royal London, *above*). Everyone loves to take a snap of the scarlet-coated guardsman standing sentinel outside the imposing Tudor gateway. ✉ *Friary Court, SW1. Tube: Green Park.*

➍ St. James's Square. One of London's oldest and leafiest squares was also the most snobbish address of all when it was laid out around 1670, with 14 resident dukes and earls installed by 1720. Since 1841, Number 14—one of the several 18th-century residences spared by World War II bombs—has housed the **London Library,** founded by Thomas Carlyle (☞ Carlyle's House *in* Chelsea and Belgravia, *below*), and which, with its million or so volumes, is considered the best private humanities library in the land. You can go in and read the famous authors' complaints in the comments book—but not the famous authors' books, unless you join, at £100 a year. ⊠ *SW1. Tube: Piccadilly Circus.*

➓ Selfridges. With its row of massive Ionic columns, this huge store was opened three years after Harry Gordon Selfridge came to London from Chicago in 1906. Now British-run, Selfridges rivals Harrods (☞ Knightsbridge, Kensington, and Holland Park, *below*) in size and stock, and it is finally rivaling its glamour, too, since investing in major face-lift operations. It stands toward the Marble Arch end of Oxford Street, close by the flagship branch of everyone's favorite chain store, **Marks & Spencer** (usually known by its pet names M&S or Marks & Sparks)—supplier of England's underwear, purveyor of woollies (sweaters, that is), producer of dishes passed off as homemade at dinner parties. This place has by far the highest turnover of stock of any shop in the country, so expect crowds at all times. ⊠ *400 Oxford St., W1,* ☎ *020/7629–1234. Tube: Marble Arch, Bond Street.*

Shepherd Market. Though it looks like a quaint and villagelike tangle of streetlets, this was anything *but* quaint when Edward Shepherd laid it out in 1735 on the site of the orgiastic, two-week-long May Fair (which gave the whole district its name). Now there are sandwich bars, pubs and restaurants, boutiques and nightclubs, and a (fading) red-light reputation in the narrow lanes. ⊠ *Curzon and Shepherd Sts., W1. Tube: Green Park.*

➓ Speakers' Corner. This corner harbors one of London's most public spectacles. Here, on Sunday afternoons, anyone is welcome to mount a soapbox and declaim upon any topic. It's an irresistible showcase of eccentricity, though sadly diminished since the death in 1994 of the "Protein Man," who thought the eating of meat, cheese, and peanuts led to uncontrollable acts of passion that would destroy Western civilization. The pamphlets he sold for four decades down Oxford Street are now collector's items. ⊠ *Cumberland Gate, Park La., W1. Tube: Marble Arch.*

★ ➌ Spencer House. Ancestral abode of the Spencers—Diana, Princess of Wales's family—this great mansion is perhaps the finest example of 18th-century elegance, on a domestic scale, extant in London. Superlatively restored by Lord Rothschild, the house was built in 1766 for the first Earl Spencer, heir to the first Duchess of Marlborough. A gorgeous Doric facade, complete with a pediment adorned with classical statues, announces at once Earl Spencer's passion for the Grand Tour and the classical antiquities of the past. Inside, James "Athenian" Stuart decorated the gilded State Rooms, including the Painted Room, the first completely Neoclassic room in Europe. The most ostentatious part of the house (and the Spencers—witness the £40,000 diamond shoe buckles the first countess proudly wore—could be given to ostentation) is the florid bow window of the Palm Room: covered with stucco palm trees, it conjures up both ancient Palmyra and modern Miami Beach. ⊠ *27 St. James's Pl., SW1,* ☎ *020/7499–8620.* ▨ *£6.* ☉ *Guided tour leaves approx. every 25 mins, Sun. 10:45 AM–4:45 (tickets on sale Sun. at 10:30). Closed Aug. and Jan. Tube: Green Park.* ✎

★ ⑮ **Wallace Collection.** Assembled by four generations of Marquesses of Hertford and given to the nation by the widow of Sir Richard Wallace, bastard son of the fourth, this collection of art and artifacts is important, exciting, under-visited—and free. As at the Frick Collection in New York, the setting here, Hertford House, is part of the show—a fine late-18th-century mansion, built for the Duke of Manchester and completely renovated during the late 1970s.

The first marquess was a patron of Sir Joshua Reynolds, the second bought Hertford House, the third—a flamboyant socialite—favored Sèvres porcelain and 17th-century Dutch painting; but it was the eccentric fourth marquess who, from his self-imposed exile in Paris, really built the collection, snapping up Bouchers, Fragonards, Watteaus, and Lancrets for a song (the French Revolution having rendered them dangerously unfashionable), augmenting these with furniture and sculpture and sending his son Richard out to do the deals. With 30 years of practice behind him, Richard Wallace continued acquiring treasures after his father's death, scouring Italy for majolica and Renaissance gold, then moving most of it to London. Look for Rembrandt's portrait of his son, the Rubens landscape, Gainsborough and Romney portraits, the Van Dycks and Canalettos, the French rooms, and of course the porcelain. The highlight is Fragonard's *The Swing,* which conjures up the 18th century's let-them-eat-cake frivolity better than any other painting around. Don't forget to smile back at Frans Hals's *Laughing Cavalier* in the Big Gallery or pay your respects to Thomas Sully's enchanting *Queen Victoria,* which resides in a rouge-pink salon (just to the right of the main entrance) that is probably the prettiest room in town. There is a fine collection of armor and weaponry in the basement in relief to all the upstairs gentility. ⊠ *Hertford House, Manchester Sq., W1,* ☎ *020/7935–0687.* ⊡ *Free.* ☉ *Mon.–Sat. 10–5, Sun. 2–5. Tube: Bond Street.* ✎

Waterloo Place. This is a long rectangle off Pall Mall, punctuated by the Duke of York Memorial Column atop the Duke of York Steps and littered with statues, among them Florence Nightingale, the "Lady with the Lamp" nurse-heroine of the Crimean War; Captain R. F. Scott, who led a disastrous Antarctic expedition in 1911–12 and is here frozen in a bronze by his wife; Edward VII, mounted; George VI; and, as usual, Victoria, here in terra-cotta. Flanking Waterloo Place looking onto Pall Mall are two of the gentlemen's clubs for which St. James's came to be known as Clubland: the **Athenaeum** and the former United Service Club, now the **Institute of Directors**, a favorite haunt of the Duke of Wellington. The latter was built by John Nash in 1827–28 but was given a face-lift by Decimus Burton 30 years later to match it up with the Athenaeum across the way, which he had designed. It's fitting that you gaze on the Athenaeum first, since it was—and is—the most elite of all the societies. (It called itself "the Society" until 1830 just to rub it in.) Most prime ministers and cabinet ministers, archbishops, and bishops have belonged; the founder, John Wilson Croker (the first to call the British right-wingers "Conservatives"), decreed it the club for artists and writers, and so literary types (Sir Arthur Conan Doyle, Rudyard Kipling, J. M. Barrie—the posh ones) have graced its lists, too. Women are barred. Most clubs will tolerate female guests these days, but few admit women members, and anyway, even if your anatomy is correct, it's almost impossible to become a member unless you have the connections—which, of course, is the whole point. ⊠ *Regent St., Pall Mall, SW1. Piccadilly Circus.*

SOHO AND COVENT GARDEN

A quadrilateral delineated by Regent Street, Coventry and Cranbourn streets, Charing Cross Road, and the eastern half of Oxford Street encloses Soho, the most fun part of the West End. This appellation, unlike the New York neighborhood's similar one, is not an elision of anything but a blast from the past—derived (as far as we know) from the shouts of "So-ho!" that royal huntsmen in Whitehall Palace's parklands were once heard to cry. One of Charles II's illegitimate sons, the Duke of Monmouth, was an early resident, his dubious pedigree setting the tone for the future: for many years, Soho was London's strip show–peep show–clip joint–sex shop–brothel center. The mid-'80s brought legislation that granted expensive licenses to a few such establishments and closed down the rest; most prostitution had already been ousted by the 1959 Street Offences Act. Only a cosmetic smear of red-light activity remains now, plus a shop called Condomania and one or two purveyors of couture fetish wear for trendy club goers.

These clubs, which cluster around the Soho grid, are the diametric opposite of the St. James's gentlemen's museums—they cater to youth, change soundtracks every month, and post tyrannical fashion police at the door. Another breed of Soho club is the strictly members-only media haunts (the Groucho, the Soho House, Fred's, Brown's, Black's), salons for carefully segregated strata of high-income hipsters. The same crowd populates the astonishing selection of restaurants, but then so do the rest of London and all its visitors—because Soho is gourmet country.

It was after the First World War, when London households relinquished their resident cooks en masse, that Soho's gastronomic reputation was established. It had been a cosmopolitan area since the first immigrant wave of French Huguenots arrived in the 1600s. More French came fleeing the revolution during the late-18th century, then the Paris Commune of 1870, followed by Germans, Russians, Poles, Greeks, and (especially) Italians, and, much later, Chinese. Pedestrianized Gerrard Street, south of Shaftsbury Avenue, is the hub of London's compact Chinatown, which boasts restaurants, dim sum houses, Chinese supermarkets, and annual February Chinese New Year's celebrations, plus a brace of scarlet pagoda-style archways and a pair of phone booths with pictogram dialing instructions.

The former Covent Garden Market became the Covent Garden Piazza, with the Central Market in the middle, in 1980, and it still functions as the center of a neighborhood—one that has always been alluded to as "colorful." It was originally the "convent garden" belonging to the Abbey of St. Peter at Westminster (later Westminster Abbey). The land was given to the first Earl of Bedford by the Crown after the Dissolution of the Monasteries in 1536. The Earls—later promoted to Dukes—of Bedford held on to the place right up until 1918, when the 11th Duke managed to off-load what had by then become a liability. In between, the area enclosed by Long Acre, St. Martin's Lane, Drury Lane, and assorted streets north of the Strand had gone from the height of fashion (until the snobs moved west to brand-new St. James's) to a period of arty-literary bohemia during the 18th century, followed by an era of vice and mayhem, once more to become vegetable provisioner to London when the market building went up in the 1830s, followed by the Flower Market in 1870 (Eliza Dolittle's alma mater in Shaw's *Pygmalion* and Lerner and Loewe's musical version, *My Fair Lady*).

Still, it was no Mayfair, what with 1,000-odd market porters spending their 40 shillings a week in the alehouses, brothels, and gambling dens that had never quite disappeared. By the time the Covent Garden Estate Company took over the running of the market from the 11th duke, it seemed as if seediness had set in for good, and when the fruit-and-veg trade moved out to the bigger, better Nine Elms Market in Vaux-hall in 1974, it left behind a decrepit wasteland. But this is one of London's success stories: the Greater London Council (now sadly de-funct) stepped in with a dream of a rehabilitation plan—not unlike the one that was tried, though less successfully, in the Parisian equivalent, Les Halles. By 1980 the transformation was complete.

Numbers in the text below correspond to numbers in the margin and on the Soho and Covent Garden map.

A Good Walk

Soho, being small, is easy to explore, though it's also easy to mistake one narrow, crowded street for another, and even Londoners go astray here. Enter from the northwest corner, Oxford Circus, and head south for about 200 yards down Regent Street, turn left onto Great Marlbor-ough Street, and head to the top of **Carnaby Street** ①. Turn right off Broad-wick Street into Berwick (pronounced "Berrick") Street, famed as central London's best fruit-and-vegetable market. Then step through tiny Walker's Court (ignoring the notorious hookers' bulletin board); cross Brewer Street, named for two extinct 18th-century breweries; and you'll have arrived at Soho's hip (and very gay) hangout, Old Compton Street. From here, Wardour, Dean, Frith, and Greek streets lead north, all of them bursting with restaurants and clubs. Either of the last two leads north to **Soho Square** ②, but head one block south instead, to Shaftes-bury Avenue, heart of theaterland, across which you'll find Chinatown's main drag, Gerrard Street. Below Gerrard Street is **Leicester Square** ③, and running along its west side is Charing Cross Road, the bibliophile's dream. You'll find some of the best of the specialist bookshops in little Cecil Court, running east just before Trafalgar Square.

The easiest way to find the **Covent Garden Piazza** ④ and market build-ing is to walk down Cranbourn Street, next to the Leicester Square tube, then down Long Acre, and turn right at James Street. Around here are **St. Paul's Church** ⑤—the actors' church—the **London Transport Mu-seum** ⑥, and the **Theatre Museum** ⑦, as well as plenty of shops and cafés. (If your aim is to shop, **Neal Street,** Floral Street, the streets around Seven Dials, and the Thomas Neal's mall all reward exploration.) From Seven Dials, veer 45 degrees south onto Mercer Street, turning right on Long Acre, then left onto Garrick Street, past the **Garrick Club** ⑧, left onto Rose Street, and right onto Floral Street. At the other end you'll emerge onto Bow Street, right next to the **Royal Opera House** ⑨ and the **Bow Street Magistrates' Court** ⑩. Continuing on and turning left onto Russell Street, you reach **Drury Lane** and the **Theatre Royal** ⑪.

At the end of Drury Lane is the Aldwych, a great big croissant of a po-tential traffic accident, with a central island on which stand three hulking monoliths: India House, Melbourne House, and the handsome 1935 Neoclassic Bush House, headquarters of the BBC World Service. Stranded on traffic islands to the west are the 1717 St. Mary-le-Strand; James Gibbs's (of St. Martin-in-the-Fields fame; ☞ Westminster and Royal London, *above*) first public building, inspired by the Baroque churches of Rome; and Wren's St. Clement Danes (with a tower ap-pended by Gibbs), whose 10 bells peal the tune of the nursery rhyme "Oranges and lemons, Say the bells of St. Clements . . ." even though the bells in the rhyme belong to the St. Clements in Eastcheap. Inside is a book listing 1,900 American airmen who were killed during World War II. Heading west, perhaps stopping at the **Courtauld Institute of Art** ⑫, walk the ¾-mi traffic-clogged **Strand** to the southern end, where you take Villiers Street down to the Thames. See the historic York Watergate and **Cleopatra's Needle** ⑬ by Victoria Embankment Gardens; cross the gardens northwest to the **Adelphi** ⑭, circumnavigating the Strand by sticking to the embankment walk; and you'll soon reach Waterloo Bridge, where (weather permitting) you can catch some of London's most glamorous views, toward both the City and Westminster around the Thames bend.

TIMING

The distance covered here is around 5 mi if you include the lengthy walk down the Strand and riverside stroll back. Skip that and it's barely a couple of miles, but you will almost certainly get lost, because the streets in both Covent Garden and Soho are winding, chaotic, and not logically disposed. Although getting lost is half the fun, it does make it hard to predict how long this walk will take. You can whiz round both neighborhoods in an hour, but if the area appeals at all, you'll want all day—for shopping, lunch, the Theatre and Transport museums, and the Courtauld Galleries. One way to do it is to start at Leicester Square at 2 PM, when the Half Price Theatre Booth opens; pick up tickets for later; and then walk, shop, and eat in between.

HOW TO GET THERE

A popular way to get to Soho is to hop on the Northern Line to Tottenham Court Road and walk south down Charing Cross Road, then west along Old Compton Street into the district proper, or eastward, by turning left at Shaftesbury Avenue, over to the Covent Garden area. The Covent Garden tube stop is on the Piccadilly Line; Leicester Square—the nearest tube to Soho—is on the Northern and Piccadilly Lines. The best Soho buses are Buses 3, 8, 10, 12, 13, 15, 23, 38, 73, 139, 159, and 176 to Charing Cross Road and Shaftesbury Avenue; for Covent Garden, get those listed above or the ones that stop along the Strand: Buses 9, 11, 13, 15, and 23.

Sights to See

⑭ **Adelphi.** This regal riverfront row of houses was the work of London's Scottish architects—all four of them. John, Robert, James, and William Adam, being brothers, gave rise to the name, from the Greek *adelphoi*, meaning brothers. All the late-18th-century design stars were roped in to beautify the interiors, but the grandeur gradually eroded, and today very few of the 24 houses remain; 1–4 Robert Street, and 7 Adam Street are the best. ✉ *The Strand, WC2. Tube: Charing Cross, Temple.*

⑩ **Bow Street Magistrates' Court.** This was where the prototype of the modern police force first operated. Known as the Bow Street Runners (because they chased thieves on foot), they were the brainchild of the second Bow Street magistrate—none other than Henry Fielding, the author of *Tom Jones* and *Joseph Andrews*. The late-19th-century edifice on the site went up during one of the market improvement drives. It now houses three courts, including that of the Metropolitan Chief Magistrate, who hears all extradition applications. ✉ *Bow Street, WC2. Tube: Covent Garden.*

❶ **Carnaby Street.** The '60s synonym for swinging London fell into a post-party depression, reemerging sometime during the '80s as the main drag of a public-relations invention called West Soho. Blank stares would greet anyone asking directions to such a place, but it is geographically logical, and the tangle of streets—Foubert's Place, Broadwick Street, Marshall Street—do cohere, at least in type of merchandise (youth accessories, mostly, with a smattering of up-and-coming, happening designer boutiques and fashionable restaurants). Broadwick Street is also notable as the birthplace, at Number 74, in 1758, of the great visionary poet and painter William Blake. At age 26 he relocated back to

Soho and Covent Garden

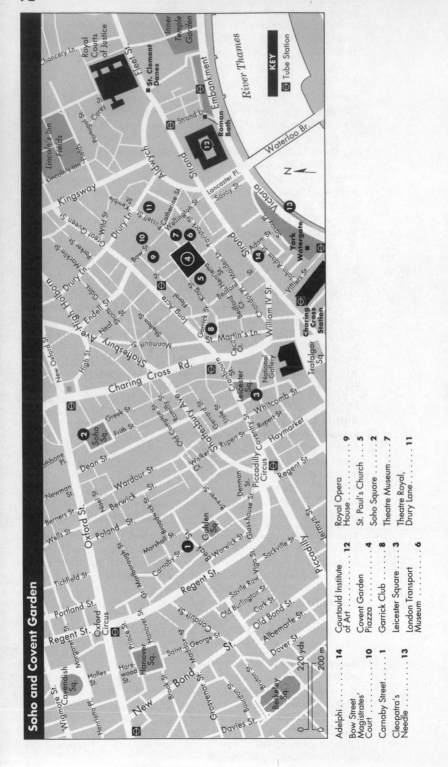

Adelphi **14**

Bow Street
Magistrates'
Court **10**

Carnaby Street **1**

Cleopatra's
Needle **13**

Courtauld Institute
of Art **12**

Covent Garden
Piazza **4**

Garrick Club **8**

Leicester Square **3**

London Transport
Museum **6**

Royal Opera
House. **9**

St. Paul's Church **5**

Soho Square **2**

Theatre Museum **7**

Theatre Royal,
Drury Lane **11**

this house for a year to sell prints next door, at Number 72 (now an ugly tower block), and then remained a Soho resident on Poland Street. ⊠ *W1. Tube: Oxford Circus.*

⑬ Cleopatra's Needle. Off the triangular-handkerchief Victoria Embankment Gardens, where office sandwich-eaters and people who call it home coexist, is London's *very oldest thing*, predating its arbitrary namesake, and London itself, by centuries. The 60-ft pink granite obelisk was erected at Heliopolis, in lower Egypt, in about 1475 BC, then moved to Alexandria, where in 1819 Mohammed Ali, the Turkish Viceroy of Egypt, rescued it from its fallen state and presented it to the British. The British, though grateful, had not the faintest idea how to get the 186-ton gift home, so they left it there for years until an expatriate English engineer contrived an iron pontoon to float it to London via Spain. The sphinxes are a later, British addition. Future archaeologists will find an 1878 time capsule underneath, containing the morning papers, several bibles, a railway timetable, some pins, a razor, and a dozen photos of Victorian pinup girls. ⊠ *Embankment, WC2. Tube: Charing Cross, Embankment.*

⑫ Courtauld Institute of Art. One of London's most beloved art collections, the Courtauld reopened in October 1998 after being closed for complete renovation. The new quarters are found in grand 18th-century classical Somerset House, alongside a vast compilation of civil servants (conjure up the red-tape-bestrewn Circumlocution Offices in Dickens's *Little Dorrit*) who still lurk inside. Founded in 1931 by the textile maven Samuel Courtauld, this is London's—and probably western Europe's—finest Impressionist and Postimpressionist collection, from Bonnard to Van Gogh (Manet's *Bar at the Folies-Bergère* is the star), with bonus post-Renaissance works thrown in. Botticelli, Breughel, Tiepolo, and Rubens are also represented, thanks to the exquisite bequest of Count Antoine Seilern's Princes Gate collection. The exciting new finds of an ancient "lost" royal palace went on show in spring 2000 at Somerset House. The relics were thought to have been lost underneath the building, but recent excavations in the parking lot have uncovered parts of the original walls of the palace—once home to Elizabeth I before she was crowned and to Charles I's and Charles II's queens. Finds from the dig, along with gold, silver, and decorative arts, are on display in the vaults of Somerset House as the Gilbert Collection (☎ 020/7845–4600). And for the first time, other interior gems are on view: the 18th-century chambers, including the Seamen's Waiting Hall, the Navy Stair, and Navy Commissioners' Barge, which has returned to its original old mooring at the Water Gate. Cafés and a restored river terrace complete the major face-lift that visitors can now reach directly from Waterloo Bridge by way of a new stone and glass footbridge across the river. ⊠ *The Strand, WC2,* ☎ *020/7848–2526.* ⊠ *Courtauld or Gilbert Collection £4; Courtauld free Mon. noon–6; combined ticket to Gilbert Collection and Courtauld £7.* ⊙ *Mon.–Sat. 10–6, Sun. noon–6 (last admission 5:15). Tube: Aldwych, Embankment, Temple.*

❹ Covent Garden Piazza. The restored 1840 market building around which Covent Garden pivots is known as the Piazza. Inside, the shops are mostly higher-class clothing chains, plus a couple of cafés and some knickknack stores that are good for gifts. There's a superior crafts market on most days, too. If you turn right, you'll reach the indoor **Jubilee Market**, with stalls selling clothing, army surplus gear, more crafts, and more knickknacks. At yet another market off to the left (on the way back to the tube), the leather goods, antiques, and secondhand clothing stalls are a little more exciting. In summer it may seem that everyone you see around the Piazza (and the crowds are legion) is a fellow tourist, but there is still plenty of office life in the area, and Londoners continue to flock here. By the church in the square, street performers—from global musicians to jugglers and mime artists—play to the crowds. ⊠ *Covent Garden, WC2. Tube: Covent Garden.*

8 **Garrick Club.** Named for the 18th-century actor and theater manager David Garrick, this club is, because of its literary-theatrical bent, more louche than its St. James's brothers, and famous actors, from Sir Laurence Olivier down, have always been proud to join—along with Dickens, Thackeray, and Trollope, in their time. Find the **Lamb & Flag** down teeny Rose Street to the left. Dickens drank in this pub, better known in its 17th-century youth as the Bucket of Blood, owing to the bareknuckle boxing matches held upstairs. (You'll find that many London pubs claim Dickens as an habitué, and it's unclear whether they exaggerate or the author was the city's premier sot.) ⊠ *15 Garrick St., WC2. Tube: Leicester Square, Covent Garden.*

3 **Leicester Square.** This square (pronounced "Lester") is showing no sign of its great age. Looking at the neon of the major movie houses, the fast-food outlets (plus a useful Häagen-Dazs café), and the disco entrances, you'd never guess it was laid out around 1630. By the 19th century it was already bustling and disreputable, and now it's usually one of the only places crowded after midnight—with suburban teenagers, Belgian backpackers, and London's swelling ranks of the homeless. That said, it is not a threatening place, and the liveliness can be quite cheering. In the middle is a statue of a sulking Shakespeare, clearly wishing he were somewhere else and perhaps remembering the days when the cinemas were live theaters—burlesque houses, but live all the same. Here, too, are figures of Hogarth, Reynolds, and Charlie Chaplin, and underneath, but not visible, is a new £22 million electrical substation. One landmark certainly worth visiting is the **Society of London Theatre ticket kiosk,** on the southwest corner, which sells half-price tickets for many of that evening's performances (☞ Theater *in* Chapter 4). On the northeast corner, in Leicester Place, stands **Notre Dame de France,** with a wonderful mural by Jean Cocteau in one of its side chapels. ⊠ *WC2. Tube: Covent Garden.*

🖐 **6** **London Transport Museum.** Housed in the old Flower Market at the southeastern corner of the Covent Garden Piazza, this museum tells the story of mass transportation in the capital, and it is much better than it sounds. It is particularly child-friendly, with lots of touch-screen interactive material; live actors in costume (including a Victorian horse-dung collector, though you should go early to see them); old rolling stock; period smells and sounds; and, best of all, a tube-driving simulator. There's also a café and a shop selling the wonderful old London Transport posters, plus mugs, socks, bow ties, and so on, printed with that elegant London tube map, designed by Harry Beck in 1933 and still in use today. The White Card is accepted. ⊠ *Piazza, WC2,* ☎ *020/7379–6344.* ⌸ *£5.50.* ☉ *Sat.–Thurs. 10–6, Fri. 11–6. Tube: Covent Garden.*

Neal Street. One of Covent Garden's most intriguing shopping streets begins north of Long Acre, catercorner to the tube station, and is closed to traffic halfway down. Here you can buy everything you never knew you needed—apricot tea, sitars, vintage aviators' jackets, silk kimonos, Alvar Aalto vases, halogen desk lamps, shoes with heel lower than toe, collapsible top hats, and so on. To the left off Neal Street, on Earlham Street, is Thomas Neal's—a new, upmarket, designerish clothing and housewares mall named after the founder (in 1693) of the star-shape cobbled junction of tiny streets just past there, called Seven Dials—a surprisingly residential enclave, with lots going on behind the tenement-style warehouse facades. The small and intimate **Donmar Warehouse Theatre** is part of the complex, and it has a radical range of theater—such as Nicole Kidman in *"The Blue Room."* Turning left onto the next street off Neal Street, Shorts Gardens, you come to Neal's Yard (note the comical, water-operated wooden clock), originally just a whole-foods wholesaler and now an entire holistic village, with therapy rooms, an organic bakery and dairy, a great vegetarian café, and a medical herbalist's shop reminiscent of a medieval apothecary. ⊠ *WC2. Tube: Covent Garden.*

🕐 **Rock Circus.** This shamelessly touristy offshoot of Madame Tussaud's waxworks (☞ *Regent's Park and Hampstead, below*) features animatronic and wax pop stars miming to their hits or frozen in time, chronologically displayed to give the impression of a museum of popular music. As some might imagine, this is strictly for younger teens. ⊠ *London Pavilion, Piccadilly Circus, W1,* ☎ *020/7734–7203.* 🎫 *£8.25.* ⊘ *Daily 10–5:30; Tues. 11–5:30. Tube: Piccadilly Circus.*

⑨ Royal Opera House. After technical teething hitches that stopped the schedule and had Falstaff hanging in the balance, the fabled home of the Royal Ballet and Britain's finest opera company reopened after seismic renovations with a gala performance on December 1, 1999. Here, in days of yore, Joan Sutherland brought down the house as Lucia di Lammermoor, and Rudolf Nureyev and Margot Fonteyn became the greatest ballet duo of all time. For such delights, seats were top dollar—nearly £100—or just one-twentieth of that lordly amount. Whatever the price, it was worth it if you loved red-and-gold Victorian decor, which always managed to give a very special feel to the hush that precedes the start of a performance. London's premier opera venue was designed in 1858 by E. M. Barry, son of Sir Charles, the House of Commons architect. This is actually the third theater on the site. The first opened in 1732 and burned down in 1808; the second opened a year later under the aegis of one John Anderson, only to succumb to fire in 1856 (Anderson, who had lost two theaters already, had an appalling record when it came to keeping the limelights apart from the curtains).

Now, the entire building has been overhauled spectacularly as a modern, practical, technologically-streamlined opera house, while keeping the magic of the grand Victorian theater. Without doubt, the glass and steel Floral Hall (so badly damaged by fire in the 1950s it was used only for storing scenery) is the most wonderful jaw-dropping feature, and visitors can wander in and drink in the atmosphere during the day. The same is true of the new Amphitheatre Bar and Piazza concourse, which give a splendid panorama across the city. The whole ethos is of a grand opening up of what was perceived as being for the elite (there are free lunchtime chamber concerts and a full educational program for schoolchildren). The ROH executive director, New Yorker Michael Kaiser, has cut ticket prices on many performances and with the new style "open house" has aimed to bring opera to the masses. Behind the scenes, conditions for the two companies have been drastically improved—the Royal Ballet has a real home with state-of-the-art rehearsal rooms, and practice rooms for the musicians. The signs are looking good for the Opera House to recover its form and shake off the shower of bad publicity that has surrounded it for far too long. At press time Kaiser announced that he would resign by the end of the 2000–01 season, so more changes may be in the works. For information about the resident troupe's performing schedules, *see* Chapter 4. ⊠ *Bow St.,* ☎ *020/7240–1066 or 020/7240–1200. Tube: Covent Garden.*

⑤ St. Paul's Church. If you want to commune with the spirits of Vivien Leigh, Noël Coward, Edith Evans, and Charlie Chaplin, this might be the place. Memorials to them and many other theater greats are found in this 1633 work of the renowned Inigo Jones, which has always been known as "the actors' church," thanks to the neighboring theater district and St. Paul's prominent parishioners (well-known actors often read the lessons at services). Fittingly, its portico was the setting for *Pygmalion*'s opening scene. St. Paul's Church (Wren's mammoth cathedral is eastward in the City) is across the Covent Garden Piazza, often picturesquely punctuated with street entertainers—those who have passed auditions for this most coveted of London's street venues. ⊠ *Bedford St., WC2. Tube: Covent Garden.*

❷ **Soho Square.** Laid out about 1680, this square was fashionable during the 18th century. Only two of the original houses still stand, plus the 19th-century central garden. It's now a place of peace and offices (among them Paul McCartney's music publishers and Bloomsbury Publishing). That isn't a Tudor landmark in the center but a Tudor-style thatch-and-daub Victorian gardener's hut—an almost fairy-tale sight to enjoy during a take-out lunch in the park. ⊠ *W1. Tube: Tottenham Court Road.*

NEED A BREAK? Take any excuse you can think of to visit either of Soho's wonderful rival patisseries: **Maison Bertaux** (⊠ 28 Greek St.) or **Pâtisserie Valerie** (⊠ 44 Old Compton St.). Both serve divine gâteaux, milles-feuilles, croissants, éclairs, and more, the former in an upstairs salon, the latter in a darkish room behind the cake counters.

Strand. Remember Judy Garland doing Burlington Bertie in Chaplin drag, walking down the Strand with gloves in hand, in *A Star Is Born*? William Hargreaves's song was a popular number in the Strand music halls that put the street on the map afresh during the early 1900s. Now its presence on maps is about all that the characterless Strand has to recommend it. ⊠ *WC2. Tube: Charing Cross.*

🐾 ❼ **Theatre Museum.** This mostly below-ground museum aims to re-create the excitement of theater itself. There are usually programs in progress allowing children to get in a mess with makeup or have a giant dressing-up session. Permanent exhibits paint a history of the English stage from the 16th century to Mick Jagger's jumpsuit, with tens of thousands of theater playbills and sections on such topics as Hamlet through the ages and pantomime—the peculiar British theatrical tradition whereby men dress as ugly women (as distinct from RuPaul) and girls wear tights and play princes. There's a little theater in the bowels of the museum and a ticket desk for "real" theaters around town, plus an archive holding video recordings and audiotapes of significant British theatrical productions. ⊠ *7 Russell St., WC2,* ☎ *020/7836–7891.* 🎫 *£4.50.* ⊙ *Tues.–Sun. 10–6. Tube: Covent Garden.*

⓫ **Theatre Royal, Drury Lane.** This is London's best-known auditorium and almost its largest. Since World War II, its forte has been musicals (*Miss Saigon* is the current resident; past ones have included *The King and I, My Fair Lady, South Pacific, Hello, Dolly!* and *A Chorus Line*)—though David Garrick, who managed it from 1747 to 1776, made its name by reviving the works of the by-then-obscure William Shakespeare. It enjoys all the romantic accessories of a London theater—a history of fires (it burned down three times, once in a Wren-built incarnation), riots (in 1737, when a posse of footmen demanded free admission), attempted regicides (George II in 1716 and his grandson George III in 1800), and even sightings of the most famous phantom of theaterland, the Man in Grey (in the Circle, matinees). The entrance is on Catherine Street. ⊠ *Catherine St., WC2. Tube: Covent Garden.*

BLOOMSBURY AND LEGAL LONDON

The character of an area of London can change visibly from one street to the next. Nowhere is this so clear as in the contrast between fun-loving Soho and intellectual Bloomsbury, a mere 100 yards to the northeast, or between arty, trendy Covent Garden and—on the other side of Kingsway—sober Holborn. Both Bloomsbury and Holborn are almost purely residential and should be seen by day. The first district is best known for its famous flowering of literary-arty bohemia, personified by the clique known as the Bloomsbury Group during this century's first three decades, and for the British Museum and the University of London, which dominate it now. The second sounds as exciting as, say, a center for accountants or dentists, but don't be put off—filled with magnificently ancient buildings, it's more interesting and beautiful than you might suppose.

Let's get the Bloomsbury Group out of the way since you can't visit them and nothing exists to mark its territory beyond a sprinkling of Blue Plaques. (London has about 400 of these government-sponsored tablets commemorating persons who enhanced "human welfare or happiness" and have been dead for at least 20 years.) There's also a plaque in Bloomsbury Square saying nothing about this elite core of writers and artists except that they lived around here. The chief Bloomsburies were Virginia Woolf, E. M. Forster, Vanessa and Clive Bell, Duncan Grant, Dora Carrington, Roger Fry, John Maynard Keynes, and Lytton Strachey, with satellites including Rupert Brooke and Christopher Isherwood. They agreed with G. E. Moore's philosophical notion that "the pleasures of human intercourse and the enjoyment of beautiful objects . . . form the rational ultimate end of social progress." True to their beliefs, when they weren't producing beautiful objects, the friends enjoyed much human intercourse, as has been exhaustively documented, not least in Virginia Woolf's own diaries. All you need do to find out more about them is to read the "Review" supplements of the Sunday broadsheets, which are forever running Bloomsbury exposés as if they were fresh gossip.

More clearly visible than those literary salons is the time-warp territory of interlocking alleys, gardens and cobbled courts, and town houses and halls where London's legal profession grew up. The Great Fire of 1666 razed most of the city but spared the buildings of legal London, and the whole neighborhood oozes history. What is best about the area is that it lacks the commercial veneer of other historic sites, mostly because it still is very much the center of London's legal profession. Barristers, berobed and bewigged, may add an anachronistic frisson to your sightseeing, but they're only on their way to work.

They are headed for one of the four "Inns of Court": Gray's Inn, Lincoln's Inn, Middle Temple, and Inner Temple. Those arcane names are simply explained. The inns were just that: lodging houses for the lawyers who, back in the 14th century, clustered together here so everyone knew where to find them and presently took over the running of the inns themselves. The temples were built on land owned by the Knights Templar, a chivalric order founded during the First Crusade in the 11th century; their 12th-century Temple Church still stands here. Few barristers (British for trial lawyers) still live in the inns, but nearly all keep chambers (British for barristers' offices) here, and all are still obliged to eat a requisite number of meals in the hall of "their" inn during training—no dinner, no career. They take exams, too.

Numbers in the text correspond to numbers in the margin and on the Bloomsbury and Legal London map.

A Good Walk

From Russell Square tube, walk south down Southampton Row and west on Great Russell Street, passing **Bloomsbury Square** on the left, en route to London's biggest and most important collection of antiquities, the **British Museum** ①. Leaving this via the back exit leads you to Montague Place, which you should cross to Malet Street, straight ahead, to reach the **University of London** ②. On the left after you pass the university buildings is the back of the Royal Academy of Dramatic Art, or RADA (its entrance is on Gower Street), where at least half of the most stellar British thespians got their training, with **University College** ③ following at the top of Malet Place. For a delightful detour, head west over to Scala Street (just one block west from the Goodge Street tube stop, then one block north on Charlotte Street) to find the delightful Victorian-era wonders of **Pollock's Toy Museum** ④. The streets surrounding here and the Adam brothers–built Fitzroy Square are known as Fitzrovia, so named by literary soaks who drank at the Fitzroy Tavern in Charlotte Street. Back around the university, head over to Gordon Street to reach Gordon Square. For the prettiest little street with picturesque 19th-century shop fronts, divert to Woburn Walk (Irish poet Yeats lived at Number 5). If you're interested in Asian art, stop in at the **Percival David Foundation of Chinese Art** ⑤; if you want to stop in at the spectacular new **British Library** ⑥, head north up to Euston Road. Otherwise, continue south down busy Woburn Place, veering left down Guilford Street to reach Coram's Fields, home of the **Thomas Coram Foundation** ⑦; then turn left south of there on Guilford Place, then right to Doughty Street and the **Dickens House Museum** ⑧. Two streets west, parallel to Doughty Street, is pretty Lamb's Conduit Street (whose pretty pub, the Lamb, Dickens inevitably frequented).

At the bottom of Lamb's Conduit Street you reach Theobalds Road, where you enter the first of the Inns of Court, **Gray's Inn** ⑨, emerging from here onto High Holborn (pronounced "Hoe-bun")—heavy with traffic, as (with the Strand) it is the main route from the City to the West End and Westminster—and Hatton Garden, running north from Holborn Circus and still the center of London's diamond and jewelry trade. Pass another ghost of former trading, **Staple Inn** ⑩, and turn left down tiny Great Turnstile Row to reach **Lincoln's Inn** ⑪, where you pass the Hall and continue around the west side of New Square to Carey Street, which leads you round into Portugal Street. Here you'll find the Old Curiosity Shop, probably one of the rare places in London Dickens did *not* frequent. Recross to the north side of Lincoln's Inn Fields to **Sir John Soane's Museum** ⑫ or walk the other way on Carey Street to reach the **Royal Courts of Justice** ⑬, which run through to the Strand. Off to the left is Fleet Street and the 1610 **Prince Henry's Room** ⑭. Cross the Strand to **Temple** ⑮ and pass through the elaborate stone arch to Middle Temple Lane, which you follow past **Temple Church** ⑯ to the Thames.

TIMING

This is a substantial walk of 3 to 4 mi, and it has two distinct halves. The first half, around Bloomsbury, is not so interesting on the surface, but it features a major highlight of London, the British Museum, where you could easily add 1 mi to your total and certainly at least two hours. The Dickens House is also worth a stop. The second half, legal London, is a real walker's walk, with most of the highlights in the architecture and atmosphere of the buildings and streets. The exception is Sir John Soane's Museum, which will absorb an extra hour. The walk alone can be done comfortably in two hours and is best on a sunny day.

HOW TO GET THERE

The best tube stops for the Inns of Court are Holborn on the Central and Piccadilly lines (surface and walk east up High Holborn, then south), or Chancery Lane on the Central Line. For the British Museum, Tottenham Court Road (Northern and Central lines) and Russell Square (Piccadilly Line) are equidistant. Bus 7 is the best bus for the BM; for the Inns of Court, get Bus 8, 17, 25, 45, 46, or 243 to High Holborn or Bus 17, 19, 38, 45, 46, 55, or 243 to Theobalds Road.

Sights to See

Bloomsbury Square. This was laid out in 1660, making it the earliest of the Bloomsbury squares, although none of the original houses remain; what is most remarkable about it now is that you can always find a parking spot in the huge underground garage. You'll find it by exiting the tube at Tottenham Court Road—a straight, very ugly street where London buys its electrical appliances, hi-fi equipment, and computer accessories—and taking Great Russell Street east. Bloomsbury is dotted with squares—Gordon, Tavistock, Bedford, and Brunswick are the names of some of the more picturesque. ⊠ *WC1. Tube: Tottenham Court Rd.*

❻ British Library. Since 1759, the British Library had always been housed in the British Museum on Gordon Square. But as Britain's greatest library was entitled to a free copy of every single book, periodical, newspaper, and map published in the United Kingdom—a gift of George II, along with his Royal Library (all this translated into 2 mi of additional shelf space per year)—space at the old library, needless to say, ran out long ago. A grand new edifice was commissioned, to rise a few blocks north of the British Museum, between Euston and St. Pancras stations. After many years and delays the great exodus of around 18 million volumes is complete. The new library has been welcoming (qualified) researchers for some time. The library's treasures, however, are on view to the general public: the Magna Carta, Gutenberg Bible, Jane Austen's writings, Shakespeare's First Folio, and musical manuscripts by Handel and Sir Paul McCartney are on show in the John Ritblat Gallery. The Pearson Gallery of Living Words is just that, with exhibits displaying the vitality of the written word; on weekends there are hands-on demonstrations of how a book comes together. Feast your eyes also on the six-story glass tower that holds the 65,000-volume collection of George III, plus a permanent exhibition of rare stamps. And if all that wordiness is just too much, you can relax in the library's piazza or restaurant. Take in one of the free concerts in the amphitheater or one of the modern ballet performances offered in the library's lobbies. ⊠ *96 Euston Rd., NW1,* ☎ *020/7412–7332.* ⊠ *Free.* ☉ *Mon. and Wed.–Fri. 9:30–6, Tues. 9:30–8, Sat. 9:30–5; Sun. 11–5. Tube: Euston, King's Cross.*

★ ☙ ❶ British Museum. With a facade like a great temple, this celebrated treasure house—filled with plunder of incalculable value and beauty from around the globe—is housed in a ponderously dignified Greco-Victorian building that makes for a suitably grand impression. Inside you'll find some of the greatest relics of humankind: the Elgin Marbles, the Rosetta Stone, the Sutton Hoo Treasure—everything, it seems, but the Ark of the Covenant. The museum is rapidly shaking off its ponderous dust as a rash of new galleries open and sections are updated, particularly with the addition of collections from the now-closed Museum of Mankind. The focal point is the unmissable Great Court, a brilliant techno-classical design with a vast glass roof, which highlights and reveals the museum's most well-kept secret—an inner courtyard—for the first time in 150 years. New galleries and exhibit space will celebrate the museum's 250th birthday in 2003 and bring it with a bang into the new century. The revered Reading Room also made a welcome comeback in 2000 after careful restoration. Beyond the new frontage, there

80

British Library 6

British Museum 1

Dickens House
Museum. 8

Gray's Inn 9

Lincoln's Inn 11

Percival David
Foundation of
Chinese Art 5

Pollock's Toy
Museum. 4

Prince Henry's
Room. 14

Royal Courts of
Justice 13

Sir John Soane's
Museum. 12

Staple Inn. 10

Temple 15

Temple Church 16

Thomas Coram
Foundation. 7

University College. . . . 3

University of
London 2

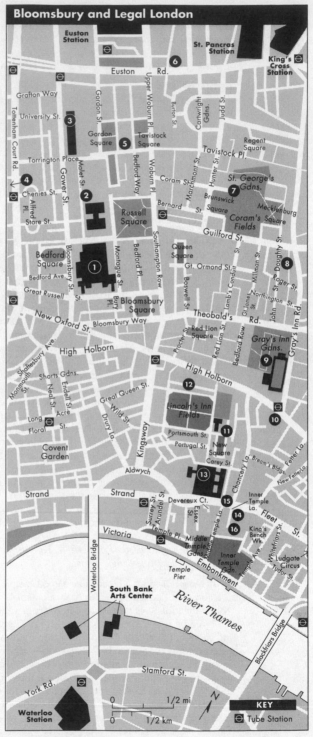

Bloomsbury and Legal London

are 2½ mi of floor space inside, split into nearly 100 galleries—so arm yourself with a free floor plan directly as you go in, or they'll have to send out search parties to rescue you.

The collection began in 1753, when Sir Hans Sloane, physician to Queen Anne and George II, bequeathed his personal collection of curiosities and antiquities to the nation. It then quickly grew, thanks to enthusiastic kleptomaniacs after the Napoleonic Wars—most notoriously the seventh Earl of Elgin, who carried off the marbles from the Parthenon and Erechtheum while on a Greek vacation between 1801 and 1804.

The enormous building, with its classical Greek-style facade featuring figures representing the Progress of Civilization, was finished in 1847, the work of Sir Robert Smirke. Wherever you go, there are marvels, but certain objects and collections are more important, rarer, older, or downright unique, and because you may wish to include these in your wanderings, here follows a highly edited résumé (in order of encounter) of the BM's greatest hits:

Close to the old entrance hall, in the south end of Room 25, is the **Rosetta Stone,** found in 1799 and carved in 196 BC with a decree of Ptolemy V in Egyptian hieroglyphics, demotic, and Greek. It was this multilingual inscription that provided the French Egyptologist Jean-François Champollion with the key to deciphering hieroglyphics.

Maybe the **Elgin Marbles** oughtn't to be here, but since they are—and they are, after all, among the most graceful and heartbreakingly beautiful sculptures on earth—you can find them in Room 8, west of the entrance in the Parthenon Galleries, renovated in 1998. The marbles are now displayed along with an in-depth high-tech exhibit of the sculptures and the Acropolis and brings to the fore the rumbling debate on whether the Greeks should reclaim their spectacular sculptural heritage. Some say aye, and voices in the Greek government respond resoundingly every so often. Above the debate are the lofty remains of the Parthenon frieze that girdled the interior of Athena's temple on the Acropolis, carved around 440 BC (the handless, footless Dionysus who used to recline along its east pediment is especially well known). While you're in the west wing, you can see one of the Seven Wonders of the Ancient World—in fragment form, unfortunately—in Room 12: the **Mausoleum of Halicarnassus.** This 4th-century tomb of Mausolus, King of Caria, was the original "mausoleum."

Upstairs are some of the most perennially popular galleries, especially beloved by children: Rooms 62–63, where the **Egyptian Mummies** live. With the opening of the Roxie Walker Galleries in May 1999, even more relics from the Egyptian Land of the Dead are on view—in addition to more mummies there is a menagerie of animal companions and fascinating items buried alongside the mummies. Scanners have helped reveal further secrets of the mummies, and some displays allow an even closer look beneath the wraps.

Proceeding clockwise, you'll come to Room 49, where the **Mildenhall Treasure** glitters in the refurbished Weston Gallery of Roman Britain. This haul of 4th-century Roman silver tableware was found beneath the sod of a Suffolk field in 1942. Next door, in Room 41, is the equally splendid **Sutton Hoo Treasure,** including swords and helmets, bowls and buckles, all encrusted with jewels—which was buried at sea with (they think) Redwald, King of the Angles, during the 7th century and excavated from a Suffolk field in 1938–39.

In Room 50 lies Pete Marsh, so named by the archaeologists who unearthed the **Lindow Man** from a Cheshire peat marsh. He was ritually slain, probably as a human sacrifice, during the 1st century and lay perfectly pickled in his bog until 1984. Some of the collections from the Museum of Mankind (now closed) have been added to the upper floors, where there are temporary exhibitions to show them off in a new light. The Chase Manhattan Gallery of **North America,** opened in June 1999, has one of the largest collections of native culture outside the North American continent, going back to the earliest hunters 10,000 years ago. Still in the upper level of the museum is the Money Gallery, which holds ancient coins and medals. The new Korean Gallery is scheduled to open in November 2000, with the royal gold crown of Silla (5th–6th century), on loan from the National Museum of Korea, as its centerpiece among ceramics and rare ancient manuscripts. ✉ *Great Russell St., WC1,* ☏ *020/7636–1555.* ⊡ *Free (suggested donation of £2).* ○ *Mon.–Sat. 10–5, Sun. noon–6. Tube: Tottenham Court Rd., Holborn, Russell Sq.* ⊗

NEED A
BREAK?

The British Museum's self-service **restaurant and café** get very crowded but serve a reasonably tasty menu beneath a plaster cast of a part of the Parthenon frieze that Lord Elgin didn't remove. The restaurant is open Monday–Saturday noon–4:30, Sunday noon–5:30; the café, Monday–Saturday 10–3.

---

❽ Dickens House Museum. This is the only one of the many London houses Charles Dickens (1812–70) inhabited that's still standing, and it would have had a real claim to his fame in any case because he wrote *Oliver Twist* and *Nicholas Nickleby* and finished *Pickwick Papers* here between 1837 and 1839. The house looks exactly as it would have in Dickens's day, complete with first editions, letters, and a tall clerk's desk (where the master wrote standing up, often chatting with visiting friends and relatives), plus a treat for Lionel Bart fans—his score of *Oliver!* Down in the basement is a replica of the Dingley Dell kitchen from *Pickwick Papers.* The museum is open on Christmas Day, so you really can celebrate *A Christmas Carol.* ✉ *48 Doughty St., WC1,* ☏ *020/7405–2127.* ⊡ *£4.* ○ *Mon.–Sat. 10–5. Tube: Chancery Lane, Russell Sq.*

❾ Gray's Inn. Although the least architecturally interesting of the four Inns of Court and the one most damaged by German bombs during the '40s, this still has its romantic associations. In 1594, Shakespeare's *Comedy of Errors* was performed for the first time in its hall—which was lovingly restored after World War II and has a fine Elizabethan screen of carved oak. You must make advance arrangements to view the Tudor-style Gray's Inn's Hall (apply in writing, in advance, to the administrator, the Under Treasurer), but you can stroll around the secluded and spacious gardens, first planted by Francis Bacon in 1606. ✉ *Gray's Inn Rd., Holborn,* ☏ *020/7458–7800.* ○ *Weekdays 10–4. Tube: Holborn, Temple.*

★ ⓫ Lincoln's Inn. There's plenty to see at one of the oldest, best-preserved, and most comely of the Inns of Court—from the Chancery Lane Tudor brick gatehouse to the wide-open, tree-lined, atmospheric Lincoln's Inn Fields and the 15th-century chapel remodeled by Inigo Jones in 1620. The wisteria-clad New Square, London's only complete 17th-century square, is not the newest part of the complex; the oldest-looking buildings are—the 1845 Hall and Library, which you must obtain the porter's permission to enter. Pass the Hall and continue around the west side of New Square, and you'll see an archway leading to Carey Street. You have just headed "straight for Queer Street." Since the bankruptcy courts used to stand here, you can divine what the old expression means. A guided tour is available. ✉ *Chancery Ln., WC2,* ☏ *020/7405–1393.* ○ *Gardens weekdays 7–7, chapel weekdays noon–2:30; public may also attend Sun. service at 11:30 in chapel during legal terms. Tube: Chancery Lane.*

⑤ **Percival David Foundation of Chinese Art.** This collection, belonging to the University of London, is dominated by ceramics from the Sung to Qing dynasties—from the 10th to the 19th century, in other words. It's on **Gordon Square**, which Virginia Woolf, the Bells, John Maynard Keynes (all, severally, at Number 46), and Lytton Strachey (at Number 51) called home for a while. ⊠ *53 Gordon Sq., WC1,* ☎ *020/7387–3909.* 🎟 *Free.* ⊘ *Weekdays 10:30–5 (sometimes closed 1–2 for lunch). Tube: Russell Sq.*

⟳ ④ **Pollock's Toy Museum.** For some, this will merit a visit whether they have children or not. A charming treasure trove of a small museum in a warren of rooms in an 18th-century town house, Pollock's is crammed with antique dolls, dolls' houses, and teddy bears. Best of all are the fabulous little toy theaters that Pollock made famous during the Victorian era—more than a few of England's most famous actors grew up playing with these cardboard delights. Even better: you can still buy reproductions of these cut-and-paste theater kits in the toy store on the premises. (Bring lots of money if you want to purchase some of the antique kits still for sale.) ⊠ *1 Scala St., W1,* ☎ *020/7636–3452.* 🎟 *£3.* ⊘ *Mon.–Sat. 10–5. Tube: Goodge St.*

⑭ **Prince Henry's Room.** This is the Jacobean half-timber house built in 1610 to celebrate the investiture of Henry, James I's eldest son, as Prince of Wales; it's marked with his coat of arms and a PH on the ceiling. It's an entrance to the lawyers' sanctum, Temple, where the Strand becomes Fleet Street, and you can go in to visit the small Samuel Pepys exhibition. ⊠ *17 Fleet St., EC4,* ☎ *020/7936–2710.* 🎟 *Free.* ⊘ *Mon.–Sat. 11–2. Tube: Temple.*

⑬ **Royal Courts of Justice.** Here is the vast Victorian Gothic pile containing the nation's principal Law Courts, with 1,000-odd rooms running off 3½ mi of corridor. And here are heard the most important civil law cases—that's everything from divorce to fraud, with libel in between—and you can sit in the viewing gallery to watch any trial you like, for a live version of *Court TV.* The more dramatic criminal cases are heard at the Old Bailey. Other sights to witness include the 238-ft-long main hall and the compact exhibition of judges' robes. ⊠ *The Strand, WC2,* ☎ *020/7936–6000.* 🎟 *Free.* ⊘ *Weekdays 9–4:30 (during Aug. there are no sittings and the public areas close at 2:30). Tube: Temple.*

★ ⑫ **Sir John Soane's Museum.** Guaranteed to raise a smile from the most blasé and footsore tourist, this museum hardly deserves the burden of its dry name. Sir John (1753–1837), architect of the Bank of England, bequeathed his house to the nation on the condition that nothing be changed. We owe him our thanks because he obviously had enormous fun with his home, having had the means to finance great experiments in perspective and scale and to fill the space with some wonderful pieces. There are also different exhibitions on subjects as broad and as varied as Sir John's interests: from early architecture to more modern art. In the Picture Room, for instance, two of Hogarth's *Rake's Progress* series are among the paintings on panels that swing away to reveal secret gallery pockets with more paintings. Everywhere mirrors and colors play tricks with light and space, and split-level floors worthy of a fairground fun house disorient you. In a basement chamber sits the vast 1300 BC Sarcophagus of Seti I, lighted by a domed skylight two stories above. When Sir John acquired this priceless object for £2,000, he celebrated with a three-day party. ⊠ *13 Lincoln's Inn Fields, WC2,* ☎ *020/7405–2107.* 🎟 *Free.* ⊘ *Tues.–Sat. 10–5; also 6–9 on the first Tues. of every month. Tube: Holborn.* 🖎

⑩ Staple Inn. Despite its name, this is not an inn of court but the former wool staple, where wool was weighed and traded and its merchants were lodged. It is central London's oldest surviving Elizabethan half-timber building and, thanks to extensive restoration, with its overhanging upper stories, oriel windows, and black gables striping the white walls, looks the same as it must have in 1586 when it was brand-new. ⊠ *Holborn, WC1.* ⊘ *Courtyard weekdays 9–5. Tube: Chancery Lane.*

⑮ Temple. The entrance to Temple—the collective name for **Inner Temple** and **Middle Temple,** and the exact point of entry into the City—is marked by a young bronze griffin, the **Temple Bar Memorial** (1880). He is the symbol of the City, having replaced (sadly) a Wren gateway (though you can't deny he makes a splendidly heraldic snapshot). In the buildings opposite is an elaborate stone arch through which you pass into Middle Temple Lane, past a row of 17th-century timber-frame houses, and on into Fountain Court. This lane runs all the way to the Thames, more or less separating the two Temples, past the sloping lawns of Middle Temple Gardens, on the east border of which is the Elizabethan **Middle Temple Hall.** If it's open, don't miss that hammer-beam roof, among the finest in the land. ⊠ *Middle Temple La.,* ☎ *020/7427–4800.* ⊘ *Weekdays 10–11:30 and (when not in use) 3–4. Tube: Temple.*

⑯ Temple Church. Featuring "the Round"—a rare circular nave—this church was built by the Knights Templar during the 12th century. The Red Knights (so called after the red crosses they wore—you can see them in effigy around the nave) held their secret initiation rites in the crypt here. Having started poor, holy, and dedicated to the protection of pilgrims, they grew rich from showers of kingly gifts, until during the 14th century they were charged with heresy, blasphemy, and sodomy, thrown into the Tower, and stripped of their wealth. You might suppose the church to be thickly atmospheric, but Victorian and post-war restorers have tamed its air of antique mystery. Still, it's a very fine Gothic-Romanesque church, whose 1240 chancel ("the Oblong") has been accused of perfection. ⊠ *The Temple, EC4,* ☎ *020/7353–1736.* ⊘ *Wed.–Sat. 10–4, Sun. 12:30–3. Tube: Temple.*

❼ Thomas Coram Foundation. Capt. Thomas Coram devoted half his life to setting up a sanctuary and hospital, which he called the Foundling Hospital, for London's street orphans. He was a remarkable man, a master mariner and shipbuilder, who, having played a major role in the colonization of Massachusetts, returned to London in 1732 to encounter sights he could not endure—babies and children "left to die on dung hills." Petitioning the lunching ladies of his day and their lords, he raised the necessary funds to set up what became the most celebrated Good Cause around, thanks partly to the sparkling benefactors he attracted. Handel donated an organ to the chapel, which he played himself at fund-raising performances of his *Messiah,* and the chapel in turn became *the* place to be seen worshiping on a Sunday. Coram's great friend William Hogarth was one of several famous hospital governors, and his portrait of the founder hangs alongside other works of art (including paintings by Reynolds and Gainsborough) and mementos in the museum, which now stands on the site of the hospital. The Foundling Museum is achieving the money to refurbish the rooms and collection and so will be closed for most of 2001–2, after which tours will operate again. ⊠ *40 Brunswick Sq., WC2,* ☎ *020/7841–3600. Currently closed to visitors; call to determine if museum has reopened. Tube: Russell Sq.*

❸ University College. Set in a satisfyingly classical edifice designed by the architect of the National Gallery, William Wilkins, the college has within its portals the **Slade School of Fine Art,** which did for many of Britain's artists what the nearby (on Gower Street) Royal Academy of Dramatic Art did for its actors. There is a fine collection of sculpture by one of the alumni, John Flaxman, on view inside. You can also see more Egyptology, if you didn't get enough at the neighboring British Museum (☞ *above*), in the **Petrie Museum** (☎ 020/7504–2884 or 020/7504–2825), accessed from Malet Place, on the first floor of the DMS Watson building. The free museum contains one of London's weirder treasures: the clothed skeleton of one of the university's founders, Jeremy Bentham, who bequeathed himself to the college. It also houses an outstanding, huge collection of fascinating objects of Egyptian archaeology—jewelry, toys, papyri, and some of the world's oldest garments. It has proved so popular with schoolchildren that it is now open on Saturday 10–1 in addition to Tuesday–Friday 1–5. ⊠ *WC1. Tube: Euston Sq., Goodge St.*

➋ **University of London.** This relatively youthful institution grew out of the need for a nondenominational center for higher education (Oxford and Cambridge both demanded religious conformity to the Church of England). It was founded by Dissenters in 1826, with its first examinations held 12 years later. Jews and Roman Catholics were not the only people admitted for the first time to an English university—women were, too, though they had to wait 50 years (until 1878) to sit for a degree. ⊠ *Russell Sq., WC1. Tube: Russell Sq.*

Wig and Pen Club. This—another of those St. James's–style affairs, this time for "men of justice, journalists, and businessmen of the City" (plus former U.S. presidents Nixon and Reagan)—has its home in the only Strand building to have survived the Great Fire of 1666. Its Legal Tours allow access to the gorgeous gardens of the Inner and Middle Temples, plus other secret sights, and include meals, refreshments, and honorary membership for the day (and women are most welcome). ⊠ *229–230 The Strand, WC2,* ☎ *020/7583–7255.* 🖰 *½-day Legal Tour £40, full day £50. Tube: Aldwych, Temple.*

THE CITY

You may have assumed you had entered the City of London when your plane touched down at Heathrow, but note that capital letter: the City of London is not the same as the city of London. The "capital-C" City is an autonomous district, separately governed since William the Conqueror's time, and despite its compact size (it's known as the Square Mile), it remains the financial engine of Britain and one of the world's leading centers of trade. The City, however, is more than just London's Wall Street: it is also home to two of London's most notable sights, the Tower of London and St. Paul's, one of the world's greatest cathedrals—truly a case of the money changers' encompassing the temple! Temple Bar marks the western edge of the district, which does cover 677 acres, though not in a remotely straight-sided fashion. The curvy shape described by its boundaries—Smithfield in the north, Aldgate and Tower Hill in the east, and the Thames in the south—resembles nothing so much as an armadillo, with Temple Bar at snout level.

The City is London's most ancient part, although there is little remaining to remind you of that beyond a scattering of Roman stones. It was Aulus Plautius, Roman ruler of Britain under Claudius, who established the Romans' first stronghold on the Thames halfway through the 1st century AD. The name "Londinium," though, probably derives from the Celtic *Lyn-dun,* meaning "fortified town on the lake," which suggests far earlier settlement. It was really only after Edward the Confessor moved his court to Westminster in 1060 that the City gathered momentum. As Westminster took over the administrative role, the City was free to develop the commercial heart that still beats strong.

The Romans had already found Londinium's position handy for trade—the river being navigable yet far enough inland to allow for its defense—but it was the establishment of crafts guilds in the Middle Ages, followed in Tudor and Stuart times by the proliferation of great trading companies (the Honourable East India Company, founded in 1600, was the star), that really started the cash flowing.

Three times the City has faced devastation—and that's not counting the "Black Monday" of 1992, when the pound sterling crashed. The Great Fire of 1666 spared practically none of the labyrinthine medieval streets—a blessing in disguise, actually, because the Great Plague of the year before had wiped (or driven) out most of the population and left a terrible mess in the cramped, downright sordid houses. With the wind in the west, they said, you could smell London from Tilbury. The fire necessitated a total reconstruction, in which Sir Christopher Wren had a big hand, contributing not only his masterpiece, St. Paul's Cathedral, but 49 other parish churches.

The third wave of destruction, after the plague and the fire, was, of course, dealt by the German bombers of the Second World War, who blitzed the City with 57 days and nights of special attention, wreaking as much havoc as the Great Fire had managed. The ruins were rebuilt, but slowly and with no overall plan, creating an awkward patchwork of the old and the new, the interesting and the flagrantly awful. The City's colorful past can be hard to visualize among today's gray reality, but there are clues. Wander through its maze of streets and you will come across ancient coats of arms and street names redolent of life in the Middle Ages: Ropemaker Street, Pudding Lane, Jewry Street, and Fish Street. During the week, the place is overrun with people—but since a mere 8,000 or so people call it home today, the City is deserted on weekends, with most restaurants shuttered and streets forlorn and windswept. It's this swing from hectic activity to near total silence that accounts for much of the City's unique atmosphere. Where else does the Lord Mayor, clad in ceremonial robes and chain of office and escorted by foot soldiers in 17th-century garb bearing pikes and muskets, ride in an 18th-century coach—during the Lord Mayor's Show, the procession held every November to celebrate the installation of a new Lord Mayor—past buildings in which satellite communications have long since become routine?

Numbers in the text correspond to numbers in the margin and on the City map.

A Good Walk

Begin at the gateway to the City—and we mean that literally. Until the 18th century there were eight such gates, of which only one survives; the others exist in name only (Cripplegate, Ludgate, Bishopsgate, Moorgate, and so on). The surviving one is Temple Bar, a bronze griffin on the Strand opposite the Royal Courts of Justice, at which the sovereign has to ask the Lord Mayor's permission to enter the City. Walk east to **Fleet Street** and turn left on Bolt Court to Gough Square and **Dr. Johnson's House** ①, passing **Ye Olde Cheshire Cheese** ② on Wine Office Court en route back to Fleet Street and the journalists' church, **St. Bride's** ③. The end of Fleet Street is marked by the messy traffic intersection called Ludgate Circus, which you should cross to Ludgate Hill to reach **Old Bailey** ④ and the Central Criminal Courts.

Continuing along Ludgate Hill, you come to **St. Paul's Cathedral** ⑤, Wren's masterpiece. There's not much else to see around here, though plans are

pending for the reinstallation of Sir Christopher Wren's 1672 Temple
Bar gateway close to its original site, which will serve as the City's western entry. Instead, retrace your steps to Newgate Street, to the road called
Little Britain, where you'll see the archway to **St. Bartholomew the Great
Church** ⑥ on the left and will come to London's meat market, Smithfield, at the end. Cross Aldersgate Street and take the right fork to London Wall, named for the Roman rampart that stood along it. It's a
dismal street, now dominated by postmodern architect Terry Farrell's
late-'80s follies, but about halfway along you can see a section of 2nd-
to 4th-century wall at St. Alphege Garden. There's another bit in an appropriate spot back at the start of London Wall, outside the **Museum of
London** ⑦; and behind that is the important arts mecca of gray concrete,
the **Barbican Centre** ⑧, and **St. Giles Without Cripplegate** ⑨. You can walk
all around there without touching the ground (well, ground level).

Back on London Wall, turn south into Coleman Street, then right onto
Masons Avenue to reach Basinghall Street and the **Guildhall** ⑩; then
follow Milk Street south to Cheapside ("cheap" derives from the Old
English via Middle English *chep,* for trade); it was on this street that
the bakers of Bread Street, the cobblers of Cordwainers Street, the goldsmiths of Goldsmith Street, and all their brothers gathered to sell their
wares. Here is another symbolic center of London, the church of **St.
Mary-le-Bow** ⑪. Walk to the east end of Cheapside, where seven roads
meet, and you will be facing the **Bank of England** ⑫. Turn your back
on the bank, and there's the Lord Mayor's Palladian-style abode, the
Mansion House, with Wren's **St. Stephen Walbrook Church** ⑬ behind
it and the **Royal Exchange** ⑭ in between Threadneedle Street and
Cornhill. Farther down Cornhill to Lime Street is **Lloyd's of London** ⑮.

Now head down Queen Victoria Street, where you'll pass the remains
of the Roman **Temple of Mithras** ⑯; then, after a sharp left turn onto
Cannon Street, you'll come upon **Monument** ⑰, Wren's memorial to
the Great Fire of London. Just south of there is **London Bridge** ⑱. Turn
left onto Lower Thames Street, for just under a mile's walk—passing
Billingsgate, London's principal fish market (until 1982) for 900 years,
and the Custom House, built early in the last century—to the **Tower
of London** ⑲, which may be the single most unmissable of London's
sights. **Tower Bridge** ⑳, just outside it, isn't bad either.

TIMING

This is a marathon. Unless you want to be walking all day without a
chance to do justice to London's most famous sights, the Tower of London and St. Paul's Cathedral—not to mention the Museum of London,
Tower Bridge, and the Barbican Centre—you should consider splitting
the walk into segments. Conversely, if you're not planning to go inside, this walk makes for a great day out, with lots of surprising vistas, river views, and history. The City is a wasteland on weekends and
after dark, so choose your time. There's a certain romantic charm to
the streets when they're deserted, but it's hard to find lunch.

HOW TO GET THERE

This is a big and confusing area, with, however, several tube stops that
will deposit you within walking distance of most of the sights. They are
the following: on the Central Line, the Bank and St. Paul's stops; on the
District and Circle lines, the Monument, Cannon Street, and Mansion
House stops (plus Blackfriars, which is a little off-center). The Moorgate and Barbican stops (Circle, Metropolitan, Hammersmith, and City
lines) are the nearest to the theaters of the Barbican Centre, while the
next stop west, Farringdon, is best for exploring Clerkenwell. Finally,
the only sensible way to get to the Tower of London is via the District
and Circle lines to the Tower Hill stop. As for buses, Numbers 4, 11, 15,

17, 23, 26, 76, and 172 deposit you centrally, by St. Paul's. For the Barbican Centre, Buses 4, 56, 172, 141, 172, and 271 to Moorgate are best.

Sights to See

⑫ **Bank of England.** Known familiarly for the past couple of centuries as "the Old Lady of Threadneedle Street," after someone's parliamentary quip, the bank, which has been central to the British economy since 1694, manages the national debt and the foreign exchange reserves, issues banknotes, sets interest rates, looks after England's gold, and regulates the country's banking system. Sir John Soane designed the Neoclassic hulk in 1788, wrapping it in windowless walls (which are all that survives of his building) to suggest a stability that the ailing economy of the post-Thatcher years tends to belie. It is ironic that an executive of so sober an institution should have been Kenneth Grahame, author of *The Wind in the Willows*. This and other facets of the bank's history are traced in the Bank of England Museum. ⊠ *Bartholomew La., EC4,* ☎ *020/7601–5545.* ▣ *Free.* ⊙ *Weekdays and Lord Mayor's Show day 10–5. Tube: Bank, Monument.*

⑧ **Barbican Centre.** Home to the Royal Shakespeare Company and its two theaters; the London Symphony Orchestra and its auditorium; the Guildhall School of Music and Drama; a major gallery for touring and its own special exhibitions; two cinemas; a convention center; and apartments for a hapless two-thirds of the City's residents (most part-time), the Barbican is an enormous concrete maze Londoners love to hate. The name comes from a defensive fortification of the City, and defensive is what Barbican apologists (including architects Chamberlain, Powell, and Bon) became when the complex was finally revealed in 1982, after 20 years as a construction site. There ensued an epidemic of jokes about getting lost forever in the Barbican bowels. A hasty rethinking of the contradictory signposts and nonsensical "levels" was performed, and navigatory yellow lines materialized, Oz-like, on the floors, but it didn't help much—the Barbican remains difficult to navigate. Time has mellowed the gray concrete into a darker blotchy brownish gray, and Londoners have come to accept if not exactly love the place, because of its contents. Actors rate the theater acoustics especially high, and the steep bank of the seating makes for a good stage view. The visiting exhibitions are often worth a trek, as are the free ones in the foyer.

Negotiating the winding walkways of the deserted residential section, then descending in elusive elevators to the lower depths of the Centre (where the studio auditorium, the aptly named Pit, lives), spotting stray sculptures and water gardens, receiving electric shocks from the brass rails—all this has its perverse charm, but there is one unadulterated success in the Barbican, though unfortunately it's not often open to the public. Secreted on an upper floor is an enormous, lush conservatory in a towering glass palace, spacious enough for full-grown trees to flourish. Tours are conducted for a minimum of 10 people and must be booked in advance. The White Card is accepted. ⊠ *Silk St., EC2,* ☎ *020/7638–8891; 020/7628–3351 RSC backstage tour.* ▣ *Barbican Centre free, gallery £5.* ⊙ *Barbican Centre Mon.–Sat. 9 AM–11 PM, Sun. noon–11 PM; gallery Mon.–Sat. 10–7:30, Sun. noon–7:30; conservatory weekends noon–5:30 when not in use for private function (call first). Tube: Moorgate, Barbican.*

NEED A BREAK?   The Barbican Centre's **Waterside Café** has salads, sandwiches, and pastries; they're unremarkable but are served in a tranquil, enclosed concrete (naturally) waterside terrace. Sometimes customers are serenaded by practice sessions of the Guildhall School of Music and Drama's orchestra next door.

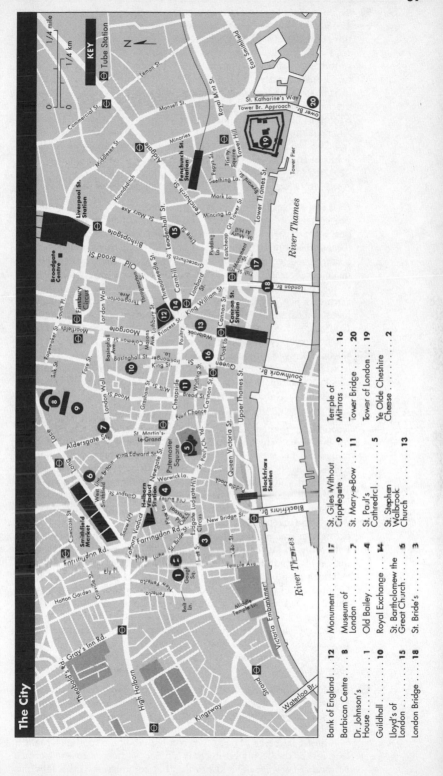

❶ **Dr. Johnson's House.** This is where Samuel Johnson lived between 1746 and 1759, while in the worst of health, compiling his famous dictionary in the attic. Like Dickens, he lived all over town, and as Dickens House is the only one of his houses still extant, this is the only one of Johnson's abodes remaining today. It is an appropriately 17th-century house, exactly the kind of place you would expect the Great Bear, as Johnson was nicknamed, to live. It is a shrine to the man possibly more attached to London than anyone else ever, and it includes a first edition of his dictionary among the Johnson and Boswell mementos. After soaking up the atmosphere, repair around the corner in Wine Office Court to the famed Ye Olde Cheshire Cheese pub (☞ *below*), once Johnson and Boswell's favorite watering hole. ⊠ *17 Gough Sq., EC4,* ☎ *020/7353–3745.* ⌺ *£3.* ⊙ *May–Sept., Mon.–Sat. 11–5:30; Oct.– Apr., Mon.–Sat. 11–5. Tube: Blackfriars, Chancery Lane.*

Fleet Street. This famous street follows the course of, and is named after, one of London's ghost rivers. The Fleet, so called by the Anglo-Saxons, spent most of its centuries above ground as an open sewer, offending local nostrils until banished below in 1766. It still flows underfoot, now a sanctioned section of London's sewer system. The street's sometime nickname, "Street of Shame," has nothing to do with the stench. It refers to the trade that made it famous: the press. Since the end of the 15th century, when Wynkyn de Worde set up England's first printing press here, and especially after 1702, when the first newspaper, the *Daily Courant,* moved in, followed by (literally) all the rest, "Fleet Street" has been synonymous with newspaper journalism. The papers themselves all moved out during the 1980s, but the British press is still collectively known as "Fleet Street." To find a relic from the old days, check out the black-glass-and-chrome Art Deco *Daily Mirror* building. ⊠ *EC4. Tube: Blackfriars, St. Paul's.*

❿ **Guildhall.** In the symbolic nerve center of the City, the Corporation of London ceremonially elects and installs its Lord Mayor as it has done for 800 years. The Guildhall was built in 1411, and though it failed to avoid either the 1666 or 1940 flames, its core survived, with a new roof sensitively appended during the 1950s and further cosmetic embellishments added during the '70s. The fabulous hall is a psychedelic patchwork of coats of arms and banners of the City Livery Companies, which inherited the mantle of the medieval trade guilds, to which we owe the invention of the City in the first place. Actually, this honor belongs to two giants, Gog and Magog, the pair of mythical beings who founded ancient Albion and who glower upon the prime minister's annual November banquet from their west-gallery grandstand in 9-ft-high painted lime-wood form. The 1970s west wing houses the **Guildhall Library**—mainly City-related books and documents, plus a collection belonging to one of the Livery Companies, the Worshipful Company of Clockmakers, with more than 600 timepieces on show, including a skull-faced watch that belonged to Mary, Queen of Scots. ⊠ *Gresham St., EC2,* ☎ *020/7606–3030.* ⌺ *Free.* ⊙ *Mon.–Sat. 9:30– 5; Clockmakers collection weekdays 9:30–4:45. Print room and bookshop closed Sat. Tube: St. Paul's, Moorgate, Bank, Mansion House.*

⓯ **Lloyd's of London.** Richard Rogers's (of Paris Pompidou Centre fame) fantastical steel-and-glass medium-rise of six towers around a vast atrium, with his trademark inside-out ventilation shafts, stairwells, and gantries, may be the most exciting recent structure erected in London. The building is best seen at night, when cobalt and lime spotlights make it leap out of the deeply boring gray skyline as though it were Carmen Miranda at a wake. The institution that commissioned this fabulous £163 million fun house has been trading in insurance for two centuries and is famous the world over for several reasons: (1) having started in a coffeehouse; (2) insuring Betty Grable's legs; (3) accepting no corporate responsibility for losses, which are carried by its investors; (4) having its "Names"—the rich people who underwrite Lloyd's losses; (5) seeming unassailable for a very long time . . . ; (6) until 1990, when it lost £2.9 billion; (7) which caused the financial ruination, and worse, of many Names. ⊠ *1 Lime St., EC3. Tube: Bank, Monument, Liverpool St., Aldgate.*

⑱ London Bridge. Dating from only 1972, this bridge replaced the 1831 Sir John Rennie number that now graces Lake Havasu City, Arizona, the impulse purchase of someone at the McCulloch Oil Corporation, who (rumor has it) was under the impression that he'd bought the far more picturesque Tower Bridge. The version before that one, the first in stone and the most renowned of all, stood for 600 years after it was built in 1176, the focus of many a gathering thanks to the shops and houses crammed along its length, not to mention the boiled and tar-dipped heads of traitors that decorated its gatehouse after being removed in the Tower of London. Before *that* the Saxons had put up a wooden bridge; it collapsed in 1014, which was probably the origin of the refrain "London Bridge is falling down." Nobody is sure of the exact location of the very earliest London Bridge—the Roman version around whose focus London grew—but it was certainly very close to the 100-ft-wide, three-span, prestressed concrete cantilever one that you see today. ⊠ *EC3, SE1. Tube: London Bridge, Monument.*

⑰ Monument. Commemorating the "dreadful visitation" of the Great Fire of 1666, this is the world's tallest isolated stone column. It is the work of Wren, who was asked to erect it "On or as neere unto the place where the said Fire soe unhappily began as conveniently may be." And so here it is—at 202 ft exactly as tall as the distance it stands from Farriner's baking house in Pudding Lane, where the fire started. Above the viewing gallery (311 steps up—a better workout than any StairMaster) is a flaming bronze urn and around it a cage for the prevention of suicide, which was a trend for a while during the 19th century. ⊠ *Monument St., EC3,* ☎ *020/7626–2717.* ▨ *£1.50.* ☉ *Daily 10–5:40 (hrs subject to change; phone before visiting). Tube: Monument*

⦿ ❷ Museum of London. If there's one place to get the history of London sorted out, it's here—although there's a great deal to sort out: Oliver Cromwell's death mask, Queen Victoria's crinolined gowns, Selfridges's Art Deco elevators, and the Lord Mayor's coach are just some of the goodies here. Various fascinating exhibitions—from London Bodies (magnetically gruesome) to early Briton king Alfred the Great and the life and times of the Rothschilds—regularly entice more crowds. The museum appropriately shelters a section of the 2nd- to 4th-century London wall, which you can view from a window inside, near the Roman monumental arch the museum's archaeologists reconstructed a mere two decades ago. Anyone with the least interest in how this city evolved will adore this museum, especially said reconstructions and the dioramas—like one of the Great Fire (flickering flames! sound effects!), a 1940s air-raid shelter, a Georgian prison cell, a Roman living room, and a Victorian street complete with fully stocked shops—as well as the Catwalk, which guides you interactively through the ages. There are special Sunday and holiday sessions for children to handle and discover many objects not on view. Galleries proceed chronologically for easy comprehension right up to the new "London Now" gallery. The White Card is accepted, and all museum tickets allow unlimited return visits for one year. ⊠ *London Wall, EC2,* ☎ *020/7600–0807.* ▨ *£5; free 4:30–5:50.* ☉ *Mon.–Sat. 10–5:50, Sun. noon–5:50.*

④ Old Bailey. This, the present-day **Central Criminal Court,** is where Newgate Prison stood from the 12th century right until the beginning of the 20th century. Few survived for long in the version pulled down in 1770. Those who didn't starve were hanged, or pressed to death in the Press Yard, or they succumbed to the virulent gaol (the archaic British spelling of "jail") fever—any of which must have been preferable to a life in the stinking, subterranean, lightless Stone Hold or to the robberies, beatings, and general victimization endemic in what the novelist Henry Fielding called the "prototype of hell." The next model lasted only a couple of years before being torn down by raving mobs during the anti-Catholic Gordon Riots of 1780, to be replaced by the Newgate that Dickens visited several times (obviously in between pubs) and described in several novels. In fact, Fagin ended up in the Condemned Hold here in *Oliver Twist,* from which he would have been taken to the public scaffold that replaced the Tyburn Tree (☞ Marble Arch *in* St. James's and Mayfair, *above*) and stood outside the prison until 1868. The Central Criminal Court replaced Newgate in 1907. The most famous and most interesting feature of the solid Edwardian building is the gilded statue of blind Justice perched on top, scales in her left hand, sword in her right. Ask the doorman which current trial is likely to prove juicy, if you're that kind of ghoul—you may catch the conviction of the next Crippen or Christie (England's most notorious wife-murderers, both tried here). Cameras are not allowed in the court. Check the day's hearings on the sign outside. There are some restrictions on entry (children under 14 are not allowed); call the information line first. ⊠ *Newgate St., EC4,* ☎ *020/7248–3277 information.* ⏲ *Public Gallery weekdays 9:30–1 and 2–4:30 (line forms at Newgate St. entrance). Tube: Blackfriars.*

⑭ Royal Exchange. Inhabiting the isosceles triangle between Threadneedle Street and Cornhill, this is the third version to have stood here but the first to have been blessed by Queen Victoria—at its 1844 opening. Sir William Tite designed the massive templelike building—its pediment featuring 17 limestone figures (Commerce, plus merchants) supported by eight sizable Corinthian columns—to house the then-thriving futures market. The market has now moved on, leaving the Royal Exchange, which you may no longer enter, as a monument to money. ⊠ *Cornhill and Threadneedle St., EC3. Tube: Bank.*

⑥ St. Bartholomew the Great Church. Reached via a perfect half-timber gatehouse atop a 13th-century stone archway, this is one of London's oldest churches. Along with its namesake on the other side of the road, St. Bartholomew's Hospital, the Norman church was founded by Rahere, Henry I's court jester. At the Dissolution of the Monasteries, Henry VIII had most of it torn down; the Romanesque choir loft is all that survives from the 12th century. ⊠ *West Smithfield, EC1,* ☎ *020/7606–5171.* ⏲ *Weekdays 8:30–5, Sat. 10:30–1:30, Sun. 2–6. Tube: Barbican.*

③ St. Bride's. From afar, study the extraordinary steeple of this church—its uniquely tiered shape gave rise, legend has it, to the traditional wedding cake. This, the first of Wren's city churches, did not escape wartime bomb damage and was reconsecrated only in 1960 after a 17-year-long restoration. As St. Paul's (in Covent Garden) is the actors' church, so St. Bride's belongs to journalists, many of whom have been buried or memorialized here, as reading the wall plaques will tell you. Even before the press moved in, it was a popular place to take the final rest. By 1664 the crypts were so crowded that diarist Samuel Pepys had to bribe the grave digger to "justle together" some bodies to make room for his deceased brother. Now the crypts house a museum of the church's rich history, and a bit of Roman sidewalk. ⊠ *Fleet St., EC4,* ☎ *020/7353–1301.* 🎟 *Free.* ⊗ *Weekdays 8–5, Sat. 9–5, Sun. between services at 11 and 6:30. Tube: Chancery Lane.*

❾ St. Giles Without Cripplegate. Standing south of the Barbican complex, this is one of the only City churches to have withstood the Great Fire, only to succumb to the Blitz bombs three centuries later. The tower and a few walls survived; the rest was rebuilt to the 16th-century plan during the 1950s, and now the little church struggles hopelessly for attention among the Barbican towers, whose parishioners it tends. Past parishioners include Oliver Cromwell, married here in 1620, and John Milton, buried here in 1674. St. Giles was the patron saint for cripples, hence Cripplegate. ⊠ *Fore St., EC2.* ⊗ *Weekdays 9:30–5:30, Sun. 8–5:30. Tube: Barbican, Moorgate.*

⓫ St. Mary-le-Bow. Wren's 1673 church has one of the most famous sets of bells around—a Londoner must be born within the sound of Bow Bells to be a true cockney. The origin of that idea was probably the curfew rung on the Bow Bells during the 14th century, even though "cockney" only came to mean Londoner three centuries later, and then it was an insult. The bow takes its name from the bow-shape arches in the Norman crypt. ⊠ *Cheapside, EC2.* ⊗ *Mon.–Thurs. 6:30–5:45, Fri. 6:30–4, weekends special services only. Tube: Mansion House.*

NEED A
BREAK?

The **Place Below** is below the church, in St. Mary-le-Bow's crypt, and gets packed with City workers weekday lunchtime—the self-service soup and quiche are particularly good. It's also open for breakfast, and Thursday and Friday evenings it features a posh and sophisticated vegetarian set dinner.

★ ☕ ❺ St. Paul's Cathedral. The symbolic heart of London, St. Paul's will take your breath away. In fact, its dome—the world's third largest—will already be familiar, since you see it peeping through on the skyline from many an angle, riding high (although now nudged by skyscrapers) over the rooftops of the City, just as it does in Canaletto's 18th-century views of the Thames. The cathedral is, of course, the masterpiece of Sir Christopher Wren (1632–1723), completed in 1710 after 35 years of building and much argument with the Royal Commission, then, much later, miraculously (mostly) spared by the World War II bombs. Wren had originally been commissioned to restore Old St. Paul's, the Norman cathedral that had replaced, in its turn, three earlier versions, but the Great Fire left so little of it standing that a new cathedral was deemed necessary.

Wren's first plan, known as the "New Model," did not make it past the drawing board, while the second, known as the "Great Model," got as far as the 20-ft oak rendering you can see here today before it, too, was rejected, whereupon Wren is said to have burst into tears. The third, however, known as the Warrant Design (because it received the royal warrant), was accepted, with the fortunate coda that the architect be allowed to make changes as he saw fit. Without that, there would be no dome, because the approved design had featured a steeple. Parliament felt that building was proceeding too slowly (in fact, 35 years is lightning speed, as cathedrals go) and withheld half of Wren's pay for the last 13 years of work. He was pushing 80 when Queen Anne finally coughed up the arrears.

When you enter and see the dome from the inside, you may find that it seems smaller than you expected. You aren't imagining things—it *is* smaller, and 60 ft lower, than the lead-covered outer dome. Between the inner and outer domes is a brick cone, which supports the familiar 850-ton lantern, surmounted by its golden ball and cross. Nobody

94

Adm.
Collingwood . 21
Adm. Howe . 20
The American
Chapel. 13
All Soul's
Chapel 1
Bishop's
Throne 18
Chapel of
Modern
Martyrs 11
Chapel of St.
Micheal and
St. George . . 27
Crypt
Entrance. . . . 19
Dean's
Vestry 16
The Donne
Effigy. 15
Dr. Johnson . . 8
Duke of
Wellington . . . 5
General Gordon
Monument . . . 4
Geometric
Staicase. . . . 28
High Altar . . 12
J.M.W
Turner 22
The Lady
Chapel. 14
Lord of Leighton
Monument . . . 3
Lord Mayor's
Stall. 17
Lord Mayor's
Vestry 6
Minor Canons'
Vestry 9
Nelson. 23
St. Dunstan's
Chapel 2
St. Paul's Watch
Memorial
Stone. 26
Sanctuary
Screens 10
Sir John
Moore 24
Sir Joshua
Reynolds 7
Staicase to
Whispering
Gallery, Dome
and Golden
Gallery 25

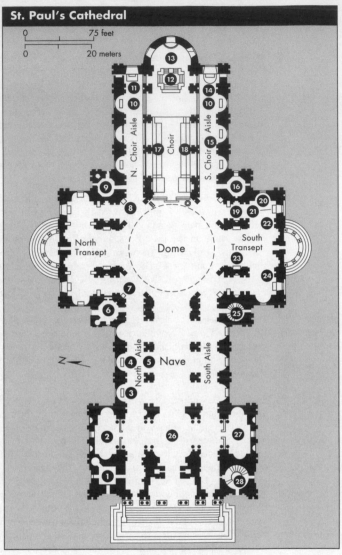

St. Paul's Cathedral

can resist making a beeline for the dome, so we'll start beneath it, standing dead center, on the beautiful sunburst floor, Wren's focal mirror of the magnificent design above.

Now climb the 259 spiral steps to the **Whispering Gallery.** This is the part of the cathedral with which you bribe children, who are fascinated by the acoustic phenomenon: whisper something to the wall on one side, and a second later it transmits clearly to the other side, 107 ft away. The only problem is identifying "your" whisper from the cacophony of everyone else's, since this is a popular game. Look down onto the nave from here, and up to the frescoes of St. Paul by Sir James Thornhill (who nearly fell off while painting them), before ascending farther to the Stone Gallery, which encircles the outside of the dome and affords a spectacular panorama of London. Up again (careful—you will have tackled 627 steps altogether), and you reach the Golden Gallery, from which you can view the lantern through a circular opening called the oculus.

Back downstairs there are the inevitable monuments and memorials to see, though fewer than one might expect because Wren didn't want his masterpiece cluttered up. The poet John Donne, who had been Dean of St. Paul's for his final 10 years (he died in 1631), lies in the south choir aisle; his is the only monument remaining from Old St. Paul's. There is Wren's own memorial, which his son (who also worked on the building) composed and which reads succinctly: LECTOR, SI MONUMENTUM REQUIRIS, CIRCUMSPICE (READER, IF YOU SEEK HIS MONUMENT, LOOK AROUND YOU). The vivacious choir-stall carvings nearby are the work of Grinling Gibbons, as is the organ, which Wren designed and Handel played. The painters Sir Joshua Reynolds and J. M. W. Turner are commemorated, as is George Washington. The American connection continues behind the high altar in the **American Memorial Chapel**, dedicated in 1958 to the 28,000 GIs stationed here who lost their lives in World War II.

A visit to the **crypt** brings you to Wren's tomb, the black marble sarcophagus containing Admiral Nelson (who was pickled in alcohol for his final voyage here from Trafalgar), and an equestrian statue of the Duke of Wellington on top of his grandiose tomb. Finally, to catch Wren's facade and dome at its most splendid, remember to make a return trip to see St. Paul's at night. ☒ *St. Paul's Churchyard, Ludgate Hill, EC4,* ☏ *020/7236–4128.* ☐ *Cathedral, crypt, ambulatory, and gallery £5.* ☉ *Cathedral Mon.–Sat. 8:30–4 (closed occasionally for special services); ambulatory, crypt, and gallery Mon.–Sat. 9:30–4:15. Tube: St. Paul's.* ☒

⑬ **St. Stephen Walbrook Church.** This is the parish church many think is Wren's best, by virtue of its practice dome, which predates the Big One at St. Paul's by some 30 years. Two inside sights warrant investigation: Henry Moore's 1987 central stone altar, which sits beneath the dome ("like a lump of Camembert," say critics), and, well, a telephone—an eloquent tribute to that genuine savior of souls, Rector Chad Varah, who founded the Samaritans, givers of phone aid to the suicidal, here in 1953. ☒ *Walbrook St., EC4.* ☉ *Mon.–Thurs. 10–4, Fri. 10–3. Tube: Bank, Cannon St.*

⑯ **Temple of Mithras.** This minor place of pilgrimage in the Roman City was unearthed on a building site in 1954 and was taken, at first, for an early Christian church. In fact, worshipers here favored Christ's chief rival during the 3rd and 4th centuries: Mithras, the Persian god of light. Mithraists aimed for all the big virtues but still were not appreciated by early Christians, from whom their sculptures and treasures had to be concealed. These devotional objects are now on display back at the Museum of London ☞ *above*, while here, on Queen Victoria Street, not far from the Bank of England, you can see the foundations of the temple itself. *Temple Court, Queen Victoria St., EC4. Tube: Bank.*

★ ☾ ⑳ **Tower Bridge.** Despite its venerable, nay, medieval, appearance, this is a Victorian youngster that celebrated its centenary in June 1994. Constructed of steel, then clothed in Portland stone, it was deliberately styled in the Gothic persuasion to complement the Tower next door, and it is famous for its enormous bascules—the "arms," which open to allow large ships through. Nowadays this rarely happens, but when river traffic was dense, the bascules were raised about five times a day.

The bridge's 100th-birthday gift was a new exhibition, **Tower Bridge Experience**, one of London's most imaginative and fun. You are conducted back in time in the company of "Harry Stoner," an animatronic bridge construction worker worthy of Disneyland, to witness the birth of the Thames's last downstream bridge. History and engineering lessons are painlessly absorbed as you meet the ghost of the bridge's architect, Sir Horace Jones; see the bascules work; and wander the walk-

96

Beauchamp
Tower 10

Bloody
Tower 12

Byward
Tower 15

Chapel of
St. John 2

Hospital
Block 5

Jewel
House 8

Martin
Tower 7

Middle
Tower 16

New
Armouries ... 4

Queen's
House 11

Royal
Armouries ... 6

St. Peter and
Vincula 9

Traitors'
Gate 14

Wakefield
Tower 13

Wardrobe
Tower 3

White
Tower 1

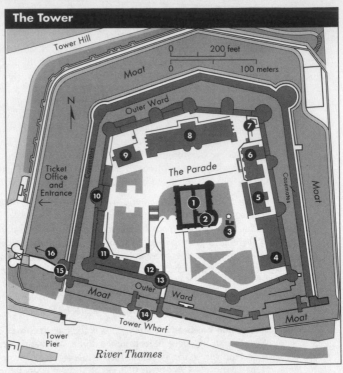

The Tower

ways with their grand upstream–downstream views annotated by interactive video displays. Be sure to hang on to your ticket and follow the signs to the Engine Rooms for part two; here the original steam-driven hydraulic engines gleam, and a cute rococo theater is the setting for an Edwardian-style music-hall production of the bridge's story. ☎ 020/7403–3761. ☜ £6.15. ☉ Apr.–Oct., daily 10–5:15; Nov.–Mar., daily 9:30–5:15 (last entry 4). Tube: Tower Hill. ☜

★ ⑲ **Tower of London.** This has top billing on many tourist itineraries for good reason. Nowhere else does London's history come to life so vividly as in this minicity of melodramatic towers stuffed to bursting with heraldry and treasure, the intimate details of lords and dukes and princes and sovereigns etched in the walls (literally in some places, as you'll see), and quite a few pints of royal blood spilled on the stones. New systems ensure that lines are minimal, so you'll be able to put in place all those grisly torture scenes you saw in the recent film *Elizabeth*. And thankfully, you need no longer spend all day in line for the prize exhibit, the Crown Jewels, since they have been transplanted to a new home where moving walkways hasten progress at the busiest times.

The reason the Tower holds the royal gems is that it is still one of the royal palaces, although no monarch since Henry VII has called it home. It has also housed the Royal Mint, the Public Records, the Royal Menagerie (which formed the basis of London Zoo), and the Royal Observatory, although its most renowned and titillating function has been, of course, as a jail and place of torture and execution.

A person was mighty privileged to be beheaded in the peace and seclusion of **Tower Green** instead of before the mob at Tower Hill. In fact, only seven people were ever important enough—among them Anne Boleyn and Catherine Howard, wives two and five, respectively, of Henry VIII's six; Elizabeth I's friend Robert Devereux, the Earl of Essex; and the nine-day queen, Lady Jane Grey, aged 17. Tower Green's other function was as a corpse dumping ground when the chapel just got too full. In 1998, the executioner's block—with its bathetic forehead-size dent—and his axe, along with the equally famous rack and the more obscure "scavenger's daughter" (which pressed a body nearly to death), plus assorted thumbscrews, "iron maidens," and so forth, took up temporary residence in the newly opened collection of the Royal Armouries in Leeds, Yorkshire; after an undetermined time, they will return to the Royal Armouries collection of the Tower of London. Fans of this horrifying niche of heavy metal might also want to pay a call on the London Dungeon attraction, just across the Thames (☞ South Bank, *below*).

Before we go any farther, you should know about the excellent free and fact-packed tours that depart every half hour or so from the Middle Tower. They are conducted by the 39 Yeoman Warders, better known as Beefeaters—ex-servicemen dressed in resplendent navy-and-red (scarlet-and-gold on special occasions) Tudor outfits. Beefeaters have been guarding the tower since Henry VII appointed them in 1485. One of them, the Yeoman Ravenmaster, is responsible for making life comfortable for Hardey, George, Hugine, Mumin, Cedric, Odin, Thor (who talks), and Gwylem—the Tower Ravens. This used to be a delicate duty, because if they were to desert the tower (goes the legend), the kingdom would fall. Today, the tower takes no chances: the ravens' wings are clipped.

In prime position stands the oldest part of the tower and the most conspicuous of its buildings, the **White Tower.** This central keep was begun in 1078 by William the Conqueror; by the time it was completed, in 1097, it was the tallest building in London, underlining the might of those victorious Normans. Henry III (1207–1272) had it whitewashed, which is where the name comes from, then used it as a barracks and as housing for his menagerie, including the first elephant ever seen in the land.

The spiral staircase—winding clockwise to help the right-handed swordsman defend it—is the only way up, and here you'll find the **Royal Armouries,** Britain's national museum of arms and armor, with about 40,000 pieces on display. One of the tower's original functions was as arsenal, supplying armor and weapons to the kings and their armies. Henry VIII started the collection in earnest, founding a workshop at Greenwich as a kind of bespoke tailor of armor to the gentry, but the public didn't get to see it until the second half of the 17th century, during Charles II's reign—which makes the Tower Armouries Britain's oldest public museum.

Here you can see weapons and armor from Britain and the Continent, dating from Saxon and Viking times right up to our own. Among the highlights are four of those armors Henry VIII commissioned to fit his ever-increasing bulk, plus one for his horse. The medieval warhorse was nothing without his *shaffron,* or head protector, and here you'll find a 500-year-old example, one of the oldest pieces of horse armor in the world. Don't miss the tiny armors on the third floor—one belonging to Henry's son (who survived in it to become Edward VI) and another just a bit more than 3 ft tall. The impressive, carved Line of Kings is not to be missed. The **New Armouries** are currently being renovated into a new restaurant.

Most of the interior of the White Tower has been much altered over the centuries, but the **Chapel of St. John the Evangelist,** downstairs from the armouries, is a pure example of 11th-century Norman—very rare, very simple, and very beautiful. The other fortifications and buildings surrounding the White Tower date from the 11th to 19th century. Starting from the main entrance, you can't miss the **moat**. Until the Duke of Wellington had it drained in 1843, this was a stinking, stagnant mush, obstinately resisting all attempts to flush it with water from the Thames. Now there's a little raven graveyard in the grassed-over channel, with touching memorials to some of the old birds (who are not known for their kind natures, by the way, and you risk a savage pecking if you try to befriend them).

Across the moat, the **Middle Tower** and the **Byward Tower** form the principal landward entrance, with **Traitors' Gate** a little farther on to the right. This is the London equivalent of Venice's Bridge of Sighs, which led to the cells in the Doge's Palace. Unlike the Venetian monument, Traitors' Gate is not architecturally beautiful but was the last walkway of daylight before condemned prisoners were doomed to darkness and death in the dungeons. During the period when the Thames was London's chief thoroughfare, this was the main entrance to the Tower.

Immediately opposite Traitors' Gate is the former Garden Tower, better known since about 1570 as the **Bloody Tower**. Its name comes from one of the most famous unsolved murders in history, the saga of the "little princes in the Tower." In 1483 the uncrowned boy king Edward V and his brother Richard were left here by their uncle, Richard of Gloucester, after the death of their father, Edward I. They were never seen again, Gloucester was crowned Richard III, and in 1674 two little skeletons were found under the stairs to the White Tower. The obvious conclusions have always been drawn—and were, in fact, even before the skeletons were discovered.

Another famous inmate was Sir Walter Raleigh, who was kept here from 1603 to 1616. It wasn't such an ordeal, as you'll see when you visit his spacious rooms, where he kept two servants, had his wife and two sons live with him (the younger boy was christened in the Tower chapel), and amused himself by writing his *History of the World*. Unfortunately, he was less lucky on his second visit in 1618, which terminated in his execution at Whitehall.

Next to the Bloody Tower is the circular **Wakefield Tower**, which dates from the 13th century and once contained the king's private apartments. It was the scene of another royal murder in 1471, when Henry VI was killed in mid-prayer. Henry founded Eton College and King's College, Cambridge, and they haven't forgotten: every May 21, envoys from both institutions mark the anniversary of his murder by laying white lilies on the site.

The most dazzling and most famous exhibits in the Tower are, of course, the **Crown Jewels**, now housed in the new **Jewel House, Waterloo Block**. In their new settings you get so close to the fabled gems you feel you could polish them (if it weren't for the wafers of bulletproof glass), and they are enhanced by laser lighting, which nearly hurts the eyes with sparkle. Before you meet them in person, you are given a high-definition-film preview, which features scenes from Elizabeth's 1953 coronation.

It's commonplace to call these baubles priceless, but it's impossible not to drop your jaw at the notion of their worth. They were, in fact, stolen once—by Col. Thomas Blood, in 1671—though only as far as a nearby wharf. The colonel was given a royal pension instead of a beating, fueling speculation that Charles II, short of ready cash as usual, had had his hand in the escapade somewhere. These days security is as fiendish as you'd expect, since the jewels—even though they would be impossible for thieves to sell—are *so* priceless that they're not insured. However, they are polished every January by the royal jewelers.

A brief résumé of the top jewels: finest of all is the **Royal Sceptre,** containing the earth's largest cut diamond, the 530-carat Star of Africa. This is also known as Cullinan I, having been cut from the South African Cullinan, which weighed 20 ounces when dug up from a De Beers mine at the beginning of the century. Another chip off the block, Cullinan II, lives on the **Imperial State Crown** that Prince Charles is due to wear at his coronation—the same one that Elizabeth II wore in her coronation procession; it was made for Victoria's coronation in 1838. Aside from its 2,800 diamonds, it features the Black Prince's ruby, which Henry V was supposed to have worn at Agincourt and which is actually an imposter—it's no ruby but, rather, a semiprecious spinel. The other most famous gem is the Koh-i-noor, or "Mountain of Light," which adorns the **Queen Mother's crown.** When Victoria was presented with this gift horse in 1850, she looked it in the mouth, found it lacking in glitter, and had it chopped down to almost half its weight.

An addendum to the major jewels in the Martin Tower is accurately called "Crowns and Diamonds." See naked crown frames—the coronation crown of George IV, George I's Imperial State Crown, Victoria's State Crown—surrounded by 12,500 loose diamonds on permanent loan from De Beers. It's a graphic illustration of how the Royals once had to rent the stones that would adorn their headpiece on the big day.

The little chapel of **St. Peter ad Vincula** can be visited only as part of a Yeoman Warder tour. The second church on the site, it conceals the remains of some 2,000 people executed at the Tower, Anne Boleyn and Catherine Howard among them. Being traitors, they were not so much buried as dumped under the flagstones, but the genteel Victorians had the courtesy to rebury their bones during renovations.

One of the more evocative towers is **Beauchamp Tower,** built west of Tower Green by Edward I (1272–1307). It was soon designated as a jail for the higher class of miscreant, including Lady Jane Grey, who is thought to have added her Latin graffiti to the many inscriptions carved by prisoners that you can see here.

Just south of the Beauchamp Tower is an L-shape row of half-timber Tudor houses, with the **Queen's House** at the center. Built for the governor of the Tower in 1530, this place saw the interrogation or incarceration of several of the more celebrated prisoners, including Anne Boleyn and the Gunpowder Plot conspirators. The Queen's House also played host to the Tower's last-ever prisoner, Rudolph Hess, the Nazi who parachuted over Scotland on a spy mission and was taken prisoner here.

Allow at least three hours to explore. Don't forget to stroll along the battlements before you leave; from them, you get a wonderful overview of the whole Tower of London. For tickets to Ceremony of the Keys (locking of main gates, nightly at 10), write well in advance to the Resident Governor and Keeper of the Jewel House (Queen's House, H. M. Tower of London, EC3). Give your name, the dates you wish to attend (including alternate dates), and number of people (up to seven) in your party, and enclose a self-addressed, stamped envelope. Yeoman Warder guides leave daily from Middle Tower, subject to weather and availability, at no charge (but a tip is always appreciated), about every 30 minutes until 3:30 in summer, 2:30 in winter. ⊠ *H. M. Tower of London, Tower Hill, EC3,* ☎ *020/7709–0765, 020/7680–9004 recorded information.* ☞ *£11.* ☉ *Mar.–Oct., Mon.–Sat. 9–5, Sun. 10–5; Nov.–Feb., Tues.–Sat. 9–4, Sun.–Mon. 10–4 (the Tower closes 1 hr after last admission time and all internal buildings close 30 mins after last admission). Tube: Tower Hill.* ✎

② **Ye Olde Cheshire Cheese.** This is one of the many places in which that acerbic compiler of the first dictionary, Dr. Johnson, drank (like Dickens, he is claimed by many a pub). This was, in fact, his "local," around the corner from his house. It retains a venerable open-fires-in-tiny-rooms charm when not too packed with tourists. Among 19th-century writers who followed Johnson's footsteps to the bar here were Mark Twain and, yes, Charles Dickens. ⊠ *145 Fleet St., EC4,* ☎ *020/7373–6170.* ☉ *Mon.–Sat. 11–11, Sun. noon–3 and 6–10. Tube: Blackfriars.*

THE EAST END

Made famous by Dickens and infamous by Jack the Ripper, the East End remains one of London's most hauntingly evocative neighborhoods. There is a good argument for considering it the real London, since East Enders are born "within the sound of Bow Bells" and are therefore cockneys through and through (not to mention models for the characters of England's favorite soap opera, *EastEnders*). The district began as separate villages—Whitechapel and Spitalfields, Shoreditch, Mile End, and Bethnal Green—melding together during the population boom of the 19th century, a boom that was shaped by French Huguenot and Jewish refugees, by poverty, and, in the past several decades, by a growing Bengali community. Whitechapel is where the Salvation Army was founded and the original Liberty Bell was forged, but, of course, what everyone remembers about it is that its Victorian slum streets were stalked by the most infamous serial killer of all, Jack the Ripper. Many outfitters offer walking tours of "Jack's London" (☞ Sightseeing Tours *in* Smart Travel Tips A to Z). Two centuries earlier, neighboring Spitalfields provided sanctuary for the French Huguenots. They had fled here after the Edict of Nantes (which had allowed them religious freedom in Catholic France) was revoked in 1685 and had found work in the nascent silk industry, many of them becoming prosperous master weavers. Today, as it turns out, Spitalfields is one of London's most cutting-edge neighborhoods, with stylish boutiques and artists setting up shop. All in all, prosperous is not really the word for the East End of today, but what the area lacks in traditional tourist attractions it makes up for in history and urban romance of a sublime sort.

Numbers in the text correspond to numbers in the margin and on the East End map.

A Good Walk

The easiest way to reach Whitechapel High Street is via the District Line to Aldgate East tube. Turn left out of the tube station. Behind 90 Whitechapel High Street once stood George Yard Buildings, where Jack the Ripper's first victim, Martha Turner, was discovered in August 1888. Nowadays you'll find the **Whitechapel Art Gallery** ① instead. Continue east until you reach Fieldgate Street on the right, where you'll find the **Whitechapel Bell Foundry** ②; then, retracing your steps, turn right onto Osborn Street, which soon becomes **Brick Lane** ③.

Brick Lane itself and the narrow streets running off it offer a paradigm of the East End's development. Its population has always been in flux, with some moving in to find refuge here as others were escaping its poverty. Just before the start of Brick Lane you can take a short detour (turn left, then right) to see the birthplace of one who did just that. Flower and Dean streets, past the ugly 1970s housing project on Thrawl Street and once the most disreputable street in London, was where Abe Sapperstein, founder of the Harlem Globetrotters, was born in 1908. On the west end of **Fournier Street** ④, see Nicholas Hawksmoor's masterpiece, **Christ Church, Spitalfields** ⑤, and some fine early Georgian houses; then follow Wilkes Street north of the church, where you'll find more 1720s Huguenot houses, and turn right onto Princelet Street, once important to the Jewish settlers. Where Number 6 stands now, the first of several thriving Yiddish theaters opened in 1886, playing to packed houses until the following year, when a false fire alarm, rung during a January performance, ended with 17 people being crushed to death and so demoralized the theater's actor-founder, Jacob Adler, that he moved his troupe to New York. Adler played a major role in founding that city's great Yiddish theater tradition—which, in turn, had a significant effect on Hollywood. The Spitalfields Centre occupies and is raising funds to restore and open to the public the house at 19 Princelet Street, which harbored French Huguenots (the upper windows are wider than usual so the Huguenot silk weavers had light to work) and, later, Polish Jews (behind its elegant Georgian door, Jacob Davidson, a shoe warehouseman, formed the Loyal United Friendly Society and a tiny synagogue). Spitalfields' grand Georgian houses were crammed with lodgings and workshops for the poor and persecuted. As you walk these quiet streets now, where many of the doors and window shutters have fresh, gleaming paint, there is an air of intellectual restoration and respect for heritage. It's an enclave of mysterious beauty.

Now you reach Brick Lane again and the **Black Eagle Brewery** ⑥. Turn left at Hanbury Street, where, in 1888, behind a seedy lodging house at Number 29, Jack the Ripper left his third mutilated murderee, "Dark" Annie Chapman. A double murder followed, and then, after a month's lull, came the death on this street of Marie Kelly, the Ripper's last victim and his most revolting murder of all. He had been able to work indoors this time, and Kelly, a young widow, was found strewn all over the room, charred remains of her clothing in the fire grate. (Of course, Jack the Ripper's identity never has been discovered, although to this day theories are still bandied about—the latest one taken up by historians fingers Francis Twomblety, an *American* quack doctor.)

Now turn onto Lamb Street and the two northern entrances to **Spitalfields Market** ⑦ or turn left on Commercial Street to Folgate Street and **Dennis Severs's House** ⑧. Elder Street, just off Folgate, is another gem of original 18th-century houses. On the south and east side of Spitalfields Market are yet more time-warp streets that are worth a wander: artillery with dinky little shops between the Indian spice emporiums, and Gun Street, where artist Mark Gertler lived at Number 32. (If you have kids, they might have fun—and learn something, too—going to **Spitalfields City Farm** ⑨ a few blocks away.) Go back west through Folgate Street to reach Shoreditch High Street, where you can catch Bus 22A, 22B, or 149 north to Kingsland Road, or get there across Bethnal Green Road, left, then right onto Club Row, to **Arnold Circus** ⑩ and then two streets north, to **Columbia Road** ⑪. Cross Hackney Road and slip up Waterson Street—that's about a ½-mi walk. On Kingsland Road, you'll come to the row of early 18th-century almshouses that are the **Geffrye Museum** ⑫. Head east about 500 yards on Hackney Road (Cremer Street, south of the museum, gets you there), and you come to the **Hackney City Farm** ⑬. Going south down Warner Place (across Hackney Road opposite the farm entrance), you come to Old Bethnal Green Road, at the end of which a right turn brings you to the **Bethnal Green Museum of Childhood** ⑭.

Now you can catch either Bus 106 or 253 or walk south about a ½ mi down Cambridge Heath Road as far as the Mile End Road. Turning left, you'll pass several historical landmarks that provide more food for thought than thrills for the senses. On the north side of the street are the former **Trinity Almshouses** ⑮, with the statue of William Booth on the very spot where the first Salvation Army meetings were held. Behind you, on the northwest corner of Cambridge Heath Road is the

Blind Beggar ⑯ pub, with the **Royal London Hospital** ⑰ a few yards to the left and its Archives behind.

TIMING

This is a long walk, and not for everyone. The East End isn't picturesque, and the sights are anything but world famous. However, those who get pleasure from discovery and an adventurous route will enjoy these hidden corners. If you visit on a Sunday morning, the East End has a festive air: about half the neighborhood sprouts hundreds of market stalls (especially in and around Middlesex Street, Brick Lane, and Columbia Road). After shopping, you could go on to take brunch among cows and sheep on a farm, then play at being Georgians in a restored, candlelit 18th-century town house. You would miss out on a few weekday-only sights, but—as a Victorian peep-show barker might say—yer pays yer money and yer takes yer choice. A weekday focus for your jaunt might well be the excellent Whitechapel Gallery, the Geffrye Museum, or the Bethnal Green Museum of Childhood, any of which will take an hour or two. Aside from visits, the walk alone is a three-hour marathon, done at a brisk pace. The suggested bus links might be appealing, since the in-between parts aren't going to win tourism awards.

HOW TO GET THERE

The best tube to start from is Whitechapel or Aldgate East on the District/Hammersmith and City lines or Aldgate on the Metropolitan and Circle lines. Buses 8, 25, 26, 35, 47, 48, and 78 are useful. To continue up into the northern part of the area, around Shoreditch and Spitalfields, including the Geffrye Museum (get the 22A or B or the 67 for that), get Buses 8, 22A, 22B, 26, 35, 47, 48, 55, 67, 78, and 242 to the junction of Shoreditch High Street and Bishopsgate.

Sights to See

⑩ **Arnold Circus.** A perfect circle of Arts and Crafts–style houses around a central raised bandstand, this is the core of the Boundary Estate—"model" housing built by Victorian philanthropists and do-gooders for the slum-dwelling locals and completed as the 20th century began. It's of special interest to architecture buffs. ⊠ *E2. Tube: Liverpool St., Old St.*

Ⓒ ⑭ **Bethnal Green Museum of Childhood.** This is the East End outpost of the Victoria and Albert Museum—in fact, this entire iron, glass, and brown-brick building was transported here from South Kensington in 1875. Since then, believe it or not, its contents have grown into the biggest toy collection in the world. The central hall is a bit like the Geffrye Museum zapped into miniature: here are doll's houses (some royal) of every period. Each genre of plaything has its own enclosure, so if teddy bears are your weakness, you need waste no time with the train sets. The museum's title is justified upstairs, in the recently opened, fascinating—and possibly unique—social-history-of-childhood galleries. Free art workshops are given for children over the age of 3. ⊠ *Cambridge Heath Rd., E2,* ☎ *020/8983–5200.* ⊡ *Free.* Ⓢ *Sat.–Thurs. 10–5:50; art workshop Sat. at 11 and 2. Tube: Bethnal Green.*

⑥ **Black Eagle Brewery.** This is the only one of the former East End breweries still standing. It is a very handsome example of Georgian and 19th-century industrial architecture, too, along with its mirrored 1977 extension. It belonged to Truman, Hanbury, Buxton & Co., which in 1873 was the largest brewery in the world (the English always did like their bitters). The building now houses the East End Tourism Trust offices and the present Truman brewery's administration. You can't go in except to look at the old stables and vat house on the east side. The old brewery canteen used to be the **Brick Lane Music Hall** (⊠ 134–146 Curtain Rd., ☎ 020/7739–9996), but this has now moved to larger

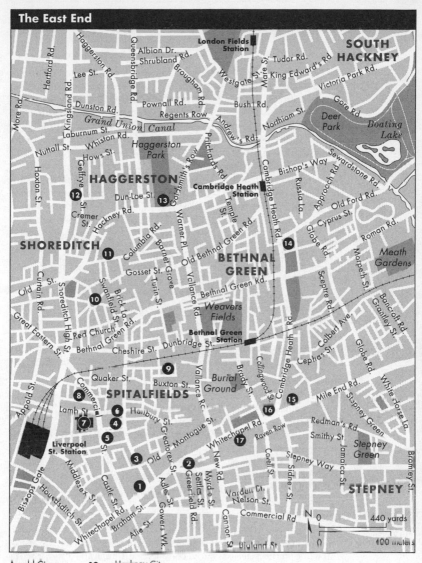

The East End

Arnold Circus **10**

Bethnal Green
Museum of
Childhood **14**

Black Eagle
Brewery **6**

The Blind
Beggar **16**

Brick Lane **3**

Christ Church,
Spitalfields **5**

Columbia Road . . . **11**

Dennis Severs's
House **8**

Fournier Street **4**

Geffrye Museum . . . **12**

Hackney City
Farm **13**

Royal London
Hospital **17**

Spitalfields City
Farm **9**

Spitalfields
Market **7**

Trinity
Almshouses **15**

Whitechapel Art
Gallery **1**

Whitechapel Bell
Foundry **2**

premises a couple of roads away; there, you'll find East End Jewish fare (latkes—potato pancakes—are a feature on most menus) and an old-fashioned laugh-a-minute cabaret show on tap. ⊠ *91 Brick La., E1. Tube: Aldgate East, Shoreditch.*

⑯ **The Blind Beggar.** This is the Victorian den of iniquity where Salvation Army founder William Booth preached his first sermon. Also, on the south side of the street stands a stone inscribed, HERE WILLIAM BOOTH COMMENCED THE WORK OF THE SALVATION ARMY, JULY 1865, marking the position of the first Sally Army platform, while back by the pub, a statue of William Booth stands where the first meetings were held. Booth didn't supply the pub's main claim to fame, though. The Blind Beggar's real notoriety dates only from March 1966, when Ronnie Kray—one of the Kray twins, the former gangster kings of London's East End underworld— shot dead rival "godfather" George Cornell in the saloon bar. The original Albion Brewery was next door, celebrated home to the first bottled brown ale. ⊠ *337 Whitechapel Rd., E1. Tube: Whitechapel.*

❸ **Brick Lane.** This street has, in its time, seen the manufacture of bricks (during the 16th century, when it was named), beer, and bagels, but nowadays it is the center of the East End's Bengali community. (You can still get the bagels, though, at Number 159, the 24-hour **Beigel Bake.**) All along here you'll see shops selling psychedelic saris and stacks of sticky Indian sweets, video stores renting Indian movies, and Bengali, Bangladeshi, and Pakistani restaurants, popular among Londoners for the most authentic and least expensive curries in town. On Sunday morning the entire street is packed with stalls in a companion market to the nearby Petticoat Lane. ⊠ *Brick Lane, E1. Tube: Aldgate East, Shoreditch.*

❺ **Christ Church, Spitalfields.** This is the 1729 masterpiece of Wren's associate, Nicholas Hawksmoor. Hawksmoor built only six London churches; this one was commissioned as part of Parliament's 1711 "Fifty New Churches Act." The idea was to score points for the Church of England against such nonconformists as the Protestant Huguenots. (It must have worked; in the churchyard, you can still see some of their gravestones, with epitaphs in French.) The Spitalfields district once flourished thanks to the silk-weaving trade of its émigré population, but as the silk industry declined (19th-century machinery had made hand weaving obsolete), the church fell into disrepair and its gardens even acquired a reputation as a tramps' ground (and the sobriquet "Itchy Park"). By 1958 the structure was crumbling to bits and had to be closed. It was saved from demolition—but only just—and reopened in 1987. Restoration work on the exterior is now complete, although the interior work continues. Opening hours are restricted to those listed below, although you can also admire the interior during the Spitalfields Festival in June and December, when there are lunchtime and evening concerts; call ☎ 020/7377–0287 for details. There is always a fine view of the colonnaded portico and tall spire from Brushfield Street to the west. ⊠ *Commercial St., E1,* ☎ *020/7247-7202.* 🖼 *Free; charge for concerts.* ☯ *Weekdays noon–2, Sun. services. Tube: Aldgate East.*

⑪ **Columbia Road.** On Sundays, this narrow street gets buried under forests of potted palms, azaleas, ivy, ficus, freesia, tiger lilies, carnations, roses, and hosts of daffodils in London's main plant and flower market. Prices are ultralow, and lots of the Victorian shop windows around the stalls are filled with wares—terra-cotta pots, vases, gardening tools, hats, and antiques. ☯ *Sun. 7–2. Tube: Old St., then Bus 55.*

★ ❽ **Dennis Severs's House.** Ever want to feel what Ebenezer Scrooge felt when the three ghosts visited him? Enter this extraordinary time machine of a house—a Georgian terrace belonging to the eponymous per-former-designer-scholar from Escondido, California, who dedicated his life not only to restoring his house but also to raising the ghosts of a fictitious Jervis family that might have inhabited it over two centuries. Severs, who died in December 1999, lived a replica of Georgian life, without electricity but with a butler in full 18th-century livery to light the candles and lay the fires—for the Jervises. His assistant still carries on the tradition. The rooms are shadowy set pieces of rose-laden Victorian wallpapers, Jacobean paneling, Georgian wing chairs, Baroque carved ornaments, "Protestant" colors (upstairs), and "Catholic" shades (downstairs). Twice a month there is an open house; reservations are essential on Monday, when the house is viewed by candlelight. Private visits by special arrangement are possible. ⊠ *18 Folgate St., E1,* ☎ *020/7247–4013.* ✉ *£10.* ⊘ *1st Sun. of month 2–5, 1st Mon. call for hrs (reservations required). Tube: Liverpool St.*

❹ Fournier Street. This contains fine examples of the neighborhood's characteristic Georgian terraced houses, many of them built by the richest of the early 18th-century Huguenot silk weavers (see the enlarged windows on the upper floors). Most of those along the north side of Fournier Street have now been restored by conservationists; others still contain textile sweatshops— only now the workers are Bengali. On the Brick Lane corner is the **Jamme Masjid,** where local Muslims worship. UMBRA SUMMUS (WE ARE SHADOWS) announces the inscription above the entrance, an apt epitaph for the successive communities that have had temporary claim on the building. Built in 1742 as a Huguenot chapel, it converted to Methodism in 1809, only to become the Spitalfields Great Synagogue when the Orthodox Machzikei Hadath sect bought it in 1897. ⊠ *E1. Tube: Liverpool St.*

★ ⑫ Geffrye Museum. This is a small and perfectly formed museum that re-creates domestic English interiors of every period from Elizabethan through postwar '50s utility, all in sequence, so that you walk through time. The best thing about the Geffrye (named after the 17th-century Lord Mayor of London whose land this was) is that its rooms are not the grand parlors of the gentry one normally sees in historic houses but copies of real family homes, as if talented movie-set designers had been let loose instead of academic museum curators. There's also a walled, scented herb garden and a full program of accessible lectures, including regular "bring a room to life" talks. A new suite of 20th-century rooms opened in November 1998. ⊠ *Kingsland Rd., E2,* ☎ *020/7739–9893.* ✉ *Free.* ⊘ *Tues.–Sat. 10–5, Sun. noon–5, Tube: Old St., then Bus 243; Liverpool St., then Bus 149, 242, or 243A.* ◑

☝ ⑬ Hackney City Farm. This one is smaller than the city farm at Spitalfields (☞ *below*), and so are its animals. Bees and butterflies are the stars here, along with the kinds of wildflowers they like, as well as an ecologically sound pond. If you're walking this route, drop in and buy a pot of London honey. ⊠ *1A Goldsmiths Row, E2,* ☎ *020/7729–6381.* ✉ *Free.* ⊘ *Tues.–Sun. 10–4:30.*

⑰ Royal London Hospital. Founded in 1740, the Royal London was once as nasty as its then-neighborhood near the Tower of London. Waste was carried out in buckets and dumped in the street; bedbugs and alcoholic nurses were problems; but according to hospital records patients didn't die—they were "relieved." Anyone who lived but refused to give thanks to both the hospital committee and God went on a blacklist, to be banned from further treatment. In 1757, the hospital moved to a new building, the core of the one you see today. By then it had become one of the best hospitals in London, and it was enhanced further by the addition of a small medical school in 1785, and again, 70 years later, an entire state-of-the-art medical college. Thomas John Barnado, who went on to found the famous Dr. Barnado's Homes for Orphans, came to train here in 1866. Ten years later, with the opening of a new wing, the hospital became the largest in the United Kingdom, and now, though mostly rebuilt since World War II, it remains one of London's most capacious. Behind it, in the crypt of St. Augustine with St. Philip's Church, on Newark Street, the **Royal London Hospital Archives** has displays of medical paraphernalia, objects, and documentation to illustrate the 250-year history of this East London institution. ☒ *Whitechapel Rd., E1,* ☎ *020/7377–7608.* ☒ *Free.* ☉ *Hospital and garden daily 9–6, archives weekdays 10–4:30. Tube: Whitechapel.*

🖐 **9** **Spitalfields City Farm.** This is just what it sounds like—a sliver of rural England squashed between housing projects. It's one of about a dozen such places in London, which exist to educate city kids in country matters. A tiny farm shop sells fresh laid eggs and farm recipes. ☒ *Pedley St., E1,* ☎ *020/7247–8762.* ☒ *Free.* ☉ *Tues.–Sun. 10:30–5. Tube: Shoreditch, Liverpool St.*

7 **Spitalfields Market.** There's been a market here since the mid-17th century, but the current version is overflowing with crafts and design shops and stalls, a sports hall, restaurants and bars (with a pan-world-palette, from Spanish tapas to Thai), and different-purpose markets every day of the week. The nearer the weekend, the busier it all gets, culminating in the Sunday arts-and-crafts and green market—the best day to go. The latest additions are an opera house and a swimming pool, and events are being staged all the time. ☒ *65 Brushfield St., E1,* ☎ *020/7377–1496.* ☒ *Free.* ☉ *Daily 10–7; market stalls weekdays 11–2, weekends 9–4. Tube: Liverpool St.*

OFF THE
BEATEN PATH

Sutton House – Homerton (part of Hackney, east of London) hasn't much to recommend it, but Sutton House has survived the ravages of modern block estates. When it was built in 1535 it was surrounded by fields and a country village. Now run by the National Trust, the mansion was first owned by Ralph Sadleir, a important courtier to Henry VIII. The Tudor linen-fold paneling in the parlor is some of the finest in London and can only be seen elsewhere in Hampton Court; the carved stone fireplaces are also original. The painted staircase with its wall friezes has been carefully preserved. The kitchen, which has fascinating cooking implements of the time, leads onto a cobbled Italianate courtyard—you could be a thousand miles from deepest Hackney. There are a café, a gift shop, and exhibitions—including a computer on which you can read a copy of a local Victorian child's diary. It's a special place that transports you light-years away from the thronging traffic and ugly apartment blocks just outside. ☒ *2 Homerton High St., E9,* ☎ *020/8986–2264. Tube: Highbury and Islington, then Bus 377 or 30; Whitechapel, then Bus 106 or 253.*

15 **Trinity Almshouses.** This is just a redbrick student hostel, but it has interesting origins, having been built (possibly with Wren's help) in 1695 for "28 decayed Masters and Commanders of Ships or ye widows of such," bombed during World War II, and restored by the London County Council. Behind, even better concealed, is the oldest Jewish cemetery in Britain, founded by the Sephardic community in 1657 after Cromwell allowed them back into the country. (If you would like to view the cemetery, call the **United Synagogues Cemetery Maintenance Department,** ☎ 020/7790–1445.) ☒ *Mile End Rd., E1. Tube: Whitechapel, Stepney Green.*

1 **Whitechapel Art Gallery.** Housed in a spacious 1901 Art Nouveau building, this has an international reputation for its shows, which are often on the cutting edge of contemporary art. The American painter Jackson Pollock exhibited here in the '50s, as did the pop artist Robert Rauschenberg in the '60s, and David Hockney had his first solo show here in the '70s. More recently, the Tate Gallery visited the Whitechapel and bought American Bill Viola's powerful video installation, the *Nantes Triptych*, which shows Viola submerged underwater, his wife giving birth on one side, his mother dying in a hospital on the other. Other exhibitions highlight the local community and culture, and there are programs of lectures, too. The Whitechapel Café serves remarkably inexpensive, home-cooked, whole-food hot meals, soups, and cakes. ⊠ *Whitechapel High St., E1,* ☎ *020/7522–7888.* ▢ *Free (fee for some exhibitions).* ⊙ *Tues. and Thurs.–Sun. 11–5, Wed. 11–8. Tube: Aldgate East.*

② **Whitechapel Bell Foundry.** It may be off the beaten track, but this working foundry was responsible for some of the world's better-known chimes. Before moving to this site in 1738, the foundry cast Westminster Abbey's bells (in the 1580s), but its biggest work, in every sense, was the 13-ton Big Ben, cast in 1858 by George Mears and requiring 16 horses to transport it from here to Westminster. The foundry's other important work was casting the original Liberty Bell (now in Philadelphia) in 1752, and both it and Big Ben can be seen in pictures, along with exhibits about bell making, in a little museum in the shop. Note: the actual foundry is off-limits, for health and safety reasons, but in the small front shop you can buy bell paraphernalia and browse through the historic photos. There are guided tours of the foundry on Saturday morning only, but bookings are usually made months in advance (2001 is already booked, although you may be lucky; call for information and fees). ⊠ *34 Whitechapel Rd., E1,* ☎ *020/7247–2599.* ⊙ *Weekdays 8:30–5:30. Tube: Aldgate East.*

OFF THE BEATEN PATH **WILLIAM MORRIS GALLERY –** An 18th-century house in northeast London where the artistic polymath William Morris (1834–96)—craftsman, painter, and writer—lived for eight years, this gallery contains many examples of his work and that of his fellow artisans in the Arts and Crafts movement. ⊠ *Water House, Lloyd Park, Forest Rd.,* ☎ *020/8527–3782.* ⊙ *Tues.–Sat. 10–1 and 2–5, 1st Sun. of the month 10–1 and 2–5. Tube: Walthamstow Central, then 15-min walk down Hoe St., turn left at Forest Rd.*

THE SOUTH BANK

That old, snide North London quip about needing a passport to cross the Thames is no longer heard on the lips of Londoners. For decades, natives never ventured beyond the watery curtain that divides the city in half; tourists, too, rarely troubled the area unless they were departing from Waterloo Station. But lately, a host of new attractions is drawing even the most ardent northerners across the great divide. The new adjunct branch of the Tate Gallery is the star attraction. Perhaps in keeping with Britain's most renowned new artist, Damien Hirst (who often uses utensils and other found objects), Tate Modern takes something functional—a 1930s power station—and makes it a place for inspiration and creativity. At the South Bank Centre, the world's largest Ferris wheel, officially called the British Airways London Eye, gives visitors a moment's flight over the city. Even looked at from a great height, the South Bank—which occupies the riverside stretch between Waterloo Bridge and Hungerford Bridge—still isn't beautiful, but if it's culture you're hunting for, this complex of theaters and museums is fantastic. Today, developers and local authorities have expanded the South Bank's potential farther east with an explosion of attractions that are turning this once-neglected district into one of London's most happening new neighborhoods. The '80s brought renovations and innovations such as Gabriel's Wharf, London Bridge City, Hay's Galleria, and Butler's Wharf; the '90s arrived, and so did such headline-making sights as the spectacular reconstruction of Shakespeare's Globe—the most famous theater in the world—the OXO Tower, and the London Aquarium. The South Bank has since become a dazzling perch for culture vultures.

Actually, it is fitting that so much of London's artistic life should once again be centered here on the South Bank—back in the days of Ye Olde London Towne, **Southwark** was the city's oldest "suburb": though just across the river from London Bridge, it was conveniently outside the City walls and laws and therefore the ideal location for the theaters, taverns, and cock-fighting arenas that served as after-hours entertainment in the Middle Ages. The Globe Theatre, in which Shakespeare acted and held shares, was one of several established here after theaters were banished from the City in 1574 for encouraging truancy in young apprentices and for being generally rowdy. In truth, the Globe was as likely to stage a few bouts of bearbaiting as the latest interpretations of Shakespeare. Today, at the reconstructed "Wooden O," of course, you can just see the latter.

Numbers in the text correspond to numbers in the margin and on the South Bank map.

A Good Walk

Start scenically at the south end of Tower Bridge, finding the steps on the east (left) side, which descend to the start of a pedestrians-only street, Shad Thames. Now turn your back on the bridge and follow this quaint path between cliffs of the good-as-new warehouses, which are now **Butler's Wharf** ① but were once the seedy, dingy, dangerous shadow lands where Dickens killed off Bill Sikes in *Oliver Twist*. See the foodies' center, the Gastrodrome, and the **Design Museum** ②; then, just before you get back to Tower Bridge, turn away from the river (along Horsleydown Lane), follow Tooley Street, take the right, follow Tooley Street, and take either the right turn at Morgan Lane to **HMS Belfast** ③ or continue to **Hay's Galleria** ④, with London Bridge and the **London Dungeon** ⑤ beyond. Next, turn left onto Joiner Street underneath the arches of London's first (1836) railway, then right onto St. Thomas Street, where you'll find the **Old St. Thomas's Operating Theatre** ⑥ and Herb Garret, with **Southwark Cathedral** ⑦ just across Borough High Street, past the organic Saturday Borough Market and past another of the South Bank's office developments, St. Mary Overie Dock, down Cathedral Street. See the west wall, with a rose-window outline of Winchester House, the palace of the Bishops of Winchester until 1626, built into it, and take a tour of the little **Golden Hinde** ⑧ and the **Clink** ⑨ next door. Continue to the end of Clink Street onto Bankside, detouring left up Rose Alley, where in 1989 the remains of a famous Jacobean theater, the Rose Theatre, were unearthed (because of office development surrounding the preserved foundations, however, there's not much to see). Just before you reach the place to imbibe culture, you come to **Vinopolis** ⑩, the world's first leisure complex to celebrate wine. Then head to the next little alley, New Globe Walk, where there is much to see: the reconstruction of that most famous of Jacobean theaters, **Shakespeare's Globe Theatre** ⑪. Next along Bankside is the 17th-century Cardinal's Wharf, where, as a plaque explains, Wren lived while St. Paul's Cathedral was being built; then Bankside Power Station, now the **Tate Modern** ⑫ at Bankside and **Bankside Gallery** ⑬. Stretching from the new Tate back across the river to the St. Paul's Cathedral steps in the City the **Millennium Bridge,** a pedestrian bridge across the Thames, opened in June 2001, at a cost of £14 million.

Now you reach your fifth bridge on this walk, Blackfriars Bridge, which you pass beneath to join the street called Upper Ground, spending some time in the Coin Street Community Builders' fast-emerging neighborhood, which features the **OXO Tower** ⑭ and Gabriel's Wharf, a marketplace of shops and cafés. Farther along Upper Ground, you reach the South Bank Centre, with the **Royal National Theatre** ⑮ first, followed by the **Museum of the Moving Image (MOMI)** ⑯ and National Film Theatre, the **Royal Festival Hall** ⑰, and the **Hayward Gallery** ⑱. Carry on round the curve of the river and you come to the Jubilee Gardens, with the magnificent **British Airways London Eye** ⑲. You'll find distractions all over this section of the walk, especially in summer— secondhand-book stalls, entertainers, and a series of plaques annotating the buildings opposite. When you've passed the South Bank Centre, look across the river for the quintessential postcard vista of the Houses of Parliament, which continues past Westminster Bridge to St. Thomas's Hospital. Much of the complex of Jubilee Gardens has been razed to make room for the 500-ft Ferris wheel, the London Eye, which opened in January 2000. Next, you reach the former County Hall, which is now the **London Aquarium** ⑳, and farther along the river, beyond the **Florence Nightingale Museum** ㉑, **Lambeth Palace** ㉒ stands by Lambeth Bridge, with the **Museum of Garden History** ㉓ in St. Mary's next door. If you take a detour to the right off Lambeth Road, you could be "doing the Lambeth Walk" down the street of the same name. A cockney tradition ever since the 17th century, when there was a spa here, the Sunday stroll was immortalized in a song from the 1937 musical *Me and My Girl,* which recently proved a hit all over again in the West End and on New York City's Broadway. A little farther east along Lambeth Road you reach the **Imperial War Museum** ㉔.

TIMING

On a fine day, this 2- to 3-mi walk makes a very scenic wander, since you're following the south bank of the great Thames nearly all the way. Fabulous views across to the north bank take you past St. Paul's and the Houses of Parliament, and you pass—under, over, or around no fewer than seven bridges. It's bound to take far longer than a couple of hours because there is so much to see. The new Tate Modern, Imperial War Museum, MOMI, Shakespeare's Globe, the Hayward Gallery, the Design Museum, and the aquarium each could take more than an hour (depending on your interests), while the London Dungeon doesn't take long, unless you have kids in tow—which is why you'd go in at all. The other museums on this route—the Clink, Garden History, Old Operating Theatre, Florence Nightingale, the South Bank Centre foyers, and the Bankside Gallery—are compact enough to squeeze together. The best thing about this walk is to finish it with a flourish by going to one of three theatres—the Lyttelton, the Cottesloe, or the Olivier—at the National Theatre complex, the National Film Theatre, or Shakespeare's Globe, but remember the theaters stay dark on Sundays. Dinner or a riverside drink at the OXO Tower Brasserie, the Gastrodrome restaurants, or the People's Palace is another idea for a big finish. Public transportation is thin on the ground here, so pick a day when you're feeling energetic; there are few shortcuts once you're under way.

HOW TO GET THERE

The tube stop to use is Waterloo on the Northern and Bakerloo lines, though you could also go to the Embankment stop (same lines, plus District and Circle) or Charing Cross (the Jubilee and Northern lines) and walk across the Charing Cross pedestrian bridge. Buses that take you into the rather confusing territory behind the South Bank Centre include Buses 1, 68, 76, 168, 171, 176, 178, and 188. For farther downstream, near Shakespeare's Globe, get the 21, 35, 40, 47, or 133 to Tooley Street, or get the tube to Blackfriars and walk across that bridge (offering a particularly scenic walk) to the stunning new Southwark station (Jubilee line, or to Mansion House and walk across Southwark Bridge. The latter is the best way to the OXO Tower.

Sights to See

⑬ Bankside Gallery. Two artistic societies—the Royal Society of Painter-Printmakers and the Royal Watercolour Society—have their headquarters here. Together they mount exhibitions of current members' work, usually for sale, alongside artists' materials and books. ⊠ *48 Hopton St., SE1,* ☎ *020/7928–7521.* ⊞ *£3.50.* ⊘ *Tues., Thurs., and Sat. 10–8; Sun. 1–5; Wed. and Fri. 10–5. Tube: Blackfriars or Southwark.*

⑲ British Airways London Eye. If you long to see London from a different perspective, this giant ride, the fourth highest structure in London, will give you the chance. The highest observation wheel in the world, this 500-ft Ferris wheel towers over the South Bank from the Jubliee Gardens next to County Hall. For 25 minutes, passengers hover over the city in a slow-motion flight, so this may not be for the fainthearted. ⊠ *Jubilee Gardens, SE1,* ☎ *0870/500–0600.* ⊞ *£7.95.* ⊘ *Apr.–Oct., daily 9–sunset; Nov.–Mar., daily 10–6.*

❶ Butler's Wharf. An '80s development that is maturing gracefully, this wharf is full of deluxe loft-style warehouse conversions and swanky new buildings housing restaurants and galleries. People flock here thanks partly to London's saint of the stomach, Sir Terence Conran (also responsible for high-profile central London restaurants Bibendum, Mezzo, and Quaglino's). He has given it his "Gastrodrome" of four restaurants (including the fabulous Pont de la Tour), a vintner's, a deli, and a bakery. ⊠ *SC1. Tube: Tower Hill, then walk across river.*

❾ The Clink. Giving rise to the term "the clink," which still refers to a jail, this institution was originally the prison attached to Winchester House, palace of the Bishops of Winchester until 1626. One of five Southwark prisons, it was the first to detain women, most of whom were called "Winchester Geese"—another euphemism meaning prostitutes. The world's oldest profession was endemic in Southwark, especially around the bishops' area of jurisdiction, which was known as "the Liberty of the Clink." Their graces' sensible solution was to license prostitution rather than ban it, but a Winchester goose who flouted the rules ended up in the Clink. Now there is a museum tracing the history of prostitution in "the Liberty" and showing what the Clink was like during its 16th-century prime. ⊠ *1 Clink St., SE1,* ☎ *020/7403–6515.* ⊞ *£4.* ⊘ *Daily 10–6. Tube: London Bridge.*

❷ Design Museum. This was the first museum in the world (it opened in 1989) to elevate everyday design and design classics to the status of art by placing it in its social and cultural context. On the top floor, the Collection traces the evolution of mass-produced goods, with showcases full of telephones and washing machines, plates and hi-fi equipment, computers and Coke bottles, and plenty of backup material, from ads to films. Alongside the Collection, the regularly revamped Review looks deeply into a particular aspect of the consumer durable. Special exhibitions are held downstairs on the first floor, and there's also a program of lectures and events, as well as the very good Blueprint Café, a funky restaurant with its own river terrace and superb views of London. ⊠ *Butler's Wharf, SE1,* ☎ *020/7403–6933.* ⊞ *£5.25.* ⊘ *Daily 11:30–6:30. Tube: Tower Hill, then walk across river.*

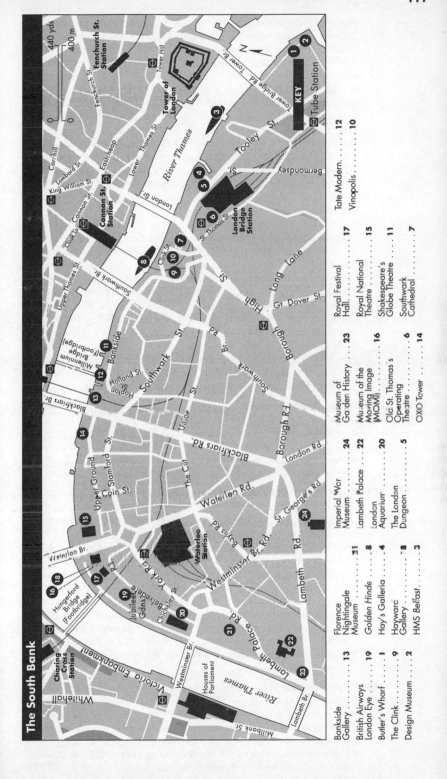

The South Bank

KEY
- ⊖ Tube Station

Scale
- 440 yds
- 400 m

Bankside Gallery.........13
British Airways London Eye....19
Butler's Wharf.........9
The Clink.............9
Design Museum.......2

Florence Nightingale Museum.......21
Golden Hinde.........8
Hay's Galleria.......4
Hayward Gallery.......8
HMS Belfast.........3

Imperial War Museum.......24
Lambeth Palace.....22
London Aquarium.....20
The London Dungeon.....5

Museum of Garden History.....23
Museum of the Moving Image (MOMI).....16
Old St. Thomas's Operating Theatre.....6
OXO Tower.....14

Royal Festival Hall.....17
Royal National Theatre.....15
Shakespeare's Globe Theatre.....11
Southwark Cathedral.....7

Tate Modern.......12
Vinopolis.........10

DULWICH PICTURE GALLERY – A highly distinguished small gallery, the Dulwich has impressive works by Rembrandt, Van Dyck, Rubens, Poussin, and Gainsborough, among others. Anyone who fell in love with Sir John Soane's house (☞ Bloomsbury and Legal London, *above*) may wish to make the trek out here, since this gallery was also designed by the visionary Sir John Soane. If you do come all this way, you'll also enjoy wandering around Dulwich Village, with its handsome 18th-century houses strung out along its main street. Most of the land around here belongs to the local, famous school, the Dulwich College Estate, founded during the early 17th century by the actor Edward Alleyn, and this keeps strict control of modern development. Opposite the gallery, Dulwich Park is a well-kept municipal park with a particularly fine display of rhododendrons in late May. ⊠ *College Rd.,* ☎ *020/8693–8000.* ▱ *£5.* ⊘ *Tues.–Fri. 10–5, weekends 1–5. British Rail: West Dulwich (from Victoria or London Bridge).*

㉑ Florence Nightingale Museum. Here you can learn all about the founder of the first school of nursing, that most famous of health-care reformers, "the Lady with the Lamp." See the reconstruction of the barracks ward at Scutari, Turkey, where she tended soldiers during the Crimean War (1854–56) and earned her nickname. Here you also find a Victorian East End slum cottage showing what she did to improve living conditions among the poor; and the famous lamp. The museum is in St. Thomas's Hospital, which was built in 1868 to the specifications of Florence Nightingale. Most of it was bombed to bits in the Blitz, then rebuilt to become one of London's teaching hospitals. ⊠ *2 Lambeth Palace Rd., SE1,* ☎ *020/7620–0374.* ▱ *£3.50.* ⊘ *Daily 10–4. Tube: Waterloo or Westminster, then walk over bridge.*

❽ *Golden Hinde.* Sir Francis Drake circumnavigated the globe in this little galleon, or one just like it. This exact replica has now finished *its* 23-year round-the-world voyage—much of it spent along U.S. coasts, both Pacific and Atlantic—and has settled here to continue its educational purpose. ⊠ *St. Mary Overie Dock, Southwark, SE1,* ☎ *020/7403–0123.* ▱ *£2.30.* ⊘ *Daily 10–6. Tube: Mansion House.*

❹ Hay's Galleria. Hay's Wharf was built by Thomas Cubitt in 1857 on the spot where the port of London's oldest wharf had stood since 1651. It was once known as "London's larder" on account of the edibles landed here until it wound down gradually, then closed in 1970. In 1987 it was reborn as this Covent Garden–esque parade of bars and restaurants, offices, and shops, all weatherproofed by an arched glass atrium roof supported by tall iron columns. The centerpiece is a fanciful kinetic sculpture by David Kemp, *The Navigators,* which looks like the skeleton of a pirate schooner crossed with a dragon and spouts water from various orifices. Inevitably, jugglers, string quartets, and crafts stalls abound. This courtyard hub of the developing London Bridge City needed all the help it could get in its early days, but it has settled in nicely now with its captive crowd of office workers from the adjacent new developments.

⓲ Hayward Gallery. This is one of the city's major art-exhibition spaces, its bias fixed firmly in the 20th century. This stained and windowless bunker tucked behind the South Bank Centre concert halls has been the brunt of most of the criticism of Thames-side buildings, enduring constant threats to flatten it and start again. But it's still here, topped by its multicolor neon tube sculpture, the most familiar feature on the South Bank skyline. ⊠ *South Bank Complex, SE1,* ☎ *020/7928–3144.* ▱ *Admission varies according to exhibition.* ⊘ *Thurs.–Mon. 10–6, Tues.–Wed. 10–8. Tube: Waterloo.*

🐾 ③ **HMS *Belfast*.** At 656 ft, this is one of the largest and most powerful cruisers the Royal Navy has ever had. It played an important role in the D-day landings off Normandy, left for the Far East after the war, and has been becalmed here since 1971. On board there's an outpost of the **Imperial War Museum** (☞ *below*), which tells the Royal Navy's story from 1914 to the present and shows you what life on board a World War II battleship was like, from mess decks and bakery to punishment cells and from operations room to engine room and armaments. ✉ *Morgan's La., Tooley St., SE1,* ☎ *020/7940–6434.* 🎟 *£4.70.* ☉ *Mid-Mar.–Oct., daily 10–6; Nov.–mid-Mar., daily 10–4:15. Tube: London Bridge.*

OFF THE BEATEN PATH

HORNIMAN MUSEUM – This educational museum of anthropology, which also manages to be fun, is set in 16 acres of gardens in south London with well-displayed ethnographic and natural history collections, a Music Gallery, and a colony of honey bees visibly at work in their glass-front hive. Other highlights are the aquarium stocked with endangered species and the new, educationally oriented Centre for Understanding the Environment. ✉ *100 London Rd., Forest Hill,* ☎ *020/8699–1872.* 🎟 *Free.* ☉ *Mon.–Sat. 10:30–5:30, Sun. 2–5:30. British Rail: Forest Hill (from London Bridge).*

㉔ **Imperial War Museum.** Despite its title, this museum of 20th-century warfare does not glorify bloodshed but attempts to evoke what it was like to live through the two world wars. Of course, there is hardware for martial-minded children—a Battle of Britain Spitfire, a German V2 rocket, tanks, guns, submarines—but there is an equal amount of war art (David Bomberg, Henry Moore, John Singer Sargent, Graham Sutherland, to name a few), poetry, photography, and documentary film footage. One very affecting exhibit is *The Blitz Experience,* which is just what it sounds like—a 10-minute taste of an air raid in a street of acrid smoke with sirens blaring and searchlights glaring. A permanent new Holocaust exhibition, funded from a generous lottery grant, has just opened. More recent wars attended by British forces are thoughtfully commemorated, too, right up to the Gulf War of 1991.

The museum is housed in an elegant domed and colonnaded building, erected during the early 19th century to house the Bethlehem Hospital for the Insane, better known as the infamous Bedlam. By 1816, when the patients were moved here, they were no longer kept in cages to be taunted by tourists (see the final scene of Hogarth's *Rake's Progress* at Sir John Soane's Museum [☞ Bloomsbury and Legal London, *above*] for some sense of how horrific it was), since reformers—and George III's madness—had effected more humane standards of confinement. Bedlam moved to Surrey in 1930. ✉ *Lambeth Rd., SE1,* ☎ *020/7416–5000.* 🎟 *£5.* ☉ *Daily 10–6. Tube: Lambeth North.*

㉒ **Lambeth Palace.** For 800 years, this has been the London base of the Archbishop of Canterbury, head of the Church of England. Much of the palace is hidden behind great walls, and even the Tudor gatehouse, visible from the street, is closed to the public, but you can stand here and absorb the historical vibrations echoing from momentous events. These include the 1381 storming of the palace during the Peasants' Revolt against the poll tax and the 1534 clash of wills when Thomas More refused to sign the Oath of Supremacy claiming Henry VIII (and not the pope) as leader of the English Church, for which he was sent to the Tower and executed for treason the following year. Adjacent to this house is the Museum of Garden History (☞ *below*). ✉ *Lambeth Palace Rd., SE1. Tube: Waterloo.*

㉒ **London Aquarium.** County Hall was the original name of this curved, colonnaded Neoclassic hulk, which, with the interference of two world wars, took 46 years (1912–1958) to build. It was once home to London's local government, the Greater London Council (GLC), which mutated out of the London County Council in 1965 and disbanded in 1986. Now, after a £25 million injection, a three-level aquarium (full of sharks and stingrays) has been installed. There are also educational exhibits and piscine sights previously unseen on these shores. It is not the biggest aquarium you've ever seen—especially if you've been to SeaWorld—but the exhibit is well arranged on several subterranean levels, with areas for different oceans, water environments, and climate zones, including a stunning coral reef, and the highlight: the rain forest, which is almost like the real thing. ⊠ *County Hall, Riverside Building, Westminster Bridge Rd., SE1,* ☎ *020/7967–8000.* ☞ *£8.* ☉ *Daily 10–6. Tube: Westminster.*

🖐 ⑤ **The London Dungeon.** Here's the most gory, grisly, gruesome museum in town, where realistic waxwork people are subjected in graphic detail to all the historical horrors the Tower of London merely tells you about. Tableaux depict famous bloody moments—like Anne Boleyn's decapitation, or the martyrdom of St. George—alongside the torture, murder, and ritual slaughter of more anonymous victims, all to a soundtrack of screaming, wailing, and agonized moaning. London's times of deepest terror—the Great Fire and the Great Plague—are brought to life, too, and so are its public hangings. And did you ever wonder what a disembowelment actually looks like? See it here. Naturally, children absolutely adore this place, but be warned—nervous kiddies may find it too truly frightening. Expect long lines. ⊠ *28–34 Tooley St., SE1,* ☎ *020/7403–7221.* ☞ *£9.50.* ☉ *Apr.–Sept., daily 10–5:30; Oct.–Mar., daily 10–5. Tube: London Bridge.*

㉓ **Museum of Garden History.** Housed in St. Mary's Church, next to Lambeth Palace, this museum was founded in 1977 (when the church was deconsecrated), by the Tradescant Trust. The trust is named after John Tradescant (circa 1575–1638), botanist extraordinaire, who brought to these shores the lilac, larch, jasmine, and a spiderwort named *Tradescantia* in his honor. In the nave are changing horticultural exhibitions, supplemented by a reconstructed—or regrown—17th-century knot garden. Tradescant's tomb in the graveyard is carved with scenes from his worldwide plant-discovery tours and surrounded with the plants he discovered. Near it, William Bligh, captain of the *Bounty,* is buried, which suits the theme—the *Bounty* was on a breadfruit-gathering mission in 1787 when the crew mutinied. ⊠ *Lambeth Palace Rd., SE1,* ☎ *020/7261–1891.* ☞ *Donations welcome.* ☉ *Early Mar.–mid-Dec., weekdays 10:30–5, Sun. 10:30–5. Tube: Waterloo.*

🖐 ⑯ **Museum of the Moving Image (MOMI).** MOMI may be the most fun of all London's museums, and many visitors will linger for a couple of hours. The main feature is a history of cinema from 4,000-year-old Javanese shadow puppets to Spielbergian special effects, and very good the displays are, too, but the supporting program is even better, and it stars *you.* Actors dressed as John Wayne or Mae West or usherettes or chorus girls pluck you out of obscurity to read the TV news or audition for the chorus line or fly like Superman over the Thames. They also perform, mime, improvise, and generally bring celluloid to life, while all around, various screens show clips from such epoch-making giants as Hitchcock and Eisenstein, plus newsreels and ads. Techies can learn focus pulling and satellite beaming; artists can try animation; eggheads can explore such ethical issues as censorship and documentary objectivity. Needless to say, this is always a big hit with kids. The

White Card is accepted. This popular attraction is attached to the National Film Theatre (or NFT), underneath Waterloo Bridge, whose two movie theaters boast easily the best repertory programming in London, favoring obscure, foreign, silent, forgotten, classic, noir, and short films over blockbusters. There's a third theater in MOMI, but if you reckon you'll just have a quick look around before you catch a movie at the NFT, think again: the museum is closed until summer 2001 for renovation. ⊠ *South Bank Centre, SE1,* ☎ *020/7401–2636.* ☒ *£6.25.* ⊙ *Daily 10–6 (last admission 5). Tube: Waterloo.*

NEED A BREAK?	The **NFT restaurant and cafeteria**—especially the big wooden tables outside—are popular for lunch or supper (and are not affected by the museum renovations) You don't have to buy a membership.

⑥ Old St. Thomas's Operating Theatre. All that remains of one of England's oldest hospitals, which stood here from the 12th century until the railway forced it to move in 1862, this was where women went under the knife. The theater was bricked up and forgotten for a century but has now been restored into an exhibition of early 19th-century medical practices: the operating table onto which the gagged and blindfolded patients were roped; the box of sawdust underneath for catching their blood, the knives, pliers, and handsaws the surgeons wielded; and—this was a theater in the round—the spectators' seats. Next door is a sweeter show: the **Herb Garret,** with displays of medicinal herbs used during the same period. ⊠ *9A St. Thomas St., SE1,* ☎ *020/7955–4791.* ☒ *£2.50.* ⊙ *Jan. 6–Dec. 14, daily 10–4. Tube: London Bridge.*

⑭ OXO Tower. This might very well turn out to be the 21st-century version of Big Ben—a wonderfully renovated Art Deco–era tower, filled with designers' workshops overlooking the Thames. Long a London landmark to the cognoscenti, the OXO has graduated from its former incarnations as a power-generating station and warehouse into a vibrant community of artists' and designers' workshops, a pair of restaurants and cafés, as well as five floors of the best low-income housing in the city, via a £20 million plan by Coin Street Community Builders. There's a rooftop viewing gallery (a balcony for observation) for the latest river vista in town, and a performance area on the first floor, which comes alive all summer long—as does the entire surrounding neighborhood. All the designers-artisans have been selected by totally nondemocratic methods, meaning the work is of incredibly high standard. They all rely on you to disturb them any time they're open. Don't be shy—they really mean it; visitors are most welcome, whether buying, commissioning, or just browsing. The biggest draw remains the OXO Tower Restaurant extravaganza for a meal or a martini (☞ Chapter 2). ⊠ *Bargehouse St., SE1,* ☎ *020/7401–3610.* ☒ *Free.* ⊙ *Studios and shops Tues.–Sun. 11–6, Tube: Blackfriars or Waterloo.*

⑰ Royal Festival Hall. This is the largest auditorium of the South Bank Centre, with superb acoustics and a 3,000-plus capacity. It is the oldest of the riverside blocks, raised as the centerpiece of the 1951 Festival of Britain, a postwar morale-boosting exercise. The London Philharmonic resides here; symphony orchestras from the world over like to visit; and choral works, ballet, serious jazz and pop, and even films with live accompaniment are staged. There is a multiplicity of foyers, with free rotating exhibitions; a good, independently run restaurant; the People's Palace; free jazz in the main foyer on Sunday, and a very fine bookstore. The next building you come to also contains concert halls, one medium and one small, the **Queen Elizabeth Hall** and the **Purcell Room,** respectively. Both offer predominantly classical recitals of international caliber, with due respect paid to 20th-century composers and the more established jazz and vocal artists. ⊠ *South Bank Centre, SE1,* ☎ *0171/960–4242. Tube: Waterloo.*

🚇 **Royal National Theatre.** When it opened in 1976, Londoners generally felt the same way about this low-slung, multilayered block the color of heavy storm clouds, designed by Sir Denys Lasdun, that they would feel a decade later about the far nastier Barbican Centre (☞ The City, *above*). But whatever its merits or demerits as a landscape feature (and architects have subsequently given it an overall thumbs-up, while rejecting the derogatory-sounding term "brutalist"), the Royal National Theatre—still abbreviated colloquially to the preroyal warrant "NT"—has wonderful insides.

There are three auditoriums in the complex. The biggest one, the **Olivier,** is named after Sir Laurence, chairman of the first building commission and first artistic director of the National Theatre Company, formed in 1962. (In between the first proposal of a national theater for Britain and the 1949 formation of that building commission, an entire century passed.) The **Lyttleton** theater has a traditional proscenium arch, while the little **Cottesloe** mounts studio productions and new work in the round. Interspersed with the theaters is a multilayered foyer with exhibitions, bars, and restaurants, and free entertainment. The whole place is lively six days a week. The Royal National Theatre Company does not rest on its laurels: it attracts many of the nation's top actors (Anthony Hopkins, for one, does time here) in addition to launching future stars. Because it is a repertory company, you'll have several plays from which to choose even if your London sojourn is short, but, tickets or not, wander around and catch the buzz. ⊠ *South Bank, SE1,* ☎ *0171/452–3000 box office.* ▤ *Tour £3.50.* ☉ *1-hr tour of theater backstage Mon.–Sat. at 10:15, 12:30, and 5:30; foyer Mon.–Sat. 10 AM–11 PM. Tube: Waterloo.*

★ 🚇 **Shakespeare's Globe Theatre.** Three decades ago, Sam Wanamaker—then an aspiring actor—pulled up in Southwark in a cab and was amazed to find that the fabled Shakespeare's Globe Playhouse didn't actually exist. Worse, a tiny plaque was the only sign on the former site of the world's most legendary theater. So appalled was he that London lacked a center for the study and worship of the Bard of Bards, Wanamaker worked ceaselessly, until his death in 1993, to raise funds for his dream—a full-scale reconstruction of the theater. The dream was realized in 1996 when an exact replica of Shakespeare's open-roof Globe Playhouse (built in 1599; incinerated in 1613) was created, using authentic Elizabethan materials and craft techniques—green oak timbers joined only with wooden pegs and mortise and tenon joints; plaster made of lime, sand, and goat's hair; and the first thatched roof in London since the Great Fire. In addition, a second, indoor theater has now been added, built to a design of the 17th-century architect Inigo Jones. The whole complex stands 200 yards from the original Globe on the appropriate site of the 17th-century Davies Amphitheatre, admittedly more a bullbaiting, prizefighting sort of venue than a temple to the legitimate stage, but at least Samuel Pepys immortalized it in his diaries.

The Globe is a celebration of the great Bard's life (1564–1616) and work, an actual rebirth of his "Great Wooden O" (see *Henry V*), where his plays are presented in natural light (and sometimes rain) to 1,000 people on wooden benches in the "bays," plus 500 "groundlings," who stand on a carpet of filbert shells and clinker, just as they did nearly four centuries ago. For any theater buff, this stunning project is unmissable. Although the open-air Globe Theatre is only open for performances during the summer season (generally mid-May to mid-September), it can be viewed year-round if you take the helpful

SHAKESPEARE LIVES! REBIRTH OF THE GLOBE THEATRE

AS IT IS SAID ABOUT THE ONE TRUE church, Britain's theater is also founded on a rock—the enduring Shakespeare. Stratford-upon-Avon remains the primary shrine, but 1997 welcomed the opening of the cathedral—London's new Globe Theatre. More than three centuries ago, the Puritans closed the first "Wooden O," for which venue Shakespeare wrote *Hamlet, King Lear,* and *Julius Caesar,* among other peerless dramas. Now, more than 350 years later, the most famous playhouse in the world has been lovingly recreated, down to its Norfolk-reed roof. The theater has been reconstructed just 200 yards from its original site—ground as holy to Shakespeare's followers as Bayreuth's is to Wagner-philes.

For sheer drama—literally—few things can top the memorable jolt of walking into the new Globe. Enter, and some Wellsian genie transports you back to Elizabethan England. Step past the entrance into a soaring 45-ft-high arena, made surprisingly intimate by three half-timber galleries picturesquely encircling the stage. Ahead of you is the "pit," or orchestra level, filling up with 500 standees—"groundlings," to use the historic term—massed in front of the high stage. Soaring overhead is a twin-gabled stage canopy—the "heavens"—framed by exquisitely painted trompe l'oeil marble columns and a "lords' gallery," all fretted with gilded bosses, painted planets, and celestial bodies. Above you is the lowering London sky, which may at any time provide an authentic mid-performance drenching!

Of course, the new Globe is not a perfect time capsule. Occasionally, Juliet's wherefores will have to compete with the roar of jets. Ladies no longer proffer oranges or stools, and yesteryear's magpie hats have been superseded by Ray-Bans and baseball caps. Some ground rules have also changed. Most performances begin in the afternoon and, while floodlighting will be used to illuminate the theater at dusk, there will be no spotlights to focus the action on stage. The audience, on view at all times, becomes as much a part of the theatrical proceedings as the actors. Elizabethans made theatergoing almost as blood-and-thunder an experience as a football game of today. You've heard of the Super Bowl: view this as the Shakespeare Bowl—go ahead and boo Iago or hiss at Macbeth; you'll have plenty of company.

The Globe Theatre is but one facet of the entire complex, which, when completed, will include the 300-seat Inigo Jones indoor theater (to be used year-round, unlike the open-air Globe, which will be open only from June to September), a restaurant, an education center (with wonderful classes and lectures year-round), a library and shop, and the largest Shakespearean exhibition in the world. The plan is to present four plays each season. Happily, even when the Globe is not open for performances, a guided tour will always include its interior—a perfect opportunity to try out your "Friends, Romans, Countrymen!"

tour offered by the **Shakespeare's Globe Exhibition Centre,** an adjacent museum that provides fascinating background material on both the Elizabethan theater and the actual construction of the new Globe. The **New Shakespeare's Globe Exhibition,** which opened in September 1999, is touted as the largest ever to focus on Shakespeare, his work, and his contemporaries; this "all-singing, all-dancing" exhibition is housed in the Undercroft, beneath the Globe site. For further information, *see* the Close-Up box "Shakespeare Lives!" ⊠ *New Globe Walk, Bankside, SE1,* ☎ *020/7902–1500; 020/7401–9919 box office; 020/ 7902–1500 New Shakespeare's Globe Exhibition,* ⊠ *020/7401–8261.* 🎫 *£6.* ☉ *Museum daily 9–4, plays May–Sept. (call for performance schedule). Tube: Southwark, then walk to Blackfriars bridge and descend the steps; Mansion House, then walk across Southwark Bridge; or Blackfriars, then walk across Blackfriars Bridge.* 🕭

❼ **Southwark Cathedral.** Pronounced "Suth-uck," this is the second-oldest Gothic church in London, after Westminster Abbey, with parts dating back to the 12th century. Although it houses some remarkable memorials, not to mention a program of lunchtime concerts, it is seldom visited. It was promoted to cathedral status only in 1905, before that having been the priory church of St. Mary Overie (as in "over the water"—on the South Bank). Look for the gaudily renovated 1408 tomb of the poet John Gower, friend of Chaucer, and for the Harvard Chapel. Another notable buried here is Edmund Shakespeare, brother of William. ⊠ *Montague Close, SE1,* ☎ *020/7367–6700.* 🎫 *Free.* ☉ *Daily 8–6. Tube: London Bridge.*

⓬ **Tate Modern.** This much-anticipated new branch of the Tate Gallery opened in May 2000 in the Bankside Power Station. Shuttered for decades, the station has glowered magnificently on its Thames-side site ever since it was built in the 1930s. Now it has been renovated by Swiss architects Herzog & de Meuron to make a dazzling venue for some of the Tate's overflowing treasures. For decades, the old Millbank Gallery of the Tate (☞ Tate Britain *in* Westminster and Royal London, *above*) had been so overstuffed the curators had to resort to a revolving menu of paintings and sculpture. The power station (designed by the same man who created the famous red telephone box) and its 8½-acre site now house the surplus, running from classic works by Matisse, Picasso, Dalí, Moore, Bacon, and Warhol to the most-talked-about British artists of today. It promises to be one of the world's finest modern art museums. ⊠ *25 Summer St., SE1 9JT,* ☎ *020/7887–8000.* 🎫 *Free.* ☉ *Sun.–Thurs. 10–6, Fri.–Sat 10–10.*

⓵⓪ **Vinopolis.** The Brits are perhaps not the first nation you would expect to erect a monument to wine, but here it is—Vinopolis, City of Wine. Spread over 2 acres between the Globe Theatre and London Bridge, its arched vaults promise multimedia tours of the world's wine cultures, tastings, retail shops, an art gallery, restaurants, and a wine school. You can learn about wine production and history, and then have a chance to put your newfound knowledge to the test in the Tasting Halls. The four restaurants claim to offer more wines by the glass than anywhere else in the city, and you can, of course, buy from an enormous selection of world vintages, many of them available for delivery. ⊠ *Axe and Bottle Court, 70 Newcomen St.,* ☎ *020/7645–3700.* 🎫 *£11.50.* ☉ *Mon.–Sat. 10–5:30.*

CHELSEA AND BELGRAVIA

Chelsea is where J. M. W. Turner painted his sunsets, John Singer Sargent his society portraits, where Oscar Wilde wrote *The Importance of Being Earnest,* and where Mary Quant cut her first miniskirt. Today,

Chelsea is a neighborhood as handsome as its real estate is costly. Strolling its streets, you will often notice gigantic windows adorning otherwise ordinary houses. They are remnants of Chelsea's 19th-century bohemian days, when they served to bring light into artists' studios; now they are mostly used to hike property values a few notches higher. This is the place—the King's Road in particular—that gave birth to Swinging '60s London, then to '70s punk youth culture. The millennial version of this colorful thoroughfare is not really the center of anything, but it's hard not to like wandering down it.

Chelsea's next-door neighborhood is aristocratic Belgravia, with the King's Road and Knightsbridge as its respective southern and northern borders, Sloane Street and Grosvenor Place its western and eastern ones, and vast Belgrave Square, home to many embassies, in the middle. Diagonally across the square, Belgrave Place will lead past grand mansions (all painted Wedgwood-white to denote that they, like every other house in this district, are the property of England's richest landowners, the Dukes of Westminster) through to Eaton Square, the aptly chosen locale for the TV series *Upstairs, Downstairs*. It is no accident that this whole neighborhood of wealth and splendor is grouped around the back of Buckingham Palace—many titled peers wished to live adjacent to the Court. Belgravia is relatively young: it was built between the 1820s and the 1850s by the builder-developer-entrepreneur Thomas Cubitt (who had as great an influence on the look of London in his day as Wren and Nash had in theirs), under the patronage of Lord Grosvenor, and was intended to rival Mayfair for spectacular snob value and expense. Today it still does.

Numbers in the text correspond to numbers in the margin and on the Chelsea and Belgravia map.

A Good Walk

Start at **Cheyne Walk** ①, stretching in both directions from Albert Bridge, going all the way west to see the statue of Thomas More, then doubling back for a left turn into Cheyne Row to reach **Carlyle's House** ②. Where the east end of Cheyne Walk runs into Royal Hospital Road, you'll find the **Chelsea Physic Garden** ③, while a right after the garden on Royal Hospital Road brings you to the **National Army Museum** ④. Royal Hospital Road takes its name from the institution next door to the museum, the magnificent **Royal Hospital** ⑤. A left turn from here up Franklin's Row and Cheltenham Terrace brings you to famous **King's Road** ⑥, which you could follow east until you reach the beginning of Belgravia: Sloane Square, named after Sir Hans Sloane, whose collection founded the British Museum (☞ Bloomsbury and Legal London, *above*) and who bought the manor of Chelsea in 1712. Cross the square more or less in a straight line, and follow Cliveden Place for a taste of Belgravia. The grand, white-stucco houses have changed not at all since the mid-19th century, and Eaton Square, which you'll soon come upon, remains such a desirable address that the rare event of one of its houses' coming on the market makes all the property pages. Its most famous residents were fictional, of course, as the enduringly popular period soap *Upstairs, Downstairs* was set here. A left turn on **Belgrave Place** ⑦ brings you to Belgrave Square, dense with embassies, but the best thing to do around here is follow your nose. Other than Palladian-perfect mansions, chic alleys, and magnificent Georgian squares—in addition to Belgrave and Eaton, the smaller Lowndes, Cadogan, Trevor, Brompton, and Montpelier—there are no particular Belgravia sights. After taking in Belgrave Place and the picturesque mews next to Eaton Place, however, you might continue eastward on Belgrave Place, walk south several blocks on Eaton Place, and head for the lovely warren of streets and alleys around Chester Row and Minerva Mews.

TIMING

This may read like a short hop, but the walk above covers a good 2 to 3 mi. If you explore side streets, you could double the figure—and exploring these streets is the best aspect of these neighborhoods, which are primarily residential and expensive. The houses along the way will detain you, and the shops will for longer; even though King's Road isn't what it used to be, it's still fruitful. In summer you'll want to spend time in the Physic Garden or around the Royal Hospital, so make sure you're heading out on one of the opening days. If you're dead set on the Physic Garden, that means Wednesday or Sunday afternoon from April to October.

HOW TO GET THERE

Chelsea is notoriously ill-served by tube stops. The best, and really the only, way into the area is to get the District and Circle lines to Sloane Square, then strike out by foot along King's Road. Or catch a bus (11, 19, 22, 137, or 211). Farther down toward the river, around World's End and Fulham, the 19, 49, 319, and 345 are the buses to look for. The edge of Belgravia farthest from Chelsea is accessible from Hyde Park Corner on the Piccadilly Line. Buses 2, 8, 9, 10, 14, 16, 19, 22, 36, 38, 52, 73, 74, 82, and 137 buses also stop there. Choose a bus that appears on both lists for travel between the two neighborhoods.

Sights to See

❼ Belgrave Place. One of the main arteries of Belgravia—London's swankiest neighborhood—Belgrave Place is lined with grand, imposing Regency-era mansions (now mostly embassies). Walk down this street toward Eaton Place to pass two of Belgravia's most beautiful mews—Eaton Mews North and Eccleston Mews, both fronted by grand Westminster-white rusticated entrances right out of a 19th-century engraving: there are few other places where London is both so picturesque and elegant.

❷ Carlyle's House. This house hosted a thriving salon of 19th-century authors, attracted by the fame of Thomas Carlyle (1795–1881)—who wrote a blockbuster, an all-but-since-forgotten history of the French Revolution, and the amusing *Sartor Resartus,* and founded the London Library—and by the wit of his wife, the poet Jane Carlyle. Dickens, Thackeray, Tennyson, and Browning were regular visitors, and you can see the second-floor drawing room where they met just as they saw it, complete with leather armchair, decoupage screen, fireplace, and oil lamps, all in ruddy Victorian hues. ✉ *24 Cheyne Row, SW3,* ☎ *020/7352–7087.* 🎟 *£3.30.* ⊙ *Apr.–Nov., Wed.–Sun. 11–4:30. Tube: Sloane Sq., then walk down King's Rd. or take Bus 11, 19, 22, 49, 219, or 249.*

❸ Chelsea Physic Garden. First planted by the Society of Apothecaries in 1673 for the study of medicinal plants, these gardens are still in use for the same purpose today. The herbs and shrubs and flowers, planted to a strict plan but tumbling rurally over the paths nevertheless, are interspersed with woodland areas, England's first rock garden, and ancient trees, some of which were tragically uprooted in a 1987 storm. In the middle stands a statue of Sir Hans Sloane, physician to Queen Anne and George II, whose collection formed the basis of the British Museum and who saved the garden from closing in 1722, making sure nobody would ever be allowed to build over it. ✉ *Swan Walk, 66 Royal Hospital Rd., SW3,* ☎ *020/7352–5646.* 🎟 *£4.* ⊙ *Apr.–Oct., Wed. noon–5 and Sun. 2–6; daily noon–5 during Chelsea Flower Show (3rd wk of May). Tube: Sloane Sq., then walk down King's Rd., or take Bus 11, 19, 22, 319, 211 or 239 (get off at Chelsea old town hall).*

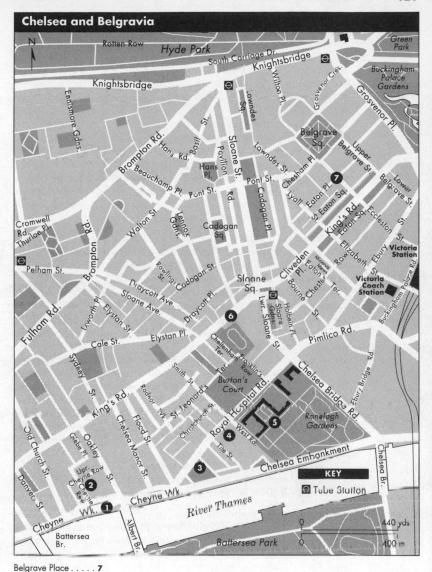

Chelsea and Belgravia

Belgrave Place **7**

Carlyle's House **2**

Chelsea Physic
Garden **3**

Cheyne Walk **1**

King's Road **6**

National Army
Museum **4**

Royal Hospital **5**

★ ❶ **Cheyne Walk.** Its name rhyming with "rainy," this street features some beautiful Queen Anne houses (particularly Norman Shaw's ornamental 1876 Cheyne House, to the right off Albert Bridge) and a storm of Blue Plaques marking famous ex-residents' abodes. George Eliot died at Number 4 in 1880; Dante Gabriel Rossetti annoyed the neighbors of Number 16 with his peacock collection (there's still a clause in the lease banning the birds); at Carlyle Mansions (after the King's Head and Eight Bells pub) Henry James died and T. S. Eliot and Ian Fleming lived. The western reaches were painters' territory, most notably of James McNeill Whistler, who lived at Number 96 and then Number 101, and J. M. W. Turner, who used Number 119 as a retreat, shielding his identity behind the name Adm. "Puggy" Booth. Also toward the western end, outside the Church of All Saints, is a golden-faced statue of **Thomas More** (who wouldn't sign the Oath of Supremacy at Lambeth Palace in 1534 and was executed as a traitor), looking pensive and beatific on a throne facing the river, in a 1969 addition to the Walk.

❻ **King's Road.** This was where the miniskirt first strutted its stuff in the '60s and where Vivienne Westwood and Malcolm McLaren clothed the Sex Pistols in bondage trousers from their shop, "Sex", in 1975, thus spawning punk rock. Westwood, one of Britain's most innovative fashion stars, still runs her shop at Number 430, where the road, fittingly, kinks. Both boutique and neighborhood are called **World's End,** possibly because Chelsea-ites believe that's what happens here. The Fulham district begins around this stretch, full of yuppie singles and more shopping opportunities. The other end of King's Road, leading into Sloane Square, has various fashion stores (no longer style-setters, on the whole) and some rather good antiques shops and markets along the way. The **Pheasantry,** at Number 152, is recognizable by some over-the-top Grecian statuary in a fancy portico. Named in its mid-19th-century pheasant-breeding days, it had a phase from 1916 to 1934 as a ballet school where Margot Fonteyn and Alicia Markova learned first position. Now it's a club-restaurant haunted by the braying breed of Chelsea yuppie dubbed "Sloane Rangers" by '80s style-watchers. The Peter Jones department store marks the exit from the north of Chelsea and the beginning of Belgravia: Sloane Square. Conran's trendy restaurant **Bluebird** is a great place to stop for lunch.

❹ **National Army Museum.** This museum covers the history of British land forces from the Yeoman of the Guard (the first professional army, founded in 1485 and ancestors of the Tower's Beefeaters) to the present. It is best explained in its current exhibit, entitled "The Rise of the Redcoat," which takes you from Henry V (1413–22) all the way to George III (1760–1820). A great deal of effort is made to convey the experience of those who lived through the wars, and a visit will enhance anyone's grasp of London's history and its personages. ⊠ *Royal Hospital Rd., SW3,* ☎ *020/7730–0717.* ▣ *Free.* ☉ *Daily 10–5:30. Tube: Sloane Sq.*

❺ **Royal Hospital.** The hospice for elderly and infirm soldiers was founded by Charles II in 1682—some say after a badgering from his soft-hearted, high-profile mistress, Nell Gwynne, but more probably as an act of expedience. His troops had hitherto enjoyed not so much as a meager pension and were growing restive after the civil wars of 1642–46 and 1648. Charles wisely appointed the great architect of burned-out City churches, Sir Christopher Wren, to design this small village of redbrick and Portland stone, set in manicured gardens (which you can visit) surrounding the Figure Court —named after the 1692 bronze figure of Charles II dressed up as a Roman soldier—and the Great Hall (dining room) and chapel. The latter is enhanced by the choir stalls of Grinling Gibbons (who did the bronze of Charles, too), the former by a vast oil of Charles on horseback by Antonio Verrio, and both are open to inspection.

No doubt you will run into some of the 400-odd residents. Despite their advancing years, these "Chelsea Pensioners" are no shrinking violets. In summer and for special occasions they sport dandy scarlet frock coats with gold buttons, medals, and natty tricorne hats, and since they are of proven good character (a condition of entry, along with old age and loyal service), they might offer to show you around—in which case you may wish to supplement their daily beer and tobacco allowance with a tip.

May is the important month at the Royal Hospital. The 29th is Oak Apple Day, when the pensioners celebrate Charles II's birthday by draping oak leaves on his statue and parading around it in memory of a hollow oak tree that expedited the king's miraculous escape from the 1651 Battle of Worcester. In the same month, the Chelsea Flower Show, the year's highlight for thousands of garden-obsessed Brits, is also held here. ⊠ *Royal Hospital Rd., SW3,* ☎ *020/7730–0161.* 🖃 *Free.* ☉ *Apr.–Sept., Mon.–Sat. 10–noon and 2–4, Sun. 2–4; Oct.– Mar., Mon.–Sat. 10–noon and 2–4. Tube: Sloane Sq.*

KNIGHTSBRIDGE, KENSINGTON, AND HOLLAND PARK

Even in these supposedly democratic days, you still sometimes hear people say that the *only* place to live in London is in the grand residential area of the Royal Borough of Kensington. True, the district is an endless cavalcade of streets lined with splendid houses redolent of stuccoed wealth and pillared porches, but there are other fetching attractions here—some of the most fascinating museums in London, stylish squares, elegant antiques shops, and Kensington Palace (formerly the home of Diana, Princess of Wales, and Queen Victoria when she was a girl)— which helped to put the district on the map. South and west of this historic edifice, you'll find the stamping grounds of the Sloane Rangers— a quintessentially London type of gilded youth whose upper-class accents make English sound like a foreign language. They tend to haunt salubrious Knightsbridge, east of Belgravia and north of Chelsea, offering as it does about equal doses of elite residential streets and ultra-shopping opportunities. To *its* east is one of the highest concentrations of important artifacts anywhere, the Museum Mile of South Kensington, with the rest of Kensington offering peaceful strolls and a noisy main street. The Holland Park neighborhood is worth visiting for its big, fancy, tree-shaded houses and its exquisite and unexpected park.

Kensington first became the *Royal* Borough of Kensington (and Chelsea) by virtue of a king's asthma. William III, who suffered terribly from the Thames mists over Whitehall, decided in 1689 to buy Nottingham House in the rural village of Kensington so that he could breathe more easily; and besides, his wife and co-monarch, Mary II, felt confined by water and wall at Whitehall. Courtiers and functionaries and society folk soon followed where the crowns led, and by the time Queen Anne was on the throne (1702–14), Kensington was overflowing. In a way, it still is, because most of its grand houses, and the Victorian ones of Holland Park, have been divided into apartments or else are serving as foreign embassies.

Numbers in the text correspond to numbers in the margin and on the Knightsbridge, Kensington, and Holland Park map.

A Good Walk

This is an all-weather walk—museums and shops for rainy days, grass and strolls for sunshine. When you surface from the Knightsbridge tube station—one of London's deepest—you are immediately engulfed by the manic drivers, professional shoppers, and ladies-who-lunch who make up the local population. If you're in a shopping mood, start with Harvey Nichols—right at the tube—and its six floors of total fashion. Sloane Street, leading south, is strung with the boutiques of big-name European designers, while **Harrods** ① is found to the west down Brompton Road; continue west down this road, pausing at Beauchamp (pronounced "Bee-chum") Place and Walton Street if shopping is your intention. Presently, at the junction of Brompton and Cromwell roads, you'll come to the pale, Italianate **Brompton Oratory** ②, which marks the beginning of museum territory, with the vast **Victoria and Albert Museum** ③ with its 11 mi of corridors and fantastic Liebeskind spiral in the process of being built (at the start of Cromwell Road), the **Natural History Museum** ④ next, and the child-friendly **Science Museum** ⑤ behind it. (The neighborhood's three large museums, incidentally, can also be reached via a long underground passage from the South Kensington tube.) Turn left to continue north up Exhibition Road, a kind of unfinished cultural main drag that was Prince Albert's conception (the **National Sound Archive** ⑥ is here, among others), toward the road after which British moviemakers named their fake blood, Kensington Gore, to reach the giant, round Wedgwood china–box of the **Royal Albert Hall** ⑦, the newly burnished **Albert Memorial** ⑧ opposite, and the **Royal College of Art** ⑨ next door.

Now follow **Kensington Gardens** (which is what this western neighbor of Hyde Park is called) west to its end, and a little farther, perhaps detouring into the park to see **Kensington Palace** ⑩ and, behind it, one of London's rare, private "Millionaires' Row" sanctuaries, **Kensington Palace Gardens** ⑪. Turn off Kensington High Street down little Derry Street, with the offices of London's local paper, the *Evening Standard,* on the left and what was once Derry and Tom's department store—it closed down in the '70s—on the right. (The best feature of the store was its magical roof garden, complete with palm trees, ponds, and flamingos; it's still there, now part of a nightclub owned by Richard Branson, the high-profile London figure also responsible for the Virgin Megastores, Virgin Atlantic Airways, etc.). Take a turn around peaceful **Kensington Square** ⑫; then, returning to High Street, either follow Kensington Church Street up to Notting Hill Gate—with the little 1870 St. Mary Abbots Church on its southwest corner and a cornucopia of expensive antiques in its shops all along the way—or take the longer, scenic route.

To do this, turn left off Kensington Church Street onto Holland Street, admiring the sweet 18th-century houses (Numbers 10, 12–13, and 18–26 remain). As you cross Hornton Street you'll see to your left an orange-brick 1970s building, the Kensington Civic Centre (donor of parking permits, home of the local council); Holland Street becomes the leafy Duchess of Bedford's Walk, with Queen Elizabeth College, part of London University, on the right. Turn left before Holland Park into Phillimore Gardens (perhaps detouring east into Phillimore Place to see Number 44, where Kenneth Grahame, author of *The Wind in the Willows,* lived from 1901 to 1908), then left again into Stafford Terrace to reach **Linley Sambourne House** ⑬. Step back to the High Street and turn right. For a tranquil time-out, head past the gates into **Holland Park** ⑭. Exit the park at the gate by the tennis courts (near the Orangery) onto Ilchester Place, follow Melbury Road a few yards, and turn right onto Holland Park Road to reach **Leighton House** ⑮. Late in the 19th century, Melbury Road was a veritable colony of artists, though the Victorian muse they followed failed to appeal to later sensibilities, and they're now an obscure bunch—except for Dickens's illustrator, Marcus Stone, who had Number 8 built in 1876. From here you could turn right onto Addison Road to see the Technicolor tiles rioting over Sir Ernest Debenham's Peacock House at Number 8 (he founded the eponymous Oxford Street department store). If you continue north, you reach plane tree–lined Holland Park Avenue, main thoroughfare of an expensive residential neighborhood that provides more pleasant strolling territory, if you feel you haven't walked enough.

TIMING
This walk is at least 4 mi long and is almost impossible to achieve without venturing inside somewhere. The best way to approach these neighborhoods is to treat Knightsbridge shopping and the South Kensington museums at one go. The rest of the tour works as a scenic walk on a fine day, because the places to see—Leighton and Linley Sambourne houses, the Commonwealth Institute, and Kensington Palace—are less time-consuming than the V&A, Natural History, and Science museums. During "term time," these are populated by more or less orderly school parties during the week, while weekends and school vacations see them fill up with more random arrangements of children. The parks are best in the growing seasons—early spring for crocuses and daffodils and summer for roses—and during fall, when the foliage show easily rivals New England's. Kensington Gardens closes its gates at sundown, though you can get into Holland Park later during the summer, thanks to the restaurant and the Open Air Theatre.

HOW TO GET THERE
There are many tubes here, but which you choose will depend on which part you want. Knightsbridge on the Piccadilly Line, Kensington High Street on District and Circle, and Holland Park on the Central Line are the best ones. The best buses between Kensington High Street and Knightsbridge are Buses 9, 10, and 52. From Kensington to Holland Park, get the 9, 27, 28, or 31.

Sights to See

8 **Albert Memorial.** The Victorian era *in excelsis*, this neo-Gothic shrine to Prince Albert has recently emerged from a decade-long renovation. Despite setbacks and cash shortages, Victoria's monument to her beloved husband has now been unsheathed from its scaffolding and restored to fine form due to the £14 million renovation. Even the 14-ft bronze statue of Albert looks as if it were created yesterday, thanks to its pure gold-leaf coat (donated by an anonymous benefactor). Albert's grieving widow, Queen Victoria, had this elaborate confection erected on the spot where his Great Exhibition had stood a mere decade before his early death from typhoid fever in 1861. ⊠ *Kensington Gore, opposite Royal Albert Hall, Hyde Park.*

2 **Brompton Oratory.** This is a late product of the English Roman Catholic revival of the mid-19th century led by John Henry Cardinal Newman (1801–90), who established this oratory in 1884 and whose statue you see outside. A then-unknown 29-year-old architect, Herbert Gribble, won the competition to design the place, an honor that you may conclude went to his head when you see the vast, incredibly ornate interior. It is punctuated by treasures far older than the church itself, like the giant Twelve Apostles in the nave, carved from Carrara marble by Giuseppe Mazzuoli during the 1680s and brought here from Siena's cathedral. ⊠ *Brompton Rd.,* ☎ *0171/808–0900.* ☞ *Free.* ☉ *Closes at 8 PM. Tube: South Kensington.*

1 **Harrods.** Just in case you don't notice it, this well-known shopping mecca frames its domed terra-cotta Edwardian outline in thousands of white lights each night. The 15-acre Egyptian-owned store's sales weeks are

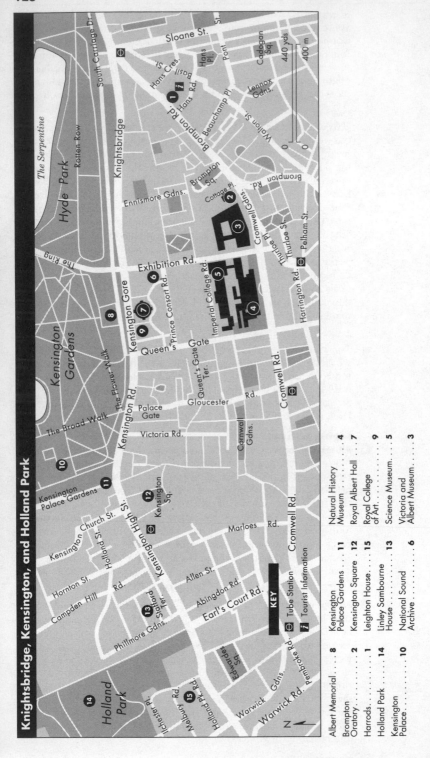

Knightsbridge, Kensington, and Holland Park

Albert Memorial **8**
Brompton
Oratory **2**
Harrods **1**
Holland Park **14**
Kensington
Palace **10**

Kensington
Palace Gardens . . . **11**
Kensington Square . **12**
Leighton House . . . **15**
Linley Sambourne
House **13**
National Sound
Archive **6**

Natural History
Museum **4**
Royal Albert Hall . . . **7**
Royal College
of Art **9**
Science Museum . . . **5**
Victoria and
Albert Museum . . . **3**

KEY

⊖ Tube Station
i Tourist Information

world class, and the environment is as frenetic as that of a stock market floor; its motto, *Omnia, omnibus, ubique* (Everything, for everyone, everywhere), is not too far from the truth. Visit the pet department, a highlight for children, and don't miss the extravagant Food Hall, with its stunning Art Nouveau tiling in the neighborhood of meat and poultry and continuing on in the fishmongers' territory, where its glory is rivaled by displays of the sea produce itself. This is the place to acquire your green-and-gold souvenir Harrods bag, as food prices are surprisingly competitive. ⊠ *87–135 Brompton Rd., SW1,* ☎ *020/7730–1234. Tube: Knightsbridge.*

NEED A BREAK? **Patisserie Valerie** (⊠ 215 Brompton Rd., ☎ 020/7832–9971), just down the road from Harrods, offers light meals and a gorgeous array of pastries. It's perfect for breakfast, lunch, or tea.

🐾 ⑭ **Holland Park.** The former grounds of the Jacobean Holland House opened to the public only in 1952. Since then, many treats have been laid on within its 60 acres. Holland House itself was nearly flattened by World War II bombs, but the east wing remains, now incorporated into a youth hostel and providing a fantastical stage for the April–September **Open Air Theatre** (☎ 020/7602–7856 box office). The glass-walled Orangery also survived to host art exhibitions and wedding receptions, while next door, the former Garden Ballroom has become the Belvedere restaurant; nearby is a lovely café. From the Belvedere's terrace you see the formal Dutch Garden, planted by Lady Holland in the 1790s with the first English dahlias. North of that are woodland walks; lawns populated by peacocks and guinea fowl and the odd, awkward emu; a fragrant rose garden; great banks of rhododendrons and azaleas, which bloom profusely in May; a well-supervised children's Adventure Playground; and even a Japanese water garden, legacy of the 1991 London Festival of Japan. If that's not enough, you can watch cricket on the Cricket Lawn on the south side or tennis on the several courts. ☉ *Daily dawn–dusk. Tube: Holland Park or High St., Kensington.*

OFF THE BEATEN PATH **KENSAL GREEN CEMETERY –** Heralding itself as "London's first Necropolis," this west London cemetery was established in 1832 and beats the more famous Highgate for atmosphere, if only because it is less populous with the living. Within its 77 acres are more freestanding mausoleums than in any other cemetery in Britain, some of them almost the size of small churches and most of them constructed while their future occupants were still alive. Those who balked at burial but couldn't afford a mausoleum of their own could opt for a position in the catacombs, and these, with their stacks of moldering caskets, are a definite highlight for seekers of the macabre, though they can only be seen as part of a tour. In the cemetery, you will find the final resting places of the novelists Trollope, Thackeray, and Wilkie Collins; of the great 19th-century engineer Isambard Kingdom Brunel; and of Decimus Burton, Victorian architect of the Athenaeum Club, the Wellington Arch, the Kew Gardens greenhouses. ⊠ *Harrow Rd., W10,* ☎ *020/8969–0152; 020/7402–2749 tours.* 🎫 *Suggested donation £2.* ☉ *Weekdays 9–4:30, weekends 10–4 (times may vary Nov.–Feb.); tours Sun. 2 PM. Tube: Kensal Green.*

★ ⑩ **Kensington Palace.** The long and regal history of this palace has been eclipsed in the last few years by its most recent—and some might say its most famous—inhabitant: the late Princess Diana. She resided here, so this was where the crowds flocked when the tragic news was heard. With millions of flowers and tributes laid outside its gates, Kensington Palace was seen on every news bulletin worldwide. Now, peace has returned, although arguments sporadically flare as to how the mother of the future king should be remembered. Plans for an immense memorial fountain in the gardens to the "people's princess" have been shelved as angry local residents have vociferously claimed the area is not able to handle the number of visitors this would generate. Of course, Kensington Palace was well known long before Diana brought it new front-page status. Kensington was put, socially speaking, on the map when King William III, "much incommoded by the Smoak of the Coal Fires of London," decided in the 17th century to vacate Whitehall and relocate to a new palace outside the center city in the "village" of Kensington. The new palace did not enjoy a smooth passage as royal residence. Twelve years of renovation were needed before William and Mary could move in, and it continued to undergo all manner of refurbishment during the successive three monarchs' reigns. By coincidence, these monarchs happened to suffer rather ignominious deaths. William III fell off his horse when it stumbled on a molehill, and succumbed to pleurisy in 1702. Then, in 1714, Queen Anne (who, you may recall, was fond of brandy) suffered an apoplectic fit thought to have been brought on by overeating. Next, George I, the first of the Hanoverian Georges, had a stroke said to have been caused by "a surfeit of melons"—admittedly not at Kensington, but in a coach to Hanover in 1727. Worst of all, in 1760, poor George II burst a blood vessel while on the toilet (the official line was, presumably, that he was on the throne).

But the royal curtain here always rang up on a remarkable new cast of characters, no more so than when the 18-year-old Princess Victoria of Kent was called from her bed in June 1837 by the Archbishop of Canterbury and the Lord Chamberlain. She was told her uncle, William IV, was dead, and she was to be queen. The state rooms where Victoria had her ultrastrict upbringing have recently been renovated, a process that still continues, gradually restoring more of the fabulous Court Dress Collection to our sight. In the meantime, the King's Apartments are the best part of the (compulsory) guided tour. Look out for Tintorettos and Van Dycks among the canvases; see the Mortlake tapestries commissioned by Charles I; and look at that ceiling in the cupola room: it appears domed but is actually as flat as a pancake. This palace is an essential stop for royalty vultures because it's the only one where you may actually catch a glimpse of the real thing. Princess Margaret, the Duke and Duchess of Gloucester, and Prince and Princess Michael of Kent all have apartments here, as did, of course, Diana, Princess of Wales, until her death. For a consoling (and expensive) cup of tea, repair to the palace's Orangery—surely one of London's most civilized settings and the festive hall where many Windsor birthday parties and weddings were held (a good number of which Princess Diana attended).

One hundred years after Queen Victoria and just a couple post-Diana, the palace has found new life in the shape of the **Royal Ceremonial Dress Collection,** which has recently reopened. Extending back centuries, the collection shows an array of state and occasional dresses, hats, and shoes worn by Britain's Royal Family. Diana-watchers will note the difference between the regal if dowdy garments of Her Majesty the queen compared to the glittering, contemporary fashions of her daughter-in-law. Other dazzlers of note are the Coronation Robes of Queen Mary and George V and a regal mantua—a 6-ft-wide court dress. ⊠ *The Broad Walk, Kensington Gardens, W8,* ☎ *020/7937–9561.* 🎫 *£9.50, including admission to the Dress Collection.* ☉ *May–Oct., daily 10–5; Nov.–Mar., Wed.–Sun. 10–3. Tube: High Street Kensington.* ✎

⑪ Kensington Palace Gardens. Starting behind Kensington Palace, this is one of London's rare private roads, guarded and gated both here and at the Notting Hill Gate end. If you walk it, you will see why it

ONE LAST TRAVEL TIP:

Pack an easy way to reach the world.

MCI WORLDCOM   WORLDPHONE.

123 456 7891 2345
J.D. SMITH

Wherever you travel, the MCI WorldCom Card℠ is the easiest way to stay in touch. You can use it to call to and from more than 125 countries worldwide. And you can earn bonus miles every time you use your card. So go ahead, travel the world. MCI WorldCom℠ makes it even more rewarding. For additional access codes, visit www.wcom.com/worldphone.

MCI WORLDCOM.

EASY TO CALL WORLDWIDE

1. Just dial the WorldPhone® access number of the country you're calling from.

2. Dial or give the operator your MCI WorldCom Card number.

3. Dial or give the number you're calling.

Austria ◆	0800-200-235
Belgium ◆	0800-10012
Czech Republic ◆	00-42-000112
Denmark ◆	8001-0022
Estonia ★	800-800-1122
Finland ◆	08001-102-80
France ◆	0-800-99-0019
Germany	0800-888-8000
Greece ◆	00-800-1211
Hungary ◆	06▼-800-01411
Ireland	1-800-55-1001
Italy ◆	172-1022
Luxembourg	8002-0112
Netherlands ◆	0800-022-91-22
Norway ◆	800-19912
Poland ⊹	800-111-21-22
Portugal ⊹	800-800-123
Romania ⊹	01-800-1800
Russia ◆ ⊹	747-3322
Spain	900-99-0014
Sweden ◆	020-795-922
Switzerland ◆	0800-89-0222
Ukraine ⊹	8▼10-013
United Kingdom	0800-89-0222
Vatican City	172-1022

◆ Public phones may require deposit of coin or phone card for dial tone.   ★ Not available from public pay phones.
▼ Wait for second dial tone.   ⊹ Limited availability.

EARN FREQUENT FLIER MILES

Limit of one bonus program per customer. All airline program rules and conditions apply. © 2000 WorldCom, Inc. All Rights Reserved. The names, logos, and taglines identifying WorldCom's products and services are proprietary marks of WorldCom, Inc. or its subsidiaries. All third party marks are the proprietary marks of their respective owners.

Bureau de change

Cambio

外国為替

In this city, you can find money on almost any street.

NO-FEE FOREIGN EXCHANGE

The Chase Manhattan Bank has over 80 convenient
locations near New York City destinations such as:

    Times Square
    Rockefeller Center
    Empire State Building
    2 World Trade Center
    United Nations Plaza

Exchange any of 75 foreign currencies

 CHASE

THE RIGHT RELATIONSHIP IS EVERYTHING.®

earned the nickname "Millionaires' Row"—it is lined with palatial white-stucco houses designed by a selection of the best architects of the mid-19th century. The novelist William Makepeace Thackeray, author of *Vanity Fair,* died in 1863 at Number 2—a building that now houses an embassy (Israel's), as do most of the others.

⑫ **Kensington Square.** Having been laid out around the time William moved to Kensington Palace up the road, this is one of London's most venerable squares. A few early 18th-century houses remain, with Numbers 11 and 12 the oldest.

NEED A
BREAK?   On Wright's Lane you'll find the **Muffin Man,** a cozy anachronism of a tea shop. Here waitresses in floral aprons serve toasted sandwiches, cream teas, and, yes, English muffins.

⑮ **Leighton House.** This was the home of Frederic Leighton (1830–96)—painter, sculptor, president of the Royal Academy. Endowed with a peerage by Queen Victoria, he unfortunately expired a month later. The prize room here is the incredible Arab Hall. George Aitchison designed this Moorish fantasy in 1879 to show off Leighton's valuable 13th- to 17th-century Islamic tile collection, and, adorned with marble columns, dome, and fountain, it is exotic beyond belief. The rest of the rooms are more conventionally, stuffily Victorian, but they do feature many paintings by Leighton, plus those of Edward Burne-Jones, John Millais, and other leading Pre-Raphaelites. ⊠ *12 Holland Park Rd., W14,* ☎ *020/7602–3316.* ☞ *Free.* ☉ *Mon.–Sat. 11–5:30. Tube: Holland Park.*

★ ⑬ **Linley Sambourne House.** Stuffed with delightful Victorian and Edwardian antiques, fabrics, and paintings, this is one of the most charming 19th-century London houses extant—little wonder it was filmed for Merchant/Ivory's *A Room with a View.* During the 1870s, it was home to the political cartoonist Edward Linley Sambourne. It has been renovated by the Victorian Society to look as it did then, complete with William Morris wallpapers and illustrations from the (now defunct) satirical magazine *Punch,* including many of Sambourne's own, adorning the walls. ⊠ *18 Stafford Terr., W8,* ☎ *020/8994–1019.* ☞ *£3.* ☉ *Mar.–Oct., Wed. 10–4, Sun. 2–5. Tube: High Street Kensington.* ☙

⑥ **National Sound Archive.** In this aural outpost of the British Library, you may listen to the queen who made this neighborhood possible: the million recordings held here include one of Victoria speaking sometime in the 1880s, but you have to book in advance to hear her, or anyone else. There's a small exhibit of early recording equipment and ephemera, too. ⊠ *British Library, 96 Euston Rd., NW1,* ☎ *0171/412–7440.* ☞ *Free.* ☉ *Mon. and Thurs. 9:30–6, Tues.–Wed. 9:30–8. Tube: Kings Cross.*

☙ ④ **Natural History Museum.** Architect Alfred Waterhouse had relief panels scattered across the outrageously ornate French Romanesque–style terra-cotta facade of this museum, depicting extant creatures to the left of the entrance, extinct ones to the right. Inside, that categorization is sort of continued in reverse, with Dinosaurs on the left and the Ecology Gallery on the right. Both these renovated exhibits (the former with life-size moving dinosaurs, the latter complete with "moonlit rain forest") make essential viewing in a museum that, realizing it was becoming crusty, has invested millions overhauling itself in recent years.

The Creepy Crawlies Gallery features a nightmarish, superenlarged scorpion yet ends up making tarantulas cute (8 out of 10 animal species, one learns here, are arthropods). Other wonderful bits include the Human

Biology Hall, which you arrive at through a birth-simulation chamber; the full-size blue whale; and the moving dinosaur diorama. The Earth Galleries are also unmissable, with ambitious exhibits about the structure of our planet: "The Power Within," "Restless Surface," and "Visions of the Earth." Understandably, this place usually resembles grade-school recess. The White Card is accepted. ⊠ *Cromwell Rd., SW7,* ☎ *020/7938–9123.* ▨ *£6.50; free weekdays 4:30–5:50 and weekends 5–5:50.* ⊙ *Mon.–Sat. 10–5:50, Sun. 11–5:50. Tube: South Kensington.*

❼ Royal Albert Hall. This domed, circular 8,000-seat auditorium (as well as the Albert Memorial, opposite) was made possible by the Victorian public, who donated funds for it. More money was raised, however, by selling 1,300 future seats at £100 apiece—not for the first night but for every night for 999 years. (Some descendants of purchasers still use the seats.) The Albert Hall is best known for its annual July–September Henry Wood Promenade Concerts (the "Proms"), with bargain-price standing (or promenading, or sitting-on-the-floor) tickets sold on the night of the world-class classical concerts. ⊠ *Kensington Gore, SW7,* ☎ *020/7589–3203.* ▨ *Fee varies according to event. Tube: South Kensington.*

❾ Royal College of Art. Housed in a glass-dominated building designed by Sir Hugh Casson in 1973, the RCA provides great contrast with the Victoriana surrounding it, including the Albert Hall next door. Famous in the '50s and '60s for processing David Hockney, Peter Blake, and Eduardo Paolozzi, the college is still one of the country's foremost art and design schools, and there's usually an exhibition, lecture, or event going on here that's open to the public. ⊠ *Kensington Gore, SW7,* ☎ *020/7584–5020.* ▨ *Free.* ⊙ *Weekdays 10–6 (call to check times). Tube: South Kensington.*

☝ ❺ Science Museum. This, the third of the great South Kensington museums, stands behind the Natural History Museum in a far plainer building. It features loads of hands-on exhibits, with entire schools of children apparently decanted inside to interact with them; but it is, after all, painlessly educational. Highlights include the Launch Pad gallery, which demonstrates basic scientific principles (try the plasma ball, where your hands attract "lightning"—if you can get them on it); the Computing Then and Now show, which gets the most crowded of all; *Puffing Billy,* the oldest train in the world; and the actual *Apollo 10* capsule. The newest attraction is the Welcome Wing, a new £45 million addition devoted to contemporary science, medicine, and technology, which also includes a 450-seat IMAX cinema. The White Card is accepted. ⊠ *Exhibition Rd., SW7,* ☎ *020/7938–8000.* ▨ *£6.50.* ⊙ *Mon.–Sat. 10–6, Sun. 11–6. Tube: South Kensington.*

★ ❸ Victoria and Albert Museum. Recognizable by the copy of Victoria's Imperial Crown it wears on the lantern above the central cupola, this institution is always referred to as the V&A. It is a huge museum, showcasing the applied arts of all disciplines, all periods, all nationalities, and all tastes, and it is a wonderful, generous place to get lost in, full of innovation and completely devoid of pretension. The collections are *so* catholic that confusion is a hazard—one minute you're gazing on the Jacobean oak 12-square-ft four-poster Great Bed of Ware (one of the V&A's most prized possessions, given that Shakespeare immortalized it in *Twelfth Night*); the next, you're in the 20th-century end of the equally celebrated Dress Collection, coveting a Jean Muir frock you could actually buy at nearby Harrods. This museum is in the process of a huge revolution: in 2001 the innovative, highly interactive new British Galleries will be opened, and in 2005 architect Daniel Liebeskind's dynamic and audacious architectural masterpiece, the spiral, will be opened, boasting stunning views of London from the top floor.

Prince Albert, Victoria's adored consort, was responsible for the genesis of this permanent version of the 1851 Great Exhibition, and his queen laid its foundation stone in her final public London appearance, in 1899. From the start, the V&A had an important role as a research institution, and that role continues today, with many resources available to scholars, designers, artists, and conservators. Two of the latest are the Textiles and Dress 20th Century Reference Centre, with ingenious space-saving storage systems for thousands of bolts of cloth, and the Textile Study Galleries, which perform the same function for 2,000 years' worth of the past.

Follow your own whims around the 7 mi of gallery space, but try to reach the new and spectacular Glass Gallery, where a collection spanning four millennia is reflected between room-size mirrors under young designer Danny Lane's breathtaking glass balustrade. The latest additions are the Raphael Galleries, where seven massive cartoons the painter completed in 1516 for his Sistine Chapel tapestries are housed, and the Silver Galleries, displaying six centuries of English silver. On Wednesdays, Late View continues—a kind of museum salon, with lectures and a wine bar. The White Card is accepted. ⊠ *Cromwell Rd., SW7,* ☎ *020/7938–8500.* 🖾 *£5; free Thurs.–Tues. after 4:30.* ⊙ *Daily 10–5:45, Wed. Late View 6:30–9:30. Tube: South Kensington.* 🐚

NEED A BREAK? Rest your overstimulated eyes in the brick-walled **V&A café,** where full meals and small snacks are available and where the Sunday Jazz Brunch (11–5), accompanied by live music and Sunday papers, is fast becoming a London institution.

HYDE PARK, KENSINGTON GARDENS, AND NOTTING HILL

The Royal Parks of Hyde Park and Kensington Gardens are among London's unique features: great swaths of green in the middle of the city, where it really is possible to decelerate from London's fast lane. Although some of this territory was covered in the Knightsbridge, Kensington, and Holland Park tour (☞ *above*), this is another option for visiting the Royal Parks (without the museums) that also takes in Portobello Road and Notting Hill. The description "royal" is somewhat paradoxical, for today, these are the most democratic of places, where Londoners from all walks of life come to relax (and let off steam as soapbox orators). Although it's probably been centuries since any major royal had a casual stroll here, these parks remain the property of the Crown, and it was the Crown that saved them from being devoured by the city's late-18th-century growth spurt. North of the pair of parks—which are separate entities, although the boundary is virtually invisible—lies Bayswater. Farther northwest lies Notting Hill, a trendsetting square mile of multiethnicity, music, and markets, with lots of see-and-be-seen-in restaurants and younger, more egalitarian, and more adventurous versions of the Cork Street commercial modern-art galleries. The style-watching media has dubbed the musician–novelist–film-biz–drug-dealer–fashion-victim local residents and hangers-out Notting Hillbillies. The whole thing has mushroomed around one of the world's great antiques markets, Portobello Road.

Numbers in the text correspond to numbers in the margin and on the Hyde Park, Kensington, and Notting Hill map.

A Good Walk

Where else would you enter Hyde Park but at **Hyde Park Corner**? The most impressive of the many entrances is the Hyde Park Screen by Apsley House, usually called **Decimus Burton's Gateway** because it was he who designed this triple-arched monument in 1828. The next gate along to the north, a gaudy unicorns-and-lions-rampant number wrought in scarlet-, cobalt-white-, and gold-painted metal, was a 90th-birthday gift to Elizabeth the Queen Mother and is therefore the **Queen Mother's Gate.** Follow the southern perimeter along the sand track called **Rotten Row,** now used by the Household Cavalry, which lives at the **Knightsbridge Barracks** to the left.

Follow Rotten Row west to the **Serpentine.** When you pass its **Bridge,** you leave Hyde Park, enter **Kensington Gardens,** and come to the **Serpentine Gallery.** En route to the formal garden at the end of the Long Water, the **Fountains,** you pass the statues of **Peter Pan** and the horse and rider called **Physical Energy.** Continuing westward, you reach the **Round Pond** and Kensington Palace (☞ Knightsbridge, Kensington, and Holland Park, *above*). Follow the Broad Walk north past the playground on the left, Bayswater Road, leaving the park by Black Lion Gate, and you are almost opposite Queensway, a rather peculiar, cosmopolitan street of ethnic confusion, late-night cafés and restaurants, a skating rink, and the Whiteleys shopping-and-movie mall. Turn left at the end into Westbourne Grove, however, and you've entered Notting Hill; you'll reach the famous **Portobello Road** after a few blocks. Turn left for the Saturday antiques market and shops, right to reach the Westway and the flea market. For Notting Hill's grandest houses, stroll over to Lansdowne Road, Crescent, and Square—two blocks west of Kensington Park Row.

TIMING

This is a route that changes vastly on weekends. Saturday is Portobello Road's most fun day, so you may prefer to start at the end and work backward, using the parks for "R and R" from your shopping exertions. Do the same on Fridays if you're a flea-market fan. Sundays, the Hyde Park and Kensington Gardens railings all along Bayswater Road are hung with very bad art, which may slow your progress; this is also prime perambulation day for locals. Whatever your priorities, this is a long walk if you explore every corner, with the perimeter of the two parks alone covering a good 4 mi, and about half as far again around the remainder of the route. You could cut out a lot of park without missing out on essential sights and walk the whole thing in a brisk three hours.

HOW TO GET THERE

For Hyde Park and Kensington Gardens, get off the Central Line at Queensway or Lancaster Gate, or enter the park from Hyde Park Corner on the Piccadilly Line. If you want Portobello Market and environs, the best tube stop is Ladbroke Grove or Westbourne Park (Hammersmith and City lines), and then ask directions; the Notting Hill stop on the District, Circle, and Central lines is also an option. Buses for the area include Buses 12, 70, and 94 for seeing anything off Bayswater Road or Buses 27, 28, 31, and 52 for penetrating the depths of Notting Hill.

Sights to See

☺ **Hyde Park.** Along with the smaller St. James's and Green parks to the east, Hyde Park started as Henry VIII's hunting grounds. He had no altruistic intent but more or less stole the land, for his own personal pleasure, from the monks at Westminster at the 1536 Dissolution of the Monasteries. James I was more generous and allowed the public in at the beginning of the 17th century, as long as they were "respectably dressed." Nowadays, as summer visitors can see, you may wear whatever you like—a bathing suit will do. Along its south side runs Rotten Row. It was Henry VIII's royal path to the hunt—hence the name, a corruption of *route du roi*. It's still used by the Household Cavalry, who live at the **Knightsbridge Barracks**—a high-rise and a long,

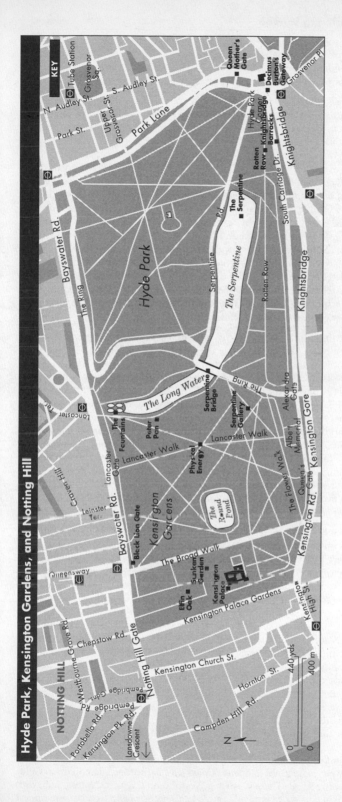

Hyde Park, Kensington Gardens, and Notting Hill

low, ugly red block—to the left. This is the brigade that mounts the guard at Buckingham Palace, and you can see them leave to perform this duty in full regalia, plumed helmet and all, at around 10:30, or await the return of the exhausted ex-guard about noon.

Kensington Gardens. More formal than neighboring Hyde Park, Kensington Gardens was first laid out as palace grounds. The paved Italian garden at the top of the Long Water, the **Fountains**, is a reminder of this, though of course **Kensington Palace** (☞ Knightsbridge, Kensington, and Holland Park, *above*) itself is the main clue to the gardens' royal status, with its early 19th-century Sunken Garden north of the palace complex, complete with a living tunnel of lime trees (i.e., linden trees) and golden laburnum. Several statues are worth looking out for: George Frampton's 1912 *Peter Pan* is a bronze of the boy who lived on an island in the Serpentine and never grew up and whose creator, J. M. Barrie, lived at 100 Bayswater Road, not 500 yards from here. Southwest of Peter at the intersection of several paths is George Frederick Watts's 1904 bronze of a muscle-bound horse and rider, entitled *Physical Energy.* By the playground close to the Round Pond is the remains of a tree carved with scores of tiny woodland creatures, Ivor Innes's *Elfin Oak.* The **Round Pond** acts as a magnet for model-boat enthusiasts and duck feeders.

Notting Hill. Currently the best place to wear sunglasses, smoke Gauloises, and contemplate the latest issue of *Wallpaper,* "the Hill" now ranks as millennial London's coolest neighborhood (for this week, at least). Centered on the Portobello Road antiques market, this district is bordered in the west by Lansdowne Crescent—address to the Hill's poshest 19th-century terraced row houses—and to the east by Chepstow Road, with Notting Hill Gate and Westbourne Grove Road marking south and north boundaries. In between, Rastafarians rub elbows with wealthy young Brits (a.k.a. "Trustafarians") and residents like fashion designer Rifat Ozbek, CNN's Christiane Amanpour, and historian Lady Antonia Fraser can be spotted at the chic shops on Westbourne Grove and the lively café on Kensington Park Road. There are no historic sites here, so explore just to savor the flavor. ⊠ *Tube: Notting Hill Gate, Ladbroke Grove.*

Portobello Road. Tempted by tassels, looking for a 19th-century snuff spoon, an ancient print of North Africa, or a dashingly Deco frock (just don't believe the dealer when he says the Vionnet label just fell off), or hunting for a gracefully Georgian silhouette of the Earl of Chesterfield? Head to Portobello Road, world famous for its Saturday antiques market (arrive at about 9 AM to find the real treasures-in-the-trash; after 10, the crowds pack in wall to wall). Actually, the Portobello Market is three markets: antiques, "fruit and veg," and a flea market. The street begins at Notting Hill Gate, though the antiques stalls start a couple of blocks north, around Chepstow Villas. Lining the sloping street are also dozens of antiques shops and indoor markets, open most days—in fact, serious collectors will want to do Portobello on a weekday, when they can explore the 90-some antiques and art stores in relative peace. Where the road levels off, around Elgin Crescent, youth culture and a vibrant neighborhood life kick in, with all manner of interesting small stores and restaurants interspersed with the fruit and vegetable market. This continues to the Westway overpass ("flyover" in British), where London's best flea market (high-class, vintage, antique, and secondhand clothing; jewelry; and junk) happens Fridays and Saturdays, then on up to Goldbourne Road. There's a strong West Indian flavor to Notting Hill, with a Trinidad-style Carnival centered along Portobello Road on the August bank-holiday weekend. ⊠ *Tube: Notting Hill Gate, Ladbroke Grove.*

Serpentine Gallery. Influential on the trendy art circuit, this gallery hangs several exhibitions of modern work a year, often very avant-garde, indeed, and always worth a look. It overlooks the west bank of the **Serpentine,** a beloved lake, much frequented in summer, when the south-shore Lido resembles a beach and the water is dotted with hired rowboats. Walk the bank, and you will soon reach the picturesque, stone **Serpentine Bridge,** built in 1826 by George Rennie, which marks the boundary between Hyde Park and Kensington Gardens. ⊠ *Kensington Gardens, W2,* ☎ *020/7402–6075.* ⊞ *Free.* ☉ *Daily 10–6. Closed Christmas wk. Tube: Lancaster Gate.*

REGENT'S PARK AND HAMPSTEAD

Regent's Park and Hampstead in north London contain some of the prettiest and most rural parts of the city, as well as some of the most aristocratic architecture in the world (thanks to the terraces and town houses of John Nash, 19th-century design whiz) and some important historical sights. For the sheer pleasure of idle exploring, these city districts are hard to beat. All told, this section covers a large area. It starts from the Georgian houses superimposed on medieval Maryburne; continues around John Nash's Regency facades and his park; stretches on into north London's canal-side youth center; climbs up the hill to the city's chicest, most expensive "village"; and finishes, fittingly, at its most famous cemetery.

Marylebone Road (pronounced "Marra-le-bun" after Queen Mary *le bon*) these days is remarkable mostly for its permanent traffic jam, some of it heading to Madame Tussaud's. At the east end is the first part of John Nash's impressive Regent's Park scheme, the elegantly curvaceous Park Crescent (1812–18), which Nash planned as a full circus at the northern end of his ceremonial route from St. James's. Like most of the other Nash houses around the park, it was wrecked during World War II, reconstructed, and rebuilt behind the repaired facade in the 1960s. Northeast of the park, Camden Town is the neighborhood that houses London's highest concentration of single people in their twenties.

The cliché about Hampstead is that it is just like a pretty little village—albeit one with designer shops, expensive French delicatessens, restaurants, cafés, cinemas, and so on. In fact, like so many other London neighborhoods, Hampstead did start as a separate village, when plague-bedeviled medieval Londoners fled the city to this clean hilltop 4 mi away. By the 18th century, its reputation for cleanliness had spread so far that its water was being bottled and sold, as the Perrier of its day, to the hoi polloi down the hill. That was the beginning of Hampstead's heyday as an artistic and literary retreat attracting many famous writers, painters, and musicians to its leafy lanes—as it still does. Just strolling around here is rewarding: not only are the streets incredibly picturesque, they also harbor some of London's best Georgian buildings.

Numbers in the text correspond to numbers in the margin and on the Regent's Park and Hampstead map.

A Good Walk

Begin at the tube station whose name will thrill the Sherlock Holmes fan: Baker Street—the **Sherlock Holmes Museum** ① is at 221B, of course. Turn left and follow the line of tour buses past **Madame Tussaud's** ② and the **London Planetarium;** then go to the end of Harley Street—an English synonym for private (as opposed to state-funded) medicine because it is lined with the consulting rooms of the country's top specialist doctors—to Park Crescent and, across the street, **Regent's Park** ③. Enter along the Outer Circle and turn left on Chester Road.

Straight ahead are Queen Mary's Gardens, the lake, and the **Regent's Park Open-Air Theatre** ④.

If you want to take a look at the winner of the Most Elegant Street in London, head straight ahead up Chester Road to **Cumberland Terrace** (1827), the porticoed white-stucco structure that overlooks the eastern edge of the park like a Grecian temple. This is one of architect Joseph Nash's most famous Regency-era creations. His most elegant urban stage set, however, is reached by continuing two blocks south, where **Chester Place** (1825) debouches into a cream-colored, magnificent triumphal arch, with its name emblazoned across the top of the arch. Nash aficionados will want to continue eight blocks to the north to see Park Village East and West, two streets that are lined with enchanting "villas" in the 19th-century mode.

If you haven't made this architectural detour outside the park to see Nash's buildings, continue within the park from Regent's Park Open-Air Theatre along Chester Road until the Broad Walk, and then make a left. Look west past the mock-Tudor prefab tearoom for one of London's rare, uninterrupted open vistas toward the London Central Mosque; and then continue on to the **London Zoo** ⑤. From here, you can take a round-trip detour on the water bus and spy on the back gardens along the **Grand Union Canal** (which everyone calls the Regent's Canal) to Little Venice. This canal is flanked with enormous white wedding-cake houses, separated from the banks with willow trees and long gardens, making it a beautiful strolling location. Alternatively you can walk along the whole canal, past the animals in the zoo down to Camden Lock, one of Britain's largest markets.

North of the zoo, cross Prince Albert Road to the man-made Primrose Hill, a high point (literally, at 206 ft) and the best place to be on the night of November 5, when London's biggest bonfire burns a Guy Fawkes effigy, and the council puts on a spectacular fireworks display. Heading east from here (the easiest route is Regent's Park Road), then left down Parkway, past the **Jewish Museum** ⑥, brings you to the center of Camden Town. Turn left at the foot of Parkway, and battle your way north along Camden High Street (actually, the crowds are unbearably dense only on the weekend) to **Camden Lock** ⑦. From here you can keep going east, although it's less scenic, to King's Cross, site of one of London's main train stations, the new British Library building, the city's highest concentration of for-hire streetwalkers, and the **London Canal Museum** ⑧.

Back at the Lock, you could walk up Haverstock Hill, or travel three stops on the Northern Line from Camden Town tube (make sure you take the Edgware branch) to Hampstead (or 181 ft below it, in London's deepest tube station). Cross High Street to Heath Street and turn right to Church Row, said to be London's most complete Georgian street. At the west end is the 1745 "village" church of St. John's, where the painter John Constable is buried. Just south of the tube, Flask Walk is another beautiful street, narrow and shop-lined at the High Street end, then widening after you pass the Flask—the pub it is named for. This place has a pretty courtyard and was described by Samuel Richardson in his 18th-century novel *Clarissa* as "a place where second-rate persons are to be found, often in a swinish condition." Lunch here, or opt for a bite at Hampstead's chic Cafe Rouge, Al Casbah, Graffiti, or the Coffee Cup. Nearby Well Walk was where a spring surfaced, its place now marked by a dried-up fountain. John Constable lived here, as well as John Keats (in, of course, **Keats House** ⑨) and, later, D. H. Lawrence. Head some blocks north to regal **Fenton House,** a National Trust treasure trove with some lovely gardens; then amble around the corner to Admiral's Walk to gaze at the house with a roof that echoes the quarterdeck of a ship immortalized in *Mary Poppins*. Farther along East Heath Road you'll find the Gothic manse (now owned by Boy George) that inspired Hell Hall in *One Hundred and One Dalmatians*. You now have two choices: if you've had enough fresh air, walk all the way down Fitzjohn's Avenue and visit the **Freud Museum** ⑩, where Sigmund Freud lived and worked, and then continue down Finchley Road to the impressive **Saatchi Collection** ⑪, a huge, cavernous gallery space; Beatles aficionados will head posthaste, instead, to the fabled **Abbey Road Studios** ⑫. If you've been blessed with a clear London day, take advantage and follow the long walk northeast up Spaniards Road, traversing **Hampstead Heath** to Hampstead Lane, to the bucolic oasis of **Kenwood House** ⑬, well worth a visit for its setting alone. To the east of Hampstead, and also topping a hill, is the former village of Highgate, which has some fine houses, especially along its Georgian High Street, and retains a peaceful period atmosphere. But it is most famous for **Highgate Cemetery** ⑭.

TIMING

You may well want to divide this tour into segments, using the (notoriously inefficient) Northern Line of the tube to jump between the Regent's Park and Hampstead neighborhoods. It will take you at least three or even four hours to cover on foot the full length of this walk.

There are several approaches. In summer, with children, you might consider a north London jaunt on Regent's Park, the zoo, Camden Lock, and a canal trip, a day's worth of sightseeing. If you wanted to add Madame Tussaud's and the planetarium, you'd have a frenetic day, especially in summer, because you might be in line for over an hour. You could start a summer's day without children at the other end, with Hampstead Heath, Kenwood House, a stroll around Hampstead, and a pub or two on the agenda. Teenagers and youth might want to spend all day shopping in Camden Town. Both Camden and Hampstead are usually fairly busy during the week as well because in addition to being shopping havens, they are residential neighborhoods. Bear in mind that much of this itinerary may be washed out by rain.

HOW TO GET THERE

For Regent's Park, go to Regent's Park tube (on the Bakerloo Line), though Camden Town on the Northern Line, with a walk up Parkway, is almost as close. Hampstead is best accessed from Hampstead tube. Make sure you get on the right branch of the Northern Line—you want the Edgware branch. Buses for Regent's Park include Buses 18, 27, and 30 along the Marylebone Road or Buses 13, 82, 113, 139, and 274 to Lord's Cricket Ground. Take the 274 for the zoo. For Hampstead, catch the 268.

Sights to See

★ ⑫ **Abbey Road Studios.** The most famous Beatles site in London, this is the fabled studio where the Fab Four recorded their entire output. The studios themselves are closed to the public, but many travelers journey here to see the famous traffic crossing used by the group on the cover of their *Abbey Road* album (☞ Close-Up box "Strawberry Beatles Forever: A Trip to Abbey Road," *below*). ⊠ *3 Abbey Rd., NW8. Tube: St. John's Wood.*

🔄 ➐ **Camden Lock.** What was once just a pair of locks on the Grand Union Canal has now developed into London's third-most-visited tourist attraction. It's a vast honeycomb of markets that sell just about everything, but mostly crafts, clothing (vintage, ethnic, and young designer), and antiques. Here, especially on a weekend, the crowds are dense, young, and relentless. You may tire of the identical T-shirts, pants, boots, vintage wear, and cheap leather on their backs and in the shops. Cam-

Abbey Road
Studios 12

Camden Lock 7

Freud Museum 10

Highgate
Cemetery 14

Jewish Museum 6

Keats House 9

Kenwood House 13

London Canal
Museum 8

London Zoo 5

Madame Tussaud's . . 2

Regent's Park 3

Regent's Park
Open-Air Theatre 4

Saatchi Collection . . . 11

Sherlock Holmes
Museum 1

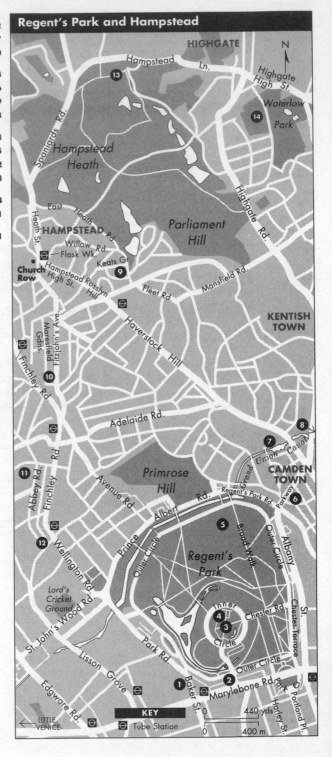

Regent's Park and Hampstead

STRAWBERRY BEATLES FOREVER:
A TRIP TO ABBEY ROAD

FOR COUNTLESS BEATLEMANIACS and baby boomers, Number 3 Abbey Road is one of the most beloved spots in London. Here, outside the legendary Abbey Road Studios, is the most famous zebra crossing in the world. Immortalized on the Beatles' *Abbey Road* 1969 album, this footpath became a Mod monument when, on August 8 of that year, John, Paul, George, and Ringo posed—walking symbolically *away* from the recording facility, incidentally—for photographer Iain Macmillan for the famous album shot.

Today, many fans venture to Abbey Road to leave their signature on the white-stucco fence that fronts the studio facility. "All You Need Is Beatles!", "God Is a Beatle!", "Imagine—John coming back!", "John Is Gone—What a Price to Pay for Being a Genius!", "Why don't you do it in the road?" and "Strawberry Beatles Forever" are a few of the flourishes left (note that these are whitewashed out every three months, by agreement with the neighborhood community, to make room for new graffiti).

The recording facility's Studio 2 is where the Beatles recorded their entire output, from "Love Me Do" onward, including, most momentously, *Sgt. Pepper's Lonely Hearts Club Band* (early 1967). Since this was, for all intents and purposes, the Beatles' professional home for much of their career, many of their most famous photos were taken here. The most celebrated, of course, was the sleeve jacket photo for the eponymous album. On Friday, August 8, 1969, at 11:35 AM, pho-tographer Macmillan balanced his Hasselblad atop a stepladder before the zebra crossing and photographed the four lads three times crossing west and three times east. Paul's sandals came off only with the third shot. Shot number 5 was the one seen around the world.

Today, tourists like to Beatle-ize themselves by taking the same sort of photo, but be careful: rushing cars make Abbey Road a dangerous intersection. Currently, there are few places in London that commemorate the Fab Four (wouldn't it be wonderful if Abbey Road Studios, now closed to the public, could become a Beatles museum one day?), so the best way Beatle-lovers can enjoy the history of the group is to take one of the smashing walking tours offered by the **Original London Walks** (☎ 020/7624–3978), including "The Beatles In-My-Life Walk" (11 AM at the Baker Street underground on Saturday and Tuesday) and "The Beatles Magical Mystery Tour" (11 AM at Dominion Theater Exit, Tottenham Court Road, on Sunday and Thursday).

Abbey Road is in the elegant neighborhood of St. John's Wood, just a 10-minute ride on the tube from central London. Take the Jubilee subway line to the St. John's Wood tube stop, head southwest three blocks down Grove End Road, and—especially if you were one of the 63 million people who tuned in to the *Ed Sullivan Show* February 8, 1964, and grew up with the Beatles—be prepared for a heart-stopping vista right out of Memory Lane.

den does have its charms, though. Gentrification has layered over a once overwhelmingly Irish neighborhood, vestiges of which coexist with the youth culture. Charm is evident in sections of the market itself as well as in other markets, including the bustling fruit-and-vegetable market on Inverness Street. Along the canal are some stylish examples of Nicholas Grimshaw architecture (architect of Waterloo station), as well as the new MTV offices with their designer graffiti. ⊠ *Camden Lock, Camden High St., NW1,* ☏ *no phone.* ☉ *Market weekends. Tube: Camden Town or Chalk Farm.*

NEED A BREAK? You will not go hungry in Camden Town. Among the countless cafés, bars, pubs, and restaurants, the following stand out for good value and good food: **Marine Ices** (⊠ 8 Haverstock Hill, past lock) has a window dispensing ice cream to strollers, and pasta, pizza, and sundaes inside. **Bar Gansa** (⊠ 2 Inverness St., near tube) offers Spanish tapas—small dishes for sharing. **Cottons Rhum Shop, Bar and Restaurant** (⊠ 55 Chalk Farm Rd., past lock) is a Caribbean island in miniature, with great rum cocktails and jerk chicken.

Fenton House. This is Hampstead's oldest surviving house. Now a National Trust property, it has an interesting collection of antiques and period interiors, along with some 17th-century-style gardens. Baroque enthusiasts can join a tour of the large collection of keyboard instruments, given by the curator. ⊠ *Hampstead Grove, NW3,* ☏ *020/ 7435-3471.* 🎫 *£4.10.* ☉ *Mar., weekends 2–5; Apr.–Oct., Wed.–Fri. 2–5, weekends 11–5:30. Tours 1st Thurs. of month. Tube: Hampstead.*

⑩ Freud Museum. The father of psychoanalysis lived here for only a few months, between his escape from Nazi persecution in his native Vienna in 1938 and his death in 1939. Many of his possessions emigrated with him and were set up by his daughter, Anna (herself a pioneer of child psychoanalysis), as a shrine to her father's life and work. Four years after Anna's death in 1982, the house was opened as a museum. It replicates the atmosphere of Freud's famous consulting rooms, particularly through the presence of *the couch.* You'll find Freud-related books, lectures, and study groups here, too. ⊠ *20 Maresfield Gardens, NW3,* ☏ *020/7435–2002.* 🎫 *£4.* ☉ *Wed.–Sun. noon–5. Tube: Swiss Cottage, Finchley Rd.*

Hampstead Heath. For an escape from the ordered prettiness of Hampstead, head to the heath—a wild park, which spreads for miles to the north and boasts stunning views of London. On the southwest corner stands the rebuilt version of a famous inn, once Dickens's favorite haunt, **Jack Straw's Castle** (⊠ North End Way, NW3, ☏ 020/7435–8885). It is named after the Peasants' Revolt leader who hid out and was captured here in 1381 after destroying Sir Robert Hales's residence and priory, the Priory of St. John. Hales was hated for enforcing the poll tax, which led to the uprising—and which, when reintroduced in 1990, proved as unpopular the second time around. Another historic pub stands off the northwest edge, on Hampstead Lane. The **Spaniard's Inn** (⊠ Spaniard's Rd., NW3, ☏ 020/8455–3276) is little changed since the early 18th century, when (they say) the notorious highwayman Dick Turpin hung out here. Keats also drank here, as did Shelley and Byron.

⑭ Highgate Cemetery. The older, west side of this sprawling early Victorian graveyard, featuring many an overwrought stone memorial, can be visited only by a tour given by the Friends of Highgate Cemetery—a group of volunteers who virtually saved the place from ruin. The shady streets of the dead, Egyptian Avenue and the Circle of Lebanon, are particularly Poe-like, but the famous graves are mostly on the newer, less atmospheric east side. This side can be wandered freely. Karl Marx's enormous black bust is probably the most-visited site, but George Eliot is also buried here. This is not London's oldest cemetery—that distinction belongs to Kensal Green (☞ Kensal Green *in* Knightsbridge, Kensington, and Holland Park, *above*), with its spine-chilling catacombs and Gothic mausoleums. ⊠ *Swains La., Highgate, N6,* ☎ *020/8340–1834.* ☜ *East side £1, west-side tour £2.* ☉ *Call for opening times and visitor information; hrs vary according to whether a funeral service is scheduled. Tube: Archway.*

NEED A
BREAK?

Lauderdale House in Waterlow Park, across Swain's Lane from Highgate Cemetery, was built during the 16th century by a master of the Royal Mint and is now a community and arts center, with a great café serving homemade hot meals as well as snacks.

⑥ Jewish Museum. This newly located museum tells a potted history of the Jews in London from Norman times, though the bulk of the exhibits date from the end of the 17th century (when Cromwell repealed the laws against Jewish settlement) and later. ⊠ *Raymond Burton House, 129 Albert St., NW1,* ☎ *020/7284–1997.* ☜ *£3.* ☉ *Sun.–Thurs. 10–4.*

⑨ Keats House. The house and gardens have recently been renovated. Here you can see the plum tree under which the young Romantic poet composed "Ode to a Nightingale," many of his original manuscripts, his library, and other possessions he managed to acquire in his short life. It was in February 1820 that Keats coughed blood up into his handkerchief and exclaimed, "I know the color of that blood; it is arterial blood. I cannot be deceived in that color. That drop of blood is my death warrant. I must die." He left this house in September, moved to Rome, and died of consumption there, in early 1821, at age 25. ⊠ *Keats House, Wentworth Pl., Keats Grove, NW3,* ☎ *020/7435–2062.* ☜ *Free.* ☉ *Apr.–Oct., weekdays 10–1 and 2–6, Sat. 10–1 and 2–5, Sun. 2–5; Nov.–Mar., weekdays 1–5, Sat. 10–1 and 2–5, Sun. 2–5. Tube: Hampstead.*

NEED A
BREAK?

Hampstead is full of restaurants, including a few that have been here forever. Try the **Coffee Cup** (⊠ 74 Hampstead High St.), serving English breakfasts all day, alongside luxurious hot chocolate, pastries, and things-on-toast, or the **Hampstead Tea Rooms** (⊠ 9 South End Rd.) for its sandwiches, pies, and its great window full of pastries and cream cakes. For a more substantial but still speedy meal, stop at the **Creperie** (⊠ Hampstead High St.), which serves authentic sweet and savory French crepes—including everything from chestnut to ham and goat cheese—on the roadside until sundown. The quaintest pub in Hampstead, complete with fireplace and timber frame, is the **Holly Bush** (⊠ 22 Holly Mount), which dates back to 1807. Tucked away on a side street, it is open until 11 each night and serves traditional English lunches and dinners, often to the accompaniment of live Irish music.

⑬ Kenwood House. Perfectly and properly Palladian, this mansion was first built in 1616 and remodeled by Robert Adam in 1764. Adam refaced most of the exterior and added the gaudy library, which, with its curved painted ceiling, rather garish coloring, and gilded detailing, is the sole highlight of the house for decor buffs. What is unmissable here is the **Iveagh Bequest,** a collection of paintings that the Earl of Iveagh gave the nation in 1927, starring a wonderful Rembrandt self-portrait and works by Reynolds, Van Dyck, Hals, Gainsborough, and Turner. Top billing goes to Vermeer's *Guitar Player,* one of the most beautiful paintings in the world. In front of the house, a graceful lawn slopes down to a little lake crossed by a trompe l'oeil bridge—all in perfect

18th-century upper-class taste. Nowadays the lake is dominated by its concert bowl, which stages a summer series of orchestral concerts, including an annual performance of Handel's *Music for the Royal Fireworks*, complete with fireworks. ⊠ *Hampstead La., NW3,* ☎ *020/8348–1286.* 🎫 *Free.* ☉ *Easter–Sept., daily 10–6; Oct.–Easter, daily 10–4. Tube: Golder's Green, then Bus 210.*

⑧ London Canal Museum. Here, in a former ice storage house, you can learn about the rise and fall of London's once extensive canal network. Outside, on the Battlebridge Basin, float the gaily painted narrow boats of modern canal dwellers—a few steps and a world away from King's Cross, which remains one of London's least salubrious neighborhoods. The quirky little museum is accessible from Camden Lock if you take the towpath. ⊠ *12–13 New Wharf Rd., N1,* ☎ *020/7713–0836.* 🎫 *£2.50.* ☉ *Apr.–Sept., Tues.–Sun. 10–3:30; call for winter hrs. Tube: King's Cross.*

☾ London Planetarium. This domed building stands right next to Madame Tussaud's (☞ *below*), but it could hardly provide greater contrast with the waxworks (though you can save a bit of cash by combining them in a single visit). Inside the dome, exact simulations of the night sky are projected by the Digistar Mark 2 and accompanied by gosh-wow-fancy-that narration. The shows, which change daily, are good enough to addict children to astronomy. There are also regular laser shows and rock music extravaganzas. ⊠ *Marylebone Rd., NW1,* ☎ *020/7935–6861.* 🎫 *£5:85, combined ticket with Madame Tussaud's £12.* ☉ *Weekdays 11:30–6, weekends 9:30–6; show every 40 mins weekdays 12:20–5, weekends 10:20–5. Tube: Baker Street.*

☾ ⑤ London Zoo. The zoo opened in 1828 and peaked in popularity during the 1950s, when more than 3 million visitors passed through its turnstiles every year. But recently it faced the prospect of closing its gates forever. Its problems started when animal-crazy Brits, anxious about the morality of caging wild beasts, simply stopped visiting. But the zoo fought back, pulling heartstrings with a "Save Our Zoo" campaign and tragic predictions of mass euthanasia for homeless polar bears. At the 11th hour it found commercial sponsorship that was generous enough not only to keep the wolves from the door (or, rather, the wolves indoors) but also to fund a great big modernization program. So successful has the zoo's revival been that it has now glitteringly expanded to include the Web of Life—a conservation and education center set in a spanking new glass pavilion. And to ensure that the celebration of life does not go unheralded, the zoo has taken on a poet-in-residence, the young but highly acclaimed Tobias Hill. If you get the chance, catch one of his readings or popular children's workshops at the zoo.

Zoo highlights (unchanged over the years) include the Elephant and Rhino Pavilion (which closely resembles the South Bank Arts Complex); the graceful Snowdon Aviary, spacious enough to allow its tenants free flight; and the 1936 Penguin Pool, where feeding time sends small children into raptures. New thrills will include the construction of a desert swarming with locusts; a rain forest alive with butterflies, bats, and hummingbirds; and a cave lighted by fireflies. This is the headquarters of the Zoological Society of London, and much work is done here in wildlife conservation, education, and the breeding of endangered species. The emphasis has been shifted onto this aspect of the exhibits. The first step along this road was the Children's Zoo, which shows how people and animals live together and features domestic animals from around the world. ⊠ *Regent's Park, NW1,* ☎ *020/7722–3333.* 🎫 *£8:50,* ☉ *Mar.–Oct., daily 10–6; Nov.–Feb., daily 10–4; pelican feed daily 1; aquarium feed daily 2:30; reptile feed Fri. 2:30; elephant bath daily 3:45. Tube: Camden Town, then Bus 74.*

② Madame Tussaud's. This—one of London's busiest sights—is nothing more and nothing less than the world's premier exhibition of lifelike wax-work models of celebrities. Madame T. learned her craft while making death masks of French Revolution victims and in 1835 set up her first show of the famous ones near this spot. Nowadays, "Super Stars" of entertainment, in their own hall of the same name, outrank any aristo in popularity, along with the newest segment, "The Spirit of London," and a "time taxi ride" that visits every notable Londoner from Shakespeare to Benny Hill. But top billing still goes to the murderers in the Chamber of Horrors, who stare glassy-eyed at visitors—one from an electric chair, one sitting next to the tin bath where he dissolved several wives in quicklime. What, aside from ghoulish prurience, makes people stand in line to invest in London's most expensive museum ticket? It is the thrill of rubbing shoulders with Shakespeare, Martin Luther King Jr., the queen, and the Beatles—most of them dressed in their very own outfits—in a single day. ✉ *Marylebone Rd., NW1,* ☎ *020/7935–6861.* 🎫 *£9:75, combined ticket with planetarium £12.* ⊙ *Sept.–June, weekdays 10–5:30, weekends 9:30–5:30; July–Aug., daily 9:30–5:30. Tube: Baker St.*

★ **③ Regent's Park.** The youngest of London's great parks, Regent's Park was laid out in 1812 by John Nash, who worked for his patron, the Prince Regent (hence the name), who was crowned George IV in 1820. The idea was to re-create the feel of a grand country residence close to the center of town, with all those magnificent white-stucco terraces facing in on the park. As you walk the Outer Circle, you'll see how successfully Nash's plans were carried out, although the focus of it all—a palace for the prince—was never actually built (George was too busy fiddling with the one he already had, Buckingham Palace). The most famous and impressive of Nash's terraces would have been in the prince's line of vision from the planned palace. **Cumberland Terrace** has a central block of Ionic columns surmounted by a triangular Wedgwood-blue pediment that is like a giant cameo. Snow-white statuary personifying Britannia and her empire (the work of the on-site architect, James Thomson) single it out from the pack. The noted architectural historian Sir John Summerson described it thus: "the backcloth as it were to Act III, and easily the most breathtaking architectural panorama in London."

As in all London parks, planting here is planned with the aim of having something in bloom in all seasons, but if you hit the park in May, June, or July, head first to the Inner Circle. Your nostrils should lead you to **Queen Mary's Gardens,** a fragrant 17-acre circle that riots with roses in summer and heather, azaleas, and evergreens in other seasons. The **Broad Walk** is a good vantage point from which to glimpse the minaret and golden dome of the **London Central Mosque** on the far west side of the park. If it's a summer evening or a Sunday afternoon, witness a remarkable recent phenomenon. Wherever you look, the sport being enthusiastically played is not cricket but softball, now Britain's fastest-growing participant sport (bring your mitt). You're likely to see cricket, too, plus a lot of dog walkers—not for nothing did Dodie Smith set her novel *A Hundred and One Dalmations* in an Outer Circle house. ✑

④ Regent's Park Open-Air Theatre. They have mounted Shakespeare productions here every summer since 1932; everyone from Vivien Leigh to Jeremy Irons has performed here. *A Midsummer Night's Dream* is the one to catch—never is that enchanted Greek wood more lifelike than it is here, augmented by genuine bird squawks and a rising moon. The park can get chilly, so bring a blanket; rain stops the play only when heavy, so an umbrella may be wise, too. ✉ *Open-Air Theatre, Regent's Park, NW1,* ☎ *020/7486–2431.* ⊙ *June–Aug., evening performances 7:30, matinees 2:30. Tube: Baker St., Regent's Park.*

⑪ **Saatchi Collection.** This blinding white space is all crisp angles and quietness, the better to contemplate the front lines of contemporary paintings, installations, and sculpture—by the likes of Lucian Freud, Paula Rego, Damian Hirst, Rachel Whiteread, Janine Antoni—collected by the advertising mogul. ⊠ *98A Boundary Rd., NW8,* ☎ *020/7624–8299.* ⊠ *Free.* ⊙ *Fri.– Sat. noon–6. Tube: Swiss Cottage.*

❶ **Sherlock Holmes Museum.** You know you've reached this museum when you see the actor dressed as a Victorian policeman outside and the sign that claims this as 221B Baker Street, the address of Arthur Conan Doyle's fictional detective. Inside, "Holmes's housekeeper" conducts you into a series of Victorian rooms full of Sherlock-abilia. By the way, the 221B, if it existed, would be down the block in the Abbey National Building Society's head office at Abbey House, 215–229 Baker Street. ⊠ *221B Baker St., NW1,* ☎ *020/7935–8866.* ⊠ *£5.* ⊙ *Daily 9:30–6. Tube: Baker St.*

2 Willow Road. Modern Movement master Erno Goldfinger put this house up in the 1930s, and the National Trust has now kindly restored it and filled it with important (and currently very trendy) Modernist furniture and art. Note that there are limited visitor hours with timed tickets because the house is small. ⊠ *2 Willow Rd., NW1,* ☎ *020/7435–6166.* ⊠ *£4.* ⊙ *Apr.–Oct., Thurs. and Fri.–Sat.; call for hrs. Tube: Hampstead.*

GREENWICH

About 8 mi downstream from central London—which means seaward, to the east—lies a neighborhood that has recently had new front-page fame thrust upon it. From a sleepy, charming self-contained village, with elegant, perfectly proportioned buildings and tall ships anchored at the river bank, Greenwich has become a byword for the millennium (and, some might say, for excesses of government spending). Yes, it is the home of the Millennium Dome, either a spectacular monument to mankind or, according to some British critics, a dazzling waste of £758 million of public money. Best just to go see for yourself what the futuristic site has to offer. Getting there is no problem—Greenwich now has more roads leading to it than Rome—but don't try driving there, as all new routes are strictly public transportation. Take the new Jubilee Line extensions, and if you're an architecture buff, get out at every stop—each one was designed by a different cutting-edge architect.

Greenwich has many attractions other than the Dome. Spreading both grandly and elegantly beside the river are the colonnades and pediments of Sir Christopher Wren's Royal Naval College and Inigo Jones's Queen's House, both of which seem to be part of a complex of Grecian temples transported to the Thames. Here, too, is the Old Royal Observatory, which measures time for our entire planet, and the Greenwich Meridian, which divides the world in two—you can stand astride it with one foot in either hemisphere. This is also where the millennium officially started (when this clock said so). The National Maritime Museum and the proud clipper ship *Cutty Sark* thrill seafaring types, and landlubbers can stroll the green acres of parkland that surround the buildings, the quaint 19th-century houses, and the weekend crafts and antiques markets.

Numbers in the text correspond to numbers in the margin and on the Greenwich map.

A Good Walk

If you arrive before the end of 2000 (when the exhibits are due to close), you can begin your Greenwich trip with a visit to the **Millennium Dome** ①. Part of the massive Millennium construction project is the

Riverside Walk, a 7-mi-long path leading from central Greenwich to the dome. You can pick up the walk at Greenwich Pier, and amble toward the massive dome, which sits on the skyline like a great spider, or take the Jubilee Line directly to the Dome.

You could also take a ferry or train directly to Greenwich proper and begin your tour with the *Cutty Sark* ②. By continuing along King William Walk, you come to the wrought-iron gates of the **Royal Naval College** ③, from the south end of which you approach the building that Wren's majestic quadrangles frame, the **Queen's House** ④, followed by the **National Maritime Museum** ⑤. Now head up the hill in Greenwich Park overlooking the Naval College and Maritime Museum to the **Old Royal Observatory** ⑥ and the **Ranger's House** ⑦. Walking back through the park toward the river, you'll enter the pretty streets of Greenwich Village to the west. There are plenty of bookstores and antiques shops for browsing and, at the foot of Crooms Hill, the modern Greenwich Theatre—a West End theater, despite its location, that mounts well-regarded, often star-spangled productions—and the **Fan Museum** ⑧ opposite. Finish up at the excellent **Greenwich Antique Market** ⑨ (Burney Street near the museum and theater) and the Victorian **Covered Crafts Market** ⑩ by the *Cutty Sark*, on College Approach.

TIMING

The boat trip takes about an hour from Westminster Pier (next to Big Ben), or 25 minutes from the Tower of London, so figure in enough time for the round-trip. Even before the Millennium made Greenwich its home, it couldn't be "done" in a day. Beyond the main new attractions, there are such riches here, especially if the maritime theme is your thing, that whatever time you allow will seem halved. If the weather's good, you'll be tempted to stroll aimlessly around the quaint villagelike streets, too, and maybe take a turn in the park. If you want to take in the markets, you'll need to come on a weekend. The antiques market is open 8–4; the crafts market, 9–5.

HOW TO GET THERE

Once, Greenwich was thought of as remote by Londoners, with only the river as a direct route. But now the new transport links to the millennium borough should make journeying there both easy and inexpensive. The Millennium Dome site itself is car-free. The Jubilee Line now links central London with a new station serving the Dome on Greenwich peninsula, North Greenwich (but this is not especially convenient to the rest of Greenwich). A shuttle service carries visitors between the Dome and Charlton railway station via the Millennium Transit Link, but travelers may experience delays along this route. A bus interchange (Buses 188 and 286) has also opened. The quickest route to Greenwich itself and all the attractions other than the Dome is the tube to Canary Wharf and the Docklands Light Rail (the toy train that carries thousands of London's hardest working and most successful to their desks in Canary Wharf each day) to the *Cutty Sark*.

The new river connections to Greenwich mean that the journey to Greenwich is fun in itself, especially if you approach by river, for you will then get the best possible vista of the Royal Naval College, with the Queen's House behind. On the way, the boat glides past famous sights on the London skyline (there's a guaranteed spine chill on passing the Tower) and the ever-changing docklands, and there's always a cockney navigator enhancing the views with wise-guy commentary. Ferries from London to Greenwich take 30–55 minutes and leave from various piers: from Charing Cross and Tower piers (☎ 020/7987–1185), from Westminster Pier (☎ 020/7930–4097), and from the Thames Barrier Pier (☎ 020/8305–0300).

Sights to See

⑩ Covered Crafts Market. You'll find this Victorian market by the *Cutty Sark,* on College Approach. As you'd expect, this one features crafts, but there are more of the sort of ceramics, jewelry, knitwear, and leather goods that you might actually want to own than is common in such places, and you get to buy them from the people who made them. ⊠ *College Approach.* ☉ *Weekends 9–5.*

② Cutty Sark. This romantic clipper was built in 1869, one of fleets and fleets of similar wooden tall-masted clippers that during the 19th century plied the seven seas, trading in exotic commodities—tea, in this case. The *Cutty Sark,* the last to survive, was also the fastest, sailing the China–London route in 1871 in only 107 days. Now the photogenic vessel lies in dry dock, a museum of one kind of seafaring life—and not a comfortable kind for the 28-strong crew, as you'll see. The collection of figureheads is amusing, too. The *Cutty Sark* gardens have also been remodeled in time for Greenwich's moment of fame. ⊠ *King William Walk,* ☎ *020/8858–3445.* ☜ *£3.50.* ☉ *Daily 10–5 (last admission 4:30).*

⑧ Fan Museum. In two newly restored houses dating from the 1820s, opposite the Greenwich Theatre, is this highly unusual museum. The 2,000 fans here, which date from the 17th century onward, compose the world's only such collection, and the history and purpose of these often exquisitely crafted objects are explained satisfyingly. It was the personal vision—and fan collection—of Helene Alexander that brought it into being in 1991, and the workshop and conservation and study center that she has also set up ensure that this anachronistic art has a future. ⊠ *10–12 Croom's Hill,* ☎ *020/8858–7879.* ☜ *£5.* ☉ *Tues.–Sat. 11–5, Sun. noon–5.*

⑨ Greenwich Antique Market. If you're visiting on the weekend, this market on Burney Street near the Fan Museum and Greenwich Theatre is open for business. It has a lot of bric-a-brac and books, too, and it's well known among the cognoscenti as a good source for vintage clothing. ⊠ *Burney St.* ☉ *Weekends 8–4.*

❶ Millennium Dome. Located on the Prime Meridian, or Longitude Zero, in Greenwich, the Millennium Dome is probably the biggest—and certainly the most expensive—monument to the advent of the new century. Looking like a futuristic sports arena, this colossus is almost 1,200 ft in diameter, with a roof 165 ft high and strong enough to support a jumbo jet. You could fit one of the Great Pyramids of Egypt inside. The doors opened on Millennium Eve (December 31, 1999), and the exhibits are spread across 14 themed Disneylandish zones, including Work—a look at how this most central of life's activities is forever changing our lives; Learn—showing the classrooms of the future and presenting the challenges facing education; and Serious Play—an exhibition focusing on leisure. The special effects in this zone are fairly spectacular and also interactive: visitors can don a Spider-Man suit that sticks to the wall to climb down, having first ascended on high via a moving platform that takes them toward huge multimedia displays. But of all the exhibits, the Body Zone is the most talked about, thanks to its larger-than-the-Statue-of-Liberty representation of the human body, which allows visitors to journey through myriad passageways to see how our bodies function. While the emphasis is on technology and the achievements of humankind, there are also zones that recognize the more spiritual side of existence. The Dreamscape zone stresses the need to relax and to let the imagination run riot with the senses. Here, you will take a seat in a boat with 16 "beds" and float along a "river of dreams."

As a look into the 21st century and what awaits us, the Millennium Dome has much to offer, but grumblings from the press, which began

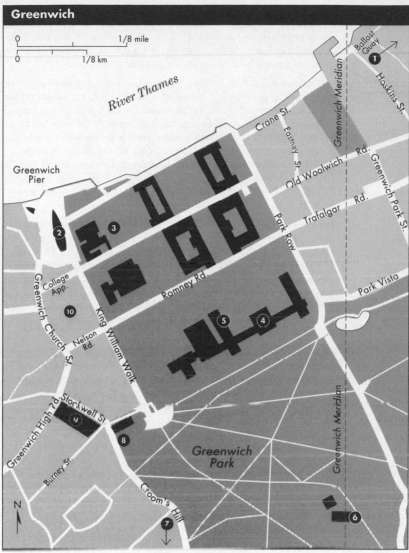

Greenwich

0 ⸻ 1/8 mile
0 ⸻ 1/8 km

River Thames

Greenwich Pier

Crane St.

Easney St.

Old Woolwich Rd.

Greenwich Meridian

Ballast Quay

Haskins St.

Greenwich Park St.

Park Row

Trafalgar Rd.

College App.

Greenwich Church St.

Nelson Rd.

King William Walk

Romney Rd.

Park Vista

Greenwich Meridian

Greenwich High Rd.

Stockwell St.

Burney St.

Groom's Hill

Greenwich Park

N

Covered Crafts
Market **10**

Cutty Sark **2**

Fan Museum **8**

Greenwich
Antique Market **9**

Millennium
Dome **1**

National Maritime
Museum **5**

Old Royal
Observatory **6**

Queen's House **4**

Ranger's House **7**

Royal Naval
College **3**

prior to its doors opening on the Millennium eve, have not ceased (some objected to the omission of Shakespeare and religion from exhibits on the achievements of mankind). The management of the dome has changed hands several times, and at press time the building itself was up for sale and all the exhibits due to close at the end of 2000.

You can not buy tickets for admission on site. Instead you can buy them wherever you can buy a a National Lottery ticket, via a direct ticket hot line, from train but not underground stations, through some coach operators, and from the Web site. All in all, while the Millennium Dome offers a great day for the whole family and is well worth a day trip, it is nowhere near to rivaling the impact and importance of its legendary predecessor, Prince Albert's 1851 Great Exhibition at the Crystal Palace. ⊠ *Drawdock St., Greenwich Peninsula,* ☎ *0870/603–2000 public information hot line.* ⌸ *£20.* ⊙ *Daily 10–6:30, peak summer months, daily 9:30–11.* ✎

☞ ❺ **National Maritime Museum.** One of Greenwich's star attractions contains everything to do with the British at sea in the form of paintings, models, maps, globes, sextants, uniforms (including the one Nelson died in at Trafalgar, complete with bloodstained bullet hole), and—best of all—actual boats, including a collection of ornate, gilded royal barges. New galleries and an immense glazed roof, creating an indoor courtyard, have revitalized this museum. ⊠ *Romney Rd.,* ☎ *020/8858–4422.* ⌸ *£5, including Queen's House and Old Royal Observatory.* ⊙ *Mon.– Sat. 10–6, Sun. noon–6.*

☞ ❻ **Old Royal Observatory.** Founded in 1675 by Charles II, this imposing institution was designed the same year by Christopher Wren for John Flamsteed, the first Astronomer Royal. The red ball you see on its roof has been there only since 1833. It drops every day at 1 PM, and you can set your watch by it, as the sailors on the Thames always have. This "Greenwich Timeball," along with the Gate Clock inside the observatory, is the most visible manifestation of Greenwich Mean Time—since 1884, the ultimate standard for time around the world. Greenwich is on the **prime meridian** at 0° longitude. A brass line laid on the cobblestones here marks the meridian, one side being the eastern, one the western hemisphere. In 1948 the Old Royal Observatory lost its official status: London's glow had grown too intense, and the astronomers moved to Sussex, while the Astronomer Royal decamped to Cambridge. They left various telescopes, chronometers, and clocks for you to view in their absence. ⊠ *Greenwich Park,* ☎ *020/8858–4422.* ⌸ *£5, including Queen's House and National Maritime Museum.* ⊙ *Daily 10–5.*

★ ❹ **Queen's House.** The queen for whom Inigo Jones began designing the house in 1616 was James I's Anne of Denmark, but she died three years later, and it was Charles I's French wife, Henrietta Maria, who inherited the building when it was completed in 1635. It is no less than Britain's first classical building—the first, that is, to use the lessons of Italian Renaissance architecture—and is therefore of enormous importance in the history of English architecture. Inside, the Tulip Stair, named for the fleur-de-lys–style pattern on the balustrade, is especially fine, spiraling up, without a central support, to the Great Hall. The Great Hall itself is a perfect cube, exactly 40 ft in all three directions, decorated with paintings of the Muses, the Virtues, and the Liberal Arts. The White Card is accepted. ⊠ *Romney Rd. SE10,* ☎ *020/8293–9618.* ⌸ *£5, including National Maritime Museum and Old Royal Observatory.* ⊙ *Daily 10–5.*

❼ **Ranger's House.** This handsome, early 18th-century mansion, which was the Greenwich Park Ranger's official residence during the 19th century, now houses collections of Jacobean portraits. Concerts are regularly given here, too. It stands just outside the park boundaries, on the southwest side of **Greenwich Park,** which is one of London's oldest Royal Parks. It had been in existence for more than 200 years before Charles II commissioned the French landscape artist Le Nôtre (who was responsible for Versailles and for St. James's Park) to redesign it in what was, in the 1660s, the latest French fashion. The flower garden on the southeast side and the deer enclosure nearby are particularly pleasant. Look also for Queen Elizabeth's Oak on the east side, around which Henry VIII and his second queen, Anne Boleyn, Elizabeth I's mother, are said to have danced. ✉ *Chesterfield Walk, Blackheath,* ☎ *020/8853–0035.* 🎫 *Free.* ☉ *Apr.–Sept., daily 10–1 and 2–6; Oct.–Mar., daily 10–1 and 2–4.*

★ ❸ **Royal Naval College.** Begun by Christopher Wren in 1694 as a home, or hospital (as in the Chelsea Royal Hospital, not Charing Cross Hospital), for ancient mariners, it became instead a school for young ones in 1873. You'll notice how the structures part to reveal the Queen's House across the central lawns. Wren, with the help of his assistant, Hawksmoor, was at pains to preserve the river vista from the house, and there are few more majestic views in London than the awe-inspiring symmetry he achieved. Behind the college are two buildings you can visit. The **Painted Hall,** the college's dining hall, derives its name from the Baroque murals of William and Mary (reigned 1689–95; William alone 1695–1702) and assorted allegorical figures, the whole supported by trompe l'oeil pillars that Sir James Thornhill (who decorated the inside of St. Paul's dome, too) painted between 1707 and 1717. In the opposite building stands the **College Chapel,** which was rebuilt after a fire in 1779 and is altogether lighter, in a more restrained, neo-Grecian style. At Christmas 1805, Admiral Nelson's body was brought from the Battle of Trafalgar to lie in state here. ✉ *Royal Naval College, King William Walk,* ☎ *020/8858–2154.* 🎫 *Free.* ☉ *Daily 2:30–4:45.* ✍

UPSTREAM FROM LONDON

The Thames is Britain's longest river. It winds its way through the Cotswolds, beyond the "dreaming spires" of Oxford and past majestic Windsor Castle—here far more the lazy, leafy country river than the dark-gray urban waterway you see in London. Once you leave the city center, going west, or upstream, you reach a series of former villages—Chiswick, Kew, Richmond, Putney—that, apart from the roar of aircraft coming in to land at Heathrow a few miles farther west, still retain a peaceful, almost rural atmosphere, especially in places where parkland rolls down to the riverbank. In fact, it was really only at the beginning of the 20th century that London proper expanded to encompass these villages. The royal palaces and grand houses that dot the area were built not as town houses but as country residences with easy access to London by river.

TIMING

Each of the places we list here could easily absorb a whole day of your time, and Hampton Court is especially huge. Access is fairly easy: the District Line of the underground runs out to Kew and Richmond, as does Network SouthEast from Waterloo, which also serves Twickenham and Hampton Court. Chiswick House can be reached by tube to Turnham Green, then the E3 bus; or by tube to Hammersmith and Bus 290. A pleasant if slow way to go is by river. Boats depart **Westminster Pier,** just by Big Ben (☎ 020/7930–4097) for Kew (1½ hours), Richmond (2–3 hours), and Hampton Court (4 hours) several times a day in summer, less frequently from October through March. As you can tell from those sailing times, the boat trip is worth taking only if you make it an integral part of your day out, and even then, be aware that it can get very breezy on the water and that the scenery going upstream is by no means constantly fascinating.

Chiswick and Kew

Chiswick is the nearest Thames-side destination to London, with Kew just a mile or so beyond it. Much of Chiswick, developed at the beginning of this century, is today a nondescript suburb. Incongruously stranded among the terraced houses, however, a number of fine 18th-century houses and a charming little village survive. The village atmosphere of Kew is still distinct, making this one of the most desirable areas of outer London. What makes Kew famous, though, are the Royal Botanic Gardens.

A Good Walk

Chiswick's **Church Street** (reached by an underpass from **Hogarth's House**) is the nearest thing to a sleepy country village street in all of London, despite its proximity to the Great West Road. Follow it down to the Thames and turn left at its foot to reach the sturdy 18th-century riverfront houses of **Chiswick Mall.** The ½-mi walk along here takes you far away from mainstream London and into a world of elegance and calm. You will pass several riverside pubs as you head along this stretch of the Thames toward Hammersmith Bridge. The **Dove** is the prettiest, if the most crowded, with its terrace hanging over the water. The food is better at the **Blue Anchor,** which you'll reach first.

There's a similarly peaceful walk to be had about 1 mi to the west along the 18th-century river frontage of **Strand-on-the-Green,** whose houses look over the narrow towpath to the river, their tidy brick facades covered with wisteria and roses in summer. Strand-on-the-Green ends at Kew Bridge, opposite which is **Kew Green,** where local teams play cricket on summer Sundays. All around it are fine 18th-century houses, and, in the center, a church in which the painters Thomas Gainsborough and John Zoffany (1733–1810) are buried.

Sights to See

★ **Chiswick House.** Built circa 1725 by the Earl of Burlington (the Lord Burlington of Burlington House, Piccadilly; home of the Royal Academy; and, of course, Burlington Arcade) as a country residence in which to entertain friends, and as a kind of temple to the arts, this is the very model of a Palladian villa, inspired by the Villa Capra near Vicenza in northeastern Italy. The house fans out from a central octagonal room in perfect symmetry, guarded by statues of Burlington's heroes, Palladio himself and his disciple Inigo Jones. Burlington's friends—Pope, Swift, Gay, and Handel among them—were well qualified to adorn a temple to the arts. Burlington was a great connoisseur, and an important patron of the arts, but he was also an accomplished architect in his own right, fascinated by—obsessed with, even—the architecture and art of the Italian Renaissance and ancient Rome, with which he'd fallen in love during his Italian grand tour (every well-bred boy's rite of passage). Along with William Kent (1685–1748), who designed the interiors and the rambling gardens here, Burlington did an awful lot to disseminate the Palladian ideals around Britain: Chiswick House sparked enormous interest, and you'll see these forms reflected in hundreds of subsequent English stately homes both small and large. ⊠ *Burlington La.,* ☎ *020/8995–0508.* ☞ *£2.50.* ☉ *Apr.–Sept., daily 10–1 and 2–6; Oct.–Mar., daily 10–1 and 2–4. Tube: Turnham Green.* ☜

Hogarth's House. This is where the painter lived from 1749 until his death in 1764. Unprotected from the six-lane Great West Road, which remains a main route to the West Country, the poor house is besieged by the surrounding traffic, but it's worth visiting for its little museum consisting mostly of the amusingly moralistic engravings for which Hogarth is best known, including the most famous of all, the *Rake's Progress* series of 1735. ✉ *Hogarth La.*, ☎ *020/8994–6757.* 🎫 *Free.* ☉ *Apr.–Sept., Mon.–Sat. 11–6, Sun. 2–6; Oct.–Mar., Mon.–Sat. 11–4, Sun. 2–4. Closed 1st 3 wks of Sept. and last 3 wks of Dec. Tube: Turnham Green.*

★ **Kew Gardens.** The Royal Botanic Gardens at Kew are a spectacular 300 acres of public gardens, containing more than 60,000 species of plants. In addition, this is the country's leading botanical institute, with strong royal associations. Until 1840, when Kew Gardens was handed over to the nation, it had been the grounds of two royal residences: the White House (formerly Kew House) and Richmond Lodge, or the Dutch House. George II and Queen Caroline lived at Richmond Lodge in the 1720s, while their eldest son, Frederick, Prince of Wales, and his wife, Princess Augusta, came to the White House during the 1730s. The royal wives were keen gardeners. Queen Caroline got to work on her grounds, while next door Frederick's pleasure garden was developed as a botanical garden by his widow after his death. She introduced all kinds of "exotics," foreign plants brought back to England by botanists. Caroline was aided by a skilled head gardener and by the architect Sir William Chambers, who built a series of temples and follies, of which the crazy 10-story **Pagoda** (1762), visible for miles around, is the star turn. The celebrated botanist Sir Joseph Banks (1743–1820) then took charge of Kew, which developed rapidly in both its roles—as a landscaped garden and as a center of study and research.

The highlights of a visit to Kew are the two great 19th-century greenhouses filled with tropical plants, many of which have been there as long as their housing. Both the **Palm House** and the **Temperate House** were designed by Sir Decimus Burton, the first opening in 1848, the second in 1899; the latter was the biggest greenhouse in the world and today contains the biggest greenhouse plant in the world, a Chilean wine palm rooted in 1846. You can climb the spiral staircase almost to the roof and look down on this and the dense tropical profusion from the walkway. The **Princess of Wales Conservatory**, the latest and the largest plant house at Kew, was opened in 1987 by Princess Diana. Under its bold glass roofs, designed to maximize energy conservation, there are no fewer than 10 climatic zones.

The **Centre for Economic Botany** is housed in the newly constructed Joseph Banks Building, the majority of which is devoted to Kew's research collection on economic botany and to its library. But the public can enjoy exhibitions here on the theme of plants in everyday life. (There is no admission charge, and the center is open Monday–Saturday 9:10–4:30 and Sunday 9:30–5:30.) The plant houses make Kew worth visiting even in the depths of winter, but in spring and summer the gardens come into their own. In late spring, the woodland nature reserve of Queen Charlotte's Cottage Gardens is carpeted in bluebells; a little later, the Rhododendron Dell and the Azalea Garden become swathed in brilliant color. High summer features glorious displays of roses and water lilies, while fall is the time to see the heather garden, near the pagoda. Whatever time of year you visit, something is in bloom, and your journey is never wasted. The main entrance is between Richmond Circus and the traffic circle at Mortlake Road. ✉ *Kew Rd.*, ☎ *020/8940–1171.* 🎫 *£5.* ☉ *Gardens Apr.–Oct., weekdays 10–6, weekends, 9:30–7:30; greenhouse Apr.–Oct., daily 9:30–5:30, Nov.–Mar., daily 10–4. Tube: Kew Gardens.* 🌿

Kew Palace. To this day quietly domestic, Kew Palace remains the smallest royal palace in the land. The palace has been closed for refurbishment, but you can glimpse the little formal gardens to its rear, redeveloped in 1969 as a 17th-century garden. It will reopen in the summer of 2001. Its brick walls have just been limewashed, and conservationists are now working on the 17th-century interior. ⊠ *Kew Gardens,* ☎ *020/8940–3321.*

NEED A BREAK?   **Maids of Honour** (⊠ 288 Kew Rd.), the most traditional of Old World English tearooms, is named for the famous tarts invented here and still baked by hand on the premises. Tea is served in the afternoon, Tuesday–Saturday 2:45–5:30.

Richmond

Named after the palace Henry VII built here in 1500, Richmond is still a welcoming and extremely pretty riverside "village," with many handsome (and expensive) houses, many antiques shops, a Victorian theater, London's grandest stately home, and, best of all, the biggest of London's Royal Parks.

Sights to See

★ **Ham House.** Ham House stands to the west of Richmond Park, overlooking the Thames and nearly opposite the oddly named Eel Pie Island. The house was built in 1610 by Sir Thomas Vavasour, knight marshal to James I, then refurbished later the same century by the Duke and Duchess of Lauderdale, who, although not particularly nice (a contemporary called the duchess "the coldest friend and the most violent enemy that ever was known"), managed to produce one of the finest houses in Britain at the time. Now that £2 million has been sunk into restoring Ham House—a project overseen by the National Trust—its splendor can be appreciated afresh. The formerly empty library has been filled with 17th- and 18th-century volumes; the original decorations in the Great Hall, Round Gallery, and Great Staircase have been replicated; and all the furniture and fittings, on permanent loan from the V&A, have been cleaned and restored. The 17th-century gardens merit a visit in their own right. You can reach Ham from Richmond on Bus 65 or 371, or by one of Greater London's most pleasant rural walks, lasting half an hour or so, along the eastern riverbank south from Richmond Bridge. ⊠ *Ham St., Richmond,* ☎ *020/8940–1950.* ▣ *House £5, gardens free.* ☉ *Mar.–Oct., Sat.–Wed. 1–5; Nov.–Dec., weekends 1–5. Tube: Richmond.* 🐾

Marble Hill House. On the northern bank of the Thames, almost opposite Ham House, stands another mansion, this one a near-perfect example of a Palladian villa. Marble Hill House was built during the 1720s by George II for his mistress, the "exceedingly respectable and respected" Henrietta Howard. Later the house was occupied by Mrs. Fitzherbert, who was secretly married to the Prince Regent (later George IV) in 1785. Marble Hill House was restored in 1901 and opened to the public two years later, looking very much like it did in Georgian times. A ferry service operates during the summer from Ham House (☞ *above*) across the river; access by foot is a half-hour walk south along the west bank from Richmond Bridge. ⊠ *Richmond Rd., Twickenham,* ☎ *020/ 8892–5115.* ▣ *£3.* ☉ *Easter–Sept., daily 10–6; Oct.–Easter, Wed.–Sun. 10–4. Tube: Richmond.*

☺ **Richmond Park.** Charles I enclosed this one in 1637 for hunting purposes, as with practically all the other parks. Unlike the others, however, Richmond Park still has wild red and fallow deer roaming its 2,470 acres of grassland and heath and the oldest oaks you're likely to see—vestiges of the medieval forests that once encroached on London from all sides. White Lodge, inside the park, was built for George II in 1729. Edward VIII was born here; now it houses the Royal Ballet School. You can walk from the park past the fine 18th-century houses in and around Richmond Hill to the river, admiring first the view from the top. At the Thames, you may notice Quinlan Terry's recent Richmond Riverside development, which met with the approval of England's architectural adviser, Prince Charles, for its classical facades and was vilified by many others for playing it safe. *Tube: Richmond.*

<table>
<tr><td>NEED A
BREAK?</td><td>The **Cricketers,** on Richmond Green, serves a good pub lunch. The modern, partially glass-roofed **Caffé Mamma,** on Hill Street, serves inexpensive Italian food. **Beeton's,** on Hill Rise, offers a good, traditional English breakfast, lunch, and afternoon tea, as well as proper dinners.</td></tr>
</table>

★ **Syon House.** Home to Their Graces the Duke and Duchess of Northumberland, this is one of England's most sumptuous stately houses; it has recently been renovated, and it is certainly the only one that's reachable by the London Underground. Several tube stops away from the center city on the District Line, the house is set in a 55-acre park landscaped by Capability Brown. The core of the house is Tudor—two of Henry VIII's queens, Catherine Howard and Lady Jane Grey, made pit stops here before they were sent to the Tower—but the house was redone in the Georgian style in 1761 by famed decorator Robert Adam. He had just returned from studying the sites of classical antiquity in Italy and created two rooms here worthy of any Caesar: the entryway is an amazing study in black and white, pairing neoclassic marbles with antique bronzes, while the Ante-Room contains 12 enormous verdantique columns surmounted by statues of gold—this, no less, was meant to be a waiting room for the duke's servants and retainers. The Red Drawing Room is covered with crimson Spitalfields silk, while the Long Gallery is one of Adam's noblest creations (it was used by Cary Grant and Robert Mitchum for a duel in the 1958 film *The Grass is Greener*). Elsewhere on the grounds are a nature center, a butterfly house, and a Victorian glass conservatory that is famous among connoisseurs for its Victorian charm. ⌗ *Syon Park, Brentford,* ☎ *020/8560–0881.* ⛨ *£5.80.* ☼ *Early Apr.–late Oct., Wed.–Thurs. and Sun. 11–5. Tube: Gunnersbury, then take Bus 237 or 267 to Brentlea stop.* ⛲

Hampton Court Palace

★ Some 20 mi from central London, on a loop of the Thames upstream from Richmond, lies one of London's oldest royal palaces, more like a small town in size and requiring a day of your time to do it justice. The magnificent Tudor brick house was begun in 1514 by Cardinal Wolsey, the ambitious and worldly lord chancellor (roughly, prime minister) of England and archbishop of York. He wanted it to be the absolute best palace in the land, and in this he succeeded so effectively that Henry VIII grew deeply envious, whereupon Wolsey felt obliged to give Hampton Court to the king. Henry moved in in 1525, adding a great hall and chapel, and proceeded to live much of his rambunctious life here. James I made further improvements at the beginning of the 17th century, but by the end of the century the palace was getting rather run-down. Plans were drawn up by the joint monarchs William III and Mary II to demolish the building and replace it with a still larger and more splendid structure, in conscious emulation of the great palace of Versailles outside Paris. However, the royal purse wouldn't stretch quite that far. It was decided to keep the original buildings but add a new complex adjoining them at the rear, for which Wren was commissioned, and his graceful south wing is one of the highlights of the whole palace. (A serious fire badly damaged some of Wren's chambers in 1986, but they were restored and opened again in 1992, with some of the Tudor features he had covered up uncovered again.) William and, especially, Mary loved Hampton Court and left their mark on the place—see their fine collections of Delftware and other porcelain.

The site beside the slow-moving Thames is perfect. The palace itself—steeped in history, hung with priceless paintings, full of echoing, cobbled courtyards and cavernous Tudor kitchens (complete with deer pies and cooking pots), not to mention the ghost of Catherine Howard screaming her innocence of adultery to an unheeding Henry VIII—is set in a fantastic array of ornamental gardens, lakes, and ponds. Among the horticultural highlights are an Elizabethan knot garden, Henry VIII's Pond Garden, the enormous conical yews around the Fountain Garden, and the Great Vine near the Banqueting House, planted in 1768 and still producing black Hamburg grapes, which you can buy in season. Best of all is the celebrated maze, which you enter to the north of the palace. It was planted in 1714 and is truly fiendish.

Royalty ceased living here with George III; poor George preferred the seclusion of Kew, where he was finally confined in his madness. The private apartments that range down one side of the palace are now occupied by pensioners of the Crown. Known as "grace and favor" apartments, they are among the most coveted homes in the country, with a surfeit of peace and history on their doorsteps. ⊠ *East Molesey,* ☏ *020/8977–8441.* ▣ *Apartments and maze £10, maze alone £2.30, grounds free.* ☉ *State apartments Apr.–Oct., Tues.–Sun. 9:30–6, Mon. 10:15–6; Nov.–Mar., Tues.–Sun. 9:30–4:30, Mon. 10:15–4:30; grounds daily 8–dusk.* ✎

2 DINING

No longer would Somerset Maugham be justified in warning, "If you want to eat well in England, have breakfast three times a day." Cool Brittania is now one of the hottest places around for restaurants of every cultural flavor, with London at its hip epicenter. Nearly everyone is passionate about food—even Lord Lloyd Webber, composer of *Cats* and *Phantom of the Opera*, has added restaurant critic to his expanding repertoire. After feasting on modern British cuisine, visit one (or two or three) of London's fabulous pubs for a nightcap. Hit the right one on the right night and watch that legendary British reserve melt away.

Updated by
Alex Wijeratna

A S ANYONE WHO READS the Sunday papers knows, London has had a restaurant boom or, rather, a restaurant atomic-bomb explosion. Natives are wondering: how far can this thing go? How many new, trendy, talked-out, flavor-of-the-month gastrodomes can the city support? Even the recent economic tightening of belts hasn't really slowed the onslaught. More than ever, London loves its restaurants—all 6,000 of them—from its be-there, wow-factor eateries to its tiny neighborhood joints, from pubs where young foodniks find their feet to swank boîtes where celebrity chefs launch their ego flights. You, too, will be smitten, since you will be spending, on average, 25% of your travel budget on eating out.

To appreciate London's rise in the culinary firmament, it helps to recall that at one time it was understood that the British ate to live while the French lived to eat. Change was slow in coming after the Second World War, when steamed puddings and overboiled brussels sprouts were still consumed on a daily basis by tweed-and-flannel-wrapped Brits. When people thought of British cuisine, fish-and-chips came to mind. The latter was a grab-and-gulp dish that tasted best wrapped in newspaper (a spoilsport bureaucracy decreed that this wasn't sanitary, so the days of peeping at the latest murder news through a film of oil came to an end). Then there was always shepherd's pie, ubiquitously available in pubs—though not made according to the song from *Sweeney Todd*, "with real shepherd in it." Visitors used to arrive in London and joke that the most compelling reason Britain conquered half the world was that its residents probably wanted some decent food. Didn't Britons invade Rajasthan just for a good curry?

Today, nearly everything on the culinary front has changed. New menus seem to evolve every five minutes as chefs outdo each other in creating hot spots that are all about the buzz of "being there." London's restaurant renaissance is credited to innovative chefs and inspired entrepreneurs. Sir Terence Conran, inventor of Habitat (British precursor to IKEA), began it all with Quaglino's, the first of the megarestaurants. His 650-seater Mezzo (☞ *below*) became the biggest restaurant in Europe when it opened in 1995, though he has since topped that with Bluebird (☞ *below*), complete with grocery store, fishmonger, florist, and produce market. His shiny Aurora and elegant Sartoria in Savile Row are just the latest additions to the string.

The biggest ego, though, probably belongs to Marco Pierre White, the first British chef to earn three Michelin stars for his restaurant, now at the Belle Epoque–flavored Oak Room (☞ *below*) at the Meridien. Although he is rumored to be hanging up his pans for good soon, his empire is everywhere: the Criterion, Mirabelle, Titanic, and Quo Vadis (☞ *below* for all) are also his creations. Another empire builder who has been or who is considering retrenching somewhat is Jean-Christophe Novelli—his staunchly modern French-Euro cuisine brings in the trendies to Novelli W8 in chic Kensington (☞ Maison Novelli, *below*), but he has pulled back after exhausting himself at the smart Les Saveurs in Mayfair.

There are moves on the haute cuisine scene, too. La Tante Claire (☞ *below*) is now at the Berkeley Hotel in Knightsbridge, and its old premises have been taken over by master chef Gordon Ramsay. There are, of course, many more stars of this new celebrity category (restaurateurs and chefs), but you'll have to read about them when you get here—which you can easily do by picking up any newspaper. To keep up with the onslaught, they have about 15 restaurant reviewers apiece. Read up on the newest places in the food supplements of the newspapers, especially the Saturday and Sunday editions.

Fortunately, London also does a good job of catering to people interested more in satisfying their appetites without breaking the bank than in following the latest food trends. We have tried to strike a balance in our listings between these extremes, and we've included hip and happening places, neighborhood spots, ethnic alternatives, and old favorites. There are about 50 cuisines on offer in London, and ethnic restaurants have always been a good bet here, especially the thousands of Indian restaurants, since Londoners see a good curry as their birthright. Londoners are busy enlarging their purview to encompass Malaysian, Spanish, and Turkish places, a drove of Thai restaurants, a new North African pack, and a wave of Japanese places. With all this going on, traditional British food, when you track it down, appears as one more exotic cuisine in the pantheon.

As for cost, the democratization of restaurants does not necessarily mean smaller checks, and London is still not an inexpensive city. Damage-control methods include making lunch your main meal—the very top places often have bargain lunch menus, halving the price of evening à la carte—and ordering a second appetizer instead of an entrée, to which few places should object. (Note that an appetizer, usually known as a "starter" or "first course," is sometimes called an "entrée," as it is in France, and an entrée in England is dubbed the "main course" or simply "mains.") Seek out fixed-price menus, and watch for hidden extras on the check: "cover," bread, or vegetables charged separately, and service. Many restaurants exclude service charges from the menu (which the law obliges them to display outside), then add 10%–15% to the check, or else stamp SERVICE NOT INCLUDED along the bottom, in which case you should add the 10%–15% yourself. Don't pay twice for service—unscrupulous restaurateurs may add service, then leave the total on the credit-card slip blank, hoping for more.

Two final caveats: first, is the roast beef of old England going to give you mad cow disease? In 1996, there was a major cull of English cattle infected with feed gone bad, with a reprise in late 1997 to early 1998. British butchers can now export their beef once more, and by the time you read this you will safely be able to enjoy succulent beef still on the bone. But most restaurants still have some form of disclaimer for the purity of their beef, and you can bet they're not lying if they say it's safe. Second, beware of Sundays. Many restaurants are closed on this day, especially in the evening; likewise public holidays. Over the Christmas period, London shuts down completely—only hotels will be prepared to feed you. When in doubt, call ahead. It's a good idea to book a table at all times, but you'll have gotten the idea by now.

For approximate costs, *see* the dining price chart, *in* Smart Travel Tips A to Z.

Mayfair

AMERICAN/CASUAL

££ ✕ **Smollensky's on the Strand.** This American-style bar-restaurant is useful for those with children in tow, especially on weekends, when the young are fed burgers, fish sticks, and "Kids' Koktails" and are taken off your hands by sundry clowns and magicians on weekend lunchtimes. The grown-ups' menu favors (fresh, additive-free) red meat, with several cuts of steak the specialty, all served with fries and a choice of sauces. There are potato skins, salads, sandwiches, and fish—from New England to New Mex—and a couple of vegetarian choices. ✉ *105 The Strand, W1,* ☎ *020/7497–2101. AE, DC, MC, V. Tube: Charing Cross.*

London Dining *(Boxes Refer to Detail Maps)*

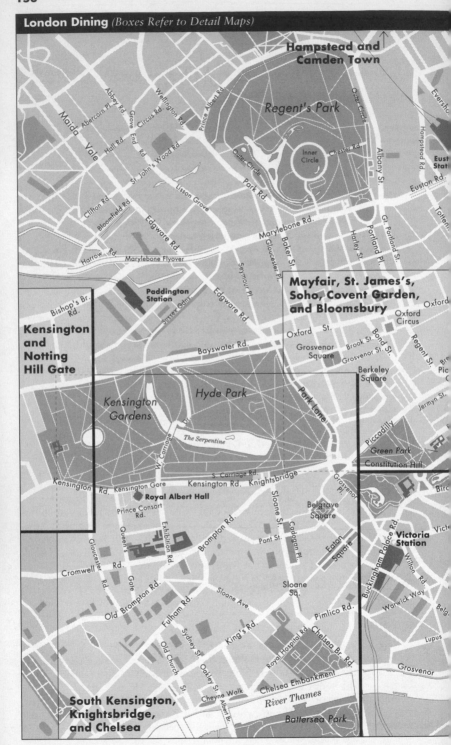

Hampstead and Camden Town

Regent's Park

Inner Circle

Maida Vale

Abbey Rd.

Abercorn Pl.

Grove End Rd.

Hall Rd.

Circus Rd.

Wellington Rd.

Prince Albert Rd.

St. John's Wood Rd.

Outer Circle

Chester Rd.

Albany St.

Eust Stat

Eversho

Hampstead Rd.

Euston Rd.

Tottenh.

Clifton Rd.

Bloomfield Rd.

Lisson Grove

Edgware Rd.

Park Rd.

Gt. Portland St.

Portland Pl.

Harley St.

Baker St.

Marylebone Rd.

Gloucester Pl.

Harrow Rd.

Marylebone Flyover

Seymour Pl.

Edgware Rd.

Paddington Station

Sussex Gdns.

Mayfair, St. James's, Soho, Covent Garden, and Bloomsbury

Oxford

Oxford St.

Oxford Circus

Bishop's Br. Rd.

Bayswater Rd.

Grosvenor Square

Brook St.

Bond St.

Grosvenor St.

Regent St.

Bre

Pic

Kensington and Notting Hill Gate

Berkeley Square

Hyde Park

Park Lane

Jermyn St.

Kensington Gardens

W. Carriage Dr.

The Serpentine

Piccadilly

Green Park

Constitution Hill

Kensington Rd.

Kensington Gore

S. Carriage Rd.

Kensington Rd.

Knightsbridge

Grosvenor Pl.

Birc

Royal Albert Hall

Prince Consort Rd.

Queen's Gate

Exhibition Rd.

Brompton Rd.

Sloane St.

Pont St.

Cadogan Pl.

Belgrave Square

Eaton Square

Buckingham Palace Rd.

Victoria Station

Vict

Wilton Rd.

Belg

Gloucester Rd.

Cromwell Rd.

Old Brompton Rd.

Fulham Rd.

Sloane Ave.

Sloane Sq.

King's Rd.

Pimlico Rd.

Warwick Way

Lupus

Sydney St.

Oakley St.

Old Church St.

Cheyne Walk

Albert Br.

Royal Hospital Rd.

Chelsea Br. Rd.

Chelsea Embankment

River Thames

Grosvenor

South Kensington, Knightsbridge, and Chelsea

Battersea Park

159

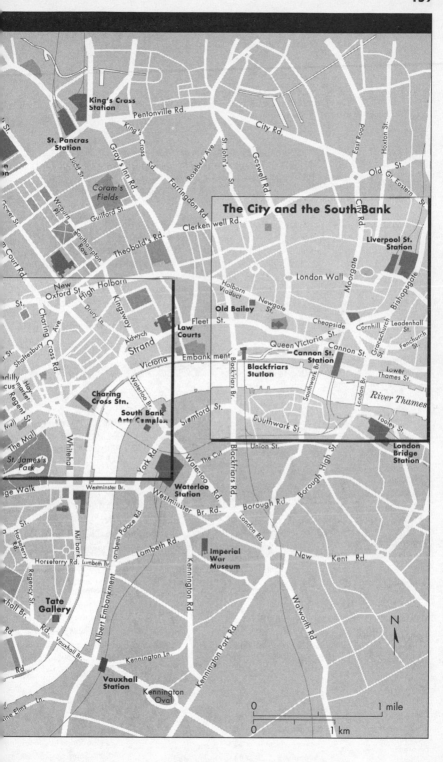

160

Dining in Mayfair, St. James's, Soho, Covent Garden, and Bloomsbury

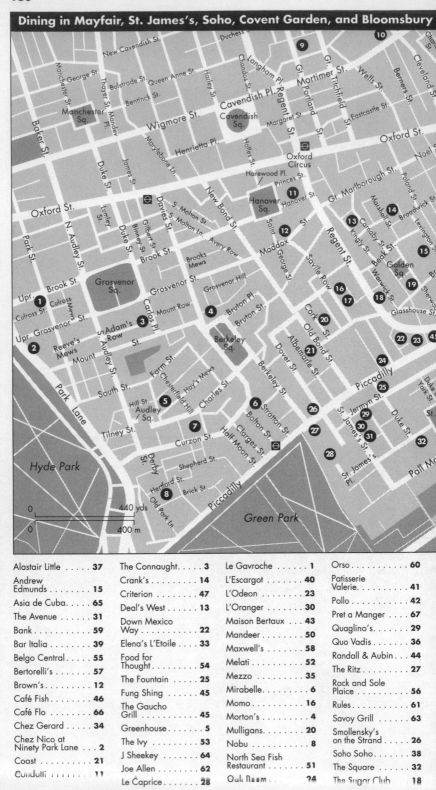

Alastair Little 37

Andrew Edmunds 15

Asia de Cuba 65

The Avenue 31

Bank 59

Bar Italia 39

Belgo Central 55

Bertorelli's 57

Brown's 12

Café Fish 46

Café Flo 66

Chez Gerard 34

Chez Nico at Ninety Park Lane . . . 2

Coast 21

Condotti 11

The Connaught 3

Crank's 14

Criterion 47

Deal's West 13

Down Mexico Way 22

Elena's L'Etoile . . . 33

Food for Thought 54

The Fountain 25

Fung Shing 45

The Gaucho Grill 45

Greenhouse 5

The Ivy 53

J Sheekey 64

Joe Allen 62

Le Caprice 28

Le Gavroche 1

L'Escargot 40

L'Odeon 23

L'Oranger 30

Maison Bertaux . . . 43

Mandeer 50

Maxwell's 58

Melati 52

Mezzo 35

Mirabelle 6

Momo 16

Morton's 4

Mulligans 20

Nobu 8

North Sea Fish Restaurant 51

Oak Room 24

Orso 60

Patisserie Valerie 41

Pollo 42

Pret a Manger 67

Quaglino's 29

Quo Vadis 36

Randall & Aubin . . 44

The Ritz 27

Rock and Sole Plaice 56

Rules 61

Savoy Grill 63

Smollensky's on the Strand 26

Soho Soho 38

The Square 32

The Sugar Club . . . 18

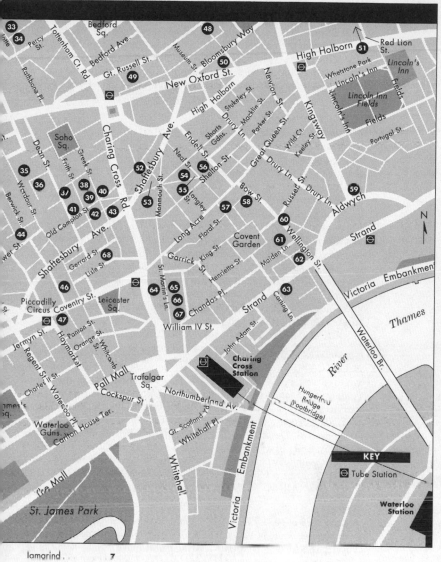

Tamarind	**7**
Titanic	**19**
Truckles of Pied Bull Yard	**48**
Villandry	**9**
Wagamama	**49**
Wok Wok	**10**
Zinc Bar & Grill . . .	**17**

£ ✕ **Condotti.** In a neighborhood not known for its casual dining options, this elegant pizzeria is like a breath of fresh air. Anyone familiar with Pizza Express will know the menu already—because this also belongs to the founder of that chain. The Veneziana (with onions, pine nuts, sultanas, and capers) is everyone's fave, and a donation goes to the Venice in Peril Fund when you order it. Or try the King Edward, with a potato base instead of bread, and check out the Paolozzis on the walls. ⊠ *4 Mill St., W1,* ☎ *020/7499–1308. AE, DC, MC, V. Tube: Oxford Circus.*

BRITISH TRADITIONAL

£££ ✕ **Greenhouse.** Tucked away behind the Mayfair mansions in a cute, cobbled mews is this elegant salon for people who like their food big and strong. You sit among extravagant topiary and men in black—with chauffeurs to match—to partake of British menus in the style of the now-departed, famous-from-TV chef Gary Rhodes: *faggots* (a type of meatball, once reviled), artichoke risotto, and trad sticky puds are all too good to miss. ⊠ *27A Hay's Mews, W1,* ☎ *020/7499–3331. Reservations essential. AE, DC, MC, V. No lunch Sat. Tube: Green Park.*

£–££ ✕ **Browns.** Unpretentious, crowd-pleasing, child-friendly English feeding is accomplished here at the former establishment of the bespoke tailors Messrs. Cooling and Wells, now converted to Edwardian style by the group behind the very successful regional Browns eateries (the Oxford and Cambridge ones are student stalwarts). The classic Browns steak and Guinness pie is still on the menu, but gravlax, *moules* (mussels), roasted peppers, salads, and pastas now predominate. ⊠ *47 Maddox St., W1,* ☎ *020/7491–4565. AE, DC, MC, V. Tube: Oxford Circus.*

CONTEMPORARY

£££ ✕ **Coast.** This former car showroom is now a posing palace of cool white curves, a piece of art that also draws a miniversion of itself (via computer) on your check. It features a *slightly* pretentious menu that careens all over the world (Spanish *planchada* bean soup; Welsh black beef, foie gras, and quail eggs; yellowfin tuna with peanut butter and Asian greens). Desserts, such as the signature dish of mille-feuille of chocolate and pistachio pastry with frozen yogurt, follow the same interesting combinations. Avoid downstairs, which is like the set from Stanley Kubrick's film *2001.* ⊠ *26B Albermarle St., W1,* ☎ *020/ 7495–5999. AE, MC, V. Tube: Green Park.*

FRENCH

££££ ✕ **Chez Nico at Ninety Park Lane.** Those with refined palates and very deep pockets would be well advised not to miss Nico Ladenis's exquisite cuisine, served in this suitably hushed and plush Louis XV dining room next to the Grosvenor House Hotel (☞ Chapter 3). Autodidact Nico is one of the world's great chefs, and he's famous for knowing it. The menu is stately with heavenly light touches. There is no salt on the table—ask for some at your peril. It's all more affordable in daylight, proffering set menus from £25 for three courses. ⊠ *90 Park La., W1,* ☎ *020/7409–1290. Reservations essential. Jacket and tie. AE, DC, MC, V. Closed Sun. and 3 wks in Aug, no lunch Sat. Tube: Marble Arch.*

££££ ✕ **Le Gavroche.** Albert Roux's son, Michel, retains many of his father's
★ "capital C" Classical dishes and has added his own style to this place, once considered London's finest restaurant. The basement dining room is comfortable and sedate, pleasing only if your idea of riveting decor is low-ceilinged and accented with potted plants and bland modern paintings. Yet again, the set lunch is relatively affordable at £37 (for canapés and three courses, plus mineral water, a half-bottle of wine, coffee, and petits fours). In fact, it's the only way to eat here if you don't have a generous expense account at your disposal—which most patrons do. You must reserve at least one week in advance. ⊠ *43 Upper Brook St., W1,*

☎ *020/7408–0881. Reservations essential. Jacket and tie. AE, DC, MC, V. Closed weekends and 10 days at Christmas. Tube: Marble Arch.*

££££ ✕ **Mirabelle.** This is Marco Pierre White doing what he does best—
★   taking over an age-old establishment, licking it into shape, and turning its fortunes round. He did it with Criterion (☞ *below*), and now he is wowing the critics with this one. The decor is in-your-face lavish, while the food is White's usual excellent interpretation of French with a hint of Italian, with fewer frills on the price. The MPW magic with seafood is in evidence, some meat creations are remarkable (steak with snails), and the range of chocolate desserts is absolutely gutsy. ⊠ *56 Curzon St., W1, ☎ 020/7499–4636. Reservations essential. AE, DC, MC, V. Tube: Green Park.*

££££ ✕ **Oak Room.** Bad boy Marco Pierre White used to enjoy Jaggerlike fame
★   from his TV appearances and gossip-column reports of his complicated love life, feuds, and random eruptions of fury. These days, he is less concerned with newsprint and more with building his substantial restaurant empire. Still, MPW's hands are often wielding the pans here (but for how much longer, nobody knows) at the restaurant of Le Meridien Piccadilly (☞ Chapter 3), which enjoys one of London's most spectacular settings—all Belle Epoque soaring ceilings and gilded bits—and palms and paintings, not to mention the crisp napery and batteries of flatware. ⊠ *Le Meridien, 21 Piccadilly, W1, ☎ 020/7437–0202. Reservations essential. Jacket and tie. AE, DC, MC, V. Tube: Piccadilly Circus.*

££££ ✕ **The Square.** Young chef Philip Howard's sophisticated set menus
★   are in the French haute tradition, with ideas from all over grafted on. Some examples will give the best idea: roast foie gras with caramelized endive and late picked muscat grapes or a velouté of truffles with *girolle* (chanterelle) tortellini (wild mushrooms are high on his shopping list); then an herb-crusted saddle of lamb with white bean puree, or a roast cod with creamed potato and truffles. All are arranged carefully and symmetrically, much like the high-ceilinged, apricot-colored room. Some desserts—like the fantastic melted chocolate cake—come on square glass plates because of the restaurant's name (which actually refers to its previous home on St. James's Square). The grown-up clientele is heavy on business types who appreciate impeccable service, complete with a friendly (and necessary—the wine list has the heft of a novel) sommelier. ⊠ *6–10 Bruton St., SW1, ☎ 020/7839–8787. Reservations essential. AE, MC, V. No lunch weekends. Tube: Green Park.*

£££ ✕ **Criterion.** This spectacular, neo-Byzantine mirrored marble hall, which first opened in 1874, is heavy on the awe factor, with dishes to match, and Marco Pierre White's team scores highly. He doesn't cook here, but some of his well-known and often-copied dishes appear on a menu whose divisions include one headed "Farinaceous Dishes"—where you'll find his ballotine of salmon with herbs and *fromage blanc,* for instance. The glamour of the soaring golden ceiling, peacock-blue theater-size drapes, oil paintings, and attentive Gallic service adds up to an elegant night out. ⊠ *Piccadilly Circus, W1, ☎ 020/7930–0488. AE, DC, MC, V. Tube: Piccadilly Circus.*

££–£££ ✕ **L'Odéon.** This contribution to London's mania for giant restaurants overlooks Regent Street in a former airline office, its long, low dimensions peculiarly reminiscent of an aircraft, despite the gauzy partitions throughout. Food is elevated French-bistro-style with the usual modish Italian additions—grilled fish and meats, wild mushrooms on brioche toast—and is far more affordable in set-menu form, available for lunch and before 7 PM. Tables by the huge arched windows are fun for people-watching. ⊠ *65 Regent St., W1, ☎ 020/7287–1400. AE, DC, MC, V. Tube: Piccadilly Circus.*

FRENCH/BRITISH TRADITIONAL

££££   ✕ **The Connaught.** This charming and very grand mahogany-paneled,
★   velvet-upholstered, and crystal-chandeliered dining room belongs to
        the absolutely exclusive eponymous hotel (☞ Chapter 3). Waiters
        wear tails, tables must be booked far in advance, and prices are fear-
        some; but the restaurant remains London's most-respected traditional
        dining room, with famed French chef Michel Bourdin still in charge
        of the kitchens after 25 years. There is nothing wild here, only the mush-
        rooms and fabulous game—venison, guinea fowl, pigeon (not local
        birds)—presented with traditional trimmings or perhaps with some con-
        fection of wild mushrooms. "Luncheon dishes" from the trolley fol-
        low a pattern according to the day of the week (if this is Wednesday,
        it must be beef) and are not as exorbitant as they seem at first, because
        the price includes a starter and dessert. The table d'hôte changes daily.
        The Connaught is by no means a fashionable place, but it is never out
        of fashion. ✉ *Carlos Pl., W1,* ☎ *020/7499–7070. Reservations essential.
        Jacket and tie. AE, DC, MC, V. Tube: Green Park.*

INDIAN

££££   ✕ **Tamarind.** Tamarind led the new wave of '90s Indian restaurants
        and seems to be keeping up the pace. The ambience in this Emily Tod-
        hunter–designed Mayfair basement is best described as sumptuous. This
        is a chic curry zone, with golden arches, framed textiles, gilded stair-
        cases, and copper plates. It is not cheap, but dishes like *hari machch*
        (John Dory with wispy deep-fried spinach) and creamy *buk har* (black
        lentils from the North West Frontier) are executed with precision. Try
        the puddings—they're all sweet and good (which doesn't always apply
        to service). Many say Tamarind does the best curry in London; lots of
        posh Indians eat here, which must be a good sign. ✉ *20 Queen St.,
        W1,* ☎ *020/7629–3561. AE, DC, MC, V. Tube: Green Park.*

IRISH

££   ✕ **Mulligans.** Mulligans is straight out of Dublin, down to the draught
        Guinness and copies of the *Irish Times* in the upstairs bar. Downstairs,
        in the upscale restaurant department, order traditional dishes such as
        steak with Guinness and oyster pie or Irish stew with homey accom-
        paniments like colcannon (buttery mashed potatoes with cabbage), then
        a big Irish pudding. ✉ *13–14 Cork St., W1,* ☎ *020/7409–1370. AE,
        DC, MC, V. Closed Sun., no lunch Sat. Tube: Green Park.*

JAPANESE

££££   ✕ **Nobu.** Nobuyaki Matsuhisa already has New York, Tokyo, and Los
        Angeles, and now he's taking London, with the same formula of new-
        style sashimi with a Peruvian influence (such as salmon, ever so slightly
        seared in sesame seed oil), plus the famous *omakase* (chef's choice) meals.
        Nobu is in the Metropolitan (☞ Chapter 3), one of London's hippest
        hotels, with staff, attitude, clientele, and prices to match, and a mini-
        malissimo decor. ✉ *Metropolitan hotel, 19 Old Park La., W1,* ☎ *020/
        7447–4747. Reservations essential. AE, DC, MC, V. No lunch week-
        ends. Tube: Hyde Park.*

MEXICAN

££   ✕ **Down Mexico Way.** London is warming up to Tex-Mex, and here
        among the usual tortillas are a few (somewhat overpriced) adventur-
        ous numbers, such as tuna with peach salsa or pollo ala Azteza (chicken
        with cocoa and chili). Look for the beautiful Spanish ceramic tiles. Avoid
        evenings here if you want a quiet night out—the place is often taken
        over by party animals. ✉ *25 Swallow St., W1,* ☎ *020/7437–9895. AE,
        DC, MC, V. Tube: Piccadilly Circus.*

St. James's

BRITISH TRADITIONAL

£ ✕ **The Fountain.** At the back of Fortnum & Mason is this old-fash-
★ ioned restaurant, as frumpy and as popular as a boarding-school ma-
tron, serving delicious light meals, toasted snacks, sandwiches, and ice
cream sodas. During the day, go for the Welsh rarebit or cold game
pie; in the evening, a no-frills rump steak is a typical option. It's just
the place for afternoon tea and ice cream sundaes after the Royal
Academy or Bond Street shopping, and for pretheater meals. ✉ *181
Piccadilly, W1,* ☎ *020/7734–8040. AE, DC, MC, V. Closed Sun.
Tube: Green Park.*

FRENCH

£££ ✕ **L'Oranger.** This offshoot of Aubergine (☞ *below*) in Chelsea fol-
★ lows a similar route of French-Mediterranean cuisine. The dishes can
reach gobsmacking precision and perfection: a ravioli of lamb and tomato
consummé; monkfish tail wrapped in crushed black pepper, spinach,
and *antiboise* (tomato, olive oil, and basil) sauce; fig *sablé* (pastry) with
spiced pear and cinnamon ice cream. The conservatory room with its
train of tables up the middle is romantic, plus there's a little courtyard
where the last duel in London was fought. The all-French waiters are
courteous and not snobby. ✉ *5 St. James's St., SW1,* ☎ *020/7839–
3774. Reservations essential. AE, DC, MC, V. Closed Sun., no lunch
Sat. Tube: Green Park.*

£–££ ✕ **Zinc Bar & Grill.** Head to the Zinc Bar (another one of Conran's restau-
★ rants) because it's fun, it's off Regent Street, it's underrated, and it kind
of works. This brasserie-rotisserie has an open (zinc) bar that heaves
with groups of music and PR girls. Try a dozen rock oysters, a juicy
plateau de fruit de mer (seafood platter), calves' liver with bacon and
gravy, or sip a "Pink Zinc"—champagne and raspberry liqueur. There
are good pre-theater and prix fixe deals. ✉ *21 Heddon St., W1,* ☎
020/7255–8899. AE, DC, MC, V. Tube: Piccadilly Circus.

FRENCH/BRITISH TRADITIONAL

££££ ✕ **Morton's.** If you're near Mayfair's clubland of Berkeley Square and
fancy an elegant meal, try Morton's. On the north side of this beautiful square, the first-floor dining room is considered one of the most
serene in London, and the classic French cooking proves worthy of the
setting. It's not cheap, mind you, not for a starter of escalope of foie
gras with muscat grapes, walnuts, and dandelion; a simple entrée of
risotto of wild mushrooms; or the tournedos Rossini (excellent though
it may be). Downstairs is a more raucous members-only bar. Watch
out for foxy Mayfair ladies of a certain age, roué business brokers, and
cufflinked wise guys on the razz. ✉ *28 Berkeley Sq., W1,* ☎ *020/7493–
7171. Reservations essential. AE, DC, MC, V. Tube: Green Park.*

££££ ✕ **The Ritz.** Constantly accused of being one of London's prettiest dining rooms, this Belle Epoque palace of marble, gilt, and trompe l'oeil
would moisten even Marie Antoinette's eye; add the view over Green
Park and the Ritz's secret sunken garden, and it seems obsolete to consider eating. But the British-French cuisine stands up to the visual onslaught, with costly morsels (foie gras, lobster, truffles, caviar, etc.) that
are superrich, all served with a flourish. Old retainers still take great
pride in this smooth operation and are still here despite the hotel's change
of ownership. Englishness is wrested from Louis XVI by a daily roast
"from the trolley." A three-course luncheon menu at £34 and a four-
course dinner at £49 make the check more bearable, but the wine list
is pricey. A Friday and Saturday dinner dance sweetly maintain a dying
tradition. ✉ *150 Piccadilly, W1,* ☎ *020/7493–8181. Reservations essential. Jacket and tie. AE, DC, MC, V. Tube: Green Park.*

MODERN BRITISH

££££ ✗ **Le Caprice.** Secreted in a small street behind the Ritz (☞ Chapter
  ★   3), Le Caprice may command the deepest loyalty of any restaurant in
       London because it gets everything right: the glamorous, glossy black
       Eva Jiricna interior; the perfect pitch of the informal but respectful ser-
       vice; the food, halfway between Euro-peasant and fashion plate. This
       food—crispy duck and watercress salad; seared scallops with bacon
       and sorrel; risotto *nero* (with squid); calves' liver with caramelized shal-
       lots, mash, and sage; grilled rabbit with black olive polenta; and di-
       vine desserts, too—has no business being so good, because the other
       reason everyone comes here is that everyone else does, which leads to
       the best people-watching in town (apart from at its sister restaurant,
       the Ivy; ☞ Covent Garden, *below*). ⊠ *Arlington House, Arlington St.,
       SW1,* ☎ *020/7629–2239. Reservations essential. AE, DC, MC, V.
       Tube: Green Park.*

£££   ✗ **The Avenue.** Huge, loud, and swanky, especially since it got permission
       to ply its City-glitzy clientele with beverages way beyond their bedtime
       (here that's until 1 AM Monday–Saturday), this was London's first restau-
       rant to be owned by committee. Unlike the horse designed by committee
       (a camel), it has worked out fairly well, emulating New York singles-
       heavy, dining-as-theater glamour, with a long, rose-pink uplighted
       glass bar and a very '80s bank of blinking TV screens at the entrance.
       The food is pretty good, generic Euro-Brit with the usual rash of Med-
       veg starters and sides. Set menus are competitively priced, but the con-
       tent does not always deliver, although the service is friendly. ⊠ *7–9 St.
       James's St., SW1,* ☎ *020/7321–2111. AE, DC, MC, V. Tube: Green
       Park.*

£££   ✗ **Quaglino's.** Now well into its first decade, Sir Terence Conran's
       original huge restaurant, "Quags," is *the* out-of-towners' posttheater
       or celebration destination, while Londoners like its late hours. To the
       cognoscenti it's *history,* but the aura never fails to impress first-timers.
       The gigantic sunken restaurant boasts a glamorous staircase, "Crustacea
       Altar," large bar, and live jazz music. The food is fashionably pan-Eu-
       ropean with some Asian trimmings—crab with mirin and soy; noodles
       with ginger, chili, and cilantro; venison with leek and prune conserve;
       roast crayfish. Desserts come from somewhere between the Paris bistro
       and the English nursery, and wine from the old world and the new, some
       bottles at modest prices. ⊠ *16 Bury St., SW1,* ☎ *020/7930–6767.
       Reservations essential. AE, DC, MC, V. Tube: Green Park.*

LATIN AMERICAN

££   ✗ **The Gaucho Grill.** Some say these are the best steaks in London, but
       that's probably overstating it. Nevertheless, this chain of four Argen-
       tinian chophouses (the other locations are Canary Wharf, Hampstead,
       and the City) are reasonably priced and unreconstructed in their rev-
       erence for meat. The steaks are shipped vacuum packed from Buenos
       Aires, and are cut to order. The biggest they've grilled is 1.8 kg (4 lbs!),
       but the standard sizes are 225 g and 300 g (8 oz and 10½ oz). There is
       not much for vegetarians, but it's great for a beef fix. ⊠ *19 Swallow
       St., W1,* ☎ *020/7734–4040. AE, DC, MC, V. Tube: Piccadilly Circus.*

NORTH AFRICAN

£££   ✗ **Momo.** Several years old now, Momo is still one of the hottest tick-
       ets in town. If you can book a table, go. Algerian-born Mourad Ma-
       zouz—Momo to his friends—has stormed beau London with his
       casbah-like, Moroccan-inspired North African restaurant, set in a cul-
       de-sac behind Regent Street. Going Momo is a real experience. The
       seats are low and placed close together, there's a resident DJ, and
       there's often live music. The Gnaouas—a Sudanese four-piece drum
       troupe—sometimes chant their way through the awestruck diners.

Downstairs is the hot and souk-like members-only Kemia Bar, and next door is Mô—a Moroccan tearoom, open to all. The restaurant menu, which is based on pastilla, tagine, and couscous, doesn't quite match the excitement of the joint; lamb merguez is recommended. Luckily, the CD of the restaurant, *Arabesque,* is now on sale. ⊠ *25 Heddon St., W1,* ☎ *020/7434–4040. Reservations essential. AE, DC, MC, V. Tube: Piccadilly Circus.*

Soho

CAFÉS

£ ✗ **Maison Bertaux.** On two floors in central Soho, this French patisserie is not in the least dainty, but it is the kind of place to refuel after a shopping trek with a savory pastry at lunchtime, or a Danish midmorning, or even an early supper (it closes at 8 PM). The ancient rivalry with Valerie (☞ *below*) around the corner still obtains. ⊠ *28 Greek St., W1,* ☎ *020/7437–6007. No credit cards. Tube: Leicester Sq.*

£ ✗ **Patisserie Valerie.** Beloved of film-biz people, students, shoppers, and just about everyone else, this dark and antique pastry shop with café is cherished because nothing has changed in years. The cakes are wondrous creations; just to drool at the window is to enter a chocoholic's paradise. Valerie has also taken over the historic eatery called the Sagne, on Marylebone High Street—the interior there has remained in a French-*sud* time warp—and at the Royal Institute of British Architects, Portland Place, which remains a favored spot for lunch. ⊠ *44 Old Compton St., W1,* ☎ *020/7437–3466. AE, DC, MC, V. Tube: Leicester Sq.*

CHINESE

££ ✗ **Fung Shing.** This comfortable, cool-green restaurant is a cut above
★ the Lisle–Wardour Street crowd in both service and ambience, as well as food. The usual Chinatown options are supplemented by some exciting dishes. Salt-baked chicken, served on or off the bone with an accompanying bowl of intense broth, is essential. Reserve a table in the conservatory-style back room. ⊠ *15 Lisle St., WC2,* ☎ *020/7437–1539. AE, DC, MC, V. Tube: Leicester Sq.*

FRENCH

£–£££ ✗ **Mezzo.** Sir Terence Conran's gargantuan 650-seater rolls on, much maligned and beloved by turns. It's not as polished as Conran's new Sartoria in Savile Row, or efficient as Zinc on Heddon Street, but young office and evening crowds still like to hang out here. Downstairs is the restaurant proper, with its huge glass-walled kitchen, its Allen Jones murals, its grand piano and dance floor, and its French menu of seafood, snails, steak frites, and fig tart. Upstairs, the bar overlooks a canteen-style operation called Mezzonine, where bowls of coconut-galangal fish soup as well as grilled squid salad, red duck curry, and deep-fried bream are the order of the day. A late-night café-patisserie-newsstand is next door. ⊠ *100 Wardour St., W1,* ☎ *020/ 7314–4000. AE, DC, MC, V. Tube: Leicester Sq.*

£–££ ✗ **Villandry.** Heaven for food lovers, Villandry occupies a food hall ideal for the foodicenti. Lined with Italian-French dark-wood shelves, this cave of wonders positively heaves with goodies—French pâtés, Continental cheeses, fruit tarts, biscuits, and breads galore are just some of the tempting offerings. If you must indulge but can't wait to take a bite, there's a tearoom café and a fashionable dining room in which to enjoy some exquisite offerings; breakfast, lunch, and dinner are served daily. ⊠ *170 Great Portland St., W1,* ☎ *020/7631–3131. AE, MC, V. Tube: Great Portland St.*

ITALIAN

£   ✗ **Bar Italia.** A beloved Frith Street landmark, this caffeine and stand-up snack stop is a favorite oasis for photographers and admen, young Soho-ites, theatergoers, and clubbers—both early and late. Strong cappuccino or espresso is the order of the day, and it comes swift and sure from waiters who have seen the eddies of London life come and go for years. ⊠ 22 *Frith St., WI,* ☎ 020/7437–4520. *No credit cards. Tube: Leicester Sq.*

£   ✗ **Pollo.** A homey, boisterous, Italian café that's been here forever, and through which all Londoners pass during their student and/or clubbing days, this does very well for a quick feed with a bottle of house plonk pretheater or for an afternoon spaghetti carbonara. Watch the crowds in the evenings, though—it's no fun unless you're 18 and in art school. ⊠ *20 Old Compton St., W1,* ☎ 020/7734–5917. *No credit cards. Tube: Leicester Sq.*

MODERN BRITISH

££–£££   ✗ **Titanic.** London's Titanic initially rode high on the crest of a media wave, yet Marco Pierre White, the noted chef who opened this—the splashiest in the tide of trend-driven dining spots—-claims it was not inspired by the blockbuster film. But like the movie, this place has pulled in the crowds, plus a clientele of the young, loud, and fashionable (Peter O'Toole, the Marquess of Londonderry). Decor is Art Deco ocean liner. Dinner is fun and casual, ranging from fish-and-chips to squid ink risotto to sticky toffee, and prices are lower than you'd expect for this corner of town. ⊠ *81 Brewer St., W1,* ☎ 020/7437–1912. *Reservations essential. AE, DC, MC, V. Tube: Piccadilly Circus.*

MEDITERRANEAN

££   ✗ **Andrew Edmunds.** One wishes this always-busy, snug, and softly lighted eatery were larger and the seats more forgiving. Tucked away behind Oxford Street and Carnaby Street, it's a favorite with the film and media bunch, who lunch on the daily-changing set menu. The place is always jammed, thanks to its talent for consistently good food at realistic prices. Starters and mains range from a taste of Ireland through the Med to the Middle East. ⊠ *46 Lexington St., W1,* ☎ 020/7437–5708. *AE, MC, V. Tube: Oxford Circus, Piccadilly Circus.*

££   ✗ **Soho Soho.** The ground floor is a lively café bar with a (no reservations) rotisserie, while upstairs is a more formal and expensive restaurant. Inspiration comes from Provence, both in the olive-oil cooking style and the decor, with its murals, primary colors, and terracotta floor tiles. The rotisserie serves omelets, salads, charcuterie, and cheeses, plus a handful of such bistro dishes as suckling pig with Provinçal potatoes; herbed, grilled silver mullet; and tart Tatin. Or you can stay in the café-bar and have just a kir or a beer. ⊠ *11–13 Frith St., W1,* ☎ 020/7494–3491. *AE, DC, MC, V. Tube: Leicester Sq.*

MODERN BRITISH

££££   ✗ **Quo Vadis.** After a bust-up between Marco Pierre White, London's most celebrated chef, and Damien Hirst, Britain's most brilliant artist, whose art once adorned this reception bar and restaurant, MPW is now going it alone here. Instead of admiring Hirst's celebrated work, you can now see Andy Warhols and MPW's very own attempts at modern art (ostrich eggs, reptile skeletons, ram heads) occupying the former house of Karl Marx. Downstairs in the restaurant proper, the kitchen is serious and good, and highlights include lobster with garlic bulbs, seafood selections, and a champagne jelly with passion fruit. Artistry does not come cheap, but there are fine fixed-price lunches for £15–£18. ⊠ *26–29 Dean St., W1,* ☎ 020/7439–4809 *Reservations essential. AE, MC, V. Tube: Leicester Sq., Tottenham Court Rd.*

£££ ✗ **Alastair Little.** Little is one of London's most original—and most imitated—chefs, drawing inspiration from practically everywhere (Thailand, Japan, Scandinavia, France, North Africa, but chiefly Italy) and sometimes bringing it off brilliantly. His restaurant is provocatively stark and sparse so all attention focuses on the menu, which changes not once but twice daily to take advantage of the best ingredients. There will certainly be fish, but other than that, it's hard to predict. Look out also for his newer, smaller, cheaper version—but with the same name—just by Ladbroke Grove tube. ✉ *49 Frith St., W1,* ☎ *020/7734–5183. AE, DC, MC, V. Closed Sun., no lunch Sat. Tube: Leicester Sq.*

££–£££ ✗ **L'Escargot.** This ever-popular media haunt serves Anglo-French food in its ground-floor brasserie and its more formal upstairs restaurant. Reasonably priced wine from a comprehensive list sets off a robust ragout of spiced lamb or a simple, fresh poached or grilled fish. With its new face-lift, this place is reliable and relaxed. ✉ *48 Greek St., W1,* ☎ *020/7437–2679. AE, DC, MC, V. Closed Sun. Tube: Leicester Sq.*

££ ✗ **Café Fish.** This cheerful, bustling restaurant has an encyclopedic selection of fish—shark and turbot join the trout, halibut, salmon, and monkfish, arranged on the menu according to cooking method (chargrilled, steamed), plus a chalkboard full of daily specials. The Mediterranean and Asian accents usually delight. Try the bar and canteen on the ground floor for a cornucopia of shellfish, while in the upstairs restaurant you can linger longer over the likes of blackened Cajun tuna. This spot is great for pretheater. ✉ *36–40 Rupert St., W1,* ☎ *020/7287–8989. AE, DC, MC, V. Tube: Piccadilly Circus.*

MALAYSIAN

££ ✗ **Melati.** What amounts to a Malaysian café featuring wooden tables and, usually, lines at the door is a very useful place when you don't want to spend too much but are looking for a taste thrill. Whole stuffed squid and a tofu omelet, stir-fried vegetables, and the inevitable *nasi goreng* (spicy fried rice with tiny shrimp, onions, garlic, etc.) are among the dishes. ✉ *21 Great Windmill St., W1,* ☎ *020/7437–2745. AE, MC, V. Tube: Leicester Sq.*

PAN-ASIAN

£££ ✗ **The Sugar Club.** Peter Gordon has been clasped warmly to the Londoner's bosom with his fresh Austral-Asian fusion cooking—seared tuna with ginger on cucumber and soba noodles; panfried cod on asparagus, Parmesan, and saffron risotto; roast English duck breast on wok-fried black beans with tomato-chili jam; grilled kangaroo. It's one of those places so loved by the native glitterati (they're still talking about the night Mick Jagger graced the joint) that you have to reserve way, way ahead—two weeks in advance is recommended. ✉ *21 Warwick St., W1,* ☎ *020/7437–7776. Reservations essential. AE, DC, MC, V. Tube: Oxford Circus, Piccadilly Circus.*

£ ✗ **Wok Wok.** A bright primary-color decor, friendly service, and a menu of fresh soups, noodles, stir-fries and rice dishes from all over the Asias—Thailand, Vietnam, Malaysia, China, Japan, and Indonesia—ensure that this central branch of a small chain should run on and on, especially given the reasonable cost. ✉ *10 Frith St., W1,* ☎ *020/7437–7080. AE, DC, MC, V. Tube: Leicester Sq.*

SEAFOOD

££ ✗ **Randall & Aubin.** R&A's consultant chef Ed Baines is shredding up
★ town as London's sexiest new TV chef. The former public-school boy, ex-Armani model, and small screen gastro-hero now needs two bodyguards to keep admirers at bay when he does celebrity demonstrations. His converted French butchers' shop (with its white tiles, meat hooks,

and slab marble table tops) is one of London's buzziest champagne-oyster bars—bang in the middle of Soho's sexland. Go for the Loch Fyne oysters or half a lobster with chips. Peak time, it can take 20 minutes at the bar waiting for a seat, but the music rocks. Watch out Thursday to Saturday for the impromptu transvestite cabaret. Another R&A has opened in Bloomsbury. ⊠ *16 Brewer St., W1,* ☎ *020/7287–4447. Reservations not accepted. AE, DC, MC, V. Tube: Piccadilly Circus.*

THAI/AMERICAN

££ ✕ **Deals West.** Viscount Linley—Princess Margaret's son—and his two partners have hit on a winning formula here (and in the two other Dealses, at Chelsea Harbour and Hammersmith): an unlikely sounding merger between America and Thailand. Off Carnaby Street in a relaxed, barn-like diner with exposed brick walls, wooden floors, and beams, loud-ish music accompanies ribs, salads, and burgers—as well as Thai curries. Cocktails, extended hours, and live soul and funk on weekends make this popular with a young, after-work crowd. ⊠ *14–16 Fouberts Pl., W1,* ☎ *020/7287–1001. AE, DC, MC, V. Tube: Oxford Circus.*

VEGETARIAN

£ ✕ **Cranks.** This is a popular vegetarian chain (there are other branches at Great Newport Street, Adelaide Street, Tottenham Street, Canary Wharf, and Barrett Street), still serving meatless meals similar to those on the menu that put the chain on the map back in the hippie, back-to-earth '60s. They are always crowded and, irritatingly, insist on closing at 8. Food can sometimes be hit or miss. ⊠ *8 Marshall St., W1,* ☎ *020/7437–9431. Reservations not accepted. No credit cards. Closed Sun. Tube: Leicester Sq.*

Covent Garden

AMERICAN

££ ✕ **Joe Allen.** Long hours (thespians flock here after the curtains fall in
★   theaterland) and a welcoming, if loud, brick-walled interior mean New York Joe's London branch is still swinging after more than two decades. The fun, Cal-Ital menu helps: roast stuffed poblano chili and black bean soup are typical starters; entrées feature barbecued ribs with black-eyed peas and London's only available corn muffins, or roast monkfish with sun-dried-tomato salsa. There are the perennial egg dishes and huge salads, too, and Yankee desserts such as grilled banana bread with ice cream and hot caramel sauce. ⊠ *13 Exeter St., WC2,* ☎ *020/ 7836–0651. Reservations essential. AE, MC, V. Tube: Covent Garden.*

£ ✕ **Maxwell's.** London's first-ever burger joint, now more than a quarter-century old, cloned itself and then grew up. Here's the result, a happy place under the Opera House serving the kind of food you're homesick for: quesadillas and nachos, Buffalo chicken wings, barbecued ribs, Cajun chicken, chef's salad, a real New York City–style Reuben, and a burger to die for. ⊠ *8–9 James St., WC2,* ☎ *020/7836–0303. AE, DC, MC, V. Tube: Covent Garden.*

ASIAN FUSION

££££ ✕ **Asia de Cuba.** The trendiest restaurant, in the trendiest hotel, in the trendiest city in the world, allegedly. Maybe it's ironic, but it takes an American, Ian Schrager, and his Philippe Starck–designed hotel to bring Cool Brittania to its apogee. Asia de Cuba is the lead restaurant at Schrager's new St. Martins Lane Hotel. Walk in at night and it feels like a dreamscape. It's sexy and it's loud; the Calvin Klein–clad waiters bop and sit by your side. There are AdeCs at Morgans in New York and the Mondrian in L.A. The food is fusion food—it comes as and when, and you're supposed to share. The Thai beef salad with Asian greens and roasted coconut is delicious, as is the lobster Mai Tai with rum and red curry. Beautiful women flock to AdeC. Ian Schrager is right: hotels (and their restaurants) are the new disco. ⊠ *St. Martins Lane Hotel, 45 St. Martin's La., WC2,* ☎ *020/7300–5588. AE, DC, MC, V. Tube: Leicester Sq.*

BELGIAN

£–££ ✗ **Belgo Centraal.** The wackiest dining concept in town started in Camden at Belgo Noord (☞ *below*) and was so adored, it was cloned uptown in a big basement space you have to enter by elevator. Have mussels and fries in vast quantities, served with your choice of 200 Belgian beers (fruit-flavored, Trappist-brewed, white, or light) by people dressed as monks in a hall like a refectory in a Martian monastery. Also eat *stoemp* (mashed potatoes and cabbage) with steak; wild boar sausages; lobster; roast chicken. The luxury index is low, but so is the check. ⊠ *50 Earlham St., WC2,* ☎ *020/7813–2233. AE, DC, MC, V. Tube: Covent Garden.*

BRITISH TRADITIONAL

£££ ✗ **Rules.** Come, escape from the 21st century. More than 200 years
★ old, this gorgeous London institution has welcomed everyone from Dickens to Charlie Chaplin to Lillie Langtry and the Prince of Wales. The menu is historic and good, even if some food critics feel it's "theme-park-y"; try the noted steak and kidney and mushroom pudding for a virtual taste of the 18th century. Happily, the decor is truly delicious: with plush red banquettes and lacquered Regency yellow walls crammed with oil paintings and framed engravings, this is probably the single most beautiful dining salon in all of London. For a main dish, try something from the list of daily specials, which will, in season, include game from Rules's own Scottish estate (venison is disconcertingly called "deer"). Rules is more than a little touristy, but that's because it's so quaint. ⊠ *35 Maiden La., WC2,* ☎ *020/7836–5314. AE, DC, MC, V. Tube: Covent Garden.*

FRENCH

£ ✗ **Café Flo.** This useful brasserie serves unpretentious chicken liver terrine, baguette sandwiches, steak frites or *poisson-frites* (fish and fries), tarts, espresso, fresh orange juice, simple set-price weekend menus . . . everything for the Francophile on a budget. There are branches in Hampstead, Islington, Fulham, Richmond, and Kensington. ⊠ *50–51 St. Martin's La., WC2,* ☎ *020/7836–8289. AE, MC, V. Tube: Covent Garden.*

FRENCH/BRITISH

££££ ✗ **Savoy Grill.** The grill continues in the first rank of power-dining locations. Politicians, newspaper barons, and tycoons like the comforting food and impeccably discreet and attentive service in the low-key, rather dull, yew-paneled salon. On the menu, an omelet Arnold Bennett (with cheese and smoked fish) is perennial, while such standards as beef Wellington and saddle of lamb are now being joined by pak choi and cèpe risotto. Play goers can split their theater menu, taking part of their meal before the show, with the rest enjoyed after the curtain. Diners can also get their dancing shoes on at the weekly "Stompin' at the Savoy." ⊠ *Strand, WC2,* ☎ *020/7836–4343. Reservations essential. Jacket and tie. AE, DC, MC, V. Closed Sun., no lunch Sat. Tube: Covent Garden.*

INTERNATIONAL

£££ ✗ **The Ivy.** This seems to be everybody's favorite restaurant—every-
★ body who works in the media or the arts, that is. In a Deco dining room with blinding-white tablecloths, and Hodgkins and Paolozzis on the walls, the celebrated and the wanna-bes eat Caesar salad, roast grouse, Thai baked sea bass, braised oxtail, and rice pudding with Armagnac

prunes or sticky toffee pudding. For star-trekking ("Don't look now, dear, but there's Ralph Fiennes") this is without a doubt the top place in London. The weekday three-course lunch is a bonus at £15.50. ✉ *1 West St., WC2,* ☎ *020/7836–4751. Reservations essential. AE, DC, MC, V. Tube: Covent Garden.*

££ ✕ **Bank.** Since Bank's successful opening in 1997, its credit rating has
★   continued to soar. City and fashionable folk flock to this vast eatery with its spectacular chandelier and equally dazzling menu. Seared fish and paillard of pheasant; spinach and puy lentils; mousses, brûlées, and nursery puds are just small examples of its fast-changing world palette, which has a definitive mod-Brit touch. Although not a steal price-wise, the dishes never fail to please. ✉ *1 Kingsway, WC2,* ☎ *020/7379–9797. Reservations essential. AE, DC, MC, V. Tube: Holborn.*

£   ✕ **Pret a Manger.** You'll fall over this sandwich chain's cafés wherever you go—even in museums and Selfridge's food hall—and you'll be grateful because the quality and freshness of the chicken breast and avocado on walnut bread, or the lox and cream cheese bagel, or the spinach quiche, lemon cake, banana bread, almond croissant, etc., are tops. There's even sushi. ✉ *78 St. Martin's La., WC2,* ☎ *020/7379–5335. No credit cards. Tube: Covent Garden.*

ITALIAN

£££ ✕ **Orso.** The Italian sister of Joe Allen (☞ *above*), this basement restaurant has the same snappy staff and a glitzy clientele of showbiz types and hacks. The Tuscan-style menu changes every day, but it always includes excellent pizza and pasta dishes—plus entrées based, perhaps, on grilled rabbit or roast sea bass and first courses of arugula with shaved Parmesan or deep-fried zucchini flowers stuffed with ricotta. Food here is never boring, much like the place itself. Orsino, in W11, is a stylish offshoot, serving much the same fare. ✉ *27 Wellington St., WC2,* ☎ *020/7240–5269. Reservations essential. AE, MC, V. Tube: Covent Garden.*

££–£££ ✕ **Bertorelli's.** Right across from the stage door of the Royal Opera House, Bertorelli's is quietly chic, the food is tempting, and the menu is just innovative enough: poached *cotechino* (highly spiced) sausage with lentils and monkfish ragout with fennel, wonder beans, Swiss chard, and lime butter are two typical dishes. A head-to-toe refurbishment has rearranged the casual versus formal options, with a big café-bar downstairs and a restaurant upstairs. Even more decorous and delicious is the branch at Charlotte Street (and do check out its amazing marble-clad rest rooms). ✉ *44A Floral St., WC2,* ☎ *020/7836–3969. AE, DC, MC, V. Closed Sun. Tube: Covent Garden.*

SEAFOOD

££££ ✕ **J Sheekey.** J Sheekey completes the golden hat trick from the team behind Le Caprice and the Ivy. Now a top-line destination, this is where the stars go when the rubbernecking at the Ivy (☞ *above*) becomes tedious. You know, Cate Blanchett, George Michael, Depp. . . . Sleek, discreet, and clublike, and slap in the heart of theaterland, this revived former fish restaurant is now a seafood haven. The walls are crammed with black and white old-school talent: Peter O'Toole, Ollie Reed, Chaplin, Coward, Olivier, Sellers. The decor charms; cracked glazed tiles, lava-rock bar tops, American oak paneling. Sample the wonderful jellied eels, pickled herrings, roll mops, Dover sole, and fish pie. To save money, try the weekday set lunch. ✉ *28–32 St. Martin's Ct., WC2,* ☎ *020/7240–2565. AE, DC, MC, V. Tube: Leicester Sq.*

£   ✕ **Rock and Sole Plaice.** The appalling pun announces central London's only fish-and-chips joint, complete with inside seating (i.e., it's not only takeout). As well as salmon, sole, and plaice, there's the usual cod and haddock, battered, deep-fried, and served with fries, ready for the salt and vinegar shakers. ⊠ *47 Endell St., WC2,* ☎ *020/7836–3785. AE, DC, MC, V. Tube: Covent Garden.*

VEGETARIAN

£ ✕ **Food for Thought.** This simple basement restaurant (no liquor license) seats only 50 and is extremely popular, so you'll almost always find a line of people down the stairs. The menu—stir-fries, casseroles, salads, and desserts—changes every day, and each dish is freshly made; there's no microwave. ⊠ *31 Neal St., WC2,* ☎ *020/7836–0239. Reservations not accepted. No credit cards. Closed 2 wks at Christmas. Tube: Covent Garden.*

Bloomsbury

BRITISH

£ ✕ **Truckles of Pied Bull Yard.** Wine bars were the hits of '70s London, though hardly any survive to tell the tale. This one's fantastic for a post–British Museum glass of something—and they purportedly serve the cheapest glass of bubbly here. The old English ham salad has gone up-scale, and southern Europe (ciabatta sandwich with goat's cheese) is more often than not on the menu. The nicest area is the courtyard with tables galore in summer. ⊠ *Off Bury Pl., WC1,* ☎ *020/7404–5338. AE, DC, MC, V. Closed Sun., no dinner Sat. Tube: Holborn.*

FRENCH

££–£££ ✕ **Elena's L'Etoile.** Elena Salvoni presided for years over L'Escargot (☞
★ *above*) in Soho, where she made so many friends among happy cus-tomers she was rewarded with her name in lights. This understated cen-tury-old place, whose only concession to trendiness of decor is a row of bentwood chairs unaccountably roped to the top of one wall, is one of London's few remaining unreconstructed French-bistro restaurants. The traditional dishes of duck braised with red cabbage, salmon fish cakes, and *poulet rôti* (roast chicken), crème brûlée, and lemon tart have now been joined by some newer treats, and most diners are guar-anteed a warm smile from Elena, even if you're not one of the politi-cian-journalist-actor regulars. ⊠ *30 Charlotte St., W1,* ☎ *020/7636–7189. AE, DC, MC, V. Closed Sun., no lunch Sat. Tube: Goodge St.*

£££ ✕ **Chez Gérard.** One of an excellent chain of steak-frites restaurants, this one has widened the choice on the utterly Gallic menu to include more for non-red meat eaters: brioche filled with wild mushrooms and artichoke hearts, for instance, plus fish dishes and even something for vegetarians, such as caramelized onion tart. Steak, served with shoestring fries and béarnaise sauce, remains the reason to visit, though. ⊠ *8 Char-lotte St., W1,* ☎ *020/7636–4975. AE, DC, MC, V. Tube: Goodge St.*

INDIAN VEGETARIAN

£ ✕ **Mandeer.** A new location hasn't altered the delicious and tranquil karma of this Indian stalwart. It's still also extremely cheap at lunchtime, when you help yourself to the buffet. ⊠ *8 Bloomsbury Way, WC1,* ☎ *020/7242 6202. AE, DC, MC, V. Closed Sun. and 2 wks at New Year's. Tube: Tottenham Court Rd.*

JAPANESE

£ ✕ **Wagamama.** London is wild for Japanese noodles in this big base-
★ ment. It's high-tech, high volume—there are always crowds, with which you share wooden refectory tables—and high turnover, with a fast-mov-ing line always at the door. You can choose ramen in or out of soup (topped with sliced meats or tempura) or "raw energy" dishes (rice, cur-ries, and so on)—all in doggy-bag sizes. So successful has this formula proved that there is now a range of clothing, so that grateful diners can

wear Wagamama. Other branches are at 10A Lexington Street (☎ 020/
7292–0990), near Oxford Circus, and 101A Wigmore Street (☎ 020/
7409–0111). ✉ *4A Streatham St., WC1,* ☎ *020/7323–9223. Reservations
not accepted. AE, DC, MC, V. Tube: Tottenham Court Rd.*

SEAFOOD

£   ✕ **North Sea Fish Restaurant.** This is the place for the British national
★   dish of fish-and-chips—battered and deep-fried whitefish with thick
fries shaken with salt and vinegar. It's a bit tricky to find—three blocks
south of St. Pancras station, down Judd Street. Only freshly caught fish
is served, and you can order it grilled—though that would defeat the
purpose. You can take out or eat in. ✉ *7–8 Leigh St., WC1,* ☎ *020/
7387–5892. AE, DC, MC, V. Closed Sun. Tube: Russell Sq.*

South Kensington

FRENCH

££££   ✕ **Bibendum.** This reconverted Michelin showroom, adorned with
★   Art Deco decorations and brilliant stained glass, remains one of London's dining showplaces, even though the great original chef, Simon
Hopkinson, is long gone. Hopkinson championed simple dishes prepared perfectly, and current chef Matthew Harris continues in a similar vein, with the same Euro-Brit flair. Try the herring with sour
cream, any of the risottos, the baked artichoke, steak au poivre, or the
sea bass and salsa verde. Here, too, are brains and tripe as they ought
to be cooked. The £27.50 set-price menu at lunchtime is money well
spent. ✉ *Michelin House, 81 Fulham Rd., SW3,* ☎ *020/7581–5817.
Reservations essential. AE, DC, MC, V. Tube: South Kensington.*

££   ✕ **Lou Pescadou.** This place is like a little slice of the South of France,
★   with the sea-theme decor and emphatically (perhaps overly) French staff.
The menu changes often and is based on fish—don't miss the *soupe
de poisson* (fish soup) with croutons and *rouille* (rose-color, garlicky
mayonnaise) if it's featured. The wine list can be on the pricey side. ✉
241 Old Brompton Rd., SW5, ☎ *020/7370–1057. Reservations essential. AE, DC, MC, V. Closed Aug. Tube: Earl's Court.*

MEDITERRANEAN

££   ✕ **Brompton Bay.** If you are shopping at Brompton Cross—Conran Shop,
★   Voyage, Joseph, Divertimenti—Brompton Bay is good for lunch or dinner. With its clean decor and odd gold-leaf wall, BB is now attracting
the "Chelsea Set" and local It(ish) Girls. The calm atmosphere is good
for a chat *à deux.* The chef, Daniel Massey, is on the rise and his light
Mediterranean cooking is well suited for those ladies who lunch. He
does great char-grilled squid with chili jam and wild rocket and wonderful monkfish in pancetta and braised Borlotti beans. It's sweet with
jazz on a balmy summers' evening. ✉ *96 Draycott Ave., SW3,* ☎ *020/
7225–2500. AE, DC, MC, V. Tube: South Kensington.*

£££   ✕ **The Collection.** Enter this former Katharine Hamnett shop through
the spotlighted tunnel over the glass drawbridge, and you're immediately engulfed in one of the most fashionable crowds in London—so
be careful about your outfit. A huge warehouse setting, adorned with
industrial wooden beams and steel cables, a vast bar, and a suspended
gallery, makes a great theater for people-watching. The loud music makes
conversation impossible anyway. Well-dressed wanna-bes and It Girls
peck at Med food seasoned with Japanese and Thai, all hoping that
Mogens Tholstrup, the owner-doré, will table-hop on over. The Belgo
Group has now taken over, although Tholstrup remains to preserve
the restaurant's signature style. ✉ *264 Brompton Rd., SW3,* ☎ *020/
7225 1212. AE, DC, MC, V. Tube: South Kensington.*

Dining in South Kensington, Knightsbridge, and Chelsea

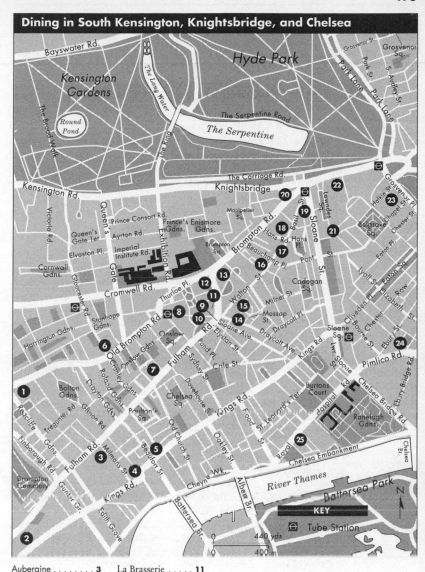

Aubergine **3**

Bibendum **9**

Bluebird **5**

Brasserie
St. Quentin **13**

Brompton Bay **14**

Cactus Blue **7**

The Capital **18**

Caravela **16**

Chelsea Bun
Diner. **4**

Chutney Mary **2**

The Collection **12**

Daquise. **8**

The Enterprise **15**

Gordon Ramsay . . . **25**

Isola **20**

La Brasserie **11**

La Poule au Pot . . **24**

La Tante Claire **22**

Lou Pescadou **1**

Pasha **6**

PJ's **10**

San Lorenzo **17**

Stefano
Cavallini **23**

Stockpot **19**

Zafferano **21**

MOROCCAN

£££ ✕ **Pasha.** Not quite a taste of old Tangiers, Pasha delivers modern Morocco and due east in a very à la mode manner. Waiters in traditional dress drift between piles of silken cushions and flickering candlelight to bring delicacies such as *pastilla* (pie) of pigeon and stylish cross-cuisine desserts (brûlée with Turkish delight). ⊠ *1 Gloucester Rd., SW7,* ☎ *020/7589–7969. Reservations essential. AE, DC, MC, V. Tube: Gloucester Rd.*

POLISH

£ ✕ **Daquise.** This venerable and well-loved Polish café by the tube station is incongruous in this neighborhood, as it is neither style-conscious nor expensive. Fill your stomach without emptying your pocketbook (or, it must be said, overstimulating your taste buds) on *bigos* (sauerkraut with garlic sausage and mushrooms), stuffed cabbage, cucumber salad, or just coffee and cake. ⊠ *20 Thurloe St., SW7,* ☎ *020/7589–6117. MC, V. Tube: South Kensington.*

Knightsbridge

FRENCH

££££ ✕ **The Capital.** This elegant, clublike dining room has greige rag-rolled walls, a grown-up atmosphere, and formal service. Chef Eric Chavot pursues traditional French cooking, and most of his fine dishes never fail to astonish. These include a gigot of rabbit and tournedos of sea bass with creamed leeks and red wine fumé. Desserts follow the same exciting route. Set-price menus at lunch (£24) make it somewhat more affordable. ⊠ *22–24 Basil St., SW3,* ☎ *020/7589–5171. Reservations essential. AE, DC, MC, V. Tube: Knightsbridge.*

££££ ✕ **La Tante Claire.** Due to the demand for its tables, one of the best
★   restaurants in London has now upped its sticks, pots, and pans and moved to the venerable and more spacious Berkeley hotel (☞ Chapter 3). Chef Pierre Koffmann still reigns over La Tante Claire, so you can expect the same blindingly brilliant standards of haute cuisine. From the *carte,* you might choose hot pâté de foie gras on shredded potatoes with a sweet wine and shallot sauce, roast spiced pigeon, or Koffmann's signature dish of pigs' feet stuffed with mousse of white meat with sweetbreads and wild mushrooms. As every expense-accounter knows, the set lunch menu (£28) is a genuine bargain. Lunch reservations must be made three to four days in advance, dinner reservations three to four weeks in advance. ⊠ *Berkeley hotel, Wilton Pl., SW1,* ☎ *020/7823–2003. Reservations essential. Jacket and tie. AE, DC, MC, V. Closed Sun., no lunch Sat. Tube: Knightsbridge.*

££ ✕ **Brasserie St. Quentin.** A very popular slice of Paris, this restaurant is frequented by French expatriates and locals alike. Every inch of the Gallic menu is explored—king prawn with foie gras, escargots, filet of beef Rossini, tart Tatin—in the bourgeois provincial comfort so many London chains (the Dômes, the Cafés Rouges) try for yet fail to achieve. ⊠ *243 Brompton Rd., SW3,* ☎ *020/7589–8005. AE, DC, MC, V. Tube: South Kensington.*

INTERNATIONAL

£ ✕ **Stockpot.** You'll find speedy service at this chain of large, jolly restaurants, often packed to the brim with young people and shoppers. The food is sometimes unstartling but filling and wholesome: try the Lancashire hot pot, for example, and the apple crumble. ⊠ *6 Basil St., SW3,* ☎ *020/ 7589–8627. No credit cards. Tube: Knightsbridge;* ⊠ *40 Panton St., off Leicester Sq.,* ☎ *020/7839–5142;* ⊠ *18 Old Compton St., Soho,* ☎ *020/ 7287–1066;* ⊠ *273 King's Rd., Chelsea,* ☎ *020/7823–3175.*

ITALIAN

££££ ✗ **Isola.** Isola is gunning to be the coolest restaurant in London, so don't be surprised to see Joseph Fiennes mooching in a corner. The brain-child of young gun Oliver Peyton (Atlantic Bar & Grill, Coast), Isola is grown-up osteria and Italian fine dining cooked by a Frenchman, Bruno Loubet. Upstairs is banquette-and-booth power dining; down-stairs is more larky and glam—diners sit at off-white leather "compromise sofas" amid the sparkle of *molto* chrome and mirrors, parquet walls, and molecular lighting. Peyton says his design rubic is "Albert Speer meets the Four Seasons." Head for the *zuppa di fagiano e farro* (pheas-ant soup with cabbage and faro) and the *faraona al forno* (wood-roasted guinea fowl with liver and mascarpone). ✉ *145 Knightbridge, SW1,* ☎ *020/7333–1234. Reservations essential. AE, DC, MC, V. Tube: Knightsbridge.*

£££ ✗ **San Lorenzo.** This well-established, well-heeled trattoria has unex-ceptional decor and is nothing special food-wise—to say the least, ac-cording to some food critics—but it may be just the ticket if you're keen to spot the occasional celebrity or to gaze into the world of ladies-who-lunch. The usual Italian dishes are here, but they often make a nod to fashion—try wood pigeon with polenta, or any of the veal dishes. ✉ *22 Beauchamp Pl., SW3,* ☎ *020/7584–1074. No credit cards. Closed Sun. Tube: South Kensington.*

££££ ✗ **Stefano Cavallini.** Gurus of banking and showbiz come to this spot set in the Halkin hotel —the sister to the more upscale Metropolitan (☞ Chapter 3 *for both*)—because there is no paparazzi and no show-ing off. Goldman-Sachs CEOs and stars like Donna Karan come for the exemplary Michelin-starred Italian cuisine. Cavallini calls it *la cucina essenziale*—old Italian recipes reinterpreted for the modern age (less cream, less fat, and more broth and olive oil). It is deeply expen-sive, and service is by Armani-clad staff ("pretentious, *moi*?"). Nev-ertheless, taste sensations include squid-ink risotto with grilled scallops and gray mullet roe, and mallard with celeriac, onion, and green beans. ✉ *Halkin hotel, 5–6 Halkin St., SW1,* ☎ *020/7333–1234. AE, DC, MC, V. Tube: Hyde Park Corner.*

£££ ✗ **Zafferano.** Princess Margaret, Eric Clapton, Joan Collins (she asked that the lights be turned down), and any number of other Cartier-brooch-wearing neighborhood Belgravians have flocked to this place, which, since 1995, has been London's best exponent of *cucina nuova*. The fire-works are in the kitchen, not in the brick-wall-and-saffron-hued decor, but *what* fireworks: pumpkin ravioli with a splash of amaretto, veni-son medallions with mash and roast cod, lentils and parsley sauce. The desserts are also *delizioso,* especially the Sardinian pecorino pastries served with undersweetened vanilla ice cream and the panettone bread-and-butter pudding. Be sure to book early: even Al Pacino was turned away one night. ✉ *15 Lowndes St., SW1,* ☎ *020/7235–5800. Reser-vations essential. AE, DC, MC, V. Tube: Knightsbridge.*

MODERN BRITISH

£–££ ✗ **The Enterprise.** One of the new luxury breed of gastro-pubs, this is a hot spot for hooray Henrys and brash bucks—near Harrods and Brompton Cross, it's filled with decorative types who complement the decor: paisley-striped wallpaper, Edwardian side tables covered with baskets and farmhouse fruit, vintage books piled up in the windows, white linen and fresh flowers on the tables. The menu isn't overly pretty—seared tuna and char-grilled asparagus, timbale of aubergine, salmon with artichoke hearts—but the ambience certainly is. ✉ *35 Walton St., SW3,* ☎ *020/7584–3148. AE, MC, V. Tube: South Kensington.*

££ ✕ **Caravela.** This narrow, lower-ground-floor place is one of London's few Portuguese restaurants. You can get *caldo verde* (cabbage soup), *bacalhau* (salt-cured cod), and other typical dishes while listening (on Friday or Saturday) to the national music, fado—desperately sad songs belted out at thrash-metal volume. ⊠ *39 Beauchamp Pl., SW3,* ☎ *020/7581–2366. AE, DC, MC, V. Tube: South Kensington.*

Chelsea

AMERICAN/CASUAL

££ ✕ **Cactus Blue.** Go for dinner or go for a weekend brunch, but go— American southwestern food is hot and happening in London these days, and this is one of the new Tex-Mex places with attitude. You can find the buzz on split levels bathed in ochre hues, with a gamut of cacti on the stairs. On offer are tequilas, beers, and Baja wines, which help slide down yummy crab stacks and quesadillas. ⊠ *86 Fulham Rd., SW3,* ☎ *020/7823–7858. AE, DC, MC, V. Tube: South Kensington.*

££ ✕ **PJ's.** The decor here evokes the Bulldog Drummond lifestyle, with wooden floors and stained glass; a vast, slowly revolving propeller from a 1940s Curtis flying boat; and polo memorabilia. A menu of all-American staples (soft-shell crab, chowder, gumbo, steaks, smoked ribs), big salads, pecan pie, brownies, and Häagen-Dazs should please all but vegetarians, and portions are big, but this place is more remarkable for ambience than for food—it's open late; it's relaxed, friendly, and efficient; and it has bartenders who can mix anything. The sister PJ's in Covent Garden (⊠ 30 Wellington St., ☎ 020/7240–7529) is worth remembering for its excellent weekend "Fun Club" for kids. ⊠ *52 Fulham Rd., SW3,* ☎ *020/7581–0025. AE, DC, MC, V. Tube: South Kensington.*

£ ✕ **Chelsea Bun Diner.** Get fed heaps of food for very little money at this hybrid of an American diner and an English greasy spoon. A huge menu of huge portions—burgers, salads, potato skins, many breakfasts, pastas, and pies—is what you get. ⊠ *9A Limerston St., SW10,* ☎ *020/ 7352–3635. Reservations not accepted. V. Tube: Sloane Sq., then Bus 11, 19, 22, or 31.*

ANGLO-INDIAN

£££ ✕ **Chutney Mary.** London's stalwart Indian restaurant provides a fantasy version of the British Raj, all giant wicker armchairs and palms. Dishes like masala roast lamb (practically a whole leg, marinated and spiced) and Malabar chicken curry (with coconut, red chili, and cinnamon) alternate with the more familiar north Indian dishes such as *dum ka murgh* (chicken, poppy seed, green chili, and onion). The best choices are certainly the dishes re-created from the kitchens of Indian chefs cooking for English palates back in the old Raj days. Service is deferential, and desserts, unheard of in tandoori places, are usually worth leaving room for. The three-course Sunday brunch is a good value at £15. ⊠ *535 King's Rd., SW10,* ☎ *020/7351–3113. Reservations essential. AE, DC, MC, V. Tube: Fulham Broadway.*

CONTEMPORARY

££–£££ ✕ **Bluebird.** From Terence Conran, the man who gave England the wok, the Habitat catalog ("one of the 10 books that changed our life," according to the *Sunday Telegraph*), and several of London's largest restaurants, now comes a full-blown gastrodome—supermarket, brasserie, florist, fruit stand, butcher shop, boutique, and café-restaurant, all housed in a mammoth King's Road former garage. The place is pale blue and white, very light, and not in the least cozy (read "noisy"), and the food is slightly formulaic: steamed mussels, coriander, lime leaf; or roasted leg of partridge, Savoy cabbage, chips; then warm chocolate cake and espresso ice cream. The menu has more than a nod in the Asia-Pacific direction. Go for the synergy and visual excitement—Conran's chefs share a tendency to promise more than they deliver. ⊠ *350 King's Rd., SW3,* ☎ *020/7559–1000. Reservations essential. AE, DC, MC, V. Tube: Sloane Sq.*

FRENCH

£££–££££ ✗ **Aubergine.** A table at Aubergine (there are only 14) was once London's toughest reservation under soccer pro turned cooking star Gordon Ramsay. Now Cumbrian chef William Drabble has taken over and is building his own reputation. His signature dishes are firm and meaty—boudin of wood pigeon with foie gras, turnip, and *jus* truffle; best-end Mansergh lamb with onions, garlic, and rosemary. The decor is alluring and bathed in the hues of Impressionist Provence. Book ahead. Lunch is a thrifty option. ⊠ *11 Park Walk, SW10,* ☎ *020/7352–3449. Reservations essential. AE, DC, MC, V. Closed Sun., no lunch Sat. Tube: South Kensington.*

££££ ✗ **Gordon Ramsay.** When the celebrated La Tante Claire (☞ *above*) moved out of its old Chelsea abode, Gordon Ramsay—considered by some to be London's greatest chef—lost no time in getting his feet under its tables. Unfortunately, his new place is on the small side, so it still takes weeks to book a seat, though not as long as at his former, even tinier Aubergine (☞ *above*). Here, Ramsay is frothing and whipping up a storm with white beans, girolles, foie gras, scallops, and truffles, and by the time you read this, he will probably have earned another 20 awards. He already has two Michelin stars. For £70 blow out on the seven-course option, for £55 you can wallow in three dinner courses, or plump for lunch (£28 for three courses) for a gentler check. ⊠ *68–69 Royal Hospital Rd., SW3,* ☎ *020/7352–4441. Reservations essential. AE, DC, MC, V. Closed weekends. Tube: Sloane Sq.*

££–£££ ✗ **La Poule au Pot.** One of London's most romantic restaurants, La Poule au Pot is superb for proposals (or assignations). Gallic and rustic, this is a corner of France in darkest Belgravia. The "Chelsea Set" love it; Americans do, too. It is candlelit at night—you could be in a rambling French country house. The country cooking is good, not spectacular. The *poule au pot* (stewed chicken) with uncut vegetables and *lapin à la moutarde* (rabbit with mustard) are strong and hearty. There are fine classics such as beef bourguignonne and French onion soup. The service comes with *bonhomie.* ⊠ *231 Ebury St., SW1,* ☎ *020/7730–7763. Reservations essential. AE, DC, MC, V. Tube: Sloane Sq.*

££ ✗ **La Brasserie.** This is a convenient spot for South Ken museum visits, and it has flexible and long opening hours, a menu of entirely French dishes—from fish soup to tart Tatin—and a good buzz on a Sunday morning, when the entire well-heeled neighborhood sits around reading the papers and sipping cappuccino. You can't do that at peak times, when you must eat, but the food's reliable, if a little overpriced. ⊠ *272 Brompton Rd., SW3,* ☎ *020/7584–1668. AE, DC, MC, V. Tube: South Kensington.*

Kensington and Notting Hill Gate

AMERICAN/CASUAL

£ ✗ **Tootsies.** A superior burger place, Tootsies is dark but cheerful. Rock music is in the background, usually accompanied by a neighborhood buzz. Alternatives to the burgers, which come with great fries, are big salads, steaks, BLTs, and chicken divertissements. The usual ice creams and pies will do for dessert. There are branches in Fulham, Chiswick, Wimbledon, Barnes, Hampstead, and Richmond. ⊠ *120 Holland Park Ave., W11,* ☎ *020/7229–8567. Reservations not accepted. AE, MC, V. Tube: Holland Park.*

The
Belvedere . . **16**

Chez Moi . . . **7**

Clarke's **14**

Costa's
Fish
Restaurant . . **11**

The Cow **1**

First Floor **3**

Geales **12**

Julie's **6**

Kensington
Place **13**

192 . . . . **4**

Pharmacy . . **10**

Prince
Bonaparte . . . **2**

Room at the
Halcyon **8**

Tootsies **9**

Wiz **5**

Wódka **15**

Yas **17**

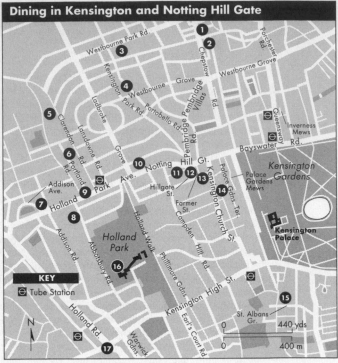

Dining in Kensington and Notting Hill Gate

KEY

⊖ Tube Station

BRITISH TRADITIONAL

£££ ✕ **Julie's.** This sweet '60s throwback has two parts: an upstairs wine bar and a basement restaurant, both decorated with Victorian ecclesiastical furniture. The cooking is sound, old-fashioned English (salmon-and-halibut terrine, roast pheasant with chestnut stuffing and wild rowan jelly). The traditional Sunday lunches are very popular, and in summer there's a garden room for open-air eating. ⊠ *137 Portland Rd., W11,* ☎ *020/7727–7985. AE, DC, MC, V. No lunch Sat. Tube: Holland Park.*

CONTEMPORARY

£££ ✕ **Clarke's.** There's no choice on the evening menu at Sally Clarke's restaurant; her four-course dinners feature ultrafresh ingredients, plainly but perfectly cooked, accompanied by home-baked breads. The plant-and-art-speckled room is similarly home-style, if home is in the big white Kensington houses you see around here. ⊠ *124 Kensington Church St., W8,* ☎ *020/7221–9225. Reservations essential. AE, DC, MC, V. Closed Sun. and 2 wks in Aug., no lunch Sat. Tube: Notting Hill Gate.*

£££ ✕ **Pharmacy.** A London scene-arena, the Pharmacy is one of those see-and-be-seen places where the bar is larger than the restaurant. In this case, the bar seats 120 and is shaped like gigantic aspirin. Yes, this spot looks just like its namesake, the wait staff is garbed like hospital orderlies, and even the menu looks fab—but then, Damien Hirst, artist-provocateur extraordinaire, was involved in setting up the place. The menu highlights "comfort food" and ranges from carpaccio of white fish with spinach tart to spit-roast Dorset lamb and suckling pig. If you can't snag a table, just have fun at the bar and order the drink called "Cough Syrup." ⊠ *150 Notting Hill Gate, W11,* ☎ *020/7221–2442, AE, DC, MC, V. Tube: Notting Hill Gate.*

££ ✕ **Wiz.** Tricky to find in the backwash of Notting Hill, Wiz is worth it when you do. A neighborhood restaurant run by TV guy Antony Worrall Thompson, it operates on tapas principles. The global-patrol menu (70 dishes) is grouped geographically (the Americas, Italy, the Subcontinent, France, United Kingdom, Mediteroccan, Far East) and diners choose from a minimenu under each heading. Some say it's a mishmash, others that the portions are tight. Nevertheless, when it works, it works. The cumin dal and tamarind chicken and coconut curry are popular, as are the Szechuan duck and seared scallops with smoked aubergine salad. Locals return time and again. ⊠ *123A Clarendon Rd., W11,* ☎ *020/7229–1500. AE, DC, MC, V. Tube: Holland Park.*

FRENCH

££££ ✕ **Room at the Halcyon.** For some of the most romantic dinners in London, check out this elegant room, favored by stars of Hollywood and rock, secreted in the leafy neighborhood of Holland Park. The kitchen is excellent and modern British. ⊠ *129 Holland Park Ave., W11,* ☎ *020/ 7221–5411. AE, DC, MC, V. No lunch Mon.–Sat. Tube: Holland Park.*

£££ ✕ **Chez Moi.** Sophisticated French food is served in a dark red and black dining room, which, with the tables widely spaced and the lighting low, demands romantic behavior. There are dishes the menu admits are "traditional" that Chez Moi's fans have depended on for a quarter century—like rack of lamb with Dijon mustard and bread crumbs, and filet mignon with port sauce—as well as more novel dishes, such as satay and seared seafood, which take their cue from Asia. The desserts are hit-or-miss, but there are ample chocolates brought with the coffee. ⊠ *1 Addison Ave., W11,* ☎ *020/7603–8267. Reservations essential. AE, DC, MC, V. Closed Sun. and 2 wks at Christmas, no lunch Sat. Tube: Holland Park.*

GREEK

£ ✕ **Costa's Fish Restaurant.** Come for good value and such down-to-earth Greek food as grilled fish and *kleftiko* (roast lamb on the bone). The atmosphere is homey and happy, and there's a tiny garden open in summer. ⊠ *14 Hillgate St., W8,* ☎ *020/7727–4310. No credit cards. Closed Sun. and 3 wks in summer. Tube: Notting Hill Gate.*

MEDITERRANEAN

££ ✕ **The Belvedere.** There can be no finer setting for a summer supper or a sunny Sunday brunch than a window table—or a balcony one if you luck out—at this stunning restaurant in the middle of Holland Park. The menu has good rib-eye Aberdeen Angus beef with snails and pommes frites, which suits the conservatory-like room—a favorite of film director and infamously demanding newspaper restaurant critic Michael Winner. ⊠ *Holland Park off Abbotsbury Rd., W8,* ☎ *020/ 7602–1238. Reservations essential. AE, DC, MC, V. No dinner Sun. Tube: Holland Park.*

MIDDLE EASTERN

£ ✕ **Yas.** Directly opposite Olympia Exhibition Centre, this friendly Per-
★ sian restaurant with terra-cotta-color walls has a beehive-shape oven by the door, from which lavish bread is brought steaming to your table. Eat this with *panir o sabzi* (soft white cheese with fresh herbs), hummus, *borani-e esfena* (yogurt and spinach), *adasi* (lentils), or any of the 15 dips and salads; then have a simple grilled chicken or lamb dish or the daily special—like Saturday's *baghali polow* (lamb shank, broad bean, dill, and rice). It's open until 5 AM every day. ⊠ *7 Hammersmith Rd., W14,* ☎ *020/7603–9148. AE, DC, MC, V. Tube: Olympia.*

MODERN BRITISH

£££ ✕ **First Floor.** This place is for well-off but artsy locals, popular both for its inventive food and its ambience—it looks like a bombed church inhabited by distressed nobility. There's a great brunch on weekends; otherwise go for Thai fish cakes, monkfish and celeriac, or pecan-encrusted lamb rump with sweet potato gratin. Sides—*petit dauphinoise* (sliced potatoes baked in cream) or Asian greens—often hit the heights, as do desserts like hazelnut and Bailey's cheesecake. ⊠ *186 Portobello Rd., W11,* ☎ *020/7243–0072. Reservations essential. AE, DC, MC, V. Tube: Notting Hill Gate.*

£££ ✕ **Kensington Place.** Being a favorite among the local glitterati keeps
★   this place packed and noisy. A huge plate-glass window and mural are backdrops to fashionable food—grilled foie gras with sweet-corn pancake and baked tamarillo with vanilla ice cream are perennials—but it's the fun buzz that draws the crowds. ⊠ *201 Kensington Church St., W8,* ☎ *020/7727–3184. AE, MC, V. Tube: Notting Hill Gate.*

£££ ✕ **192.** A noisy, buzzy wine bar–restaurant just off Portobello Road,
★   this is as much a social hangout for the local media mafia as a restaurant, especially on weekends, when you'll feel like you've gate-crashed a party—if you manage to get a table, that is. The chef likes to keep ahead of fashion and is best on the appetizer list—many people order two of these instead of an entrée. Try the pastas, the seasonal salad (perhaps romanesco, broccoli, anchovy, and gremolata), the fish (sea bass with fennel, lemon, and rosemary; scallop, chickpea, chorizo, and clam casserole), or whatever sounds unusual. ⊠ *192 Kensington Park Rd., W11,* ☎ *020/7229–0482. Reservations essential. AE, DC, MC, V. Tube: Notting Hill Gate.*

££   ✕ **The Cow.** Oh, no, not *another* Conran. This place belongs to Tom, son of Sir Terence, though it's a million miles from Quag's and Mezzo (☞ *above for both*). A tiny, chic gastro-pub, it comprises a faux-Dublin back-room bar, serving up oysters, crab salad, and seafood spaghetti. Upstairs, a serious chef whips up Tuscan-British specialties—skate poached in minestrone is one temptation. Notting Hillbillies and other stylish folk adore the house special—a half-dozen Irish rock oysters with a pint of Guinness—as well as the mixed grills and steaks that often figure on the menu. ⊠ *89 Westbourne Park Rd., W2,* ☎ *020/ 7221–5400. Restaurant reservations essential. AE, MC, V. Tube: Westbourne Park.*

£–££ ✕ **Prince Bonaparte.** This is one of the new foodie pubs that draw in the crowds. Forget bangers and mash; here you'll get blackened salmon with refried beans, a yummy toffee pudding, and a wide range of interesting beers. Singles take over during the week; young families move in on the weekends. As the night wears on, the place—accented with large windows, church pews, and farmhouse tables—becomes a lively preclub stop (complete with thumping music on weekends). ⊠ *80 Chepstow Rd., W2,* ☎ *020/7313–9491. No credit cards. Tube: Notting Hill Gate, Westbourne Park.*

POLISH

££   ✕ **Wódka.** This smart, modern Polish restaurant is the only one in the
★   world, as far as we know, to serve smart, modern Polish food. It is popular with elegant locals and a sprinkling of celebs and often has the atmosphere of a dinner party. Alongside the smoked salmon, herring, caviar, and eggplant blinis you might also find venison sausages or roast duck with *krupnik* (honey-lemon vodka). From the separate menu, order a carafe of the purest vodka in London (and watch the check inflate); it's encased in a block of ice and is hand-flavored (with bison grass, cherries, and rowanberries) by the owner, who, being an actual Polish prince, is uniquely qualified to do this. ⊠ *12 St. Alban's Grove, W8,* ☎ *020/7937–6513. Reservations essential. AE, DC, MC, V. No lunch weekends. Tube: High Street Kensington.*

SEAFOOD

£ ✕ **Geales.** This is a cut above your typical fish-and-chips joint, and
★ this is reflected in the prices. The decor is stark, but the fish will have
been swimming just hours beforehand, even the ones from the Caribbean
(grilled swordfish is a specialty). Geales is popular with the rich and
famous, not just loyal locals. ⊠ *2 Farmer St., W8,* ☏ *020/7727–7969.*
Reservations not accepted. AE, MC, V. Closed 2 wks at Christmas. Tube:
Notting Hill Gate.

The City and the South Bank

AMERICAN/CASUAL

£ ✕ **Fatboy's Diner.** One for the kids, this is a 1941 chrome trailer transplanted from the banks of the Susquehanna in Pennsylvania and now
secreted, unexpectedly, in a back street, complete with an Astroturf "garden." A '50s jukebox accompanies the dogs, burgers, and fries. ⊠ *23*
Horner Sq., Spitalfields Market, E1, ☏ *020/7375–2763. Reservations*
not accepted. No credit cards. Tube: Liverpool St.

FRENCH

£££ ✕ **Le Pont de la Tour.** Sir Terence Conran's place across the river, over-
★ looking the bridge that gives it its name, comes into its own in summer, when the outside tables are heaven. Inside there's a vintner and
baker and deli, a seafood bar, a brasserie, and this '30s diner–style restaurant, smart as the captain's table. Fish and seafood (lobster salad;
Baltic herrings in crème fraîche; roast halibut with aioli) and meat and
game (venison with juniper and Madeira sauce; veal with caramelized
endive) feature heavily—vegetarians are out of luck. Prune and Armagnac
tart or chocolate terrine could finish a glamorous—and expensive—
meal. ⊠ *36D Shad Thames, Butler's Wharf, SE1,* ☏ *020/7403–8403.*
Reservations essential. AE, DC, MC, V. Tube: Tower Hill

££–£££ ✕ **Maison Novelli.** Jean-Christophe Novelli is one of the heroes of the Mod
★ Brit movement, and his restaurant has drawn foodies from the day it opened
in up-and-buzzing Clerkenwell, near stylish Islington. These days, gladly,
Novelli is back running the kitchen after almost burning out, expanding
his empire across London and sharing his British-French cooking secrets
in the *Times.* Favorites include home-baked venison terrine and cranberry
chutney; roast filet of beef; Beaufort cheese, garlic, and tomatoes; and the
famed pig's trotter stuffed "following the mood of the day." All is not of-
fally, however—you can also come by an elegant sea bass with chorizo
or truffle oil, or steamed plaice with mussel sauce and braised cabbage.
Finish it all off, if it doesn't finish you first, with a tart Tatin with rum
and raisin ice cream or hot-and-cold chocolate cake. The cheaper brasserie
operation, Novelli EC1, is now on the ground floor. For Novelli's more
informal take, head to his wildly popular Novelli W8, in Kensington (☏
020/7229–4024). ⊠ *29–31 Clerkenwell Green, EC1,* ☏ *020/7251–*
6606. Reservations essential. AE, DC, MC, V. Tube: Farringdon.

GOAN

£ ✕ **The Eagle.** If the name makes it sound like a pub, that's because it
★ is a pub, albeit a superior one, with wooden floors, a few sofas, and
art on the walls. It does, however, belong in the "Restaurants" section
by virtue of the amazingly good-value Goan-Portuguese-Spanish food,
which you choose from the blackboard menu (or by pointing) at the
bar. There are about nine dishes, a pasta and/or risotto always among
them. There are currently quite a few places in London charging four
times the price for remarkably similar food; there's also a welcome trend
toward pubs serving good meals—one that the Eagle all but started.
⊠ *159 Farringdon Rd., EC1,* ☏ *020/7837–1353. Reservations not ac-*
cepted. No credit cards. No dinner Sun. Tube: Farringdon.

184

Bill
Bentley's 7

The Eagle . . . 4

Fatboy's
Diner. 8

fish! 10

Konditor &
Cook. 15

Livebait 13

Maison
Noveli. 2

Moro 1

Moshi Moshi
Sushi. 6

Le Pont de
la Tour. 9

OXO Tower
Brasserie and
Restaurant . . 12

People's
Palace. 14

Quality
Chop
House 3

St. John 5

Sweetings . . 11

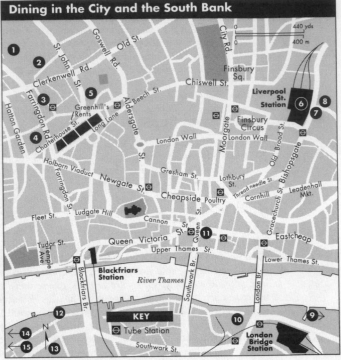

Dining in the City and the South Bank

£ ✕ **Moshi Moshi Sushi.** London is taking to sushi like New Yorkers did a decade back, and this wacky glass-walled joint above Platform One in Liverpool Street station set the ball rolling—or the fish train chugging, since the shtick here is that you pick *tekka* or *kappa maki* (tuna or cucumber seaweed rolls, respectively) or *maguro* (tuna), *sake* (salmon), *saba* (mackerel), etc.—in pairs off a conveyor belt that snakes around the counter. At the end, you count up your color-coded plates to pay. The sushi's okay, but this is not the place to go for a sophisticated evening. ⊠ *Unit 24 Liverpool St. Station, EC2,* ☎ *020/7247–3227. Reservations not accepted. AE, MC, V. Closed weekends. Tube: Liverpool St.*

MODERN BRITISH

£££ ✕ **OXO Tower Brasserie and Restaurant.** How delightful it is for London finally to get a room with a view—and *such* a view. On the eighth floor of the beautifully revived OXO Tower Wharf building near the South Bank Centre is this elegant space, run by the same people who put the chic Fifth Floor at Harvey Nichols on the map and featuring Euro-Asia food with the latest trendy ingredients (acorn-fed black pig charcuterie with tomato and pear chutney; Dover sole with sea urchin butter). The ceiling slats turn and change from white to midnight blue, but who on earth notices, with the new London Eye millennium Ferris wheel and St. Paul's dazzling you across the water? The Brasserie is slightly less expensive than the restaurant, but both have great river views. For food with a view, the terrace tables in summertime are probably the best places in London. ⊠ *Barge House St., Southbank, SE1,* ☎ *020/7803–3888. AE, MC, V. Tube: Waterloo.*

££ ✕ **Moro.** Just up the road from the City at the cusp of Clerkenwell and
★ Sadler's Wells Islington borders is Exmouth Market—a cluster of shops, an Italian church with accompanying Italian deli, and Moro,

an oasis of a restaurant that has become an award-winning outpost ever since it opened in 1997. The menu here provides a fashionable mélange of Spanish- and Moroccan-inspired flavors and even gives you a tour around North Africa. Slow-cooked spiced meats, cured serrano hams, salt cod with chick peas, and other delicacies flavored with fresh herbs are the secret to Moro's success. The only downside is the persistent hum of noise, but then, that's part of the buzz. ✉ *34–36 Exmouth Market, EC1,* ☎ *020/7833–8336. Reservations essential. AE, MC, V. Closed weekends. Tube: Farringdon.*

££ ✕ **People's Palace.** Thank goodness for this place—now you can have a civilized meal during your South Bank arts encounter. Run independently from the Royal Festival Hall et al., it has remarkably low prices considering it has the greatest river view in town (apart from OXO). There are occasional mistakes here, but the more British the dish, the more reliable it proves: roast beef, potted duck, suckling pig sandwich on granary bread, marmalade sponge, sticky toffee pudding—all these are fine. Service is a bit flaky, but the soaring space with its giant windows makes up for everything. ✉ *Royal Festival Hall, Level 3, South Bank, SE1,* ☎ *020/7928–9999. AE, DC, MC, V. Tube: Waterloo.*

££ ✕ **Quality Chop House.** This was converted from one of the most gor-
★ geous "greasy spoon" cafs in town, retaining the solid Victorian fittings (including pewlike seats, which you often have to share). It is not luxurious, but the food is a glorious parody of caf food—bangers and mash turns out to be homemade herbed Toulouse sausage with rich veal gravy and light, fluffy potatoes; egg and chips (fries) are not remotely greasy. There are also such posh things as salmon fish cakes and steak as well as desserts that change with the seasons. A further extension has added more fish to the menu: scallops, clams, jellied eels. ✉ *94 Farringdon Rd., EC1,* ☎ *020/7837–5093. Reservations essential. MC, V. No lunch Sat. Tube: Farringdon.*

££ ✕ **St. John.** This former smokehouse (ham, not cigars), converted by
★ erstwhile architect owner-chef Fergus Henderson, has soaring white walls, schoolroom lamps, stone floors, iron railings, and plain wooden chairs. Some find Henderson's chutzpah scary: one infamous appetizer is carrots and egg (a bunch of carrots with green tops intact and a boiled egg), although the imaginativeness of others—roast bone marrow and parsley salad; smoked eel, beetroot, and horseradish—excuses this silliness. Entrées (roast lamb and parsnip; smoked haddock and fennel; deviled crab) can appear shockingly nude on the plate, but they always have style. An all-French wine list has plenty of affordable bottles, plus lots of Malmseys and ports. Service is efficiently friendly, and the pastry chef's chocolate slice belongs in the brownie hall of fame. ✉ *26 St. John St., EC1,* ☎ *020/7251–0848. Reservations essential. AE, DC, MC, V. No dinner Sun. Tube: Farringdon.*

£ ✕ **Konditor & Cook.** Very useful for theatrical forays over the river, this caf in the Young Vic theater serves full meals a cut above the tired quiche and curly sandwiches you might expect. Black ravioli stuffed with crab as well as wild mushrooms on toasted brioche are the kind of dishes to expect, but the pies and cakes—from the eponymous bakery around the corner, which supplies half of London—are the standouts. ✉ *Young Vic Theatre, 66 The Cut, SE1,* ☎ *020/7620–2700. MC, V. Closed Sun. Tube: Waterloo.*

SEAFOOD

££ ✕ **Bill Bentley's.** You can see from the bare walls and the arched ceiling that this once housed a wine merchant's vaults. There are another four City-based branches in London, all equally old-fashioned in feel and all serving old-fashioned boarding school–like fish dishes and seafood platters. ✉ *Swedeland Ct., 202 Bishopsgate, EC2,* ☎ *020/7283–*

1763. Reservations essential. Jacket and tie. AE, DC, MC, V. Closed weekends; last orders 8:30 PM. Tube: Liverpool St.

££ ✕ **fish!.** fish! is one of the sensations to hit the London scene. A re-
★ markable diner—designed, sleek and modern, by Julian Wickham—it sits in the shadow of Southwark Cathedral looking for the life of it like the glass-covered innards of a giant whale. But, no, it's the Victo-rian conversion of a section of Borough Market, which still operates across the road. The fish at fish! is excellent, and PC. The langoustine are creel-caught, the salmon organic, and the scallops landed by divers. The farmed fish is GM-free. There are always at least eight types on the menu, from swordfish to brill, skate, and turbot. The splish-splosh in-and-out formula has struck a chord; six new fish! are coming on-stream. ✉ *Cathedral St., SE1,* ☎ *020/7234–3333. AE, DC, MC, V. Tube: London Bridge.*

££ ✕ **Livebait.** Perhaps no longer as truly fantastic as when it was inde-pendently run, this expanded, plain-looking fish restaurant is still packing them in, serving English seafood with a range of British ales by the pint (cockles and mussels alive-alive-o!), home-baked breads (beet-root, garlic, or turmeric, as well as olive and walnut), and all sorts of fish: broiled, in pies, baked, stewed, and generally combined in ways that are never boring. There are also branches in Covent Garden and Notting Hill. ✉ *41–43 The Cut, SE1,* ☎ *020/7928–7211. Reserva-tions essential. AE, DC, MC, V. Closed Sun. Tube: Southwark.*

££ ✕ **Sweetings.** Sweetings is uniquely *English*—a time warp from the old-school City of London, circa 1889. There are many things Sweetings doesn't do: reservations, coffee, credit cards, dinner, weekends. It does, however, do seafood. It's not far from St. Paul's, and City gents come here for "luncheon." They like the tankards for "Black Velvet" (Guin-ness and champagne) and they're reassured by the potted shrimps, fried whitebait, smoked haddock and poached eggs, Welsh rarebit, and roe on toast. The oysters are good, and the puds are old nursery-school favorites—spotted dick and steamed syrup pudding. ✉ *39 Queen Vic-toria St., EC4,* ☎ *020/7248–3062. Reservations not accepted. No credit cards. Closed weekends, no dinner. Tube: Mansion House.*

Camden Town and Hampstead

CAFÉS

£ ✕ **Coffee Cup.** A Hampstead landmark for just about as long as anyone can remember, this smoky, dingy, uncomfortable café is lovable, very cheap, and therefore always packed. You can get anything (beans, eggs, kippers, mushrooms) on toast, grills, sandwiches, cakes, fry-ups, etc.—nothing healthy or fashionable whatsoever. There are tables outside in the sum-mer but no liquor license. ✉ *74 Hampstead High St., NW3,* ☎ *020/7435–7565. Reservations not accepted. No credit cards. Tube: Hampstead.*

GREEK

££ ✕ **Lemonia.** On a very pleasant street near Regent's Park is this supe-
★ rior version of London Greek—large and light, friendly, and packed every evening. Besides the usual *mezedes* (appetizers), *souvlaki* (kebabs), *stifado* (beef stewed in wine), and so on, there are interesting specials: quail, perhaps, or *gemista* (stuffed vegetables). ✉ *89 Regent's Park Rd., NW1,* ☎ *020/7586–7454. Reservations essential. MC, V. No lunch Sat., no dinner Sun. Tube: Chalk Farm.*

Hammersmith

ITALIAN

££££ ✕ **River Café.** Often touted as having the best Italian food in Europe
★ outside Italy (some think, gasp, in all Europe), this superstar restau-

rant started a trend with its single-estate olive oils, wafer-thin pizzas, and deliriously simple roasts and pastas. Chefs Rose Gray and Ruth Rogers (wife of famed architect Richard Rogers, who created the minimalist decor) believe in the snappingly fresh ingredients, so you get your grilled salmon with imported Sicilian lemons, Tuscan bread soup with calavo nero (a black leaf cabbage) and Swiss chard, and one of London's highest checks. No matter to the food-obsessed (who swear by the famous Rogers/Gray cookbooks) and off-duty movie stars who flock here. But remember, if you're lucky enough to snag a reservation: this is in distant Hammersmith (way off our maps) and you can be stranded here if you haven't booked a taxi. ✉ *Thames Wharf Studios, Rainville Rd., W6,* ☎ *020/7381–8824. Reservations essential. AE, MC, V. Tube: Hammersmith.*

Brunch and Afternoon Tea

It is sometimes suggested that among Londoners, brunch is catching on, while the afternoon ritual (often mistakenly referred to as "high tea") is dying out. Tea, the drink, however, is so ingrained in the national character that tea, the meal, will always have a place in the capital, if only as an occasional celebration, a children's treat, or something you do when your American friends are in town. Reserve for all these, unless otherwise noted.

Brunch

✗ **The Belvedere.** This restaurant (☞ *above*) in bucolic Holland Park wins hands down for the setting, especially if you bag a rare terrace table on a rare sunny day. There is, admittedly, no official brunch, but you can fake one from the regular menu. ✉ *Holland Park off Abbotsbury Rd., W8,* ☎ *020/7602–1238. Reservations essential. AE, DC, MC, V.* ◷ *Lunch served weekends noon–3.*

Butlers Wharf Chop House. At this—yet another Terence Conran (Quaglino's, Pont de la Tour, Bibendum . . .) venture—brunch (£17 for three courses) is as British as brunch ever gets, with Dublin Bay prawns, Stilton and celery soup and such, and a fabulous Thames-side setting. ✉ *36E Shad Thames, SE1,* ☎ *020/7403–3403. AE, DC, MC, V.* ◷ *Brunch served Sun. noon–3.*

Christopher's. Imagine you're in Manhattan at this superior Covent Garden purveyor of American food, from pancakes to steak, eggs and fries, via salmon fish cakes and a Caesar salad. Two courses cost £16. ✉ *18 Wellington St., WC2,* ☎ *020/7240–4222. AE, DC, MC, V.* ◷ *Brunch served Sun. 11:30–4:30.*

✦ ✗ **Joe Allen.** This famed hangout (☞ *above*) is where to take refuge from the lovely British weather and down some Bloody Marys, and maybe a grilled chicken sandwich with Swiss chard, or a salad of spicy sausage, shrimp, and new potatoes. ✉ *13 Exeter St., WC2,* ☎ *020/7836–0651. Reservations essential. AE, MC, V.* ◷ *Brunch served Sun. noon–4.*

Veeraswamy. This restaurant has been here for years, but it's been taken over by the trendy Chutney Mary Group from Chelsea and given a modern makeover. The result is great, and what better way to try the delights here than the special Sunday brunch menu (£14 for three courses). You'll be so taken with the fresh aromatic fish and chicken dishes followed by mod-Euro/trad-Indian desserts, you'll be coming back for dinner. ✉ *Victory House, 101 Regent St., W1,* ☎ *020/7734–1401. AE, DC, MC, V.* ◷ *Brunch served Sun. noon–3.*

Afternoon Tea

Note that Claridge's and the Savoy require jacket and tie.

Brown's Hotel. Brown's does rest on its laurels somewhat, with a packaged aura and nobody around but fellow tourists who believe this to be the most famous. Still, everyone swears by the divine armchairs here. For £20 you get sandwiches, a scone with cream and jam, tart, fruit-cake, and shortbread. ✉ *33 Albermarle St., W1,* ☎ *020/7518–4108. AE, DC, MC, V.* ☉ *Tea served daily 3–6.*

Claridge's. This is the real McCoy, with liveried footmen proffering sandwiches, scones, and superior patisseries (£19 or £22) in the pala-tial yet genteel Foyer, to the sound of the resident "Hungarian orchestra" (actually a string quartet). ✉ *Brook St., W1,* ☎ *020/7629–8860. AE, DC, MC, V.* ☉ *Tea served daily 3–5:30.*

Fortnum & Mason. Upstairs at the Queen's grocers, three set teas are ceremoniously offered: standard afternoon tea (sandwiches, scone, cakes, £16.50), old-fashioned high tea (the traditional nursery meal, adding something more robust and savory, £18.50), and champagne tea (£21.50). ✉ *St. James's Restaurant, 4th floor, 181 Piccadilly, W1,* ☎ *020/7734–8040. AE, DC, MC, V.* ☉ *Tea served Mon.–Sat. 3–5:20.*

Harrods. For sweet-toothed people, the Georgian Restaurant Room at this ridiculously well known department store has a high tea that will give you a sugar rush for a week. ✉ *Brompton Rd., SW3,* ☎ *020/7730–1234. AE, DC, MC, V.* ☉ *Tea served Mon.–Sat. 3:15–5:15.*

The Orangery at Kensington Palace. This Georgian, gorgeous, sunlight-flooded (assuming the sun is out), yes, orangery is the perfect setting for a light lunch or for tea, serving homemade soups and quiche, cakes, shortbread, pastries, and pots of Earl Grey. ✉ *Kensington Gar-dens, W8,* ☎ *020/7376–0239. AE, MC, V. Closed after 5, Oct.–Easter; after 6, Easter–Sept. Tube: High Street Kensington.*

The Ritz. The Ritz's huge, stagey, and sometimes cold and overly for-mal Palm Court offers tiered cake stands, silver pots, a harpist, and Louis XVI chaises, plus a great deal of rococo gilt and glitz, all for £27. Reservations for this extremely popular tea are taken way in advance— months for a Saturday or Sunday. ✉ *150 Piccadilly, W1,* ☎ *020/ 7493–8181. Reserve 4 wks ahead, longer for weekends. AE, DC, MC, V.* ☉ *Tea served daily 2–6.*

The Savoy. The glamorous Thames-side hotel does one of the most pleas-ant teas (£19 or £26), its triple-tiered cake stands packed with good-ies, its tailcoated waiters thrillingly polite. ✉ *The Strand, WC2,* ☎ *020/ 7836–4343. AE, DC, MC, V.* ☉ *Tea served daily 3–5:30.*

Pubs

Even today, when television keeps so many people glued to their own hearth and home, the pub, or public house, or "local"—it has many aliases—is still a vital part of British life. It also should be a part of the tourist experience, as there are few better places to meet the natives in their local habitat. Sit at a table if you want privacy; better, help prop up the bar, where no introductions are needed, and watch that legendary British reserve fade away. There are hundreds of pubs in London, but the best—ever fewer of which still feature original Victorian etched glass, Edwardian panels, and Art Nouveau carvings—are listed below.

As we write, "gastro-pub" fever is still sweeping London. At many places, char-grills are being installed in the kitchen out back, while up front the faded wallpapers and the dear ole Mums are being replaced by ab-stract paintings and food mavens galore (in fact, the best of these new luxe pubs are dealt with in the restaurant reviews above). Some of the following also feature nouveau pub grub, but whether you have Mo-roccan chicken or the usually dismal ploughman's special, you'll want to order a pint. What Americans call beer Brits call lager. However, the main Brit pub drink is "bitter"—usually warm. Today, there is a flourishing movement to bring back the traditionally prepared ale that is much less gassy. There's also a vast range of other potations—stouts like Guinness and Murphy's are thick, pitch-black brews you'll either hate or love; ciders, made from apples, are an alcoholic drink in Britain (Bulmer's and Strongbow are the names to remember); shandies are a mix of lager and lemonade or orange sodas; while black and tans are a blend of lager and stout named for the distinctive uniforms worn by turn-of-the-century British troops. Discuss your choices and other arcane details of drink with the barman, turn to your neighbor, raise the glass, and utter that most pleasant of toasts, "Cheers." Note that, in some circles, women are expected to drink out of half-pint, not full-pint, glasses. Be warned if you order a drink that would normally be served with ice in the United States—ice cubes are about as common in pubs as they are in Hades.

Arcane licensing laws forbid the serving of alcohol after 11 PM (10:30 on Sunday; different rules for restaurants) and have created, some argue, a nation of alcoholics, driven to down more pints than is decent in a limited time—a circumstance you see in action at 10 minutes to 11, when the "last orders" bell signals a stampede to the bar. That noted, "lock-ins" are an old tradition—pubs that lock the front door after hours and ask remaining customers to leave by the side door—that bobbies tend to overlook. The list below offers a few pubs selected for central location, historical interest, a pleasant garden, music, or good food, but you might just as happily adopt your own temporary local.

The Albert. Positively heaving with ambience, the Albert must have been designed to be the complete and authentic London pub, with its burnished wood, walls adorned with Victorian prints about the evils of drinking, and a "division bell" (which calls back members of Parliament in time for a vote). The food in the carvery upstairs is so good reservations are usually required. ✉ *52 Victoria St., SW1,* ☎ *020/7222–5577.*
Black Friar. A step from the Blackfriars tube, this spectacular pub has an Arts and Crafts interior that is entertainingly, satirically ecclesiastical, with inlaid mother-of-pearl, wood carvings, stained glass, and marble pillars all over the place. In spite of the finely lettered temperance tracts on view just below the reliefs of monks, fairies, and friars, there are, needless to say, a nice group of beers on tap from independent brewers. ✉ *174 Queen Victoria St., EC4,* ☎ *020/7236–5650.*
Crown and Goose. This is a sky-blue-walled, art-bedecked Camden Town local, where armchairs augment the tables and coffee and herb tea the beers, and good food (steak in baguettes, smoked chicken salad with honey vinaigrette, baked and stuffed mushrooms) is served to the crowds. ✉ *100 Arlington Rd., NW1,* ☎ *020/7485–8008.*
Dove Inn. Read the list of famous ex-regulars, from Charles II and Nell Gwynn (mere rumor, but a likely one) to Ernest Hemingway as you wait for a beer at this very popular, very comely 16th-century riverside pub by Hammersmith Bridge. If it's *too* full, stroll upstream to the Old Ship or the Blue Anchor. ✉ *19 Upper Mall, W6,* ☎ *020/8748–5405.*
French House. In the pub where the French Resistance convened during World War II, Soho hipsters and eccentrics rub shoulders now—more than shoulders, actually, because this tiny, tricolore-waving, photograph-lined pub is always filled to bursting with theater luvvies and literary bods. ✉ *49 Dean St., W1,* ☎ *020/7437–2799.*
George Inn. The inn sits in a courtyard where Shakespeare's plays were once performed. The present building dates from the late 17th century and is central London's last remaining galleried inn. Dickens was a regular—the inn is featured in *Little Dorrit.* Entertainments include Shakespeare performances, medieval jousts, and morris dancing. ✉ *77 Borough High St., SE1,* ☎ *020/7407–2056.*
Island Queen. Gigantic caricature pirates leer down at you from the ceiling in this sociable Islington pub, which offers home-cooked food,

a busy pool table, and a fab jukebox. The playwright Joe Orton frequented the place; he lived—and died—next door, murdered by his lover. ✉ *87 Noel Rd., N1,* ☎ *020/7704–7631.*

Jack Straw's Castle. Straw was one of the leaders of the Peasants Revolt of 1381, and he was hanged nearby. In Tudor times this was a favorite hangout for highwaymen, but by the 19th century it had become picturesque and respectable; artists painted charming views from it, and Dickens (inevitably) stayed here. Sadly, it was blitzed during World War II but rebuilt in 1963. You can admire the views over Hampstead Heath and drink (weather permitting) in the large and lovely outside courtyard. ✉ *North End Way, NW3,* ☎ *020/7435–8885.*

The Lamb. Another of Dickens's locals is now a picturesque place for a pint in summer, when you can drink on the patio. ✉ *94 Lamb's Conduit St., WC1,* ☎ *020/7405–0713.*

Lamb & Flag. This 17th-century pub was once known as "The Bucket of Blood" because the upstairs room was used as a ring for bareknuckle boxing. Now, it's a trendy, friendly, and entirely bloodless pub, serving food (at lunchtime only) and real ale. It's on the edge of Covent Garden, off Garrick Street. ✉ *33 Rose St., WC2,* ☎ *020/7497–9504.*

Mayflower. An atmospheric 17th-century riverside inn, with exposed beams and a terrace, this is practically the very place from which the Pilgrims set sail for Plymouth Rock. The inn is licensed to sell American postage stamps. ✉ *117 Rotherhithe St., SE16,* ☎ *020/7237–4088.*

Museum Tavern. Across the street from the British Museum, this gloriously Victorian pub (although a pub has been here for centuries, and the book behind the bar details it) makes an ideal resting place after the rigors of the culture trail. With lots of fancy glass—etched mirrors and stained-glass panels—gilded pillars, and carvings, the heavily restored hostelry once helped Karl Marx to unwind after a hard day in the Library. He could have spent his *kapital* on any one of six beers available on tap. ✉ *49 Great Russell St., WC1,* ☎ *020/7242–8987.*

Pheasant and Firkin. David Bruce singlehandedly revived the practice of serving beer that's been brewed on the premises and long ago sold the thriving business. The jolly microbrewery-pubs, all named the something and Firkin (a small barrel), are now found throughout London and still serve beers called "dogbolter" or "rail ale" and sell T-shirts printed with bon mots like "I had a Pheasant time at the Firkin pub." Students like this a lot. ✉ *166 Goswell Rd., EC1,* ☎ *020/7253–7429.*

Princess Louise. This fine, popular pub has an over-the-top Victorian interior—glazed terra-cotta, stained and frosted glass, and a glorious painted ceiling. It's not all show, either; the food is a cut above normal pub grub, and there's a good selection of real ales. ✉ *208 High Holborn, WC1,* ☎ *020/7405–8816.*

Prospect of Whitby. Named after a ship, this is London's oldest riverside pub, dating to 1520. Once upon a time it was called "The Devil's Tavern" because of the low-life criminals—thieves and smugglers—who congregated here. It's ornamented with pewter ware and nautical memorabilia. ✉ *57 Wapping Wall, E1,* ☎ *020/7481–1095.*

St. James Tavern. This pretty pub is steps from Piccadilly Circus and five major West End theaters; another plus is that it also stays open until 1 AM Monday through Saturday. The decor includes lovely handpainted Doulton tiles depicting Shakespearean scenes. The kitchen is proud of its fish-and-chips. ✉ *45 Great Windmill St., W1V,* ☎ *020/ 7437–5009.*

Sherlock Holmes. This pub used to be known as "The Northumberland Arms," and Arthur Conan Doyle popped in regularly for a pint. It figures in *The Hound of the Baskervilles,* and you can see the hound's head and plaster casts of its huge paws among other Holmes memorabilia in the bar. ✉ *10 Northumberland St., WC2,* ☎ *020/7930–2644.*

Spaniards Inn. This is another historic, oak-beamed pub on Hampstead Heath, boasting a gorgeous rose garden, scene of the tea party in Dickens's *Pickwick Papers*. Dick Turpin, the highwayman, used to frequent the inn; you can see his pistols on display. Romantic poets—Shelley, Keats, Byron—hung out here, and so, of course, did Dickens. It's extremely popular, especially on Sundays, when Londoners take to the heath in search of fresh air. ✉ *Spaniards Rd., NW3,* ☎ *020/7455–3276.*

Star Tavern. In the heart of elegant Belgravia, this pub features a post-card-perfect Georgian-era facade. The inside is charming too; Victorian decor and two roaring fireplaces make this a popular spot. ✉ *6 Belgrave Mews West, SW1,* ☎ *020/7235–3019.*

Three Greyhounds. Usefully Soho-central, this welcoming, reconditioned mock-Tudor pub serves a great bar meal—homemade Scotch eggs (hard-boiled, wrapped in sausage meat, and deep-fried in bread crumbs), matzo-coated southern-fried chicken, sandwiches of home-cured ham or herring, oysters by the half dozen. Its other claim to fame is its youthful landlady's name—say hi to Roxy Beaujolais. ✉ *25 Greek St., W1,* ☎ *020/7287–0754.*

Windsor Castle. This is one to rest at on a Kensington jaunt, saving a large appetite for the food, especially on Sunday, when they do a traditional roast; other days there are oysters and salads, fish cakes and steak sandwiches. In winter there are blazing fires; in summer, an exquisite walled patio garden. ✉ *114 Campden Hill Rd., W8,* ☎ *020/ 7727–8491.*

Ye Bunch of Grapes. A traditional (which means smoky, noisy, and anti-chic) pub, popular since Victoria was on the throne, in the heart of Shepherd Market, the village-within-Mayfair, this place is still home-away-from-home for a full deck of London characters. ✉ *16 Shepherd Market, W1,* ☎ *020/7499–1563.*

Ye Olde Cheshire Cheese. Yes, it is a tourist trap, but this most historic of all London pubs (it dates from 1667) deserves a visit anyway, for its sawdust-covered floors, low wood-beam ceilings, and the 14th-century crypt of Whitefriars' monastery under the cellar bar. But if you want to see the set of 17th-century pornographic tiles that once adorned upstairs, you'll have to get special permission from the brewery to see them at the British Museum. This was the most regular of Dr. Johnson's and Dickens's many locals. ✉ *145 Fleet St., EC1,* ☎ *020/7353–6170.*

3 LODGING

Queen Elizabeth hasn't invited you this
time? No matter. Staying at one of London's
grande-dame hotels is the next best thing—
some say better—to being a guest at
the palace. Royally resplendent decor
abounds, and armies of staff are stuck in
the pampering mode—the Windsors should
have it so good. Even in more affordable
choices, inimitable British style brings
you a taste of home, with tea makers and
Queen Mum pastel wallpaper. Still not
cozy enough? Borrow some keys and
be a B&B guest.

Updated by
Roland
Chambers

S TANDING IN THE PARLORLIKE atmosphere of your lobby—burnished oak paneling, time-stained antiques, chintz-softened sofas, the distant tinkle of teacups in the air—a century seems to slip away. The concierge whispers that Queen Victoria used to visit—she, too, probably got willingly lost in the corridors and crannies. In the grand salon sit ancient Chippendale desks that once bore the concentrated energy of the empire's Kiplings and Hardys. Set near a crackling fire, a roomy leather Chesterfield beckons one to approach its quilted field. Yes, our Auld London Towne fantasies may be fading fast in the light of Blair's Britain, but when it comes time to rest your head, the old-fashioned clichés remain very enticing. Who wouldn't want to lounge in an overstuffed brocade armchair while cream tea is served by a frock-coated retainer? Or to breakfast on coffee, toast, and croissants in a handmade bed in your powder-blue and white Syrie Maugham–esque boudoir as the Thames flows lazily past your French windows? Choose one of London's heritage-rich hotels—Brown's and Claridge's supply perfect parlors; the Savoy has that river view—and these fantasies can, and always will, be fulfilled.

On the other hand, faster times are bringing more changes to the London hotel scene than there have been in years. Hotels are springing up in places not previously considered "touristy," meaning your stay need not be confined to the bustle and noise of the West End or the exclusive nabes (so exclusive you will find few Brits native to these areas) of Kensington or Knightsbridge. And the variety is not limited to location. In terms of price, the growth is at the top and bottom ends of the market. Immaculately designed, entirely contemporary hotels now are challenging luxurious, old, chintzy favorites while nationwide budget chains take on the B&B scene, offering clean and functional accommodations at friendly prices. Chain hotels with cookie-cutter decor, and—as they used to say—all mod cons (modern conveniences), tended to avoid London's center, but they're moving in now, attracted by the big increase in Chunnel travelers and other inter-Europe wayfarers. It adds another option to your vacation planning: you no longer need to blow your entire budget on your bed.

Still, if you want to do just that, London is the place. Prices can soar into the empyrean here, but many of the best hotels are worth it. Take the Connaught, a landmark whose guests wouldn't *dream* of staying anywhere else. Its Edwardian lobby, created in 1897, is unadulterated by things modern; grand and faded, it is filled with oil paintings and antiques in a way interior designers envy but can't really duplicate. In contrast to this dowager-aunt type are hotels such as the Pelham and Covent Garden—most of them renovated town houses, aglitter with sensationally atmospheric Regency-style interiors and richly endowed with stunning furnishings and guests. Designed to be the very epitome of English country-housedom, these newer boutique hotels appeal to clientele bent on revisiting the landed gentry culture. Waving the banner SMALL IS BEAUTIFUL, they have stolen a march on the genteel sleeping beauties—the Claridges, the Savoys, and the Dorchesters—who, recently awakened, have launched a broad counterattack. The Sultan of Brunei sank tens of millions into refurbishing the Dorchester; a Hunt heiress sponsored a complete makeover of the Lanesborough; and the Connaught, Savoy, and Claridge's have each been renovated to the tune of a mint. Paying top dollar, of course, does not always mean you'll get stately grandeur—several places have moved away from Regency flounces and Laura Ashleyisms into neo-Bauhaus minimalism. The Halkin was the first frill-free grand hotel; now add the Metropolitan

London Lodging *(Boxes Refer to Detail Maps)*

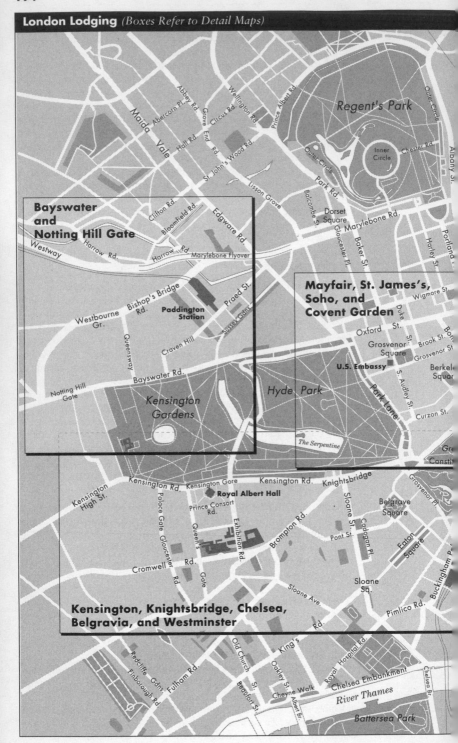

**Bayswater
and
Notting Hill Gate**

**Mayfair, St. James's,
Soho, and
Covent Garden**

**Kensington, Knightsbridge, Chelsea,
Belgravia, and Westminster**

Regent's Park

Maida Vale

Abbey Rd.
Abercorn Pl.
Grove End Rd.
Circus Rd.
Wellington Rd.
Prince Albert Rd.
Hall Rd.
St. John's Wood Rd.
Lisson Grove
Balcombe St.
Park Rd.
Outer Circle
Inner Circle
Chester Rd.
Albany St.

Westway
Harrow Rd.
Clifton Rd.
Bloomfield Rd.
Harrow Rd.
Edgware Rd.
Marylebone Flyover
Dorset Square
Marylebone Rd.
Gloucester Pl.
Baker St.
Harley St.
Portland
Wigmore St.

Bishop's Bridge Rd.
Westbourne Gr.
Paddington Station
Praed St.
Sussex Gdns.

Mayfair...
Oxford St.
Duke St.
Brook St.
Grosvenor Square
Grosvenor St.
Berkeley Square
Bond

Queensway
Craven Hill
U.S. Embassy
S. Audley St.

Bayswater Rd.
Hyde Park
Park Lane
Curzon St.

Notting Hill Gate
Kensington Gardens
The Serpentine
Gre...
Consti...

Kensington High St.
Kensington Rd.
Kensington Gore
Kensington Rd.
Knightsbridge
Grosvenor Pl.
Royal Albert Hall
Prince Consort Rd.
Palace Gate
Gloucester Rd.
Queen's Gate
Exhibition Rd.
Brompton Rd.
Sloane St.
Pont St.
Cadogan Pl.
Belgrave Square
Eaton Square

Cromwell Rd.
Sloane Ave.
Sloane Sq.
Pimlico Rd.
Buckingham P...

Redcliffe Gdns.
Finborough Rd.
Fulham Rd.
Old Church St.
Beaufort St.
King's Rd.
Oakley St.
Cheyne Walk
Albert Br.
Royal Hospital Rd.
Chelsea Embankment
Chelsea Br.
River Thames
Battersea Park

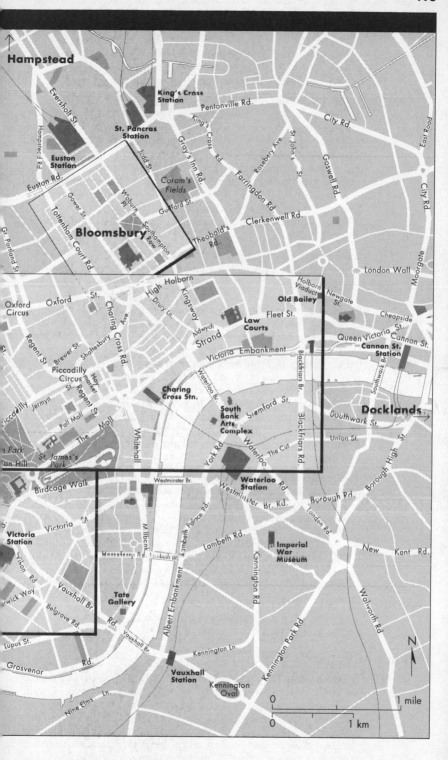

Hampstead

King's Cross Station

St. Pancras Station

Euston Station

Pentonville Rd.

City Rd.

Eversholt St.

Hampstead Rd.

King's Cross Rd.

Gray's Inn Rd.

Rosebery Ave.

St. John's St.

Goswell Rd.

City Rd.

East Road

Euston Rd.

Coram's Fields

Farringdon Rd.

Clerkenwell Rd.

London Wall

Moorgate

Gt. Portland St.

Tottenham Court Rd.

Gower St.

Woburn Pl.

Southampton Row

Judd St.

Guilford St.

Theobald's Rd.

Bloomsbury

Oxford Circus

Oxford

St.

Charing Cross Rd.

High Holborn

Kingsway

Drury Ln.

Aldwych

Law Courts

Fleet St.

Strand

Old Bailey

Holborn Viaduct

Newgate St.

Cheapside

Queen Victoria St.

Cannon St.

Cannon St. Station

Regent St.

Brewer St.

Shaftesbury

Haymarket

St.

Regent St.

Piccadilly Circus

Jermyn

Pall Mall

Piccadilly

The Mall

Victoria Embankment

Waterloo Br.

Charing Cross Stn.

South Bank Arts Complex

Stamford St.

Blackfriars Br.

Blackfriars Rd.

Southwark Br.

Docklands

Southwark St.

St. James's Park

Park

on Hill

Birdcage Walk

Whitehall

York Rd.

Waterloo Rd.

The Cut

Union St.

Borough High St.

Westminster Br.

Waterloo Station

Victoria Station

Victoria

Westminster Br. Rd.

Borough Rd.

London Rd.

New

Kent Rd.

Walworth Rd.

Millbank

Lambeth Palace Rd.

Lambeth Rd.

Imperial War Museum

Kennington Rd.

Kennington Park Rd.

on Rd.

Wilton Rd.

Warwick Way

Vauxhall Br.

Belgrave Rd.

Lupus St.

Tate Gallery

Horseferry Rd.

Lambeth Br.

Albert Embankment

Vauxhall Br.

Rd.

Grosvenor

Rd.

Nine Elms Ln.

Vauxhall Station

Kennington Ln.

Kennington Oval

N

0   1 mile

0   1 km

and the ultrafashionable Hempel. Look forward also to the Great Eastern, which offers all the advantages of an exorbitant modernity and is the first hotel in its league to be opened in London's financial nerve centre—the City. At the other end of the scale, things can be almost as trendy. In design-crazy London, even hostels have become stylish—just look into the future at the Generator.

As the city is the opposite of compact, where you stay can affect your experience significantly. For instance, the West End is equivalent to downtown, but it covers a lot of ground. There's a great deal of difference between, say, posh Park Lane and bustling, touristy Leicester Square, yet both are in the West End. Hotels in Mayfair and St. James's are central and yet distant in both mileage and atmosphere from funky, youthful neighborhoods like Notting Hill and Camden Town and from major tourist sights like the Tower of London, St. Paul's Cathedral, and the large Kensington museums. On the edges of the West End, Soho and Covent Garden have countless restaurants and late-opening bars and clubs.

South Kensington, Kensington, Chelsea, and Knightsbridge are all patrician and peaceful, which will give you a more homey feeling than anything in the West End, while Belgravia is superelegant, geographically and atmospherically about halfway between the extremes. From Bloomsbury it's a short stroll to the shops and restaurants of Covent Garden, to Theatreland, and to the British Museum. Once the preserve of family-run B&Bs, it now features that new Conran hotel on leafy Dorset Square, making Bloomsbury a more fashionable place to stay than in past years. From here, it's a short bus ride to Camden and Regent's Park, too, and Hampstead and Islington are close enough to explore easily. Bayswater is a particularly affordable haven. It's barely considered a real neighborhood by Londoners, but everywhere is accessible from there, and Hyde Park is your backyard. Notting Hill and Holland Park are worth considering as a base if you want something more down-home plus have the antiques of Portobello Road and its surrounding cutting-edge shops and restaurants on your doorstep.

The general custom these days in all but the bottom end of the scale is for rates to be quoted for the room alone (which unless otherwise noted is with bath); breakfast, whether Continental or "full English," comes at extra cost. VAT and service charges are usually included. All the hotels listed here are graded according to their weekday, high season rates from spring 2000. Remember there may be significant discounts at the weekend or off-season. Like hotels in most other European countries, British hotels are obliged by law to display a tariff at the reception desk. If you have not booked ahead, you are strongly advised to study this carefully.

Be sure to make reservations well in advance. For approximate costs, *see* the lodging price chart, *in* Smart Travel Tips A to Z.

Mayfair to Regent's Park

££££   ☒ **Athenaeum.** The welcome in this independently run baby grand opposite Green Park is in the details: from Donald, the superconcierge at his door-side desk, to the disposable camera in the minibar to the compact health spa. Rooms have distinctive custom-made leather-top mahogany and yew furniture, set against navy-and-cream drapes, Wedgwood-green walls, and ultrathick cream carpets. Without getting out of bed, you can control lighting and temperature, order free videos and CDs, and listen to your voice mail from your two phone lines. In glittering gray-marble bathrooms are power showers, mirrors angled to get the back of your head; old-fashioned Bronnley toiletries; and a hair dryer. Downstairs, there's the cozy Whisky Bar and the not-too-formal Bullochs restaurant. Rooms 201–205 face Green Park; others have a bay that affords a partial, angled view. ✉ *116 Piccadilly, W1V 0BJ,* ☎ *020/ 7499–3464,* ℻ *020/7493–1860. 111 rooms, 12 suites. Restaurant, bar, in-room VCRs, health club. AE, DC, MC, V. Tube: Green Park.* ✍

££££ 🏨 **Brown's.** Founded in 1837 by Lord Byron's "gentleman's gentleman," James Brown, this Victorian country house in central Mayfair comprises 11 Georgian houses and is occupied by many Anglophilic Americans—a habit that was established by the two Roosevelts (Teddy while on honeymoon). Bedrooms feature thick carpets, soft armchairs, brass chandeliers, and brocade wallpapers, as well as air-conditioning, while the public rooms retain their cozy oak-paneled, chintz-laden, grandfather-clock-ticking-in-the-parlor ambience. The restaurant, named 1837 in honor of the year Brown's opened, has been given a new lease on life and a chef who believes in classical French cuisine complete with an encyclopedic wine list. Right outside the door are the boutiques and art galleries of Bond and Cork streets, while in the lounge, one of London's best-known afternoon teas is served from 3 to 5:45. ✉ *34 Albemarle St., W1X 4BT,* ☎ *020/7493–6020,* ℻ *020/7493–9381. 118 rooms. Restaurant, bar. AE, DC, MC, V. Tube: Green Park.* ✍

££££ 🏨 **Churchill Inter-Continental.** Modern Park Avenue luxury came to London when the Tisch family opened this homage to Winston Churchill in the 1970s. Last year they spent £6 million on two brand-new floors. The lobby is opulent and Robert Adams–esque with a gilded ceiling and black marble columns, and the Regency-style grace notes continue throughout. Clementine's—named after the great man's wife—is the main restaurant, while the Churchill Bar and Cigar Divan, a gleaming maplewood nook, proffers private-label smokes, 75 varieties of whiskeys, and grand-piano entertainment. Business travelers and visiting VIPs like Madeleine Albright love this place; others like the Portman Square location, just two blocks from Marble Arch, the shops of Oxford Street, and the Wallace Collection. ✉ *30 Portman Sq., W1A,* ☎ *020/7486– 5800,* ℻ *020/7486–1255. 395 rooms, 40 suites. 2 restaurants, bar, meeting rooms. AE, DC, MC, V. Tube: Marble Arch.* ✍

££££ 🏨 **Claridge's.** Stay here, and you're staying at a hotel legend (founded ★ in 1812), with one of the world's classiest guest lists. The liveried staff is friendly and not in the least condescending, and the rooms are never less than luxurious, thanks to a £40 million refurbishment. Enjoy tea or coffee in the Foyer lounge (24 hours a day) with its Hungarian mini-orchestra or retreat to the stylish Claridge's bar for cocktails and canapés. The bathrooms are spacious (with enormous showerheads), as are the bedrooms, with bells (which still work) to summon either maid or valet from their station on each floor. Beds are handmade and supremely comfortable—the King of Morocco once brought his own, couldn't sleep, and ended up ordering 30 from Claridge's to take home. The grand staircase and magnificent elevator are equally impressive. ✉ *Brook St., W1A 2JQ,* ☎ *020/7629–8860 or 800/223–6800,* ℻ *020/7499 2210. 200 rooms. Restaurant, bar, beauty salon, health club. AE, DC, MC, V. Tube: Bond St.* ✍

££££ 🏨 **Connaught.** Make reservations well in advance for this *very* exclu-★ sive small hotel just off Grosvenor Square—the most understated of any of London's grand hostelries and the London home-away-from-home for guests who inherited the Connaught habit from their great-grandfathers. The bar and lounges have the air of an ambassadorial residence, an impression reinforced by the imposing oak staircase and dignified staff. Each bedroom has a foyer, antique furniture (if you don't like the desk, they'll change it), and fresh flowers. If you value privacy, discretion, and the kind of luxury that eschews labels, then you have met your

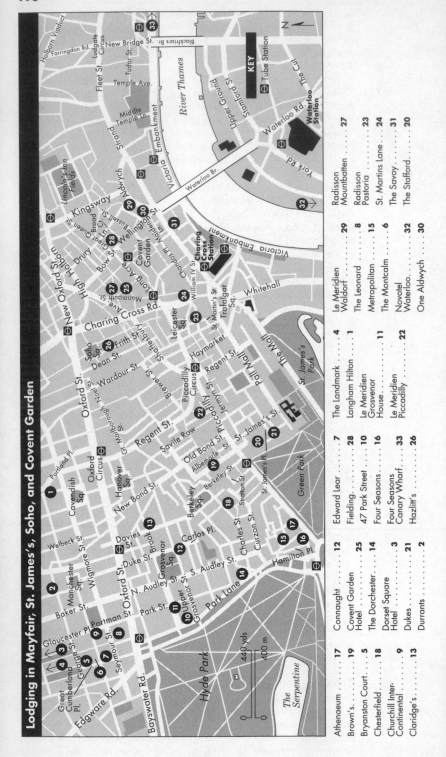

Lodging in Mayfair, St. James's, Soho, and Covent Garden

KEY
⊖ Tube Station

Athenaeum 17
Brown's 19
Bryanston Court . . . 5
Chesterfield 18
Churchill Inter-Continental . . . 9
Claridge's 13
Connaught 12
Covent Garden Hotel . . 25
The Dorchester . . . 14
Dorset Square Hotel . . 3
Dukes 21
Durrants 2
Edward Lear 7
Fielding 28
47 Park Street . . . 10
Four Seasons 16
Four Seasons Canary Wharf . . 33
Hazlitt's 26
The Landmark 4
Langham Hilton . . . 1
Le Meridien Grosvenor House . . 11
Le Meridien Piccadilly . . 22
Le Meridien Waldorf . . 29
The Leonard 8
Metropolitan 15
The Montcalm 6
Novotel Waterloo . . . 32
One Aldwych 30
Radisson Mountbatten . . 27
Radisson Pastoria . . 23
St. Martins Lane . . . 24
The Savoy 31
The Stafford 20

match here. ⊠ *Carlos Pl., W1Y 6AL,* ☎ *020/7499–7070,* FAX *020/ 7495–3262. 90 rooms. Restaurant, bar. MC. Tube: Bond St.* 🐾

££££ 🏨 **The Dorchester.** Probably no other hotel this opulent manages to be
★ this charming. A London institution since its 1931 inception, the Dorchester appears on every "world's best" list. The glamour level is off the scale: 1,500 square yards of gold leaf and 1,100 of marble gild this lily, and bedrooms (some not as spacious as you might imagine) feature Irish linen sheets on canopied beds, brocades and velvets, individual climate control, dual voltage outlets, and Italian marble and etched-glass bathrooms with Floris goodies. Decor throughout is in opulent English country-house style, with more than a hint of Art Deco, in keeping with the original 1930s building. There's a beauty spa, a nightclub, a special theater-ticket concierge, the Oriental restaurant, and the power-dining Grill Room. Taking afternoon tea, drinking, lounging, and posing are all accomplished in the catwalk-shape Promenade lounge, where you may spot one of the film-star types who will stay nowhere else (Elizabeth Taylor has been a habitué for decades— in fact, she was sitting in her tub here when that million-dollar offer to film *Cleopatra* came over the telephone). ⊠ *Park La., W1A 2HJ,* ☎ *020/7629–8888,* FAX *020/7409–0114. 195 rooms, 53 suites. 2 restaurants, bar, health club, nightclub, business services, meeting rooms. AE, DC, MC, V. Tube: Marble Arch.* 🐾

££££ 🏨 **47 Park Street.** Secreted back to back with the grand hotels of Park Lane, this dear (in every sense) little all-suite hotel has the best room service in town, with 24-hour food direct from the kitchen of Le Gavroche (☞ Chapter 2). Business services range from three personal phone lines to in-house translation facilities. Bathrooms are on the small side, but no other drawbacks are apparent in this fabulously discreet, conventionally decorated, quiet, relaxed, and homey haven—as long as you can afford it. ⊠ *47 Park St., W1Y 4EB,* ☎ *020/7491–7282,* FAX *020/7491–7281. 52 suites. Dining room, bar (jacket and tie), babysitting. AE, DC, MC, V. Tube: Marble Arch.* 🐾

££££ 🏨 **Four Seasons.** Business travelers, of course, swear by Four Seasons' standards of luxury and comfort. This hotel opened in the '70s as Inn on the Park, so if wedding-cake Victorian architecture is your thing, go elsewhere. Still, the discretion and élan of this place (situated opposite Hyde Park, off the end of Piccadilly, and on the cusp of beautiful Mayfair) inspire more-than-average loyalty in its guests. Every effort is made inside to keep up with the times—new features are constantly being added, the latest being the Lanes restaurant, which offers a sparkling menu and a view of Hyde Park to match. ⊠ *Hamilton Pl., Park La., W1A 1AZ,* ☎ *020/7499–0888 or 800/223–6800,* FAX *020/ 7493–6629. 228 rooms. Restaurant, health club. AE, DC, MC, V. Tube: Hyde Park Corner.* 🐾

££££ 🏨 **The Landmark.** In honor of its 100th anniversary, the onetime Great Central Hotel and former BritRail HQ was recently renovated to within a glitzy inch of its life. A palm-filled, eight-story glazed atrium Winter Garden forms the core, and odd-numbered rooms overlook this. If size matters to you, note that even standard rooms here are among the largest in London and have glamorous bathrooms in marble and chrome outfitted with robe and hair dryer. Despite appearances, this is one of the only London grand hotels that don't force you to dress up—even jeans are okay. The Landmark is very near Regent's Park; the West End is a 15-minute walk away. ⊠ *222 Marylebone Rd., NW1 6JQ,* ☎ *020/7631–8000,* FAX *020/7631–8080. 297 rooms. 2 restaurants, 2 bars, indoor pool, health club, business services. AE, DC, MC, V. Tube: Marylebone.* 🐾

££££ 🏨 **Langham Hilton.** Opened in 1865 by the Prince of Wales and once London's center of Victorian chic—regular guests included Toscanini, Mark

Twain, and Oscar Wilde—the Langham has recently been renovated to become the London flagship of the Hilton chain. All columns and porticoes, its exterior looks very Grand Hotel, especially at night with fairy-tale floodlighting. Inside, the lobby soars to Castle Howard heights—here you find the Chukka Bar, a stately-house salon glowing with daffodil-yellow walls, for years a fave watering spot for the BBC brass across the way. Guest rooms are done in soothing Queen Mother pastels, and many have marble-bedecked bathrooms. You're just a few blocks from the Oxford Circus tube stop and many of the big Regent Street stores. ⊠ *1C Portland Pl., W1N 3AA,* ☎ *020/7636–1000,* ℻ *020/7323–2340. 400 rooms. 2 restaurants, bar. AE, DC, MC, V.* ☜ *Tube: Oxford Circus.*

££££ ⊞ **Le Meridien Grosvenor House.** "The old lady of Park Lane" has had a recent overhaul supervised by English Heritage, the people who usually look after historic museums and stately houses. It's not the kind of place that encourages hushed whispers or that frowns on trendy Alexander McQueen outfits, despite the marble floors and wood-paneled library, open fires, oils, and fine antiques, all inspired by the Earl of Grosvenor's residence, which occupied the site during the 18th century. The hotel health club is one of the best around, thanks to its good-size pool. Bedrooms are spacious, and most of the marble bathrooms have natural light. ⊠ *Park La., W1A 3AA,* ☎ *020/7499–6363,* ℻ *020/7493–3341. 380 rooms, 70 suites, 136 apartments. 2 restaurants, bar, indoor pool, health club. AE, DC, MC, V. Tube: Marble Arch.* ☜

££££ ⊞ **Le Meridien Piccadilly.** The massive turn-of-the-century building is fin-de-siècle elegant, if slightly antiseptic in its white-marble-and-plush-carpet public areas. The vast Oak Room restaurant, however, is exquisite in limed oak paneling and gilt, and it is one of the best hotel restaurants in London, lorded over by famous chef Marco Pierre White. The hotel's second restaurant, far less formal, is a miniature Kew Gardens of arched glass, ferns, and palms. Bedrooms vary in size; a few seventh-floor ones have balconies overlooking Piccadilly. Decor is Edwardian-gent's-club with frills. The health club is the most luxurious and exclusive in London and boasts squash courts, saunas, and billiard tables, as well as a swimming pool. You can't be more central than here. ⊠ *Piccadilly, W1V 0BH,* ☎ *020/7734–8000,* ℻ *020/7437–3574. 284 rooms. 3 restaurants, bar, indoor pool, health club, library, business services. AE, DC, MC, V. Tube: Piccadilly Circus.*

££££ ⊞ **Metropolitan.** Supertrendy from the moment the DKNY-clad doormen opened the gates, this latest Park Lane grand is one of the only addresses for fashion folk, the music biz, and Hollywood youth, just as its bar is the hangout of choice (the barman even has his own column in a Sunday newspaper), and its restaurant, leased by Nobu Matsuhisa, of Nobu New York City "new style sashimi" fame, is among the swankiest in town. The lobby is sleek and postmodern (psst . . . didn't the Royalton and other N.Y.C. hotels do this long ago?). The best rooms overlook Hyde Park, but all have identical minimalist beige-and-white decor, with climate control, bedside panel-operated lighting, U.S./U.K. modem points, ISDN lines, three telephone lines, and satellite and cable TV. The minibar contains the latest alcoholic and health-boosting beverages, and the bathroom's stocked with Kiehl's goodies. Be here, and pose. ⊠ *Old Park La., W1Y 4LB,* ☎ *020/7447–1000,* ℻ *020/7447–1100. 137 rooms, 18 suites. Restaurant, bar, massage, exercise room, meeting rooms. AE, DC, MC, V. Tube: Hyde Park Corner.* ☜

££££ ⊞ **The Montcalm.** Secreted behind Marble Arch in a peaceful Georgian crescent, the Montcalm has kept a low profile since its rock-star days, but it is now back up there with the best of them, thanks to the Japanese owners, Nikko, who have made it an especially efficient, spotless, and calm hotel, with some unusual features. Here is London's only low-allergen bedroom, its only canopied water bed (not in the same room), and one of its few Japanese breakfasts, bathrooms with electronic hair dryers and bidets, and, by the conservatorylike Crescent restaurant, a CD-operated player piano serenading lunchers with a little Brahms. The duplex suites, with their cast-iron spiral staircases, are especially winning. Recently, millions of pounds have been spent to fully air-condition this state-of-the-art hotel. ⊠ *Great Cumberland Pl., W1A 2LF,* ☎ *020/7402–4288,* FAX *020/7724–9180. 120 rooms. Restaurant, bar, meeting rooms. AE, DC, MC, V. Tube: Marble Arch.* ✍

£££ 🖬 **Chesterfield.** This former town house of the Earl of Chesterfield is popular with American visitors, many of whom are repeat guests or have links with the English Speaking Union, which has its headquarters next door. It is deep in the heart of Mayfair and has welcoming wood-and-leather public rooms and spacious bedrooms. The staff is outstandingly pleasant and helpful. ⊠ *35 Charles St., W1X 8LX,* ☎ *020/7491–2622,* FAX *020/7491–4793. 110 rooms. Restaurant. AE, DC, MC, V. Tube: Green Park.* ✍

£££ 🖬 **The Leonard.** Four 17th-century buildings were combined in 1996 to create this property. Shoppers will particularly appreciate the Mayfair location, just around the corner from Oxford Street. If you stay in a two-bedroom superior suite, you can swing by Marks & Spencer's food halls for provisions, then whip up a dinner in your private kitchen—a plus for families and visitors on longer trips. All the suites have a remarkably residential feel, with sitting and bedroom areas set off by small foyers and complemented by a judicious mix of lived-in antiques and comfortable reproductions. For more elbow room, try one of the aptly named grand suites, with their palatial sitting rooms and tall windows. The welcoming lobby area is stocked with complimentary newspapers to read by the fire. ⊠ *15 Seymour St., W1H 5AA,* ☎ *020/7935–2010,* FAX *020/7935–6700. 20 suites, 9 rooms. Bar, dining room, room service, exercise room, business services. AE, DC, MC, V. Tube: Marble Arch.* ✍

££ 🖬 **Bryanston Court.** Three Georgian houses have been converted into a hotel in an historic conservation area, a couple of blocks north of Hyde Park and Park Lane. The style is traditional English—open fireplaces, comfortable leather armchairs, oil portraits—though the bedrooms are small and modern, with pink furnishings, creaky floors, and minute bathrooms. Rooms at the back are quieter and face east, so they're bright in the mornings; Room 77 is as big as a suite, but being on the lower ground floor typical of rooms in London houses, it's dark. This family-run hotel is an excellent value for the area. ⊠ *56–60 Great Cumberland Pl., W1H 7FD,* ☎ *020/7262–3141,* FAX *020/7262–7248. 56 rooms. Breakfast room, bar. AE, DC, MC, V. Tube: Marble Arch.* ✍

££ 🖬 **Dorset Square Hotel.** This special small hotel off Baker Street was
★ the first of four London addresses for husband and wife Tim and Kit Kemp, hoteliers extraordinaire. What they did was decant the English country look into a fine pair of Regency town houses and then turn up the volume. Everywhere you look are covetable antiques, rich colors, and ideas *House & Garden* subscribers will steal. Naturally, every room is different: the first-floor balconied "Coronet" rooms are the largest, and a virtue is made of the smallness of the small rooms. The marble-and-mahogany bathrooms have power showers; glossy magazines, a half bottle of claret, and boxes of vitamin C are complimentary. There's a reason for the ubiquitous cricket memorabilia: Dorset Square was the first Lord's grounds. If you want a car rental here, you get a Bentley. ⊠ *39–40 Dorset Sq., NW1 6QN,* ☎ *020/7723–7874,* FAX *020/7724–3328. 38 rooms. Restaurant, bar. AE, MC, V. Tube: Baker St.* ✍

££ 🖬 **Durrants.** A hotel since the late-18th century, Durrants occupies a quiet corner almost next to the Wallace Collection, a stone's throw from Oxford Street and the smaller, posher shops of Marylebone High

Street. It's a good value for the area, and if you like ye wood-paneled, leather-armchaired, dark-red-pattern-carpeted style of olde Englishness, this will suit you. Bedrooms, by way of contrast, are wan and motel-like but perfectly adequate—several have no bath (this disadvantage has the advantage of saving you £10 a night). Best give the baron of beef–type restaurant a wide berth. ⊠ *George St., W1H 6BH,* ☎ *020/ 7935–8131, ℻ 020/7487–3510. 92 rooms, 85 with bath. Restaurant, bar, dining rooms. AE, MC, V. Tube: Bond St.*

££ ⚄ **Novotel Waterloo.** Looking otherwise precisely like 280 other hotels in 44 countries, this French-owned, inexpensive, reliable chain hotel offers a fitness center and brasserie, conference facilities, in-room satellite TV, tea/coffeemaker, direct-dial phone, and hair dryer in very compact rooms, plus—in 40 of them—*that* view. Actually, the view is more a flagrant grandstand spying over Lambeth Palace than a river vista, though you can see from Big Ben to St. Paul's for the £5 supplement the higher-floor rooms command. Mind you, the romance rating does plummet when you can't fling open the window to catch the Thames breeze on account of the guest-room climate-control system. ⊠ *113–127 Lambeth Rd., SE1 7JL,* ☎ *020/8283–4530. 189 rooms. Restaurant, bar, health club, meeting rooms. AE, DC, MC, V. Tube: Waterloo.*

£ ⚄ **Edward Lear.** This is a good-value, family-run hotel a minute's walk from Oxford Street, in a Georgian town house that was formerly the home of writer-artist Edward Lear (famous for his nonsense verse). Rooms vary enormously in size, with some family rooms very spacious indeed and others barely big enough to get out of bed (avoid Room 14); those at the back are quieter. It's a friendly place, but there are no hotel-type facilities (although if you want a jacket pressed you're welcome to borrow the iron). The management is very proud of the English breakfasts—it uses the same butcher as the Queen. Recent letters from readers indicate the hotel has seen better days. ⊠ *28–30 Seymour St., W1H 5WD,* ☎ *020/7402–5401, ℻ 020/7706–3766. 31 rooms, 15 with shower (no toilet), 4 with full bath. Breakfast room. MC, V. Tube: Marble Arch.* ✎

St. James's

££££ ⚄ **Dukes.** This small, exclusive, Edwardian-style hotel, with its lantern-lighted entrance, is central but still quiet, as it is set in its own discreet cul-de-sac, where the Stafford (☞ *below*) also lies. A small hotel of character, it's suitably filled with squashy sofas, oil paintings of assorted dukes, and muted, rich colors and is home of the finest dry martinis in town. Its trump cards are that, for such a central location, it offers immense peace and quiet and very reasonable rates, plus personal service (they greet you by name every time), and an especially sweet suite or two, on the top floor, with views over St. James's Park. ⊠ *35 St. James's Pl., SW1A 1NY,* ☎ *020/7491–4840, ℻ 020/7493–1264. 80 rooms. Restaurant, dining room. AE, DC, MC, V. Tube: Green Park.* ✎

££££ ⚄ **The Stafford.** This hotel is most famous for its utterly amazing American Bar, where a million ties, baseball caps, and toy planes hang from a ceiling modeled, presumably, on New York's "21" Club, but it is also prized for its 12 carriage-house rooms, installed in the 18th-century stable block. Relative bargains, each of these cute and private accommodations has its own cobbled mews entrance and features gas-log fires, black-stained exposed beams, CD players, CNN, and safes. The main hotel has navy-and-gold hallways, rooms with china in cabinets or French doors to the bathrooms, and air-conditioning throughout, but the gorgeous mews remains the Stafford's best profile. ⊠ *St. James's Pl., SW1A 1NJ,* ☎ *020/7493–0111, ℻ 020/7193 7121. 72 rooms Restaurant, bar, dining rooms. AE, DC, MC, V. Tube: Green Park.* ✎

Soho and Covent Garden

££££ ⊞ **Covent Garden Hotel.** Relentlessly chic, theatrically baronial, this
★   is Tim and Kit Kemp's latest extravaganza—a former 1880s-vintage
hospital in the midst of the artsy Covent Garden district, now the London home-away-from-home for a mélange of off-duty celebrities, actors, and style mavens. The public salons will keep even the most
picky atmosphere-hunter happy: wallowing in painted silks, style
anglais ottomans, and 19th-century Romantik oils, they are perfect places
for a Hollywood star to be interviewed over a glass of sherry. Guest
rooms are *World of Interiors* stylish, each showcasing matching-but-
mixed couture fabrics to stunning effect. Antique-style desks are vast,
beds are gargantuan, and modern bathrooms even feature they-*have*-
thought-of-everything heated mirrors (steam doesn't stick). Off the lobby,
have a nibble in the Brasserie, and you'll agree: for taste, in every sense
of the word, the Covent Garden is the top. ⊠ *10 Monmouth St.,
WC2H 9HB,* ☎ *020/7806–1000,* ℻ *020/7806–1100. 46 rooms, 4
suites. Restaurant, minibars, room service, exercise room, laundry service. AE, MC, V. Tube: Covent Garden.* ✇

££££ ⊞ **Four Seasons Hotel Canary Wharf.** Magnificent, copper-roofed, re-
minding one faintly of George Orwell's Ministry of Truth, the Four
Seasons sits on a vast pedestal above a wriggling mass of throughways,
tunnels, and overpasses. The astonishing thing about this hotel, which
opened in December 1999, is the calm. Glass doors swish open; islands
of armchairs float on cool gray marble; elevators pass up and down
without a murmur. The rooms are identical, but only the more expensive
ones have the breathtaking views over the river. The beds are large and
unfussy; the windows are plate-glass rectangles, letting in light and the
view. Earthly amenities, such as data ports, TVs with Internet access,
and outlets with American voltage, are concealed. The northern Italian restaurant has a mouthwatering menu, which does not include pizza.
Come here if you are bound to the nearby City and do not love Andrew Lloyd Webber, who is far away in the West End. ⊠ *46 Westferry
Circus, E14 8R,* ☎ *020/7510–1999,* ℻ *020/7510–1990. 142 rooms.
Restaurant, bar, in-room data ports, in-room safes, minibar, room service, massage, exercise room, baby-sitting, laundry service, dry cleaning, business services. AE, D, DC, MC, V. Tube: Canary Wharf.* ✇

££££ ⊞ **Le Meridien Waldorf.** Close to the Aldwych theaters and Covent Garden, the Waldorf gleams in luscious Edwardiana, with polished marble
floors, chandeliers, and cozily comfortable period bedrooms. This is a
booking challenge for the wealthy theatergoer (Waldorf or Savoy?) and
a suitably glamorous setting for the famous Palm Court tea dances, still
going strong every weekend after nearly 90 years. ⊠ *Aldwych, WC2B
4DD,* ☎ *020/7836–2400,* ℻ *020/7836–7244. 292 rooms. Restaurant, 2 bars, brasserie, beauty salon. AE, DC, MC, V. Tube: Aldwych.*

££££ ⊞ **One Aldwych.** If stuffy Victoriana and chintz are not your scene, then
One Aldwych's understated blend of contemporary and classic might offer
the modern luxe you seek. Set in a grand Edwardian-period pile, this flaw-
lessly designed hotel with its coolly eclectic lobby, feather duvets, Italian linen sheets, and quirky touches—a TV in every bathroom—is the
ultimate in millennium style. Poised between the City and the West End
(and overlooking a major traffic intersection), the hotel comes complete
with high-style restaurants, bars, swimming pool, and holistic fitness train-
ers. There's even a high-energy espresso bar, if all this leaves you flat.
But like all good things, it comes at a price—and not a cheap one either.
⊠ *1 Aldwych, WC2 4BZ,* ☎ *020/7300–1000,* ℻ *020/7300–1001. 105
rooms. 2 restaurants, 2 bars, pool, business services, health club. AE,
MC, V. Tube: Charing Cross, Covent Garden.* ✇

££££ 🖭 **St. Martins Lane.** Philippe Starck designed Ian Schrager's hip new hotel to be theatrical, and he has succeeded. In the foyer are a Victorian chaise lounge, a row of golden molars doubling as tables, some life-size chess pieces, and the odd bowler hat. The guests are actors here, as is the staff, on display as they sit at the ice trough in the fish bar, wield their chopsticks in Asia de Cuba (☞ Chapter 2), or lounge on leather armchairs in the brasserie. Guest rooms are small, expensive, cluttered, and homogeneous, but fans of Schrager's hotels will likely be pleased. A second high-concept Schrager hotel, the Sanderson, was set to open in summer 2000. ✉ *45 St. Martins La., WC2N 4HX,* ☎ *020/7300–5500,* FAX *020/7300–5501. 204 rooms. Restaurant, bar, brasserie, in-room data ports, in-room VCRs, minibars, no-smoking rooms, room service, massage, sauna, exercise room, dry cleaning, laundry service, concierge, business services, meeting rooms, parking (fee). AE, MC, V. Tube: Leicester Sq.*

££££ 🖭 **The Savoy.** This historic, grand late-Victorian hotel is beloved by
★ wielders of international influence, now as ever. Its celebrated Grill (☞ Chapter 2) has the premier power-lunch tables; it hosted Elizabeth Taylor's first honeymoon in one of its famous river-view rooms; and it poured one of Europe's first dry martinis in its equally famous American Bar—haunted by Hemingway, Fitzgerald, Gershwin, et al. And does it measure up to this high profile? Absolutely. The impeccably maintained, spacious, elegant, bright, and comfortable rooms are furnished with antiques and serviced by valets. A room facing the Thames costs an arm and a leg and requires an early booking, but no other hotel betters that view. Bathrooms have original fittings, with the same sunflower-size showerheads as at Claridge's (☞ *above*). Though the Savoy is as grand as they come, the air is tinged with a certain naughtiness, which goes down well with Hollywood types. Others may enjoy the tea and dancing on Sundays. ✉ *Strand, WC2R 0EU,* ☎ *020/7836–4343,* FAX *020/7240–6040. 224 rooms. 3 restaurants, 2 bars, indoor pool, beauty salon, health club. AE, DC, MC, V. Tube: Aldwych.* ✺

£££ 🖭 **Hazlitt's.** The solo Soho hotel is in three connected early 18th-cen-
★ tury houses, one of which was the last home of essayist William Hazlitt (1778–1830). At press time, they were stripping away plasterboard to reveal the old Georgian paneling in the rooms. It's a disarmingly friendly place, full of personality, but devoid of such hotel features as elevators, room service (though if the staff isn't too busy, you can get ad-hoc takeouts), and porter service. Robust antiques are everywhere, assorted prints crowd every wall, plants and stone sculptures appear in odd corners, and every room has a Victorian claw-foot tub in its bathroom. There are tiny sitting rooms, wooden staircases, and more restaurants within strolling distance than you could patronize in a year. Book way ahead—this is the London address of media people, literary types, and antiques dealers. ✉ *6 Frith St., W1V 5TZ,* ☎ *020/7434–1771,* FAX *020/7439–1524. 23 rooms. AE, DC, MC, V. Tube: Piccadilly.*

£££ 🖭 **Radisson Mountbatten.** Naming the hotel after the late Lord Mountbatten, last viceroy of India and favorite uncle of Prince Charles, is probably just an excuse to go overboard with the old British Raj theme. The decor reflects Mountbatten's life: photos of the estate where he lived, Indian furnishings, silks, inlaid tables, and screens. It has a good standard of service; bedrooms in various shades of red, with chintz drapes; and bathrooms of Italian marble. A pianist performs in the comfortable bar, and there are posttheater cabarets at the Ad Lib restaurant twice a week. Two new executive floors are being built as part of a major overhaul. On a somewhat lackluster street, the hotel is a minute's walk to the Covent Garden Piazza. ✉ *20 Monmouth St., WC2H 9HD,* ☎ *020/7836–4300,* FAX *020/7340–3540. 128 rooms. Restaurant, bar. AE, DC, MC, V. Tube: Covent Garden.* ✺

££ ⊞ **Radisson Pastoria.** A less exorbitant choice for the theatergoer than the Waldorf and the rest (although rates are at the very top of this category), the Pastoria is handily situated just off Leicester Square. The building is about 70 years old, with a suitably modern decor, the bedrooms done in limed oak with light pink walls and navy blue carpets. There's a brasserie-style restaurant to dine in, but Soho, which is restaurant central, is only a few hundred yards away. ⊠ *3–6 St. Martin's St., WC2H 7HL,* ☎ *020/7930–8641,* FAX *020/7925–0551. 58 rooms. Restaurant, bar, coffee shop. AE, DC, MC, V. Tube: Leicester Sq.* ⊗

£–££ ⊞ **Fielding.** Tucked away in a quiet alley by the world's first police station (now Bow St. Magistrates' Court), and feeling far from the madding crowds of Covent Garden, this cozy hotel is so adored by its regulars that you'd be wise to book well ahead. A loyal, friendly staff maintains the place as the two founders, now retired, kept it for more than two decades. It is not uneccentric. The bedrooms are all different, shabby-homey rather than chic, and none too spacious, though you can have a suite here for the price of a chain-hotel double. There's no elevator; there are no rooms with tubs (en-suite showers only); and the restaurant has closed down. But don't despair, there are tea- and coffee-making facilities in every room, complete with biscuits for the ravenous. Cute is the word. ⊠ *4 Broad Ct., Bow St., WC2B 5QZ,* ☎ *020/7836–8305,* FAX *020/7497–0064. 24 rooms. Bar, breakfast room. AE, DC, MC, V. Tube: Covent Garden.*

Kensington

££££ ⊞ **Blakes.** Blakes is another world. It was designed by owner Anouska
★ Hempel (also known as Lady Weinberg), and each room is a fantasy packed with precious Biedermeier, Murano glass, and modern pieces inside walls of red lacquer and black, or dove-gray moiré, or perhaps—like Room 007, the movie stars' favorite suite—blood red and lily white. Cinematic mood lighting, featuring recessed halogen spots, compounds the impression that you, too, are a movie star living in a big-budget biopic. The foyer sets the tone with its piles of cushions, Phileas Fogg valises and trunks, black walls, rattan and bamboo, and a couple of love birds under a gigantic Asian parasol. Downstairs is an equally dramatic, exotic black and white restaurant. Stay away if you don't like Hollywood or the music biz. ⊠ *33 Roland Gardens, SW7 3PF,* ☎ *020/7370–6701,* FAX *020/7373–0442. 52 rooms. Restaurant. AE, DC, MC, V. Tube: South Kensington.*

£££ ⊞ **The Cranley.** New owners are refurbishing this small Georgian town-house hotel in South Ken. Anglo antiques, oils, and etchings are mixed with swagged drapery in assorted florals, but these are being replaced with more neutral schemes. The larger bedrooms have kitchens, and many are high-ceilinged and huge-windowed; renovated rooms do not have kitchens. ⊠ *10–12 Bina Gardens, SW5 0LA,* ☎ *020/7373–0123,* FAX *020/7373–9497. 33 rooms, 2 suites, 1 apartment. AE, DC, MC, V. Tube: Gloucester Rd.* ⊗

£££ ⊞ **The Gore.** Just down the road from the Albert Hall, this very friendly
★ hotel is run by the same people who run Hazlitt's (☞ *above*) and features a similar eclectic selection of prints, etchings, and antiques—the lobby looks like a set from a Luchino Visconti film. Upstairs are spectacular follylike rooms—Room 101 is a Tudor fantasy with minstrel gallery, stained glass, and four-poster bed, and Room 211, done in over-the-top Hollywood style, has a tiled mural of Greek goddesses in the bathroom. The hotel gets a fun, chic, but partying crowd—so don't be shocked if you find some cigarette butts in the hallways. ⊠ *189*

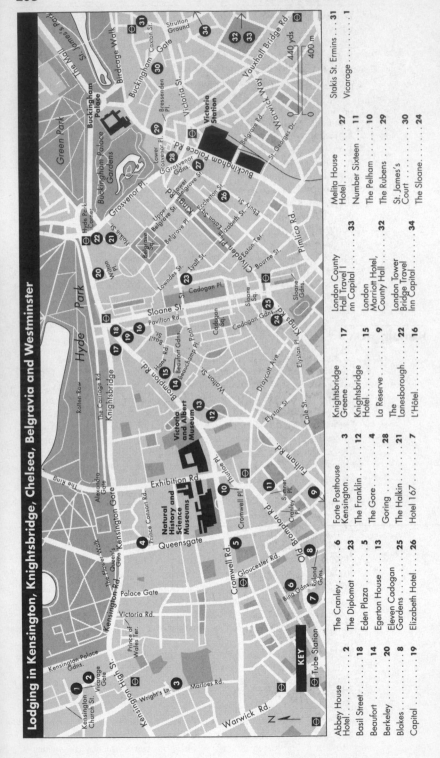

Lodging in Kensington, Knightsbridge, Chelsea, Belgravia and Westminster

Abbey House Hotel 2
Basil Street 18
Beaufort 14
Berkeley 20
Blakes 8
Capital 19

The Cranley 6
The Diplomat 23
Eden Plaza 5
Egerton House 13
Eleven Cadogan Gardens 25
Elizabeth Hotel 26

Forte Posthouse Kensington 3
The Franklin 12
The Gore 4
Goring 28
The Halkin 21
Hotel 167 7

Knightsbridge Greene 17
Knightsbridge Hotel 15
La Reserve 9
The Lanesborough 22
L'Hôtel 16

London County Hall Travel Inn Capital 33
London Marriott Hotel, County Hall 32
London Tower Bridge Travel Inn Capital 34

Melita House Hotel 27
Number Sixteen 11
The Pelham 10
The Rubens 29
St. James's Court 30
The Sloane 24

Stakis St. Ermins 31
Vicarage 1

KEY

Ⓣ Tube Station

440 yds
400 m

Queen's Gate, SW7 5EX, ☎ *020/7584–6601,* 📠 *020/7589–8127. 54 rooms. Restaurant. AE, DC, MC, V. Tube: Gloucester Rd.* ✥

£££ 🏨 **Number Sixteen.** A luxury bed-and-breakfast close to South Kensington tube and three blocks or so from the great museums, Number Sixteen stands in a white-portico row of Victorian houses, with not a sign outside to indicate it. There's no uniformity to the bedrooms except for their spaciousness and recently refitted bathrooms, but the decor overall is not so much interior-designed as understated, with new furniture and modern prints juxtaposed with yellowed oils and antiques. There's an elevator and an enticing garden complete with conservatory and fountainette. ✉ *16 Sumner Pl., SW7 3EG,* ☎ *020/7589–5232 or 800/592–5387 in U.S.,* 📠 *020/7584–8615. 36 rooms. Bar. AE, DC, MC, V. Tube: South Kensington.* ✥

££ 🏨 **Forte Posthouse Kensington.** This mammoth, fairly utilitarian hotel feels like a smaller one and boasts a few extras you wouldn't expect for the rates, at the low end of this category, and a convenient location on a quiet lane off Kensington High Street. The main attraction is the health club, with a sizable pool, two squash courts, a steam room, and a beauty salon; there's also a secluded little water garden. Standard rooms are on the small side, with plain chain-hotel built-in furniture. Some "executive" rooms are twice the size and are a particularly good value. ✉ *Wrights La., W8 5SP,* ☎ *020/7937–8170,* 📠 *020/7937–8289. 543 rooms. 3 restaurants, 2 bars, indoor pool, health club, baby-sitting. AE, DC, MC, V. Tube: High Street Kensington.*

£ 🏨 **Abbey House Hotel.** Next door to the Vicarage (☞ *below*), Abbey
★ House has been voted "Best Value, Best Quality B&B in London" in several surveys, so you'll have to book well in advance for the doubles, which go for £65 here. The place occupies a pretty, white-stucco 1860 Victorian town house—once home to a bishop and an MP before World War II—and overlooks a garden square. Rooms are spacious and have color TVs and washbasins, but every room shares a bath with another. An English breakfast is included in the rates, and a cuppa (cup of tea) is complimentary. ✉ *11 Vicarage Gate, W8,* ☎ *020/7727–2594. 16 rooms, all with shared bath. No credit cards. Tube: High Street Kensington.*

£ 🏨 **Eden Plaza.** When a hotel calls its own rooms "compact," you should imagine a double bed, then add a foot all around, and, yes, that is about the size of a room here. However, as in a cruise ship's stateroom, all you need is creatively secreted—there's a closet, mirror, satellite TV, tea/coffeemaker, and a hair dryer. Rooms are double-glazed against noisy Cromwell Road, though earplugs are useful on account of *loud* color schemes, like purple, kingfisher, and canary. The kids can share free—if you can fit a cot into these rooms—or else they get their own room at half price. The Natural History Museum is just across the street. ✉ *68–69 Queensgate, SW7 5JT,* ☎ *020/7370–6111,* 📠 *020/7370–0932. 62 rooms. Bar. AE, MC, V. Tube: Gloucester Rd.*

£ 🏨 **Hotel 167.** This friendly little bed-and-breakfast is a two-minute walk from the V&A, in a grand white-stucco Victorian corner house. The lobby is immediately cheering, with its round marble tables, wrought-iron chairs, palms, and modern paintings; it also does duty as lounge and breakfast room. Bedrooms have a hybrid Victoriana-IKEA decor, with Venetian blinds over double-glazed windows (which you need on this noisy road), plus cable TV and minibars. ✉ *167 Old Brompton Rd., SW5 0AN,* ☎ *020/7373–0672,* 📠 *020/7373–3360. 18 rooms. Breakfast room. AE, DC, MC, V. Tube: Gloucester Rd.* ✥

£ 🏨 **Vicarage.** Spend the cash you save here in the surrounding Kensington antiques shops. This has long been a favorite for the budget-minded: family-owned, set on a leaf-shaded street just off Kensington Church Street, the Vicarage is set in a large white Victorian house. The

decor is sweetly anachronistic, full of heavy and dark-stained wood
furniture, patterned carpets, and brass pendant lights, and there's a little conservatory. Many of the bedrooms now have TVs. All in all, this
still remains a charmer—but it is beginning to fray around the edges.
⊠ *10 Vicarage Gate, W8 4AG,* ☎ *020/7229–4030. 19 rooms. No credit
cards. Tube: High Street Kensington.*

Knightsbridge, Chelsea, Belgravia, Victoria, and Westminster

££££ ⬚ **Beaufort.** You can practically hear the jingle of Harrods' cash reg-
★ isters from a room at the Beaufort, the brainchild of ex–TV announcer
Diana Wallis, who employs an all-woman team to run the hotel. Actually, "hotel" is a misnomer for this elegant pair of Victorian houses.
There's a sitting room instead of reception; guests have a front door
key, the run of the drinks cabinet, and even their own phone number.
The high-ceilinged, generously proportioned rooms are decorated in
muted, sophisticated shades to suit the muted, sophisticated atmosphere—but don't worry, you're encouraged by the incredibly sweet
staff to feel at home. The rates are higher than the top range for this
category but include unlimited drinks (grand cru champagne if you
fancy), English cream tea, breakfast, and membership at a local health
club. ⊠ *33 Beaufort Gardens, SW3 1PP,* ☎ *020/7584–5252,* FAX *020/
7589–2834. 28 rooms. AE, DC, MC, V. Tube: Knightsbridge.* ⊛

££££ ⬚ **Berkeley.** The Berkeley is a successful mixture of the old and the new—
★ a luxurious, air-conditioned, double-glazed modern building with a
splendid penthouse swimming pool that opens to the sky when the
weather's good. The bedrooms have swags of William Morris prints or
are plain and masculine with little balconies overlooking the street. All
have sitting areas and big, tiled bathrooms with bidets. For the ridiculously rich, there are spectacular suites, one with its own conservatory
terrace, another with a sauna, but—such is the elegance of this place—
you'd feel almost as spoiled in a normal room. The latest feather in this
superb hotel's cap is the relocated La Tante Claire (☞ Chapter 2), one
of London's finest restaurants. After 21 years in Chelsea, chef Pierre
Koffman has come to roost here, in a restaurant designed on a camel-
lia theme, the flower that was the favorite of French fashion guru Coco
Chanel. The other restaurant is just as glittering: Vong, the Thai-French
hybrid cloned from New York, whose expensive decor, work-of-art dishes,
and exorbitant prices are going down very well with London's big
spenders. ⊠ *Wilton Pl., SW1X 7RL,* ☎ *020/7235–6000,* FAX *020/7235–
4330. 160 rooms. 2 restaurants, beauty salon, health club, pool, cinema. AE, DC, MC, V. Tube: Knightsbridge.* ⊛

££££ ⬚ **Capital.** Reserve well ahead if you want a room here—as you must
for a table in the hotel's superb restaurant (☞ Chapter 2). This grand
hotel decanted into a private house is the work of the Levin family,
who also own L'Hôtel (☞ *below*), and it exudes their irreproachable
taste, with fine-grained woods, sober prints, and shelves of books. The
10 rooms of the Edwardian Wing, with its carved wooden staircase,
enjoyed the attentions of superstar designer Nina Campbell and were
already the height of fashion in the 1920s, when this was the Squires
Hotel. ⊠ *22–24 Basil St., SW3 1AT,* ☎ *020/7589–5171,* FAX *020/
7225–0011. 48 rooms. Bar. AE, DC, MC, V. Tube: Knightsbridge.* ⊛

££££ ⬚ **The Halkin.** If you can't take any more Regency stripes, English-coun-
try florals, or Louis XV chaises, this luxurious little place is the anti-
dote. Chill out to the Milanese design: the clean-cut white marble
lobby with its royal-blue-leather bucket chairs; the arresting, curved,
charcoal-gray corridors; the "diseased mahogany" veneers; and the gray-
on-gray bedrooms that light up when you insert your electronic key.

Wealthy business and media types frequent the Halkin, so rooms feature fax machines and two phone lines with conference-call capacities, along with two touch-control pads for all the gadgets, cable TV, and VCR. The bathrooms are palaces of shiny chrome. Staying here might be like living in the Design Museum, except that this place employs some of the friendliest staff around—who look pretty good in their blue or black Armani uniforms. ✉ *Halkin St., SW1X 7DJ,* ☎ *020/7333–1000,* ℻ *020/7333–1100. 41 rooms. Restaurant, business services. AE, DC, MC, V. Tube: Hyde Park Corner.* ✎

££££ ★ 🏨 **The Lanesborough.** This very grand hotel acts for all the world as though the Prince Regent took a ride through time and is about to resume residence. Royally proportioned public rooms (not lounges but "the Library" and "the Withdrawing Room") lead one off the other like an exquisite giant Chinese box in this multimillion-pound, American-run conversion of the old St. George's Hospital opposite Wellington's house. Everything undulates with richness—brocades and Regency stripes; moiré silks and fleurs-de-lys in the colors of precious stones; magnificent antiques and oil paintings; reproductions of more gilded splendor than the originals; handwoven £250-per-square-yard carpet—as if Liberace and Laura Ashley had collaborated on the design. All you do to register is sign the visitor's book, then retire to your room, where you are waited on by a personal butler. Full-size Lanesborough toiletries, umbrellas (take them home), robes (don't), a drinks tray (pay by the inch), and even business cards with your temporary fax (in every room) and phone numbers (two lines) are waiting. If you yearn for a bygone age and are very rich, this is certainly for you. ✉ *Hyde Park Corner, SW1X 7TA,* ☎ *020/7259–5599,* ℻ *020/7259–5606. 95 rooms. 2 restaurants, bar. AE, DC, MC, V. Tube: Hyde Park Corner.* ✎

££££ 🏨 **London Marriott Hotel, County Hall.** This exceptionally grand hotel has what visitors to London most often request and which up until now has not been available—a view of the Houses of Parliament across the Thames (which means, of course, that the hotel is not in Westminster but on the south side of the river). It's in the former home of the long-defunct local governing body—a mammoth, spectacular, pedimented-and-becolumned affair—and uses the old Members' entrance, with its bronze doors and marble lobby leading into the former Council Chamber. A Marriott is a reliable thing, and this one has all the expected deluxe accoutrements—from modern, businesslike decor to almost-instantly-arriving elevators, and from conference facilities to the use of the fantastic new 24-hour Health & Fitness Spa on the top floors. ✉ *County Hall, SE1 7PB,* ☎ *020/7928–5200,* ℻ *020/7928–5300. 200 rooms. Bar, lounge, indoor pool, health club. AE, DC, MC, V. Tube: Westminster.* ✎

££££ 🏨 **The Rubens.** This hotel likes to say it treats you like royalty—after all, you're only a stone's throw from the real thing, with Buckingham Palace just across the road. And if this is how Her Majesty lives, then we've all got reason to be jealous. This elegant hotel, looking out over the Royal Mews, provides the sort of deep comfort needed to soothe away a hard day's sightseeing, with armchairs just crying out for you to sink into them with a cup of Earl Grey. With decent-size, well-appointed rooms—not quite furnished like the ones at the palace, it must be said—and a location that could not be more truly central, this hotel remains a favorite for many travelers. ✉ *39 Buckingham Palace Rd., SW1W OPS,* ☎ *020/7834–6600,* ℻ *020/7233–6037. 180 rooms. Restaurant, bar. AE, DC, MC, V. Tube: Victoria.* ✎

££££ 🏨 **St. James's Court.** You enter this Edwardian pile through a pair of enormous wrought-iron gates, which used to admit carriages into what is now the towering reception. From here, you pass ranks of green leather sofas to reach the pièce de résistance: the landscaped courtyard with its fountain and ceramic frieze of scenes from Shakespeare. Some bedrooms are disproportionately large but cost the same as standards—the reverse is also true, so beware the expensive shoe boxes—and all are plainly decorated in pallid shades with a smattering of antiques and the odd (and some are *very* odd) painting. There are two good restaurants and a business center, and many apartments offer good deals for weekly and longer stays, but unless you have business at Buckingham Palace or around Victoria, the location isn't central enough to warrant the rates. ⊠ *Buckingham Gate, SW1E 6AF,* ☎ *020/7834–6655,* FAX *020/7630–7587. 356 rooms. 2 restaurants, coffee shop, health club, business services. AE, DC, MC, V. Tube: St. James's Park.*

££££   🏨 **Stakis St. Ermins.** Smack-dab in the middle of Westminster, this hotel is just a short stroll from Westminster Abbey and minutes from Buckingham Palace and the Houses of Parliament. An Edwardian anomaly in the shadow of modern skyscrapers, the hotel is set on a tiny cul-de-sac courtyard fronted with beasts-rampant gates. The lobby is an extravaganza of Victorian Baroque—all cake-frosting stucco work in shades of baby blue and creamy white. The Cloisters restaurant features one of the most magnificent (and overlooked) dining decors in London: a 19th-century Jacobean-style salon. Guest rooms are tastefully decorated; some have snug dimensions—but are all the cozier for it. ⊠ *Caxton St., SW1H 0QW,* ☎ *020/7222–7888,* FAX *020/7222–6914. 290 rooms, 8 suites. Restaurant, bar, minibars, room service, laundry service. AE, DC, MC, V. Tube: St. James's Park.* ✎

£££   🏨 **Basil Street.** This gracious Edwardian hotel is on a quiet street behind busy Brompton Road and off (rich) shoppers' heaven, Sloane Street. It has been family-run for nearly a century, and it has always been popular with lone women travelers, who get automatic membership at the Parrot Club—an enormous lounge, with copies of *The Lady* and *Country Life* among the coffee cups. All the bedrooms are different; many are like Grandma's guest room, with overstuffed counterpanes and a random selection of furniture. You can write letters home in the peaceful gallery, which has polished wooden floors and fine Turkish carpets underneath a higgledy-piggledy wealth of antiques. Americans with a taste for period charm favor this place; some come back often enough to merit the title "Basilite"—a privileged regular offered a 15% discount. ⊠ *Basil St., SW3 1AH,* ☎ *020/7581–3311,* FAX *020/7581–3693. 80 rooms. Restaurant. AE, DC, MC, V. Tube: Knightsbridge.*

£££   🏨 **The Diplomat.** From its aristocratically elegant exterior, this hotel looks like a Cecil Beaton stage set: a Wedgwood-white "palazzo" terrace house built by the 19th-century architect Thomas Cubitt, flatiron-shape (it stands at the confluence of two streets), and often decked out with hanging flowerpots of geraniums, it is the very picture of Belgravian chic. Inside, the tiny reception area gives way to a circular staircase lighted by a Regency-era chandelier and topped by a winter-garden dome. Rooms are pleasantly decorated, some with Victorian touches; in the basement is a breakfast nook (a buffet is included in the daily rates). This hotel truly comes into its own once you step out the doorway and find yourself in the heart of Belgravia's beautiful 19th-century mansions (Baroness Thatcher is a block away) and mews. ⊠ *2 Chesham St., SW1X 8DT,* ☎ *020/7235–1544,* FAX *020/7259–6153. 27 rooms. Business services. AE, DC, MC, V. Tube: Sloane Sq., Knightsbridge.*

£££   🏨 **Egerton House.** This absolutely peaceful, private-house-style small hotel was the first in the stable that includes the Franklin and Dukes (☞ *below*), and it remains many people's favorite, appealing especially, for some reason, to bankers. Many chintzy, floral, or Regency-stripe bedrooms overlook the gorgeous gardens in back; some have quirky shapes, others have four-poster beds, still others are extra well endowed with closet space—in other words, all are different. The staff here is especially personable—and the manager would love to know what you thought of the selections in his handwritten local restaurant guide. ✉ *17–19 Egerton Terr., SW3 2BX,* ☎ *020/7589–2412,* ℻ *020/7584–6540. 30 rooms. AE, DC, MC, V. Tube: Knightsbridge.*

£££ 🏨 **Eleven Cadogan Gardens.** This aristocratic, late-Victorian gabled town house is the perfect spot for a pampered honeymoon, but it's very difficult to get into—and we're not referring to the lack of sign or reception desk. Fine period furniture and antiques, books and magazines on the tables, landscape paintings and portraits, coupled with some of that solid, no-nonsense furniture that *real* English country houses have in unaesthetic abundance make for a family-home ambience; you might be borrowing the house and servants of some wealthy friends while they're away. Take the elevator or walk up the fine oak staircase to your room, which will have mahogany furniture, a restful color scheme, and pretty bedspreads and drapes. The best rooms are at the back, overlooking a private garden. If you wish to hire a chauffeur-driven car, there is one on standby order. ✉ *11 Cadogan Gardens, Sloane Sq., SW3 2RJ,* ☎ *020/7730–3426,* ℻ *020/7730–5217. 62 rooms. AE, MC, V. Tube: Sloane Sq.* 🐾

£££ 🏨 **The Franklin.** It's hard to imagine, while taking tea in this pretty hotel overlooking a quiet, grassy square, that you're an amble away from busy Brompton and Cromwell roads and the splendors of the V&A. A few of the rooms are small, but the marble bathrooms—in which Floris toiletries and heated towel racks are standard issue—are not; the large garden rooms and suites (which fall into the ££££ category) are romantic indeed. Tea is served daily in the lounge, and there's also a self-service bar. The staff is friendly and accommodating. ✉ *28 Egerton Gardens, SW3 2DB,* ☎ *020/7584–5533,* ℻ *020/7584–5449. 47 rooms. Bar, parking (fee). AE, DC, MC, V. Tube: South Kensington.* 🐾

£££ 🏨 **Goring.** Readers love this hotel—after all, where else does the concierge offer to pack up some bread crumbs for the ducks if you're heading for a stroll in Hyde Park? This hotel is useful if you have to drop in at Buckingham Palace, just around the corner. In fact, visiting VIPs use it regularly as a conveniently close, and suitably dignified, base for royal occasions. The hotel was built by Mr. Goring in 1910 and is now run by third-generation Gorings. The atmosphere remains Edwardian: bathrooms are marble-fitted, and some of the bedrooms have brass bedsteads and the original built-in closets, many have been opulently redecorated. The bar-lounge looks onto a well-tended garden. ✉ *15 Beeston Pl., Grosvenor Gardens, SW1W 0JW,* ☎ *020/7396–9000,* ℻ *020/7834–4393. 75 rooms. Restaurant, bar. AE, DC, MC, V. Tube: Victoria.* 🐾

£££ 🏨 **L'Hôtel.** An upscale bed-and-breakfast run by the same Levins who
★ own the Capital (☞ *above*) next door, L'Hôtel is a plainer alternative— less pampering, unfussy decor. There's an air of provincial France, with white wrought-iron bedsteads, pine furniture, and delicious breakfast croissants and baguettes (included in the room rate) served in the Le Metro cellar wine bar (open to nonguests). Le Metro also serves light meals at lunchtime and in the evenings. This really is like a house— you're given your own front door key, there's no elevator, and the staff leaves in the evening. Reserve ahead—it's very popular. ✉ *28 Basil St., SW3 1AT,* ☎ *020/7589–6286,* ℻ *020/7225–0011. 12 rooms. Restaurant, wine bar. AE, V. Tube: Knightsbridge.*

£££ 🏨 **The Pelham.** The second of Tim and Kit Kemp's gorgeous hotels,
★ this place opened in 1989 and is run along exactly the same lines as the Dorset Square (☞ Mayfair to Regent's Park, *above*), except that this one looks more like the country house to end all country houses. There's 18th-century pine paneling in the drawing room—one of the most ravishingly elegant hotel salons anywhere—flowers galore, quite a bit of glazed chintz and antique-lace bed linen, and the odd four-poster and bedroom fireplace. The first-floor (American second floor) suites

are extraspacious with their high ceilings and chandeliers, while some of the top-floor rooms under the eaves have sloping ceilings and casement windows. The Pelham stands opposite the South Kensington tube stop, by the big museums, and close to the shops of Brompton Cross and Knightsbridge. ⊠ *15 Cromwell Pl., SW7 2LA,* ☎ *020/7589–8288,* FAX *020/7584–8444. 50 rooms. Restaurant. AE, MC, V. Tube: South Kensington.* 🦐

££–£££　🏨 **The Sloane.** Many hotels abuse the word "unique" to describe their identical canopied beds or garden views, but the tiny Sloane really *is* unique. It is the only hotel we know of in which you can lie in your canopied bed, pick up the phone, and buy the bed. You could buy the phone, too, but it's the covetable, tasty antiques that you might actually be tempted to take home, and these are also for sale. Nothing so tacky as a price tag besmirches the gorgeous decor—which doesn't stint on strong hues to show off the ever-changing collection of Regency armoires and occasional tables, Victorian desk lamps and crystal decanters—instead, the sweet, young Euro staff harbors a book of price lists at the desk. Room service is not 24-hour, but there's an aerie of a secret roof terrace, with upholstered garden furniture and a panorama over Chelsea, where lunch and dinner are served to guests. ⊠ *29 Draycott Pl., SW3 2SH,* ☎ *020/7581–5757,* FAX *020/7584–1348. 12 rooms. AE, DC, MC, V. Tube: Sloane Sq.* 🦐

££　🏨 **Knightsbridge Green.** This Georgian hotel is only a two-minute walk from Harrods, if that is where you wish to shop. One floor is French style, with white furniture; another English, in beech. Costing only £25 more than a double room, the suites are not overpriced, and all the rooms have trouser presses and tea/coffeemakers. There's no restaurant, but there are plenty in the area; or if you ask, they'll send the porter out to find you a sandwich. There's also coffee and cake left out in the lounge—a detail that exemplifies the friendliness of this place. ⊠ *159 Knightsbridge, SW1X 7PD,* ☎ *020/7584–6274,* FAX *020/7225–1635. 17 rooms, 11 suites. AE, MC, V. Closed 3 days at Christmas. Tube: Knightsbridge.*

££　🏨 **Knightsbridge Hotel.** When it comes to measuring location versus value, this could be considered an ideal stopping place. On a tree-lined, quiet, stately square, the Knightsbridge is just a moment from Harrods and a few blocks from the chic boutiques and restaurants of Beauchamp Place. A family-run hotel, it's set in a town house built in the early 1800s. Guest rooms are unassuming yet well furnished. ⊠ *12 Beaufort Gardens, SW3 1PT,* ☎ *020/7589–9271,* FAX *020/7823–9672. 40 rooms. Exercise room. AE, MC, V. Tube: Knightsbridge.* 🦐

£　🏨 **Elizabeth Hotel.** This elegant hotel near Victoria Station once served as the private home of aristocrats (including relatives of Edward VII). These days it offers luxuriously (for the price) appointed rooms overlooking an attractive garden square. Rooms come with a bath and/or shower, TV, and a knockout English breakfast. A less-luxurious, shared-bath single and double are also available, at a rock-bottom rate. ⊠ *37 Eccleston Sq., SW1V 1PB,* ☎ *020/7828–6812,* FAX *020/7828–6814. 38 rooms. Lounge. No credit cards. Tube: Victoria.* 🦐

£　🏨 **La Reserve.** You'll find this unusual small hotel, at the top of its price category, in the lively, classy residential neighborhood of Fulham. The varnished floorboards, black Venetian blinds, works of art (for sale), and primary-color upholstery in the public areas are contemporary and sophisticated. Bedrooms are cluttered only with the minibars, hair dryers, trouser presses, and tea/coffeemakers of more expensive places. Fulham is not within walking distance of central London, but it is two minutes from the Fulham Broadway tube, near Chelsea Football (soccer) Grounds and plenty of restaurants; there's also an in-house brasserie. ⊠ *422–428 Fulham Rd., SW6 1DU,* ☎ *020/7385–8561,* FAX

020/7385–7662. 43 rooms. Restaurant, bar, free parking. AE, DC, MC, V. Tube: Fulham Broadway.

£ ⊞ **London County Hall Travel Inn Capital.** Don't get too excited—this neighbor of the fancy new Marriott (☞ *above*) lacks the river view (it's at the back of the grand former seat of local government). Still, you get an incredible value, with the standard facilities of the cookie-cutter rooms of this chain (the phone number's the central reservation line), viz: TV, tea/coffeemaker, en suite bath/shower and—best of all for families on a budget—foldout beds that let you accommodate two kids at no extra charge. You're looking at £50 per night for a family of four, in the shadow of Big Ben. *That's* a bargain. ⊠ *Belvedere Rd., SE1 7PB,* ☎ *020/7902–1600,* ℻ *01582/400024. 312 rooms. Restaurant. AE, MC, V. Tube: Westminster.* ⬳

£ ⊞ **London Tower Bridge Travel Inn Capital.** The name may not be snappy, but the price certainly is—practically unbeatable, especially for families. Not exactly central, this brand-new hotel is based in the Tower Hill area, which has good tube connections. Despite having been around for centuries, this remains one of London's most up-and-coming neighborhoods. Bars, apartment blocks, and restaurants are pouring into this part of London, which not so long ago property developers despaired of. Those hoping for glitz should station themselves farther west, but if a bargain and a different look at London are what you want—or the Millennium Dome and the Tower of London are two of your main destinations—save your pennies and stay here. ⊠ *Tower Bridge Rd., SE1,* ☎ *01582/414341. 196 rooms. Restaurant, bar. AE, MC, V.*

£ ⊞ **Melita House Hotel.** Run by the Gabriele family for 30 years, this B&B is a short walk from Buckingham Palace and St. James's Park. It isn't fairyland, but the new pastel-blue makeover lends a freshness that puce green and beige lack. Each room is kitted out with fridge, hair dryer, safe, and direct phone line—everything, in short, the free spirit could desire—and full English breakfast is included in the tariff. ⊠ *35 Charlwood St., SW1V 2DU,* ☎ *020/7828–0471,* ℻ *020/7932–0988. 22 rooms. Breakfast room. AE, MC, V. Tube: Victoria.* ⬳

Bayswater and Notting Hill Gate

££££ ⊞ **Halcyon.** Discretion, decadent decor, and disco divas (everyone from
★ RuPaul to Snoop Doggy Dogg) make this expensive, enormous, wedding-cake Edwardian on Holland Park Avenue desperately desirable. You want film stars? They've got Johnny Depp, William Hurt, and Julia Roberts, and there are usually local residents like Sting, John Cleese, and *Absolutely Fabulous*'s Joanna Lumley haunting the absolutely excellent restaurant. But it's for perfect service and gorgeous rooms you'd follow them here. The Blue Room has moons and stars, the Egyptian Suite is canopied like a bedouin tent, one room has heraldic motifs, and the Halcyon Suite has its own conservatory. All rooms are very large, with the high ceilings and big windows typical of the grand houses here—a 10-minute tube ride to the West End and steps from London's most exquisite park. ⊠ *81 Holland Park, W11 3RZ,* ☎ *020/7727–7288,* ℻ *020/7229–8516. 42 rooms. Restaurant. AE, DC, MC, V. Tube: Holland Park.* ⬳

££££ ⊞ **The Hempel.** This is a prime contender for the "most glamorous hostelry in London" prize. Anouska Hempel did the lush and lavish Blakes, then did a 180-degree turn into these stunning, crisp, clean, white-on-white-on-white-on-white spaces—and we do mean spaces. There's nothing jarring, nothing extraneous, and no visible means of support beneath the furniture. Of course, the Hempel appeals greatly to showbizzy style hounds. Elton John (remember when he went Zen and sold all his gewgaws?) was one of the first party-throwers in the restaurant here. But beware: the minimalist decor is not for everyone. ⊠ *31–35*

Abbey
Court. 4

Adare
House 11

Columbia. . . . 7

Commodore . . 6

The Gate 3

Halcyon. 1

The
Hempel 10

Lancaster
Hall Hotel. . . . 9

London
Elizabeth 8

Pembridge
Court. 5

Portobello. . . . 2

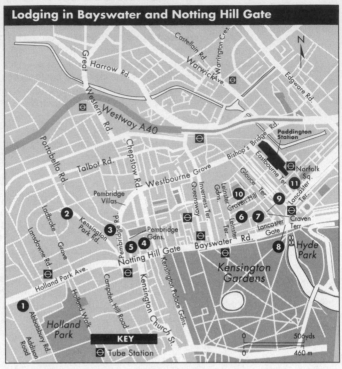

Lodging in Bayswater and Notting Hill Gate

KEY

⊖ Tube Station

Craven Hill Gardens, W2 3EA, ☎ *020/7298–9000,* FAX *020/7472–4666. 43 rooms. Restaurant, bar. AE, DC, MC, V. Tube: Lancaster Gate.*

££–£££ 🖬 **Pembridge Court.** A few doors down from the Abbey Court (☞ *below*), in a similar colonnaded white-stucco Victorian row house, is this sweet home-away-from-home of a hotel, cozy with scatter cushions and books, quirky Victoriana, and framed fans from the neighboring Portobello Market. Bedrooms have a great deal of swagged floral drapery, direct-dial phones, and satellite TV, and there's an elevator to the upper floors. Rates include English breakfast—take that into account when doing your sums, since only the half-size small twin rooms fall into the ££ category; larger ones are £10–£30 more. ⊠ *34 Pembridge Gardens, W2 4DX,* ☎ *020/7229–9977,* FAX *020/7727–4982. 25 rooms. Restaurant. AE, DC, MC, V. Tube: Notting Hill.* ✎

£££ 🖬 **Portobello.** This small, eccentric place has long been a favorite of high-style mavens in the music and design worlds, and it must be said that a tinge of the groovy early '70s still adheres to the corners, and also to the Victorian-Chinoiserie decor (which has turned a bit shabby in a few rooms, enhancing the louche and laid-back effect). The hotel consists of two adjoining Victorian houses that (as is common around here) back onto a beautiful large garden that is shared with the neighbors. The "Cabin Rooms" are minute, with everything you need is accessible by reaching out your hand from bed. Many bigger rooms have freestanding Victorian claw-foot bathtubs, though the famous round-bed suite has the pièce de résistance of the bath world—an Edwardian "bathing machine," all knobs and shiny brass pipes. Rates include breakfast, and there's a 24-hour bar-restaurant in the basement, though there are a hundred other options in this very happening area. ⊠ *22 Stanley Gardens, W11 2NG,* ☎ *020/7727–2777,* FAX *020/7792–9641. 22 rooms. Restaurant, bar. AE, DC, MC, V. Closed 10 days at Christmas. Tube: Notting Hill.* ✎

££ ⓣ **Abbey Court.** This is a very elegant little hotel that is more like a private home—albeit one with a resident designer. It's in a gracious white Victorian mansion in a quiet streetlet off Notting Hill Gate, which gives easy access to most of London. Inside, the era of Victoria is reflected in deep-red wallpapers (downstairs), Murano glass and gilt-framed mirrors, framed prints, mahogany, and plenty of antiques. Bathrooms look the part but are entirely modern in gray Italian marble, with brass fittings and whirlpool baths. There's 24-hour room service instead of a restaurant (there are plenty around here, though), and guests can relax in the sitting room or the pretty conservatory. ✉ *20 Pembridge Gardens, W2 4DU,* ☎ *020/7221–7518,* ℻ *020/7792–0858. 22 rooms. AE, DC, MC, V. Tube: Notting Hill.* ⚘

££ ⓣ **Commodore.** This peaceful hotel of three converted Victorians is close to the Columbia but deeper in the big leafy square known as Lancaster Gate. It's another find of a very different stripe, as you'll notice on entering the cozy, carpeted lounge. Try your best to get one of the amazing rooms—as superior to the regular ones as Harrods is to Kmart but priced the same. Twenty of these are split-level rooms, with sleeping gallery, all large, all different, all with something special—like a walk-in closet with its own stained-glass window. One (No. 11) is a duplex, entered through a secret mirrored door off a lemon-yellow hallway with palms and Greek statuary, with a thick-carpeted, *very* quiet bedroom upstairs and its toilet below. It's getting very popular here, so book ahead. ✉ *50 Lancaster Gate, W2 3NA,* ☎ *020/7402–5291,* ℻ *020/7262–1088. 90 rooms. Bar, business services. AE, MC, V. Tube: Lancaster Gate.* ⚘

££ ⓣ **London Elizabeth.** Steps from Hyde Park and the Lancaster Gate tube
★ (and from rows of depressing, cheap hotels) is this family-owned gem. The facade is one of the most charming in London, and the charm continues inside—foyer and lounge are crammed with coffee tables and chintz drapery, lace antimacassars, and little chandeliers. This country sensibility persists through the bedrooms done out in palest blue-striped walls, wooden picture rails and Welsh wool bedspreads, or in pink cabbage rose prints and mahogany furniture. Although rooms vary in size, there's a thoughtful tendency here to make sure that what you lose on the swings (small wedge-shape room) you gain on the roundabouts (bigger, brand-new bathroom, or a small balcony), and all have TV, direct-dial phone, and hair dryer. The exceptionally charming Anglo-Irish staff is on call around the clock, and there's a restaurant, the Rose Garden, handy in this culinary wasteland. ✉ *Lancaster Terr., W2 3PF,* ☎ *020/7402–6641,* ℻ *020/7224–8900. 55 rooms. Restaurant, bar. AE, DC, MC, V. Tube: Lancaster Gate.* ⚘

£ ⓣ **Adare House.** This is one of the most popular choices among the many B&B options in the Sussex Gardens area—not surprisingly so, since the friendly prices come with some ritzy extras. Now run by a brother-and-sister combo who maintain the friendly family atmosphere this hotel prides itself on, all rooms have en-suite showers, and the new, 24-hour reception gives guests a little more freedom than some B&Bs offer. ✉ *153 Sussex Gardens, W2 2RY,* ☎ *020/7262–0633,* ℻ *020/7706–1859. 17 rooms with shower. Restaurant. MC, V. Tube: Paddington.* ⚘

£ ⓣ **Columbia.** The public rooms in these five joined-up Victorians are as big as museum halls. Late at night they contain the hippest band du jour relaxing during their London gig, while in the morning there are sightseers sipping coffee. Indeed, this place seems to offer something for everyone in the lower price range. The clean, high-ceiling rooms, some of which are very large (three to four beds) and have park views and balconies, also offer TVs, hair dryers, tea/coffeemakers, direct-dial phones, and safes. Decor tends to teak veneer, khaki-beige-brown color schemes, and avocado bathroom suites, but who expects Regency Revival at these prices? ✉ *95–99 Lancaster Gate, W2 3NS,* ☎ *020/*

7402–0021, ⅀℻ 020/7706–4691. *103 rooms. Restaurant, bar, meeting rooms. AE, MC, V. Tube: Lancaster Gate.* ✎

£   🏠 **The Gate.** It's absolutely teeny—just a normal house at the very top of Portobello Road, off Notting Hill Gate. The plain bedrooms have refrigerators, TVs, direct-dial phones, and tea/coffee facilities, plus bath (unless you opt for a smaller, £10 cheaper, shower-only room), and you can have the inclusive Continental breakfast brought up to you, or take it in the first-floor lounge. ⊠ *6 Portobello Rd., W11 3DG,* ☎ *020/7221–2403,* ℻ *020/7221–9128. 6 rooms. AE, MC, V. Tube: Notting Hill.* ✎

£   🏠 **Lancaster Hall Hotel.** This modest hotel is owned by the German YMCA, which guarantees efficiency and spotlessness. The bargain 20-room "youth annex" has been renovated, scrubbing away any vestiges of dirt from the corners. ⊠ *35 Craven Terr., W2 3EL,* ☎ *020/7723–9276,* ℻ *020/7706–2870. 80 rooms. Restaurant, bar. MC, V. Tube: Lancaster Gate.*

Bloomsbury, Holborn, Euston, and the City

£££–££££   🏠 **Myhotel.** A hotel where tipping is discouraged and where guests brief the management on their likes and dislikes? Where you have a member of staff assigned to you personally, to see to all your needs? Where a public room is dedicated to inner karma? Yes, here it is, the work of owner Andrew Thrasyvoulou and the frighteningly omniscient Terence Conran with the help of a Feng Shui designer to check the building for negative energy. Myhotel, Conran's first hotel venture, is evidently aimed at the young, hip traveler who expects his or her hotel to be an experience in itself. Within easy walking distance of the British Museum, Soho, Covent Garden, and the West End, the brand-new Myhotel is sure to find its niche among an upmarket but open-minded breed of tourist. ⊠ *11–13 Bayley St., Bedford Sq., WC1 B3HD,* ☎ *020/7667–6000,* ℻ *020/7667–6001. 76 rooms. Bar, exercise room, library, business services. AE, DC, MC, V. Tube: Tottenham Court Rd.* ✎

£££   🏠 **The Rookery.** From the bijoux-size but beautiful rooms in this little hotel you see some of the most ancient parts of London. Set in the City district, the Rookery is just a step away from the Jerusalem Tavern, where it is said the Knights of St. John left to fight the Crusades. From the magnificent Rook's Nest, the hotel's tower that is a complete duplex suite, you can see both St. Paul's and the Old Bailey, London's famous criminal court. If you look closely, some of Dickens's characters still seem to linger around this district, if they haven't been ousted by the fashionable and wealthy young crowd now busy colonizing the area. Each double has an antique four-poster bed and period pictures, with all the modern appliances tastefully hidden away. The burgeoning nature of the neighborhood is a blessing and a drawback—there is a huge choice of restaurants but also many building sites with noisy work in progress. ⊠ *Peter's La., Cowcross St., EC1M 6DS,* ☎ *020/7336–0931,* ℻ *020/7336–0932. 33 rooms. Bar, business services. AE, MC, V. Tube: Farringdon.*

£££   🏠 **Thistle Bloomsbury.** On the main street, steps from the British Museum, this is one Edwardian-style hotel that really does feel sweetly old-fashioned, while avoiding shabbiness or stuffiness—especially since last year's £6 million refurbishment of this former temperance house (tea/coffeemakers and free in-house movies are now among the facilities). The rooms in the turret on the southwest corner, with their curved, six-window wall, are worth asking for, while executive suites have four-posters and Jacuzzis at a rate falling about halfway down the £££ category. ⊠ *Bloomsbury Way, WC1A 2SD,* ☎ *020/7212–5801,* ℻ *020/7831 0225. 138 rooms. Restaurant, bar, meeting rooms. AE, DC, MC, V. Tube: Holborn.* ✎

Academy
Town House . . 3

Alhambra
Hotel 10

Arosfa
Hotel 1

The
Generator . . 11

Great
Northern . . . 13

Jury's Inn . . . 14

La Gaffe 8

Morgan 5

Myhotel 4

Ridgemount . . 2

The
Rookery 12

St.
Margaret's . . . 7

Stakis
Islington 15

Swiss
Cottage
Hotel 9

Thistle
Bloomsbury . . 6

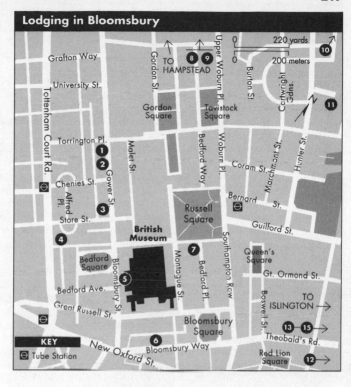

Lodging in Bloomsbury

£.£. ▦ **Academy Town House.** These three joined-up Georgian houses, boasting a little patio garden and a fashion-conscious mirrored and wood-floor basement restaurant, Alchemy, supply the most sophisticated and hotel-like facilities in the Gower Street "hotel row." The comfortable bedrooms have a TV, direct-dial phones, and tea/coffeemakers. Like most of the hotels in this section, the Academy neighbors the British Museum and University of London, a circumstance that appeals to culture vultures on a budget and affluent students. ✉ *21 Gower St., WC1E 6HG,* ☏ *020/7631–4115,* ℻ *020/7636–3442. 48 rooms. Restaurant, bar. AE, DC, MC, V. Tube: Tottenham Court Rd.* ⌘

£ ▦ **Alhambra Hotel.** One of the best bargains in Bloomsbury, this place features singles as low as £30 and doubles as low as £40. The rooms feature cheery red or blue bedspreads and magnolia wallpaper, a pleasing change from the usual B&B monochrome beige. Rooms are spotless and have TVs, though most of them lack private bathrooms. Quad rooms just bust the top of this category, but they do have en-suite shower rooms and are worth considering for a family. ✉ *17–19 Argyle St., WC1,* ☏ *020/7837–9575,* ℻ *020/7916–2476. 52 rooms. AE, DC, MC, V. Tube: King's Cross.*

£ ▦ **Arosfa Hotel.** The friendly owners, Mr. and Mrs. Dorta, mark this B&B directly opposite Dillons bookstore apart from the Gower Street pack—that, and the fact that this was once the home of Pre-Raphaelite painter Sir John Everett Millais. Rooms are simple and spotless, and they're equipped with TVs and sinks, but not necessarily with their own shower (it's about £12 extra for this; still easily within the £ category); those at the back are far quieter, though newly installed double glazing goes some way to tame the Gower Street din. ✉ *83 Gower St., WC16HJ,* ☏ *020/7636–2115,* ℻ *020/7636–2115. 15 rooms, 2 with shower. No credit cards. Tube: Goodge St.*

£ ⊞ **The Generator.** This five-year-old youth hostel is easily the grooviest in town, with a friendly, funky vibe and vibrant decor—blue neon and brushed steel downstairs, and upstairs dorm rooms painted in bright blue and orange. Talking Heads, the Internet cafe, provides handy maps and leaflets, plus a chance to get on line. The Generator Bar has cheap drinks, and the Fuel Stop cafeteria provides inexpensive meals. Rooms are simple but clean—singles run about £38, twins (there are no doubles) about £24 per person, with prices dropping very low for the ones with multiple beds in them. From October to March are bargain-rate months, too. There are no bathrooms en-suite. ⊠ *MacNaghten House, Compton Pl., WC1H 9SD,* ☎ *020/7388–7666,* 𝖥𝖠𝖷 *020/7388–7644. 217 rooms without bath. Restaurant, bar. MC, V. Tube: Russell Sq.* ☙

£ ⊞ **Morgan.** This is a Georgian row-house hotel, family run with charm
★ and panache. Rooms are small and functionally furnished yet friendly and cheerful overall, with phones and TVs. The five newish apartments are particularly pleasing: three times the size of normal rooms (and an extra £15 per night, placing them in the ££ category), complete with eat-in kitchens (gourmet cooking sessions are discouraged) and private phone lines. The tiny, paneled breakfast room (rates include the meal) is straight out of a doll's house. The back rooms overlook the British Museum. ⊠ *24 Bloomsbury St., WC1B 3QJ,* ☎ *020/7636–3735,* 𝖥𝖠𝖷 *020/7636–3045. 15 rooms with shower, 5 apartments. Breakfast room. MC, V. Tube: Russell Sq.*

£ ⊞ **Ridgemount.** The kindly owners, Mr. and Mrs. Rees, make you feel at home. The public areas, especially the family-style breakfast room, have a friendly, cluttered Victorian feel. Some rooms overlook a leafy garden, and eight have an en-suite bathroom, for an extra £10 per night. ⊠ *65 Gower St., WC1E 6HJ,* ☎ *020/7636–1141,* 𝖥𝖠𝖷 *0207/6362558. 34 rooms, 9 with bath. MC, V. Tube: Goodge Street*

£ ⊞ **St. Margaret's.** This guest house on a tree-lined Georgian street has been run for many years by a friendly Italian family. You'll find spacious rooms and towering ceilings, and a wonderful location close to Russell Square. The back rooms have a garden view. ⊠ *24 Bedford Pl., WC1B 5JL,* ☎ *020/7636–4277. 64 rooms, 10 with bath. No credit cards. Tube: Goodge St.*

Hampstead and Islington

££££ ⊞ **Stakis Islington.** This brand-new, purpose-built hotel next door to the Islington Business Design Centre has a madly colored, soaring lobby and its own neighborhood to explore, as well as easy access to central London via the tube stop a minute's walk away. One of a reliable, small Scottish chain, the hotel has ultramodern rooms with climate control, satellite TV, and trouser presses, plus, in many of them, panoramic skyline views. ⊠ *53 Upper St., N1 0UY,* ☎ *020/7354–7700,* 𝖥𝖠𝖷 *020/7354–7711. 178 rooms, 6 suites. Restaurant, bar, exercise room, meeting rooms. AE, DC, MC, V. Tube: Angel.* ☙

££ ⊞ **La Gaffe.** Another find, this is a short walk from the Hampstead tube stop. Italian Bernardo Stella has been welcoming the same guests back to these early 18th-century shepherds' cottages for more than 20 years, and his restaurant has been going for nearly 40. Make no mistake, rooms are tiny, with showers only, and the predominantly peach-and-green decor isn't luxurious, but the popular wine bar and restaurant, which (naturally) serve Italian food, are yours to lounge around in at all hours. Between the two "wings" is a raised patio for summer, and each room has TV and phone. You'll love the place if you're a fan of quaint. ⊠ *107–111 Heath St., NW3 6SS,* ☎ *020/7435–8965,* 𝖥𝖠𝖷 *020/ 7794–7592. 18 rooms with shower. Restaurant, café, wine bar. AE, MC, V. Tube: Hampstead.* ☙

££ ⌂ **Great Northern.** Walk out the back door of King's Cross Station and you'll smack straight into the Great Northern, built in 1854. It is no beauty. Claret carpets, Regency stripes, boxlike rooms, and a smoke-filled bar do not necessarily appeal to the delicate palate. But there is solid Northern sense in constructing corridors wide enough for 19th-century ladies to sweep their skirts. Each room has a television and a trouser press; drinks are available 24 hours a day from the night porter's secret hoard. Brutally convenient, without a taint of whimsy, the Great Northern is triumphantly rooted in the age of steam. ⊠ *Cheney Rd., N1 9AN,* ☎ *0171/837–5454,* 🖷 *0207/278–5270. 82 rooms. Restaurant, bar, meeting rooms. AE, DC, MC, V. Tube: King's Cross.* ☙

££ ⌂ **Swiss Cottage Hotel.** It's a little out of the way on a peaceful street behind the Swiss Cottage tube stop, but this charming hotel will suit those who like to stay in a residential district, save a little on the check, and still have their home comforts. The lounge and reception area are stuffed with antiques and reproductions and are smilingly staffed. In summer, French windows open from the bar and the breakfast room. Bedrooms are in Victorian style, most are good-size, and all come with full English breakfast, meaning the value actually falls in the £ category. ⊠ *4 Adamson Rd., NW3 3HP,* ☎ *020/7722–2281,* 🖷 *020/ 7483–4588. 54 rooms. Bar, breakfast room. AE, DC, MC, V. Tube: Swiss Cottage.* ☙

£ ⌂ **Jury's Inn.** Look no further for a no-nonsense alternative to surly receptionists and carpets that smell of wet dog. This is not a typical budget establishment. On the doorstep of fashionable Islington, there is everything here for the pragmatic traveler (including a day-return laundry service). The restaurant does breakfast and dinner; the bar serves lunch and a limited menu all day. The bedrooms have data ports, hair dryers, en-suite bathrooms, and tea- and coffee-making facilities. Oh, and there's a special hook on the outside of the door on which they hang your breakfast if you want an early start. It's spotless, pragmatic, yet remarkably inviting. ⊠ *60 Pentonville Rd., N1 9LA,* ☎ *020/7282– 5500,* 🖷 *020/7 282–5511. 229. Restaurant, bar, in-room data ports, laundry service. AE, DC, MC, V. Tube: Angel www.jurys.com.*

Bed-and-Breakfast and Apartment Agencies

££ ⌂ **Bulldog Club.** Once the most exclusive B&B club in Britain, this has recently come under new ownership, which promises the same luxe, chic, and delightful accommodations that made the Bulldog the darling of magazine editors everywhere. In days of yore, you actually got to book rooms in some of London's poshest houses, where grown-up children's rooms were converted for guests. A three-year membership is around £25, with most properties available for around £100 a night. A full British breakfast as well as other goodies are often provided. Accommodations are generally available in Knightsbridge, Kensington, and Chelsea. *14 Dewhurst Rd., W14 0ET,* ☎ *020/7371–3202,* 🖷 *020/ 7371–2015. AE, MC, V.* ☙

££ ⌂ **Uptown Reservations.** As the name implies, this B&B booking service accepts only the tonier addresses and specializes in finding hosted homes or short-term apartments for Americans, often executives of small corporations. Nearly all the 85 homes on its register are in Knights-bridge, Belgravia, Kensington, and Chelsea, with a few lying farther west in Holland Park or to the north in Hampstead. The private homes vary, of course, but all are good-looking and have private bathrooms for guests, plus full Continental breakfast. ⊠ *50 Christchurch St., SW3 4AR,* ☎ *020/7351–3445,* 🖷 *020/7351–9383. Facilities vary. Payment by bank transfer or U.S. check or credit card; 20% deposit required. AE, MC, V.*

£–££   ☎ **US B&B.** This long-established family-run agency has some truly spectacular—and some more modest—London homes that host guests, in
practically all neighborhoods of the city. Check many of them out via
its Web site before making a commitment. The staff here is most personable and helpful. ⊠ *Box 124859, San Diego, CA 92112,* ☎ *800/
872–2632. 30% deposit required.* ✍

£   ☎ **Primrose Hill B&B.** This is a small, friendly bed-and-breakfast agency
genuinely "committed to the idea that traveling shouldn't be a rip-off."
Expatriate American Gail O'Farrell has family homes (to which guests
get their own latchkeys) in or near villagey Hampstead, and all are comfortable or more than comfortable. So far this has been one of those
word-of-mouth secrets, but now that everyone knows, book well
ahead. ⊠ *14 Edis St., NW1 8LG,* ☎ *020/7722–6869. No credit cards.*

4 NIGHTLIFE AND THE ARTS

"Ladies and gentlemen, the curtain is about to rise" on London's artful pleasures: Bussell at the ballet, Domingo at the Royal Albert Hall, and the best theater in the world—perhaps Ralph Fiennes and Vanessa Redgrave doing star turns, *Oliver!* in a West End revival, and unparalleled servings of Shakespeare. Now you can see, say, *The Winter's Tale* at the reconstructed Globe Theatre, where the interaction between player and audience often goes beyond polite applause. Finish off the night at a club sizzling with comedy, cabaret, or all that jazz.

Updated by
Victoria Young

A FTER DARK, LONDON is a wonderful place to play. Shakespearean theater and Handel oratorios, chart-friendly discos and post-industrial techno-rock raves, Andrew Lloyd Webber–ish extravaganzas, the roof-rattling Proms concerts (☞ Royal Albert Hall, *below*), magnificent opera and ballet—if you're into the arts and after-hours scenes, you'll be quickly whirling to a pounding beat. Recently, the arts scene has definitely stabilized. After a period of being shunted, gypsylike, from place to place in London, the performing Muses look to be settling back into revamped, revitalized homes. The world-renowned **Royal Opera House,** after years of executive shuffling and counterblasts, reopened in time for the new millennium with a new chief, New Yorker Michael Kaiser (though he will resign by the end of the 2000–01 season). And inside the Opera House, the **Royal Ballet** has once more been given a permanent home. It was likely for a while that the **English National Opera**—or ENO, as it is called—might abandon the Coliseum, its home since 1968, but it is now sure to stay put. Other good news is that the excellent **Old Vic** theater is alive and well and continuing with a great, and often challenging, mixed calendar of programs. This coming year, the state of after-hours London looks fine indeed.

NIGHTLIFE

Nighttime London has rejuvenated itself in the past few years, with a tangible new spirit of fun abroad on the streets, and new hangouts opening at an unprecedented rate. Whatever your pleasure, there's somewhere to go. Are you a club animal? London's boîtes are famously hip, hot, and happening. Music? From indie bands (short for "independent" and referring to their record label more than their state of mind) to resident orchestras, free jazz to opera, it's everywhere. Cabaret of the traditional torch-song sort is undergoing a little revival, while comedy, which never slowed down in the first place, remains one of the city's favorite ways to wind down. The gay listing is small but gives you all you need to find the scene, and there is a fabulous scene. Just remember when you hit the town at night that regular bars (those without special extended licenses) stop serving alcohol at 11 PM (10:30 on Sunday) and the tubes stop running around midnight, although the city is reasonably well served by night buses.

Such details can inhibit the free flow of enjoyment, it has to be said. Although there's been a lot of hype about swinging London in recent years, it is no less depressing than it ever was to be thrown out of your warm and fuzzy pub corner at the sound of the bell to try to find a bar with a late license. It is worth remembering that these rather archaic licensing laws (which were made in World War II to keep working men out of the pubs) are currently under review by the Labour government, and it looks more likely than ever that they will be amended in the near future. If they are, Londoners will be denied their favorite opportunity (save the weather) to grumble, and Britain will finally be set to catch up with the rest of Europe. An optimistic start to this process was made at the beginning of the millennium when a 220-year-old law that banned dancing on Sunday was removed, meaning that nightclubs will now be allowed to open on that day. On the whole, the club scene is for under-30s. If you don't have your ear to the ground in the youth culture department, you will feel out of place in nearly all venues listed under "Clubs" in *Time Out,* the weekly magazine that updates everything to do in London. But if you must put on the glad rags and boogie, we do list a couple of places for swingers nostalgic for that action. The jazz and world-music scenes are a different matter. Live music makes for a popular night out for all ages and types. A general rule of thumb: if you like the music, you'll like the crowd.

No doubt you've heard a lot about Britpop in the past couple of years. The bands that made it big are playing the stadium venues now, of course (Wembley, principally), but one of the joys of the London music scene is discovering your own indie bands and catching the latest hype before it's hyped. Again, read between the lines in the listings magazines to find your niche. Another, completely weird trend you may choose to follow has been imitation, or "tribute," bands—Utter Madness, Björn Again, Abba Gold, Ludwig Beatles, YMCA Village People, Below Average White Band, and so on—that perform to party-animal crowds. On the opposite end of the authenticity scale, Latin and flamenco sounds are growing, and you can sometimes learn the dances in a free class before the band comes on.

Bars

The places below are stylish and perfect for sipping martinis and munching hors d'oeuvres. Londoners, however, truly come into their own at their neighborhood pubs—for a listing of the best, *see* Chapter 2.

The American Bar. Festooned with a chin-dropping array of collegiate ties, bric-a-brac, and antique toys, this is one of London's most sensational funhouse interiors. Even if you're not feeling homesick for the other side of the pond, be sure to check out this dazzler. *Stafford Hotel, St. James's Pl., SW1A,* ☏ *020/7493–0111.* ◷ *Mon.–Sat. 11:30 AM–midnight, Sun. noon–2:30 PM and 6:30–10:30. AE, MC, V. Tube: Green Park.*

The Atlantic Bar and Grill. This vast, glamorous, wood-floored basement caused a revolution when, in early 1994, it became the first central London bar to be granted a late-late alcohol license. Although there are now others, it's still popular, so that the only way to get a table on a weekend night is to book it for dinner—luckily, the food's fine. ⊠ *20 Glasshouse St., W1,* ☏ *020/7734–4888.* ◷ *Mon.–Sat. noon–3 AM, Sun. 6 PM–10:30 PM. AE, DC, MC, V. Tube: Piccadilly Circus.*

Beach Blanket Babylon. In Notting Hill, close to Portobello Market, this always-packed singles bar is distinguishable by its fanciful decor—like a fairy-tale grotto or a medieval dungeon, visited by the gargoyles of Notre-Dame. ⊠ *15 Ledbury Rd., W11,* ☏ *020/7229–2907.* ◷ *Daily noon–11 PM. AE, MC, V. Tube: Notting Hill Gate.*

The Bug Bar. Slightly out of the way if you are staying in Central London, but well worth a visit if you are in the area, this mellow bar, attached to a restaurant called Bar Humbug that serves decent food, is in the crypt of a church and offers an off-the-beaten-track opportunity to hang with some funky Londoners. An added bonus for music lovers is that various DJs often spin here for free, although there is sometimes a small cover charge. ⊠ *Brixton Hill (under St. Matthew's Church), W1,* ☏ *020/7738–3184.* ◷ *Sun.–Thurs. 7 PM–1 AM, Fri.–Sat. 8 PM–3 AM. AE, DC, MC, V. Tube: Brixton.*

Cadogan Hotel Bar. One step beyond the door here and you're back in the Edwardian era. You half-expect Lillie Langtry, the famed actress and mistress of King Edward VII, to waltz in the door—but then, she used to live upstairs at this stylish hotel. If you feel like toasting Oscar Wilde with his favorite drink, a Hock and seltzer, you'd better do it elsewhere—poor Oscar was arrested in this very bar that fateful day. ⊠ *Cadogan Hotel, Sloane St., SW1,* ☏ *020/7235–7141.* ◷ *Daily 11–11. AE, MC, V. Tube: Sloane Sq.*

Café de Paris Open since 1914 and known as the "Bower of Love," this is one of London's most glamour-puss settings. Once a haunt of royals and consorts, the boîte brought in such stars as Noel Coward,

Marlene Dietrich, Fred Astaire, and Frank Sinatra. Spot the VIP table, where diners are presented with a minimum bill of £1,000. ✉ *3–4 Coventry St., W1V 7FL,* ☎ *020/7734–7700,* 🅵🅰🅇 *020/7434–0347.* ⊙ *Weekdays 5* PM*–4* AM. 🍽 *£10–£15. AE, DC, MC, V. Tube: Piccadilly Circus.*

The Library. In this very comfortable but self-consciously "period" bar at the swanky Lanesborough hotel (☞ Chapter 3), head barman Salvatore Calabrese offers his completely eccentric collection of ancient cognacs, made in years when something important happened. A shot of this liquid history can set you back £500. Enjoy the luxe surroundings and don't ask for a brandy Alexander. ✉ *Hyde Park Corner, SW1,* ☎ *020/7259–5599.* ⊙ *Mon.–Sat. 11–11, Sun. noon–10:30. AE, DC, MC, V. Tube: Hyde Park Corner.*

The Pool. Continuing an upward trend of industrial-style, trendy bars in Shoreditch—one of London's latest up-and-coming areas—this bar derives its name from three genuine American pool tables that are usually in use. The interior is elegant, with striking lighting and colors. Drinks are fairly pricey, but the food is better than most other pub grub. ✉ *104–108 Curtain Rd., EC2,* ☎ *020/7739–9608.* ⊙ *Mon.–Sat. noon–11* PM*, Sun. noon–10:30* PM. *MC, V, DC. Tube: Old Street.*

Cabaret

Comedy Café. As well as the wide range of stand-up comedy that takes place at this popular dive in the City, there is a weekly talent night on Wednesdays and late-night dancing at the weekends. Admission charges are occasionally waived. There's food available in the evening and usually a late license (for alcohol). ✉ *66 Rivington St., EC2,* ☎ *020/7739–5706.* 🍽 *Free–£12.* ⊙ *Wed.–Thurs. 7* PM*–1* AM*, Fri.–Sat. 7* PM*–2* AM. *DC, MC, V. Tube: Old St.*

Comedy Store. Now relocated to a bigger and better space, this is the improv factory where the United Kingdom's funniest stand-ups cut their teeth. The name performers and new talent you'll see may be strangers to you, but you're guaranteed to laugh. ✉ *Haymarket House, Oxendon St., SW1,* ☎ *020/7344–4444 or 020/7344–0234.* 🍽 *£11–£25.* ⊙ *Shows Tues.–Thurs. and Sun. at 8, Fri.–Sat. at 8 and midnight. AE, MC, V. Tube: Piccadilly Circus.*

Casinos

Unfortunately for those who like a bit of spontaneity, the 1968 Gaming Act states that any person wishing to gamble *must* make a declaration of intent to gamble at the gaming house in question and *must* apply for membership in person. Membership now takes 24 hours to process. In many cases, clubs prefer that the applicant's membership be proposed by an existing member. Personal guests of existing members are, however, allowed to participate.

Crockford's. This is a civilized club, established 150 years ago, with none of the jostling for tables that mars many of the flashier clubs. It has attracted a large international clientele since its move from St. James's to Mayfair. The club offers American roulette, Punto Banco, and blackjack. ✉ *30 Curzon St., W1,* ☎ *020/7493–7771.* 🍽 *Membership £300 yearly.* ⊙ *Daily noon–4* AM. *Jacket and tie. Tube: Green Park.*

Golden Nugget. This large casino just off Piccadilly has blackjack, roulette, and Punto Banco. ✉ *22–32 Shaftesbury Ave., W1,* ☎ *020/7439–0099.* 🍽 *Membership £10 yearly.* ⊙ *Daily 2* PM*–4* AM. *Jacket required. Tube: Piccadilly Circus.*

Palm Beach Casino. In what used to be the old ballroom of the Mayfair Hotel, this is a fast-moving and exciting club attracting a large international membership. It has a red-and-gold interior, with a plush restaurant and bar. You can choose from American roulette, blackjack, casino stub poker, and Punto Banco. ⊠ *30 Berkeley St., W1,* ☎ *020/ 7493–6585.* 🎫 *One-time "membership" £25.* ☉ *Daily 2 PM–4 AM. Jacket and tie. Tube: Green Park.*

Sportsman Club. This one has a dice table as well as Punto Banco, American roulette, and blackjack. ⊠ *40 Bryanston St., W1,* ☎ *020/7414– 0061.* 🎫 *One-time "membership" £20.* ☉ *Daily 12:30 PM–4 AM. Jacket and tie. Tube: Marble Arch.*

Clubs

A mini-revolution in the London club world saw the opening in 1999 of not one but two several-story, multi-dance-floor-equipped clubs called Home and Fabric, which can accommodate hundreds of clubbers at a time. In addition to these the city is packed full of other clubs that specialize in everything from techno to garage to disco. But always call ahead, especially to the dance and youth-oriented places, because the club scene is constantly changing. One-nighters (theme nights that take place at particular clubs on the same night every week, or move around from club to club) are very popular but tend to confuse matters with erratic opening and closing times—always check the daily listings in *Time Out* for current info.

Bagley's Studio. This used to be the largest club in town. Bagley's is notable for getting in the big DJs for one-night blitzes. It doesn't come cheap, though. After surfacing at King's Cross, walk north on York Way, and turn left on Goods Way. ⊠ *King's Cross Freight Depot, N1,* ☎ *020/7278–2777.* 🎫 *£12–£15.* ☉ *Sat. 10 PM–7 AM, with other raves usually scheduled for Thurs. and Fri. No credit cards. Tube: King's Cross.*

Bar Rumba. ⊠ This steamy, sweaty dance club is almost always crammed full and hosts a different style of music each night. Saturday night is garage music, Thursday is drum and base, and Tuesday night pulsates to the rhythm of salsa music. Dress in layers, because it gets very hot. *36 Shaftesbury Ave., W1,* ☎ *020/287–2715.* 🎫 *£3–£12.* ☉ *Weeknights 5 PM–3 AM, Sat. 5 PM–6 AM, Sun. 5 PM–1:40 AM. AE, MC, V. Tube: Piccadilly Circus.*

Camden Palace. It would be difficult to find a facial wrinkle in this huge place, even if you could see through the laser lights. Try to find your way around the three floors of bars. There is live music every Tuesday. ⊠ *1A Camden High St., NW1,* ☎ *020/7387–0428.* 🎫 *£5–£20.* ☉ *Tues.–Thurs. 10 PM–2 AM, Fri.–Sat. 10 PM–6 AM. MC, V. Tube: Mornington Crescent or Camden Town.*

The Dogstar. If you happen to be in South London for the night, this club has the advantage of being attached to a spacious and atmospheric pub that is usually populated by funky locals. Frequently the club plays host to a variety of DJs throughout the week and is often free. Dress down because the atmosphere is usually quite gritty. Follow or precede your visit with a drink at the nearby Bug Bar (☞ *above*) and your sampling of local Brixton life will be complete. ⊠ *389 Coldharbour La., SW9,* ☎ *020/7733–7515.* 🎫 *Varies.* ☉ *Mon.–Thurs. noon–2:30 AM, Fri.–Sat. noon –4:30 AM. MC, V. Tube: Brixton.*

Fabric. This, along with Home (☞ *below*), really was the name on every clubbers lips when it opened in 1999. Huge and trendy, it manages to cater to vast numbers of people (with three dance floors, five sound systems, three bars, a roof terrace, etc.) while at the same time—for the moment at least—remaining cutting-edge and hip. Drinks are reasonably priced. Weekends are a hive of DJ activity, while weeknights at Fabric are usually reserved for high-profile launches and special parties. Perhaps its main selling point is a 24-hour music and dancing license that lasts from Thursday to Sunday. Another is that it is in the heart of the burgeoning East London community that is *the* place to be right now. ✉ *77A Charterhouse St., EC1,* ☎ *020/7490–0444.* 🖃 *£10–£12.* ⊙ *Weekdays vary, Fri.–Sat. 9 PM–7 AM. AE, DC, MC, V. Tube: Farringdon.*

Gardening Club. Next door to the Rock Garden, but far hipper than that ancient dive, this club has different music, ambience, and groovers on alternating nights. ✉ *4 The Piazza, WC2,* ☎ *020/7497–3154.* 🖃 *£5–£13.* ⊙ *Mon.–Thurs. 10 PM–3 AM, Fri.–Sat. 11 PM–4 AM, Sun. 8 PM–midnight. AE, DC, MC, V. Tube: Covent Garden.*

Hanover Grand. A swank and opulent big West End club, the Hanover attracts TV stars and footballers whose exploits here you can later read about in the tabloids. The "Enigma" one-nighter takes over on Friday, while Saturday's glam disco "Future Perfect" pulls in all those who want to be seen. The lines outside get long, so dress up to impress the bouncers. ✉ *6 Hanover St., W1,* ☎ *020/7499–7977.* 🖃 *£5–£15.* ⊙ *Wed. 10:30 PM–3:30 AM, Thurs.–Fri. 10:30 PM–4 AM, Sat. 10:30 PM–5 AM. AE, MC, V. Tube: Oxford Circus.*

Home. Originally an import from Sydney and soon to be opened in New York, Home is another supertrendy, cutting-edge London development. Housed in an ultramodern seven-story building in the heart of London, Home offers everything, but everything, a clubber could yearn for, starting with an impressive list of DJs, moving on to the multimedia café or the restaurant that has a bird's-eye view of the city, and ending, possibly, in the chill-out zone. If you want to party like it's 2000, then this is the place to go. Sunday is gay night. ✉ *1 Leicester Sq., WC2,* ☎ *020/8964–1999* 🖃 *£5–£15.* ⊙ *Thurs.–Fri. 10 PM–3 AM, Sat. 9 PM–3 AM, Sun. 5 PM–midnight. AE, MC, V (but only over the phone for group bookings). Tube: Piccadilly Circus or Leicester Sq.*

Ministry of Sound. This is more of an industry than a club, with its own record label, line of apparel, and, of course, DJs. Inside, there are chill-out rooms, dance floors, promotional Sony Playstations, Absolut shot bars—all the club kid's favorite things. If you are one, and you only have time for one night out, make it here. ✉ *103 Gaunt St., SE1,* ☎ *020/7378–6528.* 🖃 *£10–£15.* ⊙ *Fri. 10:30 PM–6 AM, Sat. midnight–9 AM. MC, V. Tube: Elephant and Castle.*

Notting Hill Arts Club. In one of London's trendiest neighborhoods, this is an innovative club-bar with a high-profile reputation. Saturdays showcase "Outcaste," devoted to Asian underground music; other nights include "Brazilian Love Affair" or French house beats. Art exhibitions are sometimes held here, too. ✉ *21 Notting Hill Gate, W11,* ☎ *020/ 7460–4459.* 🖃 *£3–£5.* ⊙ *Mon.–Wed. 6 PM–1 AM, Sat. 6 PM–2 AM, Sun. 4 PM–11 PM. No credit cards. Tube: Notting Hill Gate.*

Sound Republic. Dearies, isn't that Noel Gallagher of Oasis at the lead banquette? Hard to tell, what with all the strobe lights, ostrich feather hats, fake fur trim, hip DJs, and masses of London's young and restless on hand. ✉ *Swiss Center, Leicester Sq., WC2,* ☎ *020/7287–1010.* 🖃 *£12–£15; Wed. £5.* ⊙ *Wed. 7:30–midnight, Fri. 10:30–4:30, Sat. 10–4. AE, MC, V.*

Stringfellows. Peter Stringfellow's nightclub is not at all hip, but it *is* glitzy, with mirrored walls, the requisite dance-floor light show, and an expensive art deco–style restaurant. Suburbanites and middle-aged swingers frequent it. ✉ *16–19 Upper St. Martin's La., WC2,* ☎ *020/ 7240–5534.* 🖃 *Mon.–Thurs. £10 before 10 PM, Fri.–Sat. £10 before 11 PM, £15 after.* ⊙ *Mon.–Thurs. 7 PM–3:30 AM, Fri.–Sat. 8 PM–3:30 AM. AE, DC, MC, V. Tube: Charing Cross.*

Subterania. This is the place to go to hang out with London's real party people. Intimidatingly cool at times, and usually populated by the hard-core clubbing crowd, this West London club hosts nights that range from serious roots reggae to animated disco and garage. Expect a good fallout from the nearby Portobello–Notting Hill crowd, and dress down rather than up if you want to blend, which you do! ✉ *12 Acklam Rd. (under Westway), W10,* ☎ *020/8960–4590.* ✑ *Usually £5–£10.* ◷ *Mon.–Thurs. 8 PM–2 AM, Fri.–Sun. 10 PM–3 AM. AE, DC, MC, V. Tube: Ladbroke Grove.*

The Wag. This tenacious representative of Soho's club circuit takes on a different character according to the night and the DJ spinning. One extremely loud, sweaty level houses bars and dance spaces, and on a quieter, cooler floor there's a restaurant serving dinner and breakfast. ✉ *33–35 Wardour St., W1,* ☎ *020/7437–5534.* ✑ *£5–£10.* ◷ *Tues.– Thurs. 10 PM–3 AM, Fri. 10 PM–4 AM, Sat. 10 PM–5 AM. No credit cards. Tube: Piccadilly Circus.*

Jazz

Jazz Café. This palace of high-tech cool in a converted bank in bohemian Camden remains an essential hangout for fans of both the mainstream end of the repertoire and younger crossover performers. It's way north, but steps from Camden Town tube. ✉ *3–5 Parkway, NW1,* ☎ *020/ 7916–6060.* ✑ *£6–£20.* ◷ *Mon.–Thurs. 7 PM–1 AM, Fri.–Sat. 7 PM– 2 AM, Sun. 7 PM–midnight. DC, MC, V. Tube: Camden Town.*

100 Club. The best for blues, trad, and Dixie, plus the occasional straight rock-and-roll, this Oxford Street subterranean has the correct paint-peeling, smoke-choked, dance-inducing atmosphere. There's a food counter most nights. ✉ *100 Oxford St., W1,* ☎ *020/7636–0933.* ✑ *£6–£10.* ◷ *Mon.–Thurs. 7:30–midnight, Fri.–Sat. 7:30 PM–2 AM, Sun. 7:30 PM–11:30 PM. No credit cards. Tube: Oxford Circus.*

Pizza Express. It may seem strange, since Pizza Express is the capital's best-loved chain of pizza houses, but this is one of London's principal jazz venues, with music every night except Monday in the basement restaurant. The subterranean interior is darkly lighted, the lineups (often featuring visiting U.S. performers) are interesting, and the Italian-style thin-crust pizzas are great. Eight other branches also have live music; check the listings for details. ✉ *10 Dean St., W1,* ☎ *020/7437–9595 or 020/7439–8722.* ✑ *£8–£20.* ◷ *From 11:30 AM for food; music nightly 9 PM–midnight. AE, DC, MC, V. Tube: Tottenham Court Rd.*

Ronnie Scott's. Since opening in the '60s, this legendary Soho jazz club has attracted all the big names. It's usually packed and hot, the food isn't great, and service is slow—the staff can't move through the crowds, either—but the atmosphere can't be beat, and it's probably still London's best, even since the sad departure of its eponymous founder and saxophonist. Reservations are recommended. ✉ *47 Frith St., W1,* ☎ *020/7439–0747.* ✑ *£15–£20 nonmembers, £5–£9 members, annual membership £50.* ◷ *Mon.–Sat. 8:30 PM–3 AM, Sun. 7:30 PM–11:30 PM. AE, DC, MC, V. Tube: Leicester Sq.*

606 Club. In deepest Fulham, this is a civilized sit-down club with late hours, showcasing mainstream and contemporary jazz—basically, well-known British artists. You must eat a meal in order to consume alcohol. ✉ *90 Lots Rd., SW10,* ☎ *020/7352–5953.* ✑ *£7.50–£24.* ◷ *Mon.–Wed. 7:30 PM–1:15 AM, Thurs.–Sat. 8:15 PM–2 AM, Sun. 8:15 PM–11:30 PM. MC, V. Tube: Fulham Broadway.*

Rock

The Astoria. Very central and quite hip, this place hosts bands that there's a buzz about, plus it has late club nights. ✉ *157 Charing Cross Rd., W1,* ☎ *020/7434–9592.* ✑ *£8–£15.* ◷ *Check listings. No credit cards. Tube: Tottenham Court Rd.*

Barfly Club. Formerly known as the Splash Club (the people who gave Skunk Anansie, Kula Shaker, and Oasis their big breaks), this is the finest and most eclectic small club in the capital. There are three bands nightly, with events regularly scheduled by some of the top rocker magazines. ⊠ *Falcon Pub, 234 Royal College St., NW1,* ☎ *020/7482–4884.* ✆ *£3:50–£8.* ⊘ *Daily 7:30 PM–11 PM. MC, V. Tube: Camden Town.*

The Forum. This ex-ballroom with balcony and dance floor packs in the customers, and it consistently attracts the best medium-to-big-name performers, too. ⊠ *9–17 Highgate Rd., NW5,* ☎ *020/7344–0044.* ✆ *£10–£15.* ⊘ *Most nights 7–11. AE, MC, V. Tube: Kentish Town.*

The Roadhouse. True to its name, this spot pays homage to the American dream of the open road, with a Harley behind the bar and much memorabilia. Music fits into the feel-good, tuneful, middle-of-the-road end of the R&B-blues-rock-soul spectrum. ⊠ *Jubilee Hall, Covent Garden, WC2,* ☎ *020/7240–6001.* ✆ *Free–£10.* ⊘ *Mon.–Sat. 5:30 PM–3 AM, Sun. 5:30 PM–10:30 PM. AE, DC, MC, V. Tube: Covent Garden.*

Shepherd's Bush Empire. Converted from the BBC TV theater, where Terry Wogan, the United Kingdom's Johnny Carson, recorded his show for years and years, this venue now hosts names like Stevie Winwood, the Rolling Stones, and the Who. ⊠ *Shepherd's Bush Green, W12,* ☎ *020/7771–2000.* ✆ *£12–£15.* ⊘ *Most nights 7–11. MC, V. Tube: Shepherd's Bush.*

Station Tavern. For a taste of local life, head out to this recently refurbished New Orleans–style blues haven, which has played host to the likes of Tom Jones and Chaka Kahn, as well as Bob's aptly named Goodtime Blues, who have been honking here forever. The Tavern is opposite the tube, luckily. ⊠ *41 Bramley Rd., W10,* ☎ *020/7221–9921.* ✆ *Free–£5.* ⊘ *Most nights 8:30–midnight. Tube: Latimer Rd.*

The Gay Scene

Since February 1994, with the long-overdue lowering of the age of consent from 21, 18-year-old gay men in Britain have had the blessing of the law in doing what they've always done. The change did not extend to lesbians, nor did it need to, because there has never been any legislation that so much as mentions gay women—a circumstance that, believe it or not, dates from Queen Victoria's point-blank refusal to believe that women paired off with women. AIDS is, of course, a large issue, but the epidemic hasn't yet had quite as devastating an impact on the London scene as it has had in San Francisco and New York.

The whole of London has benefited hugely from the blossoming of gay nightlife. Soho, especially Old Compton Street, has gone through something of a pre-AIDS Christopher Street atmosphere, with gay shops, bars, restaurants, and even beauty salons (get your chest waxed here) jostling for space, and it has now settled into happy coexistence with club kids, restaurant patrons, and tourists. Though lesbians are included in the gay clubbing scene (as are anyone's straight friends), it's predominantly men-for-men. Lesbian chic is as trendy in London as it is in New York or Los Angeles, but it has a lower profile, generally, than the male equivalent, and it also tends to be more politically strident. Any women-only event in London attracts a large proportion of gay women.

Check the listings in *Time Out,* the weekly *MetroXtra (MX),* and the monthly *Gay Times* for events.

Bars, Cafés, and Pubs

Pub hours for the listings in this section are the same as for all London pubs, with drinks available up to 11 PM.

The Box. Modern, and très chic after a recent refurbishment, the Box has different DJs spinning every night. For peckish punters there is food before 5 PM every day. Or, for a visual feast, visit on a "Fabulous Friday" to watch the pole dancers. ⊠ *Seven Dials, 32–34 Monmouth St., WC2,* ☏ *020/7240–5828. Tube: Leicester Sq.*

The Edge. Poseurs are welcome at this hip Soho hangout, where straight groovers mix and mingle with gay men over the four floors. Get more for your money in the summer, when sidewalk tables offer an enviable view of Soho's daily street theater. Risk the vodkas infused with candy. ⊠ *11 Soho Sq., W1,* ☏ *020/7439–1313. Tube: Oxford Circus.*

Freedom. This is a popular café-bar central to the Soho scene. In addition, it has late-night music and DJs on the lower floor, which is licensed until 3 AM. There is a rigid and sometimes frigid door policy, enforced by bouncers, and a cover charge of £3–£5 after 11 PM. ⊠ *60– 66 Wardour St., W1,* ☏ *020/7734–0071. Tube: Piccadilly Circus.*

The Yard. This is Soho's best-looking and biggest café-bar, centered on the eponymous courtyard and getting very full and smoky at night. Upstairs is a little more genteel, with sofas. Get a bottomless coffee, or a club sandwich, or an entire night out here. ⊠ *57 Rupert St., W1,* ☏ *020/7437–2652. Tube: Piccadilly Circus.*

Clubs

Heaven. Aptly named, it has by far the best light show on any London dance floor, and it's unpretentious, *loud,* and huge, with a labyrinth of quiet rooms, bars, and live-music parlors. If you go to just one club, this is the one to choose. Friday is straight night. ⊠ *The Arches, Villiers St., WC2,* ☏ *020/7930–2020.* ⊑ *£1–£10.* ⊘ *Weekdays 10:30 PM– 3:30 AM, Sat. 11:30 PM–6 AM. Tube: Charing Cross.*

One-Nighters

Some of the best gay dance clubs are held once a week in mixed clubs. The following are well established and likely still to be going strong, but it's best to call first.

Jo's Original Tea Dance. A longtime fave with the girls, this is a very camp and very fun Sunday ballroom, line-dance, time-warp disco, now in a new home after many years. ⊠ *BJ's White Swan, 556 Commercial Rd., E14,* ☏ *020/7780–9870.* ⊑ *£2.* ⊘ *Sun. 5:30–midnight. Tube: Limehouse.*

Love Muscle. A steaming, mixed-gender Saturday-night party, this blast offers eight hours of dance classics at a big Brixton club. ⊠ *The Fridge, Town Hall Parade, Brixton Hill, SW2,* ☏ *020/7326–5100.* ⊑ *£6 before 11 PM, £8 11–midnight, £10 midnight–3 AM.* ⊘ *Sat. 10 PM–6 AM. Tube: Brixton.*

THE ARTS

There isn't *a* London arts scene—there are lots of them. As long as there are audiences for Feydeau revivals, drag queens, obscure teenage rock bands, hit musicals, body-painted Parisian dancers, and improvised stand-up comedy, someone will stage them in London. Commercial sponsorship of the arts is in its infancy here compared to what it is in the United States, and most major arts companies, as well as those smaller ones lucky enough to be grant-aided, are dependent, to some extent, on (inadequate) government subsidy. This ought to mean low ticket prices, but it doesn't necessarily work that way. Even so, when you consider how much a London hotel room costs, the city's arts are a bargain.

We've attempted a representative selection in the following listings, but to find out what's showing now, the weekly magazine *Time Out* (issued every Wednesday in central London) is invaluable. The *Evening Standard* also carries listings, especially in the supplement *Hot Tickets,* which comes with the Thursday edition, as do the "quality" Sun-

Theaters and Concert Halls

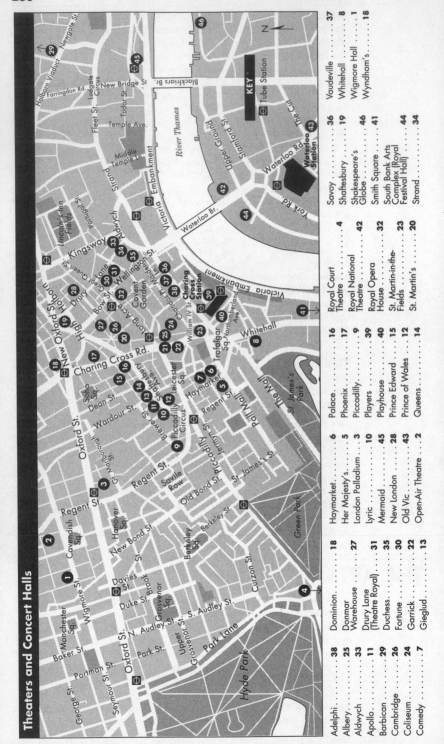

Adelphi	38
Albery	25
Aldwych	33
Apollo	11
Barbican	29
Cambridge	26
Coliseum	24
Comedy	7
Dominion	18
Donmar Warehouse	27
Drury Lane (Theatre Royal)	31
Duchess	35
Fortune	30
Garrick	22
Gielgud	13
Haymarket	6
Her Majesty's	5
London Palladium	3
Lyric	10
Mermaid	45
New London	28
Old Vic	43
Open-Air Theatre	2
Palace	16
Phoenix	17
Piccadilly	9
Players	39
Playhouse	40
Prince Edward	15
Prince of Wales	12
Queens	14
Royal Court Theatre	4
Royal National Theatre	42
Royal Opera House	32
St. Martin-in-the-Fields	23
St. Martin's	20
Savoy	36
Shaftesbury	19
Shakespeare's Globe	46
Smith Square	41
South Bank Arts Complex (Royal Festival Hall)	44
Strand	34
Vaudeville	37
Whitehall	8
Wigmore Hall	1
Wyndham's	18

KEY

⊖ Tube Station

day papers and the Saturday *Independent, Guardian,* and *Times.* You'll find leaflets and flyers in most cinema and theater foyers, too, and you can pick up the free fortnightly *London Theatre Guide* leaflet from hotels and tourist information centers.

Ballet

The Royal Opera House is once again the traditional home of the world-famous **Royal Ballet.** After 20 years of planning and a two-year closure for renovation, the stage doors finally reopened just in time for the new millennium. As well as traditional favorites like *The Nutcracker,* this year will also see a revival of the production of *CoppÈlia* that was originally presented by Dame Ninette de Valois, the founder of the Ballet. A new pricing structure means that tickets are more affordable, although bookings should be made well in advance. The **English National Ballet** and visiting international companies perform at the Coliseum— but that theater, too, is scheduled for a renovation program lasting several seasons, and resident troupes will be performing elsewhere (call the Coliseum box office for further information). In addition, the **City Ballet of London** performs at the Peacock Theatre. The newly reopened **Sadler's Wells Theatre** also hosts various other ballet companies and regional and international modern dance troupes. Modern and experimental work is best viewed at the **Place.**

Ballet Box Offices

Coliseum, ⊠ *St. Martin's La.,* WC2N 4ES, ☎ *020/7632–8300. Tube: Leicester Sq.*
Peacock Theatre, ⊠ *Portugal St.,* WC2, ☎ *020/7314–8800. Tube: Holborn.*
The Place, ⊠ *17 Duke's Rd.,* WC1, ☎ *020/7387–0031. Tube: Euston.*
Royal Festival Hall, ⊠ *South Bank Arts Complex, SE1 8XX,* ☎ *020/ 7960–4242. Tube: Waterloo or Embankment Station.*
Royal Opera House, ⊠ *Covent Garden,* WC2E 9DD, ☎ *020/7304– 4000. Tube: Covent Garden.*
Sadler's Wells, ⊠ *Rosebery Ave.,* EC1R 4TN, ☎ *020/7863–8000. Tube: Angel.*

Concerts

The ticket prices to symphony-size orchestral concerts are fortunately still relatively moderately priced, usually ranging from £5 to £35. If you can't book in advance, then arrive at the hall an hour before the performance for a chance at returns.

The London Symphony Orchestra is in residence at the **Barbican Centre,** although other top orchestras—including the Philharmonia and the Royal Philharmonic—also perform here. The **South Bank Arts Complex,** which includes the **Royal Festival Hall,** the **Queen Elizabeth Hall,** and the small **Purcell Room,** forms another major venue. The Royal Festival Hall is one of the finest concert halls in Europe. Between the Barbican and South Bank, there are concert performances almost every night of the year. The Barbican also features chamber music concerts with such celebrated orchestras as the City of London Sinfonia.

For a different concert-going experience, as well as the chance to take part in a great British tradition, try the **Royal Albert Hall** during the Promenade Concert season: eight weeks lasting from July to September. The usual chestnuts are featured, along with some novelties, but the capper is the last night, a madly jingoistic display of singing "Land of Hope and Glory," Union Jack waving, and general madness. Demand for tickets is so high that you must enter a lottery. For regular

Proms, tickets run £3–£30; special "promenade" (standing) tickets usually cost half the price of normal tickets and are available at the hall on the night of the concert. Note, too, that the concerts have begun to be jumbo-screen broadcast in Hyde Park, but even here a seat on the grass requires a paid ticket. Call ☎ 020/7589–8212 for further information. Another summer pleasure is the outdoor concert series by the lake at **Kenwood** (✉ Hampstead Heath, ☎ 020/7973–3427). Concerts are also part of the program at the open-air theater in **Holland Park** (☎ 020/7602–7856). Check the listings for details.

You should also look for the lunchtime concerts that take place all over the city in smaller concert halls, the big arts-center foyers, and churches; they usually cost less than £5 or are free and will feature string quartets, singers, jazz ensembles, or gospel choirs. **St. John's, Smith Square** and **St. Martin-in-the-Fields** are two of the more popular locations. Performances usually begin about 1 PM and last an hour.

Concert Hall Box Offices

Barbican Centre, ✉ *Barbican, EC2Y 8DS,* ☎ *020/7638–8891 or 020/7638–4141. Tube: Barbican.*

Royal Albert Hall, ✉ *Kensington Gore, SW7,* ☎ *020/7589–8212. Tube: South Kensington.*

St. John's, Smith Square, ✉ *SW1P 3HA,* ☎ *020/7222–1061. Tube: Westminster.*

St. Martin-in-the-Fields, ✉ *Trafalgar Sq., WC2N 4JJ,* ☎ *020/7839–1930. Tube: Charing Cross.*

South Bank Arts Complex, ✉ *South Bank, SE1 8XX,* ☎ *020/7960–4233. Tube: Waterloo.*

Wigmore Hall, ✉ *36 Wigmore St., W1H OBP,* ☎ *020/7935–2141. Tube: Bond St.*

Modern Dance

Contemporary dance thrives in London, with innovative young choreographers and companies constantly emerging (and then, it often seems, moving to New York). Michael Clark was one of the first of the new wave; Yolanda Snaith, Bunty Matthias, and choreographer Lea Anderson's troupe, the Cholmondeleys (pronounced "Chumleys"), are more examples of home-grown talent. In addition to the many fringe theaters that produce the odd dance performance, the following theaters showcase contemporary dance:

The Place, ✉ *17 Duke's Rd., WC1,* ☎ *020/7387–0031. Tube: Euston.*
Riverside Studios (☞ Fringe Theater, *below*).
Sadler's Wells (☞ Opera, *below,* and Ballet, *above*).

Movies

Despite the video invasion, West End movie theaters continue to do good business. Most of the major houses (Odeon, ABC, etc.) are in the Leicester Square–Piccadilly Circus area, where tickets average £8. Mondays and matinees are often cheaper, at around £4, and there are also fewer crowds. Some theaters offer student discounts, and prices drop to around £5 as you get out of the West End, becoming even lower in the suburbs, but unless you're staying there, any savings could be eaten up by transportation costs.

The few movie clubs and repertory cinemas that still exist screen a wider range of movies, including classic, Continental, and underground, as well as rare or underrated masterpieces. Some charge a membership fee of less than £1. The king is the **National Film Theatre** (✉ South Bank Arts Complex, ☎ 020/7928–3232), where the London Film Festival is based in the fall; there are also lectures and presentations. Annual membership costs £14.95 and entitles you to £1 off the ticket price. Also worth checking out are the **Everyman** (⊠ Hollybush Vale, Hampstead, ☎ 084/5606–2345), where the yearly membership is only £1; the **Rio** (⊠ Kingsland High St., Hackney E8, ☎ 020/7254–6677), though it's a bit of a trek; and the **Riverside** (☞ Fringe Theater, *below*).

Opera

The **Royal Opera** presides over the main venue for opera in London, the fabled Royal Opera House, which ranks with the Metropolitan Opera House in New York—in every way, except, surprisingly, expense. Long castigated in Britain for its outrageous ticket prices, the Opera House has adopted a new policy. Since December 1999, when a magnificent gala—and much pomp and ceremony—marked the reopening of the renovated Royal Opera House in Covent Garden, the House, as it is known, pledged to lower its ticket prices. Indeed, now the doors really are open to the masses, since the cheapest tickets are just £2 (for a ballet matinee), although prices escalate to £150 for a top-price opera. Conditions of purchase vary—call for information.

English-language productions are staged at the **Coliseum** in St. Martin's Lane, home of the English National Opera Company. Prices are lower than for the Royal Opera, ranging from £5 to £55, and productions are often innovative and exciting. The ENO sells same-day seats for as low as £2.50.

Opera Box Offices

Albert Hall (☞ Concert Hall Box Office Information, *above*).
Barbican Centre (☞ Concert Hall Box Office Information, *above*).
Coliseum, ⊠ *St. Martin's La., WC2N 4ES,* ☎ *020/7632–8300. Tube: Leicester Sq.*
Royal Festival Hall/South Bank Arts Complex (☞ Concert Hall Box Office Information, *above*).
Royal Opera House, ⊠ *Covent Garden, WC2E 9DD,* ☎ *020/7304–4000. Tube: Covent Garden.*
Sadler's Wells, ⊠ *Rosebery Ave., EC1R 4TN,* ☎ *020/7863–8000. Tube: Angel.*
Shaftesbury, ⊠ *Shaftesbury Ave., WC2H 8DP,* ☎ *020/7379–5399. Tube: Holborn.*

Theater

Although the price of a seat rarely falls below a tenner, London's West End theaters still pull in enough punters to cause a mini traffic jam each night before the house lights dim and the curtain rises. From Shakespeare's time to the umpteenth year of *Les Misérables* (or *The Glums,* as it's affectionately known), the West End has what visitors think of as London theater. But there's more to see in London than the offerings of Theatreland and the national companies.

Of the 100 or so legitimate theaters in the capital, 50 are officially "West End," while the remainder go under the blanket title of "fringe." Much like New York's off- and off-off-Broadway, fringe theater encompasses everything from off-the-wall "physical theater" pieces to first runs of new plays and revivals of old ones. A recent typical selection of fringe offerings had one Dickens, an Ibsen, a Kafka, and a couple of Molière productions, as well as several contemporary plays—all in competition. Indeed, even Hollywood's A-team now loves the fringe. At the 300-seat Almedia in Islington, big stars famously play for small bucks. The last couple of years have seen Kevin Spacey in Eugene O'Neill's *The Ice-*

man Cometh, Liam Neeson in David Hare's *Judas Kiss,* and Juliette Binoche in Pirandello's *Naked.* No star, in fact, has been too big for a small theater. Nicole Kidman wowed them in Schnitzler's *The Blue Room* at the 250-seat Donmar Warehouse; Ewan McGregor received £250 a week to star in *Little Malcolm and His Struggle Against the Eunuchs* at Hampstead's 174-seater. That's just *non*–West End.

For serious theatergoers, the top of the line are still the **Royal Shakespeare Company** and the **Royal National Theatre Company,** which perform at London's two main arts complexes, the **Barbican Centre** and the **Royal National Theatre.** Both groups mount consistently excellent productions and are usually a safe option for anyone having trouble choosing which play to see. From mid-May through mid-September, you can now see the Bard served up in his most spectacular manifestation—at the new, open-air reconstruction of **Shakespeare's Globe Theatre** (☞ Chapter 1), which opened in June 1997. In addition, Shakespeare under the stars is provided from the last week in May to the third week in September by the New Shakespeare Company at the lovely venue of the **Regent's Park Open-Air Theatre** (✉ Regent's Park Inner Circle, ☎ 020/7486–2431). Two Shakespeare plays are presented every season, along with a modern musical, from Monday to Saturday at 8 PM and on Wednesday, Thursday, and Saturday at 2 PM. Check *Time Out* for details. The renovated **Royal Court Theatre,** which has produced gritty British and international drama since the middle of the 20th century (its production of John Osborne's *Look Back in Anger* is seen as the birth of modern British drama), reopened in February 2000 with a continued dedication to new playwrights and new plays.

Most theaters have matinees twice a week (Wednesday or Thursday, and Saturday) and evening performances that begin at 7:30 or 8; performances on Sunday are rare but not unknown. Prices vary, but in the West End you should expect to pay from £10 for a seat in the upper balcony to at least £25 for a good one in the stalls (orchestra) or dress circle (mezzanine). Tickets may be booked at the individual theater box offices or over the phone by credit card (some box offices or agents have special numbers for these, marked "cc" in the phone book); most theaters still don't charge a fee for the latter. You can also book through ticket agents, such as **First Call** (☎ 020/7420–0000) or **Ticketmaster** (☎ 020/7344–0055; 800/775–2525 in the U.S.), although these usually do charge a booking fee. **Keith Prowse** has a New York office (✉ 234 W. 44th St., Suite 1000, New York, NY 10036, ☎ 212/398–1430 or 800/ 669–8687), as does **Edwards & Edwards** (✉ 1 Times Sq. Plaza, 12th floor, New York, NY 10036, ☎ 800/223–6108). If you're a theater junkie and want to put together a West End package, *The Complete Guide to London's West End Theatres* has seating plans and booking information for all the houses. It costs £9.95 (plus postage) from the Society of London Theatres (☎ 020/7557–6700). Alternatively, the SOLT Half Price Ticket Booth (no phone) on the southwest corner of Leicester Square sells up to four half-price tickets per purchaser on the day of performance for about 25 theaters, subject to availability. It's open Monday– Saturday 2–6:30, Sunday noon–3, and from noon for matinees; there is a £2 service charge, and only cash is accepted. Note that these half-price tickets are invariably for orchestra seats; for more reasonably priced seats, it may be better to go to the actual theater box office. All the larger hotels offer theater bookings, but as they tack on a hefty service charge, you would do better visiting the box offices yourself. You might, however, consider using one particular booking line that doubles the price of tickets: **West End Cares** (☎ 020/7833–3939) donates half of what it charges to AIDS charities.

Warning: Be *very* careful of scalpers outside theaters and working the line at the Half Price Ticket Booth; they have been known to charge £200 or more for a sought-after ticket (let alone the stiff fine that is levied if you are caught buying a scalped ticket). In recent years, there has been another problem: unscrupulous ticket agents, who sell tickets at four or five times their price from the ticket box offices. Although a service charge is legitimate, this type of scalping certainly isn't, especially because the vast majority of theaters have some tickets (returns and house seats) available on the night of performance.

Theater Directory

The following is a list of West End theaters:

Adelphi, ⊠ *Strand, WC2E 7NA,* ☎ *020/7344–0055. Tube: Charing Cross.*

Albery, ⊠ *St. Martin's La., WC2N 4AH,* ☎ *020/7369–1740. Tube: Leicester Sq.*

Aldwych, ⊠ *Aldwych, WC2B 4DF,* ☎ *020/7416–6003. Tube: Covent Garden.*

Apollo, ⊠ *Shaftesbury Ave., W1V 7HD,* ☎ *020/7494–5070. Tube: Piccadilly Circus.*

Apollo Victoria, ⊠ *Wilton Rd., SW1V ILL,* ☎ *020/7416–6054. Tube: Victoria.*

Arts Theatre, ⊠ *6–7 Great Newport St., WC2H 7JB,* ☎ *020/7836–2132. Tube: Leicester Sq.*

Barbican Center, ⊠ *Barbican, EC2Y 8DS,* ☎ *020/7638–8891. Tube: Moorgate.*

Cambridge, ⊠ *Earlham St., WCA 9HH,* ☎ *020/7494–5081 or 020/7494–5080. Tube: Covent Garden.*

Comedy, ⊠ *Panton St., SW1Y 4DN,* ☎ *020/7369–1741 or 020/7369–1731. Tube: Piccadilly Circus.*

Dominion, ⊠ *Tottenham Court Rd., W1 0AG,* ☎ *020/7656–1888. Tube: Tottenham Court Rd.*

Donmar Warehouse, ⊠ *41 Earlham St., WC2H 9LD,* ☎ *020/7369–1732. Tube: Covent Garden.*

Drury Lane (Theatre Royal), ⊠ *Catherine St., WC2B 5JF,* ☎ *020/7494–5060. Tube: Covent Garden.*

Duchess, ⊠ *Catherine St., WC2B 5LA,* ☎ *020/7494–5076. Tube: Covent Garden.*

Fortune, ⊠ *Russell St., WC2B 5HH,* ☎ *020/7836–2238. Tube: Covent Garden.*

Garrick, ⊠ *Charing Cross Rd., WC2H 0HH,* ☎ *020/7494–5085. Tube: Leicester Sq.*

Gielgud, ⊠ *Shaftesbury Ave., W1V 8AR,* ☎ *020/7494–5065. Tube: Piccadilly Circus.*

Globe (Shakespeare's Globe), ⊠ *New Globe Walk, Bankside, SE1,* ☎ *020/7401–9919. Tube: Mansion House, then walk across Southwark Bridge, or Blackfriars, then walk across Blackfriars Bridge.*

Haymarket Theatre Royal, ⊠ *Haymarket, SW1Y 4HT,* ☎ *020/7930–8800. Tube: Piccadilly Circus.*

Her Majesty's, ⊠ *Haymarket, SW1Y 4QR,* ☎ *020/7494–5050. Tube: Piccadilly Circus.*

London Palladium, ⊠ *8 Argyll St., W1V 1AD,* ☎ *020/7494–5020. Tube: Oxford Circus.*

Lyceum, ⊠ *Wellington St., WC2,* ☎ *020/7656–1803. Tube: Charing Cross.*

Lyric, ⊠ *Shaftesbury Ave., W1V 7HA,* ☎ *020/7494–5045. Tube: Piccadilly Circus.*

Lyric Hammersmith, ⊠ *King St., W6 0QL,* ☎ *020/8741–2311. Tube: Hammersmith.*

Mermaid, ⊠ *Puddle Dock, EC4 3DB,* ☎ *020/7236–1919. Tube: Blackfriars.*

New London, ⊠ *Drury La., WC2B 5PW,* ☎ *020/7405–0072. Tube: Covent Garden.*

Old Vic, ⊠ *Waterloo Rd., SE1 8NB,* ☎ *020/7928–7616. Tube: Waterloo.*

Open Air Theater, ⊠ *Inner Circle, Regent's Park, NW1 4NP,* ☎ *020/ 7486–2431. Tube: Baker St.*

Palace, ⊠ *Shaftesbury Ave., W1V 8AY,* ☎ *020/7434–0909. Tube: Leicester Sq.*

Phoenix, ⊠ *Charing Cross Rd., WC2H 0JP,* ☎ *020/7369–1733. Tube: Leicester Sq.*

Piccadilly, ⊠ *Denman St., W1V 8DY,* ☎ *020/7369–1734. Tube: Piccadilly Circus.*

Players, ⊠ *The Arches, Villiers St., WC2N 6NQ,* ☎ *020/7839–1134 or 020/7976–1307. Tube: Charing Cross.*

Playhouse, ⊠ *Northumberland Ave., WC2N 6NN,* ☎ *020/7839– 4401. Tube: Embankment.*

Prince Edward, ⊠ *Old Compton St., W1V 6HS,* ☎ *020/7447–5400. Tube: Leicester Sq.*

Prince of Wales, ⊠ *31 Coventry St., W1V 8AS,* ☎ *020/7839–5987. Tube: Leicester Sq.*

Queens, ⊠ *51 Shaftesbury Ave., W1V 8AS,* ☎ *020/7494–5040. Tube: Leicester Sq.*

Regent's Park Open-Air Theatre, ⊠ *Inner Circle, Regent's Park., NW1,* ☎ *020/7486–2431. Tube: Baker St., Regent's Park.*

Royal Court Theatre, ⊠ *Sloane Sq., SW1,* ☎ *020/7565–5000. Tube: Sloane Sq.*

Royal National Theatre (Cottesloe, Lyttelton, and Olivier), ⊠ *South Bank Arts Complex, SE1 9PX,* ☎ *020/7452–3000. Tube: Waterloo.*

St. Martin's, ⊠ *West St., WC2H 9NH,* ☎ *020/7836–1443. Tube: Leicester Sq.*

Savoy, ⊠ *Strand, WC2R 0ET,* ☎ *020/7836–8888. Tube: Charing Cross.*

Shaftesbury, ⊠ *Shaftesbury Ave., WC2H 8DP,* ☎ *020/7379–5399. Tube: Holborn.*

Strand, ⊠ *Aldwych, WC2B 5LD,* ☎ *020/7930–8800. Tube: Covent Garden.*

Vaudeville, ⊠ *Strand, WC2R 0NH,* ☎ *020/7836–9987. Tube: Charing Cross.*

Victoria Palace, ⊠ *Victoria St., SW1E 5EA,* ☎ *020/7834–1317. Tube: Victoria.*

Whitehall, ⊠ *14 Whitehall, SW1A 2DY,* ☎ *020/7369–1735 or 020/ 7344–4444. Tube: Charing Cross.*

Wyndhams, ⊠ *Charing Cross Rd., WC2H 0DA,* ☎ *020/7369–1736. Tube: Leicester Sq.*

Fringe

Shows can be straight plays, circus, comedy, musicals, readings, or productions every bit as polished and impressive as those in the West End—except for their location and the price of the seat. Fringe tickets are always considerably less expensive than tickets for West End productions. The following theaters are among the better-known fringe venues:

Almeida, ⊠ *Almeida St., N1 1AT,* ☎ *020/7359–4404. Tube: Angel.*

BAC, ⊠ *176 Lavender Hill, Battersea SW11 1JX,* ☎ *020/7223–2223. British Rail: Clapham Junction.*

Bush, ⊠ *Shepherds Bush Green, W12 8QD,* ☎ *020/8743–3388. Tube: Goldhawk Rd.*

Canal Café Theatre, ⊠ *Bridge House, Delamere Terr., W2,* ☎ *020/7289–6054. Tube: Warwick Ave.*

Drill Hall, ⊠ *16 Chenies St., WC1E 7EX,* ☎ *020/7637–8270. Tube: Goodge St.*

The Gate, ⊠ *The Prince Albert, 11 Pembridge Rd., W11 3HQ,* ☎ *020/7229–0706. Tube: Notting Hill Gate.*

Grace Theatre at the Latchmere, ⊠ *503 Battersea Park Rd., SW11 3BW,* ☎ *020/7223–3549. British Rail: Clapham Junction.*

Hackney Empire, ⊠ *291 Mare St., E8 1EJ,* ☎ *020/8985–2424. British Rail: Hackney Central.*

Hampstead, ⊠ *Swiss Cottage, NW3 3EX,* ☎ *020/7722–9301. Tube: Swiss Cottage.*

ICA Theatre, ⊠ *The Mall, SW1Y 5AH,* ☎ *020/7930–3647. Tube: Charing Cross.*

King's Head, ⊠ *115 Upper St., N1 1QN,* ☎ *020/7226–1916. Tube: Highbury & Islington.*

Lyric Studio, ⊠ *Lyric Theatre, King St., W6 0QL,* ☎ *020/8741–8701. Tube: Hammersmith.*

New End Theatre, ⊠ *27 New End, NW3 1JD,* ☎ *020/7794–0022. Tube: Hampstead.*

Orange Tree, ⊠ *1 Clarence St., Richmond, TW9 1SA,* ☎ *020/8940–3633. Tube: Richmond.*

Riverside Studios, ⊠ *Crisp Rd., W6 9RL,* ☎ *020/8237–1111. Tube: Hammersmith.*

Theatre Royal, ⊠ *Stratford East, E15 1BN,* ☎ *020/8534–0310. Tube: Stratford.*

Tricycle Theatre, ⊠ *269 Kilburn High Rd., NW6 7JR,* ☎ *020/7328–1000. Tube: Kilburn.*

Watermans Arts Centre, ⊠ *40 High St., Brentford, TW8 0DS,* ☎ *020/8568–1176. British Rail: Kew Bridge.*

Young Vic, ⊠ *66 The Cut, SE1 8LZ,* ☎ *020/7928–6363. Tube: Waterloo.*

5 OUTDOOR ACTIVITIES AND SPORTS

Some days you win, some you lose, and some you get rained out. But that never puts a damper on one of the liveliest sports calendars around. Tennis, of course, means Wimbledon (if center court is sold out, try for an outer-court match). In summer, Her Majesty makes an appearance at Ascot, while the world series of cricket, the Tests, are played at the fields of Lord's. In cooler weather, football (also known as soccer) takes over, and in any season you can enjoy Pilates and yoga indoors and let it rain, rain, rain.

THERE ARE THE WIMBLEDON TENNIS CHAMPIONSHIPS, and there's cricket, and then there's soccer, and that's about it for the sports fan in London, right? Wrong. London is a great city for the weekend player of almost anything. It really comes into its own in summer, when the parks sprout nets and goals and painted white lines, outdoor swimming pools open, and a season of spectator events gets under way. The listings below concentrate on facilities available to the casual visitor in a whole range of sports and on the more accessible or well-known spectator events. Bring your gear, and branch out from that hotel gym.

Updated by
Victoria Young

PARTICIPANT SPORTS AND FITNESS

If your sport is missing from those listed below, or if you need additional information, **Sportsline** (☎ 020/7222–8000), staffed weekdays 10–6, supplies details about London's clubs, events, and facilities. It's a free service.

Aerobics
You don't need to buy a membership at any of the following studios, which offer a range of classes for all levels of fitness and are open daily. The average cost for an hour of sweating is £7.

Jubilee Hall. Many are addicted to the "Fatbuster" classes, but there are plenty more, from body sculpting and step to kick boxing and jazz dance. ✉ 30 The Piazza, Covent Garden, WC2, ☎ 020/7379–0008. Tube: Covent Garden.

Porchester Center. About seven daily classes are graded from beginner to pro, with step, yoga, circuit training, and aquaerobics included in the mix. ✉ Porchester Centre, Queensway, W2, ☎ 020/7792–2919. Tube: Bayswater.

Portobello Green Fitness Club. It's under the Westway overpass, and you'll have to battle through flea-market shoppers on weekends to reach these popular classes. ✉ 3–5 Thorpe Close, W10, ☎ 020/8960–2221. Tube: Ladbroke Grove.

Bicycling
London is reasonably cycle-friendly for a big city, with special lanes marked for bicycles on some major roads, but it is never safe to ride without a helmet.

Bikepark. You can rent anything you want—mountain, hybrid, or road bike—from £10 per day, £30 per weekend, or by the week, plus a deposit of 75%–100% of the bike's value. All machines are new models and are issued with locks; accessories are available, too. Reserve ahead in summer. ✉ 11–13 Macklin St., WC2, ☎ 020/7430–0083. Tube: Holburn.

Gyms
Albany Fitness Centre. This is a deconsecrated church (buy a WORK OFF THY LAST SUPPER T-shirt), which means tons of space. There's Keiser equipment, free weights, cardio machines, and aerobics-sculpting classes. The cost is around £10 per day, with lower weekly rates negotiable. ✉ St. Bede's Church, Albany St., NW1, ☎ 020/7383–7131. Tube: Great Portland St.

Central YMCA. As you'd expect from the Y, this place boasts every facility and sport, including a great 25-meter pool and a well-equipped gym. Weekly membership is £36, a "one-day taster" £15. ✉ 112 Great Russell St., WC1, ☎ 020/7637–8131. Tube: Tottenham Court Rd.

Jubilee Hall. The day rate is £6.70, monthly £51, at this very crowded but happening and super-well-equipped central gym. ✉ 30 The Piazza, Covent Garden, WC2, ☎ 020/7379–0008. Tube: Covent Garden.

The Peak. This hotel club is expensive (£1875 per year plus £1,200 joining fee) but has top equipment, a pool, great ninth-floor views over Knightsbridge, and a sauna—with TV—in the full beauty spa. Day memberships are no longer available, but the 20-visit pass for £830 is fully transferrable, so a family can share one—as long as they use up the visits within the six-month expiration date. ⊠ *Hyatt Carlton Tower Hotel, 2 Cadogan Pl., SW1,* ☎ *020/7235–1234. Tube: Sloane Sq.*

Horseback Riding

Hyde Park Riding Stables. One of the very few public stables left for riding in Hyde Park keeps a range of horses for hacking the sand tracks. Rates are £30 for adults and £25 for children per hour. ⊠ *63 Bathurst Mews, W2,* ☎ *020/7723–2813. Tube: Lancaster Gate.*

Running

London is perfect for joggers. If you're after a crowd, more popular routes include **Green Park,** which gets a stream of runners armed with maps from Piccadilly hotels, and—to a lesser extent—adjacent **St. James's Park.** Both can get perilous with deck chairs on summer days. You can run a 4-mi perimeter route around **Hyde Park** and **Kensington Gardens** or a 2½-mi route in **Hyde Park** alone if you start at Hyde Park Corner or Marble Arch and encircle the Serpentine. Most Park Lane hotels offer jogging maps for this, their local green space. **Regent's Park** has probably the most populated track because it's a sporting kind of place; the Outer Circle loop measures about 2½ mi.

Away from the center, there are longer, scenic runs over more varied terrain at **Hampstead Heath, Kenwood,** and **Parliament Hill,** London's highest point, where you'll get a fabulous panoramic sweep over the entire city. **Richmond Park** is the biggest green space of all, but watch for deer during rutting season (October and November). Back in town, there's a rather traffic-heavy 1½-mi riverside run along **Victoria Embankment** from Westminster Bridge to the Embankment at Blackfriars Bridge, or a beautiful mile among the rowing clubs and ducks along the Malls—Upper, Lower, and Chiswick—from **Hammersmith Bridge.**

GROUP RUNS

If you don't want to run alone, call the **London Hash House Harriers** (☎ 020/8995–7879) or the **City Hash House Hotline** (☎ 020/8749–2646). They both organize noncompetitive hour-long runs around interesting bits of town, with loops and checkpoints built in. Cost is £1.

Softball

Control your mirth—the sport is huge here; in fact, it's the fastest-growing participatory sport in England. Pick up a game Sunday afternoon in **Regent's Park** or on the south edge of **Hyde Park.**

Squash

Finsbury Leisure Center. There are four squash courts in this popular sports center in the City and frequented by execs who work nearby. You can book by phone without a membership, and you're more likely to get a court if you show up to play during Londoners' regular office hours, or possibly on weekends, when courts are less busy. A court costs £7.40 for non-members and £5.90 for members, and annual membership is between £29 and £39. ⊠ *Norman St., EC1,* ☎ *020/7253–2346. Tube: Old St.* **Portobello Green Fitness Centre.** There are only three courts here, but they're inexpensive (£3 per game). An annual membership is £75. ⊠ *3–5 Thorpe Close, W10,* ☎ *020/8960–2221. Tube: Ladbroke Grove.*

Swimming

BEACHES

Hampstead Ponds. These Elysian little lakes are surrounded by grassy lounging areas. The women's one is particularly secluded—and crowded in summer, though it's open all year. Opening times vary with sunrise and sunset. The Mixed Pond is open May–September. Both have murky-looking but clean, fresh water. *Coed,* ⊠ *E. Heath Rd., NW3,* ☎ *020/7485–4491. Women only,* ⊠ *Millfield La., N6,* ☎ *020/7485–4491. British Rail: Hampstead Heath.*

Serpentine Lido. Okay, so it's a beach on a lake, but a hot day in Hyde Park is surreally reminiscent of the seaside. There are changing facilities, and the swimming section is chlorinated. ⊠ *Hyde Park, W2,* ☎ *020/7706–3422.* ☉ *July–Sept. Tube: Knightsbridge.*

INDOOR POOLS

ChelseaSports Center. This renovated, turn-of-the-century 32- by 12-meter pool is just off King's Road, so it's usually busy, and it's packed with kids on weekends. ⊠ *Chelsea Manor St., SW3,* ☎ *020/7352–6985. Tube: South Kensington.*

INDOOR/OUTDOOR POOLS

Oasis. And it is just that, with a heated pool (open year-round) right in Covent Garden, and a 32- by 12-meter one indoors. Needless to say, they both get packed in summer. ⊠ *32 Endell St., WC2,* ☎ *020/7831–1804. Tube: Covent Garden.*

SPA POOLS

Porchester Baths. Here there's a 36- by 14-meter pool for serious lap swimmers, plus a 1920s Turkish bath, sauna, and spa of gorgeous though slightly faded grandeur. It has separate sessions for men and women. ⊠ *Queensway, W2,* ☎ *020/7792–2919. Tube: Queensway.*

Tennis

Holland Park. This is the prettiest place to play, with six hard courts available all year. The cost is £9.60 for annual membership and £4.60 for each game. ⊠ *Kensington High St., W8,* ☎ *020/7602–2226. Tube: Holland Park.*

Islington Tennis Centre. It's about the only place where you don't need membership to play indoors year-round, but you need it to reserve by phone. There are two outdoor courts, too, and coaching is available. ⊠ *Market Rd., N7,* ☎ *020/7700–2100. Tube: Caledonian Rd.*

Paddington Sports Club. A surprisingly large and busy green space provides a set of 10 courts as well as squash courts and a multi-gym at this members-only club. Annual membership is £370 with a £100 joining fee, but there are no per-game charges. ⊠ *Castellain Rd., W9,* ☎ *020/7286–4515. Tube: Maida Vale.*

Yoga

Life Centre. London's best yoga school specializes in the dynamic, energetic Ashtanga Vinyasa technique. Beautiful premises enhance the experience. A huge range of holistic health therapies is available upstairs. ⊠ *15 Edge St., W8,* ☎ *020/7221–4602. Tube: Notting Hill Gate.*

SPECTATOR SPORTS

Boating

One of London's most beloved sporting events (since 1845) is also the easiest to see, and it's free. The only problem with the late-March **Beefeater Gin Oxford and Cambridge Boat Race** is securing a position among the crowds that line the Putney-to-Mortlake route (mostly at pubs along the Hammersmith Lower and Upper Malls, or on Putney Bridge). The Saturday start time varies from year to year according to the tides but is usually around 2:30 PM. The **Head of the River Race** is the professional version, only this time up to 420 crews of eight row the university course in the other direction. It usually happens the Saturday before the university race, beginning at 10 AM; the best view is from above Chiswick Bridge.

Cricket

Lord's (✉ St. John's Wood Rd., NW8, ☎ 020/7432–1066) has been hallowed turf for worshipers of England's summer game since 1811. The world series of cricket, the Tests, are played here, but tickets are hard to procure. The first stage of the process is to obtain an application form and enter the ballot (i.e., lottery) to purchase tickets. If any tickets remain (an unlikely event), they are sold over the phone in April. Standard Test Match tickets cost between £18 and £38. One-day internationals can usually be seen by lining up on the day, and top-class county matches are similarly accessible—whether the rules are is quite another matter.

The **Oval** (✉ Kennington Oval, SE11, ☎ 020/7582–6660) is a far easier place to witness the *thwack* of leather on willow. At London's second-string ground, you can see county games of very high standard.

Equestrian Events

RACING

The main events of "the Season," as much social as sporting, occur just outside the city. Her actual Majesty attends **Royal Ascot** (✉ Grand Stand, Ascot, Berkshire, ☎ 01344/622211) in mid-June, driving from Windsor in an open carriage and processing before the plebs daily at 2. You'll need to book good seats far in advance for this event, although some tickets—far away from the Royal Enclosure and winning post— can be bought on the day of the race for £8. Grandstand tickets, which must be bought well in advance, cost £37–£45, if they are available. There are also Ascot Heath tickets available for a mere £2, but these only admit you to a picnic area in the middle of the race course. You'll be able to see the horses, of course, but that's not why people come to Ascot. The real spectacle is the crowd itself: enormous headgear is de rigueur on Ladies Day—usually the Thursday of the meet—and those who arrive dressed inappropriately (jeans, shorts, tank tops) will be turned away from their grandstand seats. **Derby Day** (✉ The Grandstand, Epsom Downs, Surrey, ☎ 01372/470047), usually held on the first Saturday in June, is the other big social event of the racing calendar and one of the world's greatest races for three-year-olds.

SHOW JUMPING

The late September **Horse of the Year Show** (✉ Wembley Arena Wembley, Middlesex, ☎ 020/8900–9282) is the top international competition, with fun events held alongside the serious. Best of all are the Pony Club Games, where children perform virtual gymnastics on horseback.

Marathon

Starting at 9:30 AM on a Sunday in April, some 30,000 runners in the huge **Flora London Marathon** (☎ 020/7620–4117) race from Blackheath or Greenwich to Westminster Bridge or the Mall. Entry forms for the following year are available between August and October.

Rugby

This is not greatly different from gridiron, but team members play unpadded. It raises the British and (especially) Welsh blood pressure like no other sport. It has recently undergone a revolution, with the amateur Rugby Union and the professional Rugby League, once distinct, now playing at the same intense levels, thanks to the advent of professional sponsorship of the amateur game. The **Rugby League Challenge Cup Final** is played at **Wembley Stadium** (✉ Wembley, Middlesex, ☎ 020/8902–0902) on the last Saturday in April or the first one in

May, while the Rugby Union **Pilkington Cup** is traditionally fought a week later at the **Twickenham Rugby Football Ground** (✉ Whitton Rd., Twickenham, Middlesex, ☎ 020/8892–2000). Tickets for both are more precious than gold. But you can see international matches at Twickenham during the March–September season or catch the local Super League team, the **London Broncos,** (✉ The Stoop Memorial Ground, Langhorn Dr., Twickenham TW2, ☎ 020/8410–5000).

Soccer

To refer to the national winter sport as "soccer" is to blaspheme. It is football, and the British season culminates in the televised Wembley Stadium **FA Cup Final,** for which tickets are about as easy to get as they are for the Super Bowl. International matches at **Wembley** (☎ 020/ 8902–0902) during the August–May season are easier to attend.

For a real taste of this British obsession, though, nothing beats a match at the home ground of one of the six London clubs competing in the Premier League. More than likely you won't see a hint of the infamous hooliganism, but you will be quite carried away by the electric atmosphere only a vast football crowd can generate. **Tottenham Hotspur,** or "Spurs" (✉ White Hart La., 748 High Rd., N17, ☎ 0870/840–2468), and **Arsenal** (✉ Avenell Rd., Highbury, N5, ☎ 020/7413–3366) have north Londoners' loyalties about equally divided, while **Chelsea** (✉ Stamford Bridge, Fulham Rd., SW6, ☎ 020/7386–7799) is adored by the slightly more genteel west London fan. In the east, there is **Charlton Athletic** (✉ The Valley, Floyd Rd., SE7, ☎ 020/8333–4010), or **West Ham United** (✉ Boleyn Ground, Green St., E13, ☎ 020/8548–2700). The south boasts unglamorous **Wimbledon** (✉ Selhurst Park, Park Rd., SE25, ☎ 020/7413–3388).

Tennis

The **Wimbledon Lawn Tennis Championships**—Wimbledon is famous among fans for the green, green grass of Centre Court, for Pimms and strawberries and cream; and for rain, which always falls, despite the last-week-of-June/first-week-of-July high-summer timing. This event is, of course, one of the four Grand Slam events of the tennis year. Whether you can get tickets is literally down to the luck of the draw, because there's a ballot system (lottery) for advance purchase. To apply, send a self-addressed, stamped envelope between October and December to the All England Lawn Tennis & Croquet Club (✉ Box 98, Church Rd., Wimbledon SW19 5AE, ☎ 020/8946–2244), then fill in the application form, and hope for the best.

There are other ways to see the tennis. A block of Centre Court tickets is kept back to sell each day; fanatics line up all night for these, especially in the first week. Each afternoon tickets collected from early-departing spectators are resold (profits go to charity). These may be grandstand seats (with plenty to see—play continues till dusk), because those who can afford to care so little about tennis are often on expensive business freebies or company season tickets. You can also buy entry to the grounds to roam matches on the show courts, where even the top seeded players compete early in the fortnight. For up-to-date information, the London Tourist Board operates a **Wimbledon Information Line** (☎ 0839/123417), at a cost of 49p per minute.

6   SHOPPING

Napoléon must have known what he was talking about when he called Britain a nation of shopkeepers. The finest emporiums are in London, still. You can shop like royalty at Her Majesty's glove maker, run down a leather-bound copy of *Wuthering Heights* at a Charing Cross bookseller, find antique Toby jugs on Portobello Road, or drop in on clothier Paul Smith—a fave of Sir Paul McCartney. Whether you're out for fun or for fashion, London can be the most rewarding of hunting grounds.

Updated by
Jacqueline
Brown

WHEN IT COMES TO LONDON, shopping can be a transforming experience. It's an open secret that Cary Grant was virtually "created" by a bespoke suit from Kilgour, French, Stanbury (the tailors extended the shoulders of his jackets 6½ inches to improve his form and draped the material to slim his hips). Then there was that other fashion plate, the Duchess of Windsor—for at-home style, she couldn't be beat, thanks in part to the soigné accessories she bought at Colefax & Fowler, still purveying the "country-house look" from its shop on Brook Street. Today, London's stores continue to create icons and make styles—as you can see from a visit to Harvey Nichols, shrine of the *Absolutely Fabulous* crowd.

As befits one of the great trading capitals of the world, London's shops have been known to boast, "You name it, we sell it." If you have a yen to keep up with the Windsors, look for the BY APPOINTMENT logo, which means that this particular emporium supplies Her Majesty the Queen, the Queen Mother, Prince Philip, or the Prince of Wales—check the small print and the insignia to find out which. More fashionable types will prefer to check out the ever-expanding Browns of South Molton Street—a label hunter's heaven—while the surrounding small stores there and along quaint St. Christopher's Place aren't bad either. The most ardent fashion victims will shoot to Notting Hill, London's prime fashion location and scene of *that* movie. London's emporiums have gifts in every price range. Head to Bond Street or Knightsbridge if you're looking for the sort of thing you would find in every Rockefeller's Christmas stocking; if you're bargain-hunting, try one of the street-scene antiques fairs (it wasn't so long ago that an original Wordsworth manuscript of "When Severn's sweeping flood" was discovered in Brick Lane Market for less than $50).

If you have only limited time, zoom in on one or two of the West End's grand department stores, where you'll find enough booty for your entire gift list. Marks & Spencer is one of Britain's largest, and most beloved, chain stores, legendary primarily for its women's lingerie, its men's knitwear, and its range of food, good enough to pass off as home-cooked. Selfridges, London's answer to Macy's in New York, is a splendid pile of '20s architecture that dominates the whole of one block toward Marble Arch and is increasingly fashion-conscious and up to date. Liberty is famous for its prints—multitudes of floral designs, which you can buy as fabric, or have made into everything from book covers to dresses. It may be hokey, but Harrods is not to be missed; apart from anything else, it's one of the best free shows in the city. And though Harrods trumpets that it can supply anything to anyone anywhere in the world (once, a baby elephant to Ronald Reagan) and boasts that the queen sometimes does her Christmas shopping here, you can just pick up one of its distinctive green-and-gold-logo totes—a perfect touch of class for your marketing back home.

Credit cards are accepted virtually everywhere, but to make sure that your Cirrus or Plus card (to cite just two of the leading names) works in European ATMs, have your bank reset it to use a four-digit PIN number before your departure. Apart from bankrupting yourself, the only problem you'll encounter is exhaustion, since London is a town of many far-flung shopping areas. The farthest—in fact on the outskirts of London, at Greenhithe in the county of Kent just by the Thames—is Europe's largest gift to shopaholics, the 240-acre **Bluewater.** The mega glass-and-steel (with cute Kentish oasthouse roofs) pleasure palace by the water was designed by American architect Eric Kuhne and contains every up-market, high-street, brand-name store, department store, and chain store (more than 320) a shopper could desire. Shop-till-you-drop-pers can carry on with constant revival by numerous cappuccino stops and restaurants (which stay open until 11, long after the stores have closed), cinemas, children's play areas, a winter garden (with indoor glasshouse rain forest), and Thames-side boardwalk. Even though there is space for 13,000 cars, clever shoppers jump the jams and lines going in by taking the train, which departs frequently from Charing Cross. Shuttle buses go directly to the center from the local rail station.

A SUPER SHOPPING TOUR

For those who can make their way across the map faster than Napoléon and only have a few hours to spare, here's a suggested plan of action. Just keep in mind that you will return to your hotel room weary and wiped out, and your bathroom scale will show you've become 3 pounds lighter! Let's start with a great London trademark: **Harrods.** Be there when the doors open—this is one-stop shopping at its best (and one of the city's great sights). If you're chic to the cuticles, then make a bee-line for **Harvey Nichols,** just a block away. Harvey Nicks always has the best in modern Brit style, be it couture, menswear, or home furnishings. Want a more traditional gift that would please any Lord and Lady Fitzup-pity? Head to the nearby **General Trading Co.** on Sloane Street for that lovely Staffordshire spaniel, or run down to Pimlico to see the objets d'art and furniture of **David Linley,** the most talented royal around. For still more decorative goodies, tube or cab it over to Regent Street—one of London's main consumer heavens—and **Liberty** (which actually helped create the Arts and Crafts style of the Edwardian era). High rollers should walk east several blocks to Bond Street, Old and New. Of course, there's nothing like a visit to **Asprey & Garrard** or the other upper-crust stores here to make you acutely aware of how poor you are. *Fashion-istas* should then stroll up through Mayfair several blocks to the north-west and South Molton Street to find **Browns,** flooded with Kate Moss lookalikes, then head down Davies Street to the couture salon of **Vivi-enne Westwood.** On Davies Street you'll also find **Grays Antique Mar-ket** and **Grays in the Mews**—just the places to find a Charles II silver spoon. For gifts with gentler price tags, tube or cab it south to Piccadilly and **Hatchards**—bookseller to the royals, which still retains a trad atmosphere—or nearby **Fortnum & Mason,** the queen's grocers, to buy some tea. Speaking of which, head upstairs and collapse for the high tea here, or make a last stop at **Floris,** a few blocks south on Jermyn Street—it's one of London's prettiest parfumiers. Opt for a scent once favored by Queen Victoria or—at almost pocket-money prices—a nat-ural-bristle toothbrush. Oh, yes: if you want to add the very latest stores to this list, check out the suggestions in the monthly glossies, such as *Tatler* magazine's "I Can't Get Through the Month Without . . ." shopping pages or *World of Interiors'* "Antennae" section, or the glossy shopping sections in the Sunday newspapers. Whew! As you can see, for out-of-the-ordinary shopping, London can't be beat.

For a chart of U.S. and British clothing-size conversions, *see* the inside back cover.

Shopping Districts

Camden Town

Crafts and vintage-clothing markets and shops clustered in and around picturesque but over-renovated canal-side buildings have filled up every available space all the way up to the Roundhouse, Chalk Farm, in this frenetic mecca for the world's youth. It's a good place for boots, T-shirts, inexpensive leather jackets, ethnic crafts, antiques, and recy-cled trendy wear. Things are quieter midweek.

Chelsea

Chelsea centers on King's Road, which is no longer synonymous with ultra fashion but still harbors some designer boutiques, plus antiques and home-furnishings emporiums. The fashionable section is more off-road Chelsea, toward Belgravia, where the hot young stars of fashion are creating a haven: Lulu Guinness, Erickson Beamon, and Philip Treacy line up on Elizabeth Street.

Covent Garden

The restored 19th-century market building—in a something-for-everyone neighborhood named for the market itself—features mainly high-class clothing chains, plus good-quality crafts stalls. Neal Street and the surrounding alleys offer amazing gifts of every type—bikes, kites, tea, herbs, beads, hats . . . you name it. Floral Street and Long Acre have designer and chain-store fashion in equal measure, while Monmouth Street, Shorts Gardens, and the Thomas Neal's mall on Earlham Street offer trendy clothes for club kids. The whole area is good for people-watching, too.

Hampstead

For picturesque peace and quiet with your shopping, stroll around here midweek. Upscale clothing stores and representatives of the better chains share the half-dozen streets with cozy boutique-size shops catering to the home and stomach.

Kensington

Kensington Church Street features expensive antiques, plus a little fashion. The main drag, Kensington High Street, is a smaller, less crowded, and classier version of Oxford Street, with a selection of clothing chains and larger stores at the eastern end.

Knightsbridge

Harrods dominates Brompton Road, but there's plenty more, especially for the well-heeled and fashion-conscious. Harvey Nichols is the top clothes stop, with many expensive designers' boîtes along Sloane Street. Walton Street and narrow Beauchamp (pronounced "Beecham") Place offer more of the same, plus home furnishings and knickknacks; and Brompton Cross, at the start of Fulham Road, is the most design-conscious corner of London, with the Conran Shop and Joseph Ettudgui's store leading the field.

Marylebone

Behind the seething masses of Oxford Street lies this quiet backwater with Marylebone High Street as its main artery. Restaurants coexisted peacefully along with delis and practical stores, and it might have remained that way until the new Conran Shop and Orrery restaurant sprang up in 1997, bringing with them a retinue of smart new designer furniture stores. Satellite streets now have understated designer women's wear and menswear. Stride along a block or two to Great Portland Street and you'll arrive at the smart Villandry food emporium and the gateway to fashionable Fitzrovia.

Mayfair

Here is Bond Street, Old and New, with desirable dress designers, jewelers, plus fine art (old and new) on Old Bond Street and Cork Street. South Molton Street has high-priced, high-style fashion—especially at Browns—and the tailors of Savile Row are of worldwide renown.

Notting Hill

Branching off from the famous Portobello Road market are various enclaves of boutiques selling young designers' wares, antiques, and things for the home—now favored stops for trendsetters. Go westward and

Shopping (Map A): Mayfair, Soho, and Covent Garden

KEY

⊖ Tube Station

Accessorize **79**

Alfie's Antique
Market **2**

Aquascutum **41**

Armoury of
St. James's **45**

Asprey &
Garrard **24**

Bell, Book and
Radmall **84**

Black Market **57**

Blazer **75**

Borders **60**

British Museum
Gift Shop **54**

Browns **12**

Burberry **32**

Butler & Wilson . . . **13**

Cartier **22**

Cinema
Bookshop **53**

Colefax &
Fowler **15**

Contemporary
Applied Arts **50**

Contemporary
Ceramics **34**

Dance Books **85**

Divertimenti **4**

Droopie &
Browns **88**

Duffer of
St. George **68**

Favourbrook **43**

Fenwick **20**

Floris **47**

Forbidden Planet . . **56**

Fortnum & Mason . . **44**

Foyles **59**

Gabriel's Wharf . . . **90**

Grays Antique
Market **14**

Grosvenor Prints . . **74**

Hamleys **33**

Hatchards **42**

Herbert Johnson . . **37**

HMV **28**

Holland &
Holland **18**

Humla **3**

Janet Fitch **63**

Jigsaw **21**

Karen Millen **27**

Kilgour, French
& Stanbury **36**

Koh Samui **76**

John Lewis **6**

John Lobb **48**

Laura Ashley **30**

Liberty **31**

London Silver
Vaults **70**

Lush **81**

Malcolm Levene . . . **1**

Marchpane **87**

Marks &
Spencer **7, 29**

MDC Classic **89**

Mulberry **9**

Murder One **65**

Muji **51**

Neal St. East **73**

Neal's Yard
Remedies **72**

New Academy/
Curwen **49**

Nicole Farhi **16**

Ordning & Reda . . **100**

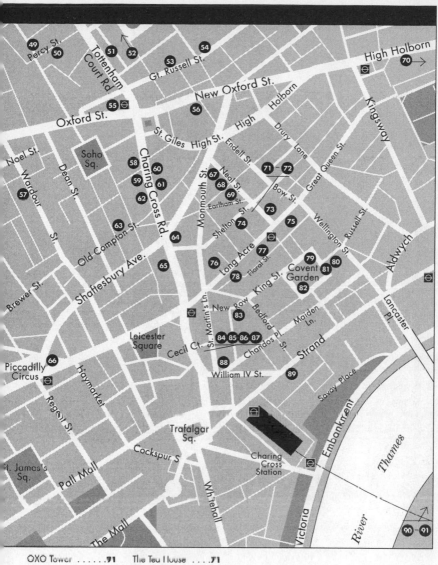

OXO Tower **91**
Ozwald Boateng . . **39**
Paddy Campbell . . . **10**
Paul Smith **77**
Penhaligon's **80**
Phillips **11**
Pleasures of
Past Times **86**
Purves & Purves . . . **52**
Selfridges **8**
Shellys **26**
Silver Moon **61**
Sotheby's **23**
Space NK **69**
Sportspages **62**
Stanfords **78**
Swaine Adeney . . . **38**
Swear **67**
Talking Bookshop . . . **5**

The Tea House **71**
Thomas Goode **19**
Tom Gilbey **35**
Top Shop/
Top Man **25**
Tower Records **66**
Turnbull & Asser . . . **46**
Vivienne
Westwood **17**
Virgin Megastore . . **55**
Waterstone's **58**
Whistles **82**
Zara **40**
Zwemmer **64**

Shopping (Map B): Kensington, Knightsbridge, and Chelsea

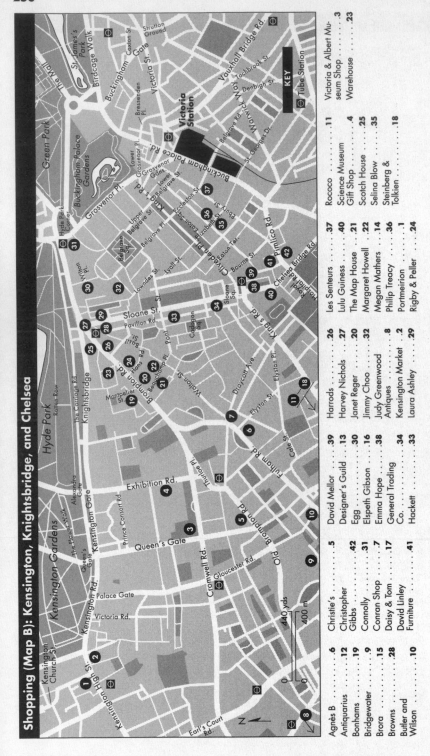

Agnès B 6
Antiquarius 12
Bonhams 19
Bridgewater 9
Brora 15
Browns 28
Butler and
Wilson 10

Christie's 5
Christopher
Gibbs 42
Connolly 31
Conran Shop 7
Daisy & Tom 17
David Linley
Furniture 41

David Mellor 39
Designer's Guild . . .13
Egg 30
Elspeth Gibson 16
Emma Hope 38
General Trading
Co. 34
Hackett 33

Harrods 26
Harvey Nichols 27
Janet Reger 20
Jimmy Choo 32
Judy Greenwood
Antiques 8
Kensington Market . .2
Laura Ashley 29

Les Senteurs 37
Lulu Guiness 40
The Map House 21
Margaret Howell . . .22
Megan Mathers 14
Philip Treacy 36
Portmeirion 1
Rigby & Peller 24

Rococo 11
Science Museum
Gift Shop 4
Scotch House 25
Selina Blow 35
Steinberg &
Tolkien 18

Victoria & Albert Mu-
seum Shop 3
Warehouse 23

KEY

⊖ Tube Station

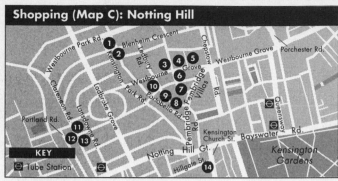

Books for Cooks . 1
Cath Kidston 13
Coach House . 3
The Cross. . . 11
Dinny Hall . . . 4
The Facade . . 5
Georgina von
Etzdorf 7
Ghost 8
Hope & Glory. 14
Nick Ashley . . 9
Shirtsmith. . . . 6
Space 10
Summerhill &
Bishop. 12
Travel
Bookshop. . . . 2

explore the Ledbury Road–Westbourne Grove axis, Clarendon Cross, and Kensington Park Road, for an eclectic mix of antiques and up-to-the-minute must-haves for body and lifestyle. To the more bohemian foot of Portobello are Ladbroke Grove and Golborne Road, where, in among the tatty stores, Portuguese cafés, and patisseries, you can bag a bargain. This is London's latest treasure trove area.

Oxford Street

Overcrowded Oxford Street is past its prime and is lined with tawdry discount shops at the Tottenham Court Road end, but many still flock here for some of London's great department stores in the run up to Marble Arch—particularly Selfridges, John Lewis, and Marks & Spencer—and the interesting boutiques secreted in little St. Christopher's Place and Gees Court.

Piccadilly

Though the actual number of shops is small for a street of its length (Green Park takes up a lot of space), Piccadilly manages to fit in several quintessential British emporiums. Fortnum & Mason is its star, and the historic Burlington Arcade is an elegant experience even for shop-phobics.

Regent Street

At right angles to Oxford Street, this wider, curvier version has several department stores, including legendary Liberty. Hamleys is the capital's toy center; other shops tend to be stylish men's chain stores or airline offices, though there are also shops selling china and bolts of English tweed. "West Soho," around Carnaby Street, stocks designer youth paraphernalia, which these days is becoming more grown up and desirable.

St. James's

Where the English gentleman shops, this district has some of the most elegant emporiums for hats, handmade shirts and shoes, and silver shaving kits and flasks. Doorways often bear Royal Warrants, and shops along Jermyn Street, like Floris, have museum-quality interiors and facades. Nothing is cheap, in any sense.

Department Stores

London's department stores range from Harrods—which every tourist is obliged to visit—through many serviceable middle-range stores, devoted to the middle-of-the-road tastes of the middle class, to a few cheapjack ones that sell merchandise you would find at a better rate back home. Most of the best and biggest department stores are grouped in the West End around Regent Street and Oxford Street, with two notable exceptions out in Knightsbridge.

🐣 **Harrods,** the only English department store classed among monuments and museums on every visitor's list, hardly needs an introduction. It is swanky and plush and as deep-carpeted as ever, its spectacular food halls are alone worth the trip, and it stands out from the pack for fashion, too. You can forgive the store its immodest motto, *Omnia, omnibus, ubique* ("Everything, for everyone, everywhere"), because there are more than 230 departments, including a pet shop rumored to supply you with anything from aardvarks to zebras on request, and the toy department—sorry, *kingdom*—which does the same for its plush versions. During the pre-Christmas period and the sale—the legendary one is during the last three weeks of January, but another storewide event, usually only one week, is held in mid-July—the entire store is a menagerie. ⊠ *87 Brompton Rd., SW1,* ☎ *020/7730–1234.* (☞ Map B)

Harvey Nichols is just a block away from Harrods, but it's not competing on the same turf, because its passion is fashion, all the way. There are nearly six floors of it, including departments for dressing homes and men, but the woman who invests in her wardrobe is the main target. Accessories are strong suits, especially jewelry, scarves, and makeup— England's first MAC counter here was 10 deep for months. The fourth floor now has a chic home design department, featuring such names as Nina Campbell, Mulberry, Ralph Lauren, and Designer's Guild. A reservation at the Fifth Floor restaurant is still coveted, too. ⊠ *109 Knightsbridge, SW1,* ☎ *020/7235–5000.* (☞ Map B)

John Lewis is a short distance from Liberty, two blocks west on Oxford Street. This store's motto is "Never knowingly undersold," and for an increasingly wide range of goods at sensible prices, John Lewis is hard to beat. The brother store, Peter Jones, in Sloane Square, has a place in Sloane Ranger history, and you will probably encounter more Barbour jackets, velvet hair bands, and pearls here than anywhere else in town—and that's just on the customers. For the visitor to London who's handy with the needle, John Lewis has a wonderful selection of dress and furnishing fabrics. Many's the American home with John Lewis drapes. ⊠ *278 Oxford St., W1,* ☎ *020/7629–7711.* (☞ Map A)

Liberty has one of London's most distinctive facades—a wonderful black-and-white mock-Tudor facade, making it a peacock among pigeons in humdrum Regent Street. Inside, it is a labyrinthine building, full of nooks and crannies stuffed with goodies, like a dream of an Eastern bazaar. Famous principally for its fabrics, it also has an Oriental department, rich with color; menswear that tends toward the traditional; and women's wear that has lately been spiced up with extra designer ranges. It is a hard store to resist, where you may well find an original gift—especially one made from those classic Liberty prints. ⊠ *200 Regent St., W1,* ☎ *020/7734–1234.* (☞ Map A)

Selfridges is near the Marble Arch end of Oxford Street, where blocks are crowded in the middle of the day and at sale time. This giant, bustling store was started early in the 20th century by an American, though it's now British-owned. If this all-rounder has one outstanding department, it has to be its Food Hall, or else its frenetic cosmetics department— one of the largest in Europe—which seems to perfume the air the whole length of Oxford Street. In recent years, Selfridges has made a specialty of high-profile popular designer fashions and has spent a lot of money sprucing up. There's also a theater ticket counter and British Airways travel shop in the basement. ⊠ *400 Oxford St., W1,* ☎ *020/ 7629–1234.* (☞ Map A)

Specialty Stores

Antiques

Investment quality or lovable junk, London has lots. Try markets first—even for pedigree silver, the dealers at these places often have the best wares and the knowledge to match. Camden Passage and Bermondsey (☞ Street Markets, *below*) are the best; the Portobello market has become a bit of a tourist trap, but its side streets are filled with interesting shops that are open outside market hours (Westbourne Grove is fast becoming the most stylish section of this part of town). Kensington Church Street is *the* antiques-shopping street, with prices and quality both high. If you know your stuff (and your price limit) head out to Tower Bridge Road, south of the river, where there are mammoth antique warehouses, some of which are open on Sunday. The Furniture Cave, at the corner of Lots Road, Chelsea, has one of the largest stocks around. Or you could try your luck at auction against the dealers. Summer is usually a quiet period, but at any other time, there are plenty of bargains to be had from £50 and beyond. Of the hundreds of stores, we list a selection to whet your appetite. Opening times will vary: many places that are open on Saturday and Sunday will close Monday or Tuesday.

Alfie's Antique Market is a huge and exciting labyrinth on several floors, with dealers specializing in anything and everything but particularly in textiles, Arts and Crafts furniture, and theater memorabilia. You won't be deliberately stiffed, but it's a caveat emptor kind of place, thanks to the wide range of merchandise. ⊠ *13–25 Church St., NW8,* ☎ *020/7723–6066. Closed Sun.–Mon.* (☞ Map A)

Antiquarius, at the Sloane Square end of King's Road, is an indoor antiques market with more than 200 stalls offering a wide variety of collectibles, including things that won't bust your baggage allowance: Art Deco brooches, meerschaum pipes, silver salt cellars. . . . ⊠ *131–145 King's Rd., SW3,* ☎ *020/7351–5353. Closed Sun.* (☞ Map B)

Christopher Gibbs attracts such leading London tastemakers as J. Paul Getty Jr. and Mick Jagger, who, the society columns note, will hardly make a move without the judgment of Mr. Gibbs's legendary eye. If you're in the market for large decorative items, such as marble busts, priceless Elizabethan embroidery, and truly one of a kind antiques from all ages, this is the place to go and dream. ⊠ *3 Dove Walk, Pimlico Rd., SW1,* ☎ *020/7730–8200. Closed weekends.* (☞ Map B)

Coach House is one reason why Westbourne Grove is one of the chicest style addresses around. A 19th-century garage has been restored by four antiques dealers, and behind a modest street facade extends a vast showroom, with neo-Gothic armoires, Arts and Crafts chairs, and lovely objets d'art. ⊠ *189 Westbourne Grove, W11,* ☎ *020/7229–8306 Closed Sun.* (☞ Map C)

Colefax & Fowler is one of the most beautiful interior decorating shops in London—the virtual birthplace of the English country-house look. John Fowler, Lady Colefax, and, most importantly, Virginia-born Nancy Lancaster together created that cozy yet grand style, and their legacy is preserved here through wonderful wallpapers, pretty painted-wood flower holders, and assorted antique accents. If you want to make your apartment back home a mini-Chatsworth, be sure to stop in here, if only to soak up the style. ⊠ *39 Brook St., W1,* ☎ *020/7493–2231. Closed weekends.* (☞ Map A)

The Facade has one of the largest eclectic collections of French and Italian chandeliers, sconces, and table lamps. Most of them aren't wired and cleaned to shining bright, and this is reflected in the reasonable prices, particularly for such an up-and-coming area. ⊠ *196*

Westbourne Grove, W11, ☎ *020/7727–2159. Closed Sun.–Mon.* (☞ Map C)

Gallery of Antique Costume and Textiles attracts numerous movie directors who come here to get the period just right, because everything on the premises, from bedspreads to bloomers, was stitched before 1930—except for the copycat brocade vests. Models and Hollywood actors find incredible (and expensive) clothes here, too. It lies off our maps, but it is easily found three blocks north of the Edgware Road tube. ⊠ *2 Church St., NW8,* ☎ *020/7723–9981. Closed Sun.*

Grays Antique Market is conveniently central and assembles dealers specializing in everything from Sheffield plates to Chippendale furniture all under one roof. Bargains are not impossible, and proper pedigrees are guaranteed. Also try Grays in the Mews (⊠ 1–7 Davies Mews, W1, ☎ 020/7629–7034) around the corner. ⊠ *58 Davies St., W1,* ☎ *020/ 7629–7034. Closed Sun.; closed Sat. Jan.–Nov.* (☞ Map A)

Hope and Glory is one of the many specialty stores in Kensington with commemorative china and glass from 1887 to the present; there are also affordable lesser pieces. Entrance on Peel St. ⊠ *131A Kensington Church St., W8,* ☎ *020/7727–8424 Closed Sun.* (☞ Map C)

Judy Greenwood Antiques beckons with its glowing red walls and a delightful selection of high-style antiques: Miss Havisham-y settees, vintage fabrics and textiles, gilded mirrors, and side tables. ⊠ *657 Fulham Rd., SW6,* ☎ *020/7736–6037. Closed Sun.* (☞ Map B)

London Silver Vaults, a basement conglomeration of around 40 dealers, is a treasure trove for the average Joe. Some pieces are spectacular, of course, but you can also pick up a set of Victorian cake forks or a dented candelabrum for less than £50. ⊠ *Chancery House, 53– 64 Chancery La., WC2,* ☎ *020/7242–3844. Closed Sun.* (☞ Map A)

Megan Mathers offers one of London's most delectable assortments of stylish antiques: decoupaged 19th-century table obelisks, mini–Nelson's Columns, Venetian blackamoor figures—perfect *touches finales* for any high-style room. ⊠ *571 King's Rd., SW6,* ☎ *020/7371–7837. Closed Sun.* (☞ Map B)

Rupert Cavendish, this most elevated of dealers, has the Biedermeier market cornered, with Empire and Deco bringing up the rear. The shop is a museum experience. ⊠ *610 King's Rd., SW6,* ☎ *020/7731–7041. Closed Sun.* (☞ Map B)

Auction Houses

The pointers on going to auction: you don't need bags of money; the catalog prices aren't written in stone; and if you are sure of what you want when you view the presale, then bid with confidence. Below, we list the main houses, which all deal in fine art and furniture. And if you find these are out of your budget, snoop around Lots Road in Chelsea, where you can find more budget-priced contemporary furniture that compares favorably with the price of new.

Bonhams is one of the more buyer-friendly places and offers many interesting collections. Graham Greene's widow recently sold her exquisite dollhouses here. Along with the antiques, Bonhams specializes in 20th-century design. There is a branch in Chelsea (Montpelier Galleries, 65–69 Lots Road, SW10). ⊠ *Montpelier St., SW7,* ☎ *020/7393–3900.* (☞ Map B)

Christie's offers some great English country-house furniture in varying states of repair, paintings, prints, carpets, lighting, plus all manner of bona fide treasures. It's amazing what can be classed as infinitely desirable: the blue door from the film *Notting Hill* and the blue pinafore dress worn by Judy Garland in *Wizard of Oz* went for a record £5,750 and £199,500 respectively in a recent sale of film memorabilia. ⊠ *85 Old Brompton Rd., SW7,* ☎ *020/7581–7611.* (☞ Map B)

Phillips conducts many specialist sales and occasionally offers an Old Master painting sale that nearly rivals Christie's. ✉ *101 New Bond St., W1,* ☎ *020/7629–6602.* (☞ Map A)

Sotheby's has a well-publicized calendar of regular auctions that are for the more well endowed. But if you just want to look, ponder on possible purchases and break for lunch in the superb new café. ✉ *34–35 New Bond St., W1,* ☎ *020/7293–5000.* (☞ Map A)

Books, CDs, and Records

Charing Cross Road is London's booksville, with a couple of dozen stores here or hereabout. The many antiquarian booksellers tend to look daunting (deceptively, as Helene Hanff found by correspondence with No. 84), but there are many new bookshops, too.

Foyles (✉ 113–119 Charing Cross Rd., WC2, ☎ 020/7437–5660) is especially large—so enormous it can be confusing—but it is the place to come to find almost anything. **Waterstone's** (✉ 121–125 Charing Cross Rd., WC2, ☎ 020/7434–4291) is part of an admirable, and expanding, chain with long hours and a program of author readings and signings. The latest monster outlet is the Waterstone's at the revamped old Simpsons store on Piccadilly. **Borders** (✉ 120 Charing Cross Rd., WC2, ☎ 020/7379–6838) has taken over the Books Etc. here with its huge and helpful range of CDs, videos, author signings and talks, children's storytime and music sessions on Sundays, and café, not forgetting the vast selection of books (an equally large store is also on Oxford Street). **Hatchards** (✉ 187–188 Piccadilly, W1, ☎ 020/7439–9921), one of London's well-established bookshops that hasn't been swallowed up by the big players, retains its old-fashioned charm and is well stocked, with helpful staff. **Books for Cooks** (✉ 4 Blenheim Crescent, W11, ☎ 020/7221–1992) and its near neighbor the **Travel Bookshop** (✉ No. 13, ☎ 020/7229–5260) are exactly what they say and worth the trip for enthusiasts (☞ Map B). Travel books and maps are the specialty of **Stanfords** (✉ 12 Long Acre, WC2, ☎ 020/7836–1321). **Cinema Bookshop** (✉ 13 Great Russell St., WC1, ☎ 020/7637–0206) has the subject taped. For art books, head for **Zwemmer** (✉ 24 Litchfield St., WC2, ☎ 020/7240–4158), just off Charing Cross Road. Sci-fi, fantasy, horror, and comic books are found by the mile at **Forbidden Planet** (✉ 71 New Oxford St., WC1, ☎ 020/7836–4179) (☞ Map A). On Charing Cross Road, **Silver Moon** (✉ 64 Charing Cross Rd., WC2, ☎ 020/7836–7906) is an accessible and friendly women's bookshop. **Sportspages** (✉ Caxton Walk, 94–96 Charing Cross Rd., WC2, ☎ 020/7240–9604) is an excellent place to start your cricket library (☞ Map A). **Murder One** (✉ 71–73 Charing Cross Rd., WC2, ☎ 020/7734–3485) is just that—from crimes of passion to fiendish horror. **Talking Bookshop** (✉ 11 Wigmore St., W1, ☎ 020/7491–4117), just behind Oxford Street, has the listening scene taped up (☞ Map A).

Just off the south end of Charing Cross is Cecil Court—a pedestrians-only lane where every shop is a specialty bookstore.

Bell, Book and Radmall (✉ 4 Cecil Ct., WC2, ☎ 020/7240–2161) offers quality antiquarian volumes and specializes in modern first editions. **Marchpane** (✉ 16 Cecil Ct., WC2, ☎ 020/7836–8661) stocks covetable rare and antique illustrated children's books. **Dance Books** (✉ 15 Cecil Ct., WC2, ☎ 020/7836–2314) has—yes—dance books. **Pleasures of Past Times** (✉ 11 Cecil Ct., WC2, ☎ 020/7836–1142) indulges the collective nostalgia for Victoriana (☞ Map A). Off our map, but unmissable if you are in the Highgate area, **Fisher & Sperr** (✉ 46 Highgate High St., N6, ☎ 020/8340–7244) is a cave of wonders of secondhand books that time forgot.

London created the great megastores that have taken over the globe, but for cutting-edge music from the clubs, there are specialty stores galore.

Black Market can be heard before you even walk in the door. Indie, house, garage, world—here you'll find the hottest club music around. ⊠ *25 D'Arblay St., W1,* ☎ *020/7437–0478.* (☞ Map A)

HMV has branches everywhere, but make a special trip to the HMV flagship store for the widest selection. There are lots of autograph sessions and free shows, too. ⊠ *150 Oxford St., W1,* ☎ *020/7631–3423.* (☞ Map A)

MDC Classic Music has the most helpful staff, who will guide you without a blink to the best deals, from Callas to Sutherland, and tell you whether the diva was on form. There's some jazz, too. ⊠ *437 Strand, WC2,* ☎ *020/7240–2157.* (☞ Map A)

Tower Records doesn't carry records—go figure. Overlook that and you'll find its specialty departments are some of the best in London. ⊠ *1 Piccadilly Circus, W1,* ☎ *020/7439–2500.* (☞ Map A)

Virgin Megastore is Richard Branson's pride and joy (though his New York City store is even bigger). It's nice to have it all under one roof, we suppose—all 8 billion selections. ⊠ *14–16 Oxford St., W1,* ☎ *020/ 7631–1234.* (☞ Map A)

China and Glass

English Wedgwood and Minton china are as collectible as they ever were, and most large department stores carry a selection, alongside lesser varieties with smaller price tags. Regent Street has several off-price purveyors, and, if you're in search of a bargain, Harrods' sale (usually held during the last three weeks of January) can't be beat—but sharpen your elbows first. And for the latest in sleek Italian, French, and Scandinavian china and glassware, check out the modern kitchenware shops, which stock the latest in young designer trends—such as Conran shops, Bluebird, Habitat, and Heal's. For handmade, signature glassware, try the Glassworks, SE1 (☞ Design, *below*).

Bridgewater (⊠ 739 Fulham Rd., SW6, ☎ 020/7371–5264) is the home of all those fruit bowls, cream jugs, and cheese platters that grace every country-style designer kitchen in London and the fashionable burbs. You can find the complete range in Emma Bridgewater's own shop (☞ Map B). **David Mellor** (⊠ 4 Sloane Sq., SW1, ☎ 020/7730–4259) has practical Dartington crystal along with more unique porcelain and pottery pieces by British craftspeople (☞ Map B). **Divertimenti** (⊠ 45–47 Wigmore St., W1, ☎ 020/7935–0689) specializes in beautiful kitchenware, unusual culinary gifts such as spoons made from polished horn, and very desirable French pottery from Provence (☞ Map A). **Portmeirion** (⊠ 13 Kensington Church St., W8, ☎ 020/7938–1891) has been around for 40 years in its tabletop form (the design inspiration for the signature china is the famed town in North Wales). If you want to delve further into your re-creation of a country kitchen, this is the place (☞ Map B). **Summerhill & Bishop** (⊠ 100 Portland Rd., W11, ☎ 020/7221–4566) is a little piece of French country kitchen right down to the ancient black bicycle with basket (which probably contains garlic strings), supplying French embroidered linen, Portuguese and Tuscan stoneware, natural candles and soaps, and all manner of authentic designer culinary ware to give ambience to sleek city kitchens (☞ Map C). **Thomas Goode** (⊠ 19 S. Audley St., W1, ☎ 020/7499–2823) is one of the world's top shops for formal china and leaded crystal. On display are dinner plates designed and made for Dame Nellie Melba, Edward VII, Queen Victoria, and the last viceroy of India (☞ Map A).

Paris, France.

Paris, Texas.

When it Comes to Getting Local Currency at an ATM, Same Thing.

Whether you're in Yosemite or Yemen, using your Visa® card or ATM card with the PLUS symbol is the easiest and most convenient way to get local currency. For example, let's say you're in France. When you make a withdrawal, using your secured PIN, it's dispensed in francs, but is debited from your account in U.S. dollars. This makes it easy to take advantage of favorable exchange rates. And if you need help finding one of Visa's 627,000 ATMs in 127 countries worldwide, visit **visa.com/pd/atm**. We'll make finding an ATM as easy as finding the Eiffel Tower, the Pyramids or even the Grand Canyon.

It's Everywhere You Want To Be.®

SEE THE WORLD
IN FULL COLOR

  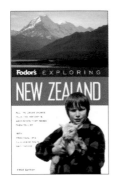

Fodor's Exploring Guides bring all the great sights vividly to life with hundreds of photographs, fascinating historical background, and colorful anecdotes. Detailed maps and practical information keep you headed in the right direction.

Pair a **Fodor's** Exploring Guide with your trusted Gold Guide for a complete planning package.

Clothing

London is one of the world's four fashion capitals (along with Paris, Milan, and New York), and every designer you've ever heard of is sold here somewhere. As well as hosting the top names, though, London retains a reputation for quirky street style, and many an exciting young designer has cut his or her teeth selling early collections at a London street market or on the borders of the central shopping streets—Notting Hill, Islington, East End. Don't just go by the label, and you could be the first to wear clothes by a future star. Traditional British men's outfitters are also rather well known. From the Savile Row suit, handmade shirt, and custom shoes to the Harris-tweeds-and-Oxford-brogues English country look that Ralph Lauren purloined, England's indigenous garments make for real investment dressing.

GENERAL

Aquascutum is known for its classic raincoats, but it also stocks the garments to wear underneath, for both men and women. Style keeps up with the times but is firmly on the safe side, making this a good bet for solvent professionals with an anti-fashion-victim attitude. ⊠ *100 Regent St., W1,* ☎ *020/7675–9050.* (☞ Map A)

Burberry tries to evoke an English Heritage ambience, with mahogany closets and stacks of neatly folded merchandise adorned with the trademark "Burberry Check" tartan. In addition to being seen on those famous raincoat linings, the tartan graces scarves, umbrellas, and even pots of passion-fruit curd and tins of shortbread. ⊠ *161–165 Regent St., W1,* ☎ *020/7734–4060;* ⊠ *18–22 The Haymarket, SW1,* ☎ *020/7730–3343.* (☞ Map A)

Connolly leather made by this elite company is the very essence of Rolls-Royce elegance and the flash of Ferrari. Drivers leave their vehicles to be made over inside, but you can content yourself with the accessories: a pair of leather driving gloves or a leather driving helmet and goggles. Prices are on a prestige basis—high—although you could settle for a smaller-statement souvenir belt or cuff links. ⊠ *32 Grosvenor Mews, SW1,* ☎ *020/7235–3883.* (☞ Map B)

Daisy & Tom is for cool kids and smart parents, who know that a happy child is an entertained child. Sadly there is no designer gear for mom to try on while her child is busy on the carousel, cuddling soft toys, or having a haircut. On one dedicated floor there are high-fashion junior clothes (Kenzo, IKKS, and Polo), shoes aplenty (for newborns to 10-year-olds), a bookshop, and a soda fountain café. What's more, it's all open on Sunday. ⊠ *181–183 King's Rd., SW3,* ☎ *020/7352–5000.* (☞ Map B)

Favourbrook tailors exquisite handmade vests, jackets, and dresses, all crafted from silks and brocades, velvets and satins, embroidered linens and chenilles. For ties and cummerbunds as well, men should kit out at 55 Jermyn Street, but from both branches you can order your own *Four Weddings and a Funeral* outfit. ⊠ *18 Piccadilly Arcade, W1,* ☎ *020/7491–2337.* (☞ Map A)

Herbert Johnson is one of a handful of gentlemen's hatters who still know how to construct deerstalkers, bowlers, flat caps, and panamas—all the classic headgear, with some Ascot-worthy hats for women, too. ⊠ *54 St James's St., W1,* ☎ *020/7408–1174.* (☞ Map A)

Holland & Holland is the place for the hunting-and-shooting fraternity. Bespoke is the byword, from guns (by appointment to the Duke of Edinburgh and the Prince of Wales) to clothing requirements for hunting, all with the Holland & Holland brand label. Tailor-made travel wear (especially of the adventure variety) is also available. The company has been in business since 1830 (rifles have been made by the same London factory since 1835) but was recently bought out by Chanel—a reason for the brighter, trendy yet practical separates aimed at the younger country set. "Sloane rangers" have their own branch at 171–172 Sloane Street. ⊠ *31–33 Bruton St., W1,* ☎ *020/7499–4411.* (☞ Map A)

Humla brought a colorful taste of Sweden to London before superstore IKEA steamrolled in. Mrs. Harris has been stocking beautifully made, quality children's clothes for 25 years and not so long ago used to make her own stripey handknits at the back of the shop. That originality is there still, although not her own work. Another branch is at 9 Flask Walk, Hampstead, where there is also a new collection of nursery furniture and timeless wooden toys. ⊠ *23 St. Christopher's Pl., W1,* ☎ *020/7224–1773.* (☞ Map A)

Kensington Market is the diametric opposite of British stiff-upper-lip anti-fashion. For more than two decades it has been a principal purveyor of the constantly changing, frivolous, hip London street style. Hundreds of stalls—some shop-size, others tiny—are crammed into this building; you can get lost for hours trying to find the good bits. ⊠ *49–53 Kensington High St., W8,* ☎ *020/7938–4343.* (☞ Map B)

Marks & Spencer is a major chain of stores that's an integral part of the British way of life—sturdy practical clothes, good materials and workmanship, and basic accessories, all at moderate, though not bargain-basement, prices. "Marks and Sparks," as it is popularly known, has never been renowned for its high style, though that is changing as it continues to bring in (anonymously) big-name designers to spice up its lines. What it *is* renowned for is underwear; all of England buys theirs here. This holds true for knitwear as well. This Marble Arch branch has the highest stock turnover of any shop in the land. ⊠ *(main store) 458 Oxford St., W1,* ☎ *020/7935–7954.* (☞ Map A)

Muji is a shortened version of the name of the Japanese store (meaning no-brand quality goods) and its range of functional, no-frills clothing (not fashion, please). Functional white cotton T-shirts, simply cut underwear (that also goes for outerwear), pants in neutral and plain colors, and navy and black sweaters are so popular they simply walk out of the shop. The merchandise is in complete harmony: white earthenware tableware on minimal, perforated-steel shelving; cream duvets on understated maple beds; gray towels and skin care products in white recyclable containers—it's a lifestyle dream that defies the cumulative heaps in most mortals' homes. ⊠ *Unit 5, 6–17 Tottenham Court Rd., W1,* ☎ *020/7436–1779.* (☞ Map A)

Mulberry outdoes Ralph Lauren in packaging the English look. This quintessentially British company makes covetable, top-quality leather bags, belts, wallets, and cases for all types of kit (even a mobile phone case and a travel case for laptop or computer organizer). Separates in fine wools, fine cotton shirts, and silk scarves and ties have widened the range. Although it is still considered traditional, Mulberry has increasingly been pursuing a quietly modern, international style niche. ⊠ *11–12 Gees Ct., St. Christopher's Pl., W1,* ☎ *020/7493–2546.* (☞ Map A)

Paul Smith is your man if you don't want to look outlandish but you're bored with plain pants and sober jackets. His well-tailored suits have a subtle quirkiness (like an outrageous, witty flash of colorful lining), his shirts and ties feature a sense of humor, and his jeans and sweats boast a good cut. Customers include Paul McCartney, Harrison Ford, and David Hockney. The boutique itself is worth seeing—it's re-created from a Victorian chemist's shop, and Smith's own range of toiletries and jewelry (women are also catered to here) adorns the shelves. The sale shop for discontinued lines is in Avery Row (W1), and the minimalist-style women's store is on fashionable Sloane Avenue (SW3). But the latest Smith buzz is Westbourne House (122 Kensington Park Rd., W11): a shop in a house designed to feel like an actual London home—a very chic one, of course—where women's, men's, and children's clothes and accessories are arranged in homelike settings. ⊠ *40–44 Floral St., WC2,* ☎ *020/7379–7133.* (☞ Map A)

Scotch House, as you'd guess, is the place to buy your kilts, tartan scarves, and argyle socks without going to Edinburgh. It's also well stocked with cashmere and accessories. ⊠ *2 Brompton Rd., SW1,* ☎ *020/7581–2151.* (☞ Map B)

Shellys offers shoes for men and women, from city slickers to clubbing, at all prices, and even at unimaginable platform heights. Also featured are the de rigueur Dr. Marten shoes—Britain's answer to Timberland. There are branches across town. ⊠ *266–270 Regent St., W1,* ☎ *020/7287–0939.* (☞ Map A)

Swaine Adeney is the most dyed-in-the-wool British and has been supplying practical kit for country pursuits since 1750. Not just for the horsey set, there are golf umbrellas, walking sticks, and hip flasks, all beautifully crafted and ingenious. One shouldn't be without the umbrella, with slim tipple-holder flask secreted inside the stick, on a frosty morning. Herbert Johnson, hatter, is housed downstairs. ⊠ *54 St. James's St., SW1,* ☎ *020/7409–7277.* (☞ Map A)

MENSWEAR

Most stores we list above under General Clothing stock excellent menswear. Try Aquascutum, Burberry, and Paul Smith. All the large department stores, too, carry a wide range of men's clothing, Selfridges and Harrods especially. There is a stealthy revolt away from the bastion of traditional made-to-order suits. Along with the flash car, young careerists want to break away from fatherly city-gent tailors. Sharp suiters, such as Ozwald Boateng, are noticeably un–Savile Row in style and demeanor.

Blazer stocks medium-price semiformal wear and separates in a more sportive vein. Clothes tend toward the classic, but with style-conscious details and rich colors. There is another branch on Oxford Street and others across town. ⊠ *117B Long Acre, WC2,* ☎ *020/7379–0456.* (☞ Map A)

Duffer of St. George has a collection of hip designers of street style, as well as its own label of sporty and dress-up lines for clubbing and posing with attitude. ⊠ *29 Shorts Gardens, WC2,* ☎ *020/7379–4660.* (☞ Map A)

Hackett started as a posh thrift shop, recycling cricket flannels, hunting pinks, Oxford brogues, and similar British wear. Now it makes its own, and it has become a genuine—and very good—gentlemen's outfitter, though polo shirts and faux sports gear are a strong theme. ⊠ *(main store) 137 Sloane St., SW3,* ☎ *020/7371–7964.* (☞ Map B)

John Lobb has a waiting list of six months plus, if you are planning to visit for your first pair of handmade shoes (after which your wooden "last," or foot mold, is kept). As well as plenty of time, you will need to have plenty of money: around £1,500. But this buys a world of choice—from finest calf to exotic elk—and they will be your finest pair of shoes ever. ⊠ *9 St. James's St., SW1,* ☎ *020/7930–3664.* (☞ Map A)

Kilgour, French & Stanbury is the classic and highly expensive bespoke tailors. Suits and shirts are custom cut (but note the cutters all go to lunch between 1:30 and 2:30 every afternoon). The 11th commandment here: you know a man looks like an English gentleman only when you do not notice that he is well dressed. ⊠ *8 Savile Row, W1,* ☎ *020/7734–6905.* (☞ Map A).

Malcolm Levene has quietly been cutting a dash in this now more trendy Marylebone district. Before he got the top job, Tony Blair used to buy here, but he is more likely to be seen now in British tailored suits. Levene's is filled with softly constructed menswear (casual weekend wear, trendy business suits, and a hint of formal evening attire) in more unusual fabrics sourced and made in Italy. The range of soft tones and styles doesn't scream fashion but shows a quiet cut of confidence. The staff is delightfully helpful. ⊠ *13–15 Chiltern St., W1,* ☎ *020/ 7487–4383.* (☞ Map A)

Nick Ashley is in the new mold of big-outdoors-goes-urban-cool, and the boutique is in one of the coolest areas of shops and restaurants in London, just west of Portobello. Ashley calls it performance wear— whether you're streaking about on a motorbike, loafing about looking cool in the city, or just keeping warm in Egyptian cotton vests and thermal long johns. The laid-back formula of chunky boots, polar fleece, and leather lookalike fabrics brings in the pop stars and young politicos. ⊠ *57 Ledbury Rd., W11,* ☎ *020/7221–1221.* (☞ Map C)

Ozwald Boateng is one of the new breed of bespoke tailors not on Savile Row but on the fringe. His made-to-measure suits are sought after (by rock luminaries George Michael, Mick Jagger and Bill Wyman, and even Lisa Stansfield) for their exclusive fabrics, fashionable detail, and shock-color lining as well as great classic cut. If bespoke is out of financial reach (around £1,000–£2,000) there is a ready-to-wear collection (from under £1,000), or the zappiest ties to be had in town (from £60). ⊠ *9 Vigo St., W1,* ☎ *020/7734–6868.* (☞ Map A)

Swear was the shoemaker for the movie *Star Wars,* which is an indicator of the style you can expect to encounter here: wild and wacky, larger-than-life platforms for daring wearers who have a head for the heights of fashion—around 4 inches and up. ⊠ *61 Neal St., WC2,* ☎ *020/7240–7673.* (☞ Map A)

Tom Gilbey is a custom tailor, but the exciting part of his shop is the Waistcoat Gallery, where exquisite vests—some in silk or brocade or embroidered by hand, others marginally plainer—are essential accessories for the dandy. ⊠ *2 New Burlington Pl., W1,* ☎ *020/7734–4877.* (☞ Map A)

Top Shop/Top Man is one of London's niftiest megachains and it's also the largest fashion store in the world. If you can circumnavigate round it, and still keep your hearing intact, head for the faux-vintage "souledout" section—the prices are as keen as any market stall. Top-notch trendsetting designers are also keeping the store one step ahead: Clements Ribeiro has produced a range for TS Design. ⊠ *214 Oxford St., W1,* ☎ *020/7636–7700.* (☞ Map A)

Turnbull & Asser is *the* custom shirtmaker. Unfortunately for those of average means, the first order must be for a minimum of six shirts, from around £100 each. But there's a range of less expensive, though still exquisite, ready-to-wear shirts, too. ⊠ *71–72 Jermyn St., W1,* ☎ *020/ 7808–3000.* (☞ Map A)

WOMEN'S WEAR

Accessorize is where shrewd shoppers find the latest high-fashion items at low prices. Beady bags, feathery jewels, devoré scarves—clever copies of each season's catwalk versions reach these stores fast. There are branches across town. ⊠ *Unit 22, The Market, Covent Garden, WC2,* ☎ *020/7240–2107.* (☞ Map A)

Agnès B has so, so pretty, understated French clothing and is conveniently close to the Bibendum restaurant (☞ Chapter 2) and the Conran Shop (☞ *below*). Many items are timelessly perfect, like fine knitwear and feminine cotton tops. Prices are mid-range and worthy for the quality—Ms. B has been a stalwart of the fashion press for years. There are branches in Marylebone High Street (W1) and Heath Street, Hampstead (NW3); Floral Street (WC2) has elegant men's suits. ⊠ *111 Fulham Rd., SW3,* ☎ *020/7225–3477.* (☞ Map B)

Brora has the very latest in cashmere and *those* shawls (about which debates on goats and their woolly coats have gone on). There are prettily dressed-up camisoles, jumpers and cardigans, practical pants, and non-cashmere items as well (picnic blankets and wash bags). Prices are surprisingly mid-range for a product that could become an endangered species—such is the current appetite. ✉ *344 King's Rd., SW3,* ☎ *020/ 7352–3697.* (☞ Map B)

Browns was the first notable store to populate the South Molton Street pedestrian mall, and it seems to sprout more offshoots every time you visit it. Well-established, collectible designers (Donna Karan, Romeo Gigli, Jasper Conran, Jil Sander, Yohji Yamamoto) rub shoulder pads here with younger, funkier names (Dries Van Noten, Clements Ribeiro, Anne Demeulemeester, Hussein Chalayan), and Browns also has its own label. Its July and January sales are famed. Menswear gets a corner, too. Bargain hunters should hotfoot it down to Browns Labels for Less at No. 50. ✉ *23–27 S. Molton St., W1,* ☎ *020/7491–7833;* ✉ *6C Sloane St., SW1,* ☎ *020/7493–4232.* (☞ Maps A and B)

Cath Kidston has the most charming, fresh ginghams and flower-sprig cotton prints. She translates these to housecoats (with matching bed linens, cushions, wallpaper, and bath wear) and nightshirts—in fact, everything you could want for a girl's bedroom in an English country cottage. The sweaters are practical, cozy handknits; the Anonymous range includes skimpy lace-edged vest tops and cardigans, and skirts in flouncy wools. There is a delightful children's wear line in the same nostalgic vein. ✉ *8 Clarendon Cross, W11,* ☎ *020/7221–4000.*

Droopie & Browns features beautifully constructed, extravagantly theatrical frocks and suits, made up in raw silks, fine linens, brocades, and velvets. Colors are strong, tailoring is unimpeachable, and kind salespeople don't turn up their noses at larger ladies. ✉ *99 St. Martin's La., WC2,* ☎ *020/7379–4514.* (☞ Map A)

Fenwick has been around for years, in a prime fashion spot, and has the most inviting windows, yet it manages to be very competitive. At sale time, it's a bargain one-stop shop, with a vast selection of bags, gloves, scarves, and shoes, and with a good selection of designers on the upper floors: Ben de Lisi, Jean Muir, Christian Lacroix, and Katherine Hamnett to name a few. ✉ *63 New Bond St., W1,* ☎ *020/7629–9161.* (☞ Map A)

Elspeth Gibson has been building up a steady following as the firm favorite of models and personalities in the glossy mags and Sunday supplements: these clothes are for the flaunty girlie in you. There are delicate beads on soft cardies; swirly, flirty, embroidered Tyrol-type skirts; and simply herds of cashmere. ✉ *7 Pont St., SW1,* ☎ *020/7235–0601.* (☞ Map B)

Emma Hope has had her shoemaking store here for many years. It's handy if you are mooching around Islington and Camden Passage antiques stalls, and since bespoke footwear has had a mini-meteoric upturn, and Hope's pretty pumps in brocades and satins have been gliding down the catwalks of Nicole Farhi and Betty Jackson, she has opened another branch in Sloane Square, SW1. ✉ *33 Amwell St., EC1,* ☎ *020/ 7833–2367.* (☞ Map B)

Egg stocks a limited choice in loosely ethnic work wear in limited colors with minimal, almost-no-fashion details—and the formula is a winner. Doherty (co-founder) worked for Issey Miyake, so you get the idea. The off-street address adds to the shop's interest factor: a former Victorian dairy tucked away in a Knightsbridge mews. ✉ *36 Kinnerton St., SW1,* ☎ *020/7235–9315.* (☞ Map B)

Georgina von Etzdorf makes scarves that positively illuminate. Made with finely woven metallic threads and delicate clusters of trapped fibers, Etzdorf's new scarves and stoles give any outfit a million-dollar shimmer through the night. Too way-out? Then drool over sumptuous deep-colored devoré velvets and crushed silks (there are irresistible silk ties for men, but they're very expensive). These phosphorescent designs also stretch to bags, shoes, and the most gorgeous jackets. It's also at 1–2 Burlington Arcade, Piccadilly, W1. ✉ *61 Ledbury Rd., W11* ☎ *020/7235–0601.* (☞ Map C)

Ghost can be found with regularity in the fashion press. The design team, led by Tania Sarne, has the feel of the moment all sewn up with willowy dresses and skirts in silks, velvets, and the ubiquitous viscose, which sculpts into wonderful crinkly textures. Indispensible little cardigans in silky weaves have been the wardrobe essential for well over a year and show no signs of fading. Pretty puff-sleeve blouses are also a strong feature. It's also at 14 Hinde Street, W1. ✉ *36 Ledbury Rd., W11,* ☎ *020/7229–1057.* (☞ Map A)

Janet Reger is still queen of the silk teddy, having become synonymous with the ultimate in luxurious negligees and lingerie many years ago. ✉ *10 Beauchamp Pl., SW3,* ☎ *020/7584–9360.* (☞ Map B)

Jigsaw is popular for its separates, which don't sacrifice quality to fashion, are reasonably priced, and suit women in their twenties to forties. There's a men's branch on Bruton Street, W1, and other branches across town. ✉ *126–127 New Bond St., W1,* ☎ *020/7491–4484.* (☞ Map A)

Jimmy Choo is the name on every supermodel's and fashion editor's feet. His exquisite, elegant designs are fantasy itself, and he's become a contender for Manolo Blahnik's crown. Obviously, these designs aren't cheap—nothing under £100—but the workmanship is out of this world. ✉ *20 Motcomb St., SW1,* ☎ *020/7235–6008.* (☞ Map B)

Karen Millen strikes a clever balance between functional working clothes with subtle fashion detailing (muted pastels and soft colors in separates), fun urban weekend wear (leather biker jackets and black-and-white ponyskin coats), and glam for evenings (little dresses with Japanese almond-sprig detail). Millen's appeal ranges from grown-up teen to forties, with mid-range prices. The successful formula has expanded to branches across the country. ✉ *262–264 Regent St., W1,* ☎ *020/7287–6158.* (☞ Map A)

Koh Samui stocks the clothing and accessories—some still steaming off the catwalk—of around 40 young designers, most of them British, some exclusive to this store, and all on the cutting edge. There are small items for under a tenner (eclectic hair clips by Japanese designer Heesoo) and drop-dead dresses for thousands of pounds (an exquisite hand-beaded dress by Berardi for £4,500). KS is the place to discover the next wave before *Vogue* gets the story. ✉ *65 Monmouth St., WC2,* ☎ *020/7240–4280.* (☞ Map A)

Laura Ashley offers design from the firm founded by the late high priestess of English traditional. Country dresses, blouses, and skirts, plus wallpapers and fabrics in dateless patterns that rely heavily on flowers, fruit, leaves, or just plain stripes have captured the nostalgic imagination of the world. (main store, ✉ *(main store) 256–258 Regent St., W1,* ☎ *020/7437–9760.* (☞ Map A)

Lulu Guinness struck a death blow to the industrial black nylon bag by bringing in bags of beads, colored silks, and the loveliest designs. Her new store is equally girlish and fun (*Vogue* covers adorn a see-through floor), with a downstairs salon where you can take tea while selecting. ✉ *3 Ellis St., SW1,* ☎ *020/7823–4828.* (☞ Map B)

Margaret Howell is the ultimate in investment, one-stop shopping. Along with Paul Smith (☞ *above*), she is the top exponent of Britishness in the Far East. Think classic fabrics—wools, silks—and perfect detail. ✉ *29 Beauchamp Pl., SW3,* ☎ *020/7584 –2462.* (☞ Map B)

Nicole Farhi suits the career woman who requires quality, cut, *and* style in a suit, plus weekend wear in summer linens and silks, or winter hand-knit woolens. Prices are on the high side, but there is some affordable wear as well, especially the sporty, casual Diversion label. Farhi offers an equally desirable men's line. The downstairs in-store restaurant, Nicole's, is not just somewhere to resuscitate between purchases; Ms. Farhi designed the space and the menu to her own taste, and it is an extension of the fashion statement, a hot spot for lunching fashionistas who like to be seen. It's wise to reserve ahead (☎ 020/7499–8408). ⊠ *(main stores) 158 Bond St., W1,* ☎ *020/7499–8368;* ⊠ *25–26 St. Christopher's Pl., W1,* ☎ *020/7486–3416;* ⊠ *27 Hampstead High St., NW3,* ☎ *020/7435–0866.* (☞ Map A)

Philip Treacy is the name that tops every fashion maven's Santa Claus list. His magnificent hats regularly grace the pages of *Harper's Bazaar;* one-half Mad Hatter, one-half Cecil Beaton, Treacy's creations always guarantee Making an Entrance. Only the most serious fashion plates need apply—truly: the atelier is open by appointment only. Cheapskates can shoot along to Debenhams department store on Oxford Street, where Treacy has a diffusion line. ⊠ *69 Elizabeth St., SW1,* ☎ *020/7259–9605.* (☞ Map B)

Rigby & Peller is for those who love pretty lingerie—many of the luxurious makes are here: La Perla and Gottex, as well the corsetières' own line. But if the right fit eludes, have one made to measure. Most of the young royal and aristo ladies buy here, not just because the store holds the Royal Appointment but because the quality and service are excellent, and much friendlier than you might expect. There is also a branch in Conduit Street, off New Bond Street, W1. ⊠ *2 Hans Rd., SW3,* ☎ *020/7584–9360.* (☞ Map B)

The **Shirtsmith** does bespoke and ready-made shirts, suits, and jackets for women, using fine cottons and Indian silks. Some designs are classic and fitted, and others are slightly outrageous. ⊠ *38B Ledbury Rd., W11,* ☎ *020/7229–3090.* (☞ Map C)

Space NK Apothecary is rapidly acquiring cult status as the cutting-edge purveyor of makeup and cosmetics. The makeup artists' lines (MAC, Bobbi Brown, and Stila) have led the alternative trend to the giant names, and new niche lines here always have the newest, hottest colors. You'll also find everything else to complete your body pampering. ⊠ *37 Earlham St., WC2,* ☎ *020/7379–7030.* (☞ Map A)

Vivienne Westwood is at the top of the British designer tree. If you want to see where it all started, the Pompadour-punk ball gowns, Lady Hamilton vest coats, and foppish landmark getups are the core of her first boutique at 430 King's Road. Westwood still represents the apex of high-style British couture, and the Davies Street boutique sells the Gold Label line of intoxicatingly glamorous creations: ready-to-wear, or made to measure. At 44 Conduit Street, the story is the sharper Red Line: hot, pared-down catwalk versions. Menswear is also on offer here—the Westwood influence is far-reaching. ⊠ *6 Davies St., W1,* ☎ *020/7629–3757.* (☞ Map A)

Whistles is a small chain stocking its own high-fashion, mid-price label, plus several selected eclectic designers. Clothes are hung in color-coordinated groupings in shops that resemble designers' ateliers. ⊠ *(main store) The Market, Covent Garden, WC2,* ☎ *020/7379–7401;* ⊠ *Heath St., Hampstead,* ☎ *020/7431–2395.* (☞ Map A)

Zara has swept across Europe and the East (the price tags carry 25 flags and related prices) and has barely been in London for two years, but the store is busy, busy. It's not hard to see why. The style is young and snappy; colors are great, with clothes sorted into color groupings for work and play; and the prices are unbelievably low. However, don't expect durability. These are fun, fashion pieces with a few basics. The whole spectrum is covered, including accessories: beady bags, wacky shoes and boots, moleskin mule slippers, jewelry. Menswear and a terrific line for kids each have their own floor. ⊠ *118 Regent St., W1,* ☎ *020/7534–9500* (☞ Map A)

Design

There's been a tremendous resurgence of interest in objects not mass-produced. The burgeoning market areas such as Spitalfields (☞ Street Markets, *below*), the state-of-the-art OXO Tower, and Lesley Craze have become the new, eclectic fashion suppliers of jewelry, clothes, and housewares, and often to personal order. These sites are not central. If you can't stretch out to these areas, then a good starting point is the Crafts Council Gallery Shop within the Victoria & Albert Museum. But forget the outmoded word "crafts"—this work is often more modern than modems.

Contemporary Applied Arts has just celebrated its 50th anniversary and has lost none of its edge in showing a huge range of work by designers and craftspeople. Regular shows and exhibitions display anything from glassware and jewelry to furniture and lighting. ⊠ *2 Percy St., W1,* ☎ *020/7436–2344.* (☞ Map A)

Contemporary Ceramics was formed by some of the best British potters as a cooperative venture to market their wares. The result is a newly modernized store that carries a wide spectrum of the potter's art, from thoroughly practical pitchers, plates, and bowls to ceramic sculptures. It's possibly the best selection of ceramics to be found in central London (just behind Oxford Street), with each piece carrying its own potted biography. There is a large range of books on the art as well. Prices range from the reasonable to way up. ⊠ *7 Marshall St., W1,* ☎ *020/ 7437–7605.* (☞ Map A)

The **Crafts Council Gallery Shop/Victoria & Albert Museum Shop** is where you will find a microcosmic selection of the wide range of British craftspeople's work (jewelry, glass, ceramics, toys). Accompanying the exhibitions in the museum are more focused displays, such as the Summer Show showcase. The Crafts Council has a smaller shop at its base in Islington (⊠ 44A Pentonville Rd., N1, ☎ 020/7806–2559), where you can source information on craftspeople and browse in the showcase gallery. ⊠ *Cromwell Rd., SW7,* ☎ *020/7589–5070.*

David Linley Furniture is the outpost for Viscount Linley—the only gentleman in the kingdom who can call the queen "Auntie" and, more importantly, one of the finest furniture designers of today. Heirlooms of the future, his desks and chairs have one foot in the 18th century, another in the 21st. The large pieces are suitably expensive, but small desk accessories and objets d'art are also available. ⊠ *60 Pimlico Rd., SW1,* ☎ *020/7730–7300.* (☞ Map B)

Designers Guild is where Tricia Guild shows her fabrics and accessories of fabulous, saturated colors. Inspirational, many designers vouch; and she has now incorporated furniture, objets d'art, and linens. ⊠ *267– 271 and 275–277 King's Rd., SW3,* ☎ *020/7351–5775.* (☞ Map B)

Glass Art Gallery/London Glassblowing Workshop is where you can find glassblowers and designers who make decorative and practical ware. The artists are British-based and display their work in the gallery. If you visit on weekdays, you can see them at work, and buy or commission your own variation. Prices can go into the thousands, but there are Saturday sales in April, July, and November–December, when many pieces go for less than £30. In the Leathermarket, which is off our map, you can also find other craftspeople, most notably a silversmith and papermaker. ⊠ *7 The Leathermarket, Weston St., SE1,* ☎ *020/7403–2800. Tube: London Bridge.*

Lesley Craze Gallery is making quite a name for itself. Craze has cornered a design market in what is now becoming a fashionable area, hot with bright new restaurants, like Maison Novelli, which is right on the doorstep here. You'll find the most exquisite jewelry to drool over, by some 100 young British designers (fashion editors source new talent here for their glossy spreads.) The adjacent Craze 2 and C2+ specialize in nonprecious metals and sumptuous scarves and textiles. ⊠ *33–35 Clerkenwell Green, EC1,* ☎ *020/7608–0393. Tube: Farringdon.*

OXO Tower is one of London's newest shopping meccas. Many and varied artisans have to pass rigorous selection procedures to set up in prime riverside workshops and make, display, and sell their work. The workshops are glass-walled, and you're invited in, even if you're just browsing or chatting. You can commission, too—anything from a cushion cover to custom-made jewelry, furniture, and sculpture. There are 23 studios in all, and a quick browse on the first floor reveals some very inviting items: hand-painted silk dresses by Nana Agyeman, handwoven textiles by Archipelago, multidiscipline design by Hive. The second floor has more of the same, including lamps, clothing, and jewelry. The very swish Harvey Nick's restaurant is on the eighth—top—floor, which has a fantastic view across the river to St. Paul's and Somerset House, and the massive London Eye millennium wheel. You don't need to pay for the view, as there is a public terrace, but beware of the wind whipping along the Thames. You'll find more craftspeople at Gabriel's Wharf, next door. ⊠ *Bargehouse St., SE1,* ☎ *020/7401–2225.* (☞ Map A)

Space has contemporary handmade furniture and other home-style designs, from beanbags and hand-embellished bed linens to sculpted candles. Owner Emma Oldham's theme focuses on mixing the affordable with the aspirational, and she has instigated an exhibition-selling space for individual artists. ⊠ *214 Westbourne Grove, W11,* ☎ *020/7229–6533.* (☞ Map C)

Walter Castellazzo Design has been getting lots of notice in the glossy interiors press with his very individual designs of modern-gothic painted furniture. His signature style is the tall bookcase (which you'll love or hate) with its gently curving pointed apex. A similar theme is used for wall and corner cabinets and mirrors. Castellazzo's shelves are filled with other craft designers' work: silk purses, metallic cushions, jewelry. His latest direction (commissions undertaken) is toward space-capsule bunk beds in brushed silver with rocket chests of drawers—a must for young space cadets. The store is off our map, in the center of Georgian Highgate Village close to the Gothic Highgate Cemetery. ⊠ *84 Highgate High St., N6,* ☎ *020/8340–3001. Tube: Archway or Highgate, then bus.*

Gifts

Of course, virtually anything from any shop in this chapter has gift potential, but these selections lean toward stores with a lot of choice, both in merchandise and price. Chances are you'll be wanting the recipients of your generous bounty to know how far you traveled to procure it for them, so our suggestions tend toward identifiable Britishness. You should also investigate the possibilities in the shops attached to the major museums, most of which offer far more than racks of souvenir postcards these days. Some of the best are at the British Museum and the V&A. For specialized gifts, the Royal Academy has great prints and cards and art paraphernalia; the London Transport Museum has transport models; the Natural History Museum has the largest selection of toy dinosaurs and real gemstones; and the new London Aquarium is top-scale for all things undersea.

The **Armoury of St. James's** offers perfect playthings for kids of all ages in the form of some of the world's finest antique and newly painted lead soldiers (most wars with British involvement can be fought in miniature), plus medals, brass buttons, uniforms, painted drums, and military prints. ⊠ *17 Piccadilly Arcade, SW1,* ☎ *020/7493–5082.* (☞ Map A)

The **British Museum** has stacks of Egyptiana, particularly cute scarabs in ceramic. You can be an archaeologist for an afternoon and buy your own ancient pottery pieces. The bookshop on the ground floor has a huge range and is a mine of historical information for adults and children. ⊠ *Great Russell St., WC1,* ☎ *020/7323–8175.* (☞ Map A)

The **Conran Shop** is the domain of Sir Terence Conran, of course, who has been informing British middle-class taste since he opened Habitat in the '60s; this is the grown-up, upmarket version. Home enhancers from furniture to stemware, both handmade and mass-produced, famous name and young designer, are displayed in a suitably gorgeous building. Bluebird (☞ Chapter 2) on King's Road and the Conran Shop on Marylebone High Street are the latest offspring with similarly beautiful wares. ⊠ *Michelin House, 81 Fulham Rd., SW3,* ☎ *020/7589–7401.* (☞ Map B)

The **Cross** is a thoughtful, ultrachic cornucopia of something to suit everyone—even your pet pooch. The idea has been around in other London shops for years, but the Cross succeeds with its ambience (bleached beach house) and hedonistic, beautiful things (silk scarves, brocade bags, embroidered chinoiserie, check housecoats, and fragrant candles and butterflies by Jade Jagger). Finally, the location: the Cross is bang in the middle of Portobello–cum–Holland Park, London's hot trend area. ⊠ *141 Portland Rd., W11,* ☎ *020/7727–6760.* (☞ Map C)

Floris is one of the most beautiful shops in London, with gleaming glass and Spanish mahogany showcases (acquired from the Great Exhibition of 1851) filled with swan's-down powder puffs, cut-glass bottles, and the elegant ivory and faux tortoiseshell combs that the shop has sold since the place opened in 1730. Queen Victoria used to daub her favorite Floris fragrance on her lace handkerchief. ⊠ *89 Jermyn St., W1,* ☎ *020/7930–2885.* (☞ Map A)

Fortnum & Mason, the queen's grocer, is, paradoxically, the most egalitarian of gift stores, with plenty of irresistibly packaged luxury foods, stamped with the gold BY APPOINTMENT crest, for less than £5. Try the teas, preserves, blocks of chocolate, tins of pâté, or a box of Duchy Originals oatcakes—like Paul Newman, the Prince of Wales has gone into the retail food business. ⊠ *181 Piccadilly, W1,* ☎ *020/7734–8040.* (☞ Map A)

General Trading Co. "does" just about every upper-class wedding gift list but caters also to slimmer pockets with merchandise shipped from farther shores (as the name suggests), but moored securely to English taste. ⊠ *144 Sloane St., SW1,* ☎ *020/7730–0411.* (☞ Map B)

Hamleys has six floors of toys and games for children and adults. The huge stock ranges from traditional teddy bears to computer games and all the latest technological gimmickry. Try to avoid it at Christmas, when police have to rope off a section of Regent Street for customers. ⊠ *188–196 Regent St., W1,* ☎ *020/7494–2000.* (☞ Map A)

Lush is crammed with fresh, pure, very wacky, handmade cosmetics. "13 Rabbit" is chocolate and spice soap for the shower; "Angels on Bare Skin" is divine lavender cleansing mush; "Banana Moon," "Dirty Boy," and "Pineapple Grunt" are soaps sliced off huge slabs like cheese and paper-wrapped as in an old-fashioned grocer; "Bath Bombs" fizz furiously, then leave the water scattered with rosebuds or scented with honey and vanilla. It's all too irresistible. ⊠ *Unit 11, The Piazza, Covent Garden, WC2,* ☎ *020/7240–4570.* (☞ Map A)

Neal Street East isn't big on British, no, but this importer of Asian everything does carry stock with universal appeal. There are several floors of what you'd expect in the way of woks, chopsticks, bowls, books, kimonos, and toys, but there are also glorious lacquered boxes, woven baskets, amber and silver jewelry, silk flowers, Japanese kites, and loads of fun gifts for less than a fiver. ⊠ *5 Neal St., WC2,* ☎ *020/7240–0135.* (☞ Map A)

Neal's Yard Remedies has exquisitely fragranced bath oils, shampoos, massage lotions, soaps, and so on, plus some of the purest essential oils money can buy, complete with burners for scenting the air back home;

all are packaged in the company's distinctive cobalt-blue apothecary bottles. ✉ *15 Neal's Yard, WC2,* ☎ *020/7379–7222.* (☞ Map A)

Ordning & Reda has the hottest colors of the moment for cool, sleek Swedish stationery and useful pieces to dress up the drabbest of desks. There are high-style rucksacks, too. ✉ *22 New Row, WC2,* ☎ *020/ 7240–8090.* (☞ Map A)

Penhaligon's was established by William Penhaligon, court barber at the end of Queen Victoria's lengthy reign. He blended perfumes and toilet waters in the back of his shop, often creating private blends for such customers as Lord Rothschild and Winston Churchill, using essential oils and natural, often exotic ingredients. You can buy the very same formulations today, along with soaps, talcs, bath oils, and accessories, with the strong whiff of Victoriana both inside and outside the pretty bottles and boxes. Although constructed only a decade ago, the shop is sumptuously outfitted with 19th-century perfumer furnishings. ✉ *(main branches) 41 Wellington St., WC2,* ☎ *020/7836– 2150;* ✉ *16 Burlington Arcade, W1,* ☎ *020/7629–1416.* (☞ Map A)

Purves & Purves is a great place if you've only a £5 note to spend and want to get something colorful and witty, too. From bubbly plastic napkin rings, toothbrushes, or clothes pegs to colonial chairs or silly soap dishes, the mundane takes on a bright new view. The store features many British designs. ✉ *80–81 and 83 Tottenham Court Rd., W1,* ☎ *020/ 7580–8223.* (☞ Map A)

Rococo is run by Chantal Coady, who writes, eats, and lives for chocolate. Vegetable fats are a forbidden word in this cocoa paradise—40% is just an average hit—and there are interesting and off-beat additions to the main chocolate recipe, such as essence of Earl Grey. ✉ *321 King's Rd., SW3,* ☎ *020/7352–5857.* (☞ Map B)

The **Science Museum** is best for the most imaginative toys and models to make, such as those darling little balsa-wood planes. The books and puzzles are extensive and will satisfy the most inquiring minds. ✉ *Exhibition Rd., SW7,* ☎ *020/7942–4455.* (☞ Map B)

Les Senteurs is an intimate, unglossy gem of a perfumery run by a French family. It sells some of the more little-known yet most wonderfully timeless fragrances in town. Sample "Creed," worn by Eugenie, wife of Emperor Napoléon III. ✉ *71 Elizabeth St., SW1,* ☎ *020/7730–2322.* (☞ Map B)

The **Tea House** purveys everything to do with the British national drink; you can dispatch your entire gift list here. Alongside every variety of tea (including strange or rare brews like orchid, banana, Japanese Rice, and Russian Caravan) are teapots in the shape of a British bobby or a London taxi, plus books, and what the shop terms "teaphernalia"— strainers, trivets, and infusers, plus some gadgets that need explaining. ✉ *15A Neal St., WC2,* ☎ *020/7240–7539.* (☞ Map A)

Jewelry

Jewelry—precious, semiprecious, and totally fake—can be had by just rubbing an Aladdin's lamp in London's West End. Of the department stores, Liberty and Harvey Nichols are particularly known for their fashion jewelry, but as well as viewing the more traditional baubles, bangles, and beads, check out the new, exceptionally creative kids on the jewelry block, such as Slim Barrett (☞ Janet Fitch, *below*), whose designs are worn by supermodels, young aristos, and TV personalities. Seek out also the new treasure trove of talent in the crafts and jewelry galleries, such as OXO Tower and Lesley Craze (☞ Design, *above*).

Asprey & Garrard has been described as the "classiest and most luxurious shop in the world." It offers a range of exquisite jewelry and gifts, both antique and modern. If you're in the market for a six-branched Georgian candelabrum or a six-carat emerald-and-diamond brooch, you won't be disappointed. Owned by the Sultan of Brunei's family, Asprey has joined forces with Garrard, which moved its operation from Regent Street in summer '98. Garrard is the royal jeweler, in charge of the upkeep of the Crown Jewels. ✉ *167 New Bond St., W1,* ☎ *020/7493–6767.* (☞ Map A)

Butler & Wilson is designed to set off its irresistible costume jewelry to the very best advantage—against a dramatic black background. It has some of the best displays in town, and it keeps very busy marketing silver, diamanté, French gilt, and pearls by the truckload. ✉ *20 South Molton St., W1,* ☎ *020/7409–2955;* ✉ *189 Fulham Rd., SW3,* ☎ *020/ 7352–8255.* (☞ Maps A and B)

Cartier exudes an exclusivity that captures the very essence of Bond Street. It combines royal connections—Cartier was granted its first royal warrant in 1902—with the last word in luxurious good taste. The store also sells glassware, leather goods, and stationery. ✉ *175 New Bond St., W1,* ☎ *020/7493–6962.* (☞ Map A)

Dinny Hall has a very simple collection of designs in mainly gold and silver. Pared-down necklaces with a single drop feature, delicate gold spot-diamond earrings, and a simple choker with delicate curls are indicative of the styles on offer—a panacea to the many other highly decorative jewels and baubles that are around right now. There is another branch in Fulham Road, SW3. ✉ *200 Westbourne Gr., W11,* ☎ *020/ 7792–3913.* (☞ Map C)

Erickson Beamon is the feather in the British cap. His highly individual style of chokers, hair decorations, and brooches contains plenty of these colored fronds along with wool and other nonmetallic material woven intricately among the jewels. McQueen and Galliano have shown Beamon's bold work to his great advantage, and his dramatic Gothic style has spawned many imitators. Costume pieces start from around £40. ✉ *38 Elizabeth St., SW1,* ☎ *020/7259–0202.* (☞ Map A)

Janet Fitch is a name that regularly hits the glossy fashion pages. This comes as no surprise, as the shop is a showcase for contemporary British designers. From cuff links to tiaras (from the above-mentioned Slim Barrett) at a great price range, you'll find a bauble or two to tempt you. Other branches are at 25A Old Compton Street and King's Road. ✉ *37A Neal St., WC2,* ☎ *020/7240–6332.* (☞ Map A)

Steinberg & Tolkien has the last word in costume jewelry from the 1920s and onward. Classic gem sets by Chanel and Schiaparelli are just two of the famous designers that you might leap on here. And if you're lucky, you may find a piece that has been signed by its creator. These pieces are sometimes cheaper than those of the top-notch jewelers, and they may be of extra interest because you know who made them. ✉ *193 King's Rd., SW3,* ☎ *020/7376–3660.* (☞ Map B)

Prints

London harbors trillions of prints, and they make great gifts—for yourself, perhaps. We list some West End stores, but try also street markets (Camden Passage in Islington, particularly) and Cecil Court (☞ Books, CDs, and Records, *above*), just north of Trafalgar Square; the intriguing shops close to the British Museum; and the Royal Academy museum shop, which has a small selection. Auction houses, such as Christie's, South Kensington, and Phillips, New Bond Street, can often prove fun hunting grounds.

Grosvenor Prints sells antiquarian prints, and 18th- and 19th-century portraits, but with an emphasis on views and architecture of London—and dogs! It's an eccentric collection, and the prices range widely, but the stock is so odd that you are bound to find something interesting and unusual to meet both your budget and your taste. ✉ *28 Shelton St., WC2,* ☎ *020/7836–1979.* (☞ Map A)

The **Map House** has antique maps (that run from a few pounds to several thousand) and excellent reproductions of maps and prints, especially of botanical subjects, cityscapes, and *Punch* cartoons and prints. ⊠ *54 Beauchamp Pl., SW3,* ☎ *020/7589–4325.* (☞ Map B)

New Academy Gallery has many prints (including originals) to browse through, with a traditional bent: landscapes and scenes of London. The partner gallery—the Curwen, at No. 4, (020/7636–1459)—has a wider selection of modern art prints. ⊠ *34 Windmill St., W1,* ☎ *020/7323–4700.* (☞ Map A)

Street Markets

London is as rich in street markets as it is in parks, and they contribute as much to the city's thriving culture. Practically every neighborhood has its own cluster of fruit-and-vegetable stalls, but we list here the bigger, specialist sort of market, which provides not only (if you luck out) a bargain but also a great day out. A Sunday morning strolling the stalls of Brick Lane and breakfasting on the native bagels (smaller than New York's, but just as good), or a Saturday antiquing on Portobello Road, is a Londoners' pastime as much as it is a tourist activity, and markets are a great way to see the city from the inside out.

Bermondsey, also known as the New Caledonian Market, is London's best antiques market, one of the largest, and the one the dealers frequent. Due to its professional needs, the Fridays-only market starts at the unearthly hour of 5 AM, and it's then that the really great buys will be snapped up. You should still be able to find a bargain or two if you turn up a bit later. ⊠ *Tower Bridge Rd., SE1. Bus 15 or 25 to Aldgate, then Bus 42 over Tower Bridge to Bermondsey Sq.; or Tube to London Bridge or Borough.* ⊘ *Fri. 5 AM–noon.*

Berwick Street is a panacea to the frenzy of Oxford Street and its chain and department stores. The hub of the market is in Berwick Street, but there is an overspill through backstreet Soho, past Raymond's Revue Bar, and onto Rupert Street. For fresh fruit and vegetables, giant slabs of chocolate, Camembert cheese on the edge of over-ripeness, and the odd clothing stalls, this is the way a London market should be, down to the stallholders who compete on who makes the loudest and most ribald way to get their cucumbers and caulis shifted. Behind the bustling stalls, there are pleasures galore: cafés, from greasy spoon to chic bar; delis with fresh meat and game; Borovik's fabrics; natty bespoke tailors; classy, risqué underwear to be found at Agent Provocateur (from Vivienne Westwood's son)—all provide a cosmopolitan, lively, delightfully brassy backdrop. ⊠ *W1. Tube to Oxford Circus or Piccadilly Circus.* ⊘ *Tues. 8–6, Sat. 9–4.*

Brick Lane is not a showcase but more a collection of bric-a-brac, and some feel it's worth a visit for the bagels from the all-night bakery and a host of bargain Bengali curry houses. The old Truman Brewery (Black Eagle Brewery) has also become a trendy retail focus, with the Vibe Bar, a cybercafé, at its hub. Arty types hang out at the Atlantis Art Shop—and Whitechapel Art Gallery is just a block away. From here it is a stone's throw to Spitalfields, the burgeoning designer market, and Columbia Road flower market, where the whole of London converges in late spring to buy trays of cheap flowers for window boxes and gardens. ⊠ *E1. Aldgate East or Shoreditch Tube, Bus 25 to Whitechapel Rd., or Bus 8 to Bethnal Green Rd.* ⊘ *Sun. 8–1.*

Camden Lock Market is the place to visit on a sunny August Sunday if you want your concept of a crowd redefined. Camden is actually several markets gathered around a pair of locks in the Regent's Canal, and it was once very pretty. Now that further stalls and a new faux warehouse have been inserted into the surrounding brick railway buildings, the haphazard charm of the place is largely lost, although the variety of merchandise is mind-blowing—vintage and new clothes (design stars have been discovered here), antiques and junk, jewelry and scarves, candlesticks, ceramics, mirrors, toys. . . . But underneath it's really a date spot for hip teens. The neighborhood is bursting with shops and cafés, and other markets, and it's a whole lot calmer, if stall-free, at midweek. ⊠ *NW1. Tube or Bus 24 or 29 to Camden Town. ⊙ Shops Tues.–Sun. 9:30–5:30, stalls weekends 8–6.*

Camden Passage, despite the name, is not in Camden but a couple of miles away in Islington, a neighborhood first gentrified by media hippies in the '60s. Around 350 antiques dealers set up stalls here Saturdays and Wednesdays, with the surrounding antiques shops open Tuesday to Saturday, 10–5 PM; even in the shops you can try your hand at price negotiation, although prices are generally fair. All in all, this remains a fruitful and picturesque hunting ground. ⊠ *Islington, N1. Bus 19 or 38 or Tube to Angel. ⊙ Wed. and Sat. 8:30–3.*

Greenwich Antiques Market. If you're planning to visit Greenwich, then combine your trip with a wander around this open-air market near St. Alfege Church. You'll find one of the best selections of secondhand and antique clothes in London—quality tweeds and overcoats can be had at amazing prices. The market for antiques is open on weekends only. ⊠ *Greenwich High Rd., SE10. British Rail to New Gate Cross, then Bus 117; or bus direct to Greenwich. ⊙ Antiques, crafts, and clothes weekends 9–5; fruit and vegetables weekdays 9–5.*

Leadenhall Market. The draw here is not so much what you can buy—plants and posh food, mainly—as the building itself. It's a handsome late-Victorian structure, ornate and elaborate, with plenty of atmosphere. ⊠ *Whittington Ave., EC3. Tube to Bank or Monument. ⊙ Weekdays 7–4.*

Petticoat Lane. Actually, Petticoat Lane doesn't exist, and this Sunday clothing and fashion market centers on Middlesex Street, then sprawls in several directions, including northeast to Brick Lane and Spitalfields. Between them, the crammed streets turn up items of dubious parentage (CD players, bikes, car radios), alongside clothes (vintage, new, and just plain tired), jewelry, books, underwear, antiques, woodworking tools, bed linens, jars of pickles, and outright junk in one of London's most entertaining diversions. ⊠ *Middlesex St., E1. ⊙ Sun. 9–2. Tube to Liverpool St., Aldgate, or Aldgate East.*

Portobello Market. London's most famous market still wins the prize for the all-round best. It sits in a most lively and multicultural part of town, the 1,500-odd antiques dealers don't rip you off (although you should haggle where you can), and it stretches over a mile, changing character completely as it goes. The top end (Notting Hill Gate) is antiques-land and more tourist-bound (with shops midweek; don't miss antiquers David and Charles Wainwright [No. 251] and Trude Weaver [No. 71]); the middle is where locals buy fruit and vegetables and hang out in trendy restaurants; the section under the elevated highway called the Westway boasts the best flea market in town; and then it tails off into a giant rummage sale among record stores, vintage-clothing boutiques, and art galleries. The bargains are to be found, here, in Golborne Road (W10) at the Ladbroke Grove end of Portobello. For original French country furniture and other pretty pieces, it is hard to beat. For refreshment, pop into one of the many Portuguese patisseries and cafés dotted around here. The western section of Portobello around the Westbourne Grove end is also worthy of exploration. ⊠ *Portobello Rd., W11. Bus 52 or Tube to Ladbroke Grove or Notting Hill Gate. ⊙ Fruit and vegetables Mon.–Wed. and Fri. 8–5, Thurs. 8–1; antiques Fri. 8–3; both food market and antiques Sat. 6–5.*

Spitalfields. Trendsville has arrived in the form of creative crafts and design shops. The scene at this old 3-acre indoor fruit market, near

Petticoat Lane, is now reminiscent of a more chic Camden Town, before the student crowds descended, and it is home to food, crafts, and clothes stalls; cafés; and performance and sports areas. On Sunday, the place really comes alive, with a host of stalls: beautiful paper lampshades, antique clothing, handmade rugs, soap filled with flowers and fruits, homemade cakes, Portuguese deli foods, and cookware. The resident stores have more beautiful things for body and home (particularly Redhouse). In the center, racks of easels are filled with the cheapest (around £10) original artwork from the Alternative Art Market. For refreshment it's possible to eat from West to East, with Spanish tapas or Thai among the bars and food stalls. Some of the oldest wine in London was recently excavated from the huge earthworks next to the market. The three-centuries-old flagons of Madeira were found in the remains of the Master Gunner's House cellar, destroyed in 1682. What's more, it was declared still lively and well balanced. For directions, *see* Petticoat Lane, *above.* ✉ *Brushfield St., E1.* ☉ *Organic market Fri. and Sun. 10–5; general market weekdays 11–3, Sun. 10–5.*

7 SIDE TRIPS FROM LONDON

Sometimes you really need to get away from Old Smoke, and just because you have only two weeks doesn't mean you won't feel the urge to see trees and sky and stately homes. Take any of these side trips and you'll feel—such is the change of pace you'll experience—as though you added another week to your vacation. England is so much more than its capital—a fact that Londoners tend to forget.

ONDONERS ARE UNDENIABLY LUCKY. Few populaces enjoy such glorious—and easily accessible—options for day-tripping. This chapter presents five of the most popular destinations: Bath, Cambridge, Oxford, Stratford-upon-Avon, and Windsor. Each can easily be done as a day trip but is also well worth considering for an overnight. For travel and visitor information, *see* Side Trips A to Z, *below*.

Updated by
Jacqueline
Brown

BATH

"I really believe I shall always be talking of Bath. . . . I do like it so very much. Oh! who can ever be tired of Bath," wrote Jane Austen in *Northanger Abbey,* and, today, thousands of visitors heartily agree with her. A remarkably unsullied Georgian city, Bath still looks as if John Wood, its chief architect, "Beau" Nash, its principal dandy, and Jane Austen (1775–1817) might be strolling on the promenade here. Stepping out of the train station plumps you right in the center, and Bath is compact enough to explore on foot. A single day is sufficient for you to take in the glorious yellow-stone buildings, tour the Roman baths, and stop for tea, though it will give only a brief hint of the cultural life that continues to thrive in this vibrant place.

A Good Walk

The first sight you come to, having followed signs from the train station, is the **Pump Room and Roman Baths,** which the Romans set about building up around the healing spring of the English goddess Aquae Sulis in AD 60, after wars with the Brits had laid the city to waste. The site became famous as a temple to Minerva, Roman goddess of wisdom. Legend has it that the first taker of these sacred waters was King Lear's leprous father, Prince Bladud, in the 9th century BC. Yes, it was claimed he was cured. The waters can still be taken, and they gush at a constant temperature of 46.5°C (116°F). Below the gorgeous and beautifully restored 18th-century Pump Room (as described in Austen's *Mansfield Park, Emma, Northanger Abbey,* et al.) is a museum of quirky objects found during excavations. ⊠ *Abbey Churchyard,* ☎ *01225/ 477784.* ⊡ *£6.90, combined ticket with Assembly Rooms (☞ below) £8.90.* ☉ *Apr.–Sept., daily 9–6; Oct.–Mar., daily 9:30–5. Last admission 30 mins before closing, but allow at least 75 mins for the museum.*

Opposite the Pump Room and Roman Baths is **Bath Abbey.** This was commissioned by God. Really. The current design came to a bishop in a dream, but it was actually built by the Vertue brothers during the 16th century. In the **Heritage Vaults** is a museum of archaeological finds, with a scale model of 13th-century Bath. Look up at the fan-vaulted ceilings in the nave and the carved angels on the newly restored West Front. *Abbey Churchyard,* ☎ *01225/422462.* ⊡ *Abbey free (suggested donation £2), Heritage Vaults £2.* ☉ *Apr.–Oct., Mon.–Sat. 9–6, Sun. 1–2:30 and 4:30–5:30; Nov.–Mar., Mon.–Sat. 9–4:30, Sun. 1–2:30 and 4:30–5:30. Heritage Vaults Mon.–Sat. 10–4. Abbey may close at short notice for special services.*

NEED A
BREAK?

After wandering around the many nooks, crannies, and secret passageways surrounding the abbey courtyard, take succor in **Sally Lunn's** (⊠ North Parade Passage, ☎ 01225/461634). Popular equally with tourists and locals, this is possibly the world's only tearoom with its own museum. A Sally Lunn is a sweet cross between an English muffin and a brioche, measuring a foot in diameter, toasted and piled with sweet toppings. ⊡ *Museum 30p, free if dining.* ☉ *Mon.–Sat. 10–6, Sun. 11–6.*

East of Bath Abbey, Bridge Street leads to the River Avon and one of the most famous landmarks of the city, **Pulteney Bridge.** This was the great Georgian architect Robert Adam's sole contribution to Bath and is, in its way, as fine as the only other bridge in the world with shops lining either side: the Ponte Vecchio in Florence.

West of Bath Abbey, the colonnades of Bath Street lead to Sawclose and the Georgian Theatre Royal on Westgate Street. Northward from here, along Barton Street and Gay streets, with a sideways look at the gracious Queen Square to the left, is the **Circus.** This pinnacle of architectural achievement is a perfectly circular ring of Bath stone houses, designed by John Wood.

On the east side of the Circus are more thrills for Austen readers: her much-mentioned **Assembly Rooms,** now containing the self-explanatory Museum of Costume. ⊠ Bennett St., 01225/477784. ▢ £4, combined ticket with Roman Baths (☞ above) £8.90. ◯ Daily 10–5. Last admission 30 mins before closing, but allow 1 hr for the museum.

West of the Circus is the most famous sight in Bath, the Royal Crescent, and you can't help but see why. Designed by John Wood the younger, it's perfectly proportioned and beautifully sited, with views sweeping over parkland. A marvelous museum at **Number 1 Royal Crescent** shows life as Beau Nash would have lived it circa 1765. ☎ 01225/ 428126. ▢ £4. ◯ Mid Feb.–Oct., Tues.–Sun. 10:30–5; Nov., Tues.–Sun. 10:30–4. House closed Dec.–mid Feb.

CAMBRIDGE

Having trouble distinguishing the two Ivy League of England college towns, Oxford and Cambridge? That's not surprising, because in the United Kingdom, the names of these two important educational institutions are often elided into the term "Oxbridge," and British people themselves—aside from Oxbridge graduates, of course—think it's another place altogether. Cambridge lies in East Anglia, a quartet of counties consisting of Norfolk, Suffolk, Essex, and Cambridgeshire. It's a city of some 100,000 souls and growing, dominated culturally and architecturally by its famous university—which is divided into colleges— and beautified by parks and gardens and the quietly flowing River Cam. Punting on the Cam is a quintessential Cambridge pursuit, followed by a stroll along the Backs, the quaintly entitled left bank of the Cam, to which Magdalene (pronounced "Maudlin"), St. John's, Trinity, Clare, King's, and Queen's colleges show their beautiful backsides.

Need a key to the city? Think Rupert Brooke, the short-lived World War I–era poet ("There is some corner of a foreign field/That is forever England"), a Cambridgeshire lad, who called his county "The shire for Men who Understand." Cambridge may be one of the most beautiful cities in Britain, but it is no museum. Even if the students are on vacation, there's a strong pulse here, and the city can trace its history back to the 1st century BC, when an Iron Age tribe settled on what's now Castle Hill. By the end of the 16th century, there were 16 colleges; there are now 31.

VISITING THE COLLEGES

College visits are certainly a highlight of a Cambridge tour, but you must remember that these are private homes and workplaces, even out of term. Some are closed to the public, and access to others is restricted to the chapels and dining rooms (called halls) and sometimes the libraries, too (and you are politely requested to refrain from picnicking in the quadrangles). Some colleges charge a small fee for the privilege of nosing around. All are closed during exams, usually from mid-April to late June, when the May Balls are held, and students let down their hair along with whatever else they can find. By far the best way to gain access without annoying anyone is to join a walking tour led by an official Blue Badge guide—in fact, many areas are off-limits unless you do. The two-hour tours leave daily from the Tourist Information Centre (☞ Side Trips A to Z, *below*). Below is a walk that takes in most of the colleges, but it's fine to set off with a map from the local tourist office and just tackle a portion of the city.

A Good Walk

On Trumpington Street is **Peterhouse,** the oldest college, founded in 1284 by the Bishop of Ely. Take a tranquil walk through its former deer park, by the river side of its ivy-clad buildings.

Near Peterhouse is East Anglia's finest art gallery, the **Fitzwilliam Museum.** This contains outstanding collections of art, including several Constable paintings, and antiquities—starring some objects from ancient Egypt. ✉ *Trumpington St.,* ☎ *01223/332900.* ⊠ *Free.* ☉ *Tues.– Sat. 10–5, Sun. 2:15–5.*

Across from Peterhouse is Pembroke College (1347), with delightful gardens and bowling greens and the chapel, young Christopher Wren's first commission. Head down Pembroke Street to reach **Emmanuel College.** John Harvard, a graduate, gave his books and his name to the new world university. A number of the Pilgrims were Emmanuel alumni, and they remembered their alma mater in naming Cambridge, Massachusetts.

Northward from Emmanuel College, along Sidney Street, is **St. John's College.** The second-largest college in Cambridge, St. John's boasts noted alumni (Wordsworth had his rooms here) and two of the finest sights in town—the School of Pythagoras, the oldest house in Cambridge; and a copy of the Bridge of Sighs in Venice that reaches across the Cam to the mock-Gothic New Court (1825), whose white crenellations have earned it the nickname the "wedding cake." From here, it's most pleasant to head south along the river and through the narrow lanes behind the colleges past Clare College, picturesque Clare Bridge, the beautiful Fellows' Gardens, and Trinity Hall to Trinity College.

Trinity College was founded by Henry VIII in 1546 and is the largest of all the colleges. Many of Trinity's features match its size, not least its 17th-century "great court" and the massive gatehouse that houses Great Tom, a giant clock that strikes each hour with high and low notes. Don't miss the wonderful library by Christopher Wren. Alumni include Newton, Byron, Tennyson, Thackeray, and the future King Charles III.

South of Trinity College is **King's College,** site of the world-famous Gothic-style (1446) **King's College Chapel,** which, with its great fan-vaulted roof supported by a delicate tracery of columns, is the final and, some would say, most glorious flowering of Perpendicular Gothic in Britain. "The noblest barn in Europe," it's truly a lovely sight and the home of the famous choristers. To cap it all, Rubens's *Adoration of the Magi* is secreted behind the altar.

Reached along the Backs and tucked away on Queen's Road, **Queens' College** (after Margaret, queen of Henry VI, and Elizabeth, queen of Edward IV) was built around 1448 and is one of Cambridge's most eye-catching colleges. Enter over the **Mathematical Bridge;** Isaac Newton fashioned this arched wooden structure without benefit of any binding save gravity. Unfortunately, the curious scholars couldn't leave well enough alone and dismantled it to find Newton's secret; they failed and had to nail it back together like any other bridge. Be sure to take in the half-timber President's Lodge. In from the river is Peterhouse. Along King's Parade is **Corpus Christi College.** If you see only one quadrangle, make it the medieval Old Court here.

OXFORD

To get Oxford fixed in your mind's eye, say the phrase "Dreaming Spires" over and over—all the tour guides do—and think *Brideshead Revisited,* Sebastian Flyte, and Evelyn Waugh, in general. Think Rhodes scholar—President Clinton was one—and think J. R. R. Tolkien, Percy Bysshe Shelley, Oscar Wilde, W. H. Auden, and C. S. Lewis. (Wait— wasn't he in Cambridge? Yes, he *studied* here but *taught* there.) Two more recent graduates are Margaret Thatcher and Kris Kristofferson. Oxford University is older than Cambridge, dating from the 12th century (only the Sorbonne in Paris is older), but once again, newcomers need to learn that the university is not one unified campus but a collection of many colleges scattered across the city.

Oxford is a bigger and much more cosmopolitan city than Cambridge, though here, too, there is no shortage of hushed quadrangles, chapels, and gardens. Bikes are propped, unlocked, against wrought-iron railings, and punting is popular along the Cherwell (rent one yourself from the foot of Magdalen Bridge), but Oxford is also a major industrial center, with large car and steel plants based in its suburbs.

VISITING THE COLLEGES

The same concerns for people's work and privacy hold here as in Cambridge (☞ *above*). Guided city walking tours leave the Oxford Information Centre (☞ Side Trips A to Z, *below*) several times a day in summer.

A Good Walk

This tour encompasses much of the city; for those with limited time, get a detailed map from the tourist office and focus on selected sights.

Any tour of Oxford should begin at its very center—a pleasant walk of 10 minutes or so east of the train station—with the splendid university church of **St. Mary the Virgin,** on High Street. From its 14th-century tower, you can get a Cinerama view of the entire city. The church's interior is crowded with 700 years' worth of funeral monuments. Just north of St. Mary the Virgin is one of Oxford's most famous sights, the **Radcliffe Camera,** which holds the august **Bodleian Library.** Not much of this—one of the planet's best book collections— is on view to non-dons, but you can see part of the 2-million plus-volume library on a tour of the Camera—a magnificent building topped by one of Britain's biggest domes—and at the former Divinity School, where there's a changing exhibit of manuscripts and rare books, and a magnificent Gothic interior. ⊠ *Broad St.,* ☎ *01865/277224.* ⊡ *£3.50, extended tour £7 (call to pre-book).* ⊙ *Tour mid-Mar.–Oct., weekdays at 10:30, 11:30, 2, and 3; Nov.–mid-Mar., weekdays at 2 and 3; Sat.-morning tours available (call for hrs).*

A minute's stroll from the Radcliffe Camera is the **Sheldonian Theatre.** Built in 1663, the Sheldonian was Sir Christopher Wren's first major work, modeled on a Roman amphitheater. Graduation ceremonies are still held here, entirely in Latin, as befits the building's spirit. Outside is one of Oxford's most striking sights—a metal fence topped with stone busts of 18 Roman emperors (modern reproductions of the originals, which were eaten away by pollution). ⊠ *Radcliffe Sq.,* ☎ *01865/ 277299.* ⊡ *£1.50.* ⊙ *Apr.–mid-Nov., Mon.–Sat. 10–12:30 and 2–4:30; mid-Nov.–Mar., Mon.–Sat. 10–12:30 and 2–3:30. Closed for 10 days* *at Christmas and Easter; also closed for degree ceremonies and events (call ahead to check).*

Along Broad Street, at the Cornmarket Street end, you can stop in at the **Oxford Story.** Take your place at a medieval student's desk as it trundles through 800 years of Oxford history. See Edmund Halley discover that comet! Watch the Scholastica's Day Riot of 1355! You can choose grown-up's or kid's commentary. ⊠ *6 Broad St.,* ☎ *01865/ 790055.* 🖭 *£5.70.* ⊙ *Apr.–June and Sept.–Oct., daily 9:30–5; July– Aug., daily 9–6; Nov.–Mar., weekdays 9–4:30, weekends 10:30–5.*

As you head westward into Cornmarket Street is the **Oxford Union,** at St. Michael's Street, where budding political heroes gave their earliest tirades. You can admire the Pre-Raphaelite (Morris, Rossetti, Burne-Jones) murals depicting the Arthurian legends.

Broad Street leads into Giles Street and prestigious **Balliol College** (1263). Outside the new (Victorian) college gates—marking the place where Archbishop Cranmer and Bishops Latimer and Ridley were burnt for their Protestant beliefs in 1555, during Mary I's reign—is a cross in the sidewalk made in cobblestones. The original college gates (which are rumored to have witnessed the scorching) hang in the library passage, between the inner and outer quadrangles. **Trinity College Chapel,** beside Balliol, is more of an architectural gem, with some superb wood carvings of Grinling Gibbons, a 17th-century master whose work is found in many an English stately home.

Westward from Giles Street, Beaumont Street is the site of the **Ashmolean Museum,** Britain's oldest public museum, in which some of the world's most precious things are stashed, all the property of the university. See Egyptian, Greek, and Roman artifacts; Michelangelo drawings; European silverware and ceramics; Asian paintings; and more. There is a café that serves snacks and meals to the culturally replete. ⊠ *Beaumont St.,* ☎ *01865/278000.* 🖭 *Free.* ⊙ *Tues.–Sat. 10–5, Sun. 2–5.*

North and across St. Giles Road from the Ashmolean Museum is **St. John's College.** This one was founded in 1555 and is worth visiting for its very large and lovely gardens.

The leading college of the southern half of Oxford is **Christ Church College,** found along the major road of St. Aldate's. Called "the House" by its modest members, Christ Church boasts the largest quadrangle in town, named **Tom Quad,** after the over-6-ton bell in the gate tower. This is where Charles Dodgson, better known as Lewis Carroll, was a math don; a shop opposite the meadows in St. Aldate's was the inspiration for the shop in *Through the Looking Glass.* Don't miss the 800-year-old chapel, nor the medieval dining hall, with its portraits of former students—John Wesley, William Penn, and 14 prime ministers. Also go to the **Canterbury Quadrangle,** whose gallery contains works by Leonardo, Michelangelo, and Rubens.

STRATFORD-UPON-AVON

Stratford-upon-Avon has become very adept at accommodating the hordes of visitors who come hoping for a taste of Shakespeare (1564–1616) and getting more than they bargained for. Stratford is a handsome town in its own right, punctuated with those distinctive black-and-white Tudor half-timber buildings that survive from its 16th-century heyday as a crafts and trading center. Shakespeare's father participated in that boom—he was a glove maker and wool dealer who rose to the rank of town bailiff. There are still fine shopping opportunities, including the Friday market, but what we're really all here for is Shakespeare.

It's difficult to avoid feeling like a herd animal as you board the Shake-speare bus, but there is something to be said for taking advantage of packaged tours like **Stratford and the Shakespeare Story,** which allows you to come and go as you please around the five Shakespeare Prop-erties, especially if your time is limited. If you can manage an overnight stay, taking in a production at one of the three Stratford theaters of the Royal Shakespeare Company (known as the RSC) will deepen your immersion in the Bard's works.

A Good Walk

Most Stratford visitors begin at **Shakespeare's Birthplace Museum.** With the Shakespeare Centre inside, this is the perfect place to start your Bard odyssey. The half-timber building in which William grew up has been a national memorial since 1847, and it is now split in half: one part is a re-creation of a typical home of the time, while the other contains a new ex-hibit about the historical characters in the Shakespeare canon, plus a history of the house itself. ⊠ *Henley St.,* ☎ *01789/204016.* ☜ *£4.90, combined ticket with Shakespeare Birthplace Trust properties (Nash's House; Hall's Croft; Anne Hathaway's Cottage; Mary Arden's House; allow at least 4 hrs, but ticket is valid for one year) £11, 3 in-town properties (not in-cluding Anne Hathaway's Cottage and Mary Arden's House) £7.50.* ☉ *Mar.–Oct., Mon.–Sat. 9–5, Sun. 10–5; Nov.–Feb., daily 9:30–4.*

High Street, which runs into Chapel Street and then Church Street, is the center road of Stratford. On the corner of Chapel Street and Chapel Lane is **Nash's House,** which belonged to Thomas Nash, first husband of Shakespeare's granddaughter, Elizabeth Hall, and now houses an exhibit charting the history of Stratford against a backdrop of period furniture and tapestries. On the grounds of Nash's House is **New Place,** the home where the Bard spent his last years and died in 1616. An Elizabethan knot garden of flower beds and topiary is set around the last remains of the house. (It was pulled down by the last owner in an attempt to stop the tide of visitors.) ⊠ *Chapel St.,* ☎ *01789/ 292325.* ☜ *£3.30, combined ticket with Shakespeare's Birthplace Trust properties £11.* ☉ ☞ *Shakespeare's Birthplace, above.*

Along Chapel Street is one of the most picturesque set pieces of Strat-ford—starting with the Guild Chapel, Schoolhouse, and Guildhall with Almshouses for the poor. Master Shakespeare learned "little Latin and less Greek" at **King Edward's Grammar School,** which is still a school but can be visited by prior arrangement (☎ 01789/293351), generally out of school hours. The Chapel, which is entered around the corner on Chapel Lane, is also used by students but is often open daily 9–5.

On the venerable road called Old Town you'll find Stratford's most beautiful Tudor town house, **Hall's Croft.** This was—almost definitely—the home of Shakespeare's daughter, Susanna, and her husband, Dr. John Hall. It's charmingly outfitted, complete with furniture of the pe-riod and the doctor's dispensary, and the walled garden is delightful. ⊠ *Old Town,* ☎ *01789/292107.* ☜ *£3.30, combined ticket with Shakespeare's Birthplace Trust properties £11.* ☉ *Mar.–Oct., Mon.–Sat. 9:30–5, Sun. 10–5; Nov.–Feb., Mon.–Sat. 10–4, Sun. 10:30–4.*

At the end of Old Town is "Shakespeare's church," **Holy Trinity,** on Trinity Street along the banks of the Avon and fronted by a beautiful avenue of lime trees. Here, in the chancel, the Bard is buried. The bust of Shakespeare is thought to be an authentic likeness, executed a few years after his death.

Perfectly positioned on the banks of the Avon not far from Holy Trin-ity church (☞ *above*), the **Royal Shakespeare Theatre** is where the Royal Shakespeare Company lives outside London, mounting several productions each season. The design of the smaller **Swan Theatre**, in the same building, is based on the original Elizabethan Globe. It's best to book well in advance, but day-of-performance tickets are nearly always available. Tours take place around performances, so call ahead. ⊠ *Waterside, Stratford-upon-Avon, CV37 6BB,* ☎ *01789/295623 ticket line; 01789/412602 tours.* ⊙ *Tours weekdays at 1:30 and 5:30; Sun. at noon, 1, 2, and 3; matinee days (usually Thurs., Sat.) at 11:30 and 5:30.*

STRATFORD ENVIRONS

The two remaining stops on the Shakespeare trail are just outside Stratford. **Anne Hathaway's Cottage** (☎ 01789/292100), the early home of the playwright's wife, is possibly the most picturesque abode in Britain—a rather substantial thatched cottage, it has been restored to reflect the comfortable middle-class Hathaway life. You can walk—it's just over a mile from downtown Stratford in Shottery. Admission is £3.90, or with one of those Shakespeare's Birthplace Trust properties combined tickets. It's also on the Stratford and the Shakespeare Story tour itinerary (☞ Guided Tours *in* Side Trips A to Z, *below*). **Mary Arden's House** (☎ 01789/293455) is probably where Shakespeare's mother was raised; you will need another £4.40 or the combined Shakespeare's Birthplace Trust properties ticket.

Some 8 mi out of town, **Warwick Castle** fulfills anyone's most clichéd Camelot daydreams, being a medieval, fortified, much-restored, castellated, moated, landscaped (by Capability Brown) castle, complete with dungeons and a torture chamber, state rooms, and the occasional battle reenactment. ⊠ *Warwick,* ☎ *01926/495421, 01926/406600 24-hr information line.* ⊡ *£9.50.* ⊙ *Apr.–Oct., daily 10–6; Nov.–Mar., daily 10–5.*

WINDSOR

The star sight of this quiet Berkshire town is, without doubt, the largest inhabited castle in the world—Windsor Castle. Windsor Great Park, however, shouldn't be forgotten; Eton College, England's most famous public school, with its old village, is also a lovely walk across the Thames; and there's the kid's paradise of Legoland.

Windsor is the only royal residence to have been in continuous royal use since the days of William the Conqueror, who chose this site to build a timber stockade soon after his conquest of Britain in 1066. It was Edward III in the 1300s who really founded the castle, building the Norman gateway, the great round tower, and new state apartments. Charles II restored the State Apartments during the 1600s and, during the 1820s, George IV—that most extravagant of kings with a mania for building—converted what was still essentially a medieval castle into the royal palace you see today. The queen uses Windsor a lot, spending most weekends here, often joined by family and friends. She's here when the Royal Standard is flown above the Round Tower but not when you see the Union Jack. Be sure to arrive early at the main entrance, as lines can be long (you will also need to line up again for both the State Apartments and the Dolls' House).

WINDSOR CASTLE

The massive citadel occupies 13 acres, but the first part you notice on entering is the **Round Tower,** on top of which the standard is flown and at the base of which is the 11th-century Moat Garden. Passing under the portcullis at the **Norman Gate,** you reach the **Upper Ward,** the quadrangle containing the State Apartments—which you may tour when the queen is out—and the sovereign's Private Apartments. Processions for foreign heads of state and other ceremonies go on here, as does the

Changing of the Guard, when the queen is in. A short walk takes you to the **Lower Ward,** where the high point is the magnificent **St. George's Chapel,** symbolic and actual guardian of the Order of the Garter, the highest chivalric order in the land, founded in 1348 by Edward III. Ten sovereigns are buried in the chapel—a fantastic Perpendicular Gothic vision, 230 ft long, complete with gargoyles, buttresses, banners, swords, and choir stalls.

The **State Apartments** are grander than Buckingham Palace's and have the added attraction of a few gems from the queen's vast art collection: choice canvases by Rubens, Rembrandt, Van Dyck, Gainsborough, Canaletto, and Holbein; da Vinci drawings; Gobelin tapestries; and limewood carvings by Grinling Gibbons. The entrance is through a grand hall holding cases crammed with precious china—some still used for royal banquets. Don't miss the outsize suit of armor in the armory, made for Henry VIII. The views across to Windsor Great Park, the remains of a former royal hunting forest, are magnificent, too. One unmissable treat—and not only for children—is **Queen Mary's Dolls' House,** a 12:1 scale, seven-story palace, complete with electricity, running water, and working elevators, designed in 1924 by Sir Edwin Lutyens. The detail is incredible—for example, some of the miniature books in the library are by Kipling, Conan Doyle, Thomas Hardy, and G. K. Chesterton, written by the great authors in their own hand. The diminutive wine bottles hold the real thing, too.

A 1992 fire started in the queen's private chapel and totally gutted some of the State Apartments. A swift rescue effort meant that, miraculously, hardly any works of art were lost, and a £37 million effort has restored the Grand Reception Room, the Green and Crimson drawing rooms, and the State and Octagonal dining rooms to their former, if not greater, glory. ⊠ *Windsor Castle,* ☎ *01753/868286, 01753/831118 recorded information with opening hours for current month.* ⊡ *£10; £8.50 Sun.* ☉ *Mar.–Oct., daily 10–5:30 (last admission at 4); Nov.– Feb., daily 10–4 (last admission at 3); St. George's Chapel closed Sun.*

SIDE TRIPS A TO Z

Arriving and Departing

All five of these places are best reached by train. Be sure to plan on an early start for all these side trips—if going by train or bus, it's a good idea to check schedules ahead of time.

By Bus
National Express coach lines (☎ 0870/580–8080) runs coaches from Victoria Coach Station (⊠ Buckingham Palace Rd., SW1) to four of the destinations. The journey time to **Bath Spa** is three hours; coaches run about every two hours. To **Cambridge** the coaches take two hours and run hourly. Several companies (including National Express) operate services to **Oxford** from Victoria Coach Station, so buses leave every 20 minutes or so. The trip takes 1 hour, 40 minutes. It takes 2 hours, 20 minutes to go to **Stratford-upon-Avon,** and there are eight coaches daily.

To **Windsor,** take the **Green Line Travel** (☎ 020/7668–7261) bus, which leaves from the Green Line Coach Station (Bullied Way, Eccleston Bridge, SW1), behind Victoria train station, *not* from Victoria Coach Station itself. Make sure you catch the fast direct service, which takes around 1 hour and runs hourly; the stopping services take up to 1 hour, 30 minutes or more.

By Train

Trains from **Paddington Station** (☎ 08457/484950, 0161/236–3522 from overseas) will take you on any of these side trips. **Bath Spa** is easily reached by hourly trains from Paddington Station (about 1 hr, 25 mins' journey time). Trains to **Cambridge** leave King's Cross Station and Liverpool Street Station every hour and take an hour. Hourly trains from Paddington Station get to **Oxford** in 55 minutes. For **Stratford-upon-Avon,** try to catch the direct train each morning from Paddington Station, or else you'll be doomed to at least one change, at Leamington Spa. There are two direct trains back from Stratford each afternoon, too, and the journey time is 2 hours, 20 minutes. **Windsor** is easy to reach by train, either from Waterloo direct to Windsor and Eton Riverside (50 mins) or from Paddington to Windsor Central, changing at Reading (45 mins); there are two trains per hour on each route.

Contacts and Resources

Guided Tours

Many people like to see Stratford from the top of an open-top double-decker bus, and the **Stratford and the Shakespeare Story Tour** run by Guide Friday is one of the better choices. It allows you to alight and reboard at any of the Bard sights on a ticket valid all day—a particularly handy mode of transport, as two of the five sights are out of town. You can pick up tours near the TIC at the Pen & Parchment pub, Bridge Foot. ✉ *14 Rother St.,* ☎ *01789/294466.* ✐ *£8 Stratford only, combined ticket with Warwick Castle £15. Note: If you have a London Pride tour ticket, you can get a £3 reduction on the Guide Friday tour, and vice versa.* ☉ *Tour May–Sept., daily every 15 mins; Oct.–Nov. and mid-Feb.–Apr., daily every 30 mins; late Nov.–mid-Feb., daily every 30 mins until 3.*

Visitor Information

The **Bath Tourist Information Centre** (☎ 01225/477101) is on Bath Street in the Colonnades.

Cambridge Tourist Information Centre is on Wheeler Street, an extension of Benet Street, off King's Parade (☎ 01223/322640).

The **Oxford Information Centre** is in the Old School, Gloucester Green (☎ 01865/726871).

Stratford Tourist Information Centre is at Bridge Foot, by the bridge (☎ 01789/293127). The **Royal Shakespeare Company (RSC)** has a ticket line (☎ 01789/295623).

Windsor's **Tourist Information Centre** (☎ 01753/743900) is in Central Station.

8 BACKGROUND AND ESSENTIALS

Portrait of London

Books and Videos

Chronology

Smart Travel Tips A to Z

THE CITY OF VILLAGES: WHAT'S WHERE

London is an enormous city—600 square mi—on a tiny island, hosting about 7 million Londoners, one-eighth of the entire population of England, Scotland, and Wales, but to many travelers, it never *really* feels big. It is fashioned on a different scale from other capital cities, as if, given the English penchant for modesty and understatement, it felt embarrassed by its size. Each of the 32 boroughs that compose the whole has its own character, lore, and rhythm. There is the heraldic splendor of Westminster, the chic of artistic Chelsea, the architectural elegance of Belgravia and Mayfair, the cosmopolitan charm of Soho, and the East End, home base of the cockney—to name just a few. You begin to wonder if there actually is such a person as a generic Londoner. Stay here long enough, and Professor Higgins's feat of deducing Eliza Dolittle's very street of birth from the shape of her vowels will seem like nothing special. It's a cliché, but London really is a city of villages.

London's contrasts can best be savored by strolling from one district to another. First pick a starting point such as Piccadilly Circus, which the British think of as the hub of the universe. Keeping your wits about you—the Circus is a swirl of traffic surrounded by grand Edwardian-era buildings—face in the direction of the area of central London you want to explore, and start moving. To the north runs Regent Street, curving up one side of ritzy, mostly residential Mayfair. To the south is Lower Regent Street, leading toward Whitehall, the parks, and the palaces. To the east are Shaftesbury Avenue and Leicester Square, for theaters and Soho; to the west is Piccadilly itself, heading out to Hyde Park and Knightsbridge. This is also a great place to board a double-decker sightseeing bus—just remember to have some sort of protective wrap handy: atop these buses it's *always* windy.

Westminster and Royal London

No matter how you first approach London—historically, geographically, emotionally—all things start at Westminster, one of the truly ancient centers of the city. There is as much history in these few acres as there is in many complete cities. The best show staged for free is in the world's most renowned ego chamber, the House of Commons. Then there is Westminster Abbey, crammed with memorials and monuments to the great, the famous, and the totally forgotten (do not allow your search for noted names to blind you to the spectacular Gothic splendor surrounding you). Whitehall is both an avenue and the heartbeat of the British government; here is the prime minister's official residence, No. 10 Downing Street, and the Horse Guards, where two mounted sentries of the queen's guard provide a memorable image. Whitehall leads to Trafalgar Square and the incomparable National Gallery (art treasures of a more modern ilk lie in the Tate Galleries, Tate Britain and Tate Modern). From the grand Admiralty Arch, the Mall leads straight to Buckingham Palace, as unprepossessing on the outside as it is sumptuous inside (as the summer tours now let you see). Naturally, in a district that regularly witnesses the pomp and pageantry of royal occasions, the streets are wide and the vistas are long. With beautifully kept St. James's Park at its center, the Westminster area exudes dignity and offers frequent glimpses of pinnacles and towers over treetops and, of course, the deep tones of Big Ben counting off the quarter hours.

Belgravia

Just a short carriage ride from Buckingham Palace is London's most splendidly aristocratic enclave: Belgravia, a grande-dame neighborhood of block after block of grand, porticoed mansions. Built in the mid-1800s, it is untouched by neon, with an authentic vintage patina. Most of its streets are lined with terraced row houses, all painted Wedgwood-china white (to signify they remain the property of the Dukes of Westminster). Pedigree-proud locations include Belgrave Square, Grosvenor Crescent, and Belgrave Place, but also check out the chic alleyways, called "mews" from the time when they housed Milord's horse and carriage. Although Belgravia remains exclusively residential, and therefore off the usual tourist path, no other spot in London will make you feel so much like warbling "On the Street Where You Live," just as Freddy Eynsford-Hill sang in *My Fair Lady*.

Bloomsbury

The literary set that made the name Bloomsbury world famous has left hardly a trace, but this remains the heart of learned London. The University of London is here; so are the Law Courts, and the British Museum—home of the Elgin Marbles, the Rosetta Stone, and the Magna Carta. With the British Library parked just north at St. Pancras, a greater number of books can probably be found in Bloomsbury than in all the rest of London. Virginia Woolf and T. S. Eliot would be pleased to note that some of London's most beautiful domestic architecture, elegant houses that would have been familiar to Dr. Johnson, still line the area's prim squares. At one, Charles Dickens worked on *Oliver Twist* at a tall upright clerk's desk.

Bloomsbury is really part of Holborn, the core of Legal London. The Inns of Court are the finest group of historic buildings in the city in an almost unspoiled setting—the closest thing to the spirit of Oxford that London has to offer. In Holborn, you'll also find Sir John Soane's Museum, a mansion that whisks you back to the mid-1800s.

Chelsea

Chelsea has always beckoned to free-thinkers and fashion-fringers—from Sir Thomas More to Isadora Duncan (she couldn't find a place to stay her first night, so she decamped to the graveyard at Chelsea Old Church, which natives *still* insist is a lovely place to stay). Major sights include Christopher Wren's magisterial Royal Hospital—now the site of the Chelsea Flower Show—and Cheyne Walk, where Henry James and Dante Gabriel Rossetti once lived. Now an extremely expensive place to live (through parted curtains you may glimpse rooms of exquisite taste), the area on Saturdays continues to draw an army of trendaholics to King's Road, whose boutiques gave birth to the paisleyed '60s and the pink-headed-punk '70s.

The City

Known as "the Square Mile," the City is to London what Wall Street is to Manhattan. And as the site of the Celtic settlement the Romans called Londinium, this is the oldest part of London. Unfortunately, thanks to blocks of high-rise apartments and steel skyscrapers, it now looks like the newest part. Yet within and around the capital-C City are some of London's most memorable attractions—St. Paul's Cathedral, the storybook Tower Bridge, and the Royal Shakespeare Company (at the Barbican Centre). Charles and Diana tied the knot at St. Paul's but they could have found other equally beautiful options here, including St. Bride's (its distinctive multitiered spire gave rise to today's wedding cakes), St. Giles-without-Cripplegate, and St. Mary-le-Bow. At the east border of the City is the legendary Tower of London, England's most perfectly preserved medieval fortress, where Sir Thomas More, Anne Boleyn, and the young Princes of the Bloody Tower all met untimely ends.

Covent Garden

In not much more than a decade, Covent Garden—which lies just to the east of Soho—has gone from a down-at-the-heels district to one of the busiest, most raffishly enjoyable parts of the city. Continental-style open-air cafés create a very un-English atmosphere. Warehouses, once cavernous and grim, now accommodate fashion boutiques and a huge variety of shops favored by the "trendoisie." A network of narrow streets, arcades, and pedestrian malls, the area is dominated by the Piazza—scene of a food market in the 1830s and a flower market in the 1870s. Today the indoor-outdoor complex overflows with clothing shops and crafts stalls, and the updated entrance to the Royal Opera House opens onto the Piazza.

The East End

In the East End, you'll find sights and sounds that are as much a part of the real London as a November fog. Its 19th-century slums—immortalized by Charles Dickens and the evocative etchings of Gustave Doré—are a relic of the past. Today the area possesses a haunting beauty and a warm spirit of humor and friendliness. Sundays you'll find 21st-century versions of the medieval fair: Spitalfields Market and Petticoat Lane. Other fascinating sights include the Geffrye Museum—an overlooked venue of wonderful historic interiors—Hawksmoor's Christ Church, and the Blind Beggar, the Victorian den of iniquity where Salvation Army founder William Booth was moved to preach his first sermon. Off the main thoroughfare, tap into the true pulse of East End life by exploring the lanes and alleys that still make up one of the world's most fascinating melting pots. If you can fit it in, take one of the evening walking tours that trace the footsteps of the infamous Jack the Ripper; at night, these mean streets still seem shrouded in a Dickensian aura.

Greenwich

A quick 8-mi jaunt down the Thames will bring you past the National Maritime Museum and the *Cutty Sark* to Greenwich's Old Royal Observatory, where, if time stood still, all the world's timepieces would be off. When you tire of straddling the hemispheres at the Greenwich Meridian, take a stroll through the acres of parkland that cover the area or, on weekends, the crafts and antiques markets.

Sir Christopher Wren's Royal Naval College and Inigo Jones's Queen House both scale architectural heights, while Richard Rogers' Millennium Dome encapsulates modern style, for better or worse. The pretty streets of Greenwich Village house numerous bookstores and antiques shops.

Hampstead

One of the great glories of England is the English village, and on the northern outskirts of London you'll find one of the most fetching: Hampstead. Today, its classic Georgian houses, its picturesque tidiness, and its expensive French delicatessens attract personages from the arts and wealthy entrepreneurs. For sheer pleasure, exploring Hampstead is hard to top, as an amble along Church Walk—possibly the finest (and certainly the prettiest) row of 18th-century houses in London—will prove. London's most beautiful painting by Vermeer is on view at Kenwood House (whose park hosts grand concerts and fireworks in the summer), and the latest Mod Brit artistic scandals are to be often seen at the Saatchi Collection. Here, too, are the Freud Museum and the Keats House; why not visit the garden where the poet penned his immortal "Ode to a Nightingale"? You can go bird-watching in the 800-plus emerald acres of Hampstead Heath. In the nearby neighborhood of St. John's Wood, you can visit Abbey Road to snap the famed crossing outside the studios where John, Paul, George, and Ringo recorded nearly all their music.

Hyde Park, Kensington Gardens

When in need of elbow room, Londoners head for Hyde Park and Kensington Gardens. They form an open swath across central London; together with St. James's Park, Green Park, and Buckingham Palace Gardens, they make up almost 600 beauty-filled acres that offer a taste of serene remoteness from the great city. The handsome trees and quiet walks will refresh you as thoroughly as, centuries ago, these grounds refreshed Henry VIII after a hard day's shenanigans. In the Regency era, splendid horseflesh and equipages were the grand attraction; today, the soapbox orators at Hyde Park Corner (most oratorical on Sunday mornings) remain grand entertainment. Sooner or later, however, everyone heads to the Long Water in Kensington Gardens for one of London's most beloved sights: the Peter Pan statue (E. M. Barrie had the sprite living on a nearby island). Then circumnavigate the Round Pond, or swim in the Serpentine, or try to catch a glimpse of the Household Cavalry on Rotten Row.

Knightsbridge and Kensington

Within the district's cavalcade of streets lined with decorous houses are tucked-away corners—small squares that would not be out of place in a sleepy cathedral town; delightful pubs nestled away in back lanes; and antiques shops, their windows aglow with the luminous colors of oil paintings. Not surprisingly, the capital's snazziest department stores are also here, Harrods and Harvey Nichols. Head first for the area's main attraction, the great museum complex of South Kensington. Raphael and Constable canvases, Ossie Clark couture, and William Morris chairs all beckon at the Victoria and Albert Museum, whose forte is the decorative arts and whose predominant audience is an especially decorative crowd. Next to the V&A come two museums devoted to science, including the Natural History Museum. Most delightful are two historic homes: Leighton House, Lord Leighton's stunning Persian extravaganza, and the Linley Sambourne House, whose elegant Edwardian interiors were featured in *A Room with a View*. Regroup at Kensington Palace—its state rooms and royal dress collection are open to view—then repair to its elegant Orangery for a pot of Earl Grey.

Notting Hill and Holland Park

These are two of London's most fashionable, coveted residential areas. Notting Hill, around Portobello Road, is a trendsetting square mile of multiethnicity, galleries, small and exciting shops, and see-and-be-seen-in restaurants. The style-watching media dubbed the natives—musicians, novelists, and fashion plates—"Notting Hillbillies." If Notting Hill is for the young, neighboring Holland Park is entirely the opposite—its leafy streets are full of expensive white-stucco Victorians that lead to bucolic Holland Park itself.

Regent's Park

Helping to frame the northern border of the city, Regent's Park is home to the much-loved zoo and the much-loved Regent's Park Open-Air Theatre. A walk around the perimeter of the park is a must for devotees of classical architecture; the payoff is a view of John Nash's Terraces, a grandiose series of white-stucco terraced houses, built around 1810 for the "People of Quality" who demanded London homes as nearly as possible resembling their grand country estates. In summer, be sure to take in the rose-bedecked Queen Mary's Gardens. Next, head over to the open-air theater for, perhaps, a picture-perfect performance of *A Midsummer Night's Dream*. Year-round, the park is a favorite spot for mothers with strollers, joggers, and hand-holding senior citizens enjoying the fresh air. Watch out for airborne objects—softballs, footballs, and cricket balls.

St. James's and Mayfair

St. James's and Mayfair form the core of the West End, the city's smartest and most desirable central area—St. James's to the south of Piccadilly and north of the Mall, Mayfair to the north of Piccadilly and south of Oxford Street. Neither is stuffed with must-sees, though there is no shortage of history and gorgeous architecture, but they *are* custom-built for window-shopping, expansive strolling, and ogling the lifestyles of London's rich and famous—18th-and 21st-century versions. Although many will say Mayfair is only a state of mind, the heart of Mayfair has shifted from the 19th-century's Park Lane to Carlos Place and Mount Street. Of course, the shops of New and Old Bond streets lure the wealthy, but the window shopping is next best to the real thing and is free. Mayfair is primarily residential, so its homes are off-limits except for two satisfyingly grand houses: Apsley House, the Duke of Wellington's home, built by Robert Adam in 1771 and once known as No. 1, London, and, on gorgeous Manchester Square, the Wallace Collection, situated in a palatial town house filled with old master paintings and fine French furniture. The district of St. James's—named after the centuries-old palace that lies at its center—remains the ultimate enclave of the old-fashioned gentleman's London. Here you'll find Pall Mall, with its many noted clubs, including the Reform Club—where Jules Verne's Phileas Fogg wagered he could go around the world in 80 days—and Jermyn Street, where you can follow in the Duke of Windsor's sartorial footsteps by purchasing a half-dozen shirts at Turnbull & Asser.

Soho and Theatreland

Once the setting for London's red-light district, Soho these days is more stylish than seedy, and it is now home to film and record bigwigs (Sir Paul McCartney's offices are here). The area is not especially rich architecturally, but it is nonetheless intriguing. The density of Continental residents around quaint Soho Square means some of London's best restaurants—whether pricey Italian, budget Chinese, or the latest opening—are in the vicinity. Shaftesbury Avenue cuts through the southern part of Soho; this is Theatreland—home to almost 50 West End theaters and a beloved of those who love Shakespeare, Maggie Smith, and *Phantom*. To the south of Theatreland lies Leicester Square, London's answer to Times Square, and Charing Cross Road, the bibliophile's dream.

The South Bank

You won't say "How very British" in this section of town across the Thames from London Bridge, which was totally rebuilt after the bombs of World War II flattened the remains of medieval Southwark (only a few stones of the Bishop of Winchester's Palace still stand). If William Shakespeare returned today, however, he would be delighted to find a complete recon-

struction of his Globe Theatre, which was inaugurated in 1996, not far from where the original closed in 1642. In fact, this side of the Thames—walk along the riverside embankment for great views of the city—has become a perch for diehard culture vultures: the Design Museum is here, and the gigantic Bankside Power Station building (hard by the Globe) has been refurbished as the Tate Modern. Also here is the South Bank Arts Complex—the country's chief arts center—with its important Museum of the Moving Image, Royal National Theatre, and Royal Festival Hall, and London's culinary hot spot, the OXO Tower Restaurant and Brasserie. And who could resist the London Dungeon—a waxwork extravaganza full of scenes featuring plenty of blood-'n'-guts and medieval dismemberments—where "a perfectly horrible experience" is guaranteed. Now towering over all is the London Eye, the tallest Ferris wheel in Europe. Under its shadow in Jubilee Gardens is the new Waterloo Pier, where you can catch ferries that plythe Thames.

The Thames Upstream

London has been Britain's power center for centuries, so it is only natural that many visitable places associated with royalty and the ruling establishment—among them, Chiswick, Kew Gardens, Osterley Park, Richmond, and Putney—should be close to the capital. The link between London and these idyllic retreats is Father Thames—who offers a river cruise as a particularly nice way to escape the city on a sweltering summer day. These palaces and country houses are enveloped with serenity and rolling greenery, which explains the astronomical prices that some of the local real estate commands. Stroll around and just enjoy the rural air or find your way out of the famous maze at Hampton Court Palace, England's version of Versailles.

WHAT TO READ & WATCH BEFORE YOU GO

London has been the focus of countless books and essays, and although there are enough books about the city to fill a library, it currently has no Richard de Combray (who recently eulogized Venice so beautifully) or Peter Mayle (who has made Provence come alive again). For sonorous eloquence, you still must reach back more than half a century to Henry James's *English Hours* and Virginia Woolf's *The London Scene*. Today, most suggested reading lists begin with V. S. Pritchett's *London Perceived* and H. V. Morton's *In Search of London*, both decades old. Two excellent books with a general compass have appeared within the last decade, however: John Russell's *London*—a sumptuously illustrated art book—and Christopher Hibbert's *In London: The Biography of a City*. With London's renaissance so much in the news these days, further tomes, it is hoped, will appear on the horizon. One current book that does much to guide the reader around modern London follows the footsteps of the Fab Four: Piet Schreuders's *The Beatles' London*.

That noted, there are books galore on the various facets of the city. *The Art and Architecture of London* by Ann Saunders is fairly comprehensive. A must for anyone who wants to track down the most beautifully historic sites of the city, *Inside London: Discovering the Classic Interiors of London*, by Joe Friedman and Peter Aprahamian, features magnificent color photographs of hidden and overlooked shops, clubs, and town houses. For a wonderful take on the golden age of the city's regal mansions, see Christopher Simon Sykes's *Private Palaces: Life in the Great London Houses*. For various other aspects of the city, consult Mervyn Blatch's helpful *A Guide to London's Churches*,

Andrew Crowe's *The Parks and Woodlands of London*, Sheila Fairfield's *The Streets of London*, Ann Saunders' *Regent's Park*, Ian Norrie's *Hampstead, Highgate Village, and Kenwood*, and Suzanne Ebel's *A Guide to London's Riverside: Hampton Court to Greenwich*. For the last word on just about every subject, see *The London Encyclopaedia*, edited by Ben Weinreb and the estimable Christopher Hibbert.

Of course, the history and spirit of the city are also to be found in biographies of great authors and British heroes and in monographs on famous architects. Peter Ackroyd's massive *Dickens* elucidates how the great author shaped today's view of the city; Martin Gilbert's magisterial, multivolume *Churchill* traces the city through some of its greatest trials; J. Mansbridge's *John Nash* elegantly details all the London buildings of this leading Regency-era architect.

Nineteenth-century London—the city of Queen Victoria, Tennyson, and Dickens—still comes alive thanks to two timeless works: *Mayhew's London*, a massive study of the London poor, and Gustave Doré's *London*, an unforgettable series of engravings of the city (often reprinted in modern editions) that detail its horrifying slums and grand avenues. When it comes to fiction, of course, Dickens's immortal works top the list. Stay-at-home detectives have long walked the streets of London, thanks to great mysteries with London settings by Sir Arthur Conan Doyle, Dorothy L. Sayers, Agatha Christie, Ngaio Marsh, and Antonia Fraser. For a little-known fictional account of London's most deadly villain, Jack the Ripper, read Marie Belloc-Lowndes's *The Lodger*.

There are any number of films—from *Waterloo Bridge* to *Georgy Girl* to

Mike Leigh's *Secrets and Lies*—that have used London as their setting. But always near the top of anyone's list are four films that rank among the greatest musicals of all time—Walt Disney's *Mary Poppins*, George Cukor's *My Fair Lady* (with its exquisite Cecil Beaton decor and costumes), Sir Carol Reed's *Oliver!*, and—yeah, yeah, yeah!—the Beatles' *A Hard Day's Night.*

LONDON AT A GLANCE

This date table parallels events in London's history with events in the world at large, especially in the Americas, to give a sense of perspective to the chronology of London. The dates of British kings and queens are those of their reigns, not of their lives.

ca. 400 BC Early Iron Age hamlet built at Heathrow (now London airport)

54 BC Julius Caesar arrives with short-lived expedition

AD 43 Romans conquer Britain, led by the emperor Claudius

AD 60 Boudicca, queen of Iceni, razes the first Roman Londinium

ca. 100 The Romans make Londinium center of their British activities, though not the capital

856 Alfred the Great (871–99), king of the West Saxons, "restored London and made it habitable"

1042 Edward the Confessor (1042–66) moves his court to Westminster and begins the reconstruction of the abbey and its monastic buildings

1066 William the Conqueror (1066–87), Duke of Normandy, wins the Battle of Hastings

1067 William grants London a charter confirming its rights and privileges

1078 The Tower of London begins with the building of the White Tower

1136 Fire destroys London Bridge (new one built 1176–1209)

1185 Knights Templar build the New Temple by the Thames

1191 First mayor of London elected

1265 First Parliament held in Westminster Abbey Chapter House

1314 Old St. Paul's Cathedral completed

1327 Incorporation of first trade guilds (which govern the City for centuries)

1348–58 The Black Death strikes London; one-third of the population dies

1382 The Peasants' Revolt destroys part of the city

1411 The Guildhall (already centuries on the same site) rebuilt

1476 William Caxton (1422–91) introduces printing to England in Westminster

1529 Hampton Court given by Cardinal Wolsey to Henry VIII; it becomes a favorite royal residence

1568 Royal Exchange founded

1588 Preparations at Tilbury to repel the Spanish invasion; the Armada defeated in the Channel

1599 Shakespeare's Globe Theatre built on the South Bank

1603 Population of London more than 200,000

1605 Unsuccessful Gunpowder Plot to blow up the Houses of Parliament

1649 Charles I (1625–49) beheaded outside the Banqueting House on Whitehall

1658 Oliver Cromwell (Lord Protector) dies

1660 Charles II (1649–85) restored to the throne (the Restoration) after exile in Europe

1665 The Great Plague; deaths probably reach 100,000 (official figure for one week alone was 8,297)

1666 The Great Fire burns for three days; 89 churches, 13,200 houses destroyed over an area of 400 streets

1675 Sir Christopher Wren (1632–1723) begins work on the new St. Paul's Cathedral

1694 The Bank of England founded

1698 Whitehall Palace destroyed by fire

1732 No. 10 Downing Street becomes the prime minister's official residence

1739–53 Mansion House built

1755 Trooping the Colour first performed for George II

1762 George III (1760–1820) makes Buckingham Palace the royal residence

1802 First gaslights on London streets

1817 First Waterloo Bridge built

1827 Marble Arch erected (in 1851 moved to the northeast corner of Hyde Park)

1829–41 Trafalgar Square laid out

1834 The Houses of Parliament gutted by fire (in 1840–52 the present Westminster Palace built)

1837 Victoria (1837–1901) comes to the throne

1838 National Gallery opens in Trafalgar Square

1845 British Museum completed

1851 The Great Exhibition, Prince Albert's brainchild, held in the Crystal Palace, Hyde Park

1863 Arrival of the Underground (the tube), first train on the Metropolitan Line

1869 Albert Embankment completed, first stage in containing the Thames's floodwaters

1897 Queen Victoria celebrates her Diamond Jubilee

1901 Victoria dies, marking the end of an era; London's population reaches about 4,500,000

1914–18 World War I—London bombed (1915) by German zeppelins (355 incendiaries, 567 explosives; 670 killed, 1,962 injured)

1939–45 World War II—air raids, between September 1940 and July 1941, 45,000–50,000 bombs (including incendiaries) are dropped on London; 1944 Flying Bomb (Doodlebug) raids; 1945 V2 raids; during the latter two series of raids, 8,938 killed, 24,504 injured. Total casualties for the whole war, about 30,000 killed, more than 50,000 injured

1946 Heathrow Airport opens

1951 The Festival of Britain spurs postwar uplift

1953 Coronation of Queen Elizabeth II (born 1926)

1956 Clean Air Act abolishes open fires and makes London's mists and fogs a romantic memory

1965 Sir Winston Churchill's funeral, a great public pageant

1974 Covent Garden fruit-and-vegetable market moves across the Thames; the original area is remodeled

1976 National Theatre opens on the South Bank

1977 Queen Elizabeth celebrates her Silver Jubilee

1981 National Westminster Tower, Britain's tallest building, opens in the City; Prince Charles marries Lady Diana Spencer in St. Paul's Cathedral

1983 The first woman lord mayor takes office

1984 The Thames Barrier, designed to prevent flooding in central London, is inaugurated

1986 The Greater London Council (the city's centralized municipal government) is abolished by Parliament; London's population now stands at approximately 6,696,000

1991 Cesar Pelli's Tower—1 Canada Square—opens at Canary Wharf and becomes Britain's tallest building

1994 The Channel Tunnel opens a direct rail link between Britain and Europe

1996 The Prince and Princess of Wales receive a precedent-breaking divorce

1997 Diana, Princess of Wales, dies at 36 in a car crash in Paris on August 31. After an extraordinary outpouring of grief, the world mourns at her Westminster Abbey funeral, televised around the globe to almost 800 million viewers. She is buried at Althorp, the Spencer family estate in Northamptonshire

2000 As Europe's most future-forward city, London welcomes in the new century with the Millennium Dome

ESSENTIAL INFORMATION

Basic Information on Traveling in London, Savvy Tips to Make Your Trip a Breeze, and Companies and Organizations to Contact

ADDRESSES

Central London and its surrounding districts are divided into 32 boroughs—33, counting the City of London, which has all the powers of a London borough. **More useful for finding your way around, however, are the subdivisions of London into postal districts.** Throughout the guide we've listed the full postal code for places you're likely to be contacting by mail, although you'll find the first half of the code more important. The first one or two letters give the location: N means north, NW means northwest, etc. Don't expect the numbering to be logical, however. You won't, for example, find W2 next to W3.

AIR TRAVEL TO AND FROM LONDON

BOOKING

When you book **look for nonstop flights** and **remember that "direct" flights stop at least once.** Try to avoid connecting flights, which require a change of plane.

CARRIERS

British Airways (☎ 800/AIRWAYS) is the national flag carrier and offers mostly nonstop flights from 18 U.S. cities to Heathrow and Gatwick airports, along with flights to Manchester, Birmingham, and Glasgow. As the leading British carrier, it offers myriad add-on options, helping to bring down ticket costs. In addition, it has a vast program of discount airfare-hotel packages.

➤ MAJOR AIRLINES: **American Airlines** (☎ 800/433–7300; 020/8572–5555 in London) to Heathrow, Gatwick. **British Airways** (☎ 800/247–9297; 0845/7222–1111 in London) to Heathrow, Gatwick. **Continental** (☎ 800/231–0856; 0800/776464 in London) to Gatwick. **Delta** (☎ 800/241–4141; 0800/414767 in London)

to Gatwick. **Northwest Airlines** (☎ 800/447–4747; 0870/507–4074 in London) to Gatwick. **United** (☎ 800/241–6522; 0845/844–4777 in London) to Heathrow. **TWA** (☎ 800/892–4141; 020/8814–0707 in London) to Gatwick. **Virgin Atlantic** (☎ 800/862–8621; 01293/747747 in London) to Heathrow, Gatwick.

CHECK-IN & BOARDING

Assuming that not everyone with a ticket will show up, airlines routinely overbook planes. When everyone does, airlines ask for volunteers to give up their seats. In return, these volunteers usually get a certificate for a free flight and are rebooked on the next flight out. If there are not enough volunteers, the airline must choose who will be denied boarding. The first to get bumped are passengers who checked in late and those flying on discounted tickets, so **get to the gate and check in as early as possible,** especially during peak periods.

Always **bring a government-issued photo I.D. to the airport.** You may be asked to show it before you are allowed to check in.

CUTTING COSTS

The least expensive airfares to London must usually be purchased in advance and are non-refundable. It's smart to **call a number of airlines, and when you are quoted a good price, book it on the spot**—the same fare may not be available the next day. Always **check different routings** and look into using different airports. Travel agents, especially low-fare specialists (☞ Discounts & Deals, *below*), are helpful.

Consolidators are another good source. They buy tickets for scheduled international flights at reduced rates from the airlines, then sell them at prices that beat the best fare available directly from the airlines, usually without restrictions. Sometimes you can even get your money back if you need to return the ticket. Carefully read the fine print detailing penalties for changes and cancellations, and **confirm your consolidator reservation with the airline.**

➤ CONSOLIDATORS: **Cheap Tickets** (☎ 800/377–1000). **Discount Airline Ticket Service** (☎ 800/576–1600). **Unitravel** (☎ 800/325–2222). **Up & Away Travel** (☎ 212/889–2345). **World Travel Network** (☎ 800/409–6753).

ENJOYING THE FLIGHT

For more legroom, **request an emergency-aisle seat.** Don't sit in the row in front of the emergency aisle or in front of a bulkhead, where seats may not recline. If you have dietary concerns, **ask for special meals when booking.** These can be vegetarian, low-cholesterol, or kosher, for example. On long flights, try to maintain a normal routine, to help fight jet lag. At night, **get some sleep.** By day, **eat light meals, drink water** (not alcohol), and **move around the cabin** to stretch your legs.

FLYING TIMES

Flying time to London is about 6½ hours from New York, 7½ hours from Chicago, 11 hours from San Francisco, and 21½ hours from Sydney.

HOW TO COMPLAIN

If your baggage goes astray or your flight goes awry, complain right away. Most carriers require that you **file a claim immediately.**

➤ AIRLINE COMPLAINTS: U.S. Department of Transportation **Aviation Consumer Protection Division** (✉ C-75, Room 4107, Washington, DC 20590, ☎ 202/366–2220, airconsumer@ost.dot.gov, www.dot.gov/airconsumer). **Federal Aviation Administration Consumer Hotline** (☎ 800/322–7873).

AIRPORTS & TRANSFERS

International flights to London arrive at either **Heathrow Airport (LHR)**, 15 mi west of London, or at **Gatwick Airport (LGW)**, 27 mi south of the capital. Most flights from the United States go to Heathrow, which is the busiest and is divided into four terminals, with Terminals 3 and 4 handling transatlantic flights (British Airways uses Terminal 4). Gatwick is London's second gateway. It has grown from a European airport into an airport that serves 21 scheduled U.S. destinations. A third, new, state-of-the-art airport, **Stansted (STN)**, is 35 mi east of the city. It handles mainly European and domestic traffic, although there is scheduled service from New York. There are fast connections from all the London airports into the capital. The cost of hotels and car rentals varies little between Heathrow and Gatwick.

➤ AIRPORT INFORMATION: **Heathrow Airport** (☎ 0870/000–0123). **Gatwick Airport** (☎ 01293/535353). **Stansted Airport** (☎ 01279/680500).

AIRPORT TRANSFERS

Airport Travel Line (☎ 0870/574–7777) has information on transfers between Heathrow and Gatwick airports and into London by rail or bus.

Heathrow, by train: the least-expensive train route into London is via the **Piccadilly line** of the **Underground** (London's subway system). Trains on the "tube" run every four to eight minutes from all four terminals; the painless 50-minute trip costs £3.40 one-way and connects with London's extensive tube system. The quickest way into London is the **Heathrow Express** (☎ 0845/600–1515), which ferries travelers in just 15 minutes to and from Paddington Station (in the city center and hub for many of London's Underground city lines). One-way tickets cost £12 for standard/express class (£22 round-trip) and £20 for first class (more space and TV screens). Service is daily, from 5:10 AM to 10:40 PM, with departures every 15 minutes.

Heathrow, by Bus: Airbus A2 (London Transport, ☎ 020/7222–1234) takes one hour and costs £7 one-way and £12 round-trip. It leaves for King's Cross and Euston, with stops at Marble Arch and Russell Square, every 30 minutes 6 AM–9:30 PM, but there are around 14 stops along the route, so it can be tedious. **National Express** (☎ 0870/580–8080) buses leave every 30 minutes to Victoria Coach Station direct, and are cheaper: £6 one-way and £8 round-trip, from 5:40 AM–9:45 PM.

Gatwick, by Train: Fast, nonstop **Gatwick Express** (☎ 0870/530–1530) leaves for Victoria Station every 15 minutes 5:20 AM–12:50 AM, then hourly 1:35 AM–6:05 AM. The 30-minute trip costs £10.20 one-way, £20.40 round-trip. A frequent local train also runs all night.

Gatwick, by Bus: National Express runs the 90-minute **Jetlink 777** (Gatwick Traveline, ☎ 0870/574–7777) from Gatwick South Terminal Coach Station to Victoria Coach Station (hourly, 5:15 AM–9:50 PM, £8 one-way, £12 round-trip), with stops at Marble Arch, Hyde Park Corner, Baker St., Finchley Rd., and Hendon Central.

Stansted, by Train: The **Stansted Skytrain** (☎ 0845/748–4950) to Liverpool Street Station runs every half hour and costs £11 one-way, £22 round-trip.

Stansted, by Bus: Hourly bus service on Jetlink 777 (8 AM–10:15 PM, ☞ *above*) to Victoria Coach Station costs £9 one-way, £13 round-trip, and takes about 1 hour and 40 minutes.

Cars and taxis drive into London on M4; the trip can take more than an hour, depending on traffic, from Heathrow. The taxi fare is about £40, plus tip. From Gatwick, the taxi is at least £60–£70, plus tip; traffic can be very heavy.

BUS TRAVEL AROUND LONDON

In central London, buses are traditionally bright red double- and single-deckers, though there are now many privately owned buses of different colors. Not all buses run the full length of their route at all times; check with the driver or conductor. Bus stops are clearly indicated; the main stops have a red LT (London Transit) symbol on a plain white background. When the word "Request" is written across the sign, you

must flag the bus down. Buses are a good way of seeing the town, but **don't take one if you are in a hurry.**

Night Buses can prove helpful when traveling in London from 11 PM to 5 AM—these buses add the prefix "N" to their route numbers and don't run as frequently or operate on quite as many routes as day buses. You'll probably have to transfer at one of the Night Bus nexuses: Victoria, Westminster, Piccadilly Circus, or Trafalgar Square. Weekly and monthly Travelcards are good for Night Buses, but One Day and Weekend Travelcards are not; Night Bus single fares are also a bit higher than daytime ones. Note: avoid sitting alone on the top deck of a Night Bus unless you want to experience the happily rare misfortune of being mugged in London.

FARES & SCHEDULES

A simpler two-fare system was introduced in January, 2000. All journeys within the central zone are £1, and all others outside are 70p. Travel from the outer to the central zone costs £1. There are numerous discount passes available, and ticket sales staff are usually helpful in choosing the best one. If you plan to make a number of journeys in one day, there is a **One Day Bus Pass** for £2.20–£2.80, which you can start using before 9:30 AM weekdays. Alternatively, **One Day Travelcards** (£3.80–£4.50) allow unrestricted travel on bus and tube after 9:30 AM and all day on weekends and national holidays. **LT Cards** (£4.80–£7.50) do not have any restricted times of travel except on N-prefixed Night Buses. Ask also about **Weekend and Family Travelcards,** which save around 25 percent on the standard fare. Traveling without a valid ticket makes you liable for an on-the-spot fine (£10 at press time), so always pay your fare before you travel. **Visitor Travelcards** (£3.90), available only in the United States in three-, four-, and seven-day versions from **Rail Europe** (✉ 226 Westchester Ave., White Plains, NY 10604, ☎ 888/274–8724), are the same as the One Day Travelcards but with the bonus of a booklet of money-off vouchers to major attractions.

➤ BUS INFORMATION: **LT Travel Information** (☎ 020/7222–1234). **LT Travel Information Centres** at Euston, Hammersmith, King's Cross, Oxford Circus, Piccadilly Circus, St. James's Park, and Victoria tube stations and at Heathrow (in Terminals 1 and 2) are open 7:15 AM–10 PM.

PAYING

On some buses you pay the conductor after finding a seat; on others you pay the driver upon boarding. Make sure you have the correct change for the fare.

SMOKING

Smoking is not permitted on any buses.

BUS TRAVEL TO AND FROM LONDON

National Express is the largest British coach operator and the nearest equivalent to Greyhound. They are fast, (particularly the Rapide services, which do not detour to make pickups and have steward service for refreshments), cheaper than trains, and comfortable (all coaches have washroom facilities on board). The network serves around 1,200 destinations and departs mainly from **Victoria Coach Station** (Victoria Coach Station, Buckingham Palace Rd., SW1), behind Victoria mainline rail station. From the underground station it is a short walk, and well signposted. Tickets can be bought from the Victoria, Heathrow, or Gatwick coach stations, by phone with a credit card, or from travel agencies. **Green Line** doesn't have as many destinations, but the airports and major tourist towns are covered.

➤ BUS INFORMATION: **Green Line** (☎ 020/8668–7261). **National Express** (☎ 0870/580–8080).

BUSINESS HOURS

Generally, businesses are closed on Sundays and national (bank) holidays (☞ Holidays, *below*). New Year's Day is a national holiday, but many major stores are open for the annual sales reductions. Many restaurants are closed over the Christmas period (☞ Mealtimes *in* Dining *below*).

BANKS & OFFICES

Banks are open weekdays 9:30–4:30; offices, 9:30–5:30.

GAS STATIONS

Most gas stations in central London are open seven days, 24 hours. As you get farther out of town, and off trunk/major roads, hours vary considerably depending on the gas company, but are usually 8 AM–8 PM.

MUSEUMS & SIGHTS

The major national museums and galleries are open daily, with shorter hours on weekends than weekdays. But there is a trend towards longer hours, such as one late-night opening a week.

PHARMACIES

Pharmacies are called chemists and are open, for the most part, Monday–Saturday 9:30 AM–5:30 PM. The leading chain drugstore, Boots, is open until 6 PM (the Oxford Street and Piccadilly Circus branches are also open Sunday) (☞ Emergencies, *below*).

SHOPS

Shops and offices in central London tend to keep longer hours than in the surrounding districts. Usual business hours are Monday–Saturday 9 AM–5:30 PM. In the main shopping streets of Oxford Street, Kensington High Street, and Knightsbridge, hours are 9:30 AM–6 PM, with late-night opening in Oxford Street on Thursday until 7:30–8 PM, and in the latter areas, on Wednesday. Many small general stores and newsagents stay open on Sunday; some chain and fashion stores in the tourist areas of Oxford Street and Piccadilly (and out-of-town shopping malls) also remain open.

CAMERAS & PHOTOGRAPHY

Don't be surprised if you are asked not to take pictures during theater, ballet, or opera productions, and in galleries, museums, and stately homes. Westminster Abbey, for example, has a particular time slot for tourists to take photos, and it's definitely not during services—when tourists are discouraged from entering, anyway. Locals are generally happy to be featured in your photos, but it's polite to ask if they mind before fixing the lens. There are many must-take sights in London, but guards on horseback in Whitehall and Big Ben are top of the list.

➤ PHOTO HELP: **Kodak Information Center** (☎ 800/242–2424). *Kodak Guide to Shooting Great Travel Pictures,* available in bookstores or from Fodor's Travel Publications (☎ 800/533–6478; $16.50 plus $5.50 shipping).

EQUIPMENT PRECAUTIONS

Always **keep your film and tape out of the sun.** Carry an extra supply of batteries, and **be prepared to turn on your camera or camcorder** to prove to security personnel that the device is real. Always **ask for hand inspection of film,** which becomes clouded after repeated exposure to airport X-ray machines, and **keep videotapes away from metal detectors.**

FILM & DEVELOPING

Film is available from pharmacies, newsagents, and supermarkets, as well as photographic stores. Kodak and Agfa are the most common brands, and prices range from £2–£4 for a roll of 36-exposure color print film. Larger drugstore branches and photographic stores stock the Advantix line. These stores provide 24-hour film developing services.

VIDEOS

Videos from the U.S. are not compatible with British and European models. If you're bringing your own video-camcorder, bring a supply of cassettes as well.

CAR RENTAL

Rental rates in London vary widely and are expensive, beginning at £50 ($80) a day and £200 ($320) a week for a small economy car (such as a sub-compact General Motors Vauxhall, Corsa, or Renault Clio), usually with manual transmission. Air-conditioning and unlimited mileage generally come with the larger-size automatic cars.

➤ MAJOR AGENCIES: **Alamo** (☎ 800/522–9696; 020/8759–6200 in the U.K.). **Avis** (☎ 800/331–1084; 800/

879–2847 in Canada; 0870/606–0100 in the U.K.; 02/9353–9000 in Australia; 09/525–1982 in New Zealand). **Budget** (☎ 800/527–0700; 0144/227–6266 in the U.K.). **Dollar** (☎ 800/800–6000; 020/8897–0811 in the U.K., where it is known as Eurodollar; 02/9223–1444 in Australia). **Hertz** (☎ 800/654–3001; 800/263–0600 in Canada; 020/8897–2072 in the U.K.; 02/9669–2444 in Australia; 03/358–6777 in New Zealand). **National InterRent** (☎ 800/227–3876; 0845/722–2525 in the U.K., where it is known as Europcar InterRent).

CUTTING COSTS

To get the best deal, **book through a travel agent who will shop around.** Do **look into wholesalers,** companies that do not own fleets but rent in bulk from those that do and often offer better rates than traditional car-rental operations. It's far cheaper to **arrange for car rental from the U.S. before you arrive,** or book an inclusive fly-drive package. Payment must be made before you leave home.

➤ WHOLESALERS: **Auto Europe** (☎ 207/842–2000 or 800/223–5555, FAX 800–235–6321, www.autocurope.com). **Europe by Car** (☎ 212/581–3040 or 800/223–1516, FAX 212/246–1458, www.europebycar.com). **DER Travel Services** (✉ 9501 W. Devon Ave., Rosemont, IL 60018, ☎ 800/782–2424, FAX 800/282–7474 for information; 800/860–9944 for brochures, www.dertravel.com). **Kemwel Holiday Autos** (☎ 800/678–0678, FAX 914/825–3160, www.kemwel.com).

INSURANCE

When driving a rented car you are generally responsible for any damage to or loss of the vehicle. Before you rent see what coverage your personal auto-insurance policy and credit cards already provide. Collision policies that car-rental companies sell for European rentals usually do not include stolen-vehicle coverage. Before you buy it, check your existing policies—you may already be covered.

REQUIREMENTS & RESTRICTIONS

In London your own driver's license is acceptable (as long as you are over

23 years old, with no endorsements or driving convictions). An International Driver's Permit is a good idea; it's available from the American or Canadian Automobile Association and, in the United Kingdom, from the Automobile Association or Royal Automobile Club. International permits are universally recognized, and having one may save you a problem with the local authorities. You may, with prior arrangement, take the car out of the U.K., even through the Channel Tunnel.

SURCHARGES

Before you pick up a car in one city and leave it in another, **ask about drop-off charges or one-way service fees,** which can be substantial. Note, too, that some rental agencies charge extra if you return the car before the time specified in your contract. To avoid a hefty refueling fee, **fill the tank just before you turn in the car,** but be aware that gas stations near the rental outlet may overcharge.

CAR TRAVEL

The best advice on driving in London is: don't. Because the capital grew up as a series of villages, there never was a central plan for London's streets, and the result is a winding mass of chaos, aggravated by a passion for one-way streets. A car is more of a liability: parking is restrictive and expensive, and traffic is tediously slow at most times of the day. Remember that Britain drives on the left, and the rest of Europe on the right. Therefore, you may want to leave your rented car in Britain and pick up a left-side drive if you cross the Channel (☞ Driving, *below*).

EMERGENCY SERVICES

The general procedure for a breakdown is to: position the red hazard triangle (which should be in the trunk of the car) a few paces away from the rear of the car. Leave the hazard warning lights on. If you are on a highway (motorway), emergency roadside telephone booths are positioned at intervals within walking distance. Contact the car rental company, or an auto club. The main automobile help groups are the Automobile Association (A.A.) and the

Royal Automobile Club (R.A.C.) If you are a member of the A.A.A. (American Automobile Association) check your membership details before you depart for Britain as, under a reciprocal agreement, roadside assistance in the U.K. should cost you nothing. You can join and receive roadside assistance from the A.A. on the spot, but the charge is higher— around £75—than a simple membership fee. For emergency A.A. roadside assistance call toll-free ☎ 0800/887766.

➤ CONTACTS: **Automobile Association** (☎ 0870/550–0600). **Royal Automobile Club** (☎ 0870/572–2722).

GASOLINE

Gasoline (petrol) is sold in liters and is increasingly expensive (75p per liter at press time). Unleaded petrol is predominant, denoted by green pump lines. Premium and Super Premium are the two varieties, and most cars run on regular premium. The old-type leaded four-star gas has been replaced by a lead-free variety for old cars not designed to take eco-friendly fuel. Supermarket pumps usually offer the best value, although they are often on the edge of the central city. Service is self-serve, except in small villages, and these gas stations are likely to be shut on Sundays and late evening. Most accept major credit cards.

PARKING

You can park at night after 6 PM or 8 PM in 30-mph zones, provided you are within 25 yards of a lighted street lamp but not within 15 yards of a road junction (within central London this includes parking on single yellow lines, but never on a double). Watch for the NO WAITING signposts on the sidewalk that tell you when restrictions are relaxed (there are different rules from street to street). To park on a bus route, you must show side (parking) lights, but you'll probably get a ticket anyway unless it's after 7 PM or whenever the signpost indicates it's permitted. On "Red Routes"— busy stretches with red lines painted in the street—you may not even stop to let a passenger out. During the day—and probably at all times—it is safest to believe that you can park nowhere except at a meter, in a garage, or where you are sure there are no lines or signs; otherwise, you run the risk of a towing cost of about £100, or a wheel clamp, which costs about the same, since you pay to have the clamp removed, plus the cost of the one or two tickets you'll have earned first. It is also illegal to park on the sidewalk, across entrances, or on white zigzag lines approaching a pedestrian crossing.

Meters have an insatiable hunger in the inner city—a 20p piece buys just 6 minutes—and some will only permit a 2-hour stay, with no return to top up. Don't try, as meter attendants in their green uniforms will pounce from nowhere, even on motorized bikes. Meters take 10p, 20p, 50p, and £1 coins. Take advantage of the many N.C.P. parking lots in the center of town, close to shopping and entertainment areas, which are often better value than daytime meters (about £2.50–£3 per hour, up to 8 hours). A London street map should have the parking lots marked. In the evening, after meter restrictions end, meter bays are free. If you must drive, an indispensable insider's reference book is the *London Parking Guide* (£4.99, Two Heads Publishing), usually found in better bookstores.

RULES OF THE ROAD

If you must risk life and limb and drive in London, note that the speed limit is 30 mph in the royal parks, as well as in all streets—unless you see the large 40 mph signs (and small repeater signs attached to lampposts) found only in the suburbs. Other basic rules: pedestrians have right-of-way on "zebra" crossings (black and white stripes that stretch across the street between two Belisha beacons—orange-flashing globe lights on posts) and it is illegal to pass another vehicle at a zebra crossing. At other crossings pedestrians must yield to traffic, but they do have right-of-way over traffic turning left at controlled crossings—if they have the nerve.

Seat belts are to be worn by law in the front and the back seats. Traffic lights sometimes have arrows directing left or right turns; try to catch a glimpse of the road markings in time, and don't get into the turn lane if you mean to go straight ahead. A right turn is not permitted on a red light. On designated bus lanes a sign at the beginning and end gives the time restrictions for use—usually during peak hours—if you are caught, you could be fined. The use of horns is prohibited between 11:30 PM and 7 AM. Drunk-driving laws are strictly enforced and it is far safer to avoid alcohol altogether. The legal limit is 80 milligrams of alcohol, which roughly translated means two units of alcohol—two glasses of wine, one pint of beer, or one glass of whiskey.

THE CHANNEL TUNNEL

Short of flying, the "Chunnel" is the fastest way to cross the English Channel: 35 minutes from Folkestone to Calais, 60 minutes from motorway to motorway, or 3 hours from London's Waterloo Station to Paris's Gare du Nord.

➤ CAR TRANSPORT: **Le Shuttle** (☎ 0870/535–3535 in the U.K.).

➤ PASSENGER SERVICE: In the U.K.: **Eurostar** (☎ 0870/518–6186), **InterCity Europe** (✉ Victoria Station, London, ☎ 0870/584–8848 for credit-card bookings). In the U.S.: **BritRail Travel** (☎ 800/677–8585), **Rail Europe** (☎ 800/942–4866).

CHILDREN AND LONDON

There is a kaleidoscope of activity for children to enjoy in London, and museums and major attractions have made great strides in special interactive features and trails (particularly during summer and Christmas holidays). In many museums children now enjoy free admission, and between the great establishments there are masses of green spaces in the London parks. During the school holiday time, bookstores run story times; cinemas, concert halls, and theaters have plenty of programs to watch—and join in on. Plan your itinerary to include places and activities that will keep children happy. When packing, include things to keep them busy en route. If you are renting a car, don't forget to **arrange for a car seat** when you reserve.

You will find up-to-date information in *Kids Out!* magazine, available monthly at better newsstands (£2) from the **Time Out** weekly listings stable, which also has a children's listings section. The information sheet *Children's London* (available free from the London Tourist Board, ✉ Tourist Information Centre, Victoria Station Forecourt, London SW1V 1JT and other London TICs) gives a complete story.

➤ LOCAL INFORMATION: **Kidsline** (☎ 020/7222–8070), open 9 AM–4 PM during summer holidays. **Visitorcall**, London Tourist Board's info line, offers two options: What's on for Children (☎ 0891/505456) and Places for Children to Go (☎ 0891/505460), both 50p per minute.

BABY-SITTING

➤ AGENCIES: **The Nanny Service** (✉ 6 Nottingham St., London W1M 3RB, ☎ 020/7935–3515). **Childminders** operates from the same address (☎ 020/7935–3000). **Nanny Connection** (✉ Collier House, 163–169 Brompton Rd., London SW3 1PY, ☎ 020/7591–4488). **Universal Aunts** (✉ Box 304, London SW4 0NN, ☎ 020/7738–8937).

FLYING

If your children are two or older, **ask about children's airfares.** As a general rule, infants under two not occupying a seat fly at greatly reduced fares or even for free. When booking, **confirm carry-on allowances** if you're traveling with infants. In general, for babies charged 10% of the adult fare you are allowed one carry-on bag and a collapsible stroller; if the flight is full, the stroller may have to be checked or you may be limited to less.

Experts agree that it's a good idea to use safety seats aloft for children weighing less than 40 pounds. Airlines set their own policies: U.S. carriers usually require that the child be ticketed, even if he or she is young enough to ride free, since the seats must be strapped into regular seats. Do **check your airline's policy about using safety seats during takeoff and landing.** And since safety seats are not allowed just everywhere in the plane, get your seat assignments early.

When reserving, **request children's meals or a freestanding bassinet** if you need them. But note that bulkhead seats, where you must sit to use the bassinet, may lack an overhead bin or storage space on the floor.

FOOD

Chinatown is welcoming, as well as being a colorful and interesting experience, and the many Italian restaurants and pasta and pizza places are practical. The key is to avoid the high class establishments unless your children are impeccable; you won't find a children's menu there, anyway. The **Pizza Express** chain is family-friendly and fun; at **Smollensky's Balloon** (✉ 1 Dover St., W1, ☎ 020/7491–1199) and **Sweeny Todds** (✉ 3–5 Tooley St., SE1, ☎ 020/7407–5267) clowns and magicians provide entertainment on the weekends. The **Hard Rock Cafe** (✉ 150 Old Park La., W1, ☎ 020/7629–0382), and **Capital Radio Cafe** (✉ Leicester Sq., WC2 ☎ 020/7484–8888) have fun, musical atmospheres. The **Rainforest Cafe** (✉ 20 Shaftesbury Ave., W1, ☎ 020/7434–3111), and **Football Football** (✉ 57–60 Haymarket, SW1, ☎ 020/7930–9970) are loud theme restaurants with decor and menus to match.

LODGING

Most hotels in London allow children under a certain age to stay in their parents' room at no extra charge, but others charge for them as extra adults; be sure to **find out the cutoff age for children's discounts.**

➤ BEST CHOICES: **Forte Hotels** (☎ 0845/740–4040). **Hart House Hotel** (✉ 51 Gloucester Pl., Marylebone, W1H 3PE, ☎ 020/7935–2288). **Basil Street Hotel** (✉ Basil St., Knightsbridge, SW3 1AH, ☎ 020/7581–3311). **Edward Lear** (✉ 30 Seymour St., Bayswater, W1H 5WD, ☎ 020/7402–5401). **Langland Hotel** (✉ 29–31 Gower St., Bloomsbury, WC1E 6HG, ☎ 020/7636–5801). **Pippa Pop-ins** (✉ 430 Fulham Rd., SW6 1DU, ☎ 020/7385–2457 or 020/7385–2458) is a hotel-kindergarten exclusively for children.

SIGHTS & ATTRACTIONS

The Tower of London, Tower Bridge Experience, London Dungeon, Madame Tussaud's, the Natural History Museum, and Pollock's Toy

Museum are just a handful of sights
to excite children. Places that are
especially appealing to children are
indicated in Chapter 1 by a rubber
duckie icon in the margin.

TRANSPORTATION

On trains and buses, children pay half
or reduced fares; children under five
ride for free. Car rental companies
may have child seats available. By
law, where there are seat belts in front
and back, children must use them, but
it is the responsibility of the driver to
ensure that they do. Children do not
need a child seat if they are over age
five and are 1.5 m in height, but they
must wear an adult seat belt. Children
must be three to sit in the front seat,
and if under 1.5 m in height will need
a child seat or adult strap, whichever
is available.

COMPUTERS ON THE ROAD

If you're traveling with a laptop,
carry a spare battery and adapter:
new batteries and replacement
adapters are expensive, although if
you do need to replace them head to
Tottenham Court Road (W1), where
the street is lined with computer
specialists. John Lewis department
store or Selfridges, in Oxford Street
(W1), also carry a limited range.
Never plug your computer into any
socket before asking about surge
protection. Some hotels do not have
built-in current stabilizers, and the
extreme electrical fluctuations and
surges can short your adapter or even
destroy your computer. IBM sells an
invaluable pen-size modem tester that
plugs into a telephone jack to check if
the line is safe to use.

CONCIERGES

Concierges, found in many hotels, can
help you with theater tickets and
dinner reservations: a good one with
connections may be able to get you
seats for a hot show or prime-time
dinner reservations at the restaurant
of the moment. You can also turn to
your hotel's concierge for help with
travel arrangements, sightseeing
plans, services ranging from aro-
matherapy to zipper repair, and
emergencies. Always, **always tip** a
concierge who has been of assistance
(☞ Tipping, *below*).

CONSUMER PROTECTION

Whenever shopping or buying travel
services in London, **pay with a major
credit card** so you can cancel payment
or get reimbursed if there's a problem. If you're doing business with a
particular company for the first time,
**contact your local Better Business
Bureau and the attorney general's
offices** in your own state and the
company's home state, as well. Have
any complaints been filed? Finally, if
you're buying a package or tour,
always **consider travel insurance** that
includes default coverage (☞ Insurance, *below*).

➤ BBBs: **Council of Better Business
Bureaus** (✉ 4200 Wilson Blvd., Suite
800, Arlington, VA 22203, ☎ 703/
276–0100, FAX 703/525–8277
www.bbb.org).

CUSTOMS & DUTIES

When shopping, **keep receipts** for all
purchases. Upon reentering the country, **be ready to show customs officials
what you've bought.** If you feel a
duty is incorrect or object to the way
your clearance was handled, note the
inspector's badge number and ask to
see a supervisor. If the problem isn't
resolved, write to the appropriate
authorities, beginning with the port
director at your point of entry.

IN AUSTRALIA

Australian residents who are 18 or
older may bring home $A400 worth
of souvenirs and gifts (including
jewelry), 250 cigarettes or 250 grams
of tobacco, and 1,125 ml of alcohol
(including wine, beer, and spirits).
Residents under 18 may bring back
$A200 worth of goods. Prohibited
items include meat products. Seeds,
plants, and fruits need to be declared
upon arrival.

➤ INFORMATION: **Australian Customs
Service** (Regional Director, ✉ Box 8,
Sydney, NSW 2001, ☎ 02/9213–
2000, FAX 02/9213–4000).

IN CANADA

Canadian residents who have been
out of Canada for at least 7 days may
bring home C$500 worth of goods
duty-free. If you've been away less
than 7 days but more than 48 hours,
the duty-free allowance drops to

C$200; if your trip lasts 24–48 hours, the allowance is C$50. You may not pool allowances with family members. Goods claimed under the C$500 exemption may follow you by mail; those claimed under the lesser exemptions must accompany you. Alcohol and tobacco products may be included in the 7-day and 48-hour exemptions but not in the 24-hour exemption. If you meet the age requirements of the province or territory through which you reenter Canada, you may bring in, duty-free, 1.14 liters (40 imperial ounces) of wine or liquor or 24 12-ounce cans or bottles of beer or ale. If you are 16 or older you may bring in, duty-free, 200 cigarettes and 50 cigars. Check ahead of time with Revenue Canada or the Department of Agriculture for policies regarding meat products, seeds, plants, and fruits.

You may send an unlimited number of gifts worth up to C$60 each duty-free to Canada. Label the package UNSOLICITED GIFT—VALUE UNDER $60. Alcohol and tobacco are excluded.

➤ INFORMATION: **Revenue Canada** (✉ 2265 St. Laurent Blvd. S, Ottawa, Ontario K1G 4K3, ☎ 613/993–0534; 800/461–9999 in Canada, FAX 613/957–8911, www.ccra-adrc.gc.ca).

IN NEW ZEALAND

Homeward-bound residents 17 or older may bring back $700 worth of souvenirs and gifts. Your duty-free allowance also includes 4.5 liters of wine or beer; one 1,125-ml bottle of spirits; and either 200 cigarettes, 250 grams of tobacco, 50 cigars, or a combination of the three up to 250 grams. Prohibited items include meat products, seeds, plants, and fruits.

➤ INFORMATION: **New Zealand Customs** (Custom House, ✉ 50 Anzac Ave., Box 29, Auckland, New Zealand, ☎ 09/359–6655, FAX 09/359–6732).

IN THE U.K.

Since **duty-free allowances were abolished within the European Union** (Belgium, Greece, the Netherlands, Denmark, Italy, Portugal, France, the Irish Republic, Spain, Germany, and Luxembourg) in June 1999, restrictions remain only for those buying

goods and importing them into the U.K. from outside the E.U. Shops within the U.K. airports run many special offers to counteract this loss of duty-free for travelers within the E.U. You may import duty-free: 200 cigarettes or 100 cigarillos or 50 cigars or 250 grams of tobacco; 2 liters of table wine and, in addition, (a) 1 liter of alcohol over 22% by volume (most spirits), (b) 2 liters of alcohol under 22% by volume (fortified or sparkling wine or liqueurs), or (c) 2 more liters of table wine; 60 milliliters of perfume; ¼ liter (250 ml) of toilet water; and other goods up to a value of £145, but not more than 50 liters of beer or 25 cigarette lighters.

Following side trips entirely within the E.U., you no longer need to go through customs on your return to the United Kingdom.

No animals or pets of any kind can be brought into the United Kingdom without a lengthy quarantine. The penalties are severe and are strictly enforced. Similarly, fresh meats, plants and vegetables, controlled drugs, and firearms and ammunition may not be brought into Great Britain.

IN THE U.S.

U.S. residents who have been out of the country for at least 48 hours (and who have not used the $400 allowance or any part of it in the past 30 days) may bring home $400 worth of foreign goods duty-free. U.S. residents 21 and older may bring back 1 liter of alcohol duty-free. In addition, regardless of your age, you are allowed 200 cigarettes and 100 non-Cuban cigars. Antiques, which the U.S. Customs Service defines as objects more than 100 years old, enter duty-free, as do original works of art done entirely by hand, including paintings, drawings, and sculptures.

You may also send packages home duty-free: up to $200 worth of goods for personal use, with a limit of one parcel per addressee per day (except alcohol or tobacco products or perfume worth more than $5); label the package PERSONAL USE and attach a list of its contents and their retail value. Do not label the package

UNSOLICITED GIFT or your duty-free exemption will drop to $100. Mailed items do not affect your duty-free allowance on your return.

➤ INFORMATION: **U.S. Customs Service** (✉ 1300 Pennsylvania Ave. NW, Washington, DC 20229, www.customs.gov; inquiries ☎ 202/354–1000; complaints c/o ✉ Office of Regulations and Rulings; registration of equipment c/o ✉ Resource Management, ☎ 202/927–0540).

DINING

The restaurants we list are the cream of the crop in each price category.

CATEGORY	COST*
££££	over £50
£££	£35–£50
££	£20–£35
£	under £20

per person for a three-course meal, excluding drinks, service, and VAT

MEALTIMES

In London, you could find breakfast all day, and perhaps all night, but breakfast is generally served between 7:30 and 9:30. Workmen's cafés and sandwich bars for office workers are sometimes open from 7:30, smarter cafés from 9–10:30. Lunch is between noon and 2 and restaurant sittings will be booked within that time. Tea—often a meal in itself—is taken between 4 and 5:30, dinner or supper between 7:30 and 9:30, sometimes earlier. In London's theaterland 6–6:30 is the time for pre-theater suppers, and 10 onwards for post-theater suppers. Many ethnic restaurants, especially Indian, serve food until midnight. Sunday is proper lunch day, and some restaurants will open just for lunch, and not for evening dinner. Unless otherwise noted, the restaurants listed in this guide are open daily for lunch and dinner, but some restaurants do not open on Sundays (or Mondays—a fish-and-chip shop worth its salt will not be open on Monday) at all.

PAYING

Most restaurants accept most major credit cards—American Express, Diner's Club, Master Card, and Visa—but do check for the signs on the window or door just in case. A pub, small café, or ethnic restaurant (such as Indian or Chinese) might not take credit cards.

RESERVATIONS & DRESS

Reservations are always a good idea: we mention them only when they're essential or not accepted. Book as far ahead as you can, and reconfirm as soon as you arrive. We mention dress only when men are required to wear a jacket or a jacket and tie.

SPECIALTIES

In London, local could mean any global flavor, but for pure Britishness roast beef probably tops the list. If you want the best value traditional Sunday lunch, go to a pub. The traditional accompaniment of Yorkshire pudding is a savory batter baked in the oven until crisp. Then you can make it go soft and soggy with rich dark gravy. There are more puddings and pies: Shepherd's Pie is trad pub fare made with stewed minced lamb and a mashed potato topping, baked until lightly browned on top. Steak-and-kidney pie is chunks of beef and pigs' kidneys braised in a thick gravy and topped with a light puff-pastry crust. Sweet bread-and-butter pudding is served hot, the layers of bread and dried fruit baked in a creamy custard until lightly crisp. The fish in fish and chips is usually cod or haddock, with thick chips. A ploughman's lunch is crusty bread, English cheese (strong flavored with bite—cheddar, blue Stilton, crumbly white Cheshire, smooth red Leicester), and pickles with a side salad garnish. For tea, choose among jam, cream, and scones, and sandwiches made with wafer-thin slices of cucumber, with plenty of tea.

WINE, BEER & SPIRITS

The cheapest and best range of alcohol is in the supermarkets, but in the middle of town, go to an informative, friendly wine merchant, or off-license shop, such as Oddbin's, which sells wine from around the world, and beer, too. For beer, bitters, or ale, go to a pub (☞ Pubs *in* Chapter 2).

DISABILITIES & ACCESSIBILITY

Compared to New York City, London has a way to go in helping people with disabilities but is moving toward making the city more accessible. Many of the tourist attractions and hotels are updating facilities. Although traveling around is a problem, there are organizations to help and advise. **Artsline** has details on access to the arts.

➤ LOCAL RESOURCES: **Artsline** (☎ 020/ 7388–2227). **Holiday Care Service** (✉ Imperial Building, Victoria Rd., Horley, Surrey RH6 7PZ, ☎ 01293/ 774535). **London Transport's Unit for Disabled Passengers** (✉ 172 Buckingham Palace Rd., London SW1W 9TN, ☎ 020/7918–3312). **Royal Association for Disability and Rehabilitation** (RADAR, ✉ 12 City Forum, 250 City Rd., London EC1, ☎ 020/7250– 3222). **Tripscope** (☎ 020/8994– 9294).

LODGING

If you book directly through Holiday Care (☎ 01293/773716), rates at some hotels with special facilities can be discounted.

➤ BEST CHOICES: **Copthorne Tara Hotel** (✉ Scarsdale Pl., Kensington, W8, ☎ 020/7937–7211). **Thistle Marble Arch** (✉ Bryanston St., W1, ☎ 020/7629–8040).

RESERVATIONS

When discussing accessibility with an operator or reservations agent, **ask hard questions.** Are there any stairs, inside *or* out? Are there grab bars next to the toilet *and* in the shower/tub? How wide is the doorway to the room? To the bathroom? For the most extensive facilities meeting the latest legal specifications, **opt for newer accommodations.**

SIGHTS & ATTRACTIONS

Tour Guides Ltd. (☎ 020/7495–5504) will tailor a tour for you. The London Tourist Board has details of more easily accessible attractions. Suggested sights might include: London Planetarium, London Transport Museum, London Zoo, National Portrait Gallery, and Natural History Museum.

TRANSPORTATION

London cabs have spacious interiors for wheelchair users. For other information, *see* Local Resources, *above*.

➤ COMPLAINTS: **Disability Rights Section** (✉ U.S. Department of Justice, Civil Rights Division, Box 66738, Washington, DC 20035-6738, ☎ 202/514–0301 or 800/514–0301; TTY 202/514–0301 or 800/514– 0301, ℻ 202/307–1198) for general complaints. **Aviation Consumer Protection Division** (☞ Air Travel, *above*) for airline-related problems. **Civil Rights Office** (✉ U.S. Department of Transportation, Departmental Office of Civil Rights, S-30, 400 7th St. SW, Room 10215, Washington, DC 20590, ☎ 202/366–4648, ℻ 202/366–9371) for problems with surface transportation.

TRAVEL AGENCIES

In the United States, the Americans with Disabilities Act requires that travel firms serve the needs of all travelers. Some agencies specialize in working with people with disabilities.

➤ TRAVELERS WITH MOBILITY PROBLEMS: **Access Adventures** (✉ 206 Chestnut Ridge Rd., Rochester, NY 14624, ☎ 716/889–9096, dltravel@ prodigy.net), run by a former physical-rehabilitation counselor. **CareVacations** (✉ 5-5110 50th Ave., Leduc, Alberta T9E 6V4, ☎ 780/986–6404 or 877/478–7827, ℻ 780/986–8332, www.carevacations.com), for group tours and cruise vacations. **Flying Wheels Travel** (✉ 143 W. Bridge St., Box 382, Owatonna, MN 55060, ☎ 507/451–5005 or 800/535–6790, ℻ 507/451–1685, thq@ll.net, www. flyingwheels.com). **Hinsdale Travel Service** (✉ 201 E. Ogden Ave., Suite 100, Hinsdale, IL 60521, ☎ 630/ 325–1335, ℻ 630/325–1342, hinstrvl@interaccess.com).

➤ TRAVELERS WITH DEVELOPMENTAL DISABILITIES: **New Directions** (✉ 5276 Hollister Ave., Suite 207, Santa Barbara, CA 93111, ☎ 805/967–2841 or 888/967–2841, ℻ 805/964–7344, newdirec@silcom.com, www.silcom. com/anewdirec/).

DISCOUNTS & DEALS

Be a smart shopper and **compare all your options** before making decisions. A plane ticket bought with a promotional coupon from travel clubs, coupon books, and direct-mail offers may not be cheaper than the least expensive fare from a discount ticket agency. And always keep in mind that what you get is just as important as what you save.

DISCOUNT RESERVATIONS

To save money, **look into discount reservations services** with toll-free numbers, which use their buying power to get a better price on hotels, airline tickets, even car rentals. When booking a room, always **call the hotel's local toll-free number** (if one is available) rather than the central reservations number—you'll often get a better price. Always ask about special packages or corporate rates.

When shopping for the best deal on hotels and car rentals, **look for guaranteed exchange rates,** which protect you against a falling dollar. With your rate locked in, you won't pay more even if the price goes up in the local currency.

➤ AIRLINE TICKETS: ☎ 800/FLY–4–LESS. ☎ 800/FLY–ASAP.

➤ HOTEL ROOMS: **Hotel Reservations Network** (☎ 800/964–6835, www.hoteldiscounts.com). **International Marketing & Travel Concepts** (☎ 800/790–4682, imtc@mindspring.com). **Steigenberger Reservation Service** (☎ 800/223–5652, www.srs-worldhotels.com). **Travel Interlink** (☎ 800/888–5898, www.travelinter-link.com).

PACKAGE DEALS

Don't confuse packages and guided tours. When you buy a package you travel on your own, just as though you had planned the trip yourself. Fly/drive packages, which combine airfare and car rental, are often a good deal. One-, three-, or six-day **London Passes,** available from the Britain Visitor Centre (☞ Visitor Information, *below*), offers local transportation, entrance to museums, movie theaters, and galleries, and tours at considerable savings.

ELECTRICITY

To use your U.S.–purchased electric-powered equipment, **bring a converter and adapter.** If your appliances are dual-voltage you'll need only an adapter, but it's best to get specific instructions from the manufacturer or retailer. The electrical current in London is 220/240 volts (coming into line with the rest of Europe at 230 volts), 50 cycles alternating current (AC); wall outlets take three-pin plugs, and shaver sockets take two round, oversize prongs. Don't use 110-volt outlets, marked FOR SHAVERS ONLY, for high-wattage appliances such as blow-dryers. If you plan to use a laptop, it's a good idea to check with your electrical supplier on the correct type of converter or adapter you should use. For converters, adapters, and advice, contact the British Airways Travel Shop 156 Regent St., W1 (☎ 020/7434–4725).

EMBASSIES

➤ AUSTRALIA: **Australia House** (✉ Strand, WC2, ☎ 020/7379–4334).

➤ CANADA: **MacDonald House** (✉ 1 Grosvenor Sq., W1, ☎ 020/7258–6600).

➤ NEW ZEALAND: **New Zealand House** (✉ 80 Haymarket, SW1, ☎ 020/7930–8422).

➤ UNITED STATES: **U.S. Embassy** (✉ 24 Grosvenor Sq., W1, ☎ 020/7499–9000); for passports, go to the **U.S. Passport Unit** (✉ 55 Upper Brook St., W1, ☎ 020/7499–9000).

EMERGENCIES

➤ DOCTORS & DENTISTS: **Dental Emergency Care Service** (☎ 020/7955–2186) directs callers to the nearest office. **Doctor's Call** (☎ 020/8900–1000) is another referral service. **Eastman Dental Hospital** (✉ 256 Gray's Inn Rd., WC1, ☎ 020/7915–1000). **Medical Express** (✉ 117A Harley St., W1, ☎ 020/7499–1991) is a private medical office with no appointments required.

➤ HOSPITALS: For emergency hospital care, with first treatment free under the National Health Service regulations contact **Royal Free Hospital** (✉ Pond St., NW3, ☎ 020/7794–0500) or **University College Hospital** (✉ Grafton Way, WC1, ☎ 020/7387–9300). Most other London hospitals also have emergency rooms.

➤ EMERGENCY SERVICES: Dial **999** for police, fire, or ambulance. **Samaritans** (☎ 020/7734–2800) is a 24-hour help line for anyone in severe emotional crisis. **Victim Support** (☎ 020/7735–9166 or 020/7582–5712 after office hours) will give emotional and practical help to victims of crime.

➤ 24-HOUR PHARMACIES: **Bliss the Chemist** (⊠ 5 Marble Arch, W1, ☎ 020/7723–6116).

ETIQUETTE & BEHAVIOR

The icy British stiff upper lip is starting to thaw, but, as in most things, it's best to play spectator and go with the flow. If you're visiting a family home, a gift of flowers is welcome. If it's for a meal, then take a bottle of wine perhaps, and maybe some candy for the children—but not necessarily all three. Kissing on greeting is still too forward and Continental for most Brits. A warm handshake is just fine. For goodbyes, if the atmosphere warrants, a quick one-cheek kiss is appropriate. The British can never say please, thank you, or sorry too often; to thank your host, a phone call or thank-you card does nicely.

BUSINESS ETIQUETTE

In business, punctuality is of prime importance, so if you anticipate a late arrival, call ahead. On dinners: it is not assumed that spouses will attend unless pre-arranged, and if you proffered the invitation it is usually assumed that you will pick up the tab. If you are the visitor, however, it's good form for the host to do the taking. Alternatively, play it safe and offer to split the check.

GAY & LESBIAN TRAVEL

The main gay communities are in the center of London (Soho, Old Compton St., and west to Kensington and Earls Court). There is a thriving social scene of clubs and cafes, and the best notice board for gay life and services is Gay's the Word (⊠ 66 Marchmount St., WC1, ☎ 020/7278–7654). The *Pink Paper,* available at libraries, large bookstores and gay cafés, and *Time Out* have comprehensive listings. Hotel front desks should serve any couples with courtesy, but using the travel agents listed below should send you in the right direction.

➤ GAY- & LESBIAN-FRIENDLY TRAVEL AGENCIES: **Different Roads Travel**

(⊠ 8383 Wilshire Blvd., Suite 902, Beverly Hills, CA 90211, ☎ 323/651–5557 or 800/429–8747, ℻ 323/651–3678, leigh@west.tzell.com). **Kennedy Travel** (⊠ 314 Jericho Turnpike, Floral Park, NY 11001, ☎ 516/352–4888 or 800/237–7433, ℻ 516/354–8849, main@kennedy-travel.com, www.kennedytravel.com). **Now Voyager** (⊠ 4406 18th St., San Francisco, CA 94114, ☎ 415/626–1169 or 800/255–6951, ℻ 415/626–8626, www.nowvoyager.com). **Skylink Travel and Tour** (⊠ 1006 Mendocino Ave., Santa Rosa, CA 95401, ☎ 707/546–9888 or 800/225–5759, ℻ 707/546–9891, skylinktvl@aol.com, www.skylink-travel.com), serving lesbian travelers.

HOLIDAYS

Holidays observed in Britain include New Year's Day, Good Friday, Easter Monday, May Day (first Monday in May), spring and summer bank holidays (last Monday in May and August, respectively), Christmas, and Boxing Day (day after Christmas). On Christmas Eve and New Year's Eve some shops, restaurants, and businesses close early, as do some museums and tourist attractions. If you want to book a hotel room during this period, make sure you do it well in advance, and check that the hotel's restaurant will be open.

INSURANCE

The most useful travel insurance plan is a comprehensive policy that includes coverage for trip cancellation and interruption, default, trip delay, and medical expenses (with a waiver for preexisting conditions).

Without insurance you will lose all or most of your money if you cancel your trip, regardless of the reason. Default insurance covers you if your tour operator, airline, or cruise line goes out of business. Trip-delay covers expenses that arise because of bad weather or mechanical delays. Study the fine print when comparing policies.

If you're traveling internationally, a key component of travel insurance is coverage for medical bills incurred if you get sick on the road. Such expenses are not generally covered by

Medicare or private policies. U.K. residents can buy a travel insurance policy valid for most vacations taken during the year in which it's purchased (but check preexisting-condition coverage). Australian citizens need extra medical coverage when traveling abroad.

Always **buy travel policies directly from the insurance company**; if you buy them from a cruise line, airline, or tour operator that goes out of business you probably will not be covered for the agency or operator's default, a major risk. Before making any purchase, **review your existing health and home-owner's policies** to find what they cover away from home.

➤ TRAVEL INSURERS: In the U.S.: **Access America** (☒ 6600 W. Broad St., Richmond, VA 23230, ☎ 804/285-3300 or 800/284-8300, FAX 804/673-1583, www.previewtravel.com), **Travel Guard International** (☒ 1145 Clark St., Stevens Point, WI 54481, ☎ 715/345-0505 or 800/826-1300, FAX 800/955-8785, www.noelgroup. com). In Canada: **Voyager Insurance** (☒ 44 Peel Center Dr., Brampton, Ontario L6T 4M8, ☎ 905/791-8700; 800/668-4342 in Canada).

➤ INSURANCE INFORMATION: In the U.K.: **Association of British Insurers** (☒ 51–55 Gresham St., London EC2V 7HQ, ☎ 020/7600-3333, FAX 020/7696-8999, info@abi.org.uk, www.abi.org.uk). In Australia: **Insurance Council of Australia** (☎ 03/9614-1077, FAX 03/9614-7924).

LODGING

London now ranks as one of the world's most expensive hotel capitals. Finding budget accommodations— especially during July and August— can be difficult; you should try to book well ahead if you are visiting during these months. Many London hotels offer special off-season (October–March) rates, however. The lodgings we list are the cream of the crop in each price category. We always list the facilities that are available—but we don't specify whether they cost extra: when pricing accommodations, always ask what's included and what costs extra.

CATEGORY	COST*
££££	over £230
£££	£160–£230
££	£100–£160
£	under £100

All prices are for a double room, VAT included.

☜ following the text of a review is your signal that the property has a Web site where you will find details and, usually, images. For a link, visit www.fodors.com/urls. Assume that hotels operate on the **European Plan** (EP, with no meals) unless we specify that they use the **Continental Plan** (CP, with a Continental breakfast), **Modified American Plan** (MAP, with breakfast and dinner), or the **Full American Plan** (FAP, with all meals).

APARTMENT RENTALS

If you want a home base that's roomy enough for a family and comes with cooking facilities, **consider a furnished rental.** These can save you money, especially if you're traveling with a group. Home-exchange directories sometimes list rentals as well as exchanges. In Britain, apartments are called flats. If you want to deal directly with local agents in Britain, get a personal recommendation from someone who has used the company, as, unlike hotels, there is no accredited system for standards. The London Tourist Board also has accommodation lists.

➤ INTERNATIONAL AGENTS: At Home Abroad (☒ 405 E. 56th St., Suite 6H, New York, NY 10022, ☎ 212/421-9165, FAX 212/752-1591, athomabrod@aol.com, http://member.aol.com/athomabrod/index.html. **Europa-Let/Tropical Inn-Let** (☒ 92 N. Main St., Ashland, OR 97520, ☎ 541/482-5806 or 800/462-4486, FAX 541/482-0660). **Hideaways International** (☒ 767 Islington St., Portsmouth, NH 03801, ☎ 603/430-4433 or 800/843-4433, FAX 603/430-4444 info@hideaways.com www.hideaways.com; membership $99). **Hometours International** (☒ Box 11503, Knoxville, TN 37939, ☎ 865/690-8484 or 800/367-4668, hometours@aol.com, http://thor.he. net/ahometour/). **Interhome** (☒ 1990 N.E. 163rd St., Suite 110, N. Miami Beach, FL 33162, ☎ 305/940-2299 or 800/882–6864, FAX 305/940–2911, interhomeu@aol.com, www.inter-home.com). **Vacation Home Rentals Worldwide** (⊠ 235 Kensington Ave., Norwood, NJ 07648, ☎ 201/767–9393 or 800/633–3284, FAX 201/767–5510, vhrww@juno.com, www.vhrww.com). **Villas and Apartments Abroad** (⊠ 1270 Avenue of the Americas, 15th floor, New York, NY 10020, ☎ 212/897–5045 or 800/433–3020, FAX 212/897–5039, vaa@altour.com, www.vaanyc.com). **Villas International** (⊠ 950 Northgate Dr., Suite 206, San Rafael, CA 94903, ☎ 415/499–9490 or 800/221–2260, FAX 415/499–9491, villas@best.com, www.villasintl.com).

➤ LOCAL AGENTS: **John D. Wood,** estate agents with short-term rentals (☎ 020/7722–3336). **The London Connection** (☎ 020/7738–8533). **Palace Court Holiday Apartments** (⊠ 1 Palace Court, Bayswater Rd., London, W2, ☎ 020/7727–3467, FAX 020/7221–7824, www.palacecourt.co.uk).

B&BS

B&Bs are often large, attractive family homes that are almost like small hotels. These aren't corporate facilities, so you should be prepared to accept some charming quirks. Choose carefully from accredited agencies, as some so-called B&Bs could be simply unfortunate hostels for refugees and the homeless. For agencies that specialize in London B&B listings, *see* Chapter 3.

HOME EXCHANGES

If you would like to exchange your home for someone else's, **join a home-exchange organization,** which will send you its updated listings of available exchanges for a year and will include your own listing in at least one of them. It's up to you to make specific arrangements.

➤ EXCHANGE CLUBS: **HomeLink International** (⊠ Box 650, Key West, FL 33041, ☎ 305/294–7766 or 800/638–3841, FAX 305/294–1448, usa@homelink.org, www.homelink.org; $98 per year). **Intervac U.S.** (⊠ Box 590504, San Francisco, CA 94159, ☎ 800/756–4663, FAX 415/435–7440, www.intervac.com; $89 per year includes two catalogues).

HOSTELS

No matter what your age, you can **save on lodging costs by staying at hostels.** In some 5,000 locations in more than 70 countries around the world, Hostelling International (HI), the umbrella group for a number of national youth-hostel associations, offers single-sex, dorm-style beds and, at many hostels, rooms for couples and family accommodations. Membership in any HI national hostel association, open to travelers of all ages, allows you to stay in HI-affiliated hostels at member rates; one-year membership is about $25 for adults (C$26.75 in Canada, £9.30 in the U.K., $30 in Australia, and $30 in New Zealand). Hostels run about $10–$25 per night. Members have priority if the hostel is full; they're also eligible for discounts around the world, even on rail and bus travel in some countries.

➤ ORGANIZATIONS: **Hostelling International—American Youth Hostels** (⊠ 733 15th St. NW, Suite 840, Washington, DC 20005, ☎ 202/783–6161, FAX 202/783–6171, www.hiayh.org). **Hostelling International—Canada** (⊠ 400–205 Catherine St., Ottawa, Ontario K2P 1C3, ☎ 613/237–7884, FAX 613/237–7868, www.hostellingintl.ca). **Youth Hostel Association of England and Wales** (⊠ Trevelyan House, 8 St. Stephen's Hill, St. Albans, Hertfordshire AL1 2DY, ☎ 01727/855215 or 01727/845047, FAX 01727/844126, www.yha.uk). **Australian Youth Hostel Association** (⊠ 10 Mallett St., Camperdown, NSW 2050, ☎ 02/9565–1699, FAX 02/9565–1325, www.yha.com.au). **Youth Hostels Association of New Zealand** (⊠ Box 436, Christchurch, New Zealand, ☎ 03/379–9970, FAX 03/365–4476, www.yha.org.nz).

HOTELS

There are several systems that grade hotels in Britain. The English Tourist Board (ETB) presently uses crowns, while the AA and RAC motoring organizations award stars. Some are awarded more for service than individual room facilities. For a good standard of comfort, look at three stars and above. Modern hotels usually have air-conditioning; if you wish to have a double bed, you should specify that. All hotels listed have private bath unless otherwise noted.

➤ TOLL-FREE NUMBERS: **Best Western** (☎ 800/528–1234, www.bestwestern.com). **Choice** (☎ 800/221–2222, www.hotelchoice.com). **Clarion** (☎ 800/252–7466, www.choicehotels.com). **Comfort** (☎ 800/228–5150, www.comfortinn.com). **Forte** (☎ 800/225–5843, www.fortehotels.com). **Four Seasons** (☎ 800/332–3442, www.fourseasons.com). **Hilton** (☎ 800/445–8667, www.hiltons.com). **Holiday Inn** (☎ 800/465–4329, www.holiday-inn.com). **Hyatt Hotels & Resorts** (☎ 800/233–1234, www.hyatt.com). **Marriott** (☎ 800/228–9290, www.marriott.com). **Le Meridien** (☎ 800/543–4300, www.lemeridienhotels.com). **Nikko Hotels International** (☎ 800/645–5687, www.nikko.com). **Quality Inn** (☎ 800/228–5151, www.qualityinn.com). **Radisson** (☎ 800/333–3333, www.radisson.com). **Renaissance Hotels & Resorts** (☎ 800/468–3571, www.hotels.com). **Sheraton** (☎ 800/325–3535, www.sheraton.com). **Wyndham Hotels & Resorts** (☎ 800/822-4200, www.wyndham.com).

MAIL & SHIPPING

Stamps may be bought from main or substation post offices (the latter are located in stores), from stamp machines outside post offices, and from many newsagent's stores and news stands. Mailboxes are known as post or letter boxes and are painted bright red; large tubular ones are set on the edge of sidewalks, while smaller boxes are set into post-office walls. Allow seven days for a letter to reach the U.S. Check the Yellow Pages telephone directory for a complete list of branches.

➤ POST OFFICES: ⊠ 17 Euston Rd., NW1; ⊠ 125–131 Westminster Bridge Rd., SW1; ⊠ 110 Victoria St., SW1; ⊠ 15 Broadwick St., W1; ⊠ 54 Great Portland St., W1; ⊠ 43 Seymour St., Marble Arch, W1; ⊠ The Science Museum, SW7; ⊠ 181 High Holborn, WC1; ⊠ 24 William IV St., Trafalgar Sq., WC2.

OVERNIGHT SERVICES

➤ MAJOR SERVICES: **DHL**(☎ 0845/710–0300). **Federal Express**(☎ 0800/123800). **Parcelforce**(☎ 0800/224466).

POSTAL RATES

Airmail letters up to 10 grams to North America, Australia and New Zealand cost 43p; postcards, 37p. Letters within Britain are 26p for first-class, 20p for second-class. Always check rates before sending mail, as they may be subject to change.

RECEIVING MAIL

If you're uncertain where you'll be staying, you can have mail sent to you c/o Poste Restante, the **London Main Post Office** at Trafalgar Square (⊠ 24–28 William IV St., London WC2N 4DL, ☎ 020/7484–9307), open weekdays 8–8, Saturday 9–8. It will hold international mail for one month. This service can be arranged at any main or substation post office (☎ 0845/774–0740). You can also collect letters at **American Express** (⊠ 6 Haymarket, London, SW1Y 4BS, ☎ 0845/774–0740) or any other branch. The service is free to cardholders and traveler's-check holders; all others pay a small fee.

SHIPPING PARCELS

Most department stores and retail outlets can ship your goods home. You should check your insurance for coverage of possible damage.

MEDIA

NEWSPAPERS & MAGAZINES

For the latest information about shops, restaurants, and arts events peruse Britain's glossy monthly magazines—*Tatler, Harpers & Queen, British Vogue, Wallpaper, British House & Garden,* the *Face,* and *Time Out London.* Many better newsstands around the world also feature the Sunday editions of the leading British newspapers, such as the *London Times,* the *Evening Standard,* the *Independent,* and the *Manchester Guardian;* the Arts sections of these papers often have advance news of future events. In addition, these London newspapers have Web sites of their own, full of tips and reviews of the hottest eateries, chicest restaurants, and newest hotels.

RADIO & TELEVISION

The main channels are BBC1 and BBC2 from the British Broadcasting Corporation. BBC2 is considered the more eclectic and artsy, with a higher proportion of alternative humor, drama, and documentaries. The independent channels are ITV (Independent Television), which is split into regional companies across the country: Carlton is the station for London and the southeast region. There are big-budget highbrow productions occasionally, but there are more mainstream soaps, both home-grown—*Brookside* and *Coronation Street* (which the Queen is rumored to watch)—and international (the Australian *Neighbors* and the U.S. daytime talk shows such as *Oprah*), and general interest shows. Channel 4 is a mixture of mainstream and off-the-wall, while Channel 5 has a higher proportion of sports and films. Rupert Murdoch's satellite dishes have sprung up like an alien culture on the London skyline—his Sky TV and a plethora of other cable channels (many of which are beamed into London hotel rooms) have increased the daily diet now available from dawn to dusk and through 'til dawn again.

Radio has seen a similar explosion, from 24-hour classics on Classic FM (100–102MHz), and rock on Branson's Virgin (105.8MHz), to nostalgic on Heart (106.2MHz), or talk-talk on Talk Radio (MW1053 kHZ)—and that is just a sample of the independents (which also include a fair smattering of pirate stations bobbing around the FM and MW wavelengths). The BBC still runs from Radios 1 to 5: 1 (FM97.6) for the young and hip; 2 (FM88) for middle-of-the-roadsters; 3 (FM90.2) for classics, jazz, and arts; 4 (FM92.4) for news, current affairs, drama, and documentary; and 5 Live (MW693 kHz) for sports and news coverage with listener phone-ins.

MONEY MATTERS

A movie in the West End costs £6–£9.50 (at some cinemas less on Mon-day and at matinees); a theater seat, from £8.50 to about £35, more for hit shows; admission to a museum or gallery, around £5 (though some are free and others request a "voluntary contribution"); coffee, £1–£2; a pint of light (lager) beer in a pub, £2 or more; whiskey, gin, vodka, and so forth, by the glass in a pub, £2.50 and up (the measure is smaller than in the United States); house wine by the glass in a pub or wine bar, around £2, in a restaurant, £3.50 or more; a Coke, around 80p; a ham sandwich from a sandwich bar in the West End, £2; a 1-mi taxi ride, £4; an average Underground or bus ride, £1.60, a longer one, £2.50. For standby theater tickets, many at half-price, go the SOLT (Society of London Theaters) booth in Leicester Square for that day's shows. It is open Monday-Saturday, 2:30–6:30; from noon on matinee days. There is a service charge of £2 or £1.25 on tickets under £12.50.

Prices throughout this guide are given for adults. Substantially reduced fees—generally referred to as "concessions" throughout Great Britain—are almost always available for children, students, and senior citizens. For information on taxes, *see* Taxes, *below*.

ATMS

A credit card or debit card (also known as a check card) will get you cash advances at ATMs worldwide if your card is properly programmed with your personal identification number. For use in London, your PIN must be four digits long or fewer.

CREDIT CARDS

Throughout this guide, the following abbreviations are used: **AE,** American Express; **DC,** Diner's Club; **MC,** Master Card; and **V,** Visa.

➤ REPORTING LOST CARDS: **American Express**(☎ 01273/696933). **Diner's Club** (☎ 0800/460800). **Master Card** (☎ 0800/964767). **Visa** (☎ 0800/895082).

CURRENCY

The units of currency in Great Britain are pound sterling (£) and pence (p): £50, £20, £10, and £5 bills; £2, £1

(100p), 50p, 20p, 10p, 5p, 2p, and 1p coins. At press time, the exchange rate was about U.S. $1.65 and Canadian $2.35 to the pound (also known as quid).

CURRENCY EXCHANGE

For the most favorable rates, **change money through banks.** Although ATM transaction fees may be higher abroad than at home, ATM rates are excellent because they are based on wholesale rates offered only by major banks. You won't do as well at exchange booths in airports or rail and bus stations, in hotels, in restaurants, or in stores. To avoid lines at airport exchange booths, **get a bit of local currency before you leave home.**

➤ EXCHANGE SERVICES: **International Currency Express** (☎ 888/278–6628 for orders, www.foreignmoney.com). **Thomas Cook Currency Services** (☎ 800/287–7362 for telephone orders and retail locations, www.us.thomascook.com).

TRAVELER'S CHECKS

Do you need traveler's checks? It depends on where you're headed. If you're going to rural areas and small towns, go with cash; traveler's checks are best used in cities. Lost or stolen checks can usually be replaced within 24 hours. To ensure a speedy refund, buy your own traveler's checks—don't let someone else pay for them: irregularities like this can cause delays. The person who bought the checks should make the call to request a refund.

PACKING

London can be cool, damp, and overcast, even in summer. You'll need a heavy coat for winter and a lightweight coat or warm jacket for summer. **Always bring an umbrella and, if possible, a raincoat.** Pack as you would for an American city: jackets and ties for expensive restaurants and nightspots, casual clothes elsewhere. Jeans are popular in London and are perfectly acceptable for sightseeing and informal dining. Blazers and sport jackets are popular here with men. For women, ordinary street dress is acceptable everywhere.

In your carry-on luggage, **pack an extra pair of eyeglasses or contact lenses** and **enough of any medication you take** to last the entire trip. You may also ask your doctor to write a spare prescription using the drug's generic name, since brand names may vary from country to country. In luggage to be checked, **never pack prescription drugs or valuables.** To avoid customs delays, carry medications in their original packaging. And don't forget to carry with you the addresses of offices that handle refunds of lost traveler's checks. If you plan to stay in budget hotels, take your own soap.

CHECKING LUGGAGE

How many carry-on bags you can bring with you is up to the airline. Most allow two, but not always, so make sure that everything you carry aboard will fit under your seat or in the overhead bin, and get to the gate early. Note that if you have a seat at the back of the plane, you'll probably board first, while the overhead bins are still empty.

If you are flying internationally, note that baggage allowances may be determined not by piece but by weight—generally 88 pounds (40 kilograms) in first class, 66 pounds (30 kilograms) in business class, and 44 pounds (20 kilograms) in economy.

Airline liability for baggage is limited to $1,250 per person on flights within the United States. On international flights it amounts to $9.07 per pound or $20 per kilogram for checked baggage (roughly $640 per 70-pound bag) and $400 per passenger for unchecked baggage. You can buy additional coverage at check-in for about $10 per $1,000 of coverage, but it excludes a rather extensive list of items, shown on your airline ticket.

Before departure, **itemize your bags' contents** and their worth, and label the bags with your name, address, and phone number. (If you use your home address, cover it so potential thieves can't see it readily.) Inside each bag, **pack a copy of your itinerary.** At check-in, **make sure that each bag is correctly tagged** with the destination airport's three-letter code. If your bags arrive damaged or fail to arrive at all, file a written report with the airline before leaving the airport.

PASSPORTS & VISAS

When traveling internationally, **carry your passport even if you don't need one** (it's always the best form of I.D.) and **make two photocopies of the data page** (one for someone at home and another for you, carried separately from your passport). If you lose your passport, promptly call the nearest embassy or consulate and the local police.

ENTERING GREAT BRITAIN

U.S. and Canadian citizens need only a valid passport to enter Great Britain for stays of up to 90 days.

PASSPORT OFFICES

The best time to apply for a passport or to renew is in fall and winter. Before any trip, check your passport's expiration date, and, if necessary, renew it as soon as possible.

➤ AUSTRALIAN CITIZENS: **Australian Passport Office** (☎ 131–232, www.dfat.gov.au/passports).

➤ CANADIAN CITIZENS: **Passport Office** (☎ 819/994–3500 or 800/567–6868, www.dfait-maeci.gc.ca/passport).

➤ NEW ZEALAND CITIZENS: **New Zealand Passport Office** (☎ 04/494–0700, www.passports.govt.nz).

➤ U.S. CITIZENS: **National Passport Information Center** (☎ 900/225–5674; calls are 35¢ per minute for automated service, $1.05 per minute for operator service).

SENIOR-CITIZEN TRAVEL

To qualify for age-related discounts, **mention your senior-citizen status up front** when booking hotel reservations (not when checking out) and before you're seated in restaurants (not when paying the bill). When renting a car, ask about promotional car-rental discounts, which can be cheaper than senior-citizen rates.

➤ EDUCATIONAL PROGRAMS: **Elderhostel** (✉ 75 Federal St., 3rd floor, Boston, MA 02110, ☎ 877/426–8056, FAX 877/426–2166, www.elderhostel.org). **Interhostel** (✉ University of New Hampshire, 6 Garrison Ave., Durham, NH 03824, ☎ 603/862–

1147 or 800/733–9753, FAX 603/862–1113, www.learn.unh.edu).

SIGHTSEEING TOURS

BY BUS

Guided sightseeing tours offer passengers a good introduction to the city from double-decker buses, which are open-topped in summer. Tours run daily and depart (9–5) from Haymarket, Baker Street, Grosvenor Gardens, Marble Arch, and Victoria. You may board or alight at any of about 21 stops to view the sights, and then get back on the next bus. Tickets (£12) may be bought from the driver. These tours include stops at places such as St. Paul's Cathedral and Westminster Abbey. Prices and pickup points vary according to the sights visited, but many pickup points are at major hotels.

➤ TOUR OPERATORS: **Evan Evans** (☎ 020/8332–2222), **Frames Rickards** (☎ 020/7837–3111), the **Original London Sightseeing Tour** (☎ 020/8877–1722), and the **Big Bus Company** (☎ 020/8944–7810). **Black Taxi Tour of London** (☎ 020/7289–4371).

BY CANAL

In summer, narrow boats and barges cruise London's two canals, the Grand Union and Regent's Canal; most vessels (they seat about 60) operate on the latter, which runs between Little Venice in the west (nearest tube: Warwick Avenue on the Bakerloo Line) and Camden Lock (about 200 yards north of Camden Town tube station). Fares are about £5 for 1½-hour cruises.

➤ CRUISE OPERATORS: **Canal Cruises** (☎ 020/7485–4433). **Jason's Trip** (☎ 020/7286–3428). **London Waterbus Company** (☎ 020/7482–2660).

BY FOOT

One of the best ways to get to know London is on foot, and there are many guided and themed walking tours from which to choose.

➤ TOUR OPERATORS: **Citisights** (☎ 020/8806–4325). **Historical Walks** (☎ 020/8668–4019). **Jack the Ripper Mystery Walks** (☎ 020/8558–9446). **Original London Walks**

(☎ 020/7624–3978). Another option is to hire your own **Blue Badge** accredited guide and tailor your own tour (☎ 020/7495–5504).

BY RIVER

All year round, but more frequently from April to October, boats cruise the Thames, offering a different view of the London skyline. Most leave from Westminster Pier, Charing Cross Pier, and Tower Pier. Downstream routes go to the Tower of London, Greenwich, and the Thames Barrier via Canary Wharf upstream; destinations include Kew, Richmond, and Hampton Court (mainly in summer). Most of the launches seat between 100 and 250 passengers, have a public-address system, and provide a running commentary on passing points of interest. Depending upon the destination, river trips may last from one to four hours.

➤ RIVER CRUISE OPERATORS: **Catamaran Cruisers** (from Charing Cross to Greenwich; ☎ 020/7839–3572). **Thames Cruises** (☎ 020/7930–3373 for the Thames Barrier and Greenwich). **Westminster Passenger Boat Services** (☎ 020/7930–4097).

A **Sail and Rail** ticket combines the modern wonders of Canary Wharf by Docklands Light Railway with a trip on the river. Tickets are available year-round from Westminster Pier or DLR stations, Canary Wharf, Island Gardens, and Tower Gateway (☎ 020/7363–9700); ticket holders also get discounted tickets to the London Aquarium at Westminster, the Tower Bridge Experience, and the National Maritime Museum, Greenwich.

EXCURSIONS

London Regional Transport, Green Line, Evan Evans, and **Frames Rickards** all offer day excursions by bus to places within easy reach of London, such as Hampton Court, Oxford, Stratford, and Bath.

STUDENTS IN LONDON

➤ I.D.s & SERVICES: **Council Travel** (CIEE; ✉ 205 E. 42nd St., 14th floor, New York, NY 10017, ☎ 212/822–2700 or 888/268–6245, FAX 212/822–2699, info@councilexchanges.org, www.councilexchanges.org) for mail

orders only, in the U.S. **Travel Cuts** (✉ 187 College St., Toronto, Ontario M5T 1P7, ☎ 416/979–2406 or 800/667–2887, www.travelcuts.com) in Canada.

TAXES

An airport departure tax of £20 (£10 for within U.K. and other EU countries) per person is payable and may be subject to more government tax increases, although it is included in the price of your ticket.

VALUE-ADDED TAX

The British sales tax (VAT, Value Added Tax) is 17½%. The tax is almost always included in quoted prices in shops, hotels, and restaurants.

Most travelers can **get a VAT refund** by either the Retail Export or the more cumbersome Direct Export method. Many large stores provide these services, but only if you request them; they will handle the paperwork. For the Retail Export method, you must ask the store for Form VAT 407 (you must have identification—passports are best), to be given to customs at your last port of departure. (Lines at major airports can be long, so allow plenty of time.) The refund will be forwarded to you in about eight weeks, minus a small service charge, either in the form of a credit to your charge card or as a British check, which American banks usually charge you to convert. With the Direct Export method, the goods go directly to your home; you must have a Form VAT 407 certified by customs, police, or a notary public when you get home and then sent back to the store, which will refund your money. For inquiries, call the local Customs & Excise office listed in the London telephone directory.

Global Refund is a V.A.T. refund service that makes getting your money back hassle-free. The service is available Europe-wide at 130,000 affiliated stores. In participating stores, **ask for the Global Refund form** (called a Shopping Cheque). Have it stamped like any customs form by customs officials when you leave the European Union. Then take the form to one of the more than 700 Global Refund counters—conveniently located at every major airport and border crossing—and your money will be refunded on the spot in the form of cash, check, or a refund to your credit-card account (minus a small percentage for processing).

➤ V.A.T. REFUNDS: **Global Refund** (✉ 707 Summer St., Stamford, CT 06901, ☎ 800/566–9828, FAX 203/ 674–8709, taxfree@us.globalrefund. com, www.globalrefund.com).

TAXIS

Those big black taxicabs are as much a part of the London streetscape as the red double-decker buses, yet many have been replaced by the new boxy, sharp- edged model, and the beauty of others is marred by the advertising they carry on their sides. Hotels and main tourist areas have cab stands (just take the first in line), but you can also flag one down from the roadside. If the yellow FOR HIRE sign on the top is lit, the taxi is available. Cab drivers often cruise at night with their signs unlit so that they can choose their passengers and avoid those they think might cause trouble. If you see an unlit, passenger-less cab, hail it: you might be lucky.

➤ TAXI FARES: Fares start at £1.40 and increase by units of 20p per 281 yards or 55.5 seconds until the fare exceeds £8.60. After that, it's 20p for each 188 yards or 37 seconds. A 60p surcharge is added on weekday nights 8–midnight and until 8 PM on Saturday. Over Christmas and on New Year's Eve, it rises to £2—and there's 40p extra for each additional passenger. Note that fares are usually raised in April of each year. Tips are extra, usually 10%–15% per ride.

TELEPHONES

AREA & COUNTRY CODES

The country code for Great Britain is 44. Since the summer of 1999, London area codes have been undergoing a major change. In order to facilitate expanded telephone access, British Telecom and other British telephone services are in the process of instituting new codes for all London telephone numbers. The former area codes of 0171 and 0181 are being merged into one London area code—020—with a new prefix, either 7 or 8, also being added before the first digit of the old phone number. Note that the new area

codes will affect London's actual telephone numbers—for example, 0171/222–3333 will now become 020/ 7222–3333, with an increase up to eight digits for the telephone number proper. Under the new system, 0800 numbers will not change; national information numbers of 0345 will change to 0845 and add a digit. Details are on the Internet at www. numberchange.org. There is help available, within England, at ☎ 0800/ 731–0202; from the U.S., at ☎ 020/ 7634–8700 (using the new system).

When dialing Great Britain from abroad, drop the initial 0 from these local area codes. The country code is 1 for the U.S. and Canada, 61 for Australia, 64 for New Zealand, and 44 for the U.K.

DIRECTORY & OPERATOR ASSISTANCE

For information anywhere in Britain, dial 192. For the operator, dial 100. For assistance with international calls, dial 155.

INTERNATIONAL CALLS

When calling from overseas to access a London telephone number, drop the 0 from the prefix and dial only 20 (or any other British area code) and then the eight-digit phone number. To give one example: Let's say you're calling Buckingham Palace—020/7839–1377 (or, in the old system, 0171/839– 1377)—from the U.S. to inquire about tours and hours. First, dial 011 (the international access code), then 44 (Great Britain's country code), then 20 (London's center city code), then the remainder of the telephone number, 7839–1377, which, under the new area code system, now includes a 7 prefix added to the old number.

LOCAL CALLS

You don't have to dial London's central area code (020) if you are calling inside London itself—just the new eight-digit telephone number.

LONG-DISTANCE CALLS

For long-distance calls within Britain, dial the area code (which begins with 01), followed by the number. The area-code prefix is only used when you are dialing from outside the city. In provincial areas, the dialing codes for nearby towns are often posted in the booth.

LONG-DISTANCE SERVICES

AT&T, MCI, and Sprint access codes make calling long distance relatively convenient, but you may find the local access number blocked in many hotel rooms. First ask the hotel operator to connect you. If the hotel operator balks, ask for an international operator, or dial the international operator yourself. One way to improve your odds of getting connected to your long-distance carrier is to travel with more than one company's calling card (a hotel may block Sprint, for example, but not MCI). If all else fails, call from a pay phone.

You can also pick up one of the many instant phonecards from newsstands, which can be used from residential, hotel, and public pay phones. You can call the U.S. for as little as 5p per minute with America First. Others with special deals are First National, Africa and Asia cards, and the Millennium Phonecard.

➤ ACCESS CODES: **AT&T Direct** (In the U.K., there are AT&T access numbers to dial the U.S. using three different phone types—Cable & Wireless: ☎ 0500/890011; British Telecom: ☎ 0800/890011; and AT&T: ☎ 0800/0130011; ☎ 800/435–0812 for other areas). **MCI WorldPhone** (In the U.K., dial ☎ 0800/890222 for the U.S via MCI; 800/444–4141 for other areas). **Sprint International Access** (In the U.K., there are Sprint access numbers to dial the U.S. using two different phone types—Cable & Wireless: ☎ 0500/890877; and British Telecom: ☎ 0800/890877; 800/877–4646 for other areas).

PHONE CARDS

Public card phones operate with special cards that you can buy from post offices or newsstands. They are ideal for longer calls; are composed of units of 10p; and come in values of £3, £5, £10, and more. To use a card phone, lift the receiver, insert your card, and dial the number. An indicator panel shows the number of units used. At the end of your call, the card will be returned. Where credit cards are taken, slide the card through, as indicated.

PUBLIC PHONES

There are three types of phones: those that accept (a) only coins, (b) only British Telecom (BT) phone cards, or (c) BT phone cards and credit cards.

The coin-operated phones are of the push-button variety; the workings of coin-operated telephones vary, but there are usually instructions in each unit. Most take 10p, 20p, 50p, and £1 coins. Insert the coins *before* dialing (minimum charge is 10p). If you hear a repeated single tone after dialing, the line is busy; a continual tone means the number is unobtainable (or that you have dialed the wrong—or no— prefix). The indicator panel shows you how much money is left; add more whenever you like. If there is no answer, replace the receiver and your money will be returned.

All calls are charged according to the time of day. Standard rate is weekdays 8 AM–6 PM; cheap rate is weekdays 6 PM–8 AM and all day on weekends, when it's even cheaper. A local call before 6 PM costs 15p for three minutes; this doubles to 30p for the same from a pay phone. A daytime call to the United States will cost 24p a minute on a regular phone (weekends are cheaper), 80p on a pay phone.

TIME

London is five hours ahead of New York City. In other words, when it is 3 PM in New York (or 12 noon in Los Angeles) it is 8 PM in London. Note that London and most European countries also move their clocks ahead for the one-hour differential when daylight saving time goes into effect (although they make the changeover several days after the U.S.).

TIPPING

Many restaurants and large hotels (particularly those belonging to chains) will automatically add a 10%–15% service charge to your bill, so **always check in advance before you hand out any extra money.** You are, of course, welcome to tip on top of that for exceptional service.

Do not tip movie or theater ushers, elevator operators, or bar staff in pubs—although you may buy them a drink if you're feeling generous.

Washroom attendants may display a saucer, in which it's reasonable to leave 20p or so.

Here's a guide for other tipping situations. **Restaurants:** 10%–20% of the check for full meals if service is not already included (when you're paying by credit card, check to see if a service tip has not already been included in the bill before you fill in the correct amount in the total box of your credit slip voucher); a small token if you're just having coffee or tea. **Taxis:** 10%–15%, or perhaps a little more for a short ride. **Porters:** 50p–£1 per bag. **Doormen:** £1 for hailing taxis or for carrying bags to check-in desk. **Bellhops:** £1 for carrying bags to rooms, £1 for room service. **Hairdressers:** 10%–15% of the bill, plus £1–£2 for the hair-washer.

TOURS & PACKAGES

Because everything is prearranged on a prepackaged tour or independent vacation, you'll spend less time planning—and often get it all at a good price.

BOOKING WITH AN AGENT

Travel agents are excellent resources. But it's a good idea to collect brochures from several agencies as some agents' suggestions may be influenced by relationships with tour and package firms that reward them for volume sales. If you have a special interest, **find an agent with expertise in that area**; ASTA (☞ Travel Agencies, *below*) has a database of specialists worldwide.

Make sure your travel agent knows the accommodations and other services of the place they're recommending. Ask about the hotel's location, room size, beds, and whether it has a pool, room service, or programs for children, if you care about these. Has your agent been there in person or sent others whom you can contact?

Do some homework on your own, too: local tourism boards can provide information about lesser-known and small-niche operators, some of which may sell only direct.

BUYER BEWARE

Each year consumers are stranded or lose their money when tour operators—even large ones with excellent reputations—go out of business. So **check out the operator.** Ask several travel agents about its reputation, and try to **book with a company that has a consumer-protection program.** (Look for information in the company's brochure.) In the United States, members of the National Tour Association and the United States Tour Operators Association are required to set aside funds to cover your payments and travel arrangements in the event that the company defaults. It's also a good idea to choose a company that participates in the American Society of Travel Agents' Tour Operator Program (TOP); ASTA will act as mediator in any disputes between you and your tour operator.

Remember that the more your package or tour includes the better you can predict the ultimate cost of your vacation. Make sure you know exactly what is covered, and **beware of hidden costs.** Are taxes, tips, and transfers included? Entertainment and excursions? These can add up.

➤ TOUR-OPERATOR RECOMMENDATIONS: **American Society of Travel Agents** (☞ Travel Agencies, *below*). **National Tour Association** (NTA; ✉ 546 E. Main St., Lexington, KY 40508, ☎ 606/226–4444 or 800/682–8886, www.ntaonline.com). **United States Tour Operators Association** (USTOA; ✉ 342 Madison Ave., Suite 1522, New York, NY 10173, ☎ 212/599–6599 or 800/468–7862, FAX 212/599–6744, ustoa@aol.com, www.ustoa.com).

TRAIN TRAVEL TO AND FROM LONDON

TRAIN INFORMATION THROUGHOUT BRITAIN

The British rail system has been totally privatized, but apart from different names, the service has not been altered radically. National Rail Enquiries (NRE) gives information and takes bookings by credit card. Please note that delays are often a national joking matter, and also that smoking is forbidden in the rail carriages. Some services offer first class, and reserved seats; this just ensures you have a seat and more space around you. Some trains have refreshment carriages. Many discounts are available, such as the young person's rail card and family travel cards, which can be bought from most mainline stations (Kings Cross, Paddington, Euston, Victoria, Waterloo) and NRE. In the U.K.: **National Rail Enquiries** (☎ 0845/748–4950); outside the U.K.: (☎ 0161/236–3522).

TRANSPORTATION AROUND LONDON

The public transport network in London covers most places you would want to go and is far easier than driving a car and having to hassle with traffic and parking.

TRAVEL AGENCIES

A good travel agent puts your needs first. Look for an agency that has been in business at least five years, emphasizes customer service, and has someone on staff who specializes in your destination. In addition, **make sure the agency belongs to a professional trade organization.** The American Society of Travel Agents (ASTA), with 27,000 agents in some 170 countries, is the largest and most influential in the field. Operating under the motto "Integrity in Travel," it maintains and enforces a strict code of ethics and will step in to help mediate any agent-client disputes if necessary. ASTA also maintains a Web site that includes a directory of agents. (If a travel agency is also acting as your tour operator, see Buyer Beware in Tours & Packages, above.)

➤ LOCAL AGENT REFERRALS: American Society of Travel Agents (ASTA; ☎ 800/965–2782 24-hr hot line, FAX 703/684–8319, www.astanet.com). Association of British Travel Agents (✉ 68–71 Newman St., London W1P 4AH, ☎ 020/7637–2444, FAX 020/7637–0713, information@abta.co.uk, www.abtanet.com). Association of Canadian Travel Agents (✉ 1729 Bank St., Suite 201, Ottawa, Ontario K1V 7Z5, ☎ 613/521–0474, FAX 613/521–0805, acta.ntl@sympatico.ca). **Australian**

Federation of Travel Agents (✉ Level 3, 309 Pitt St., Sydney 2000, ☎ 02/9264–3299, FAX 02/9264–1085, www.afta.com.au). **Travel Agents' Association of New Zealand** (✉ Box 1888, Wellington 10033, ☎ 04/499–0104, FAX 04/499–0827, taanz@tiasnet.co.nz).

UNDERGROUND TUBE TRAVEL

Known colloquially as the "tube," London's extensive Underground system is by far the most widely used form of city transportation. Its easily marked routes, crystal-clear signage, and extensive connections make it a delight to travel. Trains run both beneath and above ground out into the suburbs, and all stations are clearly marked with the London Underground circular symbol. (In Britain, the word "subway" means "pedestrian underpass.") Trains are all one class; smoking is *not* allowed on board or in the stations.

There are 10 basic lines—all named. The Central, District, Northern, Metropolitan, and Piccadilly lines all have branches, usually taking you to the outlying sections of the city, so **be sure to note which branch is needed for your particular destination.** Electronic platform signs tell you the final stop and route of the next train, and some signs conveniently indicate how many minutes you'll have to wait for the train to arrive. Begun in the Victorian era, the Underground is still being expanded and improved. The East London Line, which runs from Shoreditch and Whitechapel south to New Cross, reopened after major reconstruction in March 1998. The Jubilee Line extension opened at the end of 1999; this state-of-the-art subway sweeps from Green Park to London Bridge and Southwark, with connections to Canary Wharf and the Docklands and the Millennium Dome, and on to the east at Stratford. One of the newest lines is the Docklands Light Railway, which runs from Stratford in east London and from Bank and Tower Gateway to Island Gardens. The new DLR extension (completed at the end of 1999) passes the *Cutty Sark* in Greenwich, continues on to the Millennium Dome (North Greenwich station), and terminates at Lewisham.

FARES & SCHEDULES

For both buses and tube fares, London is divided into six concentric zones; the fare goes up the farther out you travel. Ask at Underground ticket counters for the London Transport booklets, which give details of all the various ticket options for the tube. Traveling without a valid ticket makes you liable for an on-the-spot fine (£10 at press time).

For one trip between any two stations, you can buy an ordinary single (one-way ticket) for travel anytime on the day of issue; if you're coming back on the same route the same day, an ordinary return (round-trip ticket) costs twice the single fare. Singles vary in price from £1.40 to £3.40—expensive if you're making several journeys in a day. There are several passes good for both the tube and the bus.

Several **Travelcards** for tube and bus travel are available at tube and rail stations, as well as some newsstands. These allow unrestricted travel on the tube, most buses, and national railways in the Greater London zones and are valid weekdays after 9:30 AM, weekends, and all public holidays. They cannot be used on airbuses, Night Buses, or for certain special services. Other options include the following: a **One Day Travelcard** (£3.80–£4.50); **Weekend Travelcards,** for the two days of the weekend and on any two consecutive days during public holidays (£5.70–£6.70); **Family Travelcards,** which are one-day tickets for one or two adults with one to four children (£3–£3.60 with one child, additional children cost 60p each); while the **Carnet** is a book of 10 single tickets valid for central Zone 1 (£10) to use anytime over a year. Up-to-date prices can be found on the LT Web site www.londontransport.co.uk. The **Visitor's Travelcard** may be bought in the United States and Canada for three, four, and seven days' travel; it is the same as the LT Card and has a booklet of discount vouchers to London attractions. In the United States, the Visitor's Travelcard costs $25, $32, and $49, respectively; in Canada, C$29, C$36, and C$55, respectively. Apply to travel agents or, in the United States, to **Rail Europe.**

Trains begin running just after 5 AM Monday–Saturday; the last services leave central London between midnight and 12:30 AM. On Sunday, trains start two hours later and finish about an hour earlier. Frequency of trains depends on the route and the time of day, but normally you should not have to wait more than 10 minutes in central areas.

A pocket map of the tube network is available free from most Underground ticket counters. A large map is on the wall of each platform. Within this edition, a map of the Underground system is included on the detachable Rand-McNally map found inside the back cover.

There are LT (London Transport) Travel Information Centres at the following tube stations: Euston, Hammersmith, King's Cross, Liverpool Street, Oxford Circus, Piccadilly Circus, St. James's Park, and Victoria, open 7:15 AM–10 PM; and at Heathrow (in Terminals 1, 2, and 4), open 6 AM–3 PM. For information on all London tube and bus times, fares, and so on, dial ☎ 020/7222–1234 (24 hours). For travelers with disabilities, get the free leaflet **"Access to the Underground"** (☎ 020/7918–3312).

➤ UNDERGROUND INFORMATION: **Rail Europe** (✉ 226 Westchester Ave., White Plains, NY 10604, ☎ 888/274–8724).

VISITOR INFORMATION

➤ IN THE U.S.: **British Tourist Authority** (BTA; ✉ 551 5th Ave., 7th floor, New York, NY 10176, ☎ 212/986–2200 or 800/462–2748; 625 N. Michigan Ave., Suite 1510, Chicago, IL 60611 [personal callers only]).

➤ IN CANADA: **British Tourist Authority** (✉ 5915 Airport Rd., Suite 120, Mississauga, Ontario L4V 1T1, ☎ 905/405–1840 or 800/847–4885).

➤ IN THE U.K.: **British Tourist Authority** (✉ Thames Tower, Black's Rd., London W6 9EL, ☎ 020/8846–9000).

➤ IN LONDON: Go in person to the **London Tourist Information Centre** at Victoria Station Forecourt for general information (Easter–Oct., daily 8–7; Nov.–Easter, Mon.–Sat. 8–6, Sun.

8:30–4) or to the **Britain Visitor Centre** (✉ 1 Regent St., Piccadilly Circus SW1Y 4NX) for travel, hotel, and entertainment information (July–Sept., weekdays 9–6:30, weekends 10–4; May–Sept., weekdays 9–5, Sat. 9–5).

➤ BY PHONE: The London Tourist Board's **Visitorcall** (☎ 0839/123456) phone guide to London gives information about events, theater, museums, transport, shopping, and restaurants. A three-month events calendar (☎ 0839/123401) and an annual version (☎ 0891/353715) are available by fax (set fax machine to polling mode, or press start/receive after the tone). Visitorcall charges start at 50p per minute, depending on the time of the call. Note that this service is accessible only in the U.K.

➤ U.S. GOVERNMENT ADVISORIES: **U.S. Department of State** (✉ Overseas Citizens Services Office, Room 4811 N.S., 2201 C St. NW, Washington, DC 20520, ☎ 202/647–5225 for interactive hot line, 301/946–4400 for computer bulletin board, FAX 202/647–3000 for interactive hot line); enclose a self-addressed, stamped, business-size envelope.

WEB SITES

Do check out the World Wide Web when you're planning. You'll find everything from current weather forecasts to virtual tours of famous cities. Fodor's Web site, www.fodors. com, is a great place to start your on-line travels. When you see a 🎣 in this book, go to www.fodors.com/urls for an up-to-date link to that destination's site. For more information specifically on London, visit one of the following:

The British Tourist Authority Web site is at www.visitbritain.com. Its new "gateway" Web site, www.us-agateway.visitbritain.com, focuses on information most helpful to Britain-bound U.S. travelers. The official London web site is www.londontown.com, which also supplies helpful links to other Web sites, including Evening Standard Online (www.thisislondon.com), London Transport, the Palace, No. 10 Downing Street, UK Weather, and the BBC (www.bbc.co.uk).

For London events and news months in advance, visit the following culture and entertainment Web sites: www.timeout.co.uk, www.officiallondontheatre.co.uk, and www.ukcalling.co.uk.royal-albert. For the hotel scene in London, visit www.demon. co.uk/hotel-uk. For information about millennium events throughout 2000, click on londonmillenniumcity.com. For the full array of walking tours offered by the excellent Original London Walks, try www.walks.com.

WHEN TO GO

The heaviest tourist season in Britain runs mid-April–mid-October, with another peak around Christmas—though the tide never really ebbs. The spring is the time to see the countryside and the royal London parks and gardens at their freshest; early summer to catch the roses and full garden splendor; the fall to enjoy near-ideal exploring conditions. The British take their vacations mainly in July and August, and the resorts are crowded. London in summer, though full of visitors, is also full of interesting things to see and do. But be warned: air-conditioning is rarely found in places other than department stores, modern restaurants, hotels, and cinemas in London, and on a hot summer day you'll swelter. The winter can be rather dismal and is frequently wet and usually cold, but all the theaters, concerts, and exhibitions go full speed.

CLIMATE

London's weather has always been contrary, and in recent years it has proved red hot and cool by turns. It is virtually impossible to forecast what the pattern might be, but you can be fairly certain that it will not be what you expect. The main feature of the British weather is that it is generally mild—with some savage exceptions, especially in summer. It is also fairly damp—though even that has been changing in recent years, with the odd bout of drought. The following list includes the average daily maximum and minimum temperatures for London.

➤ FORECASTS: **Weather Channel Connection** (☎ 900/932–8437), 95¢ per minute from a Touch-Tone phone.

Climate in London

Jan.	43F	6C	May	62F	17C	Sept.	65F	19C
	36	2		47	8		52	11
Feb.	44F	7C	June	69F	20C	Oct.	58F	14C
	36	2		53	12		46	8
Mar.	50F	10C	July	71F	22C	Nov.	50F	10C
	38	3		56	14		42	5
Apr.	56F	13C	Aug.	71F	21C	Dec.	45F	7C
	42	6		56	13		38	4

FESTIVALS AND SEASONAL EVENTS

Top seasonal events in and around London include the Chelsea Flower Show in May, Derby Day at Epsom Racecourse, Wimbledon Lawn Tennis Championships and Henley Regatta in June, and a new innovation, the London Arts Season, which combines many events in theater, art, and music with good deals on hotels and meals out.

There is a complete list of ticket agencies in *Britain Events,* available in person only from the **Britain Visitor Centre** (✉ 1 Regent St., Tube: Piccadilly Circus). When in London, check the weekly magazine **Time Out,** available at newsstands, for an ongoing calendar of special events. Or, for 49p per minute, call London Tourist Board's 24-hour **Visitorcall** (☎ 0839/ 123400 in U.K. only) service, which offers the latest on events throughout the city.

➤ MID-DEC.: **Olympia International Show Jumping Championships,** is an international equestrian competition in Olympia's Grand Hall. For information, ☎ 020/7370–8209. **New Year's Eve at Trafalgar Square** is a huge, freezing, sometimes drunken slosh through the fountains to celebrate the new year. Unorganized by any official body, it is held in the ceremonial heart of London under an enormous Christmas tree, which is a gift from the people of Norway that stands from early December to early January. Unlike Americans, however, most Brits celebrate New Year's Eve at home.

➤ JAN. 1: The **London Parade** is a good ole U.S.-style extravaganza complete with cheerleaders, floats, and marching bands, led by the Lord Mayor of Westminster. It starts on the south side of Westminster Bridge at 12:30, travels to Parliament Square, Whitehall, Trafalgar Square, Lower Regent Street, and Piccadilly, and finishes in Berkeley Square around 3 PM. No tickets are required.

➤ JAN. 31: **Charles I Commemoration** is held on the anniversary of the monarch's execution and brings out Londoners dressed in 17th-century garb for a march tracing his last walk from St. James's Palace to the Banqueting House in Whitehall.

➤ MID- TO LATE MAR. AND MID- TO LATE SEPT.: **Chelsea Antiques Fair** is a twice-yearly fair with wide range of pre-1830 pieces for sale. ✉ *Old Town Hall, King's Rd., Chelsea SW3 4PW,* ☎ 01444/482514.

➤ MID-MAR.: **Open House** is a rare one-day chance to view historic London interiors of buildings usually closed to the public. ☎ 020/8341– 1371.

➤ LATE MAR.: **British Antique Dealers' Association Fair,** the newest of the major fairs, is large and prestigious, with many affordable pieces. ✉ *Duke of York's Headquarters, King's Rd., Chelsea SW3,* ☎ 020/ 7589–6108.

➤ LATE MAR.: **Head of the River Boat Race** offers the spectacle of 420 eight-man crews from Oxford and Cambridge universities dipping their 6,720 oars in the Thames as they race from Mortlake to Putney. The best view is from Surrey Bank above Chiswick Bridge (tube to Chiswick); check *Time Out* for the starting time, which depends on the tide. The **Oxford Versus Cambridge University Boat Race** usually takes place the week after, over the same 4½ mi course, carrying on a tradition since around 1829. In 1912 both boats sank spectacularly.

➤ EARLY APR.: **Chaucer Festival** allows Londoners to don medieval garb and parade from Southwark Cathedral to the Tower of London, where jugglers and strolling minstrels party the day away. ☎ 01227/470379.

➤ MID-APR.: **London Marathon** is a New York–style marathon through London's streets. Runners from 68 countries start in Greenwich and Blackheath at 9–9:30 AM, then run via Docklands and Canary Wharf, to the Tower of London and Parliament Square, and finish in the Mall.

➤ APR. 21: **Queen's Birthday** earns a showy 41-gun salute at Hyde Park. In June (☞ *below*), Elizabeth II's ceremonial b-day is celebrated by Trooping the Colour.

➤ MID-MAY: **Punch and Judy Festival** is held on the second Sunday in May and offers a May Fayre Procession in the morning, services at St. Paul's Church, then puppet shows until dusk. A lovely event for children of all ages! ✉ *Covent Garden Piazza, London, WC2B,* ☎ 020/7375–0441.

➤ MID-MAY: **Royal Windsor Horse Show** is a major show-jumping event attended by some members of the Royal Family. ✉ *Show Box Office, 4 Grove Parade, Buxton, Derbyshire SK17 6AJ,* ☎ 01298/72272.

➤ LATE MAY: **Chelsea Flower Show,** Britain's most prestigious flower show, is always graced by the Royals and covers 22 acres. ✉ *Royal Hospital Rd., Chelsea SW3,* ☎ 020/7630–7422.

➤ LATE MAY–LATE AUG.: **Glyndebourne Festival Opera** is a unique opportunity to see international stars in a bucolic setting and in a brand-new theater. Tickets go fast and early. ✉ *Glyndebourne Festival Opera, Lewes, Sussex BN8 5UU,* ☎ 01273/812321.

➤ LATE MAY–LATE AUG.: **Shakespeare Under the Stars** gives you the chance to see the Bard of Bard's plays performed at Regent's Park Open Air Theatre. Performances are usually Monday–Saturday at 8 PM, with matinees on Wednesday, Thursday, and Saturday. ✉ *Inner Circle, London, NW1,* ☎ 020/7486–2431.

➤ EARLY JUNE: **Beating Retreat by the Guards Massed Bands** brings more than 500 musicians to parade at Horse Guards, Whitehall. *Tickets from Household Division Fund,* ✉ *Block 8, Wellington Barracks, Birdcage Walk, SW1E 6HQ,* ☎ 020/7414–3253.

➤ EARLY JUNE: **Derby Day** is the best-known event on the horse-racing calendar. *Information from United Racecourses Ltd.,* ✉ *Racecourse Paddock, Epsom, Surrey KT18 5NJ,* ☎ 013727/26311.

➤ MID-JUNE: The **Grosvenor House Antiques Fair** is one of the most prestigious antiques fairs in Britain. ✉ *Grosvenor House Hotel, Park La., London W1A 3AA,* ☎ 020/7499–6363.

➤ MID-JUNE: **Trooping the Colour,** Queen Elizabeth's colorful official birthday parade, is held at Horse Guards, Whitehall, usually on the second or third Saturday of June. Write for tickets *only* between January 1 and February 28, enclosing a self-addressed stamped envelope. ✉ *Ticket Office, Headquarters, Household Division, Horse Guards, London SW1A 2AX,* ☎ 020/7414 2479.

➤ MID-JUNE: **Royal Meeting at Ascot** brings the horsey set and their enormous hats out in force during the third week in June (Tuesday–Friday; Thursday is the high-fashion Ladies Day). General admission is available but reserve months in advance; for tickets (you must be sponsored) to the Royal Enclosure, write to ✉ Her Majesty's Representative, Ascot Office, St. James's Palace, London SW1 (☎ 020/7930–9882). ✉ *Ascot Racecourse, Ascot, Berkshire SL5 7JN,* ☎ 01344/622211.

➤ MID JUNE–EARLY SEPT.: **Kenwood Lakeside Concerts** offers fireworks and classical concerts under the stars in the park of London's regal stately house. ✉ *Kenwood House, Hampstead La., London, NW3,* ☎ 020/8348–1286.

➤ LATE JUNE–EARLY JULY: The **Wimbledon Lawn Tennis Championships** is held at the All England Lawn Tennis and Croquet Club in Wimbledon. Write early to enter the lottery for tickets for Centre and Number One courts; tickets for outside courts are available daily at the gate. ✉ *Church Rd., Wimbledon, London SW19 5AE,* ☎ *020/8946–2244.*

➤ LATE JUNE–EARLY JULY: **Henley Royal Regatta** is an international rowing event and top social occasion at Henley-upon-Thames, Oxfordshire. For information, ☎ 01491/572153.

➤ EARLY JULY: **Hampton Court Palace Flower Show** is a five-day event that nearly rivals the Chelsea Flower Show for glamour. ✉ *East Molesey,* ☎ *020/7834–4333.*

➤ MID-JULY–MID-SEPT.: **Henry Wood Promenade Concerts** is a marvelous series of concerts at the Royal Albert Hall. ✉ *Box Office, Royal Albert Hall, Kensington Gore, London, SW7 2AP,* ☎ *020/7589–8212.*

➤ LATE AUG.: **Notting Hill Carnival** is one of the liveliest street festivals in England. Caribbean foods, reggae music, and street parades are part of the swirling event, usually held on the last Sunday and Monday in August. For information, contact ☎ 020/8964–0544.

➤ EARLY OCT.: **Pearly Harvest Festival Service** draws a crowd of costermongers to the Church of St. Martin-in-the-Fields on the first Sunday in October. The Pearly Kings and Queens strut their famous costumes. ✉ *Trafalgar Square, London, WC2,* ☎ *020/7930–0089.*

➤ EARLY NOV.: **London to Brighton Veteran Car Run,** a run from Hyde Park in London to Brighton in East Sussex. No tickets are required. For information, ☎ 01753/681736.

➤ EARLY NOV.: **Lord Mayor's Procession and Show.** At the lord mayor's inauguration, a procession takes place from the Guildhall in the City to the Royal Courts of Justice. No tickets are required. For information, ☎ 020/7606–3030.

➤ NOV. 5: **Guy Fawkes Day** celebrates a foiled 1605 attempt to blow up Parliament. Fireworks are held throughout London, but the place to be is the bonfire festivity on Primrose Hill near Camden Town.

INDEX

Icons and Symbols

★ Our special recommen-
  dations
✕ Restaurant
🏠 Lodging establishment
✕🏠 Lodging establishment
  whose restaurant war-
  rants a special trip
🐤 Good for kids (rubber
  duck)
☞ Sends you to another
  section of the guide for
  more information
✉ Address
☎ Telephone number
🕐 Opening and closing
  times
💷 Admission prices
🔗 Sends you to
  www.fodors.com/urls
  for up-to-date links to
  the property's Web site

Numbers in white and black
circles ③ ❸ that appear on
the maps, in the margins, and
within the tours correspond
to one another.

A

Abbey Court 🏠, 215
Abbey House Hotel 🏠, 207
Abbey Road Studios, 137
Academy Town House 🏠,
  217
Accessorize (shop), 260
Adaro House 🏠, 215
Addresses, 293
Adelphi, 71
Admiralty Arch, 40, 41
Aerobics, 239
Agnès B (shop), 260
Air travel, 293–294
Alastair Little ✕, 169
The Albert (pub), 189
Albert Memorial, 39, 124,
  125
Alfie's Antique Market, 253
Alhambra Hotel 🏠, 217
All Souls Church, 65
American Bar, 223
Andrew Edmunds ✕, 168
Anne Hathaway's Cottage,
  279
Antiquarius (shop), 253
Antiques, 253–255, 320,
  321
Apartment agencies, 219–
  220
Apartment rentals, 307–308
Apsley House (Wellington
  Museum), 60, 61

Aquascutum (shop), 257
Armoury of St. James's
  (shop), 265
Arnold Circus, 101, 102
Arosfa Hotel 🏠, 217
Arts, 222, 229–237
Ashmolean Museum, 277
Asia de Cuba ✕, 170–171
Asprey & Garrard (shop),
  246, 267–268
Assembly Rooms, 274
Astoria (rock club), 227
Athenaeum (club), 68
Athenaeum 🏠, 196–197
Atlantic Bar and Grill, 223
ATMs, 310
Aubergine ✕, 179
Avenue ✕, 166

B

Bagley's Studio (nightclub),
  225
Ballet, 222, 231
Balliol College, 277
Bank ✕, 172
Bank of England, 87, 88
Bankside Gallery, 108, 110
Banqueting House, 41, 43
Bar Gansa ✕, 140
Bar Italia ✕, 168
Bar Rumba (nightclub), 225
Barbican Centre (arts
  complex), 87, 88, 231,
  232, 233, 234
Barfly Club (rock club),
  227–228
Bars, 223–224, 228–229
Basil Street 🏠, 210
Bath, 273–274
Bath Abbey, 273
Bayswater, 213–216
BBC Experience, 60, 61, 65
Beach Blanket Babylon (bar),
  223
Beaches, 240–241
Beating Retreat by the
  Guards Massed Bands, 321
Beatles, 137
Beauchamp Tower, 99
Beaufort 🏠, 208
Bed-and-breakfast agencies,
  219–220
Beeton's ✕, 153
Beigel Bake (shop), 104
Belgo Centraal ✕, 171
Belgrave Place, 119, 120
Belgravia, 118–123, 208–
  213
Bell, Book and Radmall
  (shop, 255
Belvedere ✕, 181, 187
Berkeley 🏠, 208
Berkeley Square, 61, 63
Bermondsey (street market),
  269
Bertorelli's ✕, 172

Berwick Street (street
  market), 269
Bethnal Green Museum of
  Childhood, 101, 102
Bibendum ✕, 174
Bicycling, 239
Big Ben, 47
Bill Bentley's ✕, 185–186
Black Eagle Brewery, 101,
  102, 104
Black Friar (pub), 189
Black Market (shop), 256
Blakes 🏠, 205
Blazer (shop), 259
Blind Beggar (pub), 102,
  104
Bloody Tower, 98
Bloomsbury, 77–85, 173–
  174, 216–218
Bloomsbury Square, 78, 79
Blue Anchor ✕, 150
Bluebird ✕, 178–179
Bluewater (shopping
  center), 245–246
Boat tours, 145, 149–150
Boating, 241–242
Bodleian Library, 276
Bond Street, 60, 63
Bonhams (shop), 254
Books and videos about
  London, 288–289
Books for Cooks (shop), 255
Bookshops, 255–256
Borders (shop), 255
Bow Street Magistrates'
  Court, 70, 71
Box (gay bar), 228–229
Brasserie ✕, 50
Brasserie St. Quentin ✕, 176
Brass-rubbing centers, 53,
  58
Brick Lane, 100, 104, 269
Brick Lane Music Hall, 102,
  104
Bridgewater (shop), 256
British Airways London Eye
  (Ferris wheel), 38, 109,
  110
British Antique Dealers'
  Association Fair, 321
British Library, 38, 78, 79
British Museum, 38–39, 78,
  79, 81–82, 265–266
  restaurant and café in, 82
Broad Walk, 143
Brompton Bay ✕, 174
Brompton Oratory (church),
  124, 125
Brora (shop), 260–261
Brown's ✕🏠, 162, 187–
  188, 197
Browns (shop), 246, 261
Bryanston Court 🏠, 201
Buckingham Palace, 40, 43–
  44
Bug Bar, 223

Bulldog Club (bed-and-breakfast agency), 219
Burberry's (shop), 257
Burlington Arcade (shops), 60, 63
Bus travel, 280, 296
Business hours, 296
Butler and Wilson (shop), 268
Butler's Wharf, 108, 110
Butler's Wharf Chop House ✕, 187
Byward Tower, 98

C

Cabarets, 224
Cabinet War Rooms, 40, 44
Cactus Blue ✕, 178
Cadogan Hotel Bar, 223
Café de Paris (bar), 223–224
Café Fish ✕, 169
Café Flo ✕, 171
Café-in-the-Crypt ✕, 54
Caffé Mamma ✕, 153
Cambridge, 274–276
Camden Lock, 136, 137, 139
Camden Lock Market, 269–270
Camden Palace (nightclub), 225
Camden Passage (street market), 270
Camden Town, 186, 246
Cameras and photography, 296–297
Canterbury Quadrangle (museum), 277
Capital ✕🏨, 176, 208
Car rental, 297–298
Car travel, 298–299
Caravela ✕, 178
Carlton House Terrace, 40, 44, 46
Carlyle's House, 119, 120
Carnaby Street, 70, 71, 73
Cartier (shop), 268
Cash machines. ☞ ATMs
Casinos, 224–225
Cath Kidston (shop), 261
CD shops, 256
Cenotaph (statue), 46
Central Criminal Court (Old Bailey), 92
Centre for Economic Botany, 151
Changing of the Guard, 44
Channel Tunnel, 299
Chapel of Edward the Confessor, 57
Chapel of St. John the Evangelist, 97–98
Chapter House, 58
Charles I Commemoration, 320
Chaucer Festival, 320–321
Chelsea, 118–123, 178–179, 208–213, 247
Chelsea Antiques Fair, 320

Chelsea Bun Diner ✕, 178
Chelsea Flower Show, 321
Chelsea Physic Garden, 119, 120
Chester Place, 136
Chesterfield 🏨, 201
Cheyne Walk, 119, 122
Chez Gérard ✕, 173
Chez Moi ✕, 181
Chez Nico at Ninety Park Lane ✕, 162
Children, activities for, 52, 74, 75, 76, 79, 81–82, 83, 91, 93–96, 102, 105, 106, 113, 114, 125, 127, 129, 130, 132, 134, 137, 139, 142, 143, 146, 148, 152–153, 252
Children, traveling with, 299–301
China and glass shops, 256
Chiswick, 150–152
Chiswick House, 150
Chiswick Mall (street), 150
Christ Church College, 277
Christ Church, Spitalfields, 100, 104
Christie's (shop), 254
Christopher Gibbs (shop), 253
Christopher's ✕, 187
Church Street (Kew), 150
Churches, 40, 53–54, 55–58, 65, 66, 70, 74, 75–76, 78, 84, 86–87, 92–95, 100, 104, 118, 125, 275, 276, 277, 278, 280
concerts in, 232
Churchill Inter-Continental 🏨, 197
Chutney Mary ✕, 178
Cinema Bookshop, 255
Circus (stone houses), 274
City, 85–100, 183–186, 216–218
City Ballet of London, 231
Claridges ✕🏨, 187, 197
Clarke's ✕, 180
Cleopatra's Needle (obelisk), 71, 73
Climate, 319–320
Clink (prison), 108, 110
Clock Tower, 47
Cloisters, 58
Clothing for the trip, 311
Clothing shops, 257–263
Coach House (shop), 253
Coast ✕, 162
Coffee Cup ✕, 141, 186
Colefax & Fowler (shop), 253
Coliseum (theater), 231, 233
Collection ✕, 174
College Chapel, 149
Columbia 🏨, 215–216
Columbia Road, 101, 104
Comedy Store (cabaret), 224
Commodore 🏨, 215

Computers, traveling with, 301
Concerts, 231–232, 321, 322
Concierges, 301
Condotti ✕, 162
Connaught ✕🏨, 164, 197, 199
Connolly (shop), 257
Conran Shop, 265
Consumer protection, 301
Contemporary Applied Arts (shop), 264
Contemporary Ceramics (shop), 264
Cork Street, 63
Coronation Chair, 57
Corpus Christi College, 276
Costa's Fish Restaurant ✕, 181
Costs, 310
Cottons Rhum Shop, Bar and Restaurant ✕, 140
Courtauld Institute Galleries, 70, 73
Covent Garden, 69–76, 170–173, 203–205, 247
Covent Garden Hotel 🏨, 203
Covent Garden Piazza, 70, 73–74
Covered Crafts Market, 145, 146
Cow ✕, 182
Crafts Council Gallery Shop/Victoria & Albert Museum Shop, 264
Crank's ✕, 170
Cranley 🏨, 205
Credit cards, 310
Creperie ✕, 141
Cricket, 242
Cricketers ✕, 153
Criterion ✕, 163
Crockford's (casino), 224
Cross (shop), 265
Crown and Goose (pub), 189
Crown Jewels, 98–99
Cumberland Terrace, 136, 143
Currency, 310–311
Customs and duties, 301–303
Cutty Sark (clipper ship), 145, 146

D

Daisy & Tom (shop), 257
Dance, 222, 231, 232
Dance Books (shop), 255
Dance clubs, 225–227, 229
Daquise ✕, 176
David Linley Furniture (shop), 246, 264
David Mellor (shop), 256
Deals West ✕, 170
Dean's Yard, 58
Dennis Sever's House, 101, 104–105
Department stores, 251–252

Derby Day, *321*
Design Museum, *108, 110*
Design shops, *264–265*
Designer's Guild (shop), *264*
Dickens House Museum, *78, 82*
Dining, *303.* ☞ *Also* Restaurants
Dinny Hall (shop), *268*
Diplomat ☷, *210*
Disabilities and accessibility, *303–304*
Discounts and deals, *304–305*
Divertimenti (shop), *256*
Dr. Johnson's House, *86, 90*
Dogstar (nightclub), *225*
Dorchester ☷, *199*
Dorset Square Hotel ☷, *201*
Dove Inn (pub), *150, 189*
Down Mexico Way ✕, *164*
Downing Street, *40, 46*
Droopie & Browns (shop), *261*
Duffer of St. George (shop), *259*
Dukes ☷, *202*
Dulwich Picture Gallery, *112*
Durrants ☷, *201–202*

E

Eagle ✕, *183*
East End, *100–107*
Eden Plaza ☷, *207*
Edge (gay bar), *229*
Edward Lear ☷, *202*
Edwards & Edwards (ticket agents), *234*
Egerton House ☷, *210–211*
Egg (shop), *261*
Egyptian mummies, *81*
Electricity, *305*
Elena's L'Etoile ✕, *173*
Eleven Cadogan Gardens ☷, *211*
Elfin Oak (carved tree), *134*
Elgin Marbles, *81*
Elizabeth Hotel ☷, *212*
Elspeth Gibson (shop), *261*
Embassies, *305*
Emergencies, *305–306*
Emma Hope (shop), *261*
Emmanuel College, *275*
English National Ballet, *231*
English National Opera, *222*
Enterprise ✕, *177*
Equestrian events, *242, 320, 321*
Erickson Beamon (shop), *268*
Eros (statue), *65*
Etiquette and behavior, *306*
Euston, *216–218*
Everyman (cinema), *233*
Excursions from London, *273–281*

F

Fabric (nightclub), *225–226*
Facade (shop), *253–254*

Fan Museum, *145, 146*
Faraday's Laboratory, *63*
Fatboy's Diner ✕, *183*
Favourbrook (shop), *257*
Fenton House, *136, 140*
Fenwick (shop), *261*
Festivals and seasonal events, *320–322*
Fielding ☷, *205*
Film, *232–233*
First Call (ticket agent), *234*
First Floor ✕, *181–182*
fish! ✕, *186*
Fisher & Sperr (shop), *255*
Fitness centers. ☞ Gyms and fitness centers
Fitzwilliam Museum, *275*
Fleet Street, *86, 90*
Florence Nightingale Museum, *109, 112*
Floris (shop), *246, 266*
Flower shows, *321, 322*
Food for Thought ✕, *173*
Footstool ✕, *53*
Forbidden Planet (shop), *255*
Forte Posthouse Kensington ☷, *207*
Fortnum and Mason (shop), *246, 266*
afternoon tea in, 188
47 Park Street ☷, *199*
Forum (rock club), *228*
Fountain ✕, *165*
Fountains (garden), *132, 134*
Four Seasons ☷, *199*
Four Seasons Hotel Canary Wharf ☷, *203*
Fournier Street, *100, 105*
Foyles (shop), *255*
Franklin ☷, *211*
Freedom (gay bar), *229*
French House (pub), *189*
Freud Museum, *137, 140*
Fung Shing ✕, *167*

G

Gallery of Antique Costume and Textiles (shop), *254*
Gambling, *224–225*
Gardening Club (nightclub), *226*
Gardens. ☞ Parks and gardens
Garrick Club, *70, 74*
Gate ☷, *216*
Gatwick Airport, *296*
Gaucho Grill ✕, *166*
Gay and lesbian travelers, tips for, *306*
Gay nightlife, *228–229*
Geales ✕, *183*
Geffrye Museum, *101, 105*
General Trading Co. (shop), *246, 266*
Generator ☷, *218*
George Inn (pub), *189*
Georgina von Etzdorf (shop), *261–262*
Ghost (shop), *262*

Gift shops, *265–267*
Glass Art Gallery/London Glassblowing Workshop, *264*
Globe Theatre, *108, 116, 117, 118, 234*
Glyndebourne Festival Opera, *321*
Golden Hinde (galleon), *108, 112*
Golden Nugget (casino), *224*
Gorden Ramsay ✕, *179*
Gordon Square, *83*
Gore ☷, *205, 207*
Goring ☷, *211*
Grand Union Canal, *136*
Grays Antique Market, *246, 254*
Grays in the Mews (shop), *246*
Gray's Inn, *78, 82*
Grays Mews (shop), *246*
Great Northern ☷, *219*
Greenhouse ✕, *162*
Greenwich, *144–149*
Greenwich Antiques Market, *145, 146, 270*
Greenwich Park, *149*
Grosvenor House Antiques Fair, *321*
Grosvenor Prints (shop), *268*
Grosvenor Square, *63*
Guided tours. ☞ Tour operators
Guildhall, *87, 90*
Guildhall Library, *90*
Guy Fawkes Day, *322*
Gyms and fitness centers, *239–240*

H

Hackett (shop), *259*
Hackney City Farm, *101, 105*
Halcyon ☷, *213*
Halkin ☷, *208–209*
Hall's Croft (Tudor house), *278*
Ham House, *152*
Hamleys (shop), *266*
Hammersmith, *186–187*
Hampstead, *135–144, 186, 218–219, 247*
Hampstead Heath, *137, 140–141*
Hampstead Tea Rooms ✕, *141*
Hampton Court Palace, *153–154*
Hampton Court Palace Flower Show, *322*
Hanover Grand (nightclub), *226*
Harrods (department store), *124, 125, 127, 246, 252*
afternoon tea in, 188
Harvey Nichols (department store), *246, 252*
Hatchards (shop), *246, 255*
Haymarket, *59*

Hay's Galleria, *108, 112*
Hayward Gallery, *109, 112*
Hazlitt's ⊠, *204*
Head of the River Boat Race, *241–242, 320*
Heathrow Airport, *293*
Heaven (gay club), *229*
Heinz Gallery, *63*
Hempel ⊠, *213–214*
Henley Royal Regatta, *322*
Henry VII Chapel, *57*
Henry Wood Promenade Concerts, *322*
Herb Garret (herbal museum), *115*
Herbert Johnson (shop), *257*
Heritage Vaults, *273*
Highgate Cemetery, *137, 140–141*
HMS *Belfast* (ship), *108, 113*
HMV (shop), *256*
Hogarth's House, *150–151*
Holborn, *216–218*
Holidays, *306*
Holland & Holland (shop), *257–258*
Holland Park, *124, 127, 232*
Holly Bush ✕, *141*
Holy Trinity Church, *278*
Home (nightclub), *226*
Home exchanges, *308*
Hope and Glory (shop), *254*
Horniman Museum, *113*
Horse Guards Parade, *40, 46*
Horse racing, *242*
Horseback riding, *240*
Hostels, *308*
Hotel 167 ⊠, *207*
Hotels, *193–219, 308–309.*
  ☞ *Also* Lodging
Houses of Parliament, *40, 46–48*
Humla (shop), *258*
Hyde Park, *131–135*
Hyde Park Corner (Decimus Burton's Gateway), *132*

I

ICAfé ✕, *48*
Icons and symbols, *319, 323*
Imperial State Crown, *99*
Imperial War Museum, *109, 113*
Inner Temple, *84*
Institute of Contemporary Arts (ICA), *40, 46, 48*
Institute of Directors, *68*
Insurance, *306–307*
Island Queen (pub), *189–190*
Islington, *218–219*
Isola ✕, *177*
Iveagh Bequest, *141*
Ivy, ✕, *171–172*

J

J Sheekey ✕, *172*
Jack Straw's Castle (pub), *140, 190*

Jamme Masjid, *105*
Janet Fitch (shop), *268*
Janet Reger (shop), *262*
Jazz Café (jazz club), *227*
Jazz clubs, *227*
Jermyn Street, *60, 63*
Jewel Tower, *48*
Jewelry shops, *267–268*
Jewish Museum, *136, 141*
Jigsaw (shop), *262*
Jimmy Choo (shop), *262*
Joe Allen ✕, *170, 187*
John Lewis (department store), *252*
John Lobb (shop), *259*
Jo's Original Tea Dance (gay club), *229*
Judy Greenwood Antiques (shop), *254*
Julie's ✕, *180*
Jury's Inn ⊠, *219*

K

Karen Millen (shop), *262*
Keats House, *136, 141*
Keith Prowse (ticket agents), *234*
Kensal Green Cemetery, *127*
Kensington, *123–131, 179–183, 205, 207–208, 247*
Kensington Gardens, *124, 132, 134*
Kensington Market (shop), *258*
Kensington Palace, *124, 127–128, 134*
Kensington Palace Gardens, *124, 128–129*
Kensington Place ✕, *182*
Kensington Square, *124, 129*
Kenwood House, *137, 141–142, 232*
Kenwood Lakeside Concerts, *321*
Kew, *150–152*
Kew Gardens, *151*
Kew Green, *150*
Kew Palace, *152*
Kilgour, French & Stanbury (shop), *259*
King Edward's Grammar School, *278*
King's College Chapel, *275*
King's Road, *119, 122*
Kingsley ⊠, *216*
Knightsbridge, *123–131, 176–178, 208–213, 247*
Knightsbridge Barracks, *132, 134*
Knightsbridge Green ⊠, *212*
Knightsbridge Hotel ⊠, *212*
Koh Samui (shop), *262*
Konditor & Cook ✕, *185*

L

La Brasserie ✕, *179*
La Gaffe ⊠, *218*
La Gavroche ✕, *162–163*
La Poule au Pot ✕, *179*

La Reserve ⊠, *212–213*
La Tante Claire ✕, *176*
Lamb (pub), *190*
Lamb and Flag (pub), *74, 190*
Lambeth Palace, *109, 113*
Lancaster Hall Hotel ⊠, *216*
Landmark ⊠, *199*
Lanesborough ⊠, *209*
Langham Hilton ⊠, *199–200*
Lauderdale House ✕, *141*
Laura Ashley (shop), *262*
Le Caprice ✕, *166*
Le Gavroche ✕, *162–163*
Le Meridien Grosvenor House ⊠, *200*
Le Meridien Piccadilly ⊠, *200*
Le Meridien Waldorf ⊠, *203*
Le Pont de la Tour ✕, *183*
Leadenhall Market, *270*
Legal London, *77–85*
Leicester Square, *70, 74*
Leighton House, *124, 129*
Lemonia ✕, *186*
Leonard ⊠, *201*
Les Senteurs (shop), *267*
L'Escargot ✕, *169*
Lesley Craze Gallery (shop), *264–265*
L'Hôtel ⊠, *211*
Liberty (department store), *246, 252*
Libraries, *38, 67, 78, 79, 90, 276*
Library (bar), *224*
Lincoln's Inn, *78, 82*
Lindow Man, *81–82*
Linley Sambourne House, *124, 129*
Livebait ✕, *186*
Lloyd's of London, *87, 90–91*
L'Odéon ✕, *163*
Lodging, *193–220, 307–309*
  children, 300
  disabilities and accessibility, 304
  price categories, 307
London Aquarium, *109, 114*
London Brass Rubbing Centre, *53*
London Bridge, *87, 91*
London Canal Museum, *136, 142*
London Central Mosque, *143*
London County Hall Travel Inn Capital ⊠, *213*
London Dungeon (museum), *108, 114*
London Elizabeth ⊠, *215*
London Library, *67*
London Marathon, *321*
London Parade, *320*
London Planetarium, *135, 142*
London Silver Vaults (shop), *254*
London to Brighton Veteran Car Run, *322*

London Tower Bridge Travel Inn Capital 🏨, *213*
London Transport Museum, *70, 74*
London Zoo, *136, 142*
L'Oranger ✕, *165*
Lord Mayor's Procession and Show, *322*
Lou Pescadou ✕, *174*
Love Muscle (gay club), *229*
Lower Ward, *280*
Lulu Guinness (shop), *262*
Lush (shop), *266*

M

Madame Tussaud's (museum), *135, 143*
Maids of Honour ✕, *152*
Mail and shipping, *309*
Maison Bertaux ✕, *76, 167*
Maison Novelli ✕, *182*
Malcolm Levene (shop), *259–260*
Mall (street), *40, 49*
Mandeer ✕, *173*
Map House (shop), *269*
Marathons, *242, 321*
Marble Arch, *60, 64*
Marble Hill House, *152*
Marchpane (shop), *255*
Margaret Howell (shop), *262*
Marine Ices ✕, *140*
Marks and Spencer (shop), *60, 67, 258*
Mary Arden's House, *279*
Marylebone, *247*
Mausoleum of Halicarnassus, *81*
Maxwell's ✕, *170*
Mayfair, *59–68, 157, 162–164, 196–197, 199–202, 247*
Mayflower (pub), *190*
MDC Classic Music (shop), *256*
Media, *309–310*
Megan Mathers (shop), *254*
Melati ✕, *169*
Melita House Hotel 🏨, *213*
Metropolitan 🏨, *200*
Mezzo ✕, *167*
Micro Gallery, *49*
Middle Temple, *84*
Middle Temple Hall, *84*
Middle Tower, *98*
Mildenhall Treasure, *81*
Millennium Dome, *38, 144–145, 146, 148*
Millennium Bridge, *108*
Ministry of Sound (nightclub), *226*
Mirabelle ✕, *163*
Modern dance, *232*
Momo ✕, *166–167*
Money matters, *310–311*
Montcalm 🏨, *200–201*
Monument, *87, 91*
More, Sir Thomas, statue of, *122*

Morgan 🏨, *218*
Moro ✕, *184–185*
Morton's ✕, *165*
Moshi Moshi Sushi ✕, *184*
Movies, *232–233*
Muffin Man ✕, *129*
Muji (shop), *258*
Mulberry (shop), *258*
Mulligans ✕, *164*
Murder One (shop), *255*
Museum of Garden History, *109, 114*
Museum of London, *87, 91*
Museum of the Moving Image (MOMI), *109, 114–115*
Museum Tavern, *190*
Museums and galleries, *38–39, 40, 41, 48–51, 52, 54, 55, 60, 61, 63, 66, 68, 70, 73, 74, 76, 78, 79, 81–82, 83, 87, 91, 101, 102, 105, 106–107, 110, 112, 113, 114–115, 118, 122, 129–131, 140, 141, 142, 143, 144, 146, 148, 150–151, 274, 275, 277, 278, 280*
Music festivals, *321, 322*
Myhotel 🏨, *216*

N

Nash's House, *278*
National Army Museum, *119, 122*
National Film Theatre, *115, 232–233*
National Gallery, *40, 49–50, 54*
National Maritime Museum, *145, 148*
National Portrait Gallery, *40, 50–51*
National Sound Archive, *124, 129*
Natural History Museum, *39, 124, 129–130*
Neal Street, *70, 74*
Neal Street East (shop), *266*
Neal's Yard Remedies (shop), *266–267*
Nelson's Column, *40, 51, 54*
New Academy Gallery (shop), *269*
New Armouries, *97*
New Place, *278*
NFT restaurant and cafeteria ✕, *115*
Nick Ashley (shop), *260*
Nicole Farhi (shop), *262–263*
Nightclubs, *225–226, 229*
Nightlife, *222–229*
Nobu ✕, *164*
Norman Gate, *279*
North Sea Fish Restaurant ✕, *174*
Notre Dame de France (church), *74*
Notting Hill, *134, 247, 251*

Notting Hill Arts Club (nightclub), *226*
Notting Hill Carnival, *322*
Notting Hill Gate, *179–183, 213–216*
Novotel Waterloo 🏨, *202*
Number 1 Royal Crescent, *274*
Number Sixteen 🏨, *207*

O

Oak Room ✕, *163*
Old Bailey (Central Criminal Court), *86, 92*
Old Royal Observatory, *145, 148*
Old St. Thomas's Operating Theatre, *108, 115*
Old Vic (theater), *222*
Olympia International Show Jumping Championships, *320*
One Aldwych 🏨, *203*
100 Club (jazz club), *227*
One-nighters, *229*
192 ✕, *182*
Open Air Theatre, *127*
Open House (seasonal event), *320*
Opera, *222, 233, 321*
Orangery at Kensington Palace ✕, *188*
Ordning & Reda (shop), *267*
Orso ✕, *172*
Outdoor activities. ☞ Sports and outdoor activities
Oxford, *276–277*
Oxford Story, *277*
Oxford Street, *251*
Oxford Union, *277*
OXO Tower, *109, 115*
OXO Tower (shopping center), *265*
OXO Tower Brasserie and Restaurant ✕, *184*
Ozwald Boateng (shop), *260*

P

Packing for London, *311–312*
Pagoda, *151*
Painted Hall, *149*
Pall Mall, *59, 64*
Palm Beach Casino, *224–225*
Palm House (greenhouse), *151*
Parks and gardens, *52–53, 63, 120, 127, 128–129, 132, 134, 140, 143, 149, 151, 152–153*
Pasha ✕, *176*
Passports and visas, *312*
Pâtisserie Valerie ✕, *76, 127, 167*
Paul Smith (shop), *258–259*
Peacock Theatre, *231*
Pearly Harvest Festival Service, *322*
Pelham 🏨, *211–212*

Pembridge Court 🖬, 214
Penhaligon's (shop), 267
People's Palace ✗, 185
Percival David Foundation of
    Chinese Art, 78, 83
Peter Pan (statue), 132, 134
Peterhouse College, 275
Petrie Museum, 85
Petticoat Lane (street
    market), 270
Pharmacy ✗, 180
Pheasant and Firkin (pub),
    190
Pheasantry (shop), 122
Philip Treacy (shop), 263
Phillips (shop), 255
Photographers, tips for, 297
Physical Energy (statue),
    132, 134
Piccadilly Circus, 60, 64–65,
    251
Pizza Express (jazz club),
    227
PJ's ✗, 178
Place (dance theater), 231
Place Below ✗, 93
Plane travel. ☞ Air travel
Pleasures of Times Past
    (shop), 255
Poets' Corner, 57–58
Pollo ✗, 168
Pollock's Toy Museum, 78,
    83
Pool (bar), 224
Portland Place, 65
Portmeirion (shop), 256
Portobello 🖬, 214
Portobello Market, 270
Portobello Road, 132, 134
Pret a Manger ✗, 172
Price categories
for dining, 303
for lodging, 307
Prime Meridian, 148
Primrose Hill B&B (bed-and-
    breakfast agency), 220
Prince Bonaparte ✗, 182
Prince Henry's Room, 78, 83
Princess Louise (pub), 190
Princess of Wales
    Conservatory, 151
Print shops, 268–269
Prospect of Whitby (pub),
    190
Pubs, 74, 99–100, 140,
    150, 153, 188–191
Pulteney Bridge, 274
Pump Room and Roman
    Baths, 273
Punch and Judy Festival, 321
Purcell Room (concert hall),
    231
Purves & Purves (shop), 267
Pyx Chamber, 58

Q

Quaglino's ✗, 166
Quality Chop House ✗, 185
Queen Anne's Gate, 40, 51

Queen Elizabeth Hall, 231
Queen Mary's Dolls' House,
    280
Queen Mary's Gardens, 143
Queen Mother's Crown, 99
Queen Mother's Gate, 132
Queen Victoria Memorial,
    40, 51–52
Queen's Birthday, 321
Queens' College, 275–276
Queen's Gallery, 40, 44, 52
Queen's House (Greenwich),
    145, 148
Queen's House (Tower of
    London), 99
Quo Vadis ✗, 168

R

Radcliffe Camera, 276
Radisson Mountbatten 🖬,
    204
Radisson Pastoria 🖬, 205
Rail travel, 281, 316–317
Randall & Aubin ✗, 169–170
Ranger's House, 145, 148–
    149
Record shops, 256
Reform Club, 64
Regent Street, 65, 251
Regent's Park, 135–144,
    196–197, 199–202
Regent's Park Open-Air
    Theatre, 136, 143, 234
Restaurants, 48, 50, 53, 54,
    64, 66, 76, 82, 88, 93,
    115, 127, 129, 131, 140,
    141, 152, 153, 156–191,
    273, 303
brunch and afternoon tea,
    187–188
price categories, 303
pubs, 74, 99–100, 140, 150,
    153, 188–191
Richmond, 152–153
Richmond Park, 152–153
Ridgemount 🖬, 218
Rigby & Peller (shop), 263
Rio (cinema), 233
Ritz ✗, 165, 188
River Café ✗, 186–187
River cruises, 313
Riverside Studios (cinema;
    dance theater), 232, 233
Roadhouse (rock club), 228
Rock and Sole Plaice ✗,
    172–173
Rock Circus, 75
Rock clubs, 227–228
Rococo (shop), 267
Ronnie Scott's (jazz club),
    227
Rookery 🖬, 216
Room at the Halcyon ✗, 181
Rosetta Stone, 81
Rotten Row, 132
Round Pond, 132, 134
Round Tower, 279
Royal Academy of Arts, 60,
    66

Royal Albert Hall, 124, 130,
    231, 232
Royal Armouries, 97
Royal Ballet, 222, 231
Royal Ceremonial Dress
    Collection, 128
Royal College of Art, 124,
    130
Royal Court Theatre, 234
Royal Courts of Justice, 78,
    83
Royal Crescent, 274
Royal Exchange, 87, 92
Royal Festival Hall, 109,
    115–116, 231
Royal Hospital, 119, 122–
    123
Royal London Hospital, 102,
    105–106
Royal London Hospital
    Archives, 106
Royal Mews, 52
Royal National Theatre, 109,
    116, 234
Royal Naval College, 145,
    149
Royal Opera House, 70, 75,
    222, 231, 233
Royal Sceptre, 99
Royal Shakespeare Company,
    234
Royal Shakespeare Theatre,
    278–279
Royal Windsor Horse Show,
    321
Rubens 🖬, 209
Rugby, 242–243
Rules ✗, 171
Running, 240
Rupert Cavendish (shop),
    254

S

Saatchi Collection, 137,
    144
Sadler's Wells Theatre, 231,
    232, 233
St. Bartholomew the Great
    Church, 87, 92
St. Bride's (church), 86, 92–
    93
St. George's Chapel, 280
St. George's Gardens, 63
St. Giles without Cripplegate
    (church), 87, 93
St. James Park, 52–53
St. James Tavern, 190
St. James's, 59–68, 165–
    167, 202, 251
St. James's Church, 60, 66
St. James's Court 🖬, 209–
    210
St. James's Palace, 59, 66
St. James's Square, 60, 67
St. John ✗, 185
St. John's College
    (Cambridge), 275
St. John's College (Oxford),
    277

St. John's, Smith Square (church), 53, 232
St. Margaret's ⊠, 218
St. Margaret's Church, 40, 53
St. Martin-in-the-Fields (church), 40, 53–54, 232
St. Martin's Gallery, 53
St. Martin's Lane ⊠, 204
St. Mary-le-Bow (church), 87, 93
St. Mary the Virgin (church), 276
St. Paul's Cathedral, 86–87, 93–95
St. Paul's Church, 70, 75–76
St. Peter ad Vincula (church), 99
St. Stephen Walbrook Church, 87, 95
Sally Lunn's ✕, 273
San Lorenzo ✕, 177
Savoy ⊠, 204
afternoon tea in, 188
Savoy Grill ✕, 171
Science Museum, 124, 130, 267
Scotch House (shop), 259
Selfridges (department store), 60, 67, 252
Senior-citizens, tips for, 312
Serpentine (lake), 132, 135
Serpentine Bridge, 132, 135
Serpentine Gallery, 132, 135
Shaftesbury (theater), 233
Shakespeare, William, 115, 116, 117, 277–279
Shakespeare Under the Stars, 321
Shakespeare's Birthplace Museum, 278
Shakespeare's Globe Theatre, 108, 115, 116, 117, 234
Sheldonian Theatre, 276–277
Shelly's (shop), 259
Shepherd Market, 67
Shepherd's Bush Empire (rock club), 228
Sherlock Holmes (pub), 190
Sherlock Holmes Museum, 135, 144
Shirtsmith (shop), 263
Shopping, 245–271
Sightseeing tours, 312–313
Silver Moon (shop), 255
Sir John Soane's Museum, 78, 83
606 Club (jazz club), 227
Slade School of Fine Arts, 85
Sloane ⊠, 212
Smollensky's on the Strand ✕, 157
Soccer, 243
Society of London Theatre ticket kiosk, 74
Softball, 240
Soho, 69–76, 167–170, 203–205

Soho Soho ✕, 168
Soho Square, 70, 76
Sotheby's (auction house), 255
Sotheby's Café ✕, 64
Sound Republic (nightclub), 226
South Bank, 107–118, 183–186
South Bank Arts Complex, 231, 232
South Kensington, 174, 176
Southwark Cathedral, 108, 118
Space (shop), 265
Space NK Apothecary (shop), 263
Spaniard's Inn (pub), 140, 190
Speakers' Corner, 60, 67
Spencer House, 59, 67
Spitalfields City Farm, 101, 106
Spitalfields Market, 101, 106, 270–271
Sports and outdoor activities, 239–243
Sportsman Club (casino), 225
Sportspages (shop), 255
Square ✕, 163
Squash, 240
Stafford ⊠, 202
Stakis Islington ⊠, 218
Stakis St. Ermins ⊠, 210
Stanfords (shop), 255
Staple Inn, 78, 84
Star Tavern, 191
State Apartments (art museum), 280
Station Tavern (rock club), 228
Stefano Cavallini ✕, 177
Steinberg & Tolkien (shop), 268
Stockpot ✕, 176
Strand (street), 70, 76
Strand-on-the-Green (street), 150
Stratford-upon-Avon, 277–279
Street markets, 269–271
Stringfellows (nightclub), 226
Students, tips for, 313
Subterania (nightlcub), 226–227
Subway travel. ☞ Underground tube travel
Sugar Club ✕, 169
Summer Exhibition, 66
Summerhill & Bishop (shop), 256
Sutton Hoo Treasure, 81
Sutton House, 106
Swaine Adeney (shop), 259
Swan Theatre, 278–279
Swear (shop), 260
Sweetings ✕, 186

Swimming, 240–241
Swiss Cottage Hotel ⊠, 219
Syon House, 153

T

Talking Bookshop, 255
Tamarind ✕, 164
Tate Britain, 41, 54
Tate Modern, Bankside, 38, 108, 118
Taxes, 313–314
Taxis, 314
Tea House (shop), 267
Telephones, 314–315
Temperate House (greenhouse), 151
Temple Bar Memorial, 84
Temple Church, 78, 84
Temple of Mithras, 87, 95
10 Downing Street, 40, 46
Tennis, 241, 243, 321–322
Theater, 233–237
Theater buildings, 70, 76, 115, 116, 127, 143, 276–277, 278–279
box office information, 233–237
half-price tickets, 74
Theatre Museum, 70, 76
Theatre Royal, Drury Lane, 70, 76
Thomas Coram Foundation, 78, 84
Thomas Goode (shop), 256
Three Greyhounds (pub), 191
Ticketmaster, 234
Time, 315
Tipping, 315–316
Titanic ✕, 168
Tom Gilbey (shop), 260
Tom Quad, 277
Tomb of the Unknown Warrior, 57
Tootsies ✕, 179
Top Shop/Top Man (shop), 260
Tours and packages, 316
Tower Bridge, 87, 95–96
Tower Green, 96–97
Tower of London, 39, 87, 96–99
Tower Records (shop), 256
Trafalgar Square, 40, 54–55
Train travel. ☞ Rail travel
Traitors' Gate, 98
Transportation, 317. ☞ *Also* Air travel; Bus travel; Car travel; Rail travel; Taxis; Underground tube travel
Travel agencies, 317
Travel Bookshop, 255
Traveler's checks, 311
Travellers' Club, 64
Trinity Almshouses, 101, 106
Trinity College, 275
Trinity College Chapel, 277
Trooping the Colour (parade), 321

Truckles of Pied Bull Yard ✕, *173*
Turnbull & Asser (shop), *260*
2 Willow Road, *144*

U

Undercroft, *58*
Underground tube travel, *317–318*
United Synagogues Cemetery Maintenance Department, *106*
University College, *78, 84–85*
University of London, *78, 85*
Upper Ward, *280–281*
Upstream from London, *149–154*
Uptown Reservations (bed-and-breakfast agency), *219*
US B&B (bed-and-breakfast agency), *220*

V

V.A.T. refunds, *314*
V&A Café ✕, *131*
Veeraswamy ✕, *187*
Vicarage 🖾, *207–208*
Victoria, *208–213*
Victoria and Albert Museum, *38, 124, 130–131*
Victoria Tower, *47*
Villandry ✕, *167*

Vinopolis (wine center), *108, 118*
Virgin Megastore, *256*
Visas, *312*
Visitor information, *281, 318–319*
Vivienne Westwood (shop), *246, 263*

W

Wag (nightclub), *227*
Wagamama ✕, *173–174*
Wakefield Tower, *98*
Wallace Collection, *60, 68*
Walter Castellazzo Design (shop), *265*
Warwick Castle, *279*
Waterloo Block, *98*
Waterloo Place, *68*
Waterside Café ✕, *88*
Waterstone's (shop), *255*
Weather, *319–320*
Web sites, *319*
Wellington Barracks, *40, 55*
West End Cares (tickets), *234*
Westminster, *39–58, 208–213*
Westminster Abbey, *40, 55–58*
Westminster Cathedral, *58*
Westminster Hall, *47*
Westminster Pier, *149*
Whistles (shop), *263*

White Tower, *97*
Whitechapel Art Gallery, *100, 106–107*
Whitechapel Bell Foundry, *100, 107*
Wig and Pen Club, *85*
Wigmore Hall (concert hall), *232*
William Morris Gallery, *107*
Wimbledon Lawn Tennis Championships, *321–322*
Windsor, *279–280*
Windsor Castle, *279–280*
Windsor Castle (pub), *191*
Wódka ✕, *182*
Wok Wok ✕, *169*
World's End (shop), *122*
Wren ✕, *66*

Y

Yard (gay bar), *229*
Yas ✕, *181*
Ye Bunch of Grapes (pub), *191*
Ye Olde Cheshire Cheese (pub), *86, 99–100, 191*
Yoga, *241*

Z

Zafferano ✕, *177*
Zara (shop), *263*
Zinc Bar & Grill ✕, *165*
Zoo, *136, 142*
Zwemmer (shop), *255*

NOTES

NOTES

NOTES

NOTES

FODOR'S LONDON 2001

EDITOR: Langdon Faust

Editorial Contributors: Jacqueline Brown, Roland Chambers, Anna Jefferys, Alex Wijeratna, Victoria Young

Editorial Production: Rebecca Zeiler

Maps: David Lindroth Inc., *cartographer;* Rebecca Baer and Bob Blake, *map editors*

Design: Fabrizio La Rocca, *creative director;* Guido Caroti, *art director;* Jolie Novak, *photo editor;* Melanie Marin, *photo researcher*

Cover Design: Pentagram

Production/Manufacturing: Robert Shields

ISBN 0–679–00545-5

ISSN 0149–631X

SPECIAL SALES

Fodor's Travel Publications are available at special discounts for bulk purchases for sales promotions or premiums. Special editions, including personalized covers, excerpts of existing guides, and corporate imprints, can be created in large quantities for special needs. For more information, contact your local bookseller or write to Special Markets, Fodor's Travel Publications, 280 Park Avenue, New York, NY 10017. Inquiries from Canada should be directed to your local Canadian bookseller or sent to Random House of Canada, Ltd., Marketing Department, 2775 Matheson Boulevard East, Mississauga, Ontario L4W 4P7. Inquiries from the United Kingdom should be sent to Fodor's Travel Publications, 20 Vauxhall Bridge Road, London SW1V 2SA, England.

PRINTED IN THE UNITED STATES OF AMERICA

10 9 8 7 6 5 4 3 2 1

IMPORTANT TIP

Although all prices, opening times, and other details in this book are based on information supplied to us at press time, changes occur all the time in the travel world, and Fodor's cannot accept responsibility for facts that become outdated or for inadvertent errors or omissions. So always **confirm information when it matters,** especially if you're making a detour to visit a specific place.

PHOTOGRAPHY

Adina Toby/Photo 20-20, *cover (Royal guards).*

Axiom: Alberto Arzoz, *10B, 11E.* Ian Cumming, *11D, 20C.* James Morris, *12C.*

Bibendum, *10A.*

British Museum, *26B, 30J.*

The British Tourist Authority, *3 bottom left, 19D.*

Corbis, *1, 9E, 21F, 26A, 27C, 28D, 30H.*

Crown Copyright Historic Royal Palaces, *2 top left, 8B, 29E.*

Discover Islington, *2 bottom center, 2 bottom right.*

Firmdale Hotels, *30I.*

Floris, *13F.*

The Garden Picture Library: *John McCarthy, 18B, 21D.*

Chris Gascoigne & Lifschutz Davidson, *2 top right.*

© Her Majesty Queen Elizabeth II, *3 top left, 8C.*

The Image Bank: *Chris Close, 4-5. Cralle, 32. Lisl Dennis, 8A. Tom Owen Edmunds, 30D. John Hill, 6B. Romilly Lockyer, 6A. Michael Pasdzior, 18A. Andrea Pistolesi, 9F, 20A. Leonard Rhodes, 22B. Marc Romanelli, 7D. Antonio Rosario, 13D. Guido Alberto Rossi, 7E, 12A, 23C. Paul Trummer, 30C. Alvis Upitis, 16F, 30G. Matthew Weinreb, 18C. Frank Whitney, 9D, 25C.*

Kelly/Mooney, *6C, 11F, 13E, 15C, 15D, 15E, 17G, 17I, 19E, 20B, 21E, 22A.*

La Tante Claire: *Anthony Blake, 30E.*

James Lemass, *24A.*

Liberty, *3 bottom right.*

The National Gallery, *3 top right, 2 bottom left, 14B, 30B.*

© Plum, *12B, 14A, 19F, 23E.*

Regent's Park Open-Air Theater, *25B.*

The Savoy Group, *30A, 30F.*

The Sound Republic, *25D.*

The Sugar Club, *10C.*

Three Greyhounds, *23D.*

The Victoria and Albert Museum, *17H.*

ABOUT OUR WRITERS

Every trip is a significant trip. Acutely aware of that fact, we've pulled out all stops in preparing Fodor's *London 2001*. To help you zero in on what to see in London, we've gathered some great color photos of key sights. To show you how to put it all together, we've created great itineraries and neighborhood walks. And to direct you to the places that are truly worth your time and money, we've rallied the team of endearingly picky know-it-alls we're pleased to call our writers. Having seen all corners of the regions they cover for us, they're real experts. If you knew them, you'd poll them for tips yourself.

Being a settler in London, says writer and editor **Jacqueline Brown,** is mainly different from being a true native in that one really tries to get the most out of what the city has to offer. After 20 years of living in the capital, her favorite targets are those culinary and cultural arenas which lie far beyond bully beef and Buckingham Palace. When she is not working as a freelance editor or helping to update the Exploring, Shopping, Side Trips, and Smart Travel Tips sections of this book, Jacqueline can be found strolling the parklands of a National Trust stately home with her young family.

Roland Chambers received a degree in English literature from Edinburgh University before studying directing at the Polish National Film School and film and literature at New York University. Currently living in Hackney Marshes, London, he is writing and illustrating a children's book, while pondering cause and effect—and investigating hotels for this guide.

Londoner born and bred, **Alex Wijeratna** is an old-school stalwart of fashionable Notting Hill. With his English/Sri Lankan roots, Alex is well aware that the real flavor of London is found in its ethnic diversity. He has written mainly for newspapers, including the *Times*. For this edition, he updated the dining chapter.

Don't Forget to Write

We love feedback—positive and negative—and follow up on all suggestions. So contact the London editor at editors@ fodors.com or c/o Fodor's, 280 Park Avenue, New York, New York 10017. Have a wonderful trip!

[signature]

Karen Cure
Editorial Director